Canadian History
Since Confederation
Essays and Interpretations

Canadian History Since Confederation
Essays and Interpretations

Edited by

BRUCE HODGINS

and

ROBERT PAGE
Both of the
Department of History
Trent University
Peterborough, Ontario

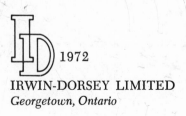 1972

IRWIN-DORSEY LIMITED
Georgetown, Ontario

First Printing, April 1972

Library of Congress Catalog Card No. 79–187063
Printed in the United States of America

Preface

THIS VOLUME has been assembled by the editors to fill a void which they experienced in teaching introductory Canadian history courses at the university level. There was no single volume to which students could be directed containing the interpretative ideas which lie behind Canadian history. Most of these ideas were outlined in key articles and books accessible only in libraries. This volume represents their attempt to overcome this deficiency.

Canadian History since Confederation makes no attempt to be a narrative survey of history but is, instead, a sampling of the ideas and interpretations which lie behind and illuminate the history of Canada since 1867. Most of the essays have stimulating and revisionist theses. Many of them lie outside the traditional political and constitutional framework and reflect the interests of many of Canada's younger historians in social and intellectual history. This collection should provide an interesting supplement to traditional textbooks and a more meaningful basis for studies in depth or for the "problems" approach to Canadian history.

In compiling this volume, the editors were unable to reproduce all of the articles desired because of the somewhat restrictive policies of certain publishers regarding republication. The editors commissioned several new articles to cover topics and interpretations not adequately covered in published materials. These were from scholars who had not yet published the fruits of their recent research. The volume also contains appropriate passages from certain books (including works of fiction) which illuminate aspects of social and intellectual history. The editors included several contemporary articles where their analysis was particularly revealing.

The editors have taken great care in attempting to determine and to gain all necessary permissions for materials republished in this book. If through any mischance they have failed to establish all obligations, they would welcome any information that would enable them to do so.

Acknowledgments

University of Toronto Press, Readings 5, 8, 10, 20, 22, 25, 32, 33; *Canadian Literature,* Reading 23; *Journal of Canadian Studies,* Readings 11, 17, 31;

Ryerson Press, Reading 26; *Queen's Quarterly*, Readings 3, 9, 12; Donald Creighton, Reading 4; Lovell Clark, Reading 15; Blair Neatby, Reading 16; F. W. Gibson, Reading 19; Canadian Political Science Association, Reading 21; W. R. Graham, Reading 24; Hugh MacLennan, Reading 27; K. W. McNaught, Reading 28; *South Atlantic Quarterly*, Reading 30.

April 1972   BRUCE HODGINS
                                                ROBERT PAGE

Contents

PART I.   THE CONFEDERATION ERA

PART II.   THE AGE OF THE NATIONAL POLICY

PART III.   LATE-VICTORIAN CANADA AND HER EXTERNAL INTERESTS

PART IV.   EARLY 20TH CENTURY CANADA

PART V.   THE INTER-WAR YEARS

PART VI.   CONTEMPORARY CANADA

part I

The Confederation Era

1

Edinburgh Review (January, 1865), Article on Proposed Federation of the British North American Colonies

WITH THE MEMORY of the "struggle" for responsible government in their minds, many students of Canadian history are not conscious of the extent to which imperial apathy was the prevailing climate of opinion in Britain in the 1860s. This apathy faced the fathers of Confederation when they negotiated the British North America Act. Free trade principles had destroyed the economic rationale of the mercantilist theory of empire. With tariff barriers abandoned they hoped that trade would be no respecter of national or imperial boundaries; therefore the costly superstructure to maintain these boundaries and colonial governments, no longer served any British purpose. Heavy defence costs were particularly annoying to the British Government and taxpayer. As independence was inevitable, Britain wanted to do nothing to impede this evolution in white settlement colonies.

This article in the *Edinburgh Review* of January 1865 is an interesting contemporary analysis of the proposals for federation. It reflected the ambivalence of British opinion to the project. With the American Civil War still raging there were many who were suspicious of the permanence and stability of any federal structure. They were also unhappy because the proposed union might turn out to be a means of keeping Britain from severing her North American responsibilities, and Canadian obligations might lead to new confrontation with the United States. Even, Sir Charles Dilke, the imperial enthusiast, urged cutting the imperial ties to Canada to improve the British people's relations with their racial cousins in the United States. The London *Times* denounced the proposed scheme of Confederation because it would "promote continual dependence upon the mother country." Thus in this period imperial ties were maintained because of the Canadian desire to retain Her Majesty's protection rather than a British determination to keep an empire. Therefore it is hardly surprising that this article should hail Confederation as "the harbinger of the future and complete independence of British North America."

ART. VII.—*Report of Resolutions adopted at a Conference of Delegates from the Provinces of Canada, Nova Scotia, and New Brunswick, and the Colonies of Newfoundland and Prince Edward's Island, held in the City of Quebec on the 10th of October, 1864, as the Basis of a proposed Confederation of those Provinces and Colonies.*

AMALGAMATION is the order of the day, the approved process by which capitalists of all classes are doubling their profits and defying their competitors. From our railway companies and millionaires the co-operative infection has spread to our mechanics and artisans. Men of all sorts and conditions, at home and abroad (theologians excepted), are seeking in union that strength with which it is proverbially identical. A colossal project of this nature has been just presented to our notice in the proposed fusion of the five provinces of British North America, "with power to add to their number" as many of the communities lying within British boundaries between the Atlantic and Pacific Oceans as may, on terms hereafter to be defined, elect to join this vast copartnership. Even to nations unconnected to political or geographical affinities with the parties more immediately concerned, the success or failure of a scheme embracing in its contingent operations an area exceeding that of Europe is no matter of indifference. To Great Britain it is impossible to over-estimate the importance and extent of the ultimate consequences depending on this crisis in the history of her Transatlantic provinces. For there are problems of colonial policy the solution of which cannot, without peril, be indefinitely delayed, and though Imperial England is doing her best to keep up appearances in the management of her five and forty dependencies, the political links which once bound them to each other and to their common centre are evidently worn out. Misgivings haunt the public mind as to the stability of an edifice which seems to be founded on a reciprocity of deception, and only to be shored up for the time by obsolete and meaningless traditions. Economists fail to comprehend the value of outlying provinces which garrison their frontiers with our troops, while they exclude our manufactures from their markets. Even orthodox politicians, who would shrink from a Colonial Emancipationist as from a pestilent heretic, cannot help asking themselves sometimes whether it is possible or desirable that these little islands of our's, whose whole area scarcely exceeds 130,000 square miles, should for ever retain, even a nominal dominion, over a fifth of the habitable globe. These hints at a possible disturbance of their existing relations very naturally shock our Colonists, who have no wish to part company with us, and think it very wicked even to talk of dismembering "an empire on which the sun never sets." It is not unnatural that the desire to maintain a connexion with the power and wealth of the mother-country should be stronger on the side of the Colonies than it is on that of the British public, for they owe almost everything to us, and we receive but little in return from them. Moreover, the existing system of colonial government enables them to combine all the advantages of local independence with the strength and dignity of a great empire. But the Imperial Government, in the meantime, has to decide, not as of old whether Great Britain is to tax the Colonies, but to what extent the Colonies are to be permitted to tax Great Britain—a question which is daily becoming more urgent and less easy of solution. To register the edicts of Provincial Legislatures is now almost the only remaining function of the Colonial Office; and in the absence of any distinct indications of public opinion at home as to the course to be pursued in the administration of our Dependencies, the smallest contributions from Colonial sources which may tend to simplify the task of the authorities in Downing Street will, no doubt, be thankfully received.

The new British American programme has arrived at a seasonable period of indecision, and this circumstance will insure for its promoters, at all events, a favourable hearing. We learn from Mr. Cardwell's despatch to Lord Monck of the 3rd December that this scheme has already received the deliberate consideration of Her Majesty's Government; and in the course of the ensuing spring it is expected that a deputation will arrive in this country for the purpose of bringing over the Quebec propositions, which will then be submitted in the form of a Bill to the Imperial Legislature. The time is therefore come when this subject must be fully discussed, and no question of greater interest is likely to come before Parliament in the session of 1865, for it raises numerous points of great novelty and complexity, and it will affect the future condition of a vast extent of territory, of a people verging on independence, and, in a less degree, of England herself.

Of all the provinces added to our empire during the last three centuries, none have on the whole proved less troublesome to the parent State than the long belt which extends from the shores of Lake Superior to the banks of Newfoundland. We have heard, it is true, in times past, of Canadian rebellions, we hear sometimes now of hostile tariffs, and it might puzzle the wisest of our statesmen if he were challenged to put his finger on any single item of material advantage resulting to ourselves from our dominions in British North America, which cost us at this moment about a million sterling a-year. But this is the sort of thing that happens to us everywhere, and we are used to it. Retainers who will neither give nor accept notice to quit our service must, it is assumed, be kept on our establishment. There are nevertheless special and exceptional difficulties which beset us in this portion of our vast field of empire. For though Kaffirs and Maories have proved more dangerous neighbours to our colonists and more costly enemies to ourselves than the Red Indians, whose race the threefold agencies of rifles, whiskey, and small-pox seem almost to have exterminated, the permanent occupation of that frontier of three thousand miles which extends from the Bay of Fundy to the Straits of San Juan presents problems more serious than any we have yet had to solve in New Zealand or at the Cape. Although half these difficulties have no place in the estimate of the sanguine prophets who predict the eternity of the American civil war, or (which is much the same thing) its duration until the utter exhaustion of both parties in the conflict, yet, even assuming for the moment that such calculations afford a safe basis of action, they afford no provision against the contingencies of an anarchy more perilous than filibustering expeditions or organised invasions, and they may fail to protect against the ambition or resentment of a powerful neighbour that vast region which, though claimed for England by our maps and guaranteed to us by our treaties, is during a seven months' winter inaccessible to our legions, and therefore indefensible by our arms. When therefore we are told that the battalions of Great Britain are the ægis under which these unapproachable provinces propose to shelter themselves against all comers from all quarters of the compass, and that they may possibly call upon us at any moment in mid-winter, as they did three years ago, for ten or a dozen regiments to protect them from the consequences of some quarrel of our own, and when we reflect how utterly inadequate such a garrison would be, unless supported by a far more efficient local militia than is now in existence, to defend those provinces from the only enemy they fear, it is scarcely surprising that any project which may offer a prospect of escape from a political situation so undignified and unsatisfactory should be hailed with a cordial welcome by all parties concerned.

The movement which culminated last October in the Quebec Conference, and in the Resolutions which have since been reported to the Home Government, novel as it may appear to us on this side of the Atlantic, represents no novel idea to our North American colonists. The scheme of a Federal Union between the Canadas and the maritime provinces was indeed ventilated six years ago, in a correspondence between the Duke of Newcastle and the Canadian Government, but the mainspring of the Federative Movement must be sought not in any past or present impulse from Imperial authorities, but in the political circumstances, necessities, and instincts of the provinces in which it has originated. It has, in fact, grown out of the crisis or (as it has been called in Canada) the "deadlock" by which the advocates of "Representation by Population" have for

some years past persistently impeded the practical operations of every
successive government which has refused to adopt their policy. When the
Canadas, which were divided into two provinces by Pitt in 1791, were
reunited in 1840, the terms of union, so far as the electoral laws of the
colony were concerned, failed to provide for the contingency which has
since arisen of a reversal of the relative proportions of population between the two provinces. West Canada, a large portion of which was then
an unreclaimed forest, has now a population of more than a million and a
half, exceeding by five or six hundred thousand that of the Eastern Province, to which nevertheless an equal voice in the Canadian parliament is
still allotted under the Act of 1840. By the leading men of Upper Canada
this state of things has been resented as an anomaly and a grievance, and
failing to obtain redress for it, they resorted to a policy of obstruction
which has proved fatal to many measures of admitted importance to all
parties and districts in the colony. The inconvenience of this position of
affairs led, not unnaturally, those who were suffering under it to look out
for the basis of a compromise which might, at all events, afford a prospect
of the Queen's Government being successfully carried on. This required
basis has been found in the project of a British American Federation in
which "Representation by Population" should be accepted as a cardinal
principle of union.

It was, therefore, no crude or capricious fancy which brought together
the delegates from Canada, Nova Scotia, and New Brunswick, who
assembled last September in Prince Edward's Island. The preliminary
gathering at Charlotte Town had for its object to establish the basis of
those negotiations which, after a further exchange of compliments between the representatives of the contracting Powers at Halifax and at St.
John's, took the more definite and detailed form in which they are now
presented to our notice, in the Resolutions passed six weeks afterwards at
the Conference of Quebec. In this last-named conclave, composed of
accredited representatives of all political parties in the five provinces of
British North America, the various topics arising out of the project they
had taken upon themselves to discuss appear to have been handled, if we
may judge from the results before us, with earnestness, vigour, and
moderation. The hearty and almost unanimous approval with which the
Quebec programme has been greeted, both in the colonies and in this
country, disinclines us, especially pending those discussions in the Imperial Parliament, which it must of course necessitate, to dwell critically
on its details. There are, nevertheless, points directly involving Imperial
interests on which, before the Executive Government is empowered by
Parliament to take action in the matter, it seems expedient that some
expression of public opinion should be invited.

It will shorten and simplify our criticisms if we assume at the outset
that these international negotiations have been undertaken with the
deliberate and honest purpose of carrying them out to their fullest conse-

quences. Let it be taken for granted that our North American fellow-subjects are as hearty as ourselves in their devotion to our Sovereign and her empire, and that no evidence is needed to prove the preamble of their project. Dismissing, therefore, from our contemplation all the *broderies* of colonial orations, banquets, balls, *déjeûners,* and receptions, which have been festooned round the council-chamber of the North American pleni-potentiaries, let us examine for a few minutes their scheme as a dry matter of business.

Their first edition only is before us. How far it may have since been amended or revised, we do not profess to know. Any alterations it may have experienced have been probably rather in the details than in the general outlines of the plan. As to its primary objects, let the delegates speak for themselves in their six opening Resolutions, which run as follows:—

That the best interests and present and future prosperity of British North America will be promoted by a Federal Union under the Crown of Great Britain, provided such Union can be effected on principles just to the several provinces.

That in the Federation of the British North American Provinces the system of Government best adapted under existing circumstances to protect the diversified interests of the several provinces and secure efficiency, harmony, and permanency in the working of the Union would be a general Government charged with matters of common interest to the whole country, and local Governments for each of the Canadas and for the provinces of Nova Scotia, New Brunswick, and Prince Edward's Island, charged with the control of local matters in their respective sections,—provision being made for the admission into the Union, on equitable terms, of Newfoundland, the North-West Territory, British Columbia, and Vancouver.

That in framing a constitution for the general Government, the Conference, with a view to the perpetuation of our connexion with the mother-country, and to the promotion of the best interests of the people of these provinces, desire to follow the model of the British Constitution so far as our circumstances will permit.

That the executive authority or government shall be vested in the Sovereign of the United Kingdom of Great Britain and Ireland, and be administered according to the well-understood principles of the British Constitution by the Sovereign personally or by representative duly authorised.

That the Sovereign or representative of the Sovereign shall be Commander-in-Chief of the land and naval militia forces.

That there shall be a General Legislature for the Federated Provinces, composed of a Legislative Council and House of Commons.

The qualifications, powers, and number of members who are to form the two Houses of the proposed Federal Parliament are then defined. The Legislative Council is to consist of seventy-six members, to be appointed by the Crown for life, in the following proportions for each province, viz.:—Twenty-four for Upper Canada, twenty-four for Lower Canada, ten for Nova Scotia, ten for New Brunswick, four for Newfoundland, and four for Prince Edward's Island. All the members of the Legislative Council to be British subjects by birth or naturalisation, of the full age of thirty years, and possessing a property qualification of four thousand dollars.

The "House of Commons" is to consist of 194 members, to be elected for five years, under the laws now in force in the several provinces respectively; the proportion of members to be returned by each province depending on the population as shown by each decennial census. At the first election each province is to be entitled to return members in the following proportions, namely:—Upper Canada, eighty-two; Lower Canada, sixty-five; Nova Scotia, nineteen; New Brunswick, fifteen; Newfoundland, eight; and Prince Edward's Island, five. It is further provided that in all re-adjustments rendered necessary by increase of population in any province, the proportion of members to electors now fixed shall be retained.

Rep by Pop

The Legislative powers proposed to be committed to the Federal Parliament are thus set forth:—

The Federal Government shall have power to make laws for the peace, welfare, and good government of the Federated Provinces (saving the sovereignty of England), and especially laws respecting the following subjects:—
1. The public debt and property. 2. The regulation of trade and commerce. 3. The imposition or regulation of duties of Customs on imports and exports, except on exports of timber, logs, masts, spars, deals, and sawn lumber, and of coal and other minerals. 4. The imposition or regulation of Excise duties. 5. The raising of money by all or any other modes or systems of taxation. 6. The borrowing of money on the public credit. 7. Postal service. 8. Lines of steam or other ships, railways, canals, and other works, connecting any two or more of the provinces together or extending beyond the limits of any province. 9. Lines of steamships between the Federated Provinces and other countries. 10. Telegraphic communication and the incorporation of telegraph companies. 11. All such works as shall, although lynig wholly within any province, be specially declared by the Acts authorising them to be for the general advantage. 12. The Census. 13. Militia, military and naval service, and defence. 14. Beacons, buoys, and lighthouses. 15. Navigation and shipping. 16. Quarantine. 17. Sea fisheries. 18. Ferries between any province and a foreign country, or between any two provinces. 19. Currency and coinage. 20. Banking and the issue of paper money. 21. Savings-banks. 22. Weights and measures. 23. Bills of exchange and promissory notes. 24. Interest. 25. Legal tender. 26. Bankruptcy and insolvency. 27. Patents of invention and discovery. 28. Copyrights. 29. Indians and lands reserved for the Indians. 30. Naturalisation and aliens. 31. Marriage and divorce. 32. The criminal law (except the constitution of courts of criminal jurisdiction), but including the procedure on criminal matters. 33. For rendering uniform all or any of the laws relative to property and civil rights in Upper Canada, Nova Scotia, New Brunswick, Prince Edward's Island, and Newfoundland, and for rendering uniform the procedure of all or any of the courts in these provinces; but any statute for this purpose shall have no force or

authority in any province until sanctioned by the Legislature thereof. 34. The establishment of a general Court of Appeal for the Federated Provinces. 35. Immigration. 36. Agriculture. 37. And generally respecting all matters of a general character not specially and exclusively reserved for the local Governments and Legislatures.[1]

The appointment of lieutenant-governors is vested in the Federal Government, together with the control over all courts of justice and the judicial patronage of the superior courts in each province, the judges of which are to hold their offices during good behaviour, and to be removable only on the Address of both Houses of the Federal Parliament.

After providing that the local Legislature of each province shall be constituted in such manner as the existing Legislature of such province shall provide in the Act consenting to the Union, it is further resolved that the local Legislatures shall have power to make laws on the following subjects:—

Direct taxation and the imposition of duties on the export of timber, logs, masts, spars, deals, and sawn lumber, and of coals, and other minerals.

Borrowing money on the credit of the province.

The establishment and tenure of local offices, and the appointment and payment of local officers.

Education; saving the rights and privileges which the Protestant or Catholic minority in both Canadas may possess as to their denominational schools at the time when the Union goes into operation.

The sale and management of public lands, excepting lands belonging to the General Government.

Sea coast and inland fisheries.

The establishment, maintenance, and management of penitentiaries, and of public and reformatory prisons.

The establishment, maintenance, and management of hospitals, asylums, charities, and eleemosynary institutions.

Municipal institutions.

Shop, saloon, tavern, auctioneer, and other licenses.

Local works.

---

[1] This last clause is obviously very loosely expressed, for what are 'matters of a general character,' and who is to decide whether a matter which may be in dispute between the Confederation and one of its members is of a general character or not? Mr. Cardwell has wisely pointed out, in his despatch of the 3rd of December, that the success of the schemes depends on giving a preponderating authority to the Federal power: and we should prefer to the foregoing enumeration of the powers of the Federal Parliament, a simple declaration that all powers are given to it except those expressly reserved to the several members of the Confederation. In the constitution of the United States the contrary principle was adopted. All powers were reserved to the several States which were not expressly made over to the Union. We think that experience has shown this to have been one of the fatal vices of the American Constitution: and if British North America is to become a great State, we hope its citizens will profit by the mistakes of their neighbours.

The incorporation of private or local companies, except such as relate to matters assigned to the Federal Legislature.

Property and civil rights, exception those portions thereof assigned to the General Legislature.

Inflicting punishment by fine, penalties, imprisonment, or otherwise for the breach of laws passed in relation to any subject within their jurisdiction.

The administration of justice, including the constitution, maintenance, and organisation of the courts, both of civil and criminal jurisdiction, and including also the procedure in civil matters.

And generally all matters of a private or local nature.

For the presumed purpose of obviating conflicts of authority between the Federal and local Legislatures it is further provided—

That in regard to all subjects over which jurisdiction belongs to both the General and Local Governments, the laws of the Federal Parliament shall control and supresede those made by the local Legislature, and the latter shall be void so far as they are repugnant to or inconsistent with the former.

All powers of taxation are reserved to the representative branches of the Federal and local Legislatures, such imposts to be in all cases first recommended by message from the Governor-General or Lieutenant-Governor as the case may be. Any Bill of the General Legislature may be reserved for the Royal Assent, and may be disallowed by her Majesty (in accordance with the present practice) within two years. All monies and securities for money belonging to each province at the time of the Union, together with all the public works, the property of such province, shall be vested in the Confederation, which shall assume all the debts and liabilities of such province, such debts not to exceed at the time of Union certain amounts fixed by the Resolutions.

After various stipulations as to the details of Intercolonial finance, the document concludes with the following provisions:—

All engagements that may be entered into with the Imperial Government for the defence of the country shall be assumed by the Confederation.

That the Federal Government will secure without delay the Completion of the Intercolonial Railway from Rivière-du-Loup through New Brunswick to Truro, in Nova Scotia.

The communications with the North-Western Territory, and the improvements required for the development of the trade of the great west with the seaboard, are regarded by this Conference as subjects of the highest importance to the Confederation, and should be prosecuted at the earliest possible period when the state of the Federal finances will permit the Legislature to do so.

The sanction of the Imperial and local Parliaments shall be sought for the union of the provinces on the principles adopted by the Conference.

The proceedings of the Conference, when finally revised, shall be signed by the delegates, and submitted by each deputation to its own Government, and the chairman is authorized to submit a copy to the Governor-General for transmission to the Secretary of State for the Colonies.[2]

Such are the leading features of this important State Paper, which will receive, no doubt, at the hands of the Imperial Government and Parliament, the careful consideration which, without prejudging the merits of the case, it may be said unquestionably to deserve. "Will it work?" is probably the first question which the statesman will ask himself as he contemplates the various cog-wheels and contrivances of this somewhat intricate political machinery. Assuming that the inventors are not mere theorists, but practical men who have an eye to their own best interests and the social and material progress of British North America, have they presented to us a scheme which will attain the objects they have in view, and which has in it the elements of permanent success? It is said, and perhaps truly, that in adopting the image and superscription of her Majesty as the frontispiece of their first edition, the authors of this Constitution prove themselves to be wise in their generation; and whatever may be the ultimate tendencies of their project, the problems which surround it are quite sufficiently numerous and perplexing, without adding to them at starting the quadrennial election of a chief magistrate, after the fashion of their Republican neighbours. It is, moreover, an evidence alike of their foresight and their tenacity of time-honoured traditions that they should have set before themselves as their model the framework of the British Constitution. Nor is it unworthy of remark, that in a project which may be said to have grown out of what we in England have regarded as a democratic movement, namely, the claim of representation by population, nearly all the changes suggested are of a distinctly "Conservative" character. The property qualification of Legislative Councillors, which is now only temporary, is to be made continuous. Instead of being elected they are to be nominated for life.[3] Though the programme contains no specific proposition respecting the franchise, it is understood that the tendency of opinion in Canada is rather towards raising than lowering the qualification of electors. We do not hear a

---

[2] A very important question on which these papers afford no information, is that relating to the future condition of those territories and dependencies of the Crown in North America which are not included within the present boundaries of the Five Provinces. We allude more particularly to the territories now held by the Hudson's Bay Company under the Crown by charter or lease. The Crown is doubtless bound to take care that the interests of its grantees are not prejudiced by these changes; but, on the other hand, an English trading company is ill qualified to carry on the government, and provide for the defence, of a vast and inaccessible expanse of continental territory. Probably the best and most equitable solution would be the cession of the whole region to the Northern Federation for a fair indemnity; and this would lead to the execution of the great Northern Pacific Railway, under the auspices of the Federal Power.

[3] This, however, is one of the two points to which Mr. Cardwell objects on the part of the Government, because it affords no remedy for a dead-lock between the two Houses.

whisper of vote by ballot, nor is it proposed to shorten the duration of the Federal Parliaments. In order to centralise authority, and to reduce as far as may be to a municipal level the local Legislatures, "all matters of a general character" are, in addition to those enumerated in the Resolutions, placed under the control of the Federal Government; and though the distinction attempted to be drawn between general and local matters is in some respects scarcely traceable in the draught minutes of the Conference, the object they had in view is sufficiently clear and intelligible. The selection of Ottawa as a metropolis has been dictated probably by the prudent principle which is said sometimes to guide republics in their choice of presidents, and prime ministers in their choice of bishops, namely, that of neutralising formidable rivalries by doing honour to insignificance. The financial arrangements as between Canada and the maritime provinces appear to have been based on the adoption by the Federal Government of the debts and liabilities of all, and the relinquishment on the part of the local Legislatures of all their revenues, except those arising from the sale of lands, and from certain export duties, the control over which each local Government respectively retains.

The concluding Resolutions, which have reference to the completion of the Intercolonial Railway and the opening of the North-West territory, are not so much items of bargain between the delegates as a recital of their common aims and interests in the prosecution to a successful issue of these important undertakings. The former has, it is well known, been the frequent subject of negotiations between the Imperial and Colonial Governments since the days of Lord Durham, and by correspondence recently laid before Parliament its accomplishment appears to depend on the result of pending applications from the North American provinces for an Imperial guarantee, to which, however, no reference is made in the document before us. This and all the undertakings contemplated for the development of the industrial resources of British America must be regulated (as the language of the Quebec Resolutions informs us) by the state of the Federal finances.

The result of these proposals, if carried into effect, would be the creation of a new State in North America, still retaining the name of a British dependency, comprising an area about equal to that of Europe, a population of about four millions, with an aggregate revenue in sterling of about two millions and a half, a debt of about sixteen millions, and carrying on a trade (including exports, imports, and intercolonial commerce) of about twenty-eight millions sterling per annum. If we consider the relative positions of Canada and the maritime provinces—the former possessing a vast and fertile back country, but no good harbours; the latter possessing good harbours but no back country—the former an unlimited supply of cereals but few minerals; the latter an unlimited supply of iron and coal but little agricultural produce—the commercial advantages of union between states so circumstanced are too obvious to need comment. The completion of the Intercolonial Railway, and the probable annexation of the fertile portions of the great North-Western territory to the new confederation, form a portion only of the probable consequences of its formation, the benefits of which will not be limited to the colonies alone, but in which Europe and the world at large will eventually participate. When the Valley of the Saskatchewan shall have been colonised, the communications between the Red River settlement and Lake Superior completed, and the harbour of Halifax united by one continuous line of railway with the shores of Lake Huron, the three missing links between the Atlantic and Pacific Oceans will have been supplied; and a political project tending however remotely to such a consummation may well challenge the all but unanimous approval it has received from the commercial community in British North America. Politically speaking, it is equally manifest that a Confederation with an aggregate population of four millions could more cheaply and effectually provide for its civil government and for its defence, if necessary, against foreign attack or internal disturbance than the five isolated communities which it is now sought to combine. There are indeed those who, anticipating the inherent difficulties of federation, desire that more complete fusion of interests which a legislative union would effect, but (with the exception, perhaps, of Mr. Dorion, and those whose opinions he represents) the objectors to the scheme belong to a class who would go beyond the plan propounded rather than thwart it or stop short of it.

The real difficulties of the proposal consist in the due adjustment of the threefold relations between the Imperial, Federal, and Local Governments which the creation of this vast confederation will involve. The colonial combinations of which we have had experience in other parts, and at other periods of our empire, furnish few analogies for our guidance under the present peculiar conditions of the North American Colonies. The consolidation of the Windward and Leeward Islands under the Governments of Barbadoes and Antigua, which took place about thirty years ago, was an arrangement devised simply with a view to official convenience, and left untouched the constitutions of the several islands so combined. In the case of New Zealand, representative institutions were given to its six provinces, which were at the same time welded into a Federal Legislature, the Local and Federal Governments having been created simultaneously by an Act of the Imperial Parliament in 1852. The present proposals of the Quebec Conference differ, however, in some important particulars from the course actually adopted by Parliament in the case of New Zealand. The Provincial Councils of that colony, though inhibited by a restrictive clause from legislating on some twelve or thirteen interdicted topics, were in all other respects left free (subject to the royal veto) to manage their own affairs. By the British American programme, on the other hand, all matters of a general character not specifically enumerated as of local or concurrent jurisdiction, are intended to be placed under the authority of the Federal Government, and thereby the risks of conflict or attempts at "nullification" on the part of the subordinate legislatures proportionally diminished. But the chief novelty, and, we may add, difficulty, presented by the Quebec scheme is in the circumstance that now for the first time in our colonial history five provinces, in all of which "responsible government" is an established rule of administration, propose to superadd to their existing parliaments a superior and central machinery, in which the same system of government by party is to prevail under the nominal rule of the Queen's representative. It will probably be admitted by all who have watched whether with favour or disapproval the working of "responsible government" in the Colonies since its first introduction in Canada five and twenty years ago, that it is, to say the least of it, a system tending to reduce to the minimum the prerogatives of the Crown. Such a result will probably be its chief praise and justification in the estimate of those who regard the political maturity and eventual independence of our colonies as the great aim and object of Imperial policy. The practical difficulties, however, which beset the working of this critically-devised machinery were foreseen by its reputed inventor in 1839, and have since been sufficiently illustrated. Neither by Lord Sydenham, nor by his three successors, was it put in action; and it was not until Lord Elgin became Governor-General in 1847, that he commenced the process of "giving his confidence" to each Executive Council in turn, retaining at the same time, through all changes of his policy, the confidence of his sovereign.

In the Australian Colonies and New Zealand, and wherever this system has been introduced, the Imperial Government has compounded for the advantages supposed to be inherent in it by a surrender of power, and by submitting to the inconveniences of a constant change in the Governor's advisers. Whether on these terms "responsible government" is a good or bad bargain, it is too late to inquire. It rests upon the doctrine by which Adam Smith justified government by party nearly a century ago. "Men desire," he says, "to have some share in the management of public affairs chiefly on account of the importance which it gives them. It is upon the power which the greater part of the leading men of every country have of preserving or defending their respective importance that the stability and duration of every system of free government depends." Whether this doctrine was rightly or wrongly applied to Canada a quarter of a century ago, we do not pretend to decide. The practical question we have now to ask is, looking at the hitches and dead-locks to which this system seems to be liable, when applied to one colony alone, how will it work when half a dozen "responsible governments" are called upon to combine in the same confederation? Assuming even that all goes smoothly, the superaddition of a Federal Parliament to the existing institutions must, of course, increase the ordinary difficulties of constitutional government in all new countries where the supply of men uniting the

qualifications of leisure, capacity, and inclination for the task of legislation is unequal to the demand. The legislative crew of the "British North
America" will not be less (including the local councils and assemblies)
than between six and seven hundred hands, all told. Allowing for the
frequent change of officers of all ranks, the question of keeping up the
complement with so slender a political reserve to fall back upon, may be
serious. This, however, is the affair of the colonists themselves. What we
have to fear, and, if possible, to guard against, is the constant peril of a
threefold conflict of authority implied in the very existence of a federation of dependencies retaining, as now proposed, any considerable share
of intercolonial independence.

In order to illustrate our argument, let us suppose the Federation to be
established, and a dispute respecting some project of law to arise
between the Parliament of Newfoundland and the officer administering
the government of that island. The dispute (as is the tendency of colonial
quarrels) grows in the constitutional struggle, and ends in a ministerial
crisis. The Lieutenant-Governor, on appealing from his intractable senate
at St. John's to the Central Executive at Ottawa, is supported in the first
instance by the Governor-General in Council, but the Newfoundland
members of the Federal House of Commons, finding perhaps that the
question at issue is one in which the maritime provinces generally are
interested, succeed in combining their being in Canada, and the result is
a vote of censure, on the Federal Executive, and a refusal to vote the
salary of the Lieutenant-Governor on the annual estimates. Under these
circumstances the Governor-General has the option of moving with the
obedience and rapidity of a marionette, in accordance with the fluctuat-
ing will of the colonial managers who pull the wires, or he may adopt the
more dignified course of submitting the whole case to the Imperial
Government, thus involving it in an arbitration between two subordinate
Legislatures, which (however it may be conducted) must end in the
disappointment of one, and may imperil the loyalty of both.

The fact is, we may schedule as we please "local" and "general" topics
of legislation; we may define with the utmost possible distinctness the
limits of each, or the concurrent authority of both Governments; we may
equitably adjust financial liabilities, and allot to the central and provincial
authorities their respective spheres of power over future redistributions
and rearrangements; but it is on the accuracy and sharpness with which
the prerogatives of the Federal Executive are defined that the success
and permanence of a constitution, necessarily clogged with checks and
counterpoises, must eventually depend. It is hardly to be expected that
the local parliaments, with their responsible "ministers," will consent at
once to be reduced to the rank of a parochial vestry, but it is by this
process alone, and by their voluntary surrender of a very large share of
the powers now left in their hands, that we can hope for a real consolidation of the provinces of British North America. If, as has been alleged, a

Legislative Union is unattainable, because inconsistent with due securities for the rights guaranteed to the French Canadians by Treaty or by the Quebec Act, and Federation is therefore the only alternative, the vital question for the framers of this Constitution is how the inherent weakness of all Federations can in this instance be cured, and the Central Government armed with a Sovereignty which may be worthy of the name. It is the essence of all good Governments to have somewhere a true Sovereign power. A Sovereignty which ever eludes your grasp, which has no local habitation, Provincial or Imperial, is, in fact, no Government at all. Sooner or later, the shadow of authority which is reflected from an unsubstantial political idea must cease to have power among men.

It has been assumed by those who take a sanguine view of this political experiment that its authors have steered clear of the rock on which the Washington Confederacy has split. But if the weakness of the central government is the rock alluded to, we fear that unless in clear water and smooth seas the pilot who is to steer this new craft will need a more perfect chart than the Resolutions of the Quebec Conference afford, to secure him against the risks of navigation. It is true that instead of a president elected every four years you have a governor-general appointed by the Queen every six. It is true also that the area of his nominal dominion presents now no topic more formidable than the expiring jealousies of race between our French and English colonists, to imperil the harmony of the British Federation. It is true that we have also now genuine aspirations of personal devotion to the sovereign, which were wanting to those who first organised the constitutions which resulted in the declaration of independence in 1776. But it is in the rapid ratio of progress at which our colonists have advanced since that period, and in their increasing sense of capacity for self-government, that we shall find our main difficulty in stranding together the thin threads of authority, which their spontaneous loyalty compels, as it were, the sovereign of Great Britain to retain. And it is evident that if this authority or its semblance is to be continued to any purpose of advantage either to the mother-country or to the provinces themselves, it can only be by gradually municipalising the local government and concentrating authority in the newly-created Federal Parliament. In the progress through its various stages of a project to which the annals of our empire present no parallel, it is more than probable that obstacles to its success now unforeseen may here and there arise, and that the present apparent unanimity may be occasionally disturbed by sectional jealousies and controversies on points now left purposely vague and undefined. On the whole, however, contemplating the future of this vast experiment, our hopes predominate over our fears. But while in the best interests of our colonists we are inclined to augur well of this enterprise, it must be remembered that the five provinces who were represented at Quebec will not be the only parties who will be called upon to sign, seal, and deliver this international indenture. By the fourth resolution of the Conference it is provided "that the Executive Authority or Government shall be vested in the sovereign of the United Kingdom of Great Britain and Ireland, and be administered according to the well-understood principles of the British Constitution, by the sovereign personally or by representative duly authorised." In other words, the Queen is invited to retain a nominal sovereignty, entailing considerable liabilities and perils, and to accept in addition the invidious functions of an arbitrator, in the event of disputes between the associated states and the Federal authorities. Imperial England is not unaccustomed to one-sided bargains with her dependencies. The sound maxim that "whoever pays the piper should order the tune," has been generally invested in the conduct of our Colonial wars. For the most part Great Britain has taken on herself the burdens, leaving to her dependencies the privileges of freedom, and the present proposal assumes accordingly that the honour and glory of empire are a full equivalent for all its accompanying embarrassments. If the Quebec project were to be regarded as in any sense a final arrangement, and the equivalent in honour or power to be derived by the Crown from the acceptance of so perilous an authority were to be weighed in the balance with the commensurate risks, the safety and dignity of the proffered position might be very questionable; but it is impossible to regard this proposed federation in any other light than that of a transition stage to eventual independence; and in this view the precise form which Imperial sovereignty may for the time being assume because a matter of comparatively secondary importance. There are those perhaps, who, if the choice were offered to them, might prefer an hereditary vice-royalty, or an independent constitutional monarchy inaugurated under a prince of the blood-royal of England, to the republic to which they believe themselves to be drifting, and which the experience of the Federal States, already burdened by a public debt not far short of that which has been accumulated by Great Britain in two centuries, proves to be rather an expensive luxury. But even if the pageantry of a court and the dignity of a peerage could be transplanted at once to an unprepared and uncongenial soil, the success of such an experiment must depend entirely on the spontaneous unanimity with which it was demanded by the colonists themselves. And whether such a course were adopted, or the present rule through the Queen's representative continued, the subsisting relations between Great Britain and her Transatlantic provinces would remain unchanged, and the responsibilities of the former practically undiminished. For with a long land frontier line swarming with marauders—with points of possible dispute bristling on all sides—with the risk of a fleet of armed American schooners covering the Canadian lakes, when the six months' notice already given of determining our treaty engagements in this behalf shall have expired—with the San Juan question still in abeyance—with the north-west boundaries of Canada still undefined—with the vast region which lies between the Red River and the Rocky Mountains left without any government at all, unless that of the irresponsible agents of the Hudson's Bay Company, at Fort Garry, be deserving of the name—with all these elements of political difficulty hanging over our Transatlantic dependencies, this is not precisely the moment when, whatever form of government they may choose, our implied engagements for some share at least of their military defence can be abruptly terminated.

The policy of retaliation, by which it was once supposed that, in the event of an invasion of Canada, we had only to bombard an American sea-port, for every inland town in our colonies that might be sacked, is, on the report of our own military engineers, now happily impracticable. At this very time it would cost, we are informed, half a million sterling to put the citadel and works of Quebec in a complete state of defence, and recent reports ordered by the Government on the North American frontier forts prove that a much larger expenditure may be necessary. In addition to these charges an armament may be required on the Lakes. It is time, therefore, to inquire by whom these expenses are to be borne? If further fortifications are deemed requisite for the protection of our North American colonists from attacks which they, it seems, do not apprehend, they may perhaps be manned, in case of necessity, by their own militia and volunteers; but whatever progress they may make in self-defence, it can scarcely be expected that, in a country so thinly peopled, and hitherto so thriftily disposed in military matters, a sudden jump from one-seventh of the total cost of their defence, which is all they now defray, to an assumption of the whole, is very likely to take place. Nor is it probable that if any prince of the blood-royal became to-morrow the adopted sovereign of British North America, any material reduction in the Imperial garrisons in those colonies would be immediately effected. But it is not in the spirit of the economist who desires to get rid, on the best possible terms, of a profitless estate, that the Government and Parliament of England will approach this important question. They have accepted, at the instance of enlightened colonial reformers at home, a fair responsibility for the defence of their dependencies abroad from perils arising from the consequences of Imperial policy. Of that responsibility they are prepared honourably to acquit themselves, until the time shall arrive when all perils traceable to that policy shall cease to threaten the distant provinces of the British Empire.

But while voluntarily accepting the burdens inseparable from their costly and now profitless inheritance, the statesmen of England, aiming no longer, as of old, to retain in helpless minority those communities of her empire which combine the powers and qualifications of free states, hail with no feelings of apprehension or regret each symptom of nascent independence as it may disclose itself. By our past colonial policy, we have surrendered the prerogatives not less absolutely than the emoluments of empire, and their relinquishment has been based on a deliberate consideration of the best interests, both of the mother-country and her provinces. The people of England have no desire to snap asunder abruptly the slender links which still unite them with their Transatlantic fellow-subjects, or to shorten by a single hour the duration of their common citizenship. On the contrary, by strengthening the ties which still remain, they would convert into a dignified alliance an undignified, because unreal, subserviency. History has warned them that it is not by futile attempts to retain in an inglorious subjection its scattered satrapies, that the real greatness of a nation can be advanced, but rather by an attitude of watchfulness for the dawning of that inevitable day, when "the years of their apprenticeship shall have been passed, and nature shall have pronounced them free." By all the tokens of rapidly increasing material prosperity, by the still more important evidences of intellectual and political development, as manifested in the records of the recent Conference at Quebec, we are led irresistibly to the inference that this stage has been well-nigh reached in the history of our Transatlantic provinces. Hence it comes to pass that we accept, not with fear and trembling, but with unmixed joy and satisfaction, a voluntary proclamation, which, though couched in the accents of loyalty, and proffering an enduring allegiance to our Queen, falls yet more welcome on our ears as the harbinger of the future and complete independence of British North America.

2

Democracy and the Ontario Fathers of Confederation*

Bruce W. Hodgins

FOR YEARS most Canadian students were nurtured on the notion that Canadian history flowed steadily and progressively, without much internal violence, toward the problem-solving present. After the explorers and the Conquest it moved, mainly constitutionally, from dependent colony to responsible, autonomous nation, from the Constitutional Act, through responsible government and Confederation, to full autonomous "status" within a British Commonwealth of Nations which was to have a glorious future. Because Canada had full autonomy and political democracy, no current internal problems seemed insurmountable, and Canada's bravery in external war had clearly been shown. Under the old view, Confederation was a corollary of responsible government, and both were democratic victories. This simplistic viewpoint has come to be called the Whig interpretation of Canadian history.

Such self-satisfied introspection, an echo of Laurier's "The twentieth century belongs to Canada," was shattered by the postwar world's insecurity and revolution, by the increasing complexity of North American life, by renewed English-French tensions within Canada, and by basic changes in the nature of historical scholarship. Each generation must rewrite its history.

Then the euphoria of Centenary Year brought back some of the old myths. The Fathers were praised for their foresight and dedication to our freedom and to our democratic principles. In this article, Bruce Hodgins argues that in fact none of the Ontario Fathers of Confederation—and the same could be said of the other Fathers—believed in democracy. Besides, they all considered, he argues, "democracy" as a bad word.

* *Profiles of a Province,* Ontario Historical Society, 1967, pp. 83–91.

As was the general style in the Ontario Historical Society's *Profiles of a Province,* it is published without footnotes. The topic is treated rather more fully in the author's "Attitudes toward Democracy during the Confederation Decade" (Queen's University M.A. Thesis, 1955).

A TENDENCY exists, particularly in this centennial year, to extoll the Fathers of Confederation for viewpoints which they in fact never possessed. They become not only fathers of our federal union, but champions of our so-called democratic way of life. In this connection the centennial euphoria builds on a well-established myth. The traditional Grade XIII history textbook states that George Brown's Grits "demanded democratic reforms such as universal suffrage and short parliaments and the secret ballot." In reality, like all of the Ontario Fathers, Brown opposed what he called "democracy" and argued that universal suffrage was one of the two major defects in the American system.

It was therefore a welcome change when Mr. Mungo James recently wrote perceptively in *Saturday Night:*

What most middle-income Canadians comfortably forget is that this country of ours was never intended to be a just, or even a democratic society. Those colonial burghers, the Fathers of Confederation, decisively rejected universal franchise at the Quebec Conference in 1864. Many of our early laws were framed in the interest of property owners, and they've proved rigidly resistant to change.

John A. Macdonald, George Brown and the other Ontario Fathers were resourceful men of their age, but they were not democrats.

Analyzing the views of the Upper Canadian Fathers with regard to democracy presents a serious problem in semantics. The Fathers claimed to oppose democracy, but what did they mean by the word? Admittedly they meant something somewhat different from what most Canadians mean by it today. Still, they opposed not only what they understood by democracy but also what we assume in using the term.

We might define general western-style political democracy as a system of government in which the concept of equality of political rights implies the notion that the people through elective machinery determine the complexion of their government. The British and Canadian versions of this democracy imply that despite the monarchical form and the constitutional supremacy of parliament, sovereignty ultimately resides in the people. American, British and Canadian democracy rests on a faith, however qualified, in the good sense of the common man and woman in the mass; it also rests on the efficacy of the principle of majority rule. In Canada federalism and constitutional guarantees have limited both parliamentary supremacy and majority rule, majority rule is also restrained by the British traditions of fair play and individual rights that predate the achievement of modern democracy. Nevertheless, majority rule has become an organic, popular part of the Ontarian's feeling about democracy. Since Ontario has always been the most populous and wealthy unit in Canada, and since the essence of federalism is apparently not deeply understood by Ontarians, an ambivalence survives as to whether majority rule tends more toward a dominant majority-backed Ontario or toward a dominant Ontarian-led, majority-backed Canada. The attitude of Ontarians both to the province of Quebec and to French Canada, which the Commission on Bilingualism and Biculturalism euphemistically describes as a second majority, constitutes an integral part of this confusion. The ambivalence played a considerable role in the story of Confederation, even though the Ontario Fathers denounced democracy.

In the mid-1860's the province of Canada, which since 1841 had linked Upper and Lower Canada in a unitary constitution, possessed internal self-rule. It operated autonomously with what contemporaries called responsible parliamentary government. The United Province preserved and fostered duality. Canada was not, however, a democracy, and no one called it such. But the working executive was picked from groups which collectively controlled a majority of the members elected to the lower house of the legislature. The Assembly was elected by a minority of the adult males of the province, roughly those heads of households who owned reasonable homes or paid substantial rents. Between the two sections of the province equality of representation rather than representation by population was the rule, and within each section gross discrepancies in the numerical size of constituencies prevailed.

But more important than these statutory divergences from what is considered democratic was the widespread elitist view of the nature of the constitution and of the limited role given to the electorate. Both George Brown and John A. Macdonald agreed that it would be unnecessary and unwise to hold an election before the implementation of Confederation. Yet union of British North America had not been an issue in the previous election, that of 1863. The idea had, however, been vaguely bandied about for several years, and Cartier and Macdonald had in 1858 unenthusiastically accepted it as part of the Conservative platform. The election of 1863 had precariously confirmed the defender of the existing constitution, John Sandfield Macdonald, as Premier of Canada and insecure leader of a temporarily reunited Reform alliance. In Upper Canada John A. Macdonald, who was later to become in the popular mind the chief architect of Confederation, had suffered a humiliating defeat. In 1865 it was left to John Sandfield Macdonald, who was now isolated and temporarily opposed to the Quebec scheme and therefore not a Father, vainly to demand the right for an expression of the popular will on the question of fundamentally changing the constitution.

Imagine the uproar a hundred years later if something similar were perpetrated. For a long time a minority of Canadians have advocated union with the United States. Imagine the Canadian government falling through the defection of a few of its erstwhile supporters. A new coalition government is formed under the titular leadership of an ancient, revered Senator. It is made up of the leadership of the former Opposition and the largest of the three roughly identifiable groups in the former government, but excluding the former Prime Minister and many of his supporters. This government then successfully negotiates union with the United States, and with the help of the party whips, secures parliamentary approval for the plan. Without an election Canadians become Americans. It would be legal but unthinkable. It would be undemocratic.

George Brown, as leader of the Grit Reformers, the largest single Upper Canadian political bloc, has often been portrayed as a democrat. Was not this British-inspired liberal the champion of representation by population, the critic of sectarian and sectional privilege, and the opponent of slavery and primogeniture? In 1865 Brown was much more moderate than he had been in the fifties, yet in 1857 he wrote in his *Globe* that "democratic theories" were inadequate "to the wants of a mixed society," and that the broader the suffrage "the more we add to the dangerous element." The extension of the franchise, he argued, had to await the "diffusion of education" and "what a mass of ignorance is still to be encountered in every constituency!" One hundred and ten years later public opinion polls and television sampling would hardly substantiate an opinion that this ignorance has been eliminated, yet we have political democracy. Long a critic of American republicanism, Brown argued that because of democracy, the American political parties had to eschew before the public all questions of high policy in favour of cant phrases and vituperative attacks. "The balance of power," he argued, "is held by the ignorant unreasoning mass; to swing them is the grand aim of the contest and as truth, character, statesmanship, honest policy, and fair argument would be thrown away upon them, both parties by consent —nay by necessity—resort to other expedients."

For Brown, the liberal-monarchist, democracy was too closely identified with American democratic republicanism. To him it involved universal suffrage, the inordinately wide use of the elective principle, a lack of respect for authority, and a tendency for government under popular impulses to go carelessly to extremes. He saw democracy as illiberal, as a threat to individualism and free institutions, as promoting the tyranny of the unreasoning majority. Yet he saw no illiberalism either in his vehement Free Kirk opposition to separate schools for the Roman Catholic minority of Upper Canada, who regarded the religiously-centred classroom as vital to its view of life, or in his own demand for province-wide representation by population without substantial safeguards for the French Canadians of Lower Canada. His acceptance in 1858 of the idea of some internal federation for the province of Canada was partial recognition that at least for political expediency some such protection was necessary to persuade even a minority of French Canadians that representation by population could be operated with justice to all. In 1850 he violently opposed, as revolutionary and republican, the radical program of the original Clear Grits; these agrarian democrats advocated the use of "elective institutions from the head of the government downward," including elective judges and justices of the peace, universal suffrage, and fixed dates for biennial parliamentary elections. Yet at the Quebec Conference in 1864, at a time when he envisioned imminent Upper Canadian and Grit dominance of a united British America, this future champion of Ontario provincial rights urged that in the provinces centrally-appointed lieutenant governors ought normally to have the right of vetoing legislation without advice; he also argued that there ought to be a fixed term of three years for the provincial legislatures and that departmental ministers ought to be directly elected and, holding office for the three years or during pleasure, not be voting members of the legislature. Like many other mid-Victorian British liberals enamoured with the idea of laissez-faire and like that great American liberal-cum-conservative Thomas Jefferson, Brown believed in the general superiority and value of the propertied man. Like Jefferson he feared the rootless urban worker. Unlike the American aristocratic democrat and more like Alexander Hamilton, Jefferson's anti-democratic city rival, Brown saw society and politics led by the aggressive urban entrepreneur. A devotee of the dominance of the lower house of parliament through a liberal evolution of the British parliamentary system, Brown effectively argued in favour of an appointed upper house for the new union so that such a chamber might be weak. He approved of not having an upper house at all for Ontario. No democrat, either as he defined the word or as it is now envisioned, Brown still accepted much of the individualistic and egalitarian spirit of nineteenth century North America.

Two of Brown's lieutenants were also Fathers, William McDougall and Oliver Mowat. Wandering Willie McDougall, as one of the founders of the original Clear Grits and in the early 'fifties editor of the *North American*, had once been a democrat. He certainly was one no longer. From 1856 almost until Confederation, McDougall partly echoed the views of Brown. Yet in 1862, McDougall showed himself less devoted than Brown to representation by population when he entered the cabinet of Sandfield Macdonald. This regime regarded representation by population as politically and ethically undesirable at the time and claimed to be devoted to the double majority, the political dualism which was anathema to Brown. Yet McDougall remained a devotee of an elected upper house and occasionally flirted with political continentalism. Brown never fully forgave McDougall for his abandonment of principle in May, 1862—though Brown himself seems partly to have shelved representation

by population in 1859 and 1860 in favour of internal provincial federa-
tion. When McDougall declined to follow him out of the Confederation
Coalition, Brown in 1867 had both McDougall and his cohort William
Howland read out of the Reform party.

From 1862 to 1864 Oliver Mowat gradually replaced McDougall as
Brown's chief lieutanant. Yet Mowat was appointed to the bench in late
1864 and was thus out of political circulation until he became Premier of
Ontario in 1872. Mowat was later to become the very personification of
Ontario provincial rights, of so-called "Grit democracy," yet his role as a
Father was not crucial. Like McDougall he had favoured an elective
upper house, but unlike McDougall he remained dedicated to representation by population. By conviction a Liberal, he was by temperament a
conservative. Certainly during the period before Confederation he was no
democrat.

During the Confederation negotiations and afterwards, John A. Macdonald was the great centralist and the great progressive and pragmatic
conservative. As early as 1844 he had declared that he did not favour
"fruitless discussion on abstract and theoretical questions of government."
Still it fell to him to frame many of the clauses of what became the British
North America Act, and he did possess underlying philosophical concepts. Like all Conservative Fathers, he rejected both the word democracy and many of those attributes now considered essential for it. He
rejected political equality, favoured privilege for the propertied and the
well-off, and seemed more concerned about protecting the rights of the
minority than providing for majority rule. He championed the autonomy
of a monarchical British Canada and the supremacy of parliament, but he
rejected the necessary logic of representation by mere numbers and the
need and wisdom of popular appeals on matters as vital as Confederation. Such an appeal, he argued, would be the device of a tyrant, would
"subvert the principles of the British Constitution," and would be an
"obvious absurdity."

Perhaps the clearest expression of his views on popular government
came in his speech to the Quebec Conference. Advancing his centralist
arguments against the principles of divided sovereignty enshrined in the
bloodily divided United States, Macdonald argued that the provinces
should only have such powers as are absolutely necessary "for local
purposes," to enable them to legislate for "sectional prejudices and interests." "Thus we shall have," he asserted, "a strong and lasting government
under which we can work out constitutional liberty as opposed to democracy, and be able to protect the minority by having a powerful central
government." The national authority would therefore be more concerned
with protecting minority rights than with providing for Grittish majority
rule. The sovereign and her governor general, advised by a responsible
ministry, would represent the whole nation rather than the mere ephemeral majority as did the American president. But although the provinces

were not the primary protectors of minority rights, the central authority ought to use its power with caution so as not to alarm the people of any section.

Here was the essence of the anti-continentalist Macdonaldian constitution. The relationship between the centre and the provinces was more an imperial than a federal one. Macdonald did not mean it to be democratic, but it could easily and logically have evolved into political democracy.

Instead, as Professor W. L. Morton has indicated, the system was overthrown before 1900 through gross deficiencies in national sentiment and through the triumph of the very ambivalent classical federalism which Macdonald and in 1864 Brown opposed. Ironically, as Canada became more politically democratic, it also, alas, became more decentralized and divided. In this reversal the Mowat-led Ontario Grits played decisive roles. Describing the 1890's, Professor Lovell Clark has pointed out how the Orangemen of Ontario inadvertently assisted their Grit political rivals. Classical federalism and continued sectionalism, coupled with the traditional parliamentary system, later helped promote the development of the broad, amorphous majority party which emphasized national unity rather than policy. Professors John Porter and Gad Horowitz have shown how this system of brokerage politics worked against political creativity and advances toward a more democratic society.

Like Brown, Macdonald favoured an appointive upper house. But though secondary to the lower house and though based on equal representation for each section (not province), it was to play a more significant role than Brown envisioned. It was to be an appropriate North American version of the House of Lords. With a materially restrictive qualification for membership, it would represent the principle of property. "The rights of the minority ought to be protected," he argued, "and the rich are always fewer in number than the poor." Such an upper house would provide "a sober second thought," even though in North America its members would necessarily be persons "springing from the people."

During the Confederation debates Macdonald argued that no one at the Quebec Conference had favoured universal suffrage, "that classes and property should be represented as well as numbers." As late as 1889, when alarmed by surging democracy and American ideas, he urged greater influence for the "monarchical idea . . . accompanied by some gradation of classes." During the election campaign of 1861, he wrote to a sympathetic Dr. Egerton Ryerson, who shared many of Macdonald's views including his distrust of Brown, that the outcome might decide whether Canada was to be "a limited Constitutional Monarchy or a Yankee Democracy." Confederation for Macdonald and others was certainly not directed against Britain. The Quebec scheme involved a deliberate attempt to establish a union with a constitution similar in principle to that of Great Britain. It involved an attempt by British American leaders to create a viable, legitimate nation apart and different from the revolutionary, republican and aggressively democratic nation to the south. In the United States democracy had allegedly resulted in a lack of moral force, in a weakening of the sense of authority and responsibility, and in government by faction. Macdonald thus disagreed most emphatically with Goldwin Smith, then of Oxford University, who in 1863 wrote: "It would seem that if Canadian monarchy differs from American democracy as painted by its worst enemies, it is only as the Irishman's ride in a sedan chair with the bottom out differed from common walking." To Macdonald democracy was unconservative, illiberal, republican and dangerous; in a phrase, it was un-British and hence un-Canadian.

Alexander Galt and T. D. McGee of Lower Canada were both more important as spokesmen for the English-Canadian Liberal Conservatives than was the other Upper Canadian Conservative, Councillor Alexander Campbell. Both Galt and McGee shared Macdonald's distrust of democracy, but Galt was considerably less anti-American and McGee was more poetic in his Canadian nationalism. During the Confederation debates, Campbell emphasized that Confederation would save a monarchical Canada from undesirable republicanism. For Campbell an appointive upper house, "conservative, calm, considerate and watchful," would check democratic tendencies not calculated "to advance the common weal."

Were there then no democrats in Upper Canada a hundred years ago? A few existed, but they had little voice in parliament. John Sandfield Macdonald of Cornwall, the titular Leader of the Opposition during the Confederation negotiations, was somewhat nearer to democracy and more North American than George Brown, his rival and fellow Reformer. A liberal or nominal Catholic who, unlike his more famous namesake or Brown, was a native Upper Canadian, Sandfield came from the undifferentiated rural masses. Although he became a most wealthy real estate lawyer and frequent backer of the promotional schemes of his entrepreneurial brothers, he never lost or ceased to use his identification with the humble folk. He has often been called a "moderate Reformer" or a "conservative Reformer" because of his opposition to Brown's Upper Canadian intransigence and because of his many French Canadian friendships. Sandfield was "moderate" in the sense that more than Brown he advocated institutional tolerance, respect for French Canadian culture, and the preservation of the organic unity of the province of Canada. He called himself a "Baldwinite" or a "Baldwin Reformer" and opposed the dogmatism and sectionalism of the Grits. Although he favoured a broad, more pragmatic Reform party, he stood to the left of Brown on most political and social matters. His advocacy of the double majority, though probably as impractical as the Southerner J. C. Calhoun's contemporary advocacy of concurrent majorities, was a faulty attempt to preserve the unity of the whole and recognize the duality of Canadian culture.

He saw in Confederation the shattering of the unity of the St. Lawrence and the Ottawa valleys, the deflection of what became eastern Ontario from its natural entrepot of Montreal in favour of the Grit and Orange-dominated west. He saw Confederation as the antithesis of retrenchment and as an unfair British device to persuade Canadians to assume a "larger burden for the defence of this country than was justified," when already it was overspending and when the now declining American threat to it stemmed primarily from its membership in the British Empire. Confederation's implementation violated the sacred rights of the people. He hailed the first New Brunswick election and its results, arguing that if its people were then "bribed" into submission, they would be unworthy of association and of being "of the race of British freeman." Although he did not always practise what he preached, he argued that in Canada the electors and not the members of parliament were supreme. Members represented their constituents, not themselves, and they had no right on their own to petition the British authorities "to destroy the constitution." Still his career hardly qualifies him as a democrat.

The radical Clear Grit movement of 1850 had had a democratic platform, an amalgam of North American agrarian democratic ideas, English chartist democracy and the old fulminations of W. L. Mackenzie. Although the sentiments survived, the movement had after 1854 been captured by Brownite metropolitan liberalism. The Clear Grit viewpoint found temporary expression in the popular utterances of the phlegmatic and demagogic George Shephard, in the *Globe* in early 1859 and at the Great Reform Convention in late 1859 where he probably expressed the attitude of a vast majority of the Grits. During the Confederation debates, it was largely without a significant spokesman. In the Assembly Joseph Rymal and in the Council James Currie and David Reesor probably represented the old viewpoint. Relatively unknown, they opposed Confederation. Yet urbanized and made more respectable and less American, this viewpoint would in future under Mowat promote Grit democracy and Ontario provincial rights. It was surely more than coincidental that Mathew Crooks Cameron, the only Ontario Conservative assemblyman to oppose Confederation, a man who vehemently denounced Brown though he favoured representation by population, a man of bitter Orange prejudices, expressed similar sentiments to those of the old Clear Grits.

The largest, most articulate and intellectual group of "democrats" in the Canadian provincial parliament were not Ontarians. They were the anti-clerical *Rouge* oppositionists from the Montreal area led by A. A. Dorion. Although decentralist and sometimes narrowly nationalistic, their criticism of Cartier and the scheme of union was often most perceptive. On the road to transformation or oblivion, in the face of increasing attacks from an increasingly ultramontane and anti-liberal and powerful Church, the *Rouges* were largely dismissed. When decades later they achieved respectability under the Gladstonian Laurier much of their constructive uniqueness, but not their decentralism, would have disappeared. Cleansed of free thought and of social democracy, they would prove fitting allies of Mowat's Grits, and unwitting supporters of Ontario Orangemen in the destruction of the Macdonaldian constitution.

Of all the colonial and British architects of Confederation, the Ontarians were most significant in establishing the governmental framework of our country. The five Ontarians were worthy Fathers of Confederation. They were not fathers of Canadian democracy.

BIBLIOGRAPHICAL NOTE

The chief primary sources for this study are the personal papers of the Fathers of Confederation and their correspondents, found mainly in the Public Archives of Canada, and also in the crucial Upper Canadian newspapers of the day. In this connection the Macdonald Papers, the Brown Papers, the Alexander Mackenzie Papers and the Toronto *Globe* are central. Also useful are the John Sandfield Macdonald Papers. The study could not be undertaken without a careful reading of the *Parliamentary Debates on the Confederation of the British North American Provinces* (Quebec, 1865; Ottawa, 1951) in the Canadian Legislature in February and March, 1865.

What follows is a short list of some of the principle secondary sources:

Careless, J. M. S., *Brown of the "Globe"* (2 vols., Toronto, 1959–63).

Cornell, P. G., *The Alignment of Political Groups in Canada, 1841–1867* (Toronto, 1962).

———, *The Great Coalition: June 1864*, Canadian Historical Association, Historical Booklets, no. 19 (Ottawa, 1966).

Creighton, D. G., *John A. Macdonald: The Young Politician* (Toronto, 1955).

Hodgins, Bruce W., "Attitudes toward Democracy during the Pre-Confederation Decade," unpublished Master's thesis, Queen's University, 1955.

———, *John Sandfield Macdonald—1812–1872* (Toronto, 1971).

———, "The Political Career of John Sandfield Macdonald to the Fall of His Administration in March, 1864: A Study in Canadian Politics," unpublished Ph.D. dissertation, Duke University, Durham, N.C., 1964.

———, and Jones, E. H., "A Letter on the Reform Party, 1860: Sandfield Macdonald and the *London Free Press*," *Ontario History*, LVII (1965), pp. 39–46.

Lower, A. R. M., "The Origins of Democracy in Canada," Canadian Historical Association, *Report*, 1930 (Ottawa, 1930), pp. 65–70.

Morton, W. L., "The Conservative Principle in Confederation," *Queen's Quarterly*, LXXI (1964), pp. 528–46.

Pope, Joseph, ed., *Confederation: Being a Series of Hitherto Unpublished Documents Bearing on the British North America Act* (Toronto, 1895).

Waite, P. B., *The Charlottetown Conference,* Canadian Historical Association, Historical Booklets, no. 15 (Ottawa, 1963).

————, *The Life and Times of Confederation: 1864–1867: Politics, Newspapers, and the Union of British North America* (Toronto, 1962).

Walker, Franklin A., *Catholic Education and Politics in Upper Canada: A Study of the Documentation Relative to the Origin of Catholic Elementary Schools in the Ontario School System* (Toronto, 1955).

Wise, S. F. and Brown, R. C., *Canada Views the United States: 19th Century Political Attitudes* (Seattle, 1967).

3

The Conservative
Principle in Confederation*†

W. L. Morton

*The conservative principle . . . is the assertion that the chief
political good is stability, the existence of order in the state and
society. The order intended, however, is not order imposed by
authority from without, but order arising from equilibrium
reached among the elements of society by usage, tradition and
law.*

IN THIS THOUGHTFUL article by one of Canada's senior
historians is found clear expression of the antithesis of the Whig or liberal
version of Canadian history. "Thus," asserts W. L. Morton, "it was not by
chance the conservative principle was the creator of the Confederation
of 1867, while the progressive principle was the undoer of that work, and
the inspirer of the loose style of federation that has prevailed since 1896."
Professor Morton here introduces the seminal concept which many other
historians have now accepted, many of whom would reject his own deep
conservatism. He argues that post-1867 Canada has in fact lived under
two constitutional systems, the conservative one which, emphasizing the
central power, stressed the unity of the whole and the "progressive" or
liberal one which emphasizes provincial rights. The watershed then is the
"disaster" of 1896, the triumph of Laurier Liberalism through the transfer
of much of the *Bleu* bloc (that dominant French-Canadian political force
which Cartier had once led) from the Conservative to the Liberal party.
Professor Morton also describes the undigestible nature of the surviving

* *Queen's Quarterly*, LXXI (Winter, 1965), pp. 528–546.

† A paper prepared for The National Conference on Canadian Goals, sponsored by
the Progressive Conservative Association of Canada, Fredericton, September 9th–12th,
1964.

French-Canadian Conservatives—people who are more often than not Ultramontanists.

While accepting much of the analysis, critics of this article have pointed out that confusion still exists between the "conservative principle" and the Conservative party. If the Whig historians tended to see Liberal Reformers as progressives and therefore "good," Professor Morton tends to see them as "bad." Some critics are also concerned with the extreme identification of the conservative principle with the unity of the whole. They fault his analysis for allegedly underestimating the importance of the divisive role of the Orange tradition in the Canadian Conservative party. Furthermore, in England and Europe, conservative forces were often noted for their resistance to the progressive centralizing of state power, and certainly American conservatism (which Professor Morton would call conservative liberalism) is identified with states rights. As Professor Don Smiley, himself a conservative thinker, has asserted (*The Canadian Political Nationality,* Toronto, 1967) centralism of a sort reached its peak under the Liberals, W. L. M. King and St. Laurent. During this latter era it was the CCF party on the left and not the Conservatives on the right that called for more concerted national action.

T HIS CONFERENCE is, I believe, a large body of uncertainty totally surrounded by question marks. Such at least the modest professions of its promoters lead one to believe. If that is so, what is needed is definition. And, lest the title of my paper should confound confusion, I hasten to attempt some definition.

I DEFINITION OF TOPIC

First please observe that it speaks of the conservative principle in Confederation; not Conservatism, nor Conservatives, nor the Conservative Party. As a matter of fact, it is quite possible to discuss the conservative principle without any reference to any or all of the three, Conservatism, Conservatives and the Conservative Party. That, by and large, is what I will do. But I shall do so in the supposition that the conservative principle may be of interest to a gathering of conservatively-minded people.

For the limited purposes of this paper, it is assumed that there may reasonably be said to be two chief and contrasting principles of political thought and action. One is the conservative principle, the other is the progressive principle. The former seeks stability as the chief political good; the latter seeks change as leading to an increase of political good. The two are in contrast, but not necessarily in opposition. At low temperature, to speak in the language of chemistry, they may go very well together, and even be harnessed by a hyphen. But at high temperature the conservative principle leads to reaction, the attempt to reverse change; and the progressive leads to anarchy, the attempt to make change incessant.

The conservative principle, then, is the assertion that the chief political good is stability, the existence of order in the state and society. The order intended, however, is not order imposed by authority from without, but order arising from equilibrium reached among the elements of society by usage, tradition and law. It is what the philosophers call an organic order, not an order mechanically contrived, but one resulting from growth from within.

Now such an order in an actually living organism or, metaphorically, in a living society results in two characteristics. One is unity, the other is wholeness. A tree, for example, lives only as one tree; branches pruned away die; and if the trunk is chopped through, the tree dies. Similarly, a society exists by means of the ligaments of language, custom, belief, law, neighbourhood. If its people should be dispersed, the society dies. What then would conserve society, the conservative principle, is the principle of the unity of a society as a whole. It is concerned with every part, with every individual element, and with the relationship of each to every other part.

It is therefore concern with the orderly unity of the parts of Canada with one another in an harmonious whole of Canada that is the conservative principle in Confederation.

II   THE HISTORICAL ORIGINS OF THE PRINCIPLE IN CANADA

So much for abstract definition. (I can only hope that the dryness of the exercise has increased your thirst for what is to follow.) Among the lands, colonies and people now called Canada, the conservative principle had, of course, actual historical origins. It came into being in actual circumstance, event and action, as a result of man's business and concern. In French Canada, for example, for all the influence of the wilderness and the Indian trade, society was profoundly orderly and conservative. A paternal authority in government, an exclusive and pervasive church, a strong tradition of paternal and masculine authority in the family and society, these were the origins of conservative principle in French society, a conservatism challenged but not really shaken until our own day.

The power of the conservative principle in French society was, if anything, intensified by the most revolutionary event of French Canadian history, the cession of New France to the United Kingdom in 1763. Not only were almost all the lay élite of New France, the traders, the soldiers, the engineers, lost to Canada; but social leadership fell almost entirely to the clergy. With their emphasis on the conservation of the faith and customs it had engendered came an inevitable emphasis on the preservation of existing rights from the hostility, or the indifference, of the conqueror. From the capitulations of Quebec and Montreal through the Treaty of Paris to the Quebec Act, the French concern was to win the recognition of existing rights, their property, their civil law, their faith, their language. These all came to be recognized and were in fact guaranteed by the conqueror. Thus one of the two main pillars of the conservative principle in Canada arose out of the conservative character of French colonial society as intensified by the conquest and its aftermath.

To this recognition of established rights in Canada there was added, as one consequence of the disruption of the first British Empire in the American Revolution, the loyalist concept of a community of allegiance. The loyalists, although called Tory by their opponents, were for the most part not less American nor less Whiggish than their compatriots who revolted. The difference between them, the rebel and the loyalist, was that one placed first in loyalty his American home with its peculiar local ties, the other the whole British community in Britain and America with its single allegiance. The loyalists saw no incompatibility between local liberty and a general imperial government, and the most thoughtful of them strove steadily to plan and implement a federal union of the colonies in union with the crown of Great Britain. It is from this line of thought, particularly as developed by William Smith, lawyer and judge in New York, and then Chief Justice of Quebec in his loyalist exile that the concept of a federation of British North America developed.

Established right, common allegiance—these were the two chief origins of the conservative principle in Canada. There was yet a third. That was the old British and old American tradition—at bottom a legal necessity—that government must be representative of the respectable elements of society, financed by money freely voted, and conducted according to known and established law. Such government had been given the American colonies from almost the first. This local self-government was no partisan matter. It was as taken for granted by Tory as by Whig. The party quarrels that were to arise were always over the conventions or the degree of self-government, never over whether there should be self-government in a community of any size. Thus the colony of Nova Scotia was as self-governing as any American state that revolted; so was loyalist New Brunswick when it was established. Indeed, the founders of New Brunswick set up very much the same kind of government as they had known before their exile.

Finally, with self-government went diversity, and in the great distances of British North America there was dispersion. The loyalists had struggled with the results of these factors of origin and distance, and they remained active in British North America after 1783, being in fact a fourth element in the conservative principle, not an element necessary to the principle, but one it had to take into account in Canada. Over the years after the ending of the War of Independence, the old colonies and the two new that sprang directly from the Revolution, New Brunswick and Upper Canada, the concept of a community of common allegiance had to become the concept of common allegiance in diversity and dispersion.

This ready and instinctive recognition of self-government in almost any colony created yet another bond of unity to strengthen that of allegiance. That was the bond of common institutions. All the British American colonies, except Lower Canada, possessed the Common Law. All enjoyed the right to trial by jury and to *habeas corpus*. All possessed representative assemblies elected on a property franchise which excluded practically no landowner. These bodies possessed in part, and to an increasing degree after 1815, control of the public expenditures.

In all this they were very like the old American colonies, but in one thing they were unlike, particularly Lower Canada and Nova Scotia, in that they did not control the local executive, the governor. They might, of course, because of identity of views, or because he chose to work with and through local people. They could not, however, affect his policies in administration if he chose to be independent of them. They did not appoint him, they could rarely obtain his recall, and they did not vote his salary.

As population increased after 1815, and as liberal ideas of popular participation in government became more general, the constitutions of the various British colonies in North America came under attack as being insufficiently responsive to popular opinion. This they undoubtedly were, but not because they were, or were designed to be, tyrannical. They were simply old-fashioned governments, in which the people's representatives were expected to share the governing of the colony with the governor and his advisors and assistants, whose job it was to carry on the routine administration.

This was a smug, yet within its limits, an admirable mode of government. But it made no provision for three things. One was that any degree of self-government creates a sense of common interest and a desire to implement it. In Lower Canada this sense had made articulate the sense of nationality in French Canada that was evident even before 1763. The second was reform, the beginning of the steady, annual flow of legislation to change the law and society which began with the industrialization and democratization of life in the last century. The third was party government, the carrying of, or the resistance to reform, by organized public opinion, that is, by party in our present sense.

Out of the needs caused by these lacks came what was called responsible government. That meant two things: first, that all decisions on Canadian matters were taken by Canadian governments, except with respect to the constitutions of the colonies, or to external affairs; and second, the conduct of parliamentary government by means of organized parties. This great change took a whole generation to complete, from roughly 1830 to 1860. When it was completed, the United Kingdom had withdrawn from matters of domestic concern in the colonies in North America, and had done so by reorganizing the old colonial constitutions along British parliamentary lines as practised in England since the Younger Pitt.

What part did the conservative principle play in these great and semi-revolutionary changes? Many actual Conservatives like Archdeacon John Strachan, and even men not professing conservatism like Egerton Ryerson, while welcoming much of the change, opposed it in its final sense of a transfer of power in domestic matters to an administration based on party. But the younger Tories, men like Henry Sherwood and John A. Macdonald, were quick to see that actually the change was a profoundly conservative one, because it gave the colonies the substance of the existing British constitution in place of the old colonial one of the colonial American model. They became the rising leaders of a conservative party that had come to terms with change in a society that was being transformed by the rise of modern industry. Change, they said in the words of Peel, was to be welcomed when the need for it was proved. Any Tory, that is, might properly welcome organic change, might welcome growth from established roots. Change for the sake of theory, or benevolence, or aspiration was quite another matter. Thus the old Tory compact, when it had made its last protest in the Rebellion Losses affair, became a modern parliamentary party in search of a majority. The conservative principle, they had realized, was in fact a fundamental part of the change from colonial to responsible government. It had given British North America British institutions of the latest model when it might have sought American ones.

In the Maritime provinces the result was the invigoration of long-established local democracies. It was indeed difficult to maintain the full conventions of parliamentary government in those small societies; it was difficult even to maintain parties. In New Brunswick, indeed, party as such had practically disappeared by the late 1850's, and government had fallen to a well-organized group of local politicians, happily known as Smashers, and fortunately led by a temperate and able politician, Samuel Leonard Tilley.

In the Canadas, however, society and parliament were larger and more complex. The inherent conservatism of French Canada had ceased to affect French Canadian politics from about 1834. The more articulate French politician, resentful of the snail-like pace of change, began to murmur and then orate in the accents of rebellion. The political voice of the French seemed to be that of Louis-Joseph Papineau and his ardent young followers, mostly not from Quebec and the conservative east, but from Montreal and the western parishes. (As so often in reading Canadian history, one is reminded of today.) Separatism at that time led to the rebellions of 1837 and 1838.

Radical solutions thus became impossible in Lower Canada, but French nationalism remained. It was organized by Louis-Hypolyte Lafontaine, a liberal as all young Frenchmen were, but a liberal who had parted company with Papineau, and now joined Robert Baldwin to seek a majority in the Parliament of the Union. The following of conservative liberals he formed remained in being, and became the cornerstone of almost every succeeding government of Canada down to 1891. French nationalism in the majority chose for fifty years to be liberal conservative. That is, it came to terms with English material development—Cartier was the greatest of the railway politicians—but it used its power to conserve the character and institutions of French society. When it carried a reform in the abolition of seignorial tenure, it did it conservatively with full care of property rights lest its opponents should do it radically.

You will recall that reform was carried, along with the abolition of the Clergy Reserves, by a coalition of Lafontaine's following headed by A. N. Morin with the Conservative Party headed by Sir Allan MacNab, soon to be succeeded by John A. Macdonald. Thus, two of the greatest reforms of the century, ending years of bitter controversy, were carried by a liberal conservative coalition. Canadian society was realizing itself through the conservative principle.

This alliance of the French liberal conservatives—called the Bleus—with the English conservative liberals who had followed Robert Baldwin and Francis Hincks and the liberal conservatives who followed Macdonald, were faced in Lower Canada by radicals called the Rouges, and in Upper Canada by another set of radicals called the Clear Grits. Both were aggressively democratic; both embodied the progressive principle in its most democratic guise; neither was capable of winning a majority in its section, or of combining readily with other groups. Like minor opposition parties in Canada since, they had many merits and were fertile in ideas, but the electorate refused to entrust them with power, at least to any degree, or for any length of time.

III THE EXPRESSION OF THE CONSERVATIVE PRINCIPLE IN CONFEDERATION

The conservative principle thus seemed to flourish in Canada before Confederation. A union, a whole of considerable proportions, a community of considerable dispersion and diversity, existed and functioned. Yet change of the greatest magnitude, change comparable with the contemporary unification of Germany and Italy and the re-unification of the United States, was forcing itself on men and events. The main causes of change were four: the growth of separatism in Upper Canada in order to win control of its domestic affairs; a need for economic expansion felt throughout every province and class of British North America; the need for defence against a possible American attack arising out of its Civil War; the desire in the wake of British military withdrawal from Canada to preserve established institutions. With the first, separatism, the adherents of the conservative principle had trouble in coming to terms, for an emphasis on local rights always threatens the unity of the whole. But with the other three it was in full accord. The upholders of the progressive principle, for their part, accepted the second, were indeed its first advocates, but they questioned the need of defence and were not unwilling to modify existing institutions.

The political problem, then, was how to meet the above needs in some adequate way in a country as deeply and evenly divided then as it is today among the main parties and two lesser ones. It was solved, you will remember, by coalition, and Confederation was planned and carried by coalition, or co-operation, of the two main parties in each of the original provinces of British North America.

IV THE EMPHASIS ON THE UNITY
OF THE WHOLE

It can, I think, be said in all objectivity that in that solution the conservative principle prevailed. It did so by making two great and wise concessions to its great competitor, one wholly, one almost, forgotten for what it was. George Brown, the chief Liberal and the chief architect of Confederation after Macdonald, insisted on the retention of his idea of a federation of the Canadas as an alternative to the confederation of all British North America, and on the separation of the Canadas as provinces within Confederation. The first never had to be resorted to; the second was taken for granted, for all the difficulty it gave rise to in the matter of education and minority rights.

Yet, if there was division at the heart of Confederation as a necessary concession to diversity, and if there always has existed, before 1867 and since, an alternative to Confederation in the shape of a loose federal union, Confederation itself was a triumphant assertion of the principle of the unity of the whole. One may quickly recite the instances of this: the maintenance of the Crown and common allegiance, with the legislative sovereignty of Parliament and the rule of law rather than popular will; the reservation of residual jurisdiction to the general government; the retention for the general government of the imperial power of disallowing any provincial act; the choice of the general parliament as the final guardian of minority rights in education in Section 93 of the BNA Act; the limited and exclusive powers assigned to the provinces; the specific, if limited, rights of the French language and law in the Province of Quebec and the Federal Parliament and Courts. In these things, after political debates and conferences of the most searching kind, the conservative principle by wise accommodation and a wise firmness restrained the tendency of the progressive principle to subordinate the whole to the urgent will of the parts. The separation of the Canadas was contained in the union of all British North America.

V THE RISE OF THE COUNTER PRINCIPLE

If Confederation itself was in 1867 a triumph for the conservative principle, it is not to be inferred that that principle was to go on in unbroken victory. Further victories it was to have, of course; the territorial completion of union; the implementation of the National Policy; the building of the Canadian Pacific Railway; the great victory of the federal power over the provincial in *Russell vs the Queen* in 1882. The very next year, however, saw the beginning of a counter-trend in *Hodge vs the Queen,* in which "provincial rights" began to prevail over federal powers.

There is, of course, no necessary connection between the progressive principle and provincial rights any more than there is between the conservative principle and federal powers. As a matter of practical development, however, there has been a logical connection in Canadian history. Just as the conservative principle, with its concern for the unity of the whole finds in the federal power the most apt and congenial agent for its object, so in the direct intensity of local democracy the progressive principle finds the appropriate agent for its peculiar concern with the claims of the individual in a society regarded as a convenience for the realization of individual aims. Thus, it was not by chance the conservative principle was the creator of the Confederation of 1867, while the progressive principle was the undoer of that work, and the inspirer of the looser style of federation that has prevailed since 1896.

The doctrine of provincial rights, as hinted above, was of course inherent in the progressive principle, and particularly in its extremer exponents, the Clear Grits and the Rouges. Both had remained opponents or at least critics of the Confederation of 1867; both influenced and even inspired the Liberal Party that was formed after that date. The groundwork for the rise of the doctrine was also laid, as may now be seen, in the leaving of the field of education and the form of responsible government to the provinces. Each could become little cultural societies, if not political nations. And in the field of jurisdiction a series of decisions of the Judicial Committee of the Privy Council, from *Hodge vs the Queen* in 1883 to the *Liquidation of the Maritime Bank vs the Attorney-General of New Brunswick* in 1892, clarified provincial powers, and finally declared the provinces sovereign within their own jurisdictions. This rise of provincial sovereignty, never admitted in Confederation, meant that popular localism, inspired by the progressive principle, was prevailing over the organic whole that was the aim of the conservative principle.

Even more important, perhaps, if less studied and much less well known, was the rise of a new kind of nationalism in French Canada. The nationalism of Papineau and the Rouges, as of Cartier and the Bleus, was a rational and democratic nationalism, sprung from the Rationalism of the eighteenth century and the French Revolution. The essential difference was that the Rouges were anti-clerical and the Bleus were not. As a result of the reaction against the French Revolution and the liberalism and nationalism of the nineteenth century, however, a new kind of nationalism had evolved in Europe and was transmitted to French Canada. It was a Catholic and clerical nationalism, profoundly conservative and anti-liberal and familial if not racial in temper. It was the child of the theological temper called ultramontane, the temper that emphasized the church and the family as against the state and the individual.

This temper came to dominate the archbishopric of Montreal and the bishopric of Trois-Rivières in the persons of Archbishop Ignace Bourget and Bishop Louis Laflèche. They clashed with the Rouges and the Institut Canadien on account of their anti-clericalism, a clash that resulted in the Guibord affair in 1869. But Confederation as an alleged attack on French Canadian nationalism and the Red River Rebellion began to bring these two extremes of anti-clerical nationalism and ultramontane nationalism together, against not only the English but also against the Bleus. The Saskatchewan Rebellion and the execution of Riel completed the alliance of the incompatibles, and the result was the nationalist government of Honoré Mercier in 1888, the forerunner of the Union Nationale in our day.

Mercier's government caused, particularly by its legislation on the Jesuit Estates, harmless as that now seems, the reaction that produced the Protestant Protective Association and the abolition of the denominational schools system in Manitoba. The result was an appeal to the Federal Government by the Catholic minority for redress of an alleged constitutional wrong. The Manitoba Schools Act of 1890 thus raised explicitly the relationship of provincial rights and federal power, and led directly to the great victory of the progressive principle over the conservative, the weakening of national power in Canada and the long predominance of the Liberal Party over the Conservative. With this crisis of 1890–96, the crux of this paper is reached.

VI THE COLLAPSE OF THE COUNTER PRINCIPLE

That crisis may be seen now as a conflict of principle. At the time it was a conflict of party and of personality, the in-fighting of actual men and events. Macdonald had barely carried the election in 1891, and had then died. His death precipitated uncertainty in the party's leadership. His Quebec lieutenant, Hector-Louis Langevin, had just been discredited by scandal. The party refused to call a much abler, but less well established French politician, Adolph Chapleau, to the leadership. It was equally impossible to call on the ablest of the younger English Conservatives, for he, Dalton McCarthy, was leading the anti-Catholic crusade that had resulted in the Manitoba Schools Act. The gifted compromise leader, Sir John Thompson, died in office. Thus the party was uncertain and divided for five years as it sought to retain its following in Quebec while not losing support in the rest of the country.

As so often, Quebec was the key to the political fetter. The long alliance of the Bleus of Quebec with the Conservatives of Ontario was ending. It was partly the result of the failure of the party to accept Chapleau as Quebec leader, on his terms, as the leader in succession to Langevin, or to find some one to challenge Chapleau. But it was more that the Bleus, worked on by Israël Tarte, a Bleu who had joined the Liberals, saw a better hope of facing the ultra-nationalism of Mercier by alliance with the Liberals rather than the Conservatives. What made such an alliance possible was the personality of Wilfrid Laurier, who had made Liberalism a respectable creed in Quebec by claiming it was of British and not of European inspiration, and who had become leader of the federal Liberal Party in 1888. His handling of the Manitoba Schools Question by supporting the legislation, but urging that the Manitoba Government be urged to compromise with Roman Catholic demands, made it possible for the Bleus to see a way to support provincial rights, a doctrine Mercier had made popular in Quebec, without abandoning their co-religionists and compatriots in Manitoba. Thus the way was cleared for the Liberals, who had carried half the seats in Quebec in 1891, to carry 49 out of 65 in 1896. (This shift of seventeen constituencies has been the cornerstone of Liberal power in Canada ever since.)

The shift meant infinitely more, however, than a party victory. It meant, first, that the attempt of the Conservative administration to obtain redress for those who lost their denominational schools in Manitoba by means of remedial legislation under Section 93 of the BNA Act had been defeated, by filibuster in Parliament and by loss of the general election. The conservative principle with its concern for the unity of the whole, and its use of the federal power to guarantee minority rights for the welfare of the whole, was thus crushingly defeated. The basic concept of the Confederation of 1867, moreover, that the central government was supreme and as such the guarantor of the welfare of the whole country, was impaired almost to the point of descruction. The constitution, as a result of this and the preceding changes touched on above, has been very different from its original substance in 1867. And, second, it meant that the Conservative Party, having lost its Bleu allies in Quebec, had to turn to the ultramontane, A. R. Angers, in 1895, and thereafter to a long line of equally ineffectual and unreliable leaders not terminated until the rise of Léon Balcer. The character of ultramontane conservatism, however, clerical, ultra-catholic, racially nationalist, made it an impossible ally for a party that sought to realize the principle of the unity of the whole.

VII   THE CHARACTER OF LAURIER LIBERALISM

This defeat of the conservative principle and crippling loss inflicted on the Conservative Party were intensified by the characteristics of Laurier liberalism.

The first was that the Liberal Party had itself become a national party to a degree it had not before reached since Confederation. With provincial rights satisfied for the time being, with policies alleged to point to annexation repudiated, Laurier and his colleagues saw fit to adopt the National Party with modifications, and to become the heirs of the Conservative Party as the promoters of national growth. At the same time, they did not repudiate their essential inheritance of individual right and local democracy. In some way yet to be traced, they found in a word Laurier used in Parliament as early, I believe, as 1893 a way of reconciling local democracy with parliamentary, indeed of re-shaping parliamentary government to make it more responsive to local democracy. That word was "mandate," the idea that the electorate when consulted gave instructions to their members, which, when interpreted by the winning party, became the policy of the government of the day. This in many ways was a revival of old Rouge and Grit doctrine, and the revival was fortified by the use of the practice in Swiss democracy and of the word in the great political struggle in the United Kingdom from 1905–1914. In the mouth of Mackenzie King, the word was to come to mean that the Prime Minister's interpretation of the results of the last election constituted an order from the sovereign people to a once sovereign parliament. Here was yet another victory for the progressive principle, one that could be used against the federal power once provincial administration began to receive mandates from sovereign political electorates, as Mr. Lesage has demonstrated.

This was in its turn the triumph of the progressive principle, the triumph of which the seeds lay in the Rouges and the Grits and of which the advent had been preparing since at least 1883, and perhaps since 1871 when the program of the ultra-French nationalists first appeared. Yet that same nationalism was not appeased by the triumph of the progressive principle. That was, after all, only a semi-triumph. The Liberal Party under Laurier was in its own way a vehicle of political nationalism; in its own way, and even if it had greatly increased the difficulty of success, it too was concerned with the unity of the whole. French nationalists might differ as to what was the whole: all Canada, French Canada, or the Province of Quebec. The greatest nationalist in Laurier's time, Henri Bourassa, was a pan-Canadian nationalist, a man any Canadian today might delight to honour. But the War, Regulation 17 in Ontario Schools, and the ending of the language clauses of the Laurier-Greenway Compromise in Manitoba, made it impossible for his kind of nationalism to satisfy the more fervent resentments of Quebec. Even more pronounced French nationalists appeared during the First World War and in the twenties, nationalists so extreme that neither the progressive principle as interpreted by the Liberal Party, nor the conservative as applied by the Conservative Party under Borden, Meighen and Bennett, could form any mutually satisfactory connection with them: the unity of the whole had ceased to rest on a harmony of parts and on acceptance by all parts of the whole.

The fact was that after 1896 the conservative principle as it had been embodied in the Confederation of 1867 had been plucked root by rootlet, out of the constitution. Decisions of the Privy Council, acts of provincial governments, the endorsation of the doctrine of provincial rights by the federal Liberal Party, had in fact converted the strong confederation of 1867 into a weak federation, into a mere alliance of provinces. The rise of the Dominion-Provincial Conference, something unknown in any other federation, was a clear indication of what had happened to the Canadian union.

The above is a statement of fact, not a deploring of a happening, however regrettable it may seem. The conservative principle has always had to recognize the facts of diversity and dispersion in Canada. What is to be noted here is that this change made it impossible for the conservative principle to embody itself again in a dominant political party, as it had done from 1867 to 1896. Borden, Meighen, Bennett, were driven to take up provincial rights, provincial and regional concerns, and stress the interests of the parts rather than the interest of the whole. The result was usually defeat, with victory as accidental as it was rare. The game was not, in fact, one Conservatives could play as well as the Liberals, for the Liberals had always a head start in any electoral race so long as provincial rights, defence and conscription fortified their hold on the great body of mildly liberal and deeply conservative French voters—the inherited mass of the Bleu vote.

In facing this Liberal margin of superiority, Conservatives had to realize that an alliance with the French ultra-nationalists was impossible. It was equally impossible to recover the Bleu vote, for the Bleus had in the Liberal Party one that both respected the rights of the provinces and also developed the national wealth without committing it to imperial adventures abroad. The best electoral showings the Conservative Party made in Quebec after 1896 were made by means of remote and uneasy electoral understanding with the continuing Conservatives and with the nationalists in 1911 and 1930. These alliances neither gave Quebec its proper voice in the national government, nor the Conservative Party a genuine footing in Quebec. After 1935 the Party had as little prospects in Quebec as the Republican Party in the Deep South before Al Smith ran for the Democrats.

When, therefore, victory perched again on the Party's standards in 1957, it was a victory won without Quebec, one might almost say, against and over Quebec. If this was a matter of deliberate tactics, as I understand it was, it was not a bad thing in itself. Politics is a matter of power, and it is well for every one who takes part in politics, even as a mere voter, to remember where, in any given community power ultimately lies. It makes for more rational behaviour all round. But such resort to force of numbers may be too brutal. In a democratic society no considerable body of voters can be merely voted down indefinitely. In Canada this would restore the conditions of 1837–43 when the French were a suppressed minority. Some part of that body of opinion must be won over by comprehension of their position and by persuasion significant to them. What was wrong with the tactics of 1957 was the subsequent failure to make the great victory of 1958 in Quebec into something more than another uneasy alliance like those of 1911 and 1930.

Here was the fundamental failure of the Diefenbaker Government, the failure to use an unexampled electoral victory to restore the Conservative Party in Quebec. To redeem that failure, without betraying its own principles, is, I venture to suggest, the chief task before the Party today. The conservative principle of the harmonious unity of the whole means, if it means anything concrete, that in Canada any national party, and any national government, must be French as well as English, English as well as French. Political parties and national governments can no more be unhyphenated than ordinary Canadians can. Culturally, Canada is two nations. Politically, it is one. Canada may be governed politically without Quebec, but the distinction between culture and politics, cannot be made a line of separation.

If this, then, is to be done, if the conservative principle is to be restored to its proper role in the national life of Canada, how is it to be done? It is necessary to ask the question; the logic of this paper requires it—it by no means follows that the questioner knows the answer. The following, however, are proffered for what they are worth, because it is believed that they also arise from the argument of this paper. They also rest on certain affirmations I choose to make, and here state bluntly. First, I believe Confederation must and will continue. I think it ought to be modified. But the supreme political power of the general government must be maintained, while allowing the provinces the means to discharge their responsibilities within the nation. I think Quebec, as a province, is a province like any other, and should remain so. I think French Canada another matter, and that it should not be identified with Quebec. I refuse to consider a special status. I deny that any province has any right to secede. I think that any such attempt should be resisted by every means, including force if necessary. I do not believe the United States would grant us union, except as a last and necessary recourse. I am convinced that Canadians must and can work out their difficulties themselves, and that Confederation will be strengthened by the process. On the argument of the paper and these just stated beliefs, what follows next?

It is first necessary to recognize cordially the cultural existence and autonomy of French Canada, in Quebec and throughout Canada. This can best be done by making the French language official in principle throughout Canada by amending Section 133 of the BNA Act, and by providing working tests of when it ought to become practically official within a province or district of it, of course by the consent of the legislature of that province.

It is next necessary to repair the disaster of 1893, and restore the Federal Government as the guarantor of minority rights and the unity of the whole nation. This should be done by amending Section 93 of the BNA Act to restore the federal power of remedial legislation for individual and minority rights, and to make the Bill of Rights fundamental law, superior to either federal or provincial statute.

Then, to make such changes possible, particularly the adoption of any law as fundamental, an amending process must be worked out. It may be possible, for example, to consider as fundamental law any section of the constitution on which the eleven legislatures of Canada, federal and provincial, are unanimous in designating as fundamental and approving as such.

With such an undertaking, which at once properly recognizes the position of the French in Canada—not, be it noted, the Province of Quebec—it would be possible to go into Quebec and campaign on the grounds both of the rights of French Canada and the interest of all Canada. But one final step remains. That is to convince French Canadians that they need not fear a national majority being used against them any more. That is their traditional fear as a minority, and it has happened to them as late as 1942—not to mention 1957—even if in the harmless form of a plebiscite. There will be no more such votes because of the deep changes that are running through all channels of Canadian life, and not in Quebec alone. The chief of those changes, as Mr. Diefenbaker sensed so well, is that we are at last, in the second half—almost the last third of the twentieth century—all Canadians on the same footing. It ao longer matters to any one what a man's origin is—English, French, German, Ukrainian, Scots, Irish, Welsh, Italian—any of all the multitudinous strains of Canadian nationality. There is no British Empire any more; there is no longer any adventitious advantage in being English, or disadvantage in not being English. Without any man having to turn his back on his past, without any fervour of conversion from one nationality to another, we have all quietly become Canadians. This means that in the future any national majority will be a varying one, a majority of opinion and not of race. Quebec is now full of men, not clericals but good Catholics, who accept the demands and welcome the fruits of North American civilization; men who have, or hope to have, much to lose in the loss of Canada; who are prepared to be thoughtful Conservatives, if approached in a thoughtful way. They would understand the above arguments. They would agree when one said: two cultural communities we have and shall maintain, but we are one political community, and will remain so.

This was the function of the conservative principle in Confederation. It is, with the changes proved necessary in a century of experience and of growth, the function of that principle today. Bring Quebec back into the unity of the whole. Restore the unity of the whole by making the whole equally significant to every Canadian and every part of Canada. Recall the nation to its senses by asserting that federal powers are even more necessary to Canada than provincial rights. The conservative principle, let us remember, exists because of what was for what is. It has no utopias to attain, only to keep up the here and now as best it can. The here and now is Canada, one of the most fortunate, most free, and most enduring of countries. Let's keep it so.

4

John A. Macdonald, Confederation and the Canadian West*

Donald Creighton

TODAY HISTORIANS and the historiography of Confederation reflect the contemporary debate on the nature of our federalism and the principles inherent in it. In this article one of Canada's senior historians attacks what he considers to be a completely new concept of federalism which is often called the "pact" theory. Based upon the concept of national cultural duality, it is claimed this theory grew out of the compact made in 1867 between the two cultures or nations of Canada. Creighton sees this new interpretation as a reflection of the rising tide of French Canadian nationalism of the 1960s and contrary to the concepts of Confederation which Macdonald and other political leaders held in the 1860s.

In this article the author attempts to establish the concepts of federalism held by Canada's first prime minister as illustrated in his handling of the integration of the West into Confederation and whether there was any evidence of this cultural duality in his words or his actions. For further expansion of Creighton's ideas on Macdonald one can turn to his famous two-volume biography. Although Creighton argues the case with his usual eloquence, his contentions would be rejected by many other Canadian historians.†

TODAY, January 11, 1967, is the 152nd anniversary of the birth of John A. Macdonald; the centenary of Confederation is less than six

---

* *Historical and Scientific Society of Manitoba*, Series III, No. 23, 1966–67.

† Ralph Heintzman, "The Spirit of Confederation: Professor Creighton, Biculturalism, and the Use of History," *Canadian Historical Review*, LII (1971), pp. 247–75.

months away; and in only three years from now the Province of Manitoba will be a hundred years old. It is appropriate for students of history to re-examine these major events of the past; and it is particularly important to do so at the present moment, for we are now confronted by a radically new interpretation of their meaning. Historians, of course, are always busy revising and modifying the accepted historical record; but I am not thinking of such minor changes in detail or emphasis.

The version of Confederation which has become current during the past few years is much more than this. It amounts, in fact, to a new theory of Canadian federalism, a theory which rests on the basic assumption that ethnic and cultural values are and ought to be recognized as fundamental in the life of the Canadian nation. The real essence of the Canadian federal union is thus the cultural duality of Canada. And Confederation becomes a compact between two cultures, two nations, English and French.

This interpretation, I have already suggested, is fairly new. The point deserves to be emphasized. In fact, the new version has been given expression mainly during the last six or, at most, the last ten years. Its increasing popularity among historians, writers, and journalists may, of course, be attributed in part to the interest in Canadian federalism which has been growing steadily as the centenary of Confederation approached. But though the centennial would naturally have revived an interest in Confederation, it would not necessarily have inspired a radical new interpretation of it. The real origins of the new theory are political; they lie in the rapid rise of French-Canadian nationalism which has come about since Jean Lesage in 1960 assumed power in Quebec. For the last half-dozen years a group of politicians, lawyers, historians and journalists, mainly French-Canadian but with some English-Canadian associates, have been disseminating a radically new view of Confederation and of French Canada's place in it. Their aims are varied and in some degree contradictory. On the one hand they have tried to improve the status and enlarge the rights of French Canadians in the nation as a whole; on the other, they have sought to emphasize the separateness and strength the autonomy of the Province of Quebec. At one and the same time they seem to believe in a bilingual, bicultural but united Canada, and a virtually independent Quebec, which, if it decides to remain in confederation at all, will have to be given a "special position" and may even become an "associate state."

Obviously, the realization of either or both these aims would mean a revolution in the present structure of Confederation. But Confederation, embodied in the law and custom of the constitution, is an inheritance from the past; and inevitably therefore, the French-Canadian nationalists and their English-Canadian associates have had to cope with the intractable problem of history. Like everybody who desires social and political change, or is merely interested in its possibility, they had to make up their minds about the past. Revolutionaries have realized this necessity

long ago and they have evolved two different, and indeed quite contradictory methods of coming to terms with history. The "quiet revolutionaries" of Quebec appropriated both. The first method is to dismiss the
past as irrelevant and meaningless for the present; the second is to
identify the past with the revolutionary aims of the present. In other
words, history can be rejected as a useless obstacle to the revolutionary
programme; or it can be re-interpreted to provide a justification for it.

The case for the dismissal of the past is not our business tonight. But
the historical re-interpretation of Confederation which the Quebec
nationalists have been so persistently offering for the last six years is
certainly worth examining. This is an historical society and I am an
historian; and we are—or should be—interested in the use, or misuse, of
history. Revolutionary re-interpretations of the past usually have a purpose. In this case, the object of the "quiet revolutionaries" was to back up
a political programme with a new theory of federalism. The old view of
confederation as a political union of several provinces must be broken
down and discredited; and the conception of Canada as a cultural
duality, as a partnership of two different cultures or "nations," must be
established in its place. The fiction of duality was to be substituted for
the fact of plurality. The true meaning of confederation, the French-
Canadian nationalists argued, has been misunderstood and its essential
spirit forgotten. Only on the surface can it be regarded as an agreement
among several provinces; in reality it was a compact between the two
cultures, the two nations, English and French, of Canada.

There is very little aid or comfort for the believers of this theory in
what we know of the aims and intentions of the Fathers of Confederation. There is no support for it at all in the lean, spare phrases of the
Quebec resolutions or the British North America Act. It is obvious that
the last thing the Fathers of Confederation wanted to do was to perpetuate duality; they hoped, through confederation, to escape from it
forever. They had seen enough, and more than enough, of duality in the
old province of Canada. There it had paralyzed governments and prevented progress for a quarter of a century. The new Dominion of Canada
was to be organized, as the arrangements for the Senate make quite clear,
not as a duality but as a triumvirate of three divisions: Quebec, Ontario,
and Atlantic provinces as a group. The distinctive cultural features of
French Canada—its language, civil code, and educational system—were
confirmed in those parts of Canada in which they had already become
established by law or custom. But that was all. They were not extended
in their application to Ontario or to the Maritime provinces. There was
nothing in the Quebec Resolutions or the British North America Act
which remotely approached a general declaration of principle that
Canada was to be a bilingual or bicultural nation.

The evidence against the two-nation theory of Confederation is so
overwhelming that some of its advocates have been driven back upon a
secondary line of defence. The bicultural compact, they admit, was only a

"tacit" or "implicit" agreement, or a "moral" commitment, when the British North America Act was framed. But later, when Canada expanded westward and the Hudson's Bay Company territories were taken over, the Fathers of Confederation honoured the moral commitments and took care to provide that the new western domain should become the joint possession, on equal terms, of both English and French-speaking Canadians. The first Conservative government after confederation established Separate Schools and gave legal status to the French language in Manitoba. The first Liberal government after confederation did exactly the same for the North-West Territories. It was a basic national policy, deliberately adopted, carefully carried out, concurred in by both parties.

This, in short, is the theory of confederation as a bicultural compact applied to Manitoba and the North-West Territories. What is its truth when tested by the actual events of the time? This is the problem which I should like to examine with you tonight.

II

John A. Macdonald was above everything else a nation builder. The union of the original British North American colonies was the first of his two greatest achievements; the expansion and integration of the new Dominion on a continental scale was the second. He was an expansionist; but he was also a realist. His purpose was to ensure that Canada would not be despoiled of her great territorial inheritance on the North American continent; he was absolutely determined that, as he himself put it, "the United States should not get behind us by right or by force and intercept the route to the Pacific." In his mind there was no doubt about Canada's ultimate destiny; but at the same time he was equally convinced that Canada should assume its great heritage slowly and prudently, a step at a time, by one firm stage after another. Even as late as March, 1865 he would have preferred to see Rupert's Land and the North-West Territories remain a crown colony under imperial control. He soon realized, however, that the march of events could not be so deliberate as he had hoped. Great Britain's urge to withdraw from her North American commitments, the British government's desire that Canada should take over its responsibilities in the north-west, and the threat of American northward expansion all helped to convince him that there could be no more delay. In the spring of 1869 the bargain with the Hudson's Bay Company was finally concluded and Canada prepared to assume the assets and liabilities of its new western Dominion.

At this point it should be emphasized that Macdonald was still trying to hold fast, as far as he was able, to his original policy respecting the North-West. He had been compelled, far earlier than he had wanted to, to assume responsibility for Rupert's Land and the Territories; but he knew very well that the problem of their government and future development was a difficult one and he had no intention of risking a hasty solution to it. The bill which he introduced in the Canadian House of Commons late in May, 1869 was characteristically entitled "For the Temporary Government of Rupert's Land." It deserves far more attention than it has yet received. It is the only document that embodies the Conservative cabinet's original policy respecting the north-west; it expresses Macdonald's original intentions, his first tentative provisional plans. And it is obvious from its few brief clauses that he was trying to keep as closely as possible to the idea of a Crown colony, the idea which he had proposed as little as four years before. The North-West was to be governed, not as a province but as a territory, by a lieutenant-governor and a small nominated council. The existing laws were to continue until altered; the public officers were to retain their posts until it was ordered otherwise. Nothing was to be changed in a hurry. Nothing new was to be introduced at once. There was no mention of either schools or languages.

Now it is usually assumed that this whole provincial plan of government was invalidated by the Red River Rising of 1869–70. It is also usually taken for granted—even less justifiably, it seems to me—that the Manitoba Act of 1870 was the only natural result, the logical and inevitable constitutional consequence of the rising. Both those assumptions, I am convinced, badly need a critical examination; and the examination ought to begin by making a clear distinction between the Red River community on the one hand and the military dictatorship of Louis Riel on the other. There is no doubt whatever about the kind of government which the Red River community would have liked to see established in the north-west. Their wishes were democratically determined in the debates of the Convention which met at Fort Garry in mid-winter 1870; and the results were embodied in the resolutions of the second "List of Rights." If this second list—the one document in which the constitutional preferences of the whole Red River community are faithfully recorded—had formed the basis of the negotiations at Ottawa, the Manitoba Act of 1870 would have been a very different statute. The Convention, against the opposition and to the intense indignation of Riel, decided against provincial status, at least for the time being. It requested equality for the English and French languages in the legislature and the courts; but it made no mention of separate or confessional schools. If the wishes of the Convention and the terms of the second "List of Rights" had been followed in drafting the Manitoba Act, there would have had no very serious departure from Macdonald's *Act for the Temporary Government of Rupert's Land* of the previous year.

But the moderate and sensible constitutional settlement was not to be. Riel was determined to prevent it. An adroit and ruthless dictator, he had no intention of permitting democracy to have its own way at Red River. His terms for the union with Canada had been openly and emphatically rejected by the Convention; but at the same time, as a final reluctant concession in the interest of political conciliation in the Settlement, the Convention had confirmed the provisional government and elected Riel as its president. At once and with purposeful energy he took over control of the negotiations with Canada. He quickly nominated Ritchot and Alfred Scott, who, he felt confident, would support his own private plans for the future of the north-west; and he persuaded the reluctant Convention to accept them as two of the three emissaries to the Canadian government. He then proceeded to make short work of the Convention's "List of Rights." The wishes of the Red River community, where they differed from his claims for his own people, the *Métis*, meant nothing whatever to him. In two quite new and increasingly detailed "Lists of Rights," drawn up in private by Riel and his lay and clerical advisers, the delegates sent to Ottawa were instructed to insist that the North-West should enter Confederation, not as a Territory, but as a Province. It must have, they demanded, an elaborate provincial constitution with an absurdly top-heavy bi-cameral legislature, including a little senate on the model of Quebec. It must also have a system of sectarian or confessional schools, again on the Quebec model. This, if you like, was a demand that biculturalism should prevail on the prairies and that French and English institutions should be combined in the government of the north-west; but it was neither a demand that was made by the community at Red River nor a plan proposed by the government of Ottawa. It was a claim exacted by Riel's dictatorship.

Why did Macdonald accept it? Why did he consent to impose such an elaborate constitution upon such an immature colony? How was he persuaded to settle all the basic institutions of a community which had not yet had time to develop its real and permanent character? The answers to these questions can never be absolutely certain, for the conclusive evidence is lacking; but the probabilities at all events are very clear. The pressures in favour of a quick settlement in the north-west were inescapable and compelling. Macdonald's foremost aim was to ensure, at almost any cost, Canada's continental destiny, her unobstructed expansion from the Atlantic to the Pacific Ocean. His greatest fear was that the United States, by deliberate policy or tragic accident, might prevent the achievement of these natural limits. He knew only too well that the acrimonious disputes which had arisen between Great Britain and the United States during the American Civil War had not yet been settled. There was evidence that both President Grant and Secretary of State Hamilton Fish were annexationists, prepared to use any method short of war to acquire all or part of British America. And finally it was clear from the beginning, that the American expansionists at St. Paul, Minnesota— the "Yankee Wire-pullers," Macdonald called them—were eager to exploit the rising at Red River, and that American citizens in the settlement were deep in Riel's councils. So long as the provisional government continued, so long as the future of the British American north-west remained uncertain and confederation was still incomplete, the threat of American intervention hung over Canada's future.

A quick settlement was urgently necessary. And its character by this time was fixed and virtually unalterable. Appeasement on any terms meant in fact appeasement on the terms demanded by the fanatical emissaries from Red River, backed up by Cartier and his French Canadian "Bleu" followers, and supported by Sir Clinton Murdoch of the British Colonial Office. It is true, of course, that the Canadian government refused to yield to Riel's vainglorious and incredible demand that the entire North-West enter Confederation as a single province; and it is also true that the request for provincial control of public lands was likewise rejected. Macdonald could limit boundaries and withhold lands, but within the restricted area of the new Province of Manitoba he had to accept a bilingual and bicultural system of rights and institutions. "The French," Sir Stafford Northcote observed, "are earnestly bent upon the establishment of a French and Catholic power in the North-West to counteract the great preponderance of Ontario." Their purpose was to fix the character and institutions of the new province at a time when French-speaking Roman Catholics formed a large part of its population, and therefore at the most favourable moment for preparing defences against the approaching influx of Protestant, English-speaking settlers.

III

The Manitoba Act did not represent the carrying-out of a solemn commitment to biculturalism which had been made at Confederation. It was not drafted in fulfilment of an ideal conception of what Canada should be; it was, to a very large extent, imposed simply by the force of circumstance. In 1869–70 a particular set of circumstances, including some very frightening external circumstances, had practically dictated a hasty policy of appeasement. But these circumstances were exceptional and transitory; they did not reappear in quite the same powerful consti-tution; and as a result the main argument in favour of biculturalism lost most of its force. This would not have mattered, of course, if the Fathers of Confederation had really felt morally committed to the ideal of a bilingual and bicultural Canada, to the conception of two nations in the Canadian national state. But the simple truth is that they did not. The French language and French-Canadian institutions had not been given legal status in any province of the original union outside Quebec; and no attempt had been made to establish the equality of the two cultures in any of the provinces that entered Confederation after Manitoba. The Manitoba Act did not lay down a national bicultural pattern which was solemnly confirmed and carefully followed thereafter. When British Columbia and Prince Edward Island joined the union, nobody so much as mentioned the great moral commitment to biculturalism.

The exception to this consistent record is, of course, the North-West Territories. And it is a very dubious exception which effectively proves the rule. It was not until the session of 1875, nearly five years after this passage of the Manitoba Act, that the Parliament of Canada finally got around to setting up a system of organized government in the western territory beyond the new province of Manitoba. The main feature of the North-West Territories bill, which the new Prime Minister Alexander Mackenzie introduced in the Commons, was a rather complicated set of clauses providing for the gradual introduction of elected members in the North-West Council as the population of the region increased. The bill contained no reference to separate or confessional schools, and no provision for the French language. If this silence could have been made to appear as a betrayal of a recognized bicultural compact, it is obvious that the Conservative opposition, in which several of the Fathers of Confederation were sitting, would have been quick to grasp the opportunity of so doing. But the Conservative member sat silent. And it was left to Edward Blake, who was not a Father of Confederation and knew nothing whatever at first hand of its purposes or principles, to move, in amendment, that separate or confessional schools should be established in the territories.

Why did Blake take up the cause of what he called "religious instruction" in the north-west? On the record, there was no reason to expect him to show any particular sympathy for the Roman Catholic *Métis* of the prairies; on the contrary, he was thought to share the critical views of *Canada First* and its representatives at Red River, Mair and Schultz. In 1871, when he had been leader of the opposition in the Ontario legislature, Blake had moved a resolution demanding that the "murderer" Riel should be brought to justice; and in the following year, after he had formed the first Liberal government in Ontario, he introduced a similar resolution offering a five thousand dollar reward for the arrest and conviction of the "murderers" of Thomas Scott. Undoubtedly he had gained a good deal of political capital from these astute moves; and political capital may well have been what he was after in the session of 1875. He was not a member of Mackenzie's government; he had been angling deviously for Mackenzie's post as Prime Minister; he was critical of Mackenzie's policies and determined to block his railway bill; and he was embarrassing him at every turn.

It was in this curious way, and with this unexpected sponsorship, that separate schools found their way into the North-West Territories Act of 1875. The grant of legal status to the French language, which was made when the statute was amended in 1877, came about in an even stranger and more accidental fashion. It was not a government amendment at all; it was proposed by a private member in the Senate. And the speech with which David Mills, the Minister of the Interior, greeted this amendment when it was brought down to the Commons effectively destroys the odd notion that the promotion of biculturalism on the prairies was the settled policy of Liberal as well as Conservative governments. Mills reminded the members that the dominant language of the region was Cree; he thought the North-West council was the only body that could properly settle the question of official languages. He regretted the Senate amendment; and he reluctantly accepted it because otherwise it would be impossible to get the revised statute through Parliament before the end of the session.

We are now in a position, it seems to me, to come to certain conclusions. The bicultural compact theory of Confederation as applied to Manitoba and the North-West Territories cannot be sustained. The idea of a solemn commitment to biculturalism, accepted in principle and deliberately implemented by both parties, is simply not borne out by the facts. The west did not get its institutions in accordance with the provisions of some long-range plan; on the contrary, the process was characterized throughout by accident and improvisation. The pressure of circumstances, the influence of certain powerful political interests, and the ambition of a few key personalities, all combined to force a series of hasty and ill-considered decisions; and the result was the abandonment of Macdonald's plan for the gradual development of government in the North-West and the premature establishment of an elaborate and cumbrous constitution. This attempt to fix the political institutions of the west before immigration and the growth of population and determined its true and permanent character was a mistake for which the whole of Canada paid dearly. By 1890—only twenty years after the Manitoba Act and fifteen years after the North-West Territories Act—the west had outgrown the inappropriate constitution that had been imposed upon it. It began suddenly and uncompromisingly to change the status of the French language and the character of its schools. The violent controversy that followed lasted for more than a quarter of a century; and it ended in the virtual extinction of biculturalism in the Canadian west.

This is an episode in our history which should not be forgotten. We should all remember it when we come to read the forthcoming report of the Royal Commission on Bilingualism and Biculturalism. The commission may possibly recommend constitutional changes designed to improve the position of the French language and of French-Canadian culture throughout the nation, including the west. These proposals should be judged critically in the light of history; and with the aid of the same clear light, westerners should examine the historical theory by which these proposals will probably be justified. The idea of a bicultural compact, of the two-nation state, has got much of its currency and its vogue during a period of profound revolution in Quebec; and this very fact ought to make it suspect. New historical interpretations which make their appearance in revolutionary times are usually the result, not of the search for truth, but of the need for historical justification. They are

invented—or partly invented—to supply historical authority for a program of radical changes. Canadians on the whole are badly equipped to
protect themselves against this kind of propaganda. For they are not as
historically minded as the English, and, unlike the Americans, they have
not been brought up in the thorough knowledge of their own history.
They cling to old myths, and are easily sold new and spurious inventions.
It would be a tragedy if, at this most critical period of their history, they
were led to damage their future irretrievably through a serious misunderstanding of their past.

5

The Genesis of
Provincial Rights*

Norman McLeod Rogers

The history of every community and every constitution may be regarded as a struggle between the action of these two forces, that which draws together and that which pushes apart, that which unites and that which dissevers.[1]

ALTHOUGH written many decades ago, this article by the late Norman McLeod Rogers still has a clear freshness and relevance about it. A great Nova Scotian and a great constitutional lawyer, Rogers was later to become a distinguished wartime federal cabinet minister and thus participate in the second great attempt at centralism. Without using the phrase, Rogers is discussing the elitest nature of the Confederation achievement. Macdonald, Monck, Tupper, and Tilley all preferred legislative union. Even Brown in 1864 was for provincial subordination. Macdonald thought that he had achieved "all the advantages of legislative union" while protecting "local institutions" in allowing "local laws" in certain sensitive and minor areas of jurisdiction. But Macdonald depended primarily on politics to make good his plans; centralizing politics depended on strong national sentiment, and this was lacking. Rogers points out that Macdonald and the others wanted the "paramount authority" to lie with Ottawa. We might say today that what these Fathers wanted for the provinces was virtually the present "Home Rule" status (minus the troubles) held by Northern Ireland in the United Kingdom.

Rogers reminds us that it was neither Quebec nor Nova Scotia but

---

* *Canadian Historical Review*, XIV (1933), pp. 9–23.
[1] James Bryce, *Studies in history and jurisprudence* (London, 1901), I, 218.

Ontario which nurtured and developed the doctrine of provincial rights, and it was this doctrine which transformed the British provinces into American-style states. Paramountcy depended on the political bravery of the federal government. This was lacking. Ontarians might more readily have accepted supervision by the judiciary rather than by the dominion executive because they could "have been lulled by the comfortable fiction that judges interpret but do not make the laws." Since Rogers wrote this article further research of a social and intellectual nature has been pushing back the location of the "Genesis" into pre-Confederation days, to the origins of the Clear Grit movement, to localism and the nature of Upper Canadian society. In this regard one should note Elwood Jones' "Ephemeral compromise: the Great Reform Convention Revisited," in *The Journal of Canadian Studies,* III (February, 1968), pp. 21–28, and his 1971 Queen's doctoral dissertation on the Convention of 1859.

I n the study of federal government the constitutional lawyer and the political theorist must sit often at the feet of the historian. Especially is this true of that central problem of federalism which is suggested by the phrase "provincial rights." A federal constitution, as Dicey observed, owes its existence to a peculiar state of feeling among the inhabitants of the several communities which have been brought together under its authority. They desire union, but do not desire unity.[2] Thus from the moment of its birth a federal state is put in a posture of competition with the states or provinces of which it is composed. If the provinces are secure in the attachment of their citizens and jealous of the letter of their rights, the federal agencies of government may be compelled to withdraw their services to the minimum permitted by a strict interpretation of the constitution. If, on the other hand, the provincial governments are lacking in the support of local sentiment, and are willing to regard themselves as subordinate partners in the business of government, the federal institutions tend to grow in influence and power with the growth of national sentiment and the diminishing importance of the provinces. The tide of the struggle may shift now this way and now that. Sometimes the federal state is in the ascendancy. At other times the provinces may win back what they have lost and even penetrate the defences of the federal power. Always, beneath the noise and clamour of particular controversies, there are changes in political consciousness and sentiment which decide the trend of the conflict. Statesmen, as they come and go, may have their

---

[2] A. V. Dicey, *Introduction to the study of the law of the constitution* (London, 8th ed., 1914), 137.

influence on events. But the area within which their influence is effective is predetermined by social forces over which their power is transient and partial. The facts which alone can illumine and explain constitutional tendencies over long periods of time must be sought in the material of history.

Although the controversy over provincial rights is inherent in every federal constitution, it was the proud boast of Sir John Macdonald that, by the wise provisions of the Quebec Conference, Canada had received a permanent immunity from this common affliction of federations. In the course of his speech on the Quebec Resolutions in the Canadian parliament, he made particular reference to the conflict over "states rights" in the United States and to the unhappy culmination of that struggle in the Civil War:

We have thus avoided that great source of weakness which has been the cause of the disruption of the United States. We have avoided all conflict of jurisdiction and authority, and if this Constitution is carried out, as it will be in full detail in the Imperial Act to be passed if the colonies adopt the scheme, we will have in fact, all the advantages of a legislative union under one administration, with, at the same time, the guarantees for local institutions and for local laws which are insisted upon by so many in the provinces now, I hope, to be united.[3]

Macdonald's optimism on this point was shared by not a few of his colleagues at the Quebec Conference. The feeling seemed to be that the origin of "states rights" in the United States lay in the wide residuary powers left to the individual states under the constitution, giving them in their own right some of the important attributes of sovereignty and thus encouraging the belief that they were the substance, and the president and Congress but the pale shadows, of sovereign authority in the nation. The expedient adopted by Canada to prevent a similar conflict between federal and provincial governments over their respective shares of jurisdiction was the simple operation of inverting the scheme of distribution of powers adopted by Canada's neighbour. As Macdonald put it in the speech just quoted (p. 35):

The United States began at the wrong end. They declared by their Constitution that each state was a sovereignty in itself, and that all the powers incident to sovereignty belonged to each state, except those powers which by the Constitution were conferred upon the General Government and Congress. Here we have adopted a different system. We have strengthened the General Government. We have given the General Legislature all the great subjects of legislation. We have conferred upon them not only specifically and in detail all the powers which are incident to sovereignty, but we have expressly declared that all subjects of general interest not distinctly and exclusively conferred upon the

[3] *Debates in the parliament of Canada on the Confederation of British North America* (Quebec, 1865), 33.

local government and local legislatures, shall be conferred upon the General Government and Legislature.[4]

Thus, as viewed by Macdonald and his associates, the bulwark against "provincial rights" in Canada was made up of those provisions in the proposed constitution which strengthened the federal government and parliament at the expense of the provincial establishments.

While Macdonald may have had some grounds for his simple faith in constitutional formulae as a safeguard against a movement for provincial rights in Canada at the close of the Quebec Conference, the events of the next two years gave little support to his evident belief that the provinces would accept voluntarily and cheerfully the subordinate position they had been destined to occupy under the proposed federal constitution. Even as the debate on the Quebec Resolutions proceeded in the Canadian parliament, there were ominous rumblings of dissent in Lower Canada, while among the English-speaking representatives such shrewd observers as Dunkin, Holton, and Huntington expressed ironical doubts regarding the supposed spirit of harmony which would prevail over the relations between the federal and provincial governments. It is significant that the resolutions which were seized upon as the chief targets for opposition were precisely those which were eulogized by Macdonald and other Canadian delegates at the Quebec Conference as safeguards against the undue assertion of provincial rights. Dorion, the leader of the opposing forces in Lower Canada, did not mince words in protesting against the wide powers granted to the dominion authorities under the Quebec scheme;

Sir, if a legislative union of the British American Provinces is attempted, there will be such an agitation in this portion of the province as was never witnessed before—you will see the whole people of Lower Canada clinging together to resist by all legal and constitutional means, such an attempt at wresting from them those institutions that they now enjoy.[5]

The point of this reference is not, of course, that legislative union was contemplated by the Quebec Resolutions, but that some of the leaders of the delegation from Upper Canada were avowedly in favour of this form of union, and having failed to secure it were assumed to have sought its partial realization through those resolutions of the Conference which favoured the central authority at the expense of the provinces. The power given to the dominion government to disallow provincial legislation was especially obnoxious to the opponents of the Quebec scheme. Both Dunkin and Dorion condemned it in outspoken terms, the former stating that it meant the disallowance of all autonomy to the provinces, and the latter complaining that it placed the provincial legislatures wholly at the

---

[4] *Ibid.*, 35.
[5] *Ibid.*, 264.

mercy of the federal government.[6] The Confederation debates abound
with similar protests on behalf of provincial autonomy and the rights of
racial and religious minorities. It was evident that even in the united
provinces, where the federal scheme commanded the most general support, there was no lack of potential opposition to the centralizing features
of the federal constitution proposed by the Quebec Conference.

In the Maritime Provinces the political situation was even less favourable to Macdonald's sanguine expectations. There the original opposition
to the Quebec scheme came not from a minority but from the great
majority of the inhabitants. The agitation, moreover, was not centred
merely upon particular features of the proposals but extended also,
especially in Nova Scotia, to the bare project of uniting the several
provinces of British North America into one federal state. The Quebec
Resolutions were never submitted to the legislature of this province for
approval. In New Brunswick the government supporting them was
defeated in a general election. In Prince Edward Island they were rejected as an unsuitable basis for union. It is doubtful if the events of the
ensuing two years indicated any widespread change in the attitude of the
people of these provinces towards the proposals for union. It is true that
the verdict of the New Brunswick electorate was reversed at a subsequent election. It is also true that the legislatures of New Brunswick and
Nova Scotia passed resolutions authorizing delegates to formulate a plan
of union in co-operation with the imperial government and delegates
from Upper and Lower Canada. Behind these apparent changes in
opinion, however, there is the shadow of imperial influence amounting
almost to coercion. The British government had committed itself definitely to a federal union of the British North American colonies and
spared no effort of diplomacy and indirect pressure to overcome the
opposition which had developed in the Maritime Provinces. The official
correspondence of the period, especially the communications which
passed between Lord Monck, the Colonial Office, and the governors of
New Brunswick, Nova Scotia, and Prince Edward Island, makes it
abundantly clear that the recalcitrant provinces were induced to enter the
union in deference to considerations of imperial policy.[7] In Nova Scotia,

---

[6] "We shall be—I speak as a Lower Canadian—we shall be at its mercy, because
it may exercise its right of veto on all the legislation of the local parliaments, and
there again we shall have no remedy" (Dorion in *ibid.*, 690). "It further allows of no
real autonomy; in fact, the only trace of uniformity it can be said to have about it
consists in its disallowance of all autonomy to the provinces" (Dunkin in *ibid.*,
502).

[7] On this subject see the very illuminating study by Chester Martin, "British policy
in Canadian Confederation" (CANADIAN HISTORICAL REVIEW, March, 1932, 3–19).
The negotiations of the period for reciprocity were also utilized by the Colonial Office
as a means of inducing the dissentient provinces to accept the proposals for federation
(*Journals of the Legislative Council, Prince Edward Island*, 1866, appendix no. 7,
180).

at least, this influence was not without its effect upon members of the legislature. But as events soon proved, the people of that province had not altered their attitude towards the proposals for federation. The Maritime Provinces, indeed, entered the union with halting and reluctant steps. In such a situation there was every prospect of a jealous assertion of provincial autonomy as against the wide powers entrusted to the new dominion under the terms of the federal constitution.

The final stages of the negotiations for union did little to allay the fears or compose the irritation of the opponents of federation in the various provinces. George Brown, the Liberal leader in the coalition which had brought about the Quebec Conference, was absent from the London Conference which formulated the definitive proposals which served as a basis for the British North America Act.[8] The Nova Scotia delegation did not represent the opinion of the majority of the inhabitants of that province. The New Brunswick delegates were pledged to insist on the Intercolonial Railway and hoped to obtain a revision of the financial terms of the Quebec scheme.[9] Cartier, it may be assumed, was fully aware that he must take account of the misgivings of many of his compatriots regarding the potential dangers which were latent in the powers assigned to the federal authority under the terms of the original Quebec Resolutions.[10] In due course the differences which divided the several provincial delegations were reconciled, but only through the revision of the Quebec scheme in several of its important features. These changes were not authorized by the legislature of the united provinces, and Macdonald took special precautions to have the British North America bill hurried through the British parliament before the details could become the subject of controversy at home.[11] Such a manoeuvre, however it may have been recommended by considerations of immediate expediency, was little calculated to commend itself to the opponents of the federal proposals in Canada. It also aroused the wrath of George Brown and weakened his advocacy of the new constitution in the years

---

[8] George Brown had resigned from the coalition government in December, 1865, the cause of his resignation being a sharp difference of opinion regarding the negotiations for reciprocity with the United States. He was not, therefore, a member of the Canadian delegation which proceeded to London in 1866 to conclude the negotiations for union (A. Mackenzie, *The life and speeches of the Hon. George Brown*, Toronto, 1882, 105).

[9] *Journals of the Legislative Assembly of New Brunswick*, 1866, 153.

[10] "It is generally believed that the most serious estrangement between [Sir John Macdonald and Sir George Cartier] occurred in London while the British North America Act was before Parliament. John A. Macdonald desired, it is said, to have it so modified that a legislative union should be substituted for the proposed federation. To this Cartier objected strongly, and made no mystery of his intention to return to Canada if his colleague persisted in his determination to alter the Constitution as it had been adopted in Quebec" (A. D. DeCelles, *Papineau Cartier*, Makers of Canada, Toronto, 1910, 102 of section on Cartier).

[11] Sir J. Pope, *Memoirs of Sir John A. Macdonald* (Ottawa, 1895), I, 307–8.

when the federal machinery was receiving the first test of practice.[12] From beginning to end the negotiations for union reflected the lack of any strong and sustained support of sentiment and opinion. Federation was essentially the work of a few master-builders. Opposition to the proposals was organized and vocal in all the provinces. The mass of the population was probably indifferent to the outcome. Certain sections of it were hostile from the outset, and their hostility was not likely to cease when the new dominion came into being.

With a background in which the high hopes of its founders were mingled with the disappointment and misgivings of its opponents, the Canadian federation entered upon its career under the direction of the statesmen who had taken a foremost part in its creation. If Sir John Macdonald had any prevision of the path which lay before him, he kept his thoughts discreetly to himself. Doubtless he had few illusions regarding the difficulties that would confront the first dominion government in establishing and maintaining harmonious relations with the provinces. But difficulties had never daunted his spirit, and it would have been strange indeed if he had been unwilling to lend himself to an enterprise in which he had invested so much of his mind and strength during the preceding years. He had taken a major part in fashioning the instrument of federal government. Now he was given the opportunity to test its utility by experience. Writing to the Honourable Ambrose Shea, one of Newfoundland's delegates at the Quebec Conference, a month before the formation of the first dominion administration, he expressed a modest faith in the outcome of the experiment:

In thirty days, for weal or woe, the Confederate Government will be inaugurated. By the exercise of common sense and a limited amount of that patriotism which goes by the name of self-interest, I have no doubt that the Union will be for the common weal.[13]

Both common sense and patriotism were required in large measure if the new dominion at the commencement of its voyage was to chart a course which would enable it to avoid the hidden reefs of racial antagonism and provincial rights.

When the first dominion government entered upon its responsibilities the plan of Macdonald and others of his associates who had favoured legislative union seemed simple in execution and by no means impossible of achievement. They believed that the success of federalism in Canada required the subordination of the provinces to the general authority of the dominion. This did not mean that the provinces were to be legislated out of existence. It simply meant that the wide constitutional powers

---

[12] The *Globe*, June 9, 1869. In a leading editorial in this issue, it is stated that the changes in the financial clauses made by the London Conference were manifestly unfair to Ontario and Quebec.

[13] Public Archives of Canada, *Macdonald letter book*, X, 575.

apparently given to the dominion government and parliament under the British North America Act were to be utilized to the utmost to secure the recognition by the provinces themselves that their proper status was one of subordination, and that, in any conflict of jurisdiction with the dominion in matters which were not covered explicitly by constitutional enactment, they must give way gracefully to the supreme authority. This doctrine of a paramount authority residing in the dominion was not regarded as a forced interpretation of the constitution. It was possible to refer to certain clauses of the British North America Act as expressly supporting such a position, as, for example, the residuary legislative authority given to the dominion parliament, the unqualified power conferred upon the dominion government to disallow provincial legislation, and the authority to appoint and presumably to instruct the lieutenant-governors of the provinces.[14] Lord Monck, the first governor-general, was known to be a vigorous advocate of legislative union, and might be expected to lend his support to any policy within the letter of the constitution which would strengthen the central government.[15] In the power of disallowance, Macdonald possessed the effective means whereby the provincial legislatures could be kept within the channels of jurisdiction which had been assigned to them by the British North America Act. The powers given to the lieutenant-governors of the provinces were so indefinite as to permit an interpretation of the status and functions of those officials which would accord with the policy of centralizing authority in the dominion.[16] These instruments and favouring conditions had for the most part a constitutional sanction behind them. It was only natural that Macdonald should take advantage of them to secure the realization of his purpose. The important object in the early years of the dominion was to habituate the provinces to a status of subordination. Once they had accepted the new régime by successive submissions to the federal authority, there was reason to believe that custom would supply the want of explicit constitutional provisions to this end.

---

[14] B.N.A. Act, sec. 58.

[15] As late as September 7, 1866, Monck proposed to Carnarvon that important changes should be made in any bill founded on the Quebec Resolutions which would have greatly strengthened the central authority in its relation to the provinces. "I am persuaded both from the internal evidence afforded by the resolutions which they drew up—and from intimate personal knowledge of most of the able men who composed the Quebec Convention, that their intention was to form out of these Provinces a solid and lasting political consolidation with a supreme central authority managing all the general interests of the people of the Union, and which would attract to itself the—so to speak—national sentiment and aspirations of the entire population" (Public Archives of Canada, *Series G*, 180 B. G, 221 A, 1856–66, Secret and confidential despatches, 212–220).

[16] Note Dufferin's opinion in 1873: "It seems to me that the true policy of the Dominion will be to subordinate the prestige and jurisdiction both of the local legislatures and their chief executive Officer, to the supreme authority of the Canadian Parliament and the Governor-General" (Public Archives of Canada, *Macdonald papers*, Governor-general's correspondence, Dufferin, V, 1872–73, 178).

To a statesman so thoroughly practised in the arts of political strategy as Sir John Macdonald, the best method of carrying forward a policy of centralization was to secure the election to both the dominion parliament and the provincial legislatures of men who had the cause of union at heart and would be prepared to work together in the service of a common cause. In the attainment of this object he was singularly favoured by fortune in every province except Nova Scotia. In that province the elections of 1867 returned a legislature which was overwhelmingly opposed to federation, and committed to make every effort to secure the repeal of the British North America Act in its application to Nova Scotia. In dealing with this difficult situation Macdonald was obliged to call upon all his resources of diplomacy and manipulation. Aided by the co-operation of the British government he succeeded at length in persuading the Nova Scotian government that it must make the most of hard necessity, providing that necessity could be rendered less harsh by a revision of the financial terms of union to the advantage of the provincial treasury. The procedure by which these "better terms" were granted to Nova Scotia was at least open to question, and aroused strong opposition in Ontario.[17] Macdonald, however, could still rely on the support of the imperial government, and was able to produce an opinion from the law officers of the crown approving of a variation of the financial conditions of union by an ordinary act of the dominion parliament.[18] With the admission of Joseph Howe to the dominion Cabinet, the opposition in Nova Scotia was reduced to modest proportions. Elsewhere the provincial administrations were in friendly hands. Sandfield Macdonald, as premier of Ontario, was willing to put his shoulder to the provincial wheel of the federal coach despite the verbal castigations he received occasionally from George Brown and the *Globe*.[19] At Quebec, Chauveau was in command with a safe majority of confederate supporters behind him. In that province Sir George Cartier could also be relied upon to deal with any embarrassing situation that might arise. In New Brunswick a favourable revision of financial terms and the influence of Tilley were effective safeguards against friction. On the whole, as the first dominion administration entered upon its task, the external evidence afforded some confirmation of Macdonald's earlier hope that the evil spirit of "provincial rights" had been exorcised from the Canadian constitution by the wise provisions of its founders.

---

[17] A resolution was passed by the Legislative Assembly of Ontario in the following terms: "That an humble Address be presented to Her Majesty praying that she may be graciously pleased to cause a measure to be submitted to the Imperial Parliament for the purpose of removing all colour for the assumption by the Parliament of Canada of the power to disturb the financial relations established by the B.N.A. Act (1867) as between Canada and the several Provinces" (*Journals of the Legislative Assembly of Ontario*, 1869, III, 33–36, 54–56).

[18] *Sessional papers, Canada*, 1870, III, no. 25.

[19] Pope, *Memoirs of Sir John A. Macdonald*, II, 20.

It is a commentary on the vanity of political calculations that before two years had elapsed Macdonald was compelled to acknowledge the failure of the precautions so carefully taken to avoid an issue on the question of provincial rights. In a letter written from Macdonald to Sir John Young shortly after his arrival in Canada as successor to Lord Monck, there is a significant reference to the antagonism towards the federal government which had become evident in some of the provinces:

It is difficult to make the local Legislatures understand that their powers are not so great as they were before the Union. In fact, the question that convulsed the United States and ended in Civil War, commonly known as the "States Rights" question, has already made its appearance in Canada![20]

Although there is nothing in this letter to indicate precisely the causes of misunderstanding with the provinces, the official communications and newspapers of the period suggest that the chief source of friction was the use made by the dominion government of its power of disallowance. As provided by the British North America Act, the power of disallowance was subject to no reservations. The dominion government was given the authority to nullify provincial legislation within a period of one year after its enactment.[21] Designed to serve as an instrument by which the provincial legislatures were to be kept to their proper channels of jurisdiction, its employment in practice depended wholly on the policy of the dominion administration. This was its inherent weakness. The provinces would have submitted to judicial decisions affecting their jurisdiction without serious protest. Any misgivings they might have entertained on this score would have been lulled by the comfortable fiction that judges interpret but do not make the law. But the dominion authorities could not escape a full measure of responsibility for every exercise of the power of disallowance. No matter how justifiable their action might be from a strict legal standpoint, every threat to disallow a provincial statute conveyed the impression of a deliberate interference with provincial autonomy. Macdonald was not long in realizing that the usefulness of his instrument would be enhanced if he could reassure the provinces that it would not be employed arbitrarily as a means of curtailing their proper legislative jurisdiction. Accordingly, on June 8, 1868, in his capacity as minister of justice, he prepared a memorandum which was designed to regularize the procedure of disallowance, and to relieve the dominion government of some of its burden of responsibility in the exercise of its powers. The memorandum expressed the view that "it is of importance that the course of Local Legislation should be interfered with as little as possible, and the power of disallowance exercised with great caution, and only in cases where the law and the general interests of the Dominion imperatively

---

[20] *Macdonald letter book*, no. 12, 443–447.
[21] B.N.A. Act, sec. 90.

demand it."[22] The memorandum then went on to propose a definite procedure for the examination of provincial legislation by the minister of justice at Ottawa. Under this procedure it was recommended that objectionable acts of the provincial legislatures should be classified under four distinct heads: (1) as being altogether illegal or unconstitutional; (2) as illegal or unconstitutional in part; (3) in cases of concurrent jurisdiction, as clashing with the legislation of the general parliament; (4) as affecting the interests of the dominion generally. As a concession to provincial susceptibilities, it was proposed that

where a measure is considered only partially defective, or where objectionable, as being prejudicial to the general interests of the Dominion, or as clashing with its legislation, communication should be had with the Provincial Government with respect to such measures, and that in such cases, the Act should not be disallowed, if the general interests permit such a course, until the Local Government has an opportunity of considering and discussing the objection taken, and the Local Legislature has also an opportunity of remedying the defects found to exist.[23]

This procedure, as adopted by the dominion government and announced to the provinces in a circular despatch, appeared to go a long way towards removing the dangers of friction. Nevertheless, it did not dispel suspicion and it failed to avoid resentment even in cases where the power of disallowance was invoked against provincial legislation which was evidently illegal or unconstitutional.

Ontario became the chief battleground in the contest over the power of disallowance. It so happened that its legislation fell under the special displeasure of the federal Department of Justice in the early years of federation. This may have been unavoidable, but the political consequences were unfortunate for the federalist party at Ottawa and ought to have been more clearly foreseen. In Ontario the opposition had a powerful newspaper organ in the *Globe* under the able editorship of George Brown. As the self-appointed guardian of provincial autonomy, it kept a vigilant watch over the provincial administration and seldom lost an opportunity to berate Sandfield Macdonald for his mistakes of judgment and his submissive attitude towards the federal authority. Its general attitude is well illustrated by the controversy over the pardoning power. In the Quebec Resolutions this power had been assigned to the lieutenant-governors of the provinces, but it was not so provided in the British North America Act.[24] When Ontario assumed the power of pardon under

---

[22] *Sessional papers, Canada*, 1869, no. 18.

[23] *Ibid.*

[24] Resolution 44 of the Quebec Conference was in the following terms: "The power of respiting, reprieving, and pardoning prisoners convicted of crimes, and of commuting and remitting sentences in whole or in part, which belongs of right to the Crown, shall be administered by the Lieutenant-Governor of each Province in Coun-

Sandfield Macdonald, the dominion authorities referred the question to the imperial government and received an opinion from Lord Granville that the power lay solely with the governor-general as the deputy of the queen.[25] The *Globe* took strong exception to this opinion, arguing that if the imperial authorities had been asked to assign the pardoning power to the lieutenant-governors of the provinces as provided for in the Quebec Resolutions, they would not have hesitated to do so.[26] Thus the responsibility which Macdonald had hoped to thrust on the law officers of the crown in England was brought back and laid on the doorstep of the federal administration at Ottawa. Whenever a centralizing tendency was evident in the policies of the Ottawa government the *Globe* was prepared to enter the lists on behalf of the provinces. Its position is summed up concisely in a brief paragraph from one of its characteristic editorials of the period:

The danger most to be feared is that men who really don't believe in Confederation at all should so seek to extend and consolidate the Federal legislative and executive power that the Local Governments and Legislatures shall be in danger of becoming mere shadows and shams, and that the recoil from such a danger may lead to the opposite extreme of ignoring national unity, and in zeal for mere local interests and specialties, the breaking up of Confederation altogether.[27]

This was a shrewd if not wholly accurate statement of the case for the provinces. It acquitted the agitation for provincial rights of any subversive efforts against the union, and even claimed for it the superior virtue of seeking to save the union from the treachery of its apparent friends. The constant reiteration of such protests could not fail to have an influence on public opinion throughout the province. The weakness of the federalist programme lay in the fact that it presupposed a general sentiment in the country which would support the dominion government in a dispute with a province. This assumption was not correct. The manner in which federation had been accomplished, and the bitter opposition it aroused in certain sections of the dominion deprived the federal government of the support of any widespread feeling of patriotic attachment. The provinces were old and familiar friends. The dominion was as yet a new and untried entity. That Macdonald himself soon came to realize this handicap of the federal authority is suggested by a passage in the letter to Sir John Young already referred to in another connection. Warning the governor-general that he might have some day a body of advisers com-

---

cil, subject to any instructions he may from time to time receive from the General Government and subject to any provisions that may be made in this behalf by the General Parliament."

[25] *Sessional papers, Canada,* 1869, no. 16.
[26] The *Globe,* July 3, 1869.
[27] *Ibid.,* April 2, 1870.

posed of "states rights" men who would look more to sectional than to general interests, he went on to say:

The natural tendency of public men is in that direction. Each member of your Government holds his position from his supposed influence in his own province, and he will be disinclined to lessen that influence by acting for the Dominion against his province should these interests come in conflict. This is more especially the case now, when the General Government is new, and the Dominion has no associations, political or historical, connected with it. We are all yet mere provincial politicians—Bye and bye, it is hoped that some of us may rise to the level of National Statesmen.[28]

At the close of Macdonald's first administration all that was needed to create an organized agitation for the assertion of provincial rights was the presence of a strong and aggressive premier in one of the provinces who would be willing to accept the leadership in a movement for the defence of provincial autonomy. Such a leader was found in the person of Oliver Mowat. A former cabinet minister of the united provinces, a member of the Canadian delegation at the Quebec Conference, a skilful lawyer with a mind well trained in constitutional precedents, he had occupied for some years following the federation of the provinces the high judicial post of vice-chancellor for Ontario.[29] The circumstances which induced him to accept the leadership of the Liberal party in Ontario are significant. The Sandfield Macdonald government, following the example of the first federal administration at Ottawa, was intended to be a non-party government composed of the friends of union. It included both Conservatives and Reformers in its ranks, but the preponderance lay with the Conservatives, and the tendency as time passed was to regard it as a Conservative administration.[30] In the legislature the opposition was led by Edward Blake and Alexander Mackenzie, both of whom held seats also in the dominion parliament under the rule of dual representation which prevailed at the time. The Ontario elections of 1871 gave a hostile verdict against the Sandfield Macdonald government, and when the legislature met in December of that year, Mr. Blake was called upon to form the first Liberal ministry of Ontario. When, however, the act abolishing dual representation was passed by the dominion parliament in the session of 1872, Blake and Alexander Mackenzie, the provincial treasurer, were obliged to choose between the dominion parliament and the provincial legislature. The situation in the dominion parliament following the general election of 1872 was such that the Liberal opposition had a reasonable hope of forming an administration at Ottawa within a short period.[31]

---

[28] *Macdonald letter book*, no. 12, 443–447.

[29] C. R. W. Biggar, *Sir Oliver Mowat* (Toronto, 1905), I, 134.

[30] *Ibid.*, 148.

[31] At the general election of 1872, Sir John Macdonald's majority in the House of Commons was reduced from 68 to 6.

If Mowat could be persuaded to accept the leadership of the Liberal party in Ontario, Blake and Mackenzie would be free to lead the forces of the party in the dominion parliament. This consideration undoubtedly had its weight in Mowat's decision, but the real reasons which impelled him to resign his judgeship for the precarious life of politics were the convictions which influenced his policy during the remainder of his public life. He was strongly of the opinion that provincial autonomy was threatened by the centralizing tendencies which he observed in the conduct of the federal administration. Holding this opinion, he was resolved to champion the cause of provincial rights as head of the government of the largest and most influential province of the dominion.[32]

The appearance of Oliver Mowat on the Canadian political scene at this juncture was the signal which opened the active conflict over provincial rights. It was an event of which Sir John Macdonald understood the full significance. In their exchange of letters after Mowat had tendered his resignation as vice-chancellor there is a note of challenge beneath the courteous phrases of congratulation and acknowledgment.

I hope [wrote Macdonald] that the relations between the Dominion Government and that of Ontario will be pleasant. There is no reason why they should not be so. Blake announced, on taking office, that he was going to pursue that course; but I fear that he allowed his double position under the dual system to affect his mind prejudicially. We all profess to have, and I have no doubt, sincerely, have the same object in view—the government of the country. We must therefore try to work the new machine, with the construction of which we have had so much to do, with as little friction as possible.[33]

To which Mowat replied:

I have ever felt greatly interested in the success of Confederation, and I agree with you that its success will be aided by proper relations being maintained between the Dominion and Local Governments as such, even when these are not in the hands of the same political party.[34]

From this common devotion to the success of Confederation, one might conclude that the relations between the dominion and Ontario were assured of harmony in the years ahead. Exactly the reverse was true. The explanation lies in the fact that Macdonald and Mowat though equally pledged to the success of the new federation, had widely different views regarding the means and methods by which that object might be attained. Macdonald held with all sincerity that the provinces must be relegated to a position of subordination in the federal scheme. Mowat, with equal sincerity, believed that the autonomy of the provinces must be

---

[32] Biggar, *Sir Oliver Mowat*, I, 152.

[33] *Macdonald papers*, Correspondence with Sir Oliver Mowat, 1852–1881, folio, 327.

[34] *Ibid.*, folio, 329.

safeguarded against federal encroachment, and that this was the only basis upon which the union could endure. Around the theories and personalities of these two men the struggle over provincial rights was to continue for twenty years. The changing tide of the conflict determined in large measure the development of the Canadian constitution in its internal aspects during this period of Canadian history.

6

The Relevance of "Canada First"*

David P. Gagan

THIS ARTICLE is a distillation of much of the author's masters' thesis on this subject for the University of Western Ontario and touches in part on his doctoral dissertation, "The Queen's Champion: the Life of George Taylor Denison III, Soldier, Author, Magistrate and Canadian Tory Patriot" (Duke, 1968). It places "Canada First" in a more realistic historical perspective than heretofore. By putting the emphasis on the earlier period, the four years beginning in April, 1868, which he considers much more significant than the later and rather feeble and idealistic third-party phase, Professor Gagan exposes Canada First for what it was: a small body of young intellectuals with an erratic desire, while defending Confederation, to display an aggressive, illiberal semi-racist nationalism or (excluding Haliburton) Ontario "imperialism." It was a nationalism quite unsuited for a pluralistic and bicultural Canada.

To R. G. Haliburton, George Denison, W. A. Foster, Charles Mair, and others, Canada through a great "rattling war" against the "weak and effeminate" United States would become the powerful home of a superior race, fashioned from the superior "races" of Northwestern Europe and fused in "the icy bosom of the frozen north," the harsh and inhospitable environment which guaranteed that the fittest would survive. When Riel resisted on the Red River, the poet Mair, who was out on the prairies, called for revenge, arguing that Canada was being held back by the stagnant medievalism of the French and the basic racial inferiority of the Indian.

This sentiment was very different from some of the later Canada Firsters who from 1872 on were deeply influenced by the doctrinaire liberal Goldwin Smith and tried unsuccessfully to launch a new puri-fied Anglophobic political party of principle. Despite the efforts of past historians, neither group now appears well suited to be Canadian heroes.

* *Journal of Canadian Studies*, V (1970), pp. 36–40.

DISCONCERTED by the aggressive ethnocentrism displayed by the "Twelve Apostles" during the Red River uprising of 1869–70, Canadian historians invariably give short shrift to this earlier, secretive phase of the Canada First movement and preoccupy themselves with the "really significant part of Canada First,"[1] the rise and decline of the Canada First Party. As a result, "Canada First" has become synonymous with the first unsuccessful incursion of the intellectuals into the political life of the new Dominion, and with the awakening of liberal nationalism in modern Canadian history. Described as a relic of the age of romantic nationalism, out of place in the age of political realism, Canada First has been both praised and criticized for its preoccupation with the visionary, rather than the practical aspects of Canada's "new nationality." But in either case, historical judgment has tended toward the view that Canada First left a legacy of farsighted policies which were eventually "plundered" by less omniscient politicians, and that it served a useful purpose in demonstrating the potential of a nonpartisan third force to elevate the normally low level of Canadian political discourse.[2]

This has been the relevance of Canada First for Canadian historiography. But Canada First did not come into being as the harbinger of a new era of liberal nationalism, or as the purveyor of constitutional theory and a pristine political morality. "Canada First" was conceived as a militantly patriotic expression of faith in the historical objectives of Confederation on the part of five young men who hoped to evoke an outpouring of "national sentiment" consistent with the immensity of the task of creating a transcontinental state. Quite capable of composing romanticized paeans to the visionary promises of a "new nationality," they were equally versed in the meaning of aggressive nationalism. Intolerant and anti-liberal toward dissenting opinion, their Procrustean bed of patriotism often resembled nothing more nor less than the aggressive exclusivism of English-Canadian nationalism. But they had an affinity with the problems of nationality which the ill-starred Canada First Party could never hope to emulate, because they understood *realpolitik*, and therein, perhaps, lies the historical relevance of Canada First.

---

[1] F. H. Underhill, *The Image of Confederation* (Toronto: CBC, 1963), p. 17.

[2] W. S. Wallace, "The Growth of Canadian National Feeling," *Canadian Historical Review*, I (June, 1920), p. 157; Underhill, *op. cit.*; G. M. Hougham, "Canada First: A Minor Party in Microcosm," *Canadian Journal of Economics and Political Science*, XIX (May, 1953), pp. 174–184, attempts to modify this view by stressing the narrow regionalism of Canada First which he sees as a model for later regional protest parties.

The story of the origins of the Canada First movement is well known; of how Charles Mair, W. A. Foster, George Taylor Denison (3rd), Henry J. Morgan, and Robert Grant Haliburton, "the old five of the corner room" as they liked to remember themselves, used to gather for a "smoke and a chat" in Morgan's rooms at Salmon's Hotel, Ottawa, in April of 1868; and of their mutual pledge to work individually or in concert, without regard for party affiliation, to place "Canada First" out of respect for the memory of D'Arcy McGee, the martyred prophet of the "new nationality."[3] The young men shared with each other, and with McGee whose grasp of the economic basis of the "new nationality" has been the subject of a recent revisionist study, something more than a rhetorical vision of national greatness. Haliburton, for example, was the author of two pamphlets, *The Coal Trade of the New Dominion* and *Intercolonial Trade: Our Only Safeguard Against Disunion,* in which he anticipated and defended transcontinental economic consolidation premised on western agricultural development, eastern industrial growth, and maritime commerce as the essential precondition of national unity and survival. Haliburton was in Ottawa, in fact, as a representative of the Nova Scotia Coal Owner's Association, and in his capacity as an ardent opponent of his province's anti-Confederates. He had dined with McGee, on the night of the assassination, to discuss these and related matters, and in the Commons that same evening McGee had made use of some of Haliburton's arguments.[4]

Similarly W. A. Foster, who was a Toronto lawyer and eventually editor of the *Monetary Times,* had written extensively for the *Westminster Review* on the historical basis of and the future prospects for the new nation whose fundamental unity and prosperity would continue to be derived from the political and economic cohesion imposed by the St. Lawrence. Foster's articles, which are reprinted in *Canada First: A Memorial of the Late W. A. Foster, Q.C.,* give some indication of his grasp of the statistical evidence at his command.[5] Mair, on the other hand, had been responsible for much of the research required for the federal government's negotiations with the Hudson's Bay Company for the transfer of the North-West to the Dominion, while George Denison, a lawyer and militia officer, for a decade prior to Confederation had conducted an energetic campaign to convince a succession of parsimoni-

---

[3] University of Western Ontario, James Coyne Papers, Morgan to Coyne, 10 Feb., 1890; George T. Denison, *The Struggle for Imperial Unity* (Toronto: Macmillan Co., 1909), pp. 10–12.

[4] PAC, Henry J. Morgan Papers, Haliburton to Morgan, 6 March, 1896; R. G. Haliburton, *The Coal Trade of the New Dominion* (Halifax, 1868) and *Intercolonial Trade: Our Only Safeguard Against Disunion* (Ottawa, 1868); Robin Burns, "D'Arcy McGee and The Economic Aspects of New Nationality," *Canadian Historical Association Annual Report, 1967* (Toronto: University of Toronto Press, 1968), pp. 95–104.

[5] *Canada First: A Memorial of the Late W. A. Foster, Q.C.* (Toronto: Hunter, Rose & Co., 1890), pp. 93–168.

ous ministries to maintain an indigenous defense establishment consistent with British North American self-determination. He was in Ottawa hoping to hold Sir John A. Macdonald, to whom he had first been introduced by McGee, to an earlier promise to nominate him as Assistant Adjutant-General of Cavalry for Ontario, perhaps with a view to putting some of his ideas into operation.[6]

The Canada Firsters, then, came together as individuals already committed to some aspect of the process of launching, consolidating, and maintaining the integrity of a new nationality. If McGee was the catalyst who had "fired [their] enthusiasm" to play a more vigorous role,[7] it was not only due to his ringing prophesies and blandishments, or to personal friendship, but equally because the Canada Firsters comprehended, and were eager to grapple with, the practical difficulties inherent in creating a transcontinental state.

Nevertheless, the Canada Firsters clearly believed that success was also dependent on the existence of a suitable atmosphere or "total environment" of national unity which would propel development forward on the crest of popular will. McGee's efforts had been stopped short of fruition by Whelan's bullet, and the young men of Canada First decided that their principal objective must be to correct the "want of vision" among Canadians about which McGee had so often complained: hence, Haliburton's forays into the major centres of population, in the early spring of 1869, to deliver a lecture on "The Men of the North and Their Place in History."

In this lecture, not Haliburton the political economist, but rather Haliburton the Fellow of the Royal Society of Northern Antiquaries of Copenhagen, interested in anthropology, ethnology, and evolution, was very much in evidence. Great nations, Haliburton maintained, invariably had enjoyed a "spring time of life, full of freshness, vigour and hope," when patriots "purified" by "fiery ordeals" had come forward to mold the nation's destiny. In contrast, he complained, Canada had "crawl[ed] into existence in . . . a humdrum, common place, matter of fact way" that had created as little excitement as the incorporation of a "joint stock company." With neither "faith in a bright future, [nor] . . . the memory of a glorious past" to sustain it, a distinctive Canadian national spirit was languishing under the "cautious indifference of old age."[8] And yet there was hope for the creation of a genuine national sentiment and national unity. Were not Canadians the descendants of the "Aryan tribes" of the German forests who had given Western civilization its superior systems

---

[6] W. L. Morton, *Alexander Begg's Red River Journal. . . . Publications of the Champlain Society*, Vol. XXXV (Toronto: University of Toronto Press, 1965), pp. 53–55; PAC, Denison Papers, 26, Diary, 15 April–26 May, 1868; *Ibid.*, I, Macdonald to Denison, 6 January, 1868; and see, for example, Denison's *A Review of the Militia Policy of the Present Administration* (Hamilton, 1863).

[7] Coyne Papers, Morgan to Coyne, 10 Feb., 1890.

[8] R. G. Haliburton, *The Men of the North and Their Place in History* (Montreal: John Lovell, 1869) p. 1.

of law and government, and who had been historically the dominant races of western Europe? Here was Canada's, "Norland's," past greatness, and the continued fusion of the Saxon, Norman, Celtic, and Teutonic races in "the icy bosom of the frozen north" was the key to a great future. *"We are the Northmen of the New World,"* Haliburton asserted, and therefore Canada's emergence as a preeminent power, the home of a superior race, was foreordained.[9]

As C. C. Berger has noted, Haliburton was the first Canadian intellectual to apply the theme of northern superiority to this country, providing the stimulus for much subsequent rhetoric about the "True North."[10] Apart from Haliburton's apparent familiarity with the writings of many early 19th-century European romantic nationalists, his choice, and the timing, of this concept of a struggle for survival against a harsh and inhospitable environment producing a superior race of northmen who would ultimately triumph over the "weak and effeminate South" were equally exhilarating in the light of contemporary American nationalism. In the United States, the isothermal theory of the German physical geographer, Alexander von Humboldt, that a *benevolent* nature had foreordained the triumph of the great American Republic, was being popularized and disseminated.[11] One wonders if Haliburton did not have a deeper political purpose in mind when he chose as a vehicle of explanation the inherent aggressiveness which stood in direct contrast to the ideology of American "manifest destiny." Certainly George Denison, whose congenital anti-Americanism knew no bounds, thought Haliburton was on the right track and predicted that Canadian national unity would be the result of a "rattling war with the United States" when "the men of the North . . . will be able to teach the Yankees that we [are] . . . the dominant race."[12]

These relatively hollow rumblings of aggressive intent were characteristic of most of the early writings, both private and public, of the Canada Firsters; and at least one scholar has suggested that a defensively imperialistic, but practically impotent, tendency on the part of new societies may be a highly desirable instrument of national unity, since it breeds cohesiveness through the apparent existence of an externalized threat.[13] As events were to prove, however, the militant impulses of the Canada Firsters were to find practical expression first in response to the Red River uprising of 1869–70, and their visceral reaction has impugned their credibility as Canadian nationalists.

---

[9] *Ibid.*, pp. 2–10.

[10] Carl Berger, "The True North Strong and Free," *Nationalism in Canada*, Peter Russell, ed. (Toronto: McGraw-Hill, 1966), pp. 5–9.

[11] Henry Nash Smith, *Virgin Land: The American West as Symbol and Myth*, Reprint (New York: Random House, 1967), pp. 42–44.

[12] Queen's University, Mair Papers, Denison to Mair, 10 March, 8 June, 1869.

[13] Joseph Schumpeter, *Social Classes: Imperialism* (New York: Meridian Books, 1964), pp. 7–21.

When Riel and his *métis* followers executed Thomas Scott, an Ontario Orangeman, in 1870 to emphasize their determination in pursuing their political objectives, it was the ever-increasing clique of Canada Firsters, or "Twelve Apostles" as they began secretly to style themselves in 1870, who led the agitation in Ontario against the *métis*. To all intents and purposes, "Canada First" became the shibboleth of the cultural and economic imperialism of English-speaking Canada, and the Apostles were able to galvanize public opinion into a bloodthirsty demand for revenge through a series of public meetings, demonstrations, and fanatical newspaper articles. Foster, who is often described as the shy and retiring intellectual of the group, took to the front page of the Toronto *Daily Telegraph* to denounce Scott's "cold-blooded murder," and Macdonald for treating with the "emissaries of murderers."[14] "Shall French Rebels Rule Our Dominion?" the Apostles' broadsheets demanded of the four thousand Orangemen who paraded in Toronto on July 12th, 1870. Denison, who organized a successful demonstration in Toronto against Sir George Cartier and Archbishop Taché the following week, went so far as to threaten civil insurrection if Macdonald pardoned Riel and abandoned the west to the *métis*.[15] It does not seem wide of the mark to suggest that the Apostles' activities were instrumental not only in providing the political justification for an expeditionary force, but in sustaining, throughout May, June, and July, Ontario's desire for revenge which produced the punitive mentality of Colonel Garnet Wolseley's troops.

Gone from the Canada First catechism was any pretense of reconciliation between Canada's two founding cultures. French Canadians, whose "Norman" ancestry previously had been adequate proof of their racial standing, now became a national liability in the eyes of the Apostles. Mair, who was in Red River before and during the uprising and who had been instrumental in recruiting John Schultz, leader of the settlement's Canadian party, for the Apostles, had supplied the necessary evidence of the "mediaeval inertia" and indolence assumed to be characteristic of the Francophone population. "In general," Mair asserted, "the Frenchman married the Indian and sank to the level of her tastes and inclinations. In general, the Englishman married the Indian and raised her to the level of his own."[16] Convinced by these and similar assertions that a reactionary, priest-ridden French society in the North-West was the principal "bar to progress, and to the extension of a great Anglo-Saxon Dominion across the Continent . . . ,"[17] the Apostles crowned their activities by organizing the *North-West Emigration Aid Society of Canada*. Ostensibly a clearing house for information directed to the prospective immigrant, in

14 Toronto *Daily Telegraph*, April 4, 1870.

15 Denison, *Struggle For Imperial Unity*, pp. 37–38; Toronto *Globe*, July 23, 1870.

16 Reprinted in George T. Denison, *Reminiscences of the Red River Rebellion of 1869* (Toronto, 1873), p. 3.

17 Toronto *Globe*, Aug. 4, 1870.

fact the society's objectives were purely political. As J. D. Edgar, supposedly a liberal nationalist and a firm believer in racial harmony,[18] told the inaugural meeting, it was their duty to insure that the west was settled, by force if necessary, by "a population liberal and intelligent, and in sympathy with" the cultural traditions of Anglo-Saxon, Protestant Ontario.[19]

Canada First's activities in 1869–70 suggest, and several commentators have asserted, that in reality the movement signified nothing more than "Ontario First," if not "Toronto First," and that the Apostles showed their true colours by reviving the older racial and religious prejudices of pre-Confederation Canada West. In a more general sense, perhaps they also exhibited some of the less appealing characteristics of modern nationalism, insofar as the Apostles were intolerant of dissenting opinion and illiberal toward minority interests. On the other hand, the Canada Firsters were demonstrably committed to the idea of Confederation as a political union for economic and strategic advantage. Confederation was a cultural accommodation only insofar as it removed past impediments to the realization of British North America's "manifest destiny." In Macdonald's handling of the territorial transfer, the Apostles, like many Canadians, thought they discerned a fundamental betrayal of trust, a willingness to delay the achievement of the "grand design" for purely political considerations which Confederation was to have rendered obsolete.[20] Thus, speaking for his colleagues in the wake of their summerlong agitation, Denison served notice on the older parties, particularly the party of Confederation, that the stifled ambitions of "Young Canada" would not tolerate for long their lack of progress. "A party is instinctively forming," he wrote,

that will uphold the honour of our Dominion; that will strive to make the name "Canadian" feared and respected; that will look to extending our territory and increasing our wealth, strength and military organization.[21]

The threat was an idle one, but it indicated the extent to which the Apostles had come to identify national greatness with an "imperialistic" image. As Denison suggested in his lecture "The Duty of Canadians to Canada" which he delivered frequently in the spring of 1871, the Apostles subscribed to the romantic notion that national sentiment properly ought to be the product of a "violent struggle for political existence."[22] In their own limited experience, that struggle had so far taken the form of a

---

[18] Robert M. Stamp, "J. D. Edgar and the Liberal Party: 1867–96," *Canadian Historical Review*, XLV (June, 1964), p. 95.

[19] Toronto *Globe*, Aug. 4, 1870.

[20] PAC, Denison Papers, 3, Mair to Denison, 17 March, 1876; Mair Papers, Denison to Mair, 20 Feb., 1876.

[21] Toronto *Globe*, Sept. 15, 1870.

[22] "The Duty of Canadians to Canada," ms. in PAC, Denison Papers, 43. Denison, *The Struggle for Imperial Unity*, pp. 52–53, offers a very expurgated version; and see Haliburton, *The Men of the North and Their Place in History*, p. 1.

limited war of attrition against forces hostile to the expansion of the Dominion, and the "patriotic" sentiment which it had aroused in some quarters, at least, seemed to verify the equation.

There were other reasons, however, for infusing national sentiment with a spirit of militarism. The resurgence of Fenian activities in 1870, England's decision to withdraw the imperial garrisons in 1871, and the increasing abrasiveness of Anglo-American relations after the Civil War had again propelled the defense question into prominence. Since, in Denison's opinion, the "pounds, shillings and pence"-conscious "school of [British] politicians" could no longer be relied upon to defend Canada's sovereignty, then militarism was an "absolutely essential" element of national policy in order to discourage potential aggressors.[23] The thrust of Denison's lecture, therefore, was that a "defensively warlike" mentality which inspired a national spirit must become a trait of the Canadian identity.

Denison's lecture represents much that is central to the early history of Canada First. It reflects, as do all of the Apostles' writings, the constantly shifting fortunes of federal union; and it attempts, equally, to define and delineate a vehicle of national sentiment, of popular will, consistent with the vicissitudes of the experiment. Thus, whereas Haliburton laboured in 1868 to formulate a national mythology for the new nation at its inception, apparently because it had none, by 1871 Denison was putting his mind to work to redefine national spirit in terms of three or four years of difficult practical experience. Whereas Haliburton could claim that a Darwinian struggle with the "stern cold North" had predetermined the course of nationhood, Denison was obliged to acknowledge that the interplay of the forces which had given rise to the idea of Confederation continued to affect national progress. Moreover, there were even a few "timid spirits" who might have to be "shown the stupidity of their conduct" and forced, willy-nilly, into a patriotic mold in order to sustain popular determination. In short, with each successive crisis the Apostles were forced to reexamine their premises of "nationality"; and while they do not appear to have lost any of their initial exuberance, it is clear that they were beginning to shed much of their youthful naivety, moving their vision of greatness into closer harmony with political realities.

Therefore, 1871 represents the high-water mark, and the turning point, of the Canada First movement. The Apostles' temporary loss of faith in Sir John A. Macdonald's capacity to solve the problems of Confederation was swiftly replaced, under the *aegis* of the Treaty of Washington, by their wholehearted, if unwitting, complicity in his political strategy; and having made that "leap of faith," the Apostles came full circle. As much as any other identifiable faction, Canada First willingly played the role written in the script for the Canadian public by the Prime Minister who,

---

23 Denison, *op. cit.*

with consummate skill, turned the ultranationalistic outburst of indignation over the Treaty of Washington into a mandate for his own "national
policy." Haliburton, who snorted angrily that the commercial concessions
granted to Canada "were about as useful as the right to shoot woodcock's
on Boston Common,"[24] circulated from England *A Review of British
Diplomacy and Its Fruits,* which indicated both the extent, and the
object, of Canada First's outrage; "The Jacobites suffered much," Haliburton bitterly complained, "but it was nothing compared to the priva-
tion and neglect with which a grateful country has repaid the United
Empire Loyalists and their descendants for their fidelity."[25]

England's callous disregard of the interests of her former colony was a
shattering revelation for the Canada Firsters, all of whom identified
loyalty to country with loyalty to Britain. For Denison, the "imperial
connexion" was the countervailing force which neutralized the United
States and created the equilibrium essential to national self-determination; it was also the necessary ingredient of his life-long belief in
Canada's political and even moral superiority over the revolutionary
society to the South.[26] But now that relationship, founded on security in
return for "loyalty," appeared to have been permanently upset, with far-
reaching implications for Canada's continued development as an independent entity on the North American continent. The upshot was the
final chapter in Canada First's attempt to delineate a firm, continuing
basis for a national sentiment which would lead to unity and progress in
spite of Canada's altered circumstances.

"Canada First: or, Our New Nationality," by W. A. Foster, first appeared in the Toronto *Globe* of 17 July, 1871, and was subsequently
issued by Canada First in pamphlet form as the first installment of a
projected series of "National Papers." While Foster's purplish prose and
convoluted syntax infused his argument for a home-grown national
sentiment with a certain loftiness, it scarcely concealed the injured pride,
the wounded sensibilities, and the disillusionment which had prompted
the essay. Reciting a catalogue of instances when Britons had sneeringly
tendered the epithet "colonist" to discredit Canadian endeavours, and
recounting at length the long history of British ingratitude for the unselfish loyalty of British North Americans, Foster concluded that Canadians could no longer bear the "equivocal associations" of their former
status. Therefore, they had no choice but to break with European tradition, to cast aside the "mummied idols of a buried past," and to find the
elements of a new nationality in Canada's North American heritage.

The task would not be easy, Foster ventured to assert, because the
problems of nationality was aggravated by "asperities of race, of creed, of

[24] Toronto Public Library, Denison Papers, Haliburton to Denison, 1 July, 1871.

[25] Copy in PAC, Sir Edward Watkins Papers, n.p.

[26] See, for example, *Imperial Federation, Report of Speech Delivered by Col. Geo.
T. Denison* (Toronto: Imperial Federation League, 1890).

interest." But he was confident that Haliburton's "northmen of the New World" would find some "common basis of agreement strong enough to counteract disintegrating tendencies." He suggested that the ingredients of a national sentiment which could exist apart from regional or cultural loyalties, apart from absolute nationality, could be found in Canada's North American historical experience, in the deeds of her heroes, in the achievements of her great men, in the spirit of her free institutions, and in a common belief in Canada's future mission, however far off, as a truly great nation.

There is a national heart which can be stirred to its depths; a national imagination that can be aroused to a fervent glow; and when noble deeds are to be done, or great triumphs of progress, enthusiasm, youth, step proudly to the front and press forward. . . .

In a word, *patriotism*—love of country, loyalty to its institutions, and simple faith in its goals—the lowest common denominator of nationalism, would be the "motive power" of the "political machine." Had the Apostles also discovered the meaning of "political nationality?"

"Canada First: or, Our New Nationality" stands as the Canada First movement's compromise with the pace and direction of national development as defined by the fathers, and the party, of Confederation. Macdonald's past sins had not been entirely forgiven. Denison, who had not received the militia appointment that he had demanded as the price of his loyalty, even ran as an independent Liberal in Algoma, in 1872, against the Conservatives who had "huckstered away" Canada's patrimony at Washington in a "disgraceful and humiliating manner."[27] The fact remains, however, that the assertion of popular will generated by the events in Washington wrote *finis*, for the time being, to the Twelve Apostles' agonizing search for an acceptable vehicle of national unity. The newly-discovered, defensively patriotic, latent pride of Canadians conformed to their own conceptions of a national sentiment arising out of a common threat, and a common determination to wage a struggle for survival. Reality had proven more reliable than myth after all.

There were those who interpreted the import of Foster's lecture in quite a different light. Professor Goldwin Smith, formerly of Oxford and Cornell Universities, the leading apostle of the "Manchester School" of economics, and a recent immigrant to Canada, possessed well-known views on the political destiny of Canada once the Empire had been dismembered and an independent Dominion was isolated in the gravitational pull of the United States. "Canada First: or, Our New Nationality" convinced him that the second stage of this dialectic had been set in motion, and that Canada First represented, in fact, an embryonic "Independence Party."[28] Equally appealing to Smith was Canada First's

27 PAC, Denison Papers, 18, *Election Manifesto*.
28 Cornell University, Smith Papers, Smith to Waring, 9 Oct., 1871.

nonpartisan image. "I must confess," he told Denison, "that I am unable to see the dividing line between parties here, or to feel decided allegiance to either of them."[29] Inevitably, Goldwin Smith moved into the ever-widening "magic circle" of Canada Firsters, primarily as a contributor to the *Canadian Monthly and National Review*, a journal initiated in 1872 "to give the intellectual life of Canada an organ,"[30] and then, to all intents and purposes, as the movement's resident intellectual.

In the meantime, the "old five of the corner room," for a variety of reasons, gradually lost control of Canada First. Denison took up a series of appointments as Ontario's Commissioner for Immigration in London; Mair returned to the west to become a shopkeeper in Portage La Prairie; and Haliburton decided to stay in England. Similarly, at least two more of the movements earliest and most militant recruits abandoned the Apostles. Edgar returned to the Liberal fold, while Schultz entered Parliament as the M.P. for Lisgar in 1871. That left Foster and a group of Torontonians, Liberals and lawyers for the most part, to direct the fortunes of the movement under the tutelage of Goldwin Smith, whose political commentary, appearing in the *Canadian Monthly*, was a weathercock of Canada First's new directions. "[So] far as we can see," ran one article,

party can have no permanent justification, no lasting guarantee against corruption. . . . Party without principle inevitably becomes faction; and faction as inevitably supports itself by intrigue, demagogism, and corruption.[31]

The innate wisdom of that, and similar, pronouncements seemed to have been thoroughly validated when the "Pacific Scandal" was revealed to the public in the spring of 1873; and when it subsequently appeared that Macdonald and his "corruptionists" must resign, Foster, Smith, and the others decided upon a rather bold, to say the least, course of action. "A number of us have determined to try," Foster wrote to his brother-in-law, James Coyne,

if a new political party could be made to take hold of public favour—a party that will be more distinctly national if not patriotic than the present ones. . . . We intend to break out ere long: Meantime the Canadian Monthly is ploughing up the ground. We think of running Goldwin Smith for West Toronto if Crawford accepts the Lt. Governorship.[32]

John Crawford, Liberal-Conservative M.P. for West Toronto, did accept the Lt. Governorship of Ontario from Macdonald in the dying days of his administration, and the resultant by-election which was to be fought in

---

[29] TPRL, Denison Papers, Smith to Denison, 2 Sept., 1872.

[30] Smith Papers, Smith to Waring, 9 Oct., 1871.

[31] "The Late Session of the Parliament of Ontario," *Canadian Monthly and National Review*, I (April, 1872), p. 322.

[32] Coyne Papers, Foster to Coyne, 30 Sept., 1873.

December was to be a test of strength between Grits and Tories prior to a general election.

Smith, however, conveniently departed for England, leaving Foster without a candidate, so the obvious solution was a public nomination meeting. In the first week of December, broadsheets were distributed inviting all who felt the need for a new political party to attend such a meeting on December 6, sponsored by the "Canada First" Party and its parent organization, The Canadian National Association.[33]

There, confusion reigned supreme. Foster's law partner and the Liberal candidate, Thomas Moss, was in attendance as were many of his supporters. But an equally large faction of Tories also appeared, and after a confusing opening address by William Howland, the chairman, who expended half an hour condemning Canadian "toadyism" to Britain and British traditions, the meeting devolved into a bitter procedural wrangle between Tories, Grits, and Canada Firsters over whose resolutions and amendments took precedence. When the smoke had cleared, the new "Canada First" Party found itself publicly committed to support Thomas Moss.[34]

On the day of the nomination meeting, the *Mail* had demanded: "What are we to understand by 'Canada First'?" After the meeting, the party journals felt no more enlightened, perhaps fortunately for Canada First. Liberal newspapers tended to withhold comment, in any case, since their candidate enjoyed Canada First's support. Liberal-Conservative organs speculated that Canada First might be the protectionist wing of the Liberal Party, the Liberal wing of the Grit Party, or, on the strength of Howland's anti-British remarks, probably an incipient independence, republican, or "know-nothing" party.[35] Only the editors of the Montreal *Gazette*, who remembered Foster's patriotic "Canada First: or, Our New Nationality," thought that an independent political movement under his direction had real merit. Therefore, they asked, why had Canada First compromised itself by supporting the Liberal Party?[36] There could be no answer, of course, because it had not been Foster's intention to support Moss. Canada First had been the victim of superior political tactics and the ineptitude of its own leaders.

Rather than admit failure, however, they decided to make yet another attempt to launch their party. On January 8, 1874 (in the same week that Mackenzie called a general election), Canada First issued a new manifesto designed to clear the air. The broadsheet, *Canada First: Address of the Canadian National Association to the People of Canada*,[37] com-

---

33 Toronto *Mail*, Dec. 6, 1873.

34 This account of the meeting is from the Toronto *Globe*, Dec. 8, 1873.

35 See clippings in *W. A. Foster's Canada First Scrapbook* (Canadian Library Association Microfilm).

36 Montreal *Gazette*, Dec. 10, 1873.

37 In *W. A. Foster's Canada First Scrapbook;* reprinted in *Canada First: Memorial*, pp. 48–56, but without the platform.

plained at length that Canada First's motives had been unfairly impugned and assailed by "fortune-tellers" and "sycophantic partisans" for no other reason than to make political capital at the expense of the new party! That in itself, the authors implied, was good and sufficient reason for a new party which would not engage in the bitter partisanship characteristic of Grit and Tory, labels "merely synonymous with cat and dog," "ins and outs."

But the principal argument for a new party, they contended, lay in the sorry pass to which national unity and standards of political morality had been brought by "despotic individuals" who had chained progress to the "chariot wheels" of party, and circumscribed patriotism in the interest of political advantage. What was needed was a new party dedicated only to the "cultivation of a Canadian national sentiment." Canada First put itself forward as the most hopeful light on the horizon. Moreover, it now offered a firm platform consisting of eleven planks that ranged from blatant contradictions (imperial consolidation and protectionism) through improbable schemes (political union with the British West Indies) to benign puerility ("pure and economic administration of public affairs").

"Delightfully innocent," crowed the editor of the *Globe*.

There is not a man in Canada . . . who would not be ashamed to put his name to such an abortion. Let these sucking politicians . . . go to school and study the alphabet of politics in the meantime, while they "tarry at Jericho till their beards are grown."[38]

Just as unceremoniously, and with equal derision, the other party organs hooted Canada First off the political stage, and once again the movement turned in upon itself, waiting for the moment when its fortunes might be revived. There were many who speculated that Canada First's millenium had arrived in October, 1874, when Edward Blake, the *enfant terrible* of the Liberal Party, incorporated much of the Canadian National Association's platform in his celebrated "Aurora Speech."[39] But Foster chose to believe that Blake had stolen Canada First's thunder and that the movement had suffered for it.[40] In the meantime, the association had launched its own paper, the *Nation*, which survived only until 1876, and a more enduring edifice, the National Club, now the rendezvous of Toronto's financial establishment. The National Club was intended as the headquarters of the Canadian National Association, modelled upon London's Carleton and Reform Clubs. Perhaps it has even regained that legitimacy. But in any event, within a year of its opening the club was chiefly distinguished for its "good functions—excellent pub—nice com-

---

[38] Toronto *Globe,* Jan. 9, 1874.

[39] See the newspaper commentary appended to Hon. Edward Blake, M.P., "*A National Sentiment!*" (Ottawa: E. A. Perry, 1874), pp. 23–88.

[40] Morgan Papers, Foster to Morgan, 5 Sept., 1877.

pany—best of liquor. . . ."[41] Foster might bravely maintain that "Canada First is well" somewhere within the confines of the National Club, but in fact it was never heard from again.

Denison and Mair, who had abandoned Canada First when it lost sight of its original purpose, thoroughly understood the decline and fall of this "Grit Frankenstein" whose "audacious theorists" had traded in abstrusities when development demanded action. If ever Canada First was to be revived,

it must be in a new dress, under a new name, and in some time of public excitement when some great rallying cry can form a pivot around which the young men can gather.[42]

For the time being, however, they were both prepared to place their trust in Sir John A. Macdonald's "national policy" as the closest approximation to Canada First's vision of nationality.

Considered in relation to the history of the earlier movement, the significance of the Canada First party, which one contemporary aptly dismissed as a "flash in the pan,"[43] seems open to serious qualification. The "Twelve Apostles," for all of their romantic cant and sophomoric irresponsibility, comprehended the political and economic ramifications of Confederation, and were prepared to resort to "blood and iron" to achieve the objectives of union. But once Canada First became a political party, when it turned away from the shibboleths of aggressive nationalism to pursue intellectual platitudes and nice political theories, when it ceased to be a mirror of popular hopes and fears and swamped itself, to borrow a phrase from D'Arcy McGee, in an "exhalation of self-opinion," it rapidly disintegrated. The real significance of "Canada First," if it has any at all, would appear to reside with the young militants who venerated Mazzini, Garibaldi, and Friedrich Schiller's legendary Swiss patriots, and whose single objective was to promote the real, as well as the visionary, promises of Confederation in order to create *"ein einig Volk von Brüdern."*[44]

---

41 Mair Papers, Foster to Mair, 10 June, 1875.

42 Mair Papers, Denison to Mair, 20 Feb., 1876; PAC, Denison Papers, Mair to Denison, 17 March, 1876.

43 James Young, *Public Men and Public Life in Canada*, Vol. II (2 vols, Toronto: William Briggs, 1912), p. 211.

44 "A single nation of brothers"; the phrase is Schiller's, from *Wilhelm Tell.*

7

The Wake*

Ralph Connor

FOR THE STUDENT of history, the novel is often a useful complement to the works of historians. The novel can provide stimulating insights into the social history of an era, re-creating passions and prejudices with meaning and emotion in a way which is very difficult for those writing narrative or analytical history. As there are few works yet in Canadian social history, some novels can help to fill this void providing they are written with skill and close knowledge of the period and people described.

This chapter taken from Ralph Connor's *The Man from Glengarry* illustrates several important social questions for these highland settlements in eastern Ontario. Connor in real life was the Rev. Charles Gordon, a prominent Presbyterian minister of the social gospel tradition who in his work and in his writing emphasized the moral aspects of religion in Victorian Canada. For so many Canadians religion was the paramount interest in their lives and debates such as this one over salvation for the soul must have been frequent. Hell and damnation were of overriding significance to such people. In this section, before the coffin of a brave young hero, the stern Calvinist of traditional Presbyterianism, is challenged from the outside by the concept of saving love and the emphasis on morality. Later in life the author, as moderator of the Presbyterian church, helped to push the bulk of that denomination into the United Church with the anti-Calvinist Methodists. Like many of the popular novels of the day, there is an element of the sermon in the message of the novel something which Canadians relished. His crusading moralism was a true reflection of Victorian Canada.

In this chapter Connor describes vividly one of the old social customs. A son of the Camerons has been drowned in a logging accident and the

---

* From *The Man from Glengarry*, pp. 97–107.

friends gather with the family for the night-long "Wake" prior to the funeral.

T HE WAKE was an important feature in the social life of the people of Indian Lands. In ancient days, in the land of their forefathers, the wake had been deemed a dire necessity for the safeguarding of the dead, who were supposed to be peculiarly exposed to the malicious attacks of evil spirits. Hence, with many lighted candles, and with much incantation, friends would surround the body through the perilous hours of darkness. It was a weird and weary vigil, and small wonder if it appeared necessary that the courage and endurance of the watchers should be fortified with copious draughts of "mountain dew," with bread and cheese accompaniments. And the completeness of their trust in the efficacy of such supports was too often evidenced by the condition of the watchers toward the dawn of the morning. And indeed, if the spirits were not too fastidious, and if they had so desired, they could have easily flown away, not only with the "waked," but with the "wakers" as well.

But those days and those notions had long passed away. The wake still remained, but its meaning and purpose had changed. No longer for the guarding of the dead, but for the comfort of the living, the friends gathered to the house of mourning and watched the weary hours. But Highland courtesy forbade that the custom of refreshing the watchers should be allowed to die out, and hence, through the night, once and again, the whisky, bread, and cheese were handed around by some close friend of the family, and were then placed upon the table for general use. It was not surprising that, where all were free to come and welcome to stay, and where anything like scantiness in providing or niggardliness in serving would be a matter of family disgrace, the wake often degenerated into a frolic, if not a debauch. In order to check any such tendency, it had been the custom of late years to introduce religious services, begun by the minister himself and continued by the elders.

As the evening fell, a group of elders stood by the back door of Long John Cameron's sorrow-stricken home, talking quietly over the sad event and arranging for the "exercises" of the night. At a little distance from them sat Yankee, with Ranald beside him, both silent and listening somewhat indifferently to the talk of the others. Yankee was not in his element. He was always welcome in the homes of his comrades, for he was ready with his tongue and clever with his fingers, but with the graver and religious side of their lives he had little in common. It was, perhaps, this feeling that drew him towards Macdonald Dubh and Ranald, so that for weeks at a time he would make their house his home. He had "no use for wakes," as he said himself, and had it not been that it was one of the gang that lay dead within, Yankee would have avoided the house until all was over and the elders safely away.

Of the elders, only four were present as yet: Donald Ross, who was ever ready to bring the light of his kindly face to cheer the hearts of the mourners; Straight Rory, who never by any chance allowed himself to miss the solemn joy of leading the funeral psalm; Peter McRae, who carried behind his stern old face a heart of genuine sympathy; and Kenny Crubach, to whom attendance at funerals was at once a duty and a horror.

Donald Ross, to whom all the elders accorded instinctively the place of leader, was arranging the order of "the exercises."

"Mr. McCuaig," he said to Straight Rory, "you will take charge of the singing. The rest of us will, in turn, give out a psalm and read a portion of Scripture with a few suitable remarks, and lead in prayer. We will not be forgetting, brethren," said old Donald, "that there will be sore hearts here this night."

Straight Rory's answer was a sigh so woeful and so deep that Yankee looked over at him and remarked in an undertone to Ranald, "He ain't so cheerful as he might be. He must feel awful inside."

"It is a sad and terrible day for the Camerons," said Peter McRae.

"Aye, it is sad indeed," replied Donald Ross. "He was a good son and they will be missing him bad. It is a great loss."

"Yes, the loss is great," said Peter grimly. "But, after all, that is a small thing."

Straight Rory sighed again even more deeply than before. Donald Ross said nothing.

"What does the old duck mean, anyhow?" said Yankee to Ranald.

The boy made no reply. His heart was sick with horror at Peter's meaning, which he understood only too well.

"Aye," went on Peter, "it is a terrible, mysterious Providence, and a heavy warning to the ungodly and careless."

"He means me, I guess," remarked Yankee to Ranald.

"It will perhaps be not amiss to any of us," said Kenny Crubach sharply.

"Indeed, that is true," said Donald Ross, in a very humble voice.

"Yes, Mr. Ross," said Peter, ignoring Kenny Crubach, "but at times the voice of Providence cannot be misunderstood, and it will not do for the elders of the church to be speaking soft things when the Lord is speaking in judgement and wrath."

Donald was silent, while Straight Rory assented with a heart-rending "Aye, aye," which stirred Yankee's bile again.

"What's he talkin' about? He don't seem to be usin' my language," he said, in a tone of wrathful perplexity. Ranald was too miserable to answer, but Kenny was ready with his word.

"Judgement and wrath," he echoed quickly. "The man would require to be very skilful whatever in interpreting the ways of Providence, and very bold to put such a meaning into the death of a young man such as Malcolm yonder." The little man's voice was vibrating with feeling.

Then Yankee began to understand. "I'll be golblamed to a cinder!" he exclaimed, in a low voice, falling back upon a combination that seemed more suitable to the circumstances. "They ain't sendin' him to hell, are they?" He shut up the knife with which he had been whittling with a sharp snap, and rising to his feet, walked slowly over to the group of elders.

"Far be it from me to judge what is not to be seen," said Peter. "But we are allowed and commanded to discern the state of the heart by the fruits."

"Fruits?" replied Kenny quickly. "He was a good son and brother and friend; he was honest and clean, and he gave his life for another at the last."

"Exactly so," said Peter. "I am not denying much natural goodness, for indeed he was a fine lad; but I will be looking for the evidence that he was in a state of grace. I have not heard of any, and glad would I be to hear it."

The old man's emotion took the sharpness out of Kenny's speech, but he persisted stoutly, "Goodness is goodness, Mr. McRae, for all that."

"You will not be holding the Armenian doctrine of works, Mr. Campbell?" said Peter severely. "You would not be pointing to good works as a ground of salvation?"

Yankee, who had been following the conversation intently, thought he saw meaning in it at last.

"If I might take a hand," he said diffidently, "I might contribute somethin' to help you out."

Peter regarded him a little impatiently. He had forgotten the concrete, for the moment, in the abstract, and was donning his armour for a battle with Kenny upon the "fundamentals." Hence he was not too well pleased with Yankee's interruption. But Donald Ross gladly welcomed the diversion. The subject was to him extremely painful.

"We will be glad," he said to Yankee, "to hear you, Mr. Latham."

"Well," said Yankee slowly, "from your remarks I gathered that you wanted information about the doings of—" he jerked his head towards the house behind him. "Now, I want to say," he continued confidentially, "you've come to the right shop, for I've ate and slept, I've worked and fought, I've lived with him by day and by night, and right through he was the straightest, whitest man I ever seen, and I won't except the boss himself." Yankee paused to consider the effect of this statement, and to allow its full weight to be appreciated; and then he continued: "Yes, sir, you may just bet your—you may be right well sure," correcting himself, "that you're safe in givin'"—here he dropped his voice, and jerked his head towards the house again—"in givin' the highest marks, full value, and no discount. Why," he went on, with an enthusiasm rare in him, "ask any man in the gang, any man on the river, if they ever seen or heard of his doin' a mean or crooked thing, and if you find any feller who says he did, bring him here, and, by"—Yankee remembered himself in time— "and I give you my solemn word that I'll eat him, hat and boots." Yankee brought his bony fist down with a whack into his hand. Then he relapsed into his lazy drawl again. "No, siree, hoss! If it's doin's you're after, don't you be slow in bankin' your little heap on *his* doin's."

Donald Ross grasped Yankee's hand and shook it hard. "I will be thanking you for that word," he said earnestly.

But Peter felt that the cause of truth demanded that he should speak out. "Mr. Latham," he said solemnly, "what you have been saying is very true, no doubt, but 'if a man is not born again he cannot see the kingdom of God.' These are the words of the Lord himself."

"Born again!" said Yankee. "How! I don't seem to get you. But I guess the feller that does the right thing all round has got a purty good chance."

"It is not a man's deeds, we are told," said Peter patiently, "but his heart."

"There you are," said Yankee warmly, "right again, and that's what I always hold to. It's the heart a man carries round in his inside. Never mind your talk, never mind you actin' up for people to see. Give me the heart that is warm and red, and beats proper time, you bet. Say! you're all right." Yankee gazed admiringly at the perplexed and hopeless Peter.

"I am afraid you are not remembering what the Apostle Paul said, Mr. Latham," said Peter, determined to deal faithfully with Yankee. " 'By the deeds of the law shall no flesh be justified.' "

It was now Yankee's turn to gaze helplessly at Peter. "I guess you have dropped me again," he said slowly.

"Man," said Peter, with a touch of severity, "you will need to be more faithful with the Word of God. The Scriptures plainly declare, Mr. Latham, that it is impossible for a man to be saved in his natural state."

Yankee looked blank at this.

"The prophet says that the ploughing and sowing, the very prayers, of the wicked are an abomination to the Lord."

"Why, now you're talkin', but look here." Yankee lowered his tone. "Look here, you wouldn't go for to call"—here again he jerked his head towards the house—"wicked, would you? Fur if you do, why, there ain't any more conversation between you and me."

Yankee was terribly in earnest.

" 'There is none righteous, no, not one,' " quoted Peter, with the air of a man who forces himself to an unpleasant duty.

"That's so, I guess," said Yankee meditatively, "but it depends some on what you mean. I don't set myself up for any copy-bood head-line, but as men go—men, say, just like you here—I'd put—I'd put him alongside, wouldn't you? You expect to get through yourself, I judge?"

This was turning the tables somewhat sharply upon Peter, but Yankee's keen, wide-open eyes were upon him, and his intensely earnest manner demanded an answer.

"Indeed, if it will be so, it will not be for any merit of my own, but only because of the mercy of the Lord in Christ Jesus." Peter's tone was sincerely humble.

"Guess you're all right," said Yankee encouragingly; "and as for—as for—him—don't you worry about that. You may be dead sure about his case."

But Peter only shook his head hopelessly. "You are sorely in need of instruction, Mr. Latham," he said sadly. "We cannot listen to our hearts in this matter. We must do honour to the justice of God, and the word is clear, 'Ye must be born again.' Nothing else avails." Peter's tone was final.

Then Yankee drew a little nearer to him, as if settling down to work.

"Now look here. You let me talk awhile. I ain't up in your side of the business, but I guess we are tryin' to make the same point. Now supposin' you was in for a hoss race, which I hope ain't no offence, seein' it ain't likely but suppose, and to take first money you had to perdoose a two-fifteen gait. 'Purty good lick,' says you; 'now where will I get the nag?' Then you sets down and thinks, and, says you, 'By gum,' which of course you wouldn't, but supposin' says you, 'a Blue Grass bred is the hoss for that gait,' and you begin to inquire around, but there ain't no Blue Grass bred stock in the country, and that race is creeping up close. One day just when you was beginnin' to figure on takin' the dust to the hull field, you sees a colt comin' along the road hittin' up a purty slick gait. 'Hello,' says you, 'that looks likely,' and you begin to negotiate, and you finds out that colt's all right and her time's two-ten. Then you begin to talk about the weather and the crops until you finds out the price, and you offer him half money. Then, when you have fetched him down to the right figure, you pulls out your wad, thinkin' how that colt will make the rest look like a line of fence-posts. 'But hold on,' says you, 'is this here cold Blue Grass bred?' 'Blue Grass! Not much. This here's Grey Eagle stock, North Virginny' says he. 'Don't want her,' says you. 'What's the matter with the colt?' says he. 'Nothin', only she ain't Blue Grass. Got to be Blue Grass." 'But she's got the gait, ain't she?' 'Yes, the gait's all right, action fine, good-looking, too, nothing wrong, but she ain't Blue Grass bred.' And so you lose your race. Now what kind of a name would you call yourself?"

Peter saw Yankee's point, but he only shook his head more hopelessly than before, and turned to enter the house, followed by Straight Rory, still sighing deeply, and old Donald Ross. But Kenny remained a moment behind the others, and offering his hand to Yankee, said "You are a right man, and I will be proud to know you better."

Yankee turned a puzzled face to Kenny. "I say," he inquired, in an amazed voice, "do you think he didn't catch on to me?"

Kenny nodded. "Yes, he understood your point."

"But look here," said Yankee, "that don't hold that—that he is—" Yankee paused. The thought was too horrible, and these men were experts, and were supposed to know.

"It's hard to say," said Kenny diplomatically.

"See here," said Yankee, facing Kenny squarely, "you're a purty level-headed man, and you're up in this business. Do you think with them? No monkeying. Straight talk now." Yankee was in no mood to be trifled with. He was in such deadly earnest that he had forgotten all about Ranald, who was now standing behind him waiting, with white face and parted lips, for Kenny's answer.

"Whisht!" said Kenny, pointing into the kitchen behind. Yankee looked and saw Bella Peter and her father entering. But Ranald was determined to know Kenny's opinion.

"Mr. Campbell," he whispered eagerly, and forgetting the respect due to an elder, he grasped Kenny's arm, "do you think with them?"

"That I do not," said Kenny emphatically, and Yankee, at that word, struck his hand into Kenny's palm with a loud smack.

"I knew blamed well you were not any such dumb fool," he said, softening his speech in deference to Kenny's office and the surrounding circumstances. So saying, he went away to the stable, and when Ranald and his uncle, Macdonald Bhain, followed a little later to put up Peter McGregor's team, they heard Yankee inside, swearing with a fluency and vigour quite unusual with him.

"Whisht, man!" said Macdonald Bhain sternly. "This is no place or time to be using such language. What is the matter with you, anyway?"

But Macdonald could get no satisfaction out of him, and he said to his nephew, "What is it, Ranald?"

"It is the elders, Peter McRae and Straight Rory," said Ranald, sullenly. "They were saying that Mack was—that Mack was—"

"Look here, boss," interrupted Yankee, "I ain't well up in Scriptures, and don't know much about these things, and them elders do, and they—some of them, anyway—are sending Mack to hell. Now, I guess you're just as well up as they are in this business, and I want your solemn opinion." Yankee's face was pale, and his eyes were glaring like a wild beast's. "What I say is," he went on, "if a feller like Mack goes to hell, then there ain't any. At least none to scare me. Where Mack is will be good enough for me. What do you say, boss?"

"Be quiet, man," said Macdonald Bhain gravely, but kindly. "Do you not know you are near to blasphemy there? But I forgive you for the sore heart you have; and about poor Mack yonder, no one will be able to say for certain. I am a poor sinner, and the only claim I have to God's mercy is the claim of a poor sinner. But I will dare to say that I have hope in the Lord for myself, and I will say that I have a great deal more for Mack."

"I guess that settles it all right, then," Yankee, drawing a big breath of content and biting off a huge chew from his plug. "But what the blank blank," he went on savagely, "do these fellers mean, stirring up a man's feelin's like that? Seem to be not a bad sort, either," he added meditatively.

"Indeed, they are good men," said Macdonald Bhain, "but they will not be knowing Mack as I knew him. He never made any profession at all, but he had the root of the matter in him."

Ranald felt as if he had wakened out of a terrible nightmare, and followed his uncle into the house with a happier heart than he had known since he had received Yankee's letter.

As they entered the room where the people were gathered, Donald Ross was reading the hundred and third psalm, and the words of love and pity and sympathy were dropping from his kindly lips like healing balm upon the mourning hearts, and as they rose and fell upon the cadences of "Coleshill," the tune Straight Rory always chose for this psalm, the healing sank down into all the sore places, and the peace that passeth understanding began to take possession of them.

Softly and sweetly they sang, the old women swaying with the music:

> For, as the heaven in its height
> The earth surmounteth far,
> So great to those that do him fear,
> His tender mercies are.

When they reached that verse, the mother took up the song and went bravely on through the words of the following verse:

> As far as east is distant from
> The west, so far hath he
> From us removed, in his love,
> All our iniquity.

As she sang her last words her hand stole over to Bella, who sat beside her quiet but tearless, looking far away. But when the next words rose on the dear old minor strains,

> Such pity as a father hath
> Unto his children dear—

Bella's lip began to tremble, and two big tears ran down her pale cheeks, and one could see that the sore pain in her heart had been a little eased.

After Donald Ross had finished his part of the "exercises," he called upon Kenny Crubach, who read briefly and without comment the exquisite Scottish paraphrase of Luther's "little gospel":

> Behold the amazing gift of love
> The Father hath bestowed
> On us, the sinful sons of men,
> To call us sons of God—

and so on to the end.

All this time Peter McRae, the man of iron, had been sitting with hardening face, his eyes burning in his head like glowing coals; and when Donald Ross called upon him for "some words of exhortation and comfort suitable for the occasion," without haste and without hesitation the old man rose, and trembling with excitement and emotion, he began abruptly: "An evil spirit has been whispering to me, as to the prophet of old, 'Speak that which is good,' but the Lord hath delivered me from mine enemy, and my answer is, 'As the Lord liveth, what the Lord said unto me, that will I speak,' and it is not easy."

As the old man paused, a visible terror fell upon all the company assembled. The poor mother sat looking at him with the look of one shrinking from a blow, while Bella Peter's face expressed only startled fear.

"And this is the word of the Lord this night to me," the elder went on, his voice losing its tremor and ringing out strong and clear: " 'There is none righteous, no, not one, for all have sinned and come short of the glory of God. He that believeth shall be saved, and he that believeth not shall be damned.' That is my message, and it is laid upon me as a sore burden to hear the voice of the Lord in this solemn Providence, and to warn one and all to flee from the wrath to come."

He paused long, while men could hear their hearts beat. Then, raising his voice, he cried aloud: "Woe is me! Alas! it is a grievous burden. The Lord pity us all, and give grace to this stricken family to kiss the rod that smites."

At this word the old man's voice suddenly broke, and he sat down amid an awful silence. No one could misunderstand his meaning. As the awful horror of it gradually made its way into her mind, Mrs. Cameron threw up her apron over her head and rocked in an agony of sobs, while Long John sat with face white and rigid. Bella Peter, who had been gazing with a fascinated stare upon the old elder's face while he was speaking his terrible words, startled by Mrs. Cameron's sobs, suddenly looked wildly about as if for help, and then, with a wild cry, fled towards the door. But before she had reached it a strong hand caught her and a great voice, deep and tender, commanded her: "Wait, lassie, sit down here a meenute." It was Macdonald Bhain. He stood a short space silent before the people, then, in a voice low, deep, and thrilling, he began: "You have been hearing the word of the Lord through the lips of his servant, and I am not saying but it is the true word; but I believe that the Lord will be speaking by different voices, and although I hev not the gift, yet it is laid upon me to declare what is in my heart, and a sore heart it is, and sore hearts hev we all. But I will be thinking of a fery joyful thing, and that is that 'He came to call, not the righteous, but sinners,' and that in His day many sinners came about Him and not one would He turn away. And I will be remembering a fery great sinner who cried out in his dying hour, 'Lord, remember me,' and not in vain. And I'm thinking that the Lord will be making it easy for men to be saved, and not hard, for He was that anxious about it that He gave up His own life. But it is not given me to argue, only to tell you what I know about the lad who is lying yonder silent. It will be three years since he will be coming on the shanties with me, and from the day he left his mother's door till he came back again, never once did he fail me in his duty in the camp, or on the river, or in the town, where it was fery easy to be forgetting. And the boys would be telling me of the times that he would be keeping them out of those places. And it is not soon that Dannie Ross will be forgetting who it was that took him back from the camp when the disease was upon him and all were afraid to go near him, and for seex weeks, by day and by night, watched by him and was not thinking of himself at all. And sure am I that the lessons he would be hearing from his mother and in the Bible class and in the church were not lost on him whatever. For on the river, when the water was quiet and I would be lying in the tent reading, it is often that Mack Cameron would come in and listen to the Word. Aye, he was a good lad,"—the great voice shook a little—"he would not be thinking of himself, and at the last, it was for another man he gave his life."

Macdonald stood for a few moments silent, his face working while he struggled with himself. And then all at once he grew calm and, throwing back his head, he looked through the door and pointing into the darkness said: "And yonder is the lad, and with him a great company, and his face is smiling, and oh! it is a good land, a good land!" His voice dropped to a whisper, and he sank into his seat.

"God preserve us!" Kenny Crubach ejaculated; but old Donald Ross rose and said, "Let us call upon the name of the Lord." From his prayer it was quite evident that for him at least all doubts and fears as to poor Mack's state were removed. And even Peter McRae, subdued not so much by any argument of Macdonald Bhain's as by his rapt vision, followed old Donald's prayer with broken words of hope and thanksgiving; and it was Peter who was early at the manse next morning to repeat to the minister the things he had seen and heard the night before. And all next day, where there had been the horror of unnamable fear, hope and peace prevailed.

The service was held under the trees, and while the mother and Bella Peter sat softly weeping, there was no bitterness in their tears, for the sermon breathed of the immortal hope, and the hearts of all were comforted. There was no parade of grief, but after the sermon was over the people filed quietly through the room to take the last look, and then the family, with Bella and her father, were left alone a few moments with their dead, while the Macdonald men kept guard at the door till the time for "the lifting" would come.

After Long John passed out, followed by the family, Macdonald Bhain entered the room, closed the lid down upon the dead face, and gave the command to bear him forth.

So, with solemn dignity as befitted them, they carried Big Mack from his home to Farquhar McNaughton's light wagon. Along the concession road, past the new church, through the swamp, and on to the old church-yard the long procession slowly moved. There was no unseemly haste, and by the time the last words were spoken and the mound decently rounded, the long shadows from the woods lay far across the fields. Quietly the people went their ways homeward, back to their life and work, but for many days they carried with them the memory of those funeral scenes. And Ranald, though he came back from Big Mack's grave troubled with questions that refused to be answered, still carried with him a heart healed of the pain that had torn it these last days. He believed it was well with his friend, but about many things he was sorely perplexed, and it was this that brought him again to the minister's wife.

part II

*The Age of the
National Policy*

8

The Political Career of
Sir Hector Louis Langevin*†

Barbara Fraser

"REGIONALISM," wrote Barbara Fraser, "is not a factor which
can be overlooked in Quebec politics." In this important article Miss
Fraser, whose untimely death ended a budding career, describes the
peculiar machinations and divisions which were Quebec politics in the
late 19th century. This is done through an examination of the career of Sir
Hector Langevin, who on Cartier's death became Sir John A. Macdonald's chief lieutenant in Quebec. The article shows why Langevin was
never able to hold securely *le manteau de Cartier,* and it describes how it
was pulled from him. Besides regionalism, there is depicted here within
the Conservative party in Quebec, the great battle between the Ultramontanists and the so-called moderates, the clash of ambitious personalities, the roll of railways, and the conflicting desires of federal and
provincial politicians. Joseph-Adolphe Chapleau, who was the Montreal
leader of the "moderates," ultimately portrayed Langevin, his rival, as the
spokesman of the Quebec City Ultramontanists. The article strongly
asserts that Langevin was no Ultramontanist, that he did not even understand Ultramontanism and that indeed, unlike Chapleau, he could not
think in ideological terms; Langevin favoured a broadly based and all
inclusive Conservative party for Quebec. Nevertheless, deserted by his
own Quebec City lieutenant, J-I Tarte, the tragic Langevin became,
malgré lui, the leader of the Ultramontanists, and the Ultramontanists
lost.
The article also alludes to the battle within the Liberals between the

* *Canadian Historical Review,* XLII (June, 1961), pp. 93–132.

† The research on which this article is based was made possible by a grant from the
Committee which administers the Rockefeller Foundation at the University of
Toronto.

Rouges and the "moderates" and asserts again the strong catalytic effect on French-Canadian politics and Canadian federalism of the execution of Louis Riel. Though the Liberal-Ultramontanist coalition under Honoré Mercier temporarily won the day in provincial politics, the destruction in Quebec of the Conservative coalition which accompanied the destruction of Langevin ultimately paved the way for the transfer of most of Chapleau's and Tarte's "moderates" to the Laurier Liberal fold.

Miss Fraser describes Langevin's aloof aristocratic character as being in the Cartier tradition. Perhaps if she were writing today, when social and intellectual history seems to hold greater attention than it did in 1961, she might have given emphasis to the fact that the more national- istic Chapleau was the son of a humble stone mason who could identify with and appeal to the French-Canadian populace at the dawn of the era of mass democracy.

M ANY OF CANADA's political leaders have acquired a label. There has been a Firebrand, a Prophet in Politics, an Old Chieftain, a Credible Canadian, and an Incredible Canadian. No such tag has ever been at- tached to Sir Hector Langevin, but if one were, it might well be the Forgotten French Canadian. Langevin was a member of Parliament for thirty-one years, and a Cabinet Minister for twenty-three; he was a father of Confederation, leader of the House of Commons, and dispenser of the immense patronage of the Public Works Department. At the height of his career, he was second only to Sir John and his acknowledged suc- cessor. He had inherited from Sir George-Etienne Cartier the leadership of the powerful French-Canadian wing on which so much of the strength of the Liberal-Conservative party depended. His was a position of en- trenched power and yet, within three months of Macdonald's death, Langevin's career had come to an end. A scandal which had been long brewing in his department removed him from public life and his last fifteen years were spent in the virtual oblivion in which he has been left, even by Quebec historians. His memory has been overshadowed by such younger and more colourful rivals as Honoré Mercier and Joseph- Adolphe Chapleau. Yet his career had a solidity and substance which theirs lacked.

Born in 1826 in Quebec City, Langevin came of a family which had begun to co-operate with the English almost before the ink on the treaty had dried. Several generations of moderate prominence were climaxed by Sir Hector's own which produced a bishop of Rimouski, a vicar general, a Cabinet Minister, and a Clerk of the Senate. Sir Hector's path to power began in the Seminary of Quebec, and then led through the offices of

Montreal lawyers A.-N. Morin and G.-E Cartier.[1] He was called to the Bar in 1850 but, although he continued to work in Cartier's office, he does not seem to have seriously contemplated a career in law. Like Cartier he looked to railways and politics. Unlike his employer he became involved in the affairs of a city whose metropolitan dream failed, and of a railway which was still-born.

This was the North Shore Railway—a route designed to join Quebec and Montreal and tap the western trade.[2] The ubiquitous Quebec politician, J.-E. Cauchon, was its president, and Langevin became secretary-treasurer. Alas for their hopes. The railway was not built for twenty years, and came too late to assist Quebec's metropolitan aspirations. Yet these seemed less hopeless in 1853 than they do now, for Quebec was then a political capital, a university city, a ship-building centre, and a great port. A railway seemed to be the key to the trade of the continent, and Langevin lent his efforts to the attempt to seize control of the St. Lawrence traffic. His ideas received their most dramatic expression in an essay which took a prize at the Paris Exposition of 1855.[3] It contains an exhaustive description of Canada, but its most remarkable feature is surely the shining belief expressed in the future of the St. Lawrence River system which is compared to that of the Danube. Like this river, the St. Lawrence, with the addition of more canals and railroads, was to carry the commerce of a continent. Navies would navigate its length carrying produce and immigrants for both Canada and the United States. The development of the St. Lawrence would take work, but the results would be worth it.

More than essays were needed to effect such development, however, and Quebec was not alone in her metropolitan hopes. Not until 1856 did the time seem ripe to undertake the promotion of the North Shore Railway.[4] Then in one year of furious activity Langevin ran for alderman in Quebec, founded *Le Courrier du Canada,* ceaselessly promoted himself and his railway, and climaxed the year by becoming, almost simultaneously, Mayor of Quebec and member for Dorchester.

Langevin had run as a ministerialist, but his record was erratic in terms of party.[5] He preferred to put the welfare of his railway, his city, and Lower Canada ahead of the welfare of the Cartier-Macdonald

---

[1] The Collection Chapais in the Archives of the Province of Quebec has some material on this early part of Hector Langevin's life.

[2] Province of Canada, *Statutes, 1852–1853,* 16 Vic., c. 100.

[3] H. L. Langevin, *Le Canada, ses institutions, resources, produits, manufactures, etc., etc.* (Quebec, 1855).

[4] This was as a result of the passing of a new land grant act from which the North Shore Railway might hope to benefit, *Statutes, 1856,* 18 Vic., c. 34.

[5] *Microfilm copy of newspaper account of debates in the Legislative Assembly and Legislative Council, 1846–1867, and the House of Commons, 1867–1874,* from various newspapers, including the *Mirror of Parliament,* 1846–1862; and *Le Courrier du Canada.*

ministry. His course was consistent in his own view, but sometimes surprising to others, as when he first helped defeat the Ministry and then proposed the vote of no confidence on which its successor—the brief Brown-Dorion experiment—was chased out of office.[6] The independence did not endear him to Cartier and Macdonald, and sometimes hindered his plans for his railway and his city. As befitted a minister from Montreal Cartier resisted any suggestion for a land grant to the North Shore Railway, and only the intervention of Charles Baring, then in Toronto, forced the Ministry to accede to legislation which was essential to preserve Quebec City from immediate bankruptcy.[7] Langevin persisted, and at last secured both permission to use Quebec credit to finance his railway, and the indispensable land grant.

Two energetic years had been spent in these activities, but at last the railway had reached the point at which foreign capital must be secured. In 1859 Langevin brought his project to London where he presented it to Barings—the bankers who so often aided Canadians in search of money. Barings were reluctant to undertake such a dubious railway scheme, but they did their best. London investors, however, were not interested. Suddenly the railway was a failure, and with it all Langevin's other schemes for Quebec. Montreal forged ahead as a railway port to attain a quite conclusive commercial dominance; Quebec sank into a depression, which resulted eventually in the bankruptcy Langevin had foreseen.[8] The result was quite final. In November, 1860, Langevin announced that he would not run again for mayor, and turned decisively to provincial politics.

In the Assembly, Langevin's method was to talk, predictably, monotonously, but above all, frequently. He continued a flirtation with the Sicotte Liberals, but refused in 1862 to have his name put forward as a candidate for Speaker in opposition to Cartier's choice.[9] In 1863 he joined wholeheartedly in the Conservative attack on the Reform Ministry, and when the Conservatives regained office in 1864, Langevin was solicitor general. The decision to back Cartier, probably made in 1863, had paid handsomely. He had reached the Cabinet just in time to become a part of the Great Coalition dedicated to constitutional reform.

Langevin was an enthusiastic, if largely unnoticed, delegate to all the

6 *Ibid.*

7 Baring Papers, Letters received from British North America, 1196, C. Baring to T. Baring, March 17, 1859, and 1204, April 12, 1859. All manuscripts are in the Public Archives of Canada unless otherwise noted. Also, Collection Chapais, Langevin to Mme Langevin, May 5, 1859; Langevin to his father, May 5, 1859.

8 *Le Courrier du Canada,* Jan. 27, 1860, Annual Report of the Mayor of Quebec; Baring Papers, Letters received from British North America, 1764, report on Quebec, May 25, 1865.

9 Collection Chapais, Sicotte to Langevin, Jan. 9, 1858, and Feb. 21, 1859; L. Bilodeau to Langevin, Feb. 19, 1859, and Feb. 26, 1859; Langevin to Cartier, March 18, 1862; Macdonald Papers, 337, Alleyn to Macdonald, Sept. 22, 1862; *La Minerve,* March 20, 1862, and May 17, 1862.

conferences of the next few years. Not until the Confederation Debates of 1865 did he secure a recorded part. His contribution here shows a particular awareness of the economic advantages which Confederation would bring. He was confident that it would also serve as a guarantee of Quebec particularism. Concerning the office of lieutenant governor, he was confident if confused; somewhat prophetically, he assured his hearers that the federal government would recall any lieutenant governor who exceeded his duties in the province. In addition he assumed responsibility for disposing of the question of marriage and divorce. Provision had had to be made for the latter, he informed his hearers, but it had been made as difficult as possible.[10]

There was one more session before Confederation would come into effect, and Galt had been promised a new education act for Lower Canada which was to protect the Protestants of the new province of Quebec. Langevin took charge of the bill, describing it in French primarily as a measure for securing proportionate distribution of provincial funds to the various sorts of schools. Galt supported it, in English, as a measure which would permit a separate Protestant school system in the province.[11] As introduced it was a moderate and unexceptionable measure. However the Catholics of Upper Canada believed it more generous than their own settlement and immediately introduced a companion bill of their own. In the resulting resurrection of religious and sectional strife, the Government was forced to withdraw its bill. Langevin was furious and considered resignation.[12] Galt had counted on the educational autonomy guaranteed in the bill and did resign. He and his constituents felt themselves betrayed and remained ominously ready to distrust the good intentions of any French Canadian who had not supported the bill.

London and the final conferences with the Colonial Office and the Maritime provinces were the next step towards Confederation. The possibility of leaving Langevin and Howland at home was briefly debated, but when the delegation sailed, Langevin went with it. In London, his contribution remains obscure, and can be gauged only from his few letters home. The Maritime bishops harangued lengthily on the importance of separate schools, and Tilley seemed ready to bargain. The intermediate steps are not reported although Langevin thought that in the end what the bishops wanted had been secured. Maritime problems seemed to interest him, probably because they were unfamiliar, but his main concern was French Canada. He opposed any arrangement for enlarging the federal senate which might upset the delicate balance of

10 Province of Canada, Legislative Assembly, *Parliamentary Debates on the Subject of the Confederation of the British North American Provinces* (Quebec, 1865), 362–92, 691–2.

11 *Globe* (Toronto), Aug. 1, 1866.

12 Collection Chapais, Langevin to Edmond Langevin, Aug. 3, 6, and 7, 1866.

interests which Lower Canada had achieved in its half of the Legislative Council. He rejoiced that the French language had been made as secure as humanly possible, and that he had preserved French Canadian sensibilities by assuring the Celebration of Marriage to the provinces, while preserving Marriage and Divorce to the federal government. The final draft of the bill had his unqualified support, and he recommended it to his constituents in Lower Canada for their approval.[13]

More important for Langevin's future, however, was that he had established himself as an important political leader before Confederation, and that, in London, he and Macdonald had what seems to have been their first chance to become well acquainted.

When the Fathers of Confederation returned to Canada, their first task was the selection of a new federal Cabinet. This did not concern Langevin. He himself became Secretary of State, and urged Galt to come into the Government,[14] but his main concern was in Quebec. The new provincial Cabinet was in the hands of Belleau, Cartier, Chapais, and Langevin. As a first step Belleau was rewarded for his services with the lieutenant-governorship to the gratification of French Canada which hailed his appointment as evidence of Quebec's autonomy. The next step was to enlist J.-E. Cauchon as premier. Cauchon refused at first and then, stipulating that he would accept no salary for his work, yielded to Langevin's persuasions.[15] The cause of his reluctance is not known, but perhaps Cauchon foresaw the opposition to his leadership that arose among the English.

Quebec Cabinets, like federal Cabinets, must achieve a subtle balance among interests and regions. Not least important of these in Quebec was the English of the Eastern Townships. But Mr. Dunkin, their representative, refused to enter a Cabinet under Cauchon without specific guarantees of educational autonomy.[16] Cauchon had opposed the Langevin bill of 1866 describing it as an insult to the well-known generosity of French Canadians. Not unexpectedly he also refused Dunkin's condition, but the

---

13 *Ibid.*, Langevin to Edouard Langevin, Nov. 22, 1866; Langevin to Mme Langevin, Nov. 27, 1866; Mgr. Connolly to Langevin, Dec. 15, 1866; Langevin to Edmond Langevin, Dec. 27, 1866; Langevin to J.-C. Chapais, Feb. 14, 1867.

14 O. D. Skelton, *The Life and Times of Sir Alexander Galt* (Toronto, 1920), 417, Langevin to Galt, April 5, 1867.

15 Collection Chapais, Langevin to Cartier, July 5 and 6, 1867; *Le Canadien*, Jan. 3, 1868, Cauchon to Belleau, and Belleau to Couchon, July 5, and July 6, 1867.

16 *Le Canadien*, Jan. 3, 1868, Dunkin to Cauchon, July 9, 1867, and July 13, 1867. Both R. Rumilly, *Histoire de la Province de Quebec* (29 vols., Montreal, 1940–56), I, 56–9 and C. M. Boissonault, *Histoire Politique de la Province de Quebec, 1867–1920* (Quebec, 1936), 3, suggest that Cauchon failed to form his government because of the extreme hostility of Cartier, Galt, and Langevin in particular. Both authors reject Dunkin's assertions that the English distrusted Cauchon after his opposition to the education bill of 1866. While it would be a mistake to suggest that Cauchon was really popular with the ministers, it seems likely that Cartier and Langevin were quite genuine in urging him to accept the premiership, and that it really was English distrust which prevented him from forming a government.

adamant Dunkin would not place his trust in either Cauchon or the generous sentiments of French Canada. Negotiations broke down on this point, and Cauchon resigned. He was replaced by P.-J.-O. Chauveau, the deputy Commissioner of Education, who had drafted the Langevin bill, and was acceptable to the English. Under the tender guidance of Langevin and Cartier, he succeeded in forming a Cabinet, which was sworn in on July 15, 1867.

Through the troublesome post-Confederation years, Langevin moved serenely in the shadow of Cartier. He recognized that such safety might not always be his, and looked anxiously to a future in which he would have to take the lead.[17] But Cartier continued to lead, and Langevin accepted his pragmatic Conservatism based on a French-English co-operation dedicated to nation-building, railways, and survival. Langevin represented, however, not the prosperous Montreal and South Shore regions, but the depressed Quebec and northeastern regions. Politics in this area came to sound an aggrieved and sometimes Liberal note. Liberalism in the whole province was attempting to cast off its anti-clerical, radical past, and to build a new strength based on a dislike for federal power and for the Conservative party. New currents stirred Conservatives too, and began to threaten Cartier's control of "ses moutons." Ultramontanism, inappropriately imported from France in opposition to *rougism*, attempted to create a less tolerant, more exclusive Conservatism. New divisions revealed themselves in the last years of Cartier's reign. Had he lived he might or might not have suppressed them, but he died leaving the problem of party schism to Langevin.[18]

These problems did not appear immediately, however, and Langevin had several years in which to build for himself a reputation as a capable administrator and a first-rate parliamentary manager. He was no orator —a handicap in an age which took its oratory seriously—and regarded a speech as one of the higher forms of popular entertainment. He had neither voice, gesture, nor poignant phrase. But both friends and enemies admitted his finesse, ability, good temper, and discretion in the handling of a legislature. His energy and competence were rewarded in December, 1869, with promotion to the powerful ministry of Public Works, making him one of the senior Ministers. Of the men who had been in the Cabinet of March, 1864, only he, Cartier, Chapais, and Macdonald were left. *La Minerve,* the voice of Cartier, hailed Langevin as the successor to Cartier, and other papers repeated the claim. Tacit recognition of this legacy was given at a political banquet in Chambly where Langevin

17 Collection Chapais, Langevin to Edmond Langevin, Dec. 29, 1867.

18 J. I. Cooper, "The Political Ideas of George-Etienne Cartier," *Canadian Historical Review,* XXIII (1942), 286–94; J. I. Cooper, "French Canadian Conservatism in Principle and Practice, 1873–1891," unpublished Ph.D. thesis (McGill, 1938); M. Ayearst, "The *Parti Rouge* and the Clergy," *Canadian Historical Review,* XV (1934), 390–405.

was described as the heir in Cartier's presence.[19] But in 1870 Cartier's need of an heir did not seem immediate. He and Macdonald continued to deal with problems in their own fashion. When the crisis arose in the West Langevin was used only as an intermediary when the Government wished to communicate with Mgr. Taché through Mgr. Langevin. It was possibly this quite legitimate connection which led McDougall to accuse him of secretly abetting the Métis. Langevin, like many French Canadians, was probably sympathetic to the Métis but not to the point of embarrassing the Government. Nor did he accept the appeal of L. Beaubien to form a French *bloc,* both Conservative and Liberal, to resist the despatch of troops to quiet the West.[20] The acquisition of the new territory had to proceed without the intervention of *le parti national.*

Four years of comparative electoral peace had followed Confederation, but in 1871 provincial elections were due. In Quebec a militant wing of the Conservative party was organized under the title *le programme catholique.* This was the lay, political wing of ultramontanism, and its *programme* stated that it was the religious and political duty of each voter to support the candidate "qui offre des garanties sérieuses aux intérêts religieux."[21] Such candidates were only to be found in the Conservative party, but not all Conservatives qualified. The doubtful voter could seek guidance from his curé, who spoke the thoughts of his bishop, whose words were inspired by the directives of the (newly) infallible Pope. Doctrinal infallibility was thereby extended to all ranks. Neither the hierarchy nor the party considered the *programme* an unmixed blessing. Quebec clerical politics were complicated enough already without the laity joining in, and the Conservative party was unwilling to make a particular brand of religious orthodoxy a requirement for membership. The *Programmistes* were undismayed, enchanted as they were by the logic of ultramontanism.[22] Admittedly the doctrine has a charm, and the basic premises once accepted, its conclusions are inescapable, but it is supremely unsuited for mixed societies such as Canada. The Archbishop of Quebec urged his flock to eschew religious quarrels, Bishop Langevin firmly dissociated himself from the *programme,* Cartier joined battle with the ultramontane Bishop of Montreal, Langevin told his constituents in Quebec Centre that "jamais je ne ferai, en travaillant pour mes électeurs, de distinctions de race ni de religion."[23]

---

19 *Le Canadien,* Nov. 2, 1870.

20 Collection Chapais, L. Beaubien to Langevin, April 5, 1870.

21 First printed in *Le Journal des Trois-Rivières,* April 20, 1871, and copied in almost the entire French-Canadian press; Rumilly, *Histoire,* I, 153–9.

22 The best Canadian statement of this doctrine is perhaps the widely circulated joint *mandement* of Sept. 22, 1875, *Mandements, lettres pastorales, circulaires et autres documents publiées dans le diocèse de Montréal depuis son érection* (13 vols., Montreal, 1887), VII, 203–24.

23 *La Minerve,* June 12, 1871.

This speech—accepting an acclamation—was an important statement. Langevin dealt amiably with Quebec railways, colonization, agriculture, and industry. Then provincial election or not, he discussed the projected Pacific railway. The Government would not, he assured his listeners, give money or raise taxes to support the railway. Only land would be given to the private companies which would build it. Finally he essayed what was to be the Government line on the Washington Treaty. Sir John, he said, had always protested the fisheries clauses, and the treaty had been signed on the condition that these clauses would not come into effect until ratified by the Canadian Parliament. In this matter the Government had retained its full liberty of action. If this was not quite exact, it pleased Macdonald who wrote Langevin, "Your speech is all that could be desired. Without going into too much detail to forestall my remarks, it has stated the case in a manner to prepare the public mind favourably."[24]

Despite several promising issues, and the conflicts stirred up by the *Programmistes*, the Conservative Government was securely returned. Langevin who had been helping supervise the election, hurried off to inspect the newly acquired province of British Columbia. He consulted with Lieutenant Governor Trutch on appointments, examined existing and projected public works in which the Dominion might participate, made innumerable pleasant speeches, and enjoyed himself immensely. He returned with a truly significant report on the Pacific province, comprehensive, authoritative, and optimistic.[25] His return to the east was marked by a lively political banquet at which Quebec City honoured her famous son, and Cartier and Langevin made buoyant speeches about the future. The immediate future, however, contained a federal general election.

Once again *programmiste* cries were heard, this time on the question of the New Brunswick schools. Langevin had supported federal nonintervention, and Mgr. Langevin supported his brother, but the *Programmistes* were undaunted. In Montreal Cartier found his election complicated by several factors including the *programme* and some resentful young Conservatives. For both men it was a difficult election marked by party indiscipline. Cartier lost his own election, but the province was won for the Conservatives by work and money. Unfortunately too much of the latter had come from Sir Hugh Allan.

Immediate re-organization was necessary. The insurgent sections must be pacified, and the party held together for federal electoral purposes. But Cartier was no longer able to whip his province into line. Bright's disease was killing him, and he was forced to leave the task to Langevin.[26] The legacy Langevin had feared in 1868 was now his. Nor was it

24 Macdonald Papers, 518, Macdonald to Langevin, June 13, 1871.

25 Canada, Parliament, *Sessional Papers*, 1872, VI (10), "Report on British Columbia."

26 Collection Chapais, Cartier to Langevin, Feb. 8, 1873, and Feb. 20, 1873.

questioned. Even from the rival centre of Montreal came assurance. J.-A. Chapleau, already emerging as that city's next boss, wrote accepting "avec plaisir l'honneur de servir sous un Chef de la ville de Champlain."[27] There was much to do. Five years had passed since Belleau's appointment to Spencer Wood, and despite his pleas for re-appointment he was firmly evicted. Nor were the tarnished Cauchon or the weary Chauveau permitted the plum. Instead, distinguished, moderate, and dependable R.-E. Caron was drafted from the Bench to serve as lieutenant governor and shed an aura of respectability over the administration.[28] Cabinet reorganization took longer. Chauveau wished to retire, and Beaubien and de Boucherville were leaving with him. This left a serious weakness in Montreal Cabinet representation, and Montrealers willingly offered their advice. In the end Langevin selected pretty well the Cabinet he wanted, ignoring the advice of Chapleau, and of Dansereau of *La Minerve*. His choice—Ouimet, Chapleau, and Ross—was predominately moderate, and a rebuff to the *Programmistes* who had supported the ultramontane de Boucherville and Chauveau.[29]

Langevin completed his re-organization in Quebec just in time to meet the blast of the Huntington revelations. As the situation grew worse, their own supporters disowned the guilty Cartier, Langevin, and Macdonald. At last, yielding to the plea of Tilley, Pope, and Langevin that possibly neutral members not be forced to a choice in Parliament, Macdonald resigned. The new administration called an election, and in Quebec Langevin fell heir to the dead Cartier's political debits as well as his own. His task was impossible, but the job and the guilt were indisputably his. The suggestion of *Le Castorisme, Voilà l'ennemi*[30] that Langevin was one of several candidates and that he was imposed on the party by the ultramontanes of *Le Nouveau Monde* simply ignores the facts. Of the three possible candidates Masson had everything except ambition, Chapleau lacked the necessary prestige and authority, and Cauchon had already started his pilgrimage towards the Liberals. None of them could muster the political assets—the Public Works Department, a pre-Confederation reputation, and Cartier's patronage—that Langevin could. Quite literally, even had the leadership been particularly desirable in 1873, Langevin had no serious competition. Finally the *Nouveau-*

---

27 *Ibid.*, Chapleau to Langevin, Jan. 25, 1873. The Chapleau-Langevin correspondence in the Collection Chapais has been edited by Fernand Ouellet in the *Rapport de l'Archiviste de la province de Québec pour 1959–1960: No. 40* since this article went to press [Ed.].

28 *Ibid.*, Dansereau to Langevin, Jan. 28, 1873; Langevin to Belleau, Feb. 5, 1873; Cartier to Langevin, Feb. 8, 1873; *Le Journal de Quebec* (ed. Cauchon), 1872–3.

29 Collection Chapais, Chapleau to Langevin, Jan. 25, 1873; Dansereau to Langevin, Feb. 14, 1873; Chapleau to Langevin (wire), Feb. 22, 1873; Macdonald Papers, 226, Ouimet to Macdonald, Oct. 12, 1880.

30 *Le Castorisme, Voilà l'ennemi, par un vrai Conservateur* (Montreal, 1892), 3, Public Archives of Canada Pamphlets, vol. II, no. 1766.

Mondistes had no reason to prefer Langevin, who had not shown himself to be particularly sympathetic to them.

The Quebec Conservatives campaigned under Langevin's leadership, but he decided not to run himself. The voters were much too disposed to discuss the $32,000 that he had received from Allan. The party itself was impoverished, shamefaced, and far from sympathetic to the federal railways policy. The election was a Conservative disaster. It was no less a disaster for Langevin. There was no offer of a safe seat from which to enter Parliament. Instead there was mutual agreement among the friends that Langevin had best avoid publicity until the voters had forgotten the scandal. Chapleau was rumoured to be manoeuvring for himself.[31] A thoroughly demoralized party was prey to dissension and coalition. It was a dark period for Langevin. Nevertheless he continued to represent, as no one else did, the Cartier concept of a federal Conservative party which transcended race and religion. To this end Langevin resisted the numerous suggestions of a coalition between Conservatives and Liberals to form a purely French party devoted to French-Canadian interests.

As if a federal scandal had not sufficiently weakened the Conservative party, the Quebec administration was detected in a shady land deal.[32] Liberals in Quebec proclaimed its downfall. Langevin moved swiftly to reform the Ministry and prevent a Liberal coup. Premier Ouimet and most of his colleagues were forced to resign for the good of their party.[33] This left a serious shortage of untarnished Cabinet material, but an administration was formed headed by de Boucherville and supported by some of the ultramontanes whose political integrity was unquestioned. The charge, however, that this wing had engineered the whole affair for this purpose, and that Langevin was at the least a willing tool of the *Nouveau-Mondistes* seems unrealistic.[34] Most ultramontanes were painfully honest. The extremists, such as those of *Le Nouveau Monde* and *Le Journal des Trois-Rivières*, were actually on a coalitionist tack in the name of upright government, although they usually eschewed Liberalism and all its works. Consequently the new Cabinet met with disapproval from the *Nouveau-Mondistes*.[35] What had been chosen, however, was a staunchly Conservative, unquestionably honest team with which to undertake the provincial general election of 1875. Not surprisingly political morality was an important issue in the campaign. But in spite of furious Liberal efforts, the Conservatives maintained their stronghold, and backed by this victory, Langevin decided that it was time for him to re-enter political life.

---

[31] Mackenzie Papers, Cauchon to Mackenzie, Jan. 30, 1874.

[32] The story of this scandal is in Rumilly, *Histoire*, I, 276–337.

[33] Macdonald Papers, 226, Ouimet to Macdonald, Oct. 12, 1880.

[34] *Le Castorisme, Voilà l'ennemi*, 4.

[35] *Le Nouveau Monde*, July 22, 1874, Aug. 18, 1874, and Aug. 20, 1874.

He decided to run just in time to get caught in the great debate on the meaning of the "undue influence" clause in the new act relegating contested elections to the courts. Could priestly influence be "undue"? And if so, could the courts take cognizance of it? For the Liberals—condemned as anti-clericals—the question was of the utmost importance. For the Conservatives—divided between the ultramontanes and the moderates—it was hardly less so, particularly as it affected their English wing which was nervously jibing at the claims of ultramontanism. Langevin's election became a classic case in the interpretation of "undue influence."

The county was Charlevoix—bailiwick of the ubiquitous Cauchon. It was open because the election of the member, P.-A. Tremblay, had just been disallowed on the grounds of the most undue physical, financial, and spiritual influence. Elections in Charlevoix were run with old time zest, and candidates ran the risk of personal injury. Cauchon made certain that the county supported his candidate, whether as a Conservative, Independent, or Liberal. Charlevoix would be a particularly fitting trophy to mark Langevin's return. Both Langevin and Tremblay introduced clerical influence into the campaign. Langevin enlisted the support of his brother's clergy, in whose diocese the county lay; Cauchon, managing Tremblay's campaign, by-passed the local clergy but sought and found support in the notably Liberal archiepiscopal palace of Quebec.[36] He did not rely on spiritual force alone, however, but ordered, quite illegally, the Quebec river police to assist in the election.[37] Langevin had on his side, not only his brother's clergy, but the political genius of ultramontane J.-I. Tarte of *Le Canadien*, and the financial strength of Thomas McGreevy.[38] The combination proved unbeatable. Langevin was delighted, both for himself and for his party. "L'exemple que nous venons de donner à Charlevoix," he exulted to J.-C. Chapais, "fait voir ce que nous pouvons faire avec de l'énergie, de l'activité, et de la détermination d'une bonne cause."[39]

Victory was not to be so easily won. The results had scarcely been declared before the Liberals announced their intention of contesting the election on the ground of undue clerical influence. Other aspects of both campaigns had been dubious, but it was on this point that the Liberals chose to fight. Certainly some curés had been promising their parishioners innumerable sorrows if they failed to vote for Langevin. But the curés believed that their actions were neither improper nor actionable in

---

36 Mackenzie Papers, Cauchon to Mackenzie, Jan. 7, 1876.

37 Canada, House of Commons, *Debates*, 1876, 177–81.

38 L. LaPierre, "Joseph-Israël Tarte: A Dilemma in Canadian Politics, 1874–1896," unpublished M.A. thesis (Toronto, 1957), 25–7; Canada, House of Commons, *Journals*, 1891, Appendix I, 1290, traces McGreevy's financial interest in Langevin back as far as this campaign.

39 Collection Chapais, Langevin to J.-C. Chapais, Jan. 28, 1876.

a civil court. The Liberals hoped to establish both these principles. On their side the Conservatives hailed the pacifying and purifying influence of the clergy. Protestant ministers, *La Minerve* stated, did not hesitate to offer political advice from the pulpit.[40] Clerical influence had been enlisted on both sides. In fact Langevin sent a protest to the Archbishop concerning two priests who had acted for the Liberals. Taschereau investigated, but declined to do more than require an apology from the curés involved, although he subsequently issued a *mandement* declaring both parties to be on an equal footing vis-à-vis the Church.[41]

The case of the Charlevoix by-election was heard by Judge Routhier, an old friend of Langevin and an ultramontane. Illness, and possibly distaste for the case, delayed his decision. Nearly a year later Routhier announced that he was unable to believe that the result of the election had been unduly influenced, or that he had a right to deal with evidence involving the actions of clergy in the performance of clerical duties.[42] He awarded the election to Langevin, and the Liberals promptly appealed to the newly established Supreme Court. The decision was of the utmost importance. As Mackenzie pointed out to Brown, whose *Globe* was showing a disturbing tendency to support clerical intervention in elections, "At the present moment a desperate effort is made by the priests to defeat every Liberal candidate . . . if Langevin retains his seat we cannot win ten seats in Quebec at the coming general election. That power must now be firmly met and conquered or it will conquer us."[43] For Langevin the outcome meant a future in politics, or possible obscurity.

The Supreme Court moved more swiftly than the lower court had. On February 23, 1877, the Charlevoix election was annulled, and Langevin was charged $6,000 costs. The verdict was written by Judge Taschereau, a Liberal and brother of the Archbishop of Quebec. He began by admitting the dilemma of a Catholic judge faced by a case involving the Roman Catholic clergy, but held that a case affecting the civil government belonged in the civil courts despite the difficulties involved. Further, he held that the evidence showed that Langevin had consented to the curés becoming his agents, and was therefore responsible for their

---

[40] *Le Canadien*, July 29, 1876; *La Minerve*, Aug. 31, 1876.

[41] Collection Chapais, Langevin to Mgr. Taschereau, Jan. 31, 1876, and April 26, 1876; Mgr. Taschereau to Langevin, Feb. 4, 1876, and April 26, 1876; *Le Canadien*, Jan. 29, 1876; *Mandements, lettres pastorals et circulaires des evêques de Québec* (Quebec, 1889), n.s. I, 403–9; Rumilly, *Histoire*, II, 146.

[42] *The Quebec Law Reports; Rapports judiciaires de Québec*, published by the Bar of the Province of Quebec, section of the district of Quebec (Quebec, 1876, repr. 1877), II, 323–72; son Honneur le juge Routhier, *Jugement sur la contestation de l'Hon. Hector Langevin, député fédéral du comté de Charlevoix: O. Brassard et al., petitionnaires* (Quebec, 1876), P.A.C. Pamphlets, vol. I, no. 4128; Rumilly, *Histoire*, II, 56–8.

[43] Mackenzie Papers, Mackenzie to Brown, Jan. 25, 1877.

acts. These acts included sermons which could create in the minds of docile and ill-taught parishioners a fear of committing an important sin, or of being denied the sacraments, should they vote Liberal. Such sermons might not unduly influence the educated and intelligent part of the congregation, but must constitute the most undue influence on the others. The secret ballot made it impossible to prove that more than six or eight votes had been affected, but even one vote, unduly influenced, was ground for annulling an election. The evidence suggested wholesale intimidation; four curés were particularly guilty, and their acts as agents bound their principal. The court was unanimous in annulling the election.[44]

The decision was a serious setback, and the costs, in addition to what the election had already involved, were staggering. Thomas McGreevy kindly assumed the considerable burden of Langevin's debts,[45] and Charlevoix being again open, Langevin ran again and was elected. His victory was immediately contested, but Judge Routhier rejected the plea on a preliminary objection, and the Supreme Court refused to entertain it. Langevin was back in Parliament, and ready to resume his role of *chef*. He was fortunate that no other undisputed leader had yet emerged. The powerful Cauchon had defected to the Liberals. Masson refused to sacrifice his health and his country life to politics. Mousseau and Caron suffered from youth and unsteadiness. Chapleau was the ablest but had still to acquire the prestige that would overcome his poor background and comparative youth. If the Conservatives won the next election, Langevin had every prospect of reclaiming the position he had held prior to the Pacific Scandal.

Liberals in Quebec continued their fight for political freedom, and began to receive support from English Protestants who found the clamour of the ultramontanes frightening. Laurier's speech on political Liberalism was designed not only to proclaim the religious neutrality of Canadian Liberals, but also to woo the English from their normal allies in the Conservative party. It was in this latter sense that Langevin under stood Laurier, and his speech a few days later at Baie St. Paul included an eulogy of the happy history of French-English co-operation in the bosom of the Conservative party. He praised the alliance of English and French, Protestant and Catholic, on which the Conservative party both in Canada and in Quebec was and should be founded. Such a tradition had no existence in the Liberal party, and Laurier was merely imposing one

---

44 E. R. Cameron, *Notes and Annotations upon the Reports of the Judgments of the Supreme Court of Canada* (Toronto, 1925), I (1876–7), 145–234 (actual text of evidence and decision); C. Lindsey, *Rome in Canada: The Ultramontane Struggle for Supremacy over the Civil Authority* (Toronto, 1877), 284–6 (summary); Rumilly, *Histoire*, II, 70–1. Most of the evidence was also printed in *Le Canadien*, Sept. 16–22, 1876.

45 *Journals*, 1891, Appendix I, 1015, 1100. This debt was still unpaid in 1891.

to appeal to the English. The English however, Langevin was certain, would not be so easily fooled. Apart from this statement of the dualism of the Conservative party, the speech leaned heavily on figures showing the unfair distribution of Public Works, and of unemployment and distress in Canada. Langevin's remedy was protection to encourage industry and keep Canadians at home.[46]

Other Conservatives paid more attention to the problem of clerics in politics, and it was not only the Liberals and the English who found ultramontanism dismaying. Chapleau made a spirited attempt to oust the Castors from the Conservative party, and proposed a coalition with moderate Liberals for the purpose. He succeeded in inciting a bitter quarrel between *La Minerve* and *Le Canadien,* Tarte's ultramontane organ. Langevin tried to reconcile the two, but both Chapleau and Tarte remained convinced of the other's error.[47] The Conservative rift was widening, and Chapleau had managed to establish his leadership of the provincial moderates. Internal struggles were abandoned, however, when Laurier was forced to seek re-election in Drummond-Arthabaska, Conservatives of all shades of *bleu* united to secure his defeat, nor were they unduly disheartened when they failed to stop his second attempt in Quebec East. The first victory had been very sweet.

The Quebec administration which Langevin had selected for its honesty proved too honest for its own good. Crisis threatened, and Langevin found it necessary to persuade de Boucherville to be more accommodating to the friends of the Government.[48] His efforts were in vain. Within a month the Government had been dismissed by a Liberal and irate Lieutenant Governor. Disaster was not, however, undiluted. The new Liberal administration had eked out the scantiest of victories in its hastily called election, and the crisis offered a superb theme on which to ring the changes of provincial autonomy. "I really believe," Langevin assured Macdonald, "that our Province will give a much better account of itself than it did in the local general elections."[49]

During the election of 1878, Chapleau began his long series of complaints about the organization of Quebec district. It is true that almost any politician in Quebec could have taken lessons from Chapleau when it came to organization, but it was not so widely recognized that Quebec district—depressed, abandoned by railways, and discontented with fed-

[46] H. L. Langevin, *Les Conservateurs et les Libéraux, discours pronocé à Baie St. Paul, le 5 août 1877* (Quebec, 1877), an unnumbered pamphlet in the Public Archives of Canada.

[47] Collection Chapais, Langevin to Chapleau, Sept. 11, 1877; Langevin to Masson, Sept. 15, 1877; Chapleau to Langevin, Sept. 15, 1877.

[48] Macdonald Papers, 200, A.-P. Caron to Macdonald, Jan. 26, 1878; 226, Langevin to Macdonald, Nov. 29, 1877, and Jan. 28, 1878; Collection Chapais, Macdonald to Langevin, Jan. 26, 1878.

[49] Macdonald Papers, 226, Langevin to Macdonald, June 19, 1878.

eral policy—was inherently more difficult for Conservative organizers. Chapleau might have managed it better, but on this occasion Langevin was likely right in saying that everything that could be done was being done.[50] The party results were good, but Langevin failed to carry Rimouski. There is no record as to why, except that he apparently counted on the county as safe, and devoted his time to the rest of the election. Sympathetic friends urged him not to delay entering Parliament and offered him seats.[51] There was plenty of time as Mackenzie dallied over his resignation, and Macdonald debated his Cabinet choices. Langevin was held to be certain for the ministry of Public Works, Chapleau was determined to finish the defeat of the Liberals in Quebec before considering a federal position, and a superfluity of Montrealers wrangled over their ambitions.[52] When the new Cabinet was announced at last, Quebec had four Ministers—Masson, Pope, Baby, and Langevin, but Langevin had been demoted to postmaster general. Undaunted he moved to Ottawa, establishing the home which he shared, from time to time in the next thirteen years, with his good friend, Thomas McGreevy.

The federal success was regarded as but the first step in restoring Quebec to Conservatism. Provincial Conservatives were determined to secure the dismissal of Lieutenant Governor Letellier, and the defeat of Premier Joly. The evidence suggests that, in the beginning at least, Langevin was more propelled by, than propellor of the Latellier-must-go movement. However, he apparently decided to put himself at the head of so important an agitation, and when it was determined to consult the Colonial Office, Macdonald was happy to send Langevin on the mission, and to urge the Colonial Office (secretly) not to hurry about returning him with the answer.[53] Langevin fretted in vain, anxious to return and take up the work of his newly acquired Department of Public Works. The Colonial Office dallied as long as it could, then returned the chalice to Macdonald. Langevin returned with an air of triumph, and Macdonald reluctantly dismissed Letellier.

The past months had seen a great improvement in Langevin's position. He was senior leader of the victorious Quebec Conservatives, and the holder of a major spending Department. He had triumphantly, if rather needlessly, negotiated with the Colonial Office. Letellier had been dis-

[50] Macdonald Papers, 204, Chapleau to Macdonald, Aug. 8, 1878; 226, Langevin to Macdonald, Aug. 22, 1878; Collection Chapais, Macdonald to Langevin, Aug. 12, 1878.

[51] Collection Chapais, Chapleau to Langevin (wire), Sept. 19, 1878; T. H. Allen to Langevin, Sept. 24, 1878.

[52] *Ibid.*, Chapleau to Langevin, Oct. 3, 1878.

[53] *Ibid.*, Chapleau to Langevin, Nov. 28, 1878 and Dec. 20, 1878; Tarte to Langevin, April 10, 1879; Macdonald Papers, 226, Langevin to Macdonald, April 4, 1879; J. T. Saywell, *The Office of Lieutenant-Governor* (Toronto, 1957), 242 ff., Lorne to Hicks Beach, April 3, 9, 1879; *Debates,* 1879, 331–7; Rumilly, *Histoire,* II, 183–4.

missed, and Chapleau was using every means he could muster to destroy Joly. Chapleau had emerged by now as the leading provincial Conservative, and his work in this battle marked him as master of the legislature. But he continued to rely on Langevin's friendly assistance for advice on parliamentary techniques, for federal aid, and for much of his communication with Macdonald and the rest of the Ministry.[54] Concluding one lament Chapleau wrote, "Je ne vous demanderai pas même de présenter mes amitiés à Sir John, ni à Masson, ni même à Caron—Je me bornerai à vous offrir les miennes en vous remerciant de votre inaltérable bienveillance à mon égard."[55]

When Joly's beleaguered garrison at last surrendered, and the Conservatives resumed control at Quebec, Langevin continued to assist Chapleau in various ways. The first necessity was to restore the province to financial health. A provincial dream of expansion had led to immense debts incurred in the name of railway development. Rehabilitation was complicated, and the only solution seemed to lie in the sale of the provincial railway.[56] This would be a dangerously controversial move, particularly while the party remained so divided. Not only did the ultramontanes oppose Chapleau's rule, but some of his friends, like J.-A. Mousseau, were willing to usurp his position. From Langevin, however, he received sympathy, support, and active assistance.[57] In time geography, rival ambitions, and differing concepts of Quebec Conservatism would separate these men, but in these years Chapleau needed Langevin's strength and experience at Ottawa just as Langevin needed Chapleau's hard-working political leadership in Quebec. They could work together and reinforce each other. Their followers were less amiable. The struggle between ultramontanes and moderates was never successfully terminated. J.-I. Tarte, ultramontane mouthpiece, set out to secure the recognition he believed he deserved, and to undermine the moderate Chapleau. In March, 1880, he could be observed discussing coalition for this end with Liberals Thibaudeau, Goeffrion, and Beausoleil.[58] When this failed he attempted to use Langevin's position to bolster the ultramontane cause. After all the ultramontanes had given Langevin much support, and in a series of open letters in *Le Canadien* Tarte explained to Langevin his duty to follow an ultramontane line.[59] He was ingratiating

[54] Collection Chapais, Chapleau to Langevin, Aug. 20, 1879, Aug. 28, 1879, and Sept. 28, 1879.

[55] *Ibid.*, Sept. 25, 1879.

[56] *Ibid.*, Chapleau to Langevin, Dec. 14, 1879, Jan. 19, 1880, Feb. 4, 9, 22, 1880, and May 20, 1880.

[57] *Ibid.*, Chapleau to Langevin, Jan. 19, 1880; Dansereau to Langevin, Oct. 31, 1880; Macdonald Papers, 253, Mousseau to Macdonald, Nov. 22, 1880.

[58] *L'Etendard*, Sept. 7, 1883, published the correspondence relating to a series of coalition discussions.

[59] J.-I. Tarte, *Lettres à l'hon. H. L. Langevin* (Quebec, 1880), P.A.C. Pamphlets, vol. II, no. 245. These letters also appeared in *Le Canadien*, Aug. 4–7, 1880.

and flattering showing no sign of the Tarte who a decade later would pull down Langevin's career in ruins.[60] If Langevin was impressed, he did not show it. He knew that the Roman Catholic Church was important, he agreed that Liberals were wrong, but that he had either sympathy for, or even a full understanding of, ultramontanism is doubtful. His first interest was the federal Conservative party designed to support "John A. and his friends." Langevin accepted ultramontane support, as he accepted the support of any group which would vote for the Conservatives. But he could not accept their thesis, which was of doubtful value in Quebec, and pernicious in Ottawa. Nevertheless he became branded with an ultramontane label that Tarte had applied, and the moderates who wished to oppose ultramontanism found their leader in Chapleau. Each section sought to eliminate the other, and did not hesitate to seek Liberal coalition for that purpose.[61] The Liberals of Quebec were no less divided—doctrinaire Liberals like Thibaudeau vied with moderate Liberals like Mercier and federal Liberals like Laurier. The federal wings of both parties deplored coalition, and usually managed to prevent it, but the doctrinaires of each shared a chronic honesty, while the moderates had other interests in common.

A Conservative truce was declared briefly in the fall of 1880. Mousseau, who had been inciting trouble among Chapleau's followers, was silenced by a transfer to Ottawa where he replaced the retiring Masson, on the condition that when Chapleau might wish his place he would go to the Bench.[62] It is improbable that Langevin wished to see Chapleau move to Ottawa, for, as long as the younger man stayed in Quebec, and maintained a stable administration, his power enhanced Langevin's.[63] Peace was marked by one of those great demonstrations which every one attended and made interminable speeches about unity and progress. Thus united the party approached the federal session in which Macdonald intended to introduce his railway bill. On this occasion Langevin made one of his few great speeches. He followed Blake, and defended the bill against the latter's attack. Langevin stressed the urgency, inevitability, and future of the railway. To critics of the terms, he pointed out that compromise between the various parties involved was inevitable, but that Canada was a nation founded on compromise. Finally he spoke of the greatness of the idea of a Canada separate from the United States—pros-

---

[60] *Autour d'une carrière politique: Joseph-Israël Tarte, 1880–1897* (Montreal, 1897).

[61] *L'Etendard*, Sept. 7, 1883; Alphonse Desjardins collected and printed many relevant documents in an Appendix to the Quebec Legislative Assembly *Debates*, 1883; Rumilly, *Histoire*, III.

[62] Collection Chapais, Chapleau to Langevin, Jan. 1, 1880; Dansereau to Langevin, Oct. 31, 1880; Macdonald Papers, 253, Mousseau to Macdonald, Nov. 22, 1880.

[63] Collection Chapais, Dansereau to Langevin, Oct. 31, 1880.

perous, happy, and free under the British flag. The railway was a great measure, a crowning act of the Government.[64] The opposition differed, but the contract was approved, and the provinces began to total up what each would gain or lose individually on the project.

The process was acutely painful in Quebec. As chartered, the C.P.R. would neither spend money in Quebec, nor join up with existing Quebec railways. Obviously the solution was for the C.P.R. to acquire the provincial railway.[65] Railways were not properly the concern of the Minister of Public Works, but Quebec was. His sympathies were divided between the C.P.R. whose problems he knew all too well, and Quebec whose problems were also familiar. He hesitated to press claims that the C.P.R. could not entertain. Nor was the sale universally acceptable in Quebec. Ultramontanes clung to a railway associated with the almost sacred colonization policy. Its sale to an English concern was heresy. Their outcry drove moderates of both parties into coalition discussions, but no agreement was reached,[66] and the railway continued to trouble politics in Quebec.

Langevin could overlook these difficulties. Macdonald's Cabinet was enjoying a prosperous season, and Langevin shared in the general success of the Government. Even in Ontario, his part in the railway debate had attracted favourable notice. His ability in the House and in his department were well known. In 1881 he received the K.C.M.G. Briefly, perhaps, but undeniably he was Quebec's premier political leader, and all factions of his party recognized and sought to capitalize on it. Quebec City celebrated the knighthood with a banquet. Tilley, Bowell, O'Connor, Chapleau, Mousseau, Ross, Lynch, Garneau, and others were there. Speeches were long and ornate enough for the most exacting. Sir Hector, however, was brief. He dwelt on the success of the tariff, the advantages of immigration, the brilliance of the railway policy, and the general good fortune of the country. As was becoming his characteristic, he omitted any appeal to specifically French-Canadian feelings.[67] This was the beginning of a summer of triumphant speeches as Langevin toured Quebec, Ontario, and the Maritimes. In December his native city again hosted him, this time at a more intimate banquet celebrating the twenty-fifth anniversary of his entry into politics, as alderman of the Palace ward.

The serenity of the Ottawa scene was not reflected at Quebec. There provincial railway became the subject of a furious debate. Not that

---

[64] *Debates*, 1880–1, 132–41.

[65] Macdonald Papers, 204, Chapleau to Macdonald, Feb. 26, 1881; Collection Chapais, Chapleau to Langevin, Feb. 15, 1881, Feb. 27, 1881, and March 6, 1881.

[66] *L'Etendard*, Sept. 7 1883; *Le Canadien*, Sept. 10, 1883.

[67] *Le Courrier du Canada*, May 5, 1881.

Chapleau had any doubts about selling the Québec, Montréal, Ottawa et Ouest.[68] But the suggestion had brought the whole history of provincial railways under review. The Liberals joyously uncovered evidence of Government boodling.[69] The ultramontanes followed the Liberals in their hot pursuit of corruption, and varied the theme with charges of betrayal of sacred Quebec interests. Chapleau was unshaken in his determination to sell the railway and balance the provincial budget. The project had Langevin's approval, and he offered to convey Chapleau's wishes to the C.P.R.[70] But the C.P.R. was in no position to purchase the Q.M.O.&O., even in the face of threats to sell it to such rivals as the Northern Pacific or Grand Trunk. Lack of a market did not deter Chapleau or his opponents. In an attempt to silence the ultramontanes once and for all, Chapleau called a mid-winter election on the railway issue. Ultramontanes contined hot on the track of the moderates right down to nomination day, when ranks abruptly closed. Newspapers which had all but forgotten their political allegiance in quarrelling over the railway (and assorted politico-religious issues) resumed their support of the Conservative administration. Firmly supported by moderates and ultramontanes alike the Government scored an overwhelming success—53 seats out of 65. Ignoring the mixed basis of his electoral support Chapleau regarded the result as a personal victory for himself, his railway policy, and his moderates. The figures are probably somewhat misleading however, as the real battle in this election was fought before nomination day. Figures for Chapleau's success in this phase of the election are not easily available, but there clearly remained more opposition within the Conservative party than he cared to admit.

The ultramontanes continued to protest the sale of the railway,[71] but the province was in serious financial straits. Chapleau sold the Q.M.O.&O. for what it would bring—the Ottawa-Montreal section to the C.P.R., and the Quebec-Montreal section to a Montreal syndicate headed by L.-A. Sénécal. The split within the party came out into the open again when J.-J. Ross resigned from the Cabinet, and in the Assembly J.-I. Tarte organized an opposition to the sale to such effect that Chapleau was forced to pause. Both men appealed to Langevin for help. Chapleau was particularly annoyed to see Langevin's self-proclaimed supporters in the forefront of his opposition.[72] Langevin apparently came to Chapleau's

---

[68] The railway in question is the successor to the old North Shore Railway, plus an Ottawa extension, built as a public work, and currently referred to as the Q.M.O.&O.

[69] See particularly Laurier's article "La Caverne des Quarante Voleurs," *L'Electeur*, April 4, 1881; Rumilly, *Histoire*, III, 63–5.

[70] Collection Chapais, Langevin to Chapleau, Oct. 19, 1881.

[71] *Ibid.*, Tarte to Langevin, Dec. 20, 1881; *Le Monde*, Dec. 28, 1881.

[72] Collection Chapais, Tarte to Langevin, March 17, 1882; Chapleau to Langevin, March 22, 1882; Macdonald Papers, 204, Chapleau to Macdonald, March 25, 1882.

aid, and months later Tarte had not forgiven him for it.[73] *La Minerve* discounted the ideologies involved, and coolly put her finger on the regional nature of the dispute. Regionalism is not a factor which can be overlooked in Quebec politics, and the eastern end of the province was displeased with the terms of the sale and aggrieved over the disposition of patronage. The provision for three places for Quebec citizens on the syndicate did much to lessen Chapleau's opposition.[74] The railway resolutions were passed, and Chapleau felt that he had finished mastering his province. He looked for further fields, and to the standing offer of a Cabinet post at Ottawa. Langevin and Macdonald decided, however, that he should not leave Quebec until the incipient general federal elections should be over.[75] But as soon as this last obstacle had been overcome, Chapleau headed for Ottawa. At last the field was set for a struggle which would become famous as Chapleau attempted to dominate the federal scene as he had mastered the provincial. Against these pretensions Langevin maintained a steadfast resistance. The "inalterable bienveillance" which Chapleau had once hailed could not survive at such close quarters. But this could not be foreseen in the summer of 1882 when Chapleau arrived in Ottawa.

II

The summer passed in a deceptive atmosphere of peace brought on by the return of prosperity and a successful election. But within the Quebec wing of the party serious changes were in progress. The relatively peaceful combination of Langevin at Ottawa and Chapleau at Quebec came to an end, as the younger man joined his colleague in the federal Cabinet. Chapleau had every intention of being first in Ottawa as he had been at Quebec, and the co-operation which had been possible between the two men was now replaced by a rivalry augmented by the existing divisions in the party. Each man had already become identified with one section, and the split which Langevin had striven to abolish from Ottawa was now firmly established there.

Chapleau took his seat in the Cabinet at the expense of J.-A. Mousseau despite what seems to have been a spirited attempt by Langevin to sacrifice Caron instead.[76] Chapleau, however, was insistent that Mousseau should take his place as Premier of Quebec, and refused to sympa-

---

[73] The evidence is vague, but Tarte clearly believed it, and said as much: *Le Canadien*, Dec. 15, 1882; and the paper generally believed to express the Ministers' views, *Le Courrier du Canada*, came to Chapleau's support.

[74] *La Minerve*, March 17, 1882; Collection Chapais, Chapleau to Langevin, March 22, 1882.

[75] Macdonald Papers, 524, Macdonald to Chapleau, May 22, 1882.

[76] *Ibid.*, 524, Macdonald to Chapleau, June 30, 1882.

thize with him. "Few men," he claimed inaccurately, "have had such an opportunity of the leadership of a party, with such a majority and such a well disciplined House."[77] In truth Mousseau faced a difficult task, involving considerable re-organization. He was without experience in the Assembly, and Chapleau offered no assistance. Langevin came down to advise in the delicate matter of appointments, and under his guidance Mousseau selected a completely moderate Cabinet, excluding the ultramontanes from even the one portfolio they had expected. This alarmed them, and a Castor contested Mousseau's own election. On the other side, the moderate press which Chapleau and Sénécal controlled was also unfriendly. Caught in this cross-fire, Mousseau clung to Langevin.[78]

The Liberal press speculated hopefully on these developments. Prospects for Conservative chaos seemed much brighter, and coalition was again discussed as both wings of the Conservative party approached the Liberals. Mousseau, however, was unwilling to become involved, and Langevin, returning from one of his western trips, put a stop to the negotiations.[79] Within the party the moderates continued to fight with the Castors, while as federal leader, Langevin worked for peace and unity. But he could not afford to obtain this by reading Conservative supporters out of the party and enlisting the support of Liberal moderates to pursue a purely French-Canadian policy—as Chapleau was willing to do. Instead he suggested that the ultramontanes be pacified by inviting J.-J. Ross to re-enter the Cabinet. The gesture was not enough. Ultramontanes had been long and faithfully *bleu*. They had resented Mousseau and his all-moderate Cabinet, as they had resented Chapleau's struggles against them. They were prepared to fight. The moderates, in turn, had no liking for the ultramontanes or for Mousseau. The latter was in as difficult a position as can be imagined.

Winter was a period of uneasy peace, as Chapleau took his bronchial tubes in search of warmer weather, and Langevin continued to counsel conciliation. In the spring Mousseau faced his Assembly with a misplaced confidence. A hoped-for federal subsidy did not materialize, and the aura of peace was quickly dispelled. At the end of a difficult session Liberals and Castors joined in a loose coalition for electoral purposes, and opposed Mousseau's candidates in the by-elections. Masson, Langevin, and Mousseau tried and failed to quell this movement. The local organizations seem to have been completely out of hand. At length Langevin and

[77] *Ibid.*, 204, Chapleau to Macdonald, July 7, 1882.

[78] *Ibid.*, 226, Langevin to Macdonald, July 27, 1882, July 29, 1882 (wire), and July 30, 1882; Mousseau to Langevin, Aug. 2, 1882 (wire); 253, Mousseau to Macdonald, Aug. 4, 1882; Rumilly, *Histoire*, IV, 12.

[79] Ontario Department of Public Records and Archives, Blake Papers, Laurier to Blake, July 31, 1882, Sept. 12, 1882, and Nov. 27, 1882; Pacaud to Blake, July 27, 1882; Langelier to Blake, Nov. 4, 1882; Blake to Langelier, Nov. 9, 1882 (copy).

Macdonald sent Chapleau, who was in some measure responsible for Mousseau, to take a hand in Quebec.[80] His assistance was fatal.

Although Chapleau had acquiesced in the attempt to conciliate the Castors, his opinion of them had not changed. He went to Quebec to smash them.[81] To what extent Mousseau assented to this is unknown. Certainly conciliation had failed for him. Perhaps he hoped that Chapleau would rally the moderates to his support. But Chapleau's speech at St. Laurent served only to inflame and complete the alienation of the Castors, without securing any alternative strength to the helpless Mousseau. From Ottawa, Langevin continued his attempt to hold moderates and ultramontanes together. As a federal Conservative his task was to convince as many voters as possible that the party of "John A. and his friends" best satisfied their needs, and in his opinion this could only be done by persuading all who wore the Conservative label to work and vote together regardless of political philosophy. Since Mousseau had notably failed to hold the Quebec party together, Langevin determined to replace him.[82] This move had a brief success. The Castors were quieted, and Chapleau affirmed his complete support of Sir Hector at a banquet given in the latter's honour and to mark party solidarity. All shades of party opinion were represented, and Langevin addressed them plainly. In a speech which embodied the traditional elements of his long years of service rendered without regard to nationality or province, and of the brilliant future awaiting the Canadian nation, Langevin also underlined the importance of the party system, and in particular the importance of the "parti qui soutient le gouvernement."[83] He did not succeed, however in impressing the Conservatives with the importance of solidarity.

The ideal successor to Mousseau would have been Masson, who declined the honour. The premiership was hard to fill, but at length, Chapleau and Langevin patched together a compromise Cabinet under the durable but reluctant J.-J. Ross. The immediate problem of inadequate finances faced Quebec, and the traditional solution of a raid on the federal treasury was proposed. When the federal Government balked at this, the Quebec members retired to their committee room, and refused their support to the Government at a crucial moment. It was a quite successful tactic, and Langevin grimly negotiated the Government sur-

---

[80] Macdonald Papers, 525, Macdonald to Masson, June 30, 1883, 226, Langevin to Macdonald, July 12, 1883, July 23, 1883, and Aug. 2, 1883; 229, Masson to Macdonald, July 5, 1883, and July 29, 1883; 253, Mousseau to Macdonald, July 23, 1883, and Aug. 13, 1883; Collection Chapais, Macdonald to Langevin, July 17, 1883.

[81] Macdonald Papers, 204, Chapleau to Macdonald, May 6, 1883, May 20, 1883, and Aug. 13, 1883.

[82] Collection Chapais, Mousseau to Langevin, Oct. 25, 1883; Macdonald Papers, 317, Mousseau to Macdonald, Dec. 5, 1883.

[83] *Le Monde,* Oct. 19, 1883, and Oct. 25, 1883.

render.[84] This incident is of interest less as an example of the successful coercion of the federal Government by a provincial government aided by the M.P.'s from that province, than as an episode in which the Conservative M.P.'s from Quebec briefly but decisively abandoned Langevin's leadership to pursue a policy which seemed more productive of immediate provincial gain.

Unfortunately the terms of the surrender could not be implemented immediately, and a portion of the Conservative press continued to attack the Goverment, and Langevin in particular. Among the angry editors was J.-I. Tarte who had commenced his long pilgrimage away from ultramontanism.[85] Rumour implicated Chapleau in the attack, but Langevin refused to credit this.[86] Once again he succeeded in patching up a peace, aided by Thomas McGreevy who pacified *Le Monde* by purchasing it.[87] But unity was a precarious thing at best. Castors and moderates continued to distrust each other, and the pressure to maintain a united front for federal purposes only annoyed provincial leaders, convinced that Quebec interests were being sacrificed to the interests of the rest of Canada.

Quebec matters were in this uneasy condition when the news of fresh troubles in the West began to reach eastern Canada. The north-west was of only peripheral concern to the Department of Public Works, but Langevin was not only a French Canadian—and presumably a friend of the Métis—he was also the Minister who had travelled most widely within Canada. Mgrs. Grandin and Taché appealed to him at length, and a deputation of Métis met him at Qu'Appelle in the summer of 1884 to present their grievances in person.[88] In November, 1884, Langevin, having received another complaint from Mgr. Grandin, warned Macdonald that Riel constituted "a permanent danger. However we must take care not to make a martyr out of him and thus increase his popularity. Some cessions to and good treatment of the half-breeds will go a long way to settle matters."[89] Whether Langevin, had he been the Minister responsible, would have taken his own advice in time cannot be known. But the matter was not in his hands, and the Government delayed action, permitting Riel to continue in a course which resulted in the establishment of a Métis provisional government.

---

[84] Collection Chapais, Chapleau to Langevin, Feb. 11, 1884; Langevin to Chapais, Feb. 25, 1884.

[85] For details concerning Tarte's chequered career see LaPierre, "Joseph-Israël Tarte."

[86] Macdonald Papers, 227, Langevin to Macdonald, Aug. 2, 1884, and Aug. 18, 1884.

[87] *Ibid.;* Caron Papers, 4752, P. Landry to Caron, Oct. 16, 1884; *Journals,* 1891, Appendix I, 1101–2.

[88] Concerning the Métis see M. Giraud, *Le Métis canadien, son rôle dans l'histoire des provinces de l'ouest* (Paris, 1945).

[89] Macdonald Papers, 227, Langevin to Macdonald, Nov. 6, 1884.

English and French Canada joined loyally in putting down the rebellion. In Parliament Langevin and Chapleau maintained silence, while Caron as Minister of Militia enjoyed the limelight, and the Liberals began to censure the Government policy which had led to this danger. Riel was captured, and a long Parliamentary session dragged on without extracting any comment on the rebellion from Langevin. Perhaps he agreed with the Liberal censure of Government policy, but was too loyal to say so. His only intervention was to assure Parliament that the Government was indeed considering the matter of the government of the Territories, but that no action could be taken until the census returns were complete.[90]

In Regina, Riel was tried, convicted, and sentenced to death. Tempers rose in eastern Canada, but the eventual hysteria was not foreseen. Macdonald attributed the manifestations in Quebec to *rouge* activity and assumed they would disappear.[91] The C.P.R. was more important. Its solvency was at last ensured, and the problem of its connection with Quebec City was solved under Langevin's tactful management. But the C.P.R. was not going to get the Ministry out of the grief of the Riel affair, even though Riel had saved the C.P.R.

Parliament prorogued, and the ministers scattered—some as far as France. Langevin stayed in Ottawa and watched the crisis develop. He has been accused of actually encouraging this hysteria in Quebec for the purpose of forcing Macdonald to commute Riel's sentence, or at least of failing to direct the press and guide French Canadians in a way that would have made Riel's death tolerable to Quebec. The evidence for this role is scant and inconclusive. The Conservative press, and especially *Le Monde*—regarded as the voice of Langevin—seemed convinced that Riel would not hang.[92] Tassé of *La Minerve* complained of a lack of direction, and when all was over T.-C. Casgrain insisted that had the press been used to put French Canadians in possession of the true facts of the case it would have been impossible for them to sympathize with Riel. In December, Chapleau wrote that "avec un peu de travail on aurait prévenu le mouvement qui a suivi la mort de Riel," but in September he had rather sympathized with that sentiment in Quebec which he regarded as admirable if mistaken. On balance it seems likely that Langevin may have encouraged *Le Monde* to believe that Riel would not hang, that he left the press free to follow its own line, and that he made no attempt to quell the tumult in Quebec, unless the message in his son-in-law's paper on the day of the hanging, "Riel sur l'échafaud ne personnifie pas pour

---

90 *Debates*, 1885, 3405–6.

91 Macdonald Papers, 106, Macdonald to Lord Lansdowne, Aug. 28, 1885.

92 *Le Monde* took this line as late as Nov. 13, 1885; see also Rumilly, *Histoire*, V, 55, 78.

nous la race canadienne-française, pas même la race métisse," was inspired by him.[93]

The evidence does not make it clear whether the Sanity Commission which Langevin urged on Macdonald was intended to placate French Canada, or to obtain clemency for Riel. It was, however, probably the latter, since he assured a friend that in it lay the best chance of saving Riel's life.[94] It was, however, a very long chance since it seems fairly clear that Macdonald had no intention of interfering to save Riel from the due process of law.[95] Whether his colleagues realized this is another matter. Once again the evidence is not clear, but it is possible, and it would be in accord with what is known of his actions and character, that Langevin believed he could persuade Macdonald to spare Riel. Langevin may have believed that his position and his long years of friendship and service combined with the distress in Quebec would be the lever to pry Riel out of the hangman's hands. If he believed this he was mistaken. But if he believed this Macdonald allowed him to continue in his error until November 11 when it was already too late to attempt to reconcile Quebec. A powerful current was sweeping over the province. Perhaps if it had been taken seriously early enough the Conservatives might have been able to guide it. As it was, only the Liberals would benefit from it.

At last Macdonald warned his colleagues that Riel must die, and that he would, if forced, govern without Quebec. He may even have threatened to hold an election, on what would, necessarily, have been a straight issue of race.[96] No wonder the French-Canadian ministers submitted! Years later Tupper credited Langevin's acquiescence to a promise of the succession to Macdonald. Professor Creighton attributes it to simple loyalty to his chief.[97] Loyalty was almost certainly a factor. A problematical future prime ministership might have affected the issue. Langevin himself states quite simply that he decided that the whole of French Canada could not be sacrificed for one criminal. Riel was clearly guilty. He had incited rebellion, had roused the savages against harmless citizens, including priests, and had been responsible for death and devastation. In conscience Langevin felt that the law must be allowed to

[93] Macdonald Papers, 421, Tassé to Macdonald, Nov. 2, 1885; Collection Chapais, Casgrain to Sir Alexander Campbell, Nov. 17, 1885; Chapleau to Langevin, Dec. 17, 1885, and Sept. 22, 1885; *Le Courrier du Canada,* Nov. 16, 1885; R. W. Cox, "The Quebec Provincial General Election of 1886," unpublished M.A. thesis (McGill, 1948), discusses this question.

[94] Collection Chapais, Langevin to L.-H. Huot, n.d.

[95] Donald G. Creighton, *John A. Macdonald,* II. *The Old Chieftain* (Toronto, 1955), 432–7.

[96] J.-I. Tarte, *1892, Procès Mercier, les causes qui l'ont provoqué: Quelques faits pour l'histoire* (Montreal, 1892), 21, P.A.C. Pamphlet, vol. II, no. 1767.

[97] W. A. Harkins, ed., *The Political Reminiscences of the Rt. Hon. Sir Charles Tupper, Bart.* (London, 1914), 147; Creighton, *Macdonald,* II, 437.

take its course. "Il est possible que nous perdions l'appui de la majorité des députés français mais notre conscience nous appuie et l'avenir dira que nous n'avons fait que notre devoir." Resignation would not have saved Riel. It would merely create an impassable gulf between the Government and French Canada. Even yet Riel's crime might be the cause of a war of nationalities.[98]

The evidence does not show whether Langevin ever threatened to resign, but that he considered the possibility is clear from his letters to his brother. His decision to stay was less publicized, but just as important as Chapleau's. Langevin's resignation would have almost forced his colleagues to resign also, and race would have been set against race. As it was the normal channels of co-operation remained open. His critics accused him of clinging to office, but he was also clinging to a long tradition, established by Lafontaine and Cartier, that in Canada, French and English could and must live peacefully together. He accepted the painful responsibility for Riel's death so that his compatriots might be spared a greater evil.[99] But his action cost him much personal support, especially among the more ultramontane Conservatives who had once hailed his leadership most vociferously.

Even members of Parliament repudiated the decision of Caron, Chapleau, and Langevin to accept Riel's execution, and in Quebec the hanging was followed by an hysterical outburst and the formation of *le parti national*. Ultramontanes ignored the attempts of the hierarchy to contain this reaction and joined leading Liberals in the task of convincing the voters of Quebec that Ottawa, as they had long suspected, did indeed discriminate against them. "Si Riel avait été un métis anglais protestant il n'aurait pas été pendu,"[100] they proclaimed with much justice. Langevin was attacked for failing to save Riel, for not resigning, and for shirking his duty to French Canada. Few recognized that his refusal to be stampeded had preserved more for French Canada than it had lost. As the tumult rose Langevin remained quiet. He correctly predicted the return of the Quebec deputies to the Conservative fold,[101] but made no estimate of the reaction of the constituencies. Chapleau made a largely ineffectual attempt to counter the work of *le parti national* in the counties, and Conservative deputies who had once repudiated all responsibility hurried off to placate their electors. Conservative efforts were far from successful and Senator Bolduc reported unhappily that he feared lest "dans quelques comtés, le mal soit irréparable; ce sont les libéraux qui en profiteront. Il est à espérer que les journaux se montreront plus prudents une autre fois."[102]

---

[98] Collection Chapais, Langevin to Edmond Langevin, Nov. 16, 1885, and Nov. 20, 1885.

[99] *Ibid.*, L.-H. Huot to Langevin. Nov. 16, 1885.

[100] *Ibid.*, anonymous enclosure in letter from Gelinas to Langevin, Dec. 1, 1885.

[101] Macdonald Papers, 227, Langevin to Macdonald, Nov. 19, 1885.

[102] Collection Chapais, Joseph Bolduc to Langevin, Dec. 11, 1885.

Before facing Parliament the French-Canadian ministers wanted time for the reaction to fade, and Chapleau, in particular, wanted the rewards of loyalty and the symbols of power to assure the French Canadians of their importance in the Cabinet. Chapleau urged the necessity of this on Langevin who alone might be able to influence Sir John.[103] Time Macdonald was willing to grant, but a promotion for Chapleau was not forthcoming, although three English Canadians were appointed to senior Cabinet posts.

When Parliament met the management of the inevitable debate on Riel was left to Langevin. A back-bencher, P. Landry, moved censure on the Government for permitting Riel to hang. Here was a motion on which English and French Liberals could not hope to agree. Langevin rose swiftly to defend the Government and himself, pointing out that he was in the Cabinet as a representative not of French Canadians alone but of all Canadians for all of whom it was his duty to seek justice. Then as had been agreed with Macdonald, he moved the previous question.[104] No amendments were possible, and the whole question of Government policy in the northwest was closed. Thereafter it was merely a matter of securing priority for the motion. When the vote came only seventeen French-Canadian Conservatives—three less than Langevin had predicted—opposed the Government. The arguments of Caron, Chapleau, Langevin, and Mgr. Taché had been effective.[105]

In Quebec the Assembly repulsed the attacks of *le parti national* with equal success, and if there had not been both a provincial and a federal general election due within the year, these two defeats might have ended the matter. But the issue was too useful for Mercier and his *parti national*. The provincial election campaign was conducted almost exclusively on the Riel crisis. Ross lost his majority, but since the opposition was not united, it was hoped that the Conservatives might be able to stay in office, at least until after the federal election. But Conservative machinations failed, and when the Assembly met Mercier assumed office supported by a group of ex-ultramontanes.[106]

The provincial defeat was serious both for the coming federal election, and for Langevin personally. The relationship between federal and provincial politics was peculiarly close in Quebec, and without solid provincial support neither Langevin nor Chapleau could hope to advance federally. The blow was particularly severe for Langevin. The party which he had mended so often was broken. The ultramontanes whom he had so often protected from Chapleau had deserted. His concept of party

---

[103] *Ibid.*, Chapleau to Langevin, Dec. 17, 1885.

[104] *Debates*, 1886, 77.

[105] Mgr. Taché actually sat in the gallery and lobbied the members. *Le Courrier du Canada*, Jan. 22, 1887, printed a letter from Taché to Laflèche, March 3, 1886.

[106] Details of this episode are in Saywell, *Office of Lieutenant-Governor*, 97–9; and in Rumilly, *Histoire*, V, 204 ff.

organization, in which *les bleus*—whatever their differences of opinion—remained intact as a voting group, had failed. He had resisted all attempts by moderates to form a party with purely Quebec interests. Now the Castors, many of whom had once decried Liberalism in all its forms, had confused race, religion, and party. They had deserted the non-racial alignment of the Conservative party for a cry of French-Canadian unity and a slightly disguised Liberal party. Macdonald may have believed that the Riel affair had increased Langevin's stature.[107] Chapleau and Langevin knew better what had been lost. The Castors had defected, and the moderates had always preferred Chapleau.

The election campaign further handicapped Langevin. His talent lay in the management of a parliamentary party, in raising funds, soothing deputies, and juggling patronage. But these talents were not suited to a hard-fought campaign. Langevin was no orator who could sway the hearts and votes of the crowds as Mercier, Laurier, and Chapleau could. Langevin dared not participate in one of the popular *assemblées contradictoires*. Chapleau, on the other hand, was one of the best speakers in Lower Canada and his ability won him a popular support that Langevin never had. This was his opportunity to exploit Langevin's weakness.

Chapleau's first step was to secure absolute control of the Montreal district organizations. He wrote to Macdonald warning him that two distinct Conservative factions contested the Montreal scene, and that this must cease. He wanted the sole direction, and urged Macdonald to "see Langevin about this and have it well understood, because I tell you frankly if things do not work out that way I shall withdraw absolutely from the direction of the election and confine myself to my own constituency."[108] This first protest seems to have been ignored because Langevin and his paper *Le Monde* continued to participate in Montreal affairs, and in January Chapleau tried again. Langevin's senior position irritated him, and at an *assemblée* "il a accusé le Ministère de lui être déloyal, depuis longtemps qu'il apercevait qu'on voulait le jeter par dessus bord et comme il représente le plus beau district de la Province, il mérite la plus belle position,"[109] and reinforced his claims with a threat to resign.[110] An alarmed Macdonald and Langevin consulted while the crisis dragged on, but Chapleau's terms were plain: a free hand in Montreal district and suppression of *Le Monde*. Cession was inevitable and when Chapleau insisted that his resignation be communicated to the Governor General, his claims were accepted.[111] This may

---

[107] Creighton, *Macdonald*, II, 505.

[108] Macdonald Papers, 205, Chapleau to Macdonald, Oct. 31, 1886.

[109] Collection Chapais, J. Lessard to Langevin, Jan. 22, 1887.

[110] *Ibid.*, Macdonald to Langevin, Jan. 15, 1887.

[111] Macdonald Papers, 205, Chapleau to Macdonald, Jan. 20, 1887 (It is an index to Chapleau's mood that he addresses Macdonald in French in this letter); later the same day; 527, Macdonald to Chapleau, Jan. 21, 1887.

have been partly a tactical withdrawal on Langevin's part, since his paper continued to operate in Montreal, although more discreetly. But the surrender infuriated him to a point where he contemplated the unusual step of making his anger public. A few months later only Macdonald's firm intervention prevailed upon Langevin to uphold party solidarity and attend a banquet held in Chapleau's honour.

Conservative misgivings about the election results were justified. They suffered a net loss of fifteen or twenty members, leaving the Quebec contingent almost evenly divided between the parties. Chapleau enjoyed tremendous success in Montreal district, and his name became almost synonymous with electoral vistory. Langevin's district showed a dismaying tendency to vote Liberal, although he himself was safely returned. The contrast between the Montreal and Quebec districts was dismal, but Chapleau was probably guilty of over-estimating his personal responsibility for the results in Montreal. Montreal was a wealthy region, blessed by the federal railway policy, while Quebec was chronically impoverished, and convinced that federal railway policy was discriminatory. Economic dissatisfaction in Quebec probably helped the Liberals. Whatever his responsibility Chapleau failed to secure the prize for which he had worked. In Ottawa Langevin continued to enjoy the trappings if not the fact of leadership.

This election marks it seems the true end of Langevin's career. Never after this time can he be seen hurrying down to Quebec to impose order on a fractured party. Organization was left to others, primarily Chapleau. Langevin stayed in Ottawa, secure in office, and still master of an enviable power, patronage, and prestige. The Riel crisis and its aftermath had cost Langevin much. In 1885 he had been a *chef*, assaulted but assured. Like Cartier he had worked towards the sort of politics in which French Canadians would be safe, since divisions were made on other issues than race. Yet now Canada threatened to divide along racial lines, although it was to prevent this that he had supported Macdonald over Riel. In spite of him Mercier had formed a *parti national* from Castors and Liberals. The only slightly less *national* moderates were backing Chapleau, whose oft proposed coalition of moderates would have resulted in a similar *bloc*. Chapleau was a proven crowd-pleaser and vote-getter. Langevin's political techniques were demonstrably inadequate. His approach to party, and politics, had been rejected by his countrymen. This is what he must have known when he yielded to Chapleau in January, and when he read the election returns in March. In Quebec he had nothing left, but he would be hard to dislodge from Ottawa.

The first attempt to remove him came almost immediately. "I am only sorry," wrote Chapleau, "that one of us, Langevin, Caron or I is not *forced* to go to the Senate."[112] Nor was the Senate the only refuge for a

---

[112] *Ibid.*, 205, Chapleau to Macdonald, April 18, 1887.

surplus French-Canadian minister. Spencer Wood was available, and a spirited movement developed to draft Langevin for that spot. This clique centred on Caron, Tarte, Casgrain, and Turcotte who wished to get rid of Langevin whom they suspected of aspirations for the prime minister-ship.[113] Their animadversions were without effect, and when Langevin was offered the post, he declined. Macdonald then suggested that Chapleau might like to be Lieutenant Governor of his native province. Chapleau hesitated rather longer, and then also refused.[114] The bitter-ness that had developed in January, 1887, was not to be rooted out of the Cabinet so easily. What solution Macdonald would have preferred can-not be known. Langevin had lost support in Quebec, but he was an amiable and capable colleague. Chapleau was a far less good-natured and competent Cabinet Minister, but he wielded an indispensable power in Quebec. Of course, he could have exercised the latter effectively, if unconstitutionally, from Spencer Wood. As it was, Macdonald was not prepared to force a decision. A lieutenant governor of the utmost recti-tude was found in A.-R. Angers, and a surface truce was arranged in the Cabinet.[115]

Amidst the lively politics of the later eighties, Langevin scarcely moved. The federal Government's war with Mercier was left in Thomp-son's capable hands, and Langevin confined himself to the work of his Department. Macdonald remained loyal to his old friend, and at one of the innumerable banquets which characterized Quebec politics took occasion to refer to Sir Hector in glowing terms. He traced the history of their association, draped Cartier's mantle over Langevin's shoulders, lauded his loyalty, sincerity, wisdom, and prudence, and concluded "et vous gens de Québec, vous devez être fiers qu'il vienne d'au milieu de vous. Aucun homme en Canada, n'occupe une place plus élevée dans l'estime du parti conservateur et de ceux qui le connaissent comme homme privé ou homme public, que mon collegue et ami Sir Hector Langevin."[116] Such a demonstration undoubtedly contributed to the feeling of discontent and frustration in Ottawa which led Chapleau to consider "une politique provinciale qui s'occupe enfin des intérêts du Bas-Canada, sans consulter les convenances ou les besoins d'Ottawa."[117] Ottawa, however, held him fast, and he continued to work to strengthen the Conservative party.

Langevin had abdicated from that aspect of politics, but his work as

---

[113] Caron Papers, 10883, Turcotte to Caron, May 29, 1887; Tarte to Caron, May 30, 1887; Casgrain to Caron, May 30, 1887.

[114] Macdonald Papers 205, Chapleau to Macdonald, June 20, 1887.

[115] Le Courrier du Canada, Nov. 23, 1887; La Minerve, Nov. 25, 1887; L'Elec-teur, Nov. 25, 1887.

[116] Le Courrier du Canada, Feb. 13, 1888. (Sir John, of course, spoke in English, and the translation is courtesy of the newspaper.)

[117] Rumilly, Histoire, VI, 15, Chapleau to Nantel, April 30, 1888.

Minister of Public Works took him to all parts of Canada, and before all sorts of audiences. He had developed a pleasant, undramatic style in either French or an accented English. He expertly invoked such reliable topics as the War of 1812, the British North America Act, Cartier, and British liberties. He continued to uphold the idea of one Canada in which all should share, while also advocating a large degree of autonomy for the provinces. He was completely orthodox on protection, while advocating more extended trade relations with both the United States and the United Kingdom. He deprecated any step which might lead to annexation or to imperial federation since these would involve a sacrifice of Canadian rights and liberties. In general, he seemed to find the status quo quite satisfactory, and assured his listeners: "Nous vivions à l'ombre du drapeau britannique, nous sommes heureux et prospères."[118]

Goaded by the threat of Mercier, Conservatives attempted to re-enlist the ultramontanes who had deserted to *le parti national*. This was just the sort of alignment on which Langevin had always insisted, but this time he left the negotiations to his old colleagues, Chapleau, Caron, Taillon, and de Boucherville. He did not even attend the banquet which, as usual, marked the conclusion of an agreement.[119]

In the session of 1890, a move to remove the guarantees to the French language in the Northwest Territories Act galvanized Langevin to an unaccustomed activity. He spoke vehemently, and he spoke in English that that portion of his audience might be sure of understanding him. He described the motion as unjust, and said it raised a "question of race and nationality . . . a question of self-preservation," a question on which if necessary all French Canadians would join together to preserve autonomy, language, and institutions.[120] It was a stirring speech for the French Canadians, but not likely to conciliate the English Canadians in the House. As the motion made its way through the House Langevin voted with a French-Canadian *bloc*. Curiously Chapleau voted with the English Canadians. It was left for Thompson to work out an acceptable compromise.

The speech was an odd one for Langevin to make. He had so often stressed his responsibility to all his compatriots, saying "Je ne resterai dans le gouvernement si je devais representer une seule race." His French Canadians had shown, however, that impartiality was not what they expected of their leaders. The frankly *national* appeal of Mercier and Chapleau had been far more successful in Quebec. Previously, Langevin had said, "je sais qu'il faut deux partis, l'un qui soutient le gouvernement

---

[118] *Le Courrier du Canada*, Aug. 9–11, 1888.

[119] Caron Papers, 12868, Beaubien to Caron, March 1, 1889, April 24, 1889, May 10, 1889, and June 11, 1889; *Le Courrier du Canada*, May 31, 1889; Rumilly, *Histoire*, VI, 88.

[120] *Debates*, 1890, 602–12.

et l'autre qui le combat; les deux partis sont importants, . . ."[121] Now he advocated the submergence of party, and the formation of a *bloc!* Was this speech one last attempt to rally support in Quebec? On no other interpretation does it make sense. For many years, and on far harder issues, Langevin had held fast to the Conservative party as the bastion of French Canada's safety. But a virulent racism was evident in both French and English Canada. The Conservative party, and the concept of mutual tolerance and co-operation, must have seemed a less sure stronghold. In one of his last important utterances Langevin returned to the attitude of the young member from Dorchester who had always voted "en faveur du Bas-Canada."

Even as Langevin made this speech, the scandal which would drive him from office was starting to unfold. The long co-operation of the McGreevy brothers to secure profitable government contracts for the firm of Larkin, Connolly, and Co., in return for large contributions at election time, had come to an end. Early in 1889 Thomas took Robert into court in an attempt to extract a larger share of the profits from his brother. Just why he did so insane a thing, has never been explained, but once the case was blazoned in the press the rest of the McGreevy affair was well nigh inevitable.

Aggrieved by Thomas' prosecution, Robert McGreevy assembled a dossier convicting his brother of conduct unbecoming to a member of Parliament. The evidence in the dossier involved activities of Thomas McGreevy's good friend, the Minister of Public Works. Robert took his papers to Macdonald who questioned Langevin and McGreevy who denied all guilt.[122] Balked, Robert turned the papers over to Tarte, all unaware he claimed of the feud which existed between the latter and Thomas. Tarte again took the papers to Macdonald, and when nothing happened began, in spite of Roberts' stipulation for secrecy, to publish titillating bits in *Le Canadien.* Thomas sued Tarte for libel, and the scandal continued to unroll. The matter was introduced into Parliament by Laurier, in spite of protests from Mercier who had also enjoyed the McGreevy largesse.[123] Laurier attested to general Liberal innocence and wanted to know what truth there was in *Le Canadien*'s articles. Langevin upheld the virtue of himself and his department, and there the matter rested.[124] But Tarte was not finished. His revelations continued in a series entitled "Les Coulisses de McGreevéisme," and on November 19 he

---

[121] *Banquet offert à Sir Hector L. Langevin, C.B., K.C.M.G., ministre des Travaux publics, par les citoyens de Montréal à l'Hotel Windsor le jeudi, 18 octobre 1883* (Montreal, 1883).

[122] *Journals,* 1891, Appendix I, 725, 1092. On the scandal see the detailed study in LaPierre, "Joseph-Israël Tarte;" B. Fraser, "The Political Career of Sir Hector Langevin," M.A. Thesis (Toronto, 1959).

[123] Laurier Papers, Mercier to Laurier, March 29, 1890.

[124] *Debates,* 1890, 4827, 4935.

published the first document involving the Minister. It was a statement that Larkin, Connolly, and Co. had given Thomas McGreevy $5,000 for Sir Hector Langevin.

Tarte's attack was an external evidence of the struggle that was raging, more or less privately, in the Cabinet. Caron and Chapleau, both of whom had probably given Tarte at least tacit approval, were at loggerheads with Langevin, but Macdonald, who was after all in a position to almost guarantee it, was sure that Langevin would not be compromised, and continued to support him.[125] Chapleau, on the other hand, found Macdonald singularly difficult to deal with. Appointments which he sought were not forthcoming, and when he protested in his vehement fashion, Macdonald answered coldly, demanding explanations of intemperate expressions, and advising immediate reforms in the Printing Bureau unless Chapleau wanted his management to undergo Parliamentary investigation.[126] In his difficulty, Chapleau turned continuously to Thompson who was noncomittally sympathetic.[127] But Thompson was not his only confidant. Friends reported to Langevin that Chapleau had been seen in consultation with Tarte, Nantel, and Mercier.[128] There was no evidence that Chapleau was engaged in improper dealings with these old friends of his, but the possibility amounting to probability exists. Macdonald and Langevin presumably thought so for they blandly delayed the appointment, so vital in Chapleau's scheme of things, of Dansereau as Postmaster of Montreal.[129]

The press attack and the Cabinet struggles were a bad omen for the oncoming election, and Macdonald made an attempt to resolve the strife in Quebec. Langevin was again offered the refuge of Spencer Wood for the purpose, according to Tupper, of reconciling Tarte who would halt his attack if Langevin would leave the Cabinet. Langevin would not retreat, and after further discussion, Macdonald faced the election with the Quebec difficulties unresolved.[130]

Chapleau led and organized the Conservatives in Quebec, and under his amiable guidance party lines tended to blur, as candidates changed

[125] Macdonald Papers, 530, Macdonald to Anger, Dec. 26, 1890.

[126] Thompson Papers, Chapleau to Thompson, Dec. 12, 1890; Chapleau to Macdonald, Dec. 22, 1890 (copy enclosed in above); Macdonald Papers, 205, Chapleau to Macdonald, Dec. 28, 1890; 530, Macdonald to Chapleau, Dec. 31, 1890.

[127] Thompson Papers, Chapleau to Thompson, Jan. 2, 1891.

[128] Macdonald Papers, 227, Langevin to Macdonald, Jan. 11, 1891.

[129] Collection Chapais, Chapleau to Langevin, Jan. 3, 1891; Langevin to Chapleau, Jan. 5, 1891; Macdonald Papers, 227, Langevin to Macdonald, Jan. 5, 1891 (enclosing a translation of Chapleau to Langevin, Jan. 3, 1891).

[130] Macdonald Papers, 530, Macdonald to Angers, Jan. 19, 1891; 186, Angers to Macdonald, Jan. 22, 1891; 530, Macdonald to de Boucherville, Feb. 2, 1891; 205, Chapleau to Macdonald, Feb. 8, 1891, and Feb. 10, 1891; Harkins, ed., *Reminiscences of Sir Charles Tupper*, 152.

allegiance, and leaders politely traded acclamations. Langevin concentrated on his own re-election in Trois-Rivières, but seems to have quite innocently upset Chapleau's arrangements when Richelieu also insisted on nominating him, although Laurier and Chapleau had "paired" the county with Verchères. Chapleau complained, Macdonald advised tact, but Langevin was returned for both counties.[131] An ominous symptom was Tarte's election in Montmorency. He had decided to enter Parliament for the purpose of directly attacking the Minister of Public Works, and campaigned on a platform of further revelations. These included the testimony of the head of the Quebec Harbour Commission that the misappropriations in the Quebec harbour contracts were the direct responsibility of Langevin.[132] When Parliament met, Tarte introduced these charges, and demanded an investigation into the actions of Thomas McGreevy, Sir Hector Langevin, and the Department of Public Works. The Minister categorically denied the charges in the name of himself, his officers, and his department. McGreevy also denied the charges, although the evidence against him was already damning, and the affair was referred to the Standing Committee on Elections and Privileges.[133]

Almost before the Committee could begin work, the Canadian political world was upset by the death of Macdonald. The election had been a terrible strain from which he had not recovered, and on May 29, Langevin announced Macdonald's illness to the House. That he would not return became obvious at once, and the party began to speculate about a successor. Various names were mentioned: Tupper, Abbott, Langevin, and Thompson; but there was no clear choice, and Macdonald himself offered no guidance. On June 8, Langevin briefly announced his friend's death, saying, "having spent half my life with him as his follower and his friend, his departure is the same as if I lost half my existence." He managed a few more sentences about Macdonald before he broke down, and was forced to conclude quickly, "Mr. Speaker, I would have wished to speak of our dear departed friend, and spoken to you about his goodness of heart the witness of which I have been so often, but I feel that I must stop! My heart is full of tears. I cannot proceed further."[134] The last sentence was twice true. Deprived of Macdonald's unfailing support, smeared by the muck of the McGreevy scandal, Langevin could indeed proceed no further. His end would be a little more drawn out, but no less certain.

Without the scandal Langevin, as senior Minister and Macdonald's oldest and ever loyal friend, might have claimed the office of prime

---

[131] Macdonald Papers, 530, Macdonald to Langevin, Feb. 13, 1891; 205, Chapleau to Langevin, March 17, 1891; Collection Chapais, Macdonald to Langevin, Feb. 15, 1892 (should be 1891); Chapleau to Langevin, Feb. 17, 1891.

[132] *L'Electeur*, Feb. 18, 1891.

[133] *Debates*, 1891, 146, 153.

[134] *Ibid.*, 883–4.

minister.[135] As it was he was ineligible in the eyes of all save a few Quebec papers such as *Le Monde*. Probably this was just as well, for in the nature of things, he could never have secured a united Cabinet, and his rule might have been personally disastrous. The scandal, however, saved him from the need for decision. Under the circumstances he decided to resign at the end of the session,[136] and apparently let the Cabinet negotiations proceed without his intervention. A compromise Prime Minister was found in Abbott, the business of the session was resumed, and the investigation into the Department of Public Works dragged on through the heat of an Ottawa summer. Langevin, himself, appeared twice before the Committee, and defended himself with considerable skill, but the evidence itself, in spite of its curious gaps, is quite conclusive.[137] The Department of Public Works had woefully failed to protect the public interest, and had let contracts, that on the friendliest estimate, allowed an unjustifiable profit amounting to at least five per cent.[138] Nor, in spite of a majority report exonerating him, could Langevin have been unaware of the malversation of funds under his control. The corrupt contracts had been arranged through McGreevy, and Thomas McGreevy was Langevin's old friend, creditor, and party manager.

McGreevy is, in fact, one of the most curious actors in this whole affair. His uncommunicative presence was frequently felt in Quebec political affairs. He supported either party, as it suited him,[139] and extracted his tithe from any project he could get a grip on. Tarte described him, with what accuracy it is impossible to say, as a sort of all-powerful puppet master manipulating politicians to his will.[140] McGreevy was actually guilty of starting the whole investigation, since without his prosecution of Robert, Tarte's attack on Langevin would have been impossible. On the face of it, taking his brother into court was sheer foolishness, unless McGreevy, like Tarte, was also in the process of a political re-alignment. The fact remains that in his long years as Langevin's friend, and as treasurer of the Quebec Conservatives, McGreevy had undoubtedly raised money by using the Minister's name. He had traded contributions for contracts, and Langevin had clearly condoned, or more probably, encouraged this. Sheer political realism demands that a party treasurer be successful in raising money. It might also suggest that he be neither a member of Parliament nor too closely connected with one of the big spending departments of the Government.

---

[135] J. T. Saywell, "The Crown and the Politicians: The Canadian Succession Question: 1891–1896," *Canadian Historical Review*, XXXVII (1956), 310.

[136] Collection Chapais, Abbott to Langevin, July 28, 1891.

[137] *Journals*, 1891, Apendix I; see also Apendix II for the account of the investigation conducted at the same time into the building of the Langevin Block.

[138] *Debates*, 1891, 5784.

[139] Laurier Papers, Tarte to Laurier, Oct. 7, 1890.

[140] *Debates*, 1891, 5796.

The Committee was less successful in finding out where the money went. For the most part, the witnesses were uncommunicative. McGreevy refused to answer, and Tarte, who as one of Langevin's ex-organizers had probably had the spending of some of it, also pleaded political honour. *Le Monde* absorbed a good deal of money,[141] and a subsequent investigation into another scandal unearthed some of McGreevy's election accounts.[142] Presumably the money was for party purposes, but there is little evidence as to how it was spent, or for which party.

Both Conservatives and Liberals on the Committee were much disturbed by all these revelations, and Langevin eventually traded an immediate resignation for a favourable majority report.[143] The minority report condemned him, but the majority report clearing him of personal corruption was accepted by a straight party vote.[144] This marked the end of his career. His party could not even retire him to some peaceful but remunerative post. Spencer Wood went to Chapleau within a year and a half, but Langevin continued to sit in the House until the next election. At that time he retired to the obscurity in which he remained until he died of a stroke and pneumonia on June 12, 1906. After almost forty years in politics, after a career characterized by loyalty,[145] Langevin died with his name a by-word for corruption.

III

Langevin's life had been an interesting one. If he himself did not quite make the first rank politically, he was intimately associated with two who did, Cartier and Macdonald. In addition, his political relationship with the irrepressible Chapleau and with the ultramontane group is worth considering.

Ever since 1873 ambitious Quebec politicians have claimed the "manteau de Cartier." Some have even been awarded this garment. Langevin like the others asserted his title to the cloak. His right to it, however, was frequently challenged, and in the later years of his career Chapleau made a determined effort to wrest it from him. There were many who believed that Langevin had no right to the mantle.[146] Certainly he lacked the political strength that had characterized Cartier. At the height of his career Cartier had dominated the politics of his province. This Langevin was never able to do, but in so many other ways he was a very real

---

141 *Ibid.*, 5813.

142 *Sessional Papers*, 1893, no. 27, 90–229.

143 Collection Chapais, Abbott to Langevin, Sept. 5, 1891; Langevin to Abbott, Sept. 7, 1891. He had resigned previously on Aug. 11, 1891, but it had not been officially accepted, *ibid.*, Langevin to Abbott, and Abbott to Langevin, Aug. 11, 1891.

144 *Debates*, 1891, 6125–6.

145 J. Willison, *Reminiscences, Political and Personal* (Toronto, 1919), 194.

146 Tarte, *Procès Mercier*, 19; and LaPierre, "Joseph-Israël Tarte," 126.

successor to Cartier. To begin with Cartier had chosen him. The suggestion that Chapleau was the natural successor, trained in fact by Cartier,[147] is negated by evidence which suggests that Cartier was in fact deliberately ignoring the young Conservative in Montreal.[148] After a brief fling with rather *nationaliste* politics, "en faveur du Bas-Canada," and a flirtation with the Sicotte moderate Liberals, Langevin had settled down modestly in Cartier's *équipe*. Here he imbibed many of the ideas of his leader. Indeed he and Cartier had already shown tastes in common. Had not Langevin attempted to build a railway, tap the western trade, and make a great metropolis of Quebec? Cartier's successful association with the Grand Trunk in just such an endeavour is well known. Chapleau's later interest in railways was quite different. His railway policy remained provincial, and inextricably mixed up with the colonization of Quebec province. After the death of Cartier, Langevin continued to forward the development of the national railway and the opening of the West, whereas Chapleau rather approved of the threat in 1884 to stop the C.P.R. unless provincial demands were met.[149] This was not only an attack on national development, but also a step in the direction of the dangerous *bloc* politics.

Cartier always advocated the insurance of French-Canadian particularism by means of co-operation with the English Canadians. Langevin too, paid continuous service to this ideal, and sponsored projects designed to insure racial amity such as the Langevin education bill of 1866. He apparently did not even consider leading his province on a religious crusade in 1872 over the matter of the New Brunswick schools, or on a *nationaliste* crusade in 1885 over Riel. Chapleau, on the other hand, was quite able to propose sulkily a *politique provinciale*, when he failed to get his own way in the Cabinet.

Cartier and Langevin were both apparently well liked by their English colleagues, whereas Chapleau was distrusted. In 1879 he was unable to muster a single English vote in the Conservative Legislative Council to help him in his battle with Letellier and Joly. His flamboyant oratory did not please the English either. Langevin and Cartier, however, without being orators of any note, won the respect of their English colleagues by their skill in parliamentary management.

Like Cartier too, and quite unlike Chapleau, Langevin was mildly aristocratic. He came from an old family which could afford to educate its own offspring. Chapleau, of course, the son of a stone mason, had been educated by the Masson family, and had never forgiven them for it. His background helped Chapleau appeal to the large crowds before which he loved to speak. This was an aspect of politics to which Cartier

[147] *Le Castorisme, Voilà l'ennemi*, 3.
[148] Collection Chapais, Dansereau to Langevin, Sept. 7, 1872.
[149] LaPierre, "Joseph-Israël Tarte," 91.

and Langevin devoted little attention. Both of them were accustomed to deal with the professional politicians of Quebec rather than with the populace.[150] Cartier had a generally conservative attitude toward law, society, and property. Even in his youth, Langevin had questioned the wisdom of extending the franchise to paupers whose vote would then equal that of wealthy men.[151]

A difference between the two men is sometimes found in their attitude towards the Church. Langevin is described as "très religieux."[152] He is accused of an alliance with the ultramontanes.[153] Cartier, on the other hand, is described as a religious moderate, with anti-clerical leanings. Yet this distinction is unfair. Cartier was quite willing to make use of the Church, and this was essentially Langevin's position in regard to the ultramontanes. Even his critics admit that he was not one himself. There is no record of his making an ultramontane speech, or even understanding ultramontanism. To Langevin, they were a group whose voting power had always belonged to the Conservative party, and whose support should still be enlisted. He believed in the Church, of course, and French Canada's special interests, but he was primarily interested in the ultramontanes as a political, not a religious, group. His troubles arose when other Conservatives attempted to exclude the ultramontanes—a step of which Cartier's very inclusive Conservatism, would have never approved.

Chapleau, on the other hand, for ideological reasons wished to detach the Castors from his supporters and coalesce with the moderate Liberals. Langevin was unable to appreciate the ideologies involved, and could only see that such a step would so confuse party in Quebec as to endanger the federal Conservatives. He insisted that the Conservative party be kept together. Chapleau reluctantly acquiesced, and from 1878 to 1882 despite the widening rift in the party, the two leaders were usually able and willing to co-operate. The same was not true of the two wings of the party, and when Chapleau arrived at Ottawa his strength no longer complemented Langevin's and the two men became competitors. Already the Castors had identified their cause with Langevin, and this identification remained, while the moderates in their turn had lined up behind Chapleau. It was a competition which Chapleau won. Here it is that Langevin differs most radically from Cartier. Cartier was accustomed to win his battles, but it can be suggested that Cartierism as practised by the master himself would have broken down under the impact of new ways and issues.[154] It was in the ascendancy he held over his province

---

[150] Cox, "The Election of 1886," 49.

[151] Collection Chapais, Langevin to Edmond Langevin, Aug. 13, 1850.

[152] L. O. David, *L'Union des Deux Canadas, 1841–1867* (Montreal, 1898), 170.

[153] LaPierre, "Joseph-Israël Tarte," 126.

[154] Cox, "The Election of 1886," 5.

that Chapleau finds his best title to the "manteau de Cartier," and even here he did not equal the old leader.

The other specific characteristic in which Langevin failed to follow Cartier was in his inability to achieve a position of equality with Macdonald. Cartier had not been a mere lieutenant in the Cabinet. Langevin was. He was invaluable in directing Quebec affairs, and Macdonald leaned heavily on him, but he was never responsible for policy. As he gained much of his political ideas and orientation from Cartier,[155] so he gained much of his political strength from Macdonald. It was not entirely a coincidence that Langevin's downfall came at a time when Macdonald was ill, and that he was forced out of the Cabinet within two months of the latter's death.

Langevin was one of those Quebec politicians who on arrival at Ottawa became identified with the national scene. Cartier accomplished this without losing his Quebec identification. Langevin lost touch, and in 1887 was forced to admit it. Chapleau, on the other hand, was never quite at home in Ottawa. Langevin and Cartier were much alike—both pragmatic, hard-working men, unaccustomed to theorizing. To the extent that he was able, Langevin followed Cartier. He was perhaps an unworthy follower, but he was closer in many ways than any of the others who have claimed that mantle. The two men had one final touch in common. Both saw their careers end in a scandalous revelation of corruption entered into for the sake of party.

---

[155] Cooper, "Political Ideas of Cartier," is the source for the statements on Cartier's position.

9

Some Historical and Theoretical Comment on Canada's National Policies*

John H. Dales

It is high time that someone should write the history of Canada since Confederation as a triumph of the forces of economic and political development over the policies of Macdonald and his successors.

IN THIS CONTROVERSIAL article of revisionist economic history, John H. Dales sets out to destroy some of the patriotic myths regarding the contribution of the National Policy to the economic development of the country. Setting his sights at the historians in particular, he uses the arguments of an economist to attack the basic assumptions of the need for a protective tariff. Here he is attacking the works of H. A. Innis, Donald Creighton, J. B. Brebner, and other leading historians. These men emphasized the positive role of the National Policy which by fostering secondary industry, transcontinental railways, and western settlement produced a national interdependent economy with one section of the country supplying the needs of the others.

Dales is the latest of a long series of low-tariff critics of Macdonald's policy but by far the most sophisticated in terms of economic analysis. Dales examines the various ingredients in the National Policy—tariff, land settlement, railways—and assesses the weaknesses as he sees them. He sees the economic cost to Canada of these policies as a serious hindrance to her development. Hence from 1896 on, Canada prospered in spite of, not because of, the National Policy.

* Queen's Quarterly (1964), p. 297–316.

I

To the infant industry argument for protectionism Canadians have added an infant nation argument. Among Canadian academic historians, journalists, and citizens at large there seems to be a dangerous unanimity of opinion that Canada is a transparently artificial entity whose very existence has always depended on something called a national policy. Canada, in this view, is a denial of geography and a travesty of economics that stands as living proof of the primacy of politics in the affairs of men. Critical comment to the effect that most Canadian manufacturers still depend on protective tariffs is very apt to be greeted first by astonishment that anyone would think the comment worth making, and then by patient explanation that of course many parts of the Canadian economy—not only manufacturing—have *always* depended on government bounty in one form or another, and that Canada simply wouldn't exist as a nation if public support were not continuously made available to key sectors of the economy. Such a policy is necessary, the explanation continues, both in order to overcome the outrageous geography of the country and in order to defend the nation's economy against the formidable efficiency, and thus the natural expansionism, of the American economy. In Canada infant industries are not *expected* to grow up.

I reject this view of Canada. It seems to me to be subversive not only of the nation's wealth but also of the nation's pride. National pride and economic performance I believe to be positively, not negatively, correlated; both efficiency and honour, as the parable of the talents teaches, come from making the most of what one has, not from having the most. And yet Canadian economic policy—and, what is more important, the economic policy of so many developing nations to-day—aims consistently at maximizing the purse, Gross National Product, rather than the performance, Gross National Product per citizen.

Sir John A. Macdonald gave us our first national policy, and our first lessons in the irrelevance of economics. Western lands, he argued, must be controlled by the Dominion because provincial land policies "might be obstructive to immigration," i.e. provinces might actually try to sell land rather than give it away. Canadian railways, in Macdonald's view, were not to be thought of primarily as business enterprises; they were instruments of national development and served this end by providing both attractive objects of government expenditure and reliable sources of party support. As for the tariff, Macdonald rang all the changes on the protectionist fallacies and promised that *his* tariff would benefit everyone, the teachings of the dismal science notwithstanding. Macdonald was the first great Canadian non-economist; he was also an endearing figure, full of robust good humour, who practised with zest what he preached.

It is hard to believe, though, that Macdonald deserves the whole credit for the low esteem in which economics and economists are held in Canada to-day. Macdonald has in any event had powerful support from Canadian historians, of both the political and economic persuasions, who have rationalized his national policy and have encouraged Canadians to believe that by disregarding economics they could build a nation that would represent a victory over mere materialism. The national policy originally consisted of government support for three main ventures: railway building, Western settlement, and manufacturing development. (We adopt the original convention of using "national policy" for the famous trinity of Canadian nation-building policies, and of reserving "National Policy" for the protective tariff policy.") The mutual consistency of Western settlement and railway building was perhaps fairly obvious; land grants helped to finance railways, and railway companies encouraged settlement. From an economist's point of view, however, the rationalization has been carried a little far. The government has been praised for using valuable lands as a loss-leader, while the C.P.R. has been praised for selling land to immigrants at prices considerably below those charged by other land owners, and for showing great initiative in developing uneconomic irrigation projects.

What was at first difficult for historians to discover was the consistency between Macdonald's tariff policy and the other two prongs of his national policy. The late Professor H. A. Innis seems to have provided the connecting argument. The role of the tariff in the Canadian economy, he taught, was to inhibit Canadian-American trade, to promote East-West trade in Canada, and in this way to provide revenue for Canadian transcontinental railways. Though I cannot resist a long footnote on the subject, I do not want to make a full textual analysis of Innis's writings in order to try to find out whether he believed that his tariff-railway link was (a) the *ex post* result of the two policies—the way things worked out, or (b) the *ex-ante* design—the way things were intended to work out, or (c) either or both of these combined with the opinion that the link was felicitous. (See Appendix.) I wish only to suggest that once the Innis link was forged the way was wide open for a full-scale rationalization of the national policy. Thus D. G. Creighton:

[The tariff] was intimately and vitally related to the other national policies. By means of the tariff, the settlement of the west would provide a national market; and this national market would supply east-west traffic for Canadian transcontinental railways and areas of exploitation for eastern Canadian industry. (*Dominion of the North*, 1944, 346.)

And J. B. Brebner:

Looking backward from the present, it is easy to see that the very existence of both the Province and the later Dominion of Canada as entities separate from the United States has depended on such expensive transportation services that a large proportion of their cost has had to be met from the public purse . . .

it was [in the exuberant 1850's] that Canadians . . . began systematically to adopt the *only* procedure by which they could surmount this handicap, that is, the imposition of quite high tariffs on manufactured goods. (*North Atlantic Triangle*, 1945, 158, my italics.)

W. T. Easterbrook and H. G. Aitken:

[The detailed program of Canadian nation building] appeared slowly and in piecemeal fashion but by 1879 . . . the parts of the comprehensive and more or less complete pattern had fallen into place: a transcontinental railway, protective tariffs, land settlement policy, the promotion of immigration. (*Canadian Economic History*, 1956, 383.)

And the present author, who providentially has written very little on the subject:

The Dominion immediately proceeded to fulfil its purposes. A transcontinental railway system was constructed, an energetic settlement policy was adapted to the needs of the West, and the tariff was designed to develop Canadian industry and stimulate Canadian trade. These policies proved effective in the period of prosperity which began towards the end of the nineteenth century. (J. H. Dales, *Engineering and Society*, Part II, 1946, 246.)

Two features of the historians' stereotype of the national policy should be noted. First, much emphasis is placed on the consistency of the three pillars of the program, while inconsistencies are either ignored or glossed over. Among the authors I have consulted, several mention the regional inconsistency inherent in the policy. V. C. Fowke, in particular, interprets the national policy as a program designed by and for Central Canadians. The national policy is therefore seen not as national at all but rather as a policy of Central Canadian Imperialism. Fowke comes dangerously close to shattering the whole myth of the national policy, yet in the end he refuses to be an iconoclast. Thus his glosses that the national policy was "prerequisite to western development" and that "the groundwork [for western development] . . . was laid . . . by the institution of the 'National Policy' of tariff protection . . ."[1] seem wildly inconsistent with his main position, particularly in view of his insistence that Macdonald's railway policy was *not* prerequisite to western development: "As far as the western provinces are concerned . . . Canadian railways are expensive alternatives to American railways rather than to no railways at all."[2] Brebner and Careless both hint at the logical inconsistency inherent in protectionism, namely, the attempt to build a wealthy nation by lowering the standard of living of its population. Thus Careless notes that "A protective

---

[1] V. C. Fowke, *Canadian Agricultural Policy* (Toronto, 1946), 8. Fowke may mean that the National policy was a prerequisite from Central Canadians' point of view, i.e., that Central Canada would not have "invested" in the West without it. At the same time he would not argue that Eastern investment was a *sine qua non* of Western development; see footnote 2.

[2] V. C. Fowke, *The National Policy and The Wheat Economy* (Toronto, 1957), 69.

tariff plainly meant that goods would cost more to buy in Canada," yet after a token flirtation with this line of reasoning he surrenders to the stereotype on the following page and concludes that "as far as Canada is concerned the protective tariff system that was adopted under Macdonald . . . did much in the long run to develop the wealth and encourage the industry of the Dominion." (*Canada*, 1953, 277–8.) He then goes on to paint the usual picture of the wonderful consistency among Canada's railway, settlement and tariff policies.

None of the authors I have examined has flatly challenged the national stereotype of the beneficence of the national policy. W. A. Mackintosh, however, writes very cautiously about this subject. He outlines the "Basic National Decisions" and their interrelations in Chapter II of his *The Economic Background of Dominion-Provincial Relations,* but adds at the end of the chapter: "It is not suggested that these national decisions were taken by governments, or still less by electorates, in full consciousness of their implications, nor that the inter-relations among them were fully appreciated. They were in large measure the outcome of conflicts of interest and, to some extent, of political expediency" (p. 21). Later he notes the regional conflicts occasioned by the national policies, and the tendency of these policies to rigidify the economy by creating "vested interests, regional and sectional, which would resist readjustment" (p. 37). Also two other authors, both political historians, have distinguished themselves by refusing to have anything to do with the standard patter. Chester Martin disdains even to mention the tariff in his *Foundations of Canadian Nationhood;* A. R. M. Lower bluntly refers to the National Policy as being a "frank creation of vested manufacturing interests living on the bounty of government," and in exasperation writes that "Macdonald's way of imposing the new tariff was simple: he just invited anyone who wanted a duty to come to Ottawa and ask for it." (*Colony to Nation*, 1946, 373–4.)

The stereotype of the national policy is powerful enough not only to bridge logical inconsistencies but also to abridge time. To its defenders the national policy was both a well designed and a powerful engine of nation-building. Yet it refused to function for some twenty or thirty years. Many authors simply ignore this awkward gap in timing, as does Dales in the quotation above. Others mention it and then ignore it, as for example Easterbrook and Aitken: "The three decades following Confederation . . . seemed to many a prolonged period of marking time . . . Not until the turn of the century did the program of nation-building begin to pay off . . ." (381). After a long account of the Time of Troubles in both its economic and political aspects, Careless finds himself concluding that "conservative nationalism was played out," and thus in imminent danger of rending the stereotype beyond repair. But he draws back at the very brink of the abyss, and proclaims in strident tones that "Macdonald nationalism had not failed. It was the age that had failed . . ." (295).

Why can we not bring ourselves to say quite simply that the national policy was a dismal failure? Everyone admits, for example, that the land settlement policy was a failure before 1900. After 1900 the demand for Western land was so brisk, and the C.P.R. and various land companies so zealous in attracting settlers to the region, that it is hard to believe that the homestead policy was in any sense necessary as a means of settling the West. It was, indeed, probably undesirable. After writing of the efficiency and enterprise of the private land companies, Martin notes that "The general opening of 'Dominion lands,' even- and odd-numbered sections alike, to homestead entry after 1908 brought a deluge of less selective migration to Western Canada. In vain the government had sought to reserve vast areas with marginal rainfall in 'Palliser's triangle' for grazing and other purposes. In the queues which formed up at the land offices prospective settlers, as one observer records, 'held their place in the line day and night for two or three weeks to enable them to file on certain lands,' and places in the queue were frequently bought and sold for 'substantial sums of money.'" Uneconomically low prices inevitably produce queues. No one, I suggest, really believes that without the homestead policy in particular, and the settlement policy in general, the West would not have been settled. These policies were powerless to promote settlement before 1900; after 1900 their chief effect was to promote not settlement but *rapid* settlement, and there is much evidence to suggest that the rapidity of settlement did much short term and long term harm in Western Canada. Martin's trenchant criticism of the homestead system certainly permits one to believe that Canada would have been better off without this member of the ntaional policy trilogy.

As with land settlement policy so with tariff policy; later in this paper, when I comment on international trade theory, I shall suggest that we would have been much better off still if we had never tangled with the National Policy. Historically it need only be noted that manufacturing was developing in Canada well before the tariff of 1879; Mackintosh notes that the "Census of 1871 reveals that Canada had made some progress along the path of industrialization," and that "The new protectionist policy intensified, broadly speaking, industrial trends already visible. (*The Economic Background of Dominion Provincial Relations*, 1939, 17 and 20.) Moreover Canadian manufacturing grew less rapidly than American manufacturing both before and after the tariff and net emigration from Canada was a feature of the decades both before and after 1879. To the extent that the National Policy was intended to reverse, or even to reduce, the disparity in Canadian and American growth rates it was clearly a failure. After 1900 the Canadian economy, including Canadian manufacturing, grew more rapidly than the American economy for a dozen years, and Canadian historians have not hesitated to attribute this surge to the beneficial, if somewhat delayed, effects of the National Policy. As Careless wrote, it was the "age that had failed" before 1900 and the rise of a prosperous age after 1900 that "spelt success at long last for the National Policy . . ." (295 and 312). In Canadian history it is heads the National Policy wins, and tails the age loses.

There remains the curious case of the C.P.R. While a Canadian transcontinental railway, as Fowke argues, was not prerequisite to Western development, economists and political scientists can agree that as a matter of political economy such a railway was an essential adjunct of nationhood for the new Dominion. The railway had to be built for political reasons, whatever the subsidy involved; sensible economic policy required only that the subsidy be kept as low as possible. The C.P.R. was in fact heavily subsidized. Still, given the lack-lustre performance of Canadian settlement and tariff policies before the middle 1890's one might have expected, on the basis of the national policy stereotype in general and the Innis link in particular, that the C.P.R. would have been unable to survive its first bleak decade. Surely no one would wish to argue that the population of Western Canada in 1895 (perhaps a third of a million people, an increase of something over 100,000 since the completion of the C.P.R.) was able to supply either enough wheat or a large enough market for manufactured goods to make a paying proposition out of even so heavily subsidized a transcontinental railway as the C.P.R. Yet the C.P.R. was profitable from the minute it was completed and began to pay dividends on its common stock in 1889. The Wheat Boom that began in the closing years of the century was only the frosting on the cake that allowed the Company to raise dividends from 4% in 1897 to 10% in 1911, despite large decreases in railway rates around the turn of the century. The chronology of C.P.R. earnings thus raises a nagging doubt about whether the C.P.R. ever *needed* to be subsidized indirectly by the tariff as well as directly by grants of money and a kingdom in land. Professor Fogel's conclusion that the Union Pacific Railway would have been profitable *without* subsidies, despite unanimous opinion, before the fact, that it would not be,[3] suggests a need for testing the hypothesis that the C.P.R. would have been profitable with direct subsidies alone, or even, subversive thought, without *any* subsidy! Careful analysis of this matter seems to be an urgent necessity. The core of the national policy has always been the protective tariff, and although to-day the tariff is more and more often brazenly defended simply on the grounds that we must protect the vested interests we have built up, the argument of last resort is still that the tariff is the defender of the railways, and thus of the East-West economy. The defence retains its appeal since the railways still carry a great deal of freight, if not many passengers, and the Innis link remains persuasive. If it were possible to deny the validity of the Innis argument that without the tariff there would be no C.P.R., it would be much more difficult for present-day nationalists to argue that if there were no tariff there would be no Canada.

---

[3] R. W. Fogel, *The Union Pacific Railroad* (Baltimore, 1960), Passim.

There are, therefore, reasonable grounds for questioning the validity of the historians' stereotype of the national policy. To stress the consistency of the national policy as an interrelated whole is to ignore all too cavalierly its inconsistencies. And to write as if the wisdom and power of a nation-building program that is ineffective for two or three decades is somehow "proved" or "demonstrated" by a subsequent period of great prosperity is to mislead the public with a monstrous example of the *post hoc ergo propter hoc* fallacy. Moreover, the whole tortuous exercise is so unnecessary, for a much more reasonable, and very much simpler, explanation of the Great Canadian Boom is also standard fare in our textbooks. This explanation runs in terms of a number of world events and developments in the last decade of the nineteenth century, all of which reacted favourably on the Canadian economy—the "closing" of the American frontier, rising world prices, falling shipping rates, the development of the gradual reduction process for milling wheat, and the development of the technique of making paper from wood pulp are perhaps the principal items in the list. None of these factors owed anything to the national policy.

Why, then, do historians insist on overdetermining their explanation of the Great Boom by trying to fit a perfectly straightforward argument into the national policy stereotype, as Fowke, for example, does when he writes that "This conjuncture of world circumstances created the opportunity for Canadian expansion, but a half-century of foundation work along the lines of the national policy had prepared Canada for the opportunity" (70). Economic man does not need to be prepared by government policy before he reacts to opportunities for making profits. Is it crude hero worship, or an unconscious human predisposition to human explanations of history that leads Canadians to believe that what success they have enjoyed "must" reflect Macdonald's wise nation-building policies? Or are we all of us merely prisoners of our own history—as it has been written? It is very odd that, enjoying one of the highest standards of living in the world, Canadians in all walks of life should nevertheless believe that their economy is a frail, hothouse creation, whose very survival depends on the constant vigilance of a government gardener well provided with props and plant food. Who but historians could have created this chasm between reality and belief? It is high time that someone should write the history of Canada since Confederation as a triumph of the forces of economic and political development over the national policies of Macdonald and his successors.

II

We turn, now, on the economic theorists. Was it not Keynes who insisted that we were all of us likely to be prisoners, not of plausible history, but of outmoded economic theory? And what branch of economic theory could be more outmoded than international trade theory, which still hews to the Ricardian line that factors of production never move from one country to another? A theory based on the absurd assumption that men, capital, and knowledge never cross national borders is guaranteed to produce conclusions that are irrelevant to the real world. Did Ricardo imagine that his assumption was the only possible way in which to distinguish international trade from any other trade? Our present-day mathematical ethic enables us to see clearly enough that there is no qualitative difference between international trade, interregional trade, inter-city trade and inter-household trade. The realities of national differences in monetary units and monetary and fiscal policies, in immigration policies and tariff policies, not to mention international differences in tastes and natural resources, surely provide sufficient justification for treating international trade as an institutionally distinct branch of economic theory; it seems a work of supererogation to create an additional unrealistic distinction between domestic trade and international trade.

Be that as it may, the Ricardian assumption has stultified international trade theory in at least one major respect; it has prevented the development of any long run theory of international trade, and thus of any long run theory of protectionism. The long run in economics is defined as the time during which supplies of the factors of production adjust to changes in price; thus the assumption that national supplies of factors of production never change means—to overstate the matter somewhat—that we have no theory of the long run effects of international trade. The theory of international trade is thereby distinguished from all other branches of economic theory by its inability to say anything about changes in capacity to produce.[4] It is no doubt for this reason that the short run theorems of international trade have been so little heeded by politicians, who have always been able to reply, "Ah, yes, but in the long run . . ." infant industries will grow and reap the economies of scale, the labour force will be transformed from low-productivity agriculture to high-productivity manufacturing, G.N.P. will grow, the population will increase, we will be

---

[4] Writings in the field of international trade are not, of course, entirely devoid of discussions of international factor movements; recent literature on the subject is summarized in R. C. Caves, *Trade and Economic Structure* (Cambridge, 1960), Ch. V. The literature has concentrated to a large extent on the question of whether, and to what extent, factor movements are substitutes for goods movements in international trade; interest has thus been focussed on the short run effects on trade of the movement of factors, rather than on the long run effects of the factor movements on a country's capacity to produce. This is particularly true of the literature on capital movements which has been concerned largely with the "transfer problem" and thus, as Caves writes, "with the monetary and short run disturbances accompanying the capital transfer" (p. 133). The international trade literature on labour migration comes closer to the problem of long run changes in capacity to produce; see the summary of this work, pp. 139–14. It remains true, I think, that work on the long run effects of international trade on a country's capacity to produce is still fragmentary and not integrated into the main body of trade theory.

more self-sufficient, and so on and on. International trade theory has failed conspicuously to provide any check on the long run "theorizing" of the man in the street and in government.

In principle it is clearly possible for a protective tariff to create a sustained change in the terms at which domestic goods relative to imported goods are available to domestic consumers. This change in relative prices, consumers' tastes remaining unchanged, will affect the factor supplies available to the domestic economy—just as a sustained change in the prices of two domestic goods will affect the factor supplies available to each of the two industries producing them. But while in a free price system resources will flow *away* from the industry whose product has risen in price, as a result of an increase in the real costs of producing it, artificial distortion of relative prices by government policy may make at least some resources flow up-hill *to* a high-cost industry. Suppose the state were to "protect" the production of hand-made cigars by making illegal the sale of machine-made cigars. The cost of producing cigars, and consequently their price, would rise. If, however, the demand for cigars were inelastic, consumption would fall less than proportionately, the value of output of the industry would rise, and, with the more labour-intensive method of production, at least one factor of production, labour, would flow to the industry. It is not my purpose to develop here a full theory of the effects of a protective tariff on domestic factor supplies, but I do suggest that the tariff case may prove to have certain similarities to the cigar example, including the conclusion of negative economic progress to which the example points. My studies of the Canadian economy have led me to believe that in the long run the Canadian tariff: (1) tends to increase the supplies of labour and capital in the country and thus to raise G.N.P.; (2) tends to keep the standard of living—G.N.P. per capita—lower than it would otherwise be; and (3) may lower the average quality of the Canadian labour force by promoting the immigration of workers with average, or perhaps lower than average, skill levels, and the emigration of those who may, more confidently, be supposed to have above average levels of education and training. I shall not here attempt fully to support these views, but I shall comment briefly on each of them merely in order to suggest that they are sensible hypotheses that merit the attention of international trade theorists.

We must first of all exorcise a widely-held but erroneous assumption. Discussions of the economic effects of tariffs are usually based on the implicit assumption that the tariffs on the law books always produce their intended effects on the economy; in fact, many actual tariffs constitute a species of economic "blue laws" that have no economic effect whatever. Tariffs can have a variety of economic effects, but we are here interested only in their effect on the allocation of resources within a country. We therefore define *an effective tariff* as one that directly affects resource allocation, and refer to all other tariffs as being *ineffective*. Ineffective tariffs are of various kinds: (1) a tariff that is exactly matched by an excise or sales tax on domestic production of the good in question; (2) a tariff on goods that are not domestically produced—the tariff is then just a tax on the consumption of a particular commodity, and has no direct effect on domestic resource allocation; and (3) a tariff on a good that is produced so efficiently at home that even in the absence of the tariff imports could not compete with domestic production—the tariff then has no effect on prices, government revenues or resource allocation and is the sort of "blue law" tariff referred to above.

Consideration of the third type of ineffective tariff leads us to a surprising conclusion. If a domestic producer exports regularly and in significant volume we can be sure that he is a low-cost producer by international standards and that he has nothing to fear from import competition; accordingly sustained exports of a good provide *prima facie* proof that a domestic tariff on that good is ineffective. Since the United States during the first half of this century was a large exporter of a very wide range of manufactured goods, we can conclude that, in general, tariff protection of manufacturing in the United States during this period did not exist, and that American tariffs on most manufactured goods were of the "blue law" variety. It is important to note, however, that both the second and third types of ineffective tariffs may, without any change in the law, become effective. If the prospective domestic costs of producing an article that is not now produced domestically fall secularly relative to the costs of producing that article elsewhere, a time will come when domestic costs of production are marginally lower than world costs plus the domestic tariff; domestic entrepreneurs will then begin to produce the good under the protection of the tariff, and the ineffective "revenue" tariff (type two above) will be transformed into an effectively protective tariff. In the reverse case, when domestic costs of production rise relative to foreign costs of production a "blue law" tariff (type three above) can easily become an effective tariff. In view of the great reduction achieved in the costs of producing manufactured goods in Western Europe and in Japan in recent years, one might hazard the guess that many American tariffs which were "blue laws" a decade ago are now effective, i.e., protective in fact.

This discussion serves to remind us that a given tariff may provide any degree of protection from zero to infinity at a point of time, and a degree of protection that may vary, again from zero to infinity, over time. The upshot is that it is not only very difficult to measure the economic effects of a protectionist policy; it is also very difficult to find out whether it has any effect at all! Generally, it is clear that a protectionist policy with respect to manufacturing will do little harm either to countries with manufacturing capacity that is low cost by world standards, e.g., the United States in the first half of this century, or to countries with such a large comparative disadvantage in manufacturing that even with high tariffs little manufacturing develops in the country. The countries that suffer from protectionism are the countries where tariffs are effective, i.e., countries where manufacturing costs are only moderately above world costs, and thus lie below world costs plus domestic tariff rates. These countries suffer, in brief, because their tariffs really work. On the basis of a considerable amount of statistical work contained in an unpublished study, I am satisfied that the Canadian tariff *has* been effective over the period since 1926, the beginning date for the central part of the statistical study. More generally, it seems very likely that the National Policy has been effective, and probably strongly so, during most of the past eighty-five years.

We return now to our alleged long run effects of protectionism. An effective tariff, we claim, will lead on the one hand to an increase in a country's supplies of labour and capital, and on the other, as traditional theory argues, to a reduction in income per capita. Since it may seem odd to argue that the same force that leads to a decrease in income per head will also lead to a growth of population, we must pause to note the institutional assumptions that make this result possible. In the first place we assume that the major, and normal, mechanism of population adjustment is change in net migration; there is statistical evidence that such has been the case in Canadian development.[5] The second assumption is statistically untested, but I think it gives a fair representation of Canada's historical experience with respect to both immigration and emigration. It is that migration is responsive not only to differences in per capita income levels between countries, but also to differences in the volume of job opportunities between countries. Accordingly, immigration to a country may rise so long as job opportunities in the country are increasing, provided only that the standard of living in the country, though falling, remains above the standard of living in the country of emigration; conversely emigration from a country may fail to rise, even if the standard of living in the country is falling, if employment opportunities are scarce in countries of prospective emigration, i.e., those countries where the standard of living is higher. By creating jobs, even if they be jobs in uneconomic industries, an effective tariff can, under certain conditions, promote net immigration and population growth. Granted that effective protectionism in general, and the Canadian National Policy in particular, actually does tend to raise a country's population and G.N.P., we can see why any proposal to move from protection to free trade is so unattractive politically. Politicians dearly love big populations and big national incomes; the only question seems to be how far they are willing to depress

---

[5] In an unpublished paper D. J. Daly has shown that gross immigration has been much more important as a proportion of population change in Canada than in the United States, and that changes in net migration have been more important than changes in natural increase of population in determining changes in total Canadian population. (D. J. Daly "Kuznets Cycles in Canada," paper presented to the Ottawa Chapter, Canadian Political Science Association, March 13, 1962, Charts 2 and 3).

their electorate's standard of living in order to add another thousand people and another two or three millions of dollars to the total magnitudes.

Our third statement about protection alleges, in effect, that an effective tariff policy may lower the average quality of a country's labour force. We have argued that protection is likely to lead to net immigration, the increased labour force being absorbed in the growing manufacturing sector and associated service industries. I shall simply assume that the average skill level required in these employments is the same as the average skill level in the country's labour force before protection. Under this assumption, protection leaves the quality of the labour force unchanged so far as immigration is concerned. But what of emigration?

Let us continue to consider the manufacturing sector of the economy to be the main "beneficiary" of protection. I suggest that protected industries impose a low ceiling on the careers available to their executive personnel, and thus severely cramp the style of ambitious members of the business élite. The reason is that protected industries, which by definition produce at costs above world costs, are thereby prevented from exporting and are confined to the home market. (In passing we should note that it is far closer to the truth to say that the domestic tariff confines industries to the home market than to say that foreign tariffs do so. Tariffs throughout the world restrict trade but they do not reduce it to zero. The market available to any business is always the world market; if a protected manufacturer of widgets in Canada is undersold in third markets by a manufacturer of widgets in Sweden *given existing tariffs,* an abolition of all foreign tariffs will be of no benefit whatever to the Canadian widget producer because he will *still* be undersold in foreign markets by his Swedish competitor.) Home markets have never been large enough to contain the energies of the best businessmen. Having gained experience in a protected industry, and having bumped his head on the ceiling of the home market, the ambitious executive is likely to move to some other country where his industry is *not* protected, and where he can get into the international swim. Thus there is some reason to expect the average quality of business leadership in protected industries to be below that in non-protected industries. I leave it to other investigators, more courageous than I, to test this hypothesis empirically in Canada, perhaps by comparing the quality of business leadership in Canada's export industries with that in the protected industries. The export of brains from Canada is certainly not to be explained entirely, or even mainly, in terms of protectionism, but I think it probable that the National Policy acts as a selective mechanism tending to increase the proportion of second-grade business executives in Canada, and thus to lower the average quality of business leadership in the country. It might be noted, finally, in view of the current interest in investment in human capital as an attractive avenue to economic development, that there is little point in a society's striving to increase its supply of highly-trained businessmen if it can offer an increased demand for them only by expanding its protected production; top-flight people on the average display high mobility.

III

In this paper I have questioned the adequacy of conventional historical interpretations of Canada's nation-building policies, and especially of Canadian protectionism, by reference to simple economic theory and have questioned the adequacy of conventional tariff theory by reference to the economic history of Canada and to some speculation about the contemporary Canadian economy. If my hunches about the long run costs of protectionism to the Canadian economy turn out on further investigation not to be grossly exaggerated, the probable economic cost of the National Policy to Canada in terms of a general, and perhaps progressive, weakening of economic efficiency and economic morale, will be heavy indeed—of an order of magnitude entirely different from the "cost of the tariff" as conventionally calculated under the Ricardian assumption.[6] Moreover there should be charged to Canada's national policy a heavy cost in terms of political obfuscation, for it is a serious matter in a democracy when the purposes of economic policy are confused. All three Canadian nation building policies have been intended to increase the size of the economy. Whatever political attraction this goal may have it has no economic justification; economics has to do with the maximizing of income from given resources, not with the maximizing of resources. In practice it may very well happen that the size of an economy can only be increased at the expense of the quality of its economic life. In Canada our National Policy leads us to think even to-day in terms of size rather than quality, greatly to the detriment, in my opinion, of our national life. It is perhaps time for Canadian historians to take economic theory seriously; and for international trade theorists to accept the historical record of large-scale movements of men and capital across international borders as a challenge to develop a theory that will elucidate the long run effects of protectionism on a country's capacity to produce. It is possible that both groups would then have something of value to tell developing nations about the long run dangers of national policies in general, and of the protectionist route to economic salvation in particular.

APPENDIX

The Innis link was derived from Galt's argument, made in reply to protests from British manufacturers against his raising of the Canadian tariff in the late 1850's, that increased tariff revenue was necessary to help

---

[6] J. H. Young, *Canadian Commercial Policy* (Ottawa, 1957), Ch. 7; H. G. Johnson, "The Cost of Protection and the Scientific Tariff" in *Journal of Political Economy*, August, 1960, 327–345.

pay for Canadian canals and railways that could not be profitably built by private concerns, and that British manufacturers ought to be pleased with the arrangement because the cheaper cost of transportation would lower the price of British manufactured goods in Canada and thus increase the market for them. Innis accepted as profound this economic doubletalk of a suave politician, though with a certain amount of incredulity about its source: ". . . whether or not [Galt's] explanation was one of rationalization after the fact, or of original theoretical analysis, reliance on the customs was undoubtedly the only solution." Surely it wasn't the only solution; if the canals had been paid for by domestic taxation, or by import duties that were no heavier than domestic excise duties, the British manufacturers would have been at least as well off, and Canadians would have been better off. A subsidy is always to be preferred to a tariff on both economic grounds and political grounds; on economic grounds because direct payments distort resource allocation less than indirect payments, and on political grounds because direct payments involve less deception than indirect payments.

Galt was talking *mainly* of revenue tariffs. Innis extended the Galt argument to tariffs that were mainly protective, and thereby compounded Galt's error. "The National Policy was designed not only to increase revenue from customs [as in Galt's argument] but also to increase revenue from traffic from the standpoint of the railways. The increasing importance of railways has tended to emphasize the position of protection rather than revenue." As economic theory this is absurd, not only because the railways, like the canals, could have been financed more efficiently by subsidy than by tariff, but also because a tariff cannot at the same time maximize both protection and revenue; the greater the protective effect of a tariff the less the revenue will provide. The charitable interpretation of this passage is that Innis was indulging in "rationalization after the fact." In the article in which these passages occurred, Innis at any rate doubted the *future* application of his argument: "Dependence on the application of mature technique, especially in transport, to virgin natural resources must steadily recede in importance as a basis for the tariff. It will become increasingly difficult to wield the tariff as the crude but effective weapon by which we have been able to obtain a share of our natural resources."

All of the above quotations are taken from an article by Innis published in 1931, and reprinted in H. A. Innis, *Essays in Canadian Economic History* (Toronto, 1956), pp. 76–7. Two years later Innis was in a deep quandary about the effect of the Canadian tariff. "Inflexibility of the tariff downward contributed to the difficulties during the period of prosperity which began . . . in 1896 . . ." (ibid., p. 91). On the following page he wrote that "During a period of prosperity the tariff should be raised to act as a brake . . . . If railroad rates are lowered at the beginning of a period of prosperity tariff rates should be raised accordingly . . . .

Lowering the tariff during the period of a depression and raising the tariff during a period of prosperity might do much to alleviate the problem of a staple-producing area" (pp. 92–3). The only way I can see of resolving the contradiction between these two quotations is to suppose that in the first Innis was thinking of the combined effect on C.P.R. revenues of the wheat boom and the continued support of the tariff, and the consequent effect of swollen railway revenues in promoting a new, and uneconomically large, railway building program in Canada: had the tariff been lowered, and the C.P.R.'s profits thereby dampened, the incentive to build *two* new transcontinental railways in Canada would have been reduced; and that in the second he was thinking of the Western farmer: the wheat boom might have been dampened by raising farm cost by means of *increased* tariff rates in order to offset the advantages that farmers gained by lowered railway rates. Since the final part of the second quotation recommends a counter-cyclical tariff policy (Innis must have known how politically impracticable *this* was!), with no qualification about how railway rates should be changed, one can only make sense out of this passage by supposing that by 1933 Innis was willing to sacrifice the railways to the farmers during depression and the farmers to the railways during prosperity; his recommended policy would be counter-cyclical for farmers and pro-cyclical for railways! Perhaps the subtlety, or the confusion, was covering a retreat. Realizing that a high tariff may "become inadequate" during depressions (p. 91), and suggesting that the period of resource expansion in Canada had ended, Innis in fact repudiated his linking of the National Policy and railways by reverting to the lesser economic confusions of Galt's position: "Assuming relative stability in the production of raw materials as a result of exhaustion of natural resources the tariff must assume to an increasing extent the position of a toll, as Galt originally planned, and should approximate the deficit on transportation finance" (p. 93). Unfortunately the damage had been done, for text book writers cannot spare the time to assess qualifications to, or second thoughts on, powerful generalizations.

10

Literary Taste in Central Canada during the Late Nineteenth Century*†

C. T. Bissell

CANADIAN intellectual and literary history is a field which still requires a great amount of primary research and writing to isolate the ideas and assumptions which lie behind our past. The present generation of scholars take this field much more seriously; with works such as this, an important start has been made.

One of the fascinating questions for the intellectual historian is the very one which Bissell poses here: "What is the literary taste of a given era?" If we can answer this question it helps to explain a great deal about any society. The novels people read tend to reflect the ethics and mores they espoused.

The interrelationship between politics and literature is another theme which inevitably emerges from this study. The links between this paper and the nationalist "Canada First" movement are obvious. Confederation which gave such an impetus to nationalism also gave an indirect impetus to its cultural forms. The poet Charles Mair was a rabid nationalist in his writings and his political activism in Red River. Goldwin Smith, a towering intellectual figure brooding over the Toronto scene from "The Grange," was himself a leading agitator for continental union.

The Maritimes and French Canada experienced a vibrant period in

* *Canadian Historical Review*, XXXI (September, 1950), pp. 237–251.

† This is the second of three papers, printed in this issue, which were presented at the Regional Conference, Humanities Research Council of Canada, Kingston, June 10, 1950, in a symposium on the cultural and intellectual development of Central Canada in the nineteenth century.

their literary development equal to the one outlined here for the English-speaking of central Canada.

I~~T WOULD BE POSSIBLE~~, no doubt, to undertake the study of Canadian literary taste by analysing what we might call the primary literature—the published works of those writers whom we dignify in our handbooks as poets, novelists, essayists, dramatists. Many of our early nineteenth-century poets, for instance—I am thinking particularly of Sangster, McLachlan, and Mair—leave on their work the heavy imprint of their reading, so that a volume of their poetry resembles an anthology of Romantic and Victorian verse compiled by an editor who has relied for his texts on the promptings of an energetic but erratic memory. During the late nineteenth century, however, the poets do not yield up their secrets so casually. Most of these later poets have assimilated their sources more thoroughly and a few of them have developed an individual style. Still, even with one of the better poets, Charles G. D. Roberts, it is easy enough to trace in his work the almost immediate deflection of current taste; as one moves through his series of published volumes, one can hear in orderly chronological succession the voices of Keats, Tennyson, Browning, Oscar Wilde, William Sharpe, W. E. Henley, W. B. Yeats, and others. But this method of determining literary taste is, at best, uncertain. Even if we were willing to risk the spiritual enervation that overcomes critics unduly concerned with influences, we would find, in adopting this method, that we had thereby cut ourselves off from many currents of taste that do not find their way directly into the creative literature of the time. At the opposite extreme, we could look for our evidence among readers who have no deep concern for literature, but who have been moved to express in newspapers, in letters, and in journals the unreflecting convictions of the heart. Even if this were feasible, it would have only a mild sociological significance. The student of literary taste must, it seems to me, take up his position on middle ground. He must search out the direct comment made by writers who have either a professional or a personal interest in literature and who are addressing themselves to an audience that clearly shares their interest. He will find such comment most clearly, therefore, in periodicals that have an obvious literary bias. Admittedly we are here dealing with a coterie; but I think we may take it for granted that the very existence of a colonial or Dominion literature depends upon the activities of a coterie. The most fruitful period in the literature of Central Canada for a study conducted on this basis is the seventies and eighties. For the first time there was a vitality and density to literary life that can make the study of taste something more than an arid documentation of the banal.

I do not want to suggest, however, that, with the eighties, there was in Central Canada a sudden, spontaneous generation of literary life. Indeed, the first considerable attempt in Central Canada to maintain a periodical devoted primarily to the cultivation of literature, *The Literary Garland* published in Montreal, enjoyed a longer life span than most of its successors. For thirteen years, from 1838 to 1851, the *Literary Garland* miraculously remained alive and managed, according to the testimony of Mrs. Moodie, perhaps its most distinguished contributor, to pay rather well.[1]

Curiously enough, this production of a raw and sparsely populated colony was aggressively *belle-lettre* in tone and liked to think of itself as a soothing antidote to the recent political troubles that had culminated in rebellion. Like the poetry of the time, there was something forced and precociously imitative about the *Literary Garland*, as if its editor and his associates felt that they were reproducing some of the elegance and grace of the parent literature. Between 1851 and 1870 a number of periodicals made brief, apologetic appearances and then speedily and quietly withdrew. With the seventies, however, the periodical emerged as one of the dominant expressions of the time.

The usual reason assigned for this reawakening of cultural life, of which the flourishing of the periodical constitutes only one symptom, was the achievement of Confederation and the accompanying growth in Central Canada, at least, of a national consciousness and pride. We must, however, be careful not to establish a simple causal relationship. Confederation was not so much a solution as a posing of the national problem. To many observers, the factional manœuvering that had preceded Confederation and the grave problems that immediately followed it made it apparent that national unity had to be founded on something more stable than the niceties of political compromise. Was it not possible, they asked, to sink political divergence in a disinterested concern for the cultural life of the new nation? This was the query that the Canada First movement addressed to the nation during the seventies. In his "Address to the Canadian National Association" (1875), William Foster, the prophet of Canada First, quoted with approval the following analysis of the origin and nature of the movement: "That movement was at the outset an intellectual movement. It was the revolt of educated and thoughtful men against the inanity, and worse than inanity, of what was offered to them as political discussion. It was a direct product, in some

---

[1] Mrs. Moodie recounts how early efforts to earn money by writing for American periodicals had been frustrated by her inability to pay the postage on manuscripts. When she explained this situation to the editor of the *Literary Garland*, "in the most liberal manner, he offered to pay the postage on all manuscripts to his office, and left me to name my own terms of remuneration" (*Roughing It in the Bush*, New York, n.d., 476). It is obvious that during their stay in the bush, the Moodie family was supported almost entirely by Mrs. Moodie's literary labours.

measure, of that higher culture which the universities and colleges of our land are steadily promoting."[2] Almost all of those who could be described as members of the movement were, in the broad sense of the term, men of letters, more adept in the arts of propaganda than in the skills of political warfare. It had from the outset the embarrassingly powerful endorsement of Goldwin Smith, who had just taken up residence in Toronto. It had in Charles Mair its official poet, described by Foster with a pardonable touch of exaggeration as "The Canadian Keats." And Robert Grant Haliburton gave the movement the prestige of a great literary name and the service of a ringing, rhetorical style. Politically, of course, the Canada First movement was only a minor incident; its members moved off rapidly in a number of directions—toward Imperial Federation, towards national independence, and even towards annexation. But culturally, I am convinced, the movement had wide and deep implications. It was the outward and visible sign of a widespread conviction that Canadian intellectual life was not necessarily circumscribed by "responsible government," "rep. by pop.," and the thin ideological conflict between Grits and Tories. Writers who gave expression to this conviction were not contemptuous of politics and history. But they were constantly seeking to transcend party controversy, in the words of one of their most distinguished mentors, to turn "a stream of fresh and free thought upon our stock notions and habits."

The leaders of this modest cultural renaissance found a means of giving currency to their ideas in a group of periodicals that flourished most vigorously in the seventies and eighties. Two of these periodicals were primarily political in character: *The Nation* (1874–6), which was the official organ of Canada First, and *The Bystander* (1880–2; 1890–1), which was little more than a political broadsheet, albeit a brilliant one, inspired and largely written by Goldwin Smith. Two of them, however, were conceived in broader terms: *The Canadian Monthly and National Review* (1872–82) and *The Week* (1883–96). Each was, to use the subtitle of the *Week,* "a Canadian Journal of Politics, Society, and Literature." And each betrayed signs of Canada First parentage, although only the *Canadian Monthly* could be described as a legitimate offspring. An editorial pronouncement in the first number of the *Canadian Monthly* sounded a note of vibrant patriotism and referred confidently to "the general awakening of national life."[3] Towards the end of its span, however, as economic difficulties crowded in, the mood changed and the *Canadian Monthly* ended with a bitter and despairing valedictory. But the defunct monthly had accomplished much. Most important, it had gathered together a group of practised writers, who were to transfer their allegiance en bloc to the *Week.*

---

[2] *Canada First, a Memorial of the Late William A. Foster, Q.C.* (Toronto, 1890), 77.
[3] I (Jan., 1872), 1.

At the centre of this group was, of course, Goldwin Smith. About Goldwin Smith, political commentator and political prophet, there is room for the liveliest divergence of opinion; about Goldwin Smith, intellectual and man of letters, there can be only one considered judgment. He was a quickening force in the intellectual life of Canada. By a chain of circumstances that still resists logical analysis, the brilliant young writer for the *Saturday Review*, the one time Regius Professor of History at Oxford, the friend and intimate of the Victorian great, came to Toronto, and for some forty years devoted himself to "The Canadian question." To have in their midst a man who by training, natural endowments, and the pleasant fruits of a judicious marriage could lead uninterruptedly the life of a Victorian man of letters was in itself a stimulus to local writers. But in addition Goldwin Smith gave his literary services and his financial support to a long series of periodicals and newspapers, and he attracted to himself and set his imprint upon a group of serious journalists. Two of the best of these, Graeme Mercer Adam and Theodore Arnold Haultain, were both employed at various times by Goldwin Smith in the capacity of literary assistant. In the launching of the *Canadian Monthly* and the *Week*, Goldwin Smith played a prominent role. Although he was a dominating voice in the columns of the *Week* only during the first few years of its publication, it is clear that his outlook and his critical standards left a permanent impress. The *Week* proclaimed the following policy: an insistence upon independence in politics and on the right and indeed the duty to criticize freely; a concern with the national scene but, at the same time, a due regard for what was happening in the United States and in Europe. The *Week* liked to think that both in conception and by achievement it could take its place beside the great literary periodicals of the day. This was, at least, not a fantastic contention. For our purpose, it will be sufficient to argue more modestly that the *Week* was for its time the least tarnished mirror of Central Canadian culture and as such gave the clearest reflection of current literary taste.

The *Week* was published in Toronto and certainly did not take issue with those correspondents who asserted that Toronto was the intellectual centre of the Dominion. But local and even provincial matters did not bulk large in its columns. For a brief period after its inception it was edited by the promising young poet from the Maritimes, Charles G. D. Roberts. Although Roberts speedily discovered that his Canadian accent had not been formed in the school of Goldwin Smith and severed his official connection with the *Week*, he continued to be a contributor. Its major writers were drawn from all parts of Central Canada. Montreal contributed John Reade, poet, essayist, and literary critic of the *Montreal Gazette*, and William Douw Lighthall, patron of letters, writer, and anthologist. Ottawa was well represented by John Henry Brown and William Dawson LeSueur, both, like Lampman, employed in the federal Post Office Department, and both vigorous advocates of advanced ideas in religion and politics. Kingston and eastern Ontario sent a feminine contingent: Agnes Maude Machar, who under the pen name of "Fidelis" wrote novels, poetry, and literary criticism; and Louisa Murray, a veteran romancer and a self-made bluestocking. From the western Ontario town of Brantford came Sara Jeannette Duncan, the liveliest and most urbane writer in the *Week*. In spite of the wide dispersion of its contributors throughout Central Canada, the general literary tone was remarkably uniform. The main reason for this was that the central corps of writers were born in the United Kingdom and received their education there; it is only natural to assume that they owed to their early training many of the qualities that they displayed when they entered upon the Canadian literary scene. Goldwin Smith was, of course, a product of Eton and Orford; Adam was educated in Edinburgh, Reade was born in Ireland and educated at Queen's College, Belfast. Yet, in journalism and literature, as in academic life, there were signs that the native product was not wholly without flavour. LeSueur and Haultain were both graduates of the University of Toronto, and Sara Jeannette Duncan did not find the Toronto Normal School a barrier to the literary life.

On the whole, I would suggest that the *Week* is a better source for material illustrative of cultivated literary taste than most of the Canadian periodicals that have appeared since it ceased publication. In its pages one finds a synthesis of the academic and the literary that has since broken down with the split between the learned journal and the little magazine, on the one hand, and the general magazine designed for careless reading, on the other. It is admittedly the vehicle of the intellectuals and the high-brows, but it is not the effusion of a coterie nor the unbending spokesman of the learned.

True to its non-partisan ideals, the *Week* accepted contributions from writers who represented a conflicting variety of tastes. Still, one can pick out trends and emphases, and it is to this task, admittedly a hazardous one, that I should now like to turn.

We may safely begin with an estimate of the range and timeliness of the literary comment. The *Week's* proclaimed devotion to the principle of cosmopolitanism was not an empty gesture. Although the space given to Canadian literature gradually increased with the publication during the eighties of major volumes by Cameron, Lampman, Carman, Roberts, Campbell, and a great cloud of minor songsters, the *Week* never permitted patriotic zeal to mar its perspective. The emphasis rested where it belonged on the literature of older and more culturally mature countries. Outside of England and the United States, France received the greatest attention. An attempt was made to keep an orderly check on contemporary French books, if only to draw comforting conclusions about the superior morality of Anglo-Saxon civilization. The novels of Tolstoi, then appearing in English translation, were made the subject of long and generally laudatory reviews; to be called "The Russian George Eliot" was certainly not at that time to be damned with faint praise.[4] Between the literatures of the two great English-speaking countries, it would be difficult to say where the heavier emphasis lay. Certainly reviewers attached the greater prestige to English names; but it is, I think, increasingly apparent that general reading habits were being shaped by the more immediate influences from across the border. Sara Jeannette Duncan pointed out that if a comparison were made "of the number of English and American contemporary writers familiar to the present generation, the latter would be found to preponderate in almost anybody's experience." She went on to observe that "any bookseller in the city will tell us that for one reader of Blackmore or Meredith he finds ten of Howells and James."[5] The American centres to which the commentators in the *Week* turned for literary news were, of course, Boston and New York. Boston was still the city of the great names, of Holmes and Lowell, and their younger and more active contemporaries, Aldrich and Howells. But the shift to New York was duly reflected in the *Week*. The Canadian periodical manifested a discreet interest, both through its reviews and comments and through its selections from contemporary American fiction and poetry, in the typical work of New York writers, particularly in light society verse and in novels that aspired to be bright and sophisticated.

In turning over the pages of the *Week,* one is not oppressed by the consciousness of a time-lag, to use a phrase much favoured by our literary diagnosticians. If anything, the *Week* was too quick to catch on to the popular fashions. This anxiety to keep abreast of the times often led to a flurry of excited critical comment that had to be revised later when more sober judgments prevailed. Its columns were filled with the praise of authors who now rarely creep out of footnotes and bibliographies into the text of even the most comprehensive literary histories—Americans such as Julian Hawthorne, Edgar Fawcett, F. Marion Crawford, and "Charles Egbert Craddock"; English writers such as Sir Francis Hastings, Charles Doyle, William Black, and Sir Edwin Arnold. Yet, one is struck less by this understandable deference to fashionable taste than by the frequency with which writers who have safely survived the critical scrutiny of half a century were singled out for praise. It is well to remember that the task of the literary critic during the last three decades of the nineteenth century was a particularly difficult one. Most of the old Victorian masters had departed and the stage was now crowded with a multitude of clever aspirants for their roles.

The questions I have just discussed—the range of comment, the relative weight given to the literatures of other countries, the response to

---

[4] See "Notes from the Continent," II (Oct. 15, 1885), 727 and "The Review of *Anna Karenina,*" III (April 22, 1886), 338.

[5] "American Influence on Canadian Thought," IV (June 7, 1887), 518.

fashionable taste—all rest on factual data that can be fairly easily established. A more difficult task lies ahead. Is there apparent in this mass of wide-ranging comment a clear pattern of taste? And if there is, what are some of the dominant ideas, principles, assumptions upon which it rests?

Fortunately the search for ideas in the *Week* is not a difficult process that demands a willingness on the part of the reader to draw generous deductions from inhospitable material. Indeed its tone was intellectual and aggressively controversial—a characteristic that appeared no less markedly in its predecessor, the *Canadian Monthly*. The great question to which almost every issue of the *Week* made some contribution was this: how was it possible to bring about a reconciliation between a world view that was shaped by orthodox Christian theology and that alone, it was thought, could give authoritative sanction to a strong morality, and a world view that incorporated the findings of science and that seemed to many to threaten the very basis of morality? This, of course, was the peculiar problem that exercised the minds of the earnest Victorians. Here, it might be said, is some evidence of a time-lag, for in contemporary England the centre of emphasis was beginning to shift noticeably from religious to social and economic controversy. Certainly this shift was not so clearly apparent in Canada; but it should be pointed out that the *Week* was by no means indifferent to changes in economic and social thought, although its awareness usually took the form of petulant outbursts against the fantastic theories of a Henry George or a William Morris.

In the religious and ethical conflict the *Week* consistently strove to establish a compromise that would retain the spirit of the old and at the same time incorporate the truths of the new. Although it emphatically rejected a boldly naturalistic interpretation, it believed in the necessity for the gradual assimilation of the findings of science and of the higher criticism. A writer like LeSueur, a devoted disciple of positivism who sought to replace Christian theism with the religion of humanity, was a valued contributor to the *Week*. Editorial discretion demanded only that from time to time he be gently admonished for his vivacities. What the *Week* admired in critics like LeSueur was their deep seriousness, their insistence that they were not so much rejecting the ethics of Christianity as giving it a new philosophical basis. "The scepticism which now prevails," said the *Week* editorially, "is not that light and sensual scepticism, the nature and source of which are betrayed in Voltaire and Diderot by its union with the vilest obscenities. . . . In these men it does not prevent the character from remaining reverent, and even in a certain sense religious; especially when they invest scientific law with such attributes as to make it practically another name for God."[6]

In the light of this attitude towards the central issue of the age, it is

---

6 III (Nov. 11, 1886), 800.

clear why two of the authors who dominated the cultivated taste of the late nineteenth century were George Eliot and Matthew Arnold. In the novels of George Eliot and the poetry and prose of Matthew Arnold the *Week* found the spirit of serious scepticism and reverent innovation that it so much admired. The deification of George Eliot had already taken place in the *Canadian Monthly,* which was appearing during the last ten triumphant years of her life. Her death occurred shortly before the *Week* began publication, and the comments on her novels in that periodical had some of the sobriety of retrospective judgment.[7] But Matthew Arnold was for the *Week* not only a contemporary man of letters; he was in himself a public question in the same category with Imperial Federation, Irish Home Rule, and the Scott Act. Tennyson and Gladstone might be real and imposing figures against an English backdrop, but Matthew Arnold had actually been seen and heard during the winter of 1884 in Toronto, Ottawa, Montreal, and Quebec. In the *Week* Arnold was treated always with respect, usually with deference.[8]

Although Arnold was a respected figure in the *Week,* it is clear that his message was only partially understood. His Canadian disciples emphasized strongly the hebraic side of his teaching, and largely ignored the hellenic. He was hailed for his "earnest aspirations and large humanity,"[9] and for his skill as a literary critic in bringing poets "to the tests of truth and righteousness."[10] The only contributor to the *Week* who clearly caught the spirit of Arnold's attack on the middle class was Sara Jeannette Duncan. To her the province of Ontario was "one great camp of the Philistines," whose intellectual diet was made up of "politics and vituperation, temperance and vituperation, religion and vituperation."[11]

The same conflict between the old and the new reflected in the comments on the literature of thought appeared also in the comments on the literature of imagination. The *genre* about which writers showed the

---

[7] The appearance of Cross's *Life and Letters* inspired reviews on the general significance of George Eliot's contributions to literature and thought. She was praised less as an artist and more as a great "preceptress of agnosticism teaching through character-lessons, and at the same time, perhaps, as a herald of the transition from a literary to a scientific era" ("Topics of the Week," II (April 9, 1885), 292).

[8] Arnold has not left any extended record of his impressions of English-speaking Canadian society. But the following passage indicates clearly that he thought of that society as possessing all the shortcomings that he attributed to the English middle classes: "You know the conversation which reigns in thousands of middle-class families at this hour, about nunneries, teetotalism, the confessional, eternal punishment, ritualism, disestablishment. It goes wherever the class goes which is moulded on the Puritan type of life. In the long winter evenings of Toronto Mr. Goldwin Smith has had, probably, abundant experience of it." ("Equality" in *Mixed Essays* (London, 1904), 80.) The essay was written before Arnold visited Canada, but I suspect that he was never tempted to revise this passage in the light of his Canadian experience.

[9] G. M. Adam, "Matthew Arnold," *Week,* V (April 26, 1888), 347.

[10] "Review of *Essays in Criticism, Second Series,*" *Week,* VI (Dec. 7, 1888), 12.

[11] "Saunterings," *Week,* III (Sept. 30, 1886), 707.

sharpest awareness of the nature of basic principles was, curiously enough, the novel—the *genre* in which the native effort was weakest, both quantitatively and qualitatively. In briefest terms, the conflict in this area was between those who espoused the traditional novel of complicated plot stiffened by abundant passages of generalized description and of a wholesome morality—what its devotees liked to describe as "the romantic and imaginative novel"—and those who defended the novel that scorned the machinery of plot, strove for a calm objectivity, substituted close analysis of character and motives for elaborate background descriptions, and aimed to trouble the mind rather than to strengthen the moral fibre. The former novel was associated with a settled society, conservative and aristocratic in its social theory, orthodox and absolutist in its religious and ethical teaching; its characteristic writers were Scott, Bulwer-Lytton, Dickens, and even George Eliot. The latter novel was associated with an unsettled society that made a gospel of democracy and with scientific experimentalism that was concerned only with uncovering the data of experience; its practitioners fall into two categories—the French naturalists presided over by Zola, and the American realists of whom Howells and James were the leaders. Even the most liberal writer in the *Week* found it impossible to admit the French naturalists into the republic of letters. For James and Howells, however, there was courteous acceptance, occasionally, spirited support.[12]

The lines between the "romanticists" and the "realists" were sharply drawn. Where common ground could be found, however, was in the generally enthusiastic attitude towards American local colour novelists. George W. Cable and Sarah Orne Jewett were two early favourites. But Mary N. Murfree, who wrote about the Tennessee mountain region under the unpleasant pen name of "Charles Egbert Craddock," received the greatest attention. The local colour novel seems to have been the form in which the current interest in realism was most palatable to the Cana-

---

[12] The two most vigorous upholders of "the romantic and imaginative novel" were G. M. Adam and Louisa Murray. In a review, "Some Books of the Last Year," Adam referred to "the intellectual vivisection methods of the American schools of James and Howells, or, worse still, the loathsome realism and putridity of the school of Zola and France" (II (Jan. 15, 1885), 103). Louisa Murray in an article "Democracy in Literature" argued that the cult of democracy led in the novel to an emphasis on "the prosaic details of commonplace life, with every vestige of poetry carefully eliminated," and to a dreary pessimism. She concluded that "all books are mean that do not make us think nobly of human nature and the heights to which it may attain." (VI (Aug. 2, 1889), 550.) In a lively essay entitled "Outworn Literary Methods," Sara Jeannette Duncan vigorously defended the new novel. "The novel of today," she explained, "may be written to show the culminative action of a passion, to work out an ethical problem of everyday occurrence, to give body and form to a sensation of the finest or of the coarsest kind, for almost any reason which can be shown to have a connection with the course of human life, and the development of human character." (IV (June 9, 1887), 45.) Miss Duncan was thinking primarily of the novels of James and Howells. For an example of intelligent comment on James, see the review of *The Princess Cassamassima* (IV (March 3, 1887), 223–4).

dian reader. This novel demanded close observation of regional types, but observation tempered by "a sunny gleam of humour" and "a general sympathy."[13] Above all, it demanded elaborate natural description in which details were walled about by generalization and edifying comment. All these characteristics produced what one critic aptly called "picturesque realism."[14]

When we turn to the comment on poetry, we find a disturbing absence of critical principles. The general position, however, is abundantly clear: writers in the *Week* were opposed, sometimes belligerently, to poetry that was experimental either in technique or in subject-matter. Even Browning, although he was spoken of with the respect befitting one of the eminent Victorians, was not looked upon as an authentic poetic voice. Agnes E. Wetherald, one of the more sprightly literary autocrats of the time, wittily expressed the common dislike for Browning's obscurity: " 'What is not clear,' says Voltaire, 'is not French.' Apparently Browning thinks it is English. . . ."[15] When in 1889 the newly appointed professor of English at the University of Toronto, W. J. Alexander, published his *Introduction to the Poetry of Robert Browning*, he may very well have looked upon it as an epistle to the Philistines. If Browning earned a grudging respect, Walter Whitman, America's most notable literary eccentric, was usually linked with Zola as beneath serious critical consideration. Whitman's offence was a double one: he expressed himself in a form that "so far from being poetry . . . is not even verse," and he was guilty in his general outlook of a "rampant bestiality."[16] In all fairness, one should add that there were dissenting voices. The *Week* for May 16, 1890 had on one page a statement that Whitman "is not even original in these days, nor improper—simply dull,"[17] and on the next page printed a sonnet by J. H. Brown, always a spokesman of the enlightenment, in which Whitman was apostrophized as "great democrat, great poet, and great man."

It is clear then what in poetry the Canadian literary world mainly disliked: technical experimentation, the intellectual, any suggestion of the commonplace and the realistic. The positive ideal is more difficult to establish, but its general characteristics may be suggested. Its animating conceptions as they emerge by implication in the *Week* were elegance of diction, nobility of sentiment, and clarity and picturesqueness of observation. The good poem embodies either a clear picture or a general sentiment expressed in measured verse and in unambiguous language. The

---

[13] "Charles Egbert Craddock," *Week*, III (Oct. 26, 1886), 767.

[14] *Ibid.*

[15] "One Vice of the Poets," *Week*, III (May 27, 1886), 414.

[16] These phrases are from a review in the *Canadian Monthly and National Review* (I (March, 1872), 279), but they might very well have come from the *Week*.

[17] VII, 375. The most discerning critique of Whitman published in the *Week* was that by Charles G. D. Roberts in his "Notes on Some of the Younger Poets" (I (April 24, 1884), 328).

poets who received consistent praise—Austin Dobson, Oliver Wendell Holmes, and Thomas Bailey Aldrich—were all exponents of these ideals of Victorian neo-classicism.

So far this analysis of Canadian literary taste has been based entirely on comment and criticism of non-Canadian writers. I have done this not merely because the literatures of other countries offered a richer field for the exercise of literary judgment, but because taste in the native literature was deficient even in those modest powers of discrimination that I have been trying to describe. Canadian critics were not unaware of the problems posed by the noxious mixture of colonialism and nationalism and they could, at times, be attractively ruthless when writing about native poets and novelists.[18] But, on the whole, it would be at best only a well-intentioned distortion if I were to suggest that criticism of Canadian writing showed powers of careful selection and rejection and that a distinct preference was shown for, say, the nature poetry of Lampman as against the rhymed jingles of any number of versifiers now mercifully forgotten.[19]

---

[18] The early issues of the *Week* contained a number of articles analysing the plight of Canadian literature and calling for a tough, uncompromising criticism. The ultimate note in cynical despair was struck by J. E. Collins when he observed that "the fiction and *belles-lettres,* generally, have the limits of the municipality and the flavour of the log-hut" ("English-Canadian Literature," I (Aug. 28, 1884), 614). In the next issue "Barry Dane" (John E. Logan) warned against the dangers of a "flattering and fulsome praise" and declared that many of the reviews of Canadian books were as "reliable as patent medicine advertisements, and probably as fostering to good literature" ("National Literature," I (Sept. 4, 1884), 633). Occasionally, Canadian criticism was equal to its task and did not scorn the tools of analysis. A long review of John Hunter-Duvar's *De Roberval, a Drama* struck this opening note: "The opening is weak, the growth tedious, the climax doubtful, the fall is unproportioned, and the close is only redeemed from bathos by a chorus" (VI (Feb. 15, 1889), 170). Unfortunately such remarks are as rare as they are refreshing. W. D. Lighthall, writing in the *Week* just at the time when his much-praised anthology, *Songs of the Great Dominion,* was appearing (1889), selected for especial commendation a passage from a poem on Laura Secord by a certain Mrs. Curzon, the first lines of which are as follows:

"I stood on Queenston Heights;
And as I gazed from tomb to cenotaph,
From cenotaph to tomb, adown and up,
My heart grew full, much moved with many thoughts."

[19] For a few years after the publication of *Among the Millet* (1888) Lampman was given special attention in the *Week,* and there is some reason for concluding that he was more highly esteemed than his contemporaries. *Among the Millet* was given two long reviews, laudatory but not uncritical, each by one of the leading *littérateurs* of the day: "Seranus" (Mrs. J. F. Harrison) in VI (Dec. 28, 1888), 59, and "Fidelis" (Miss A. M. Machar) in VI (March 22, 1889), 251–2. *Among the Millet* inspired two poetic tributes, one by D. C. Scott, "Written in a Copy of Archibald Lampman's Poems" (VI (Oct. 4, 1889), 689), and one by C. M. Holmes, "*Among the Millet*—by Lampman" (VIII (April 10, 1891), 298). The highest tribute to be paid Lampman in the *Week* was his inclusion in the series "Prominent Canadians," a series given over for the most part to the great in politics, law, and finance. The writer of the sketch, Lilly F. Barry, obviously feels that Lampman is the great Canadian poet. "His success," she writes, "is a matter of national importance" (VIII (April 10, 1891), 298–300). From this time on, however, Lampman was a less prominent figure in the *Week* both as contributor and as the subject for the literary essay.

I do not want to give the impression that the not unrespectable standards of taste that determined the reception of European, English, and American literatures ceased to operate in the field of Canadian literature and that they bear witness merely to the existence of a surface cosmopolitanism. Where they reappeared, indirectly but none the less powerfully, was in the best creative literature of the day, in the poetry of Lampman, Cameron, Scott, and Campbell—all poets who lived and worked in Central Canada; and, to a lesser extent, in the poetry of Roberts and Carman—poets who were subjected to more diverse influences and could draw from another and more distinctive regional culture. The poetry of Lampman, to take one of this group, is the poetry of a man who expresses the serious tastes of his cultural environment. The demonstration of such a thesis belongs to a separate study to which this analysis of taste is, in a sense, a prologue. At the conclusion of this paper, I can suggest only the broad outlines of the argument.

Archibald Lampman belonged to the family compact of intellectuals and men of letters that, as we have seen, grew up in Central Canada during the later part of the nineteenth century. It was far more benevolent and, unfortunately, far less powerful than the more famous compact that moves ambiguously through the history of Upper Canada, and it did not exact from its numbers the same rigid qualifications. Lampman's career, however, gives us a pattern of the normal development. It is founded on a family tradition that stresses devotion to things British, to the Church, and to classical literature. It is subsequently toughened by exposure to the world of politics and education, and by immersion in journalism. Lampman, for instance, came from a clerical home, took his university degree in classics, and had a brief, unhappy experience as a teacher. After 1882, when he entered the Post Office Department at Ottawa, he was a horrified observer of the political scene, and from the time of his student days he was an active part-time journalist aspiring to be a full-time man of letters. All of his close friends were journalists and writers, most of them associated at some time with the *Week*—J. E. Collins, E. W. Thomson, W. D. LeSueur, J. H. Brown, Duncan Campbell Scott, and Wilfred Campbell. Many of his early poems appeared in the *Week;* he himself wrote critical articles for that periodical,[20] and for a little over a year beginning in February, 1892, he conducted in the *Globe* (Toronto), in association with Campbell and Scott, a literary column known as "At the Mermaid Inn."

---

[20] Lampman did not write much prose for the *Week*. He was, however, an occasional reviewer. (See a review of *Lyrical Translations* by Charles J. Parkam in V (Dec. 8, 1887), 22, and a review of *Old Man Savarin, and Other Stories* by his friend E. W. Thomson in XII (Aug. 9, 1895), 880–1.) The bulk of his prose work is to be found in "At the Mermaid Inn," where, incidentally, he singled out the *Week* as the one contemporary Canadian periodical in which he had confidence. (See the *Globe*, Oct. 1, 1892.) The most extended piece of critical prose written by Lampman is the lecture, "Two Canadian Poets," reprinted in the *University of Toronto Quarterly*, XIII (July, 1944), 406–23.

What then is abundantly evident is that Lampman was no pale recluse but an active participator and an acknowledged leader in the intellectual and cultural life of Central Canada. In his poetry, it seems to me, you will find the concrete embodiment of the standards of taste that animate critical comment in the *Week*. It is poetry of "picturesque realism," at its best in natural description where a large, general effect is fused with sharply observed detail. Less successfully, it is poetry of thought and sentiment that may, at times, recall the sermons of a liberal-minded clergyman with a dignified presence and a monotonous voice, but never, as does so much of the thoughtful verse of his Canadian contemporaries, the high-school commencement address or the recitation at the "box social." And in his final volume, *Alcyone*, it is poetry that voices the religious doubts and yearnings of the age with a subdued melancholy and a stoic calm that echoes "the eternal note of sadness" of the great English contemporary who was his declared master.[21] In the poetry of Lampman the cultivated taste of the age finds its most eloquent apology.

---

[21] At first Lampman was under the spell of Keats. "Keats has always," he wrote, "had such a fascination for me and has so permeated my whole mental outlet, that I have an idea that he has found a sort of faint reincarnation in me." (Quoted by Duncan Campbell Scott in the Introduction to Lampman's *Lyrics of Earth*, Toronto, 1925, 32.) But Matthew Arnold was always a favourite and he gradually rose to the top of Lampman's hierarchy of poets. After hearing Arnold in Ottawa in the winter of 1884, he wrote to his friend J. A. Ritchie: "I went to hear Matthew Arnold and was filled with an abiding sense of reverence and affection for that splendid old fellow, who looks and acts and speaks as nobly as he writes." (Quoted by Carl Y. Connor in *Archibald Lampman, Canadian Poet of Nature*, Montreal, 1929, 76.) His fullest estimate of Arnold concludes as follows: "He who has been reading Browning till his head spins with the multitude of subtleties and splendid tours de force, or he who is ever weary, if such a thing may be, of the rounded perfections of Tennyson, betakes himself to Matthew Arnold, and then he seems to have reached the hills. With a mind blown clear as by the free wind of heaven he surveys the extent of life. He passes through an atmosphere where only the noblest emotions, life, beauty and thought possess him. He becomes gentle and majestic as the mind of the master who commands him. I believe that the time will come when Matthew Arnold will be accounted the greatest poet of his generation, and one of the three or four noblest that England has produced." (Quoted by Duncan Campbell Scott, *Lyrics of Earth*, 34–5.)

11

Riel*

Léandre Bergeron

BY SELLING OUT the Franco-Manitobans in 1896, Laurier showed his treason toward his people, a treason which would be confirmed in international and national events of the future. So concludes Léandre Bergeron in the section on Riel in his volume of radical and anticlerical historiography which has recently been extremely popular in labour and student circles in Quebec. It is not the history most English-speaking Canadians have known. Before the Quiet Revolution it would hardly have been acceptable in Quebec. No longer is Confederation defended as a pact later violated by *les Anglais*. Instead, the French-Canadian people, broken by the events of 1837–38, were dragged into Confederation by the treachery of Cartier, the clergy, and the English-speaking capitalists—the forces *les plus anti-démocratiques de la societé canayenne*. Virtually all the important powers were given to the central level where Quebec representation fell from one half to less than a third. The heroes of that dark hour were clearly the *Rouges*.

Referring to earlier events, Bergeron makes the important point that the "Explorers" were not "Discoverers." To call them such is to show the profound racism which has infected white men for centuries. According to Bergeron, they explored and conquered territories by force, practising a genocide as barbaric as that of Hitler against the Jews.

Before the Rebellions, Papineau showed his naivete by believing that English oppression could be ended by declarations, economic boycotts, and union with the United States. He failed, according to Bergeron, to comprehend that liberation of a people under economic "imperialism" requires armed struggle; he really did not want a revolution which would bring the habitants to power, he wanted an evolution which would give

* From *The History of Quebec: A Patriot's Handbook* (Toronto, New Canada Press, 1971), translated from the original *Petit manuel d'histoire du Québec* (Montréal, Editions Québécoises, 1970).

power to *la petite bourgeois canayenne*. Besides those who fell during the struggle, the real heroes were the 12 simple men whom the tyrant Colbourne publicly executed in November 1838 as an "example." As for Lafontaine, he and his like allied themselves with the clergy and collaborated with the enemy while negatively resisting assimilation. They manufactured myths to make the people forget their situation and to ensure the continued supremacy of *l'élite clérico-bourgeoise*.

In the section reproduced here, the sad but brave story of the French-speaking people of the North-West is recounted from a radical and popular perspective. Louis Riel, the hero, emerges as the Ché Guevara of the Plains.

CONFEDERATION was only a few years old when the Manitoba crisis revealed that its main purpose was really to make Quebec into a kind of "reserve" for the Canayens. The English would fight to the death before they would allow the Canayens and the Canayen Métis on the Red River to create a French-speaking province west of Ontario. One province of Quebec was already too much for the English-Canadians. They had to nip in the bud any Métis coalition on the Plains. They had to massacre them if necessary, and bring in the English to make Manitoba at all costs an English-speaking province.

Ottawa organized and carried out this project, efficiently, right through to the murder of Louis Riel in 1885.

In the West, the Hudson Bay Company had been exploiting the fur-trade. The Red men, the Canayen Métis, and the Canayen trappers are the *cheap-labour* of this trade. The 10,000 Métis and the few thousand Canayens are evenly settled along the Red River and its tributaries, according to the Quebec system of settlement—strips of narrow lands stretching from the river deep into the hinterland. They also concentrated at St. Boniface, where Bishop Plessis sent missionaries as early as 1818. On the other side of the Red River a few thousand Scottish settlers, who had come over with Lord Selkirk in 1812, are cultivating the fertile lands of the region. The majority of the population is Canayen Métis and very conscious of its identity.

The Hudson's Bay Company, like all the monopoly companies at this time, has fantastic privileges. It has established a virtual political administration in the region. It nominates a governor and a Council, which has dictatorial powers over the population. The Company gets along well with the Scottish settlers who restrict themselves to agriculture; but it shamefully exploits the Métis. Already in 1826–27 the Métis had revolted against its tyranny.

In 1849 the Company prosecuted, before its own "court of justice," a Métis accused of illegal fur-trading. What this Métis had done in fact was to sell his furs to some Americans who offered him more than he would normally have received from the Company. During his "trial" before an agent of the Company, a group of Métis invaded the court-room and forced the acquittal of their comrade. Jean-Louis *Riel*, a miller from St. Boniface and father of Louis Riel, was the leading figure in this insurrection.

During the 1850s and '60s a few thousand Canayens who are forced to leave Quebec but do not care to emigrate to the United States, go to settle along the Red River and devote themselves to clearing the lands, engaging in agriculture, and founding parishes.

Meanwhile the Americans, who are expanding to the Pacific, have their own designs on these rich plains. And the English from Ontario are reading anti-Canayen articles by George Brown and William McDougall, who want to make the Prairies an extension of Ontario. They see clearly that they must put a stop to the Canayens organizing a society there, and at the same time prevent the Americans from annexing the region to the United States.

In 1864, the promoters of Confederation meet in Quebec, and discuss the admission of that region then called the North-West Territories (present-day Manitoba, Saskatchewan, Alberta, the Yukon, and Keewatin). When the Métis learn that their fate is being decided without consulting them, their resentment increases.

In 1868, Ottawa illegally sends a road construction team into the Red River district, ostensibly to give work to the Métis, whose economic situation is desperate due to grass-hoppers ruining the harvest. The following summer Canadian land-surveyors began to mark out the roads without regard to the Métis' strips of farms along the river. They contemptuously ridicule the Métis protests. And when Prime Minister Macdonald hears of these protests, all he does is utter injurious remarks about the Métis. He treats them as "half-castes," as degenerates.

Negotiations between Ottawa and the Hudson's Bay Company are concluded. On December 1, the territory is officially handed over to Canada for a sum of £300,000 sterling. The Canadian government nominates a governor and a council for the region. William McDougall is named governor to take up his post as of December 1st. All the members of the Council, except for one sellout Canayen, are militant anti-Canayen Protestants.

The Métis, however, have been organizing their resistance since October.

On October 11, the young Louis Riel at the head of a group of Métis disperses a team of surveyors.

On October 20, the Métis meet and elect a Provisional Government modelled on their organization for buffalo hunting. John Bruce, a Scottish

Métis, is elected president, and Riel, secretary. Their goal is to gain recognition of their rights from Canada before December 1, the day on which the territory is to be handed over to Canada by the Company.

The Council of Assiniboia, the local Company council, summons Riel to appear before it and explain himself. Riel appears, and defends the rights of the Métis by protesting against any government over them originating in Canada without their consent.

Meanwhile McDougall and his Council make their way to the Red River via the United States. At Pembina, in American territory, a Métis representative warns them not to cross the border. On October 30, McDougall tries to cross, but a Métis commando group under the command of Ambroise Lépine stops him. On the same day, Riel seizes Fort Garry, the main Company trading post, in the name of the Provisional Government.

Meanwhile Colonel Dennis, leader of the surveying team, tries to organize a *coup d'état* to get McDougall in by force. On November 6, Riel invites the Scottish parishes to choose representatives to meet with the Canayen Métis on November 16.

But on that day MacTavish, governor of the Company, issues a proclamation protesting the decision of the Provisional Government and demanding a return to "legality." In other words, he would like to get rid of the Provisional Government, but does not dare say so for fear of the people's reaction. One of his English colleagues proposes a solution: both English and Métis should get together to form a new Council to negotiate with Ottawa.

Riel considers accepting, but smells the rat in time. On the 23rd of November, he and his troops seize the provisions and funds of Fort Garry, and take command of all its entrances and exits.

At the end of November, McDougall, who is still waiting at the border, receives a letter from Prime Minister Macdonald, telling him not to try to move in to this "foreign country" by force. But at the same time, Colonel Dennis, with 20 Canadians and 70 Red-men, tries to attack Fort Garry and overthrow the Provisional Government. They fail miserably.

On December 5th, Louis Riel publishes his *List of Rights*, in which he proclaims the necessity of consulting the Métis people as to whether or not they wish to join Canada. On December 9th, he arrests the leaders of the pro-Canadian Party and locks them up in Fort Garry. He hoists the Provisional Government's flag, a shamrock and a fleur-de-lis. The supporters of the pro-Canadian Party hardly dare to show their flag, which is nothing but the Union Jack with *Canada* embroidered on it.

The Canadian government is really vexed: the coveted territory is not falling into its hands like an apple from a tree. Macdonald decides to send two well-chosen emissaries—a priest, Father Thibault, who has spent 27 years in the region, and Charles de Salaberry, son of the hero of

Chateauguay. A third character, Donald Smith, the Hudson Bay Company manager, carries with him a little bag—and in it the money needed to buy off the rebel leaders. The plan is to offer the Métis two seats on a Council, two-thirds of which will be elected by the population of the colony; to promise to respect property titles; and to offer Riel a post in the territory's police force.

All these promises are to be accompanied by hard cash, "to construct," as Macdonald puts it, "a bridge of gold over which McDougall can cross into the territory."

On December 6, a royal proclamation urges the Métis to lay down their arms and promises an amnesty.[1]

Riel assumes the presidency of the Provisional Government. When the representatives of the expansionist Canadian government arrive, he prevents them from speaking to the people, but agrees to engage in discussion with them. The Métis leaders do not allow themselves to be bought off. Riel demands that Ottawa recognize his Provisional Government as the only constituted body that could negotiate the entrance of the Red River region as a full-fledged province into Confederation.

The Ottawa emissaries are obliged to recognize the Provisional Government officially on the 20th of February, so that Ottawa also recognizes it *de facto.* The Provisional Government at this point agrees to send in return a delegation of three men to Ottawa: Father Ritchot for the Canayen Métis; Judge John Black for the English-speaking Métis, and Alfred H. Scott for the American and English colonists.

During these discussions between the representatives of Ottawa and the Métis leaders, the supporters of the pro-Canadian Party resolve to raid the fort and slaughter all the Métis in it. They are utterly unable to accept that the Métis, whom they so despise, are carrying out the negotiations with the federal government.

Among this gang of blood-thirsty colonizers is Thomas Scott who managed to escape from Fort Garry where he had been imprisoned by Riel on December 7 along with other leaders of the pro-Canadian Party.

During the night of February 14, this group under the command of a Major Boulton descends on Fort Garry, but soon withdraws when Riel promises to do them no harm if they disperse. Upon leaving, these cowards cannot restrain themselves from attacking a Métis named Parisien and taking him prisoner. Parisien escapes and the next day shoots an English colonist, who he believes is following him. The Métis leader Lépine surrounds the Boulton gang and locks them up in the fort. Boulton goes before the Provisional Government's War Council, and is condemned to be shot. The emissary Smith intercedes on his behalf and manages to get him a suspended sentence.

---

[1] *Amnesty:* a special law granting pardon.

Thomas Scott is brought to trial, and he too is condemned to be shot. Again Smith tries to intercede, but this time it is wasted effort. Scott had tried to murder the chief surveyor Snow when he worked under him, and was one of the leaders agitating against the Métis. During his earlier imprisonment, he had not for a moment ceased to insult Riel and his Provisional Government. He had escaped in January, and was now the instigator of this new attack against the Provisional Government, recognized even in Ottawa. The War Council cannot go back on its decision. Thomas Scott is executed on March 4th.

His execution further inflames the conflict. The Ontario aggressors are fuming with rage. Bishop Taché, immediately recalled from Rome by Macdonald, uses all his influence to persuade the Métis leaders to give in to the pressures from Ottawa. Riel regards him as an agent of the Canadian government, but nevertheless frees the rest of the prisoners on March 16th, proclaims peace on April 9th, and on April 23rd replaces the Provisional Government's flag on the Fort with the Union Jack. The Provisional Government remains in control, with Ottawa's consent, until the arrival of the new governor.

The three representatives of the Provisional Government, on their way to Ottawa to negotiate their country's entry into Confederation, are arrested in Toronto on the instigation of Thomas Scott's brother. They have to be released, however, when the Ontario government is unable to prosecute them.

After a month of negotiation between Ottawa and the Provisional Government, the Province of Manitoba is created. The federal government holds on to public lands in exchange for small concessions to the Métis. Denominational schools, Protestant and Catholic, are guaranteed. French and English are both to be official languages. The Métis get what they fought for, but fall into a trap anyway. They have won their cause only on paper: Manitoba becomes a province, and not merely an extension of Ontario. But in reality the Métis will not gain much from the rights they acquire with the creation of the new province, because the English will chase them out, modify the school laws and take control in order to make Manitoba a white Anglo-Saxon Protestant province like Ontario.

On July 15, 1870, Manitoba officially becomes a Canadian province. Under the orders of Colonel Wolseley, Lieutenant-Governor Archibald arrives with an armed force. The Métis do not understand the need for this display of military might. They think the question is settled: Manitoba is a province, with laws guaranteeing their rights. Besides, Riel and his troops have already withdrawn from the Fort when Wolseley arrives.

Repression begins. Smith sends out a warrant for the arrest of Riel and other Métis leaders. Immigrants arriving by the thousand from Ontario begin a Métis-hunt. The Métis are persecuted and murdered. Even Governor Archibald is forced to admit this. In a letter to his boss, Macdonald, he writes: "Many of the French half-breeds have been so beaten and outraged by a small but noisy section of the people that they feel as if they were living in a state of slavery." He adds that the newcomers from Ontario "seem to feel as if the French half-breeds should be wiped off the face of the globe."

The new colonists from Ontario are allowed to chase the Métis off their ancestral lands, burn their houses and take over their farms. Killing Métis becomes a sport, as killing Blacks is for the Southern Whites in the United States. Two soldiers from the "Ontario Rifles" shoot down Elzéar Goulet like an animal. Instead of being arrested they are encouraged and commended for their bravery.

The Métis reaction to this persecution is to emigrate further west and north. Riel and Lépine are now somewhat isolated. Governor MacTavish calls on them to combat the Fenians—Irish refugees in the United States who were attacking Canada in order to weaken England and thus help to liberate their homeland from English domination. And Riel and Lépine actually recruit about 300 Métis for this purpose in October, 1871. Bishop Taché has indeed managed to convince Riel that collaboration with and submission to Canadian authority is the only answer for every Manitoban Christian.

In the Federal elections of 1871, Riel is elected for the district of St. Boniface. Cartier, who has lost in a Montreal east-end riding because the Canayens there find him a disgusting sell-out, manages to convince Riel to give up his seat so that he, Cartier, can become Member of Parliament for St. Boniface instead. Bishop Taché and Cartier both shamefully manipulate Riel. He is a believer whose religious sentiments can easily be exploited by these two characters for their own ends.

In 1873 Lépine is arrested, judged, and condemned to death. Bishop Taché protests against a government that breaks its promise of amnesty. Lépine's sentence is commuted to two years in prison. But he loses his civil rights. This same Bishop Taché hands over some money from Macdonald and Cartier to Louis Riel to encourage him to get lost in the United States.

The death of Cartier in that same year, however, leaves the riding of St. Boniface vacant. Riel is re-elected in 1874. But how can he sit in Ottawa, when the entire population of Ontario is out to get him? A price is put on his head: $5,000 to the person who arrests him and places him in the hands of the Ontario authorities.

Despite this danger, Riel presents himself in Ottawa and takes the oath as a Member of Parliament. Such hysteria ensues, however, that he is expelled from the House of Commons. We can see that the laws of democracy work only for the masters, the English gentlemen. According to their own tradition a duly elected Member of Parliament is supposed to be protected from arrest when exercising his functions. This is what is called parliamentary immunity. But Louis Riel has no right to it. The masters make their laws for their own benefit, and prevent their colonized subjects from taking advantage of them. Riel is chased from the House of Commons like a bum. And in order to justify this action the members from Ontario officially declare him a fugitive from justice.

The British democratic circus is not yet over: in 1875 a Royal Commission of Inquiry is created to find out if the rebels had indeed been granted amnesty. This Royal Commission concludes that Scott had been judged and executed by a legal government, the Provisional Government recognized by Ottawa; that an amnesty had in fact been granted according to the promises of Macdonald, Cartier and Co., as proved by the fact that Governor Archibald had called on Riel and Lépine to help fight the Fenians. This Commission of Inquiry mildly chastises the government, in order to clear its conscience. To say that things should have been otherwise is but a petty "mea culpa" after the crime.

Now that the Métis are subdued, the Federal government has nothing to lose by saying that it should have been nicer to their leaders.

Acting on the report of the commission, the government decrees a general amnesty for all the rebels except Riel, Lépine, and a certain O'Donaghue. These are all exiled for five years.

Lépine freed from prison in 1876, goes to Batoche on the Saskatchewan River, where many Métis sought refuge from persecution by the English who had stolen their lands on the Red River.

Riel seeks refuge in Quebec with the fanatic Catholic Alphonse Desjardins. In this period he has mystical visions. Desjardins has him confined to asylums in Longue Pointe and Beauport from 1875 to 1878. Riel emerges from time to time, to speak for the Métis cause. He leaves Beauport in 1878, and makes his way toward the American west. He settles at the Jesuit mission of St. Pierre in Montana, marries a Métis and teaches at the local school. He becomes a U.S. citizen in 1883, but still does not renounce the Métis cause.

The creation of the province of Manitoba does not solve all the problems on the prairies. The Métis have taken refuge west of Manitoba along the Saskatchewan River. As for the English who have grabbed Manitoba, they are still not satisfied. They need the entire territory, all the way to the Pacific. Colonialism has no limits.

The Métis, who hunt buffalo for food, witness the disappearance of their food supply. The Americans slaughter entire herds for skins or simply for sport; in addition, the Canadian Pacific Railway and more colonists penetrate into their hunting territory. The Métis repeatedly complain to Ottawa about the slaughter of the buffalo and about the speculators who are stealing their property, but Ottawa turns a deaf ear. In fact, Ottawa encourages speculation, hoping for higher property taxes to help defray the enormous costs of railway construction. The fate of the Métis has no importance in Ottawa.

So once again the surveyors begin to subdivide the Métis lands and chase them out. The Métis send a petition to Ottawa. Nothing happens. There is finally nothing left but self-defence.

In the spring of 1884, a delegation composed of Gabriel Dumont, Moise Ouellet, James Isbister, and Michel Dumas make their way to Montana, to urge Riel to come back and organize the struggle. Riel accepts. He even hopes to establish a new Métis nation west of Manitoba.

He arrives in the region in July, and immediately has the support of the Métis, the Red men and some of the Whites. He demands recognition of the Métis, property rights on all Métis lands, and proposes the creation of the provinces of Alberta and Saskatchewan.

Sometimes he has fantastic visions: the creation of a society in the west free from exploitation where poverty and misery would disappear, where men would love each other, work together and create an ideal society together. Some of these ideas come close to Ché Guevara's concept of the "new man." These visions frighten the missionaries, for whom man is necessarily an evil being who must live in misery, guilt, and fear in order to earn his place in heaven. A man who speaks of a better society in this world is to be dreaded. Father André refuses Riel the sacraments, considers him crazy and thinks about trying to get him to leave the country.

Father André is present at the negotiations between the Federal government and Riel at the end of 1885. Riel agrees to return to the United States if the government gives him $35,000 for the lands he would be abandoning. The government refuses all compensation, and instead reinforces the Royal North-West Mounted Police,[2] a force created expressedly for the repression of the Métis. It tries to buy off the Métis leaders by offering them jobs. Isbister and Dumas are offered posts as agricultural instructors for the Red men, while Gabriel Dumont is offered a ferry license.

Riel understands that the federal government once again is seeking to buy him off. So he asks for sums the government cannot pay.

In February, 1885, he organizes secret meetings in which he prepares his men for guerrilla warfare. When the priests hear of these preparations, they quickly oppose and condemn all action that is not legal or constitutional. Riel replies, "The spirit of God is in me" and "Rome has fallen."

The priests take these words as proof that Riel must be crazy. How could God be in the heart of a man who takes up arms to defend the rights of his compatriots, and dares to claim that Rome has fallen when it is well-known that Rome and the Catholic Church, like the British Empire, extends its grasp over a large part of the earth?

But Riel is right. He speaks the language of simple and brutal truth. If we agree that the word "God" is a synonym for love, for life, for fulfill-

---

[2] This special army of repression in the name of the Federal government is later to be called 'the RCMP.'

ment, then Riel really has God in him. He is a leader who wants to take his people through a liberation struggle and create a better society, where love, justice and a free and full life will prevail. And he is right in saying that "Rome has fallen" because the Catholic Church, founded by a revolutionary who wanted to establish a kingdom of love, has become an exploitative capitalist institution, power-hungry and permeated with the spirit of oppression, domination, and colonialism. The Church gets along well with the bourgeois class, the imperialist British government and the aspiring imperialists in Ottawa. Is not Father André himself in favour of Canadian expansion in the west as long as he can keep his job as evangelist among the Métis?

If his words are given their true meaning, Riel's religious-political declarations show us a man fired by a revolutionary vision of the world. He is among that category of men who, realizing the misery that comes with the exploitation of man by man whether in its pharisaic or capitalist form, engage in a struggle to the death against this repression and do not back down, even if they are forced to pay the supreme sacrifice.

On March 17, 1885, Riel establishes the Provisional Government of Saskatchewan at St. Laurent. Riel is president, Dumont adjutant.

On March 18, Riel seizes the church at Batoche. Father Moulin protests. Riel gently pushes him aside, referring to him as a "Protestant" comrade, and takes a few prisoners.

On the 21st of March Riel draws up an ultimatum to be sent to Major Crozier, commander of the Mounted Police at Carleton and Battleford. He threatens a war of extermination, and demands that Crozier hand over the police stations and withdraw from the country.

On March 6, about 30 Métis had prevented soldiers from entering Carleton. The police counter-attacked but had to abandon the fight and leave twelve dead, after an assault by Gabriel Dumont and his buffalo hunters. The armed struggle has begun.

Riel tries to win over the English colonists, at least to neutrality if not to the cause, by promising to prevent the Red men from entering the conflict. But the colonists remember George Custer's defeat at the hands of the Sioux in the American West.

This fear of seeing the Red men join their brothers, the Métis, to demand their rights brings out a military expedition from the Ottawa government to crush both the Red men and the Métis. This will be easier than in 1870, because the Canadian Pacific now links Winnipeg to Edmonton and Calgary, and the telegraph links Ottawa to the smallest station in the West.

To bolster the hundreds of Mounties, Ottawa sends 5,000 militia from Ontario, Quebec, Nova Scotia, and Manitoba. The militia from Ontario think they are engaged in a holy war against "the French and Indian rebels," and the Québécois who participate in this expedition believe that they are going to fight a crazy heretic and his "savage" allies.

The Crees and the Stoneys join with Riel. Big Bear's Crees execute two Catholic missionaries and five traders. Poundmaker and his Stoneys lay siege to Battleford.

The rebels, Métis and Red men, number about 700 in all. Several times, they ambush advancing army columns of 5,000. Gabriel Dumont's guerrilla warfare spreads terror among the Canadian ranks.

In spite of everything, the Métis stronghold, Batoche, falls on May 12. Riel surrenders to two scouts. The generals telegraph to Ottawa to say that they have "captured" him.

Ten days later, Poundmaker gives himself up. The Rebellion is crushed. Canadian oppression is victorious.

The expedition and the repression cost $4,500,000. The Hudson's Bay Company, which supplied the provisions and land transportation, claims $1,737,032.00; the Canadian Pacific $852,231.32.

We see that Canadian propaganda managed to raise troops in Quebec by making Canayens believe that the Métis and their allies, the Red men, are all vicious savages. But with Riel's surrender this same propaganda shows its real face: this war of repression is directed against the Canayens settled in Manitoba and against their Métis cousins. A Toronto newspaper writes, "Riel should be strangled with a French flag." The federal government prosecutes Riel on July 20 in Regina, on a charge of high treason.

The Canayens, deceived not only by Canadian propaganda but also by their own clerical-bourgeois elite about the war of repression against the Métis, are now becoming aware of the reality of the situation. The Canadians want Riel's head because he dared to conceive the idea of making the West a French-speaking province of Canayen Métis. Riel is now seen as the symbol of the Canayen people.

A campaign to save Riel is organized. Even though journalists like L. O. David consider Riel the spiritual heir of the Patriotes of 1837, the campaign becomes a mere political football when the Liberals grab it to attack Macdonald's Conservative government.

Riel's trial is a monumental judicial farce. From the beginning the dice are loaded against him. He is judged by an English magistrate assisted by a French Justice of the Peace before a jury of six men, all English colonists and English merchants.

Riel's English secretary, William Henry Jackson, who insists that he shares responsibility with Riel, is tried during one of Riel's own trial adjournments. Jackson is declared insane in half an hour and locked up in an asylum, from which he easily escapes to the United States. From this incident we can see clearly that Canadian justice had no intention of prosecuting an English person, even when he declares his solidarity with an individual accused of high treason.

Riel himself asks for the Deputy Minister of the Interior, who has his official documents and the Métis petitions. The judge rejects the request.

Riel demands that his personal papers seized at Batoche be returned to him. The judge denies this request too, since the Crown Attorneys are busy using the papers to prepare their case against Riel.

The lawyers for the accused, intimidated in advance or already sold out for some time, try to prove that Riel is a mental case whose wild conduct should be excused. Dr. Roy from the Beauport asylum is a witness for this plea, but he loses all credibility under cross-examination when he cannot express himself in English. Dr. Jukes of the Mounted Police declares Riel sane.

With remarkable eloquence, Riel repudiates all his own lawyers' arguments, assuring the court that he is sane. He explains how as *founder of Manitoba and prophet of the New World* he wanted to make the West a free country for all the oppressed nations, not only for the Métis and Red men but also for the oppressed peoples of Europe.

He recalls the schemings of Macdonald and Cartier to try to buy him off, the provocations of the Mounted Police, the promises to the Métis that the government never kept. He attacks the Clergy for its complicity with the government, and ends with a call for a trial before a complete jury, and an examination before a medical commission.

Seven days later, the jury returns a verdict of guilty with a recommendation for clemency. But on August 1, the judge condemns Riel to be hanged on September 18 in Regina. Riel appeals to the Manitoba Court of the Queen's Bench, which confirms the verdict, and then to the Privy Council, which refuses to hear the case.

During all this time a great campaign is in full swing in Ontario for the execution of the sentence. In Quebec, on the other hand, a campaign is organized to obtain a pardon for Riel. Despite the Clergy's warnings, the Canayens recognize that Riel is one of them, and that he is valiantly struggling against Ottawa for all the oppressed people of the West.

In Ottawa, the question is settled. Has not Macdonald proclaimed, "Riel must swing."

As a matter of procedure, the government grants three stays of execution to give the condemned man time to make his various appeals. In addition, a medical commission is set up. It finds that Riel is not insane, in the eyes of the law, and is therefore fit to hang.

In the end the government refuses to commute the sentence on November 12, and Riel is executed in Regina on November 16th. The justice of the masters, the colonizers, has run its course; again the agents of imperialism have put down the indigenous people by perpetrating the necessary murders, though at the same time clearing their own consciences with a mock-show of justice, judges, law-court, lawyers and legal parlance, the whole masquerade needed to cover up the most shameful political crime of the era.

The murder of Riel occasions a considerable political backlash in

Quebec. The majority of the population rise up in protest against Macdonald. His Canayen ministers are burned in effigy. On November 22, a huge popular assembly (50,000 strong) is held on the *Champs-de-Mars* in Montreal. The fever is at its pitch. Not since 1837 has the indignation of the Canayen people risen so high.

Unhappily, the spokesmen at this rally are not up to the situation. They cannot provide the leadership necessary to mobilize the people, arm them and begin again the struggle for liberation. They are not even worthy of addressing the people, for they are in fact mere petty politicians anxious to exploit the situation for their own personal ambitions.

Wilfrid Laurier, the Liberal, claims "If I had been on the banks of the Saskatchewan I too would have shouldered my musket." But why then did he not go and join Riel on the shores of the Saskatchewan? Couldn't he afford a ticket to get there? Didn't he have a gun? Riel could have supplied him with everything—ticket, gun, bullets, buffalo coat and pemmican. . . .[3] But no such thing happened. Laurier really was one of that race of weak little men who exploit the gestures and even the deaths of others, to make political capital. This high-sounding rhetoric is nothing but bad literature, well-turned phrases to pass himself off as a different kind of man. He steals Riel's heroism, and conceals his own underhandedness. Behind these lovely words is written large, "Vote Liberal, Vote for Me, I want to be Prime Minister of Canada." And we will see, when he does become Prime Minister, how his handling of the Manitoba school question confirms his utter baseness.

The second speaker is the arch-Catholic leader of the *Ultramontains*, F. X. Trudel. According to this fanatic, Riel died defending a Catholicism that was threatened in the West by Protestants of all kinds. According to Trudel the Canayens, like the medieval knights, with a sword in one hand and a cross in the other.

The third speaker, the Liberal Honoré Mercier, had prepared in advance the Resolutions of the *Champs-de-Mars* as the basis of a new national political party with him as leader. He too exploits Riel's murder to his own ends. He claims that Riel was "a victim of fanaticism and treason!" This reference to fanaticism and treason only proves that Mercier does not at all understand the nature of imperialism and its Canadian agents. Ottawa wanted to take the West, to exploit it economically. The fanaticism of the Ontario English was only the outward trapping of this exploitation. As for treason, where was it if not in Mercier's foggy mind and literary expressions?

The English-Canadian bourgeois were not betraying anyone in conquering the West. They were being most faithful to their colonialist mentality. They could hardly be said to have betrayed the Canayens,

---

[3] *Pemmican:* dried meat, pulverized and mixed with melted fat.

since they never promised them anything other than oppression and subjugation.

The Canayens, ready for action, are greatly disappointed in their so-called leaders. Yet they continue to hold meetings all over Quebec; they sing the *Marseillaise*, and proclaim Riel a national hero.

The Clergy is really running scared, and gathers all its strength to combat this national movement that is taking a revolutionary turn. Bishop Taché of St. Boniface, Riel's advisor until he took up arms, now calls Riel a "miserable fool and a sectarian."

The *Ultramontain* movement is torn between two factions. The bishops are all against Riel and consequently for the Conservative Macdonald. But opposing them is the zealot Trudel who supports the rebel, Riel.

Laurier loses no time in dissociating himself from Mercier and the movement. The movement has served its purpose for him, helping to fill the ranks of the Liberal Party with his supporters. This goal accomplished, he puts the brakes on.

When Parliament opens again in Ottawa in 1886, the Riel question is first on the agenda. A Canayen Conservative, the sell-out Philippe Landry, makes a motion of deepest regret for Riel's execution. That is to say, the murderers wish to apologize for having killed Riel. But in fact they regret nothing. They simply have to prevent the Liberals from exploiting the affair any further.

Bishop Taché, who follows the debate in the public gallery, advises all the Canayen Conservative members to vote for Landry's motion. This indicates that some Canayen Conservatives still had a few principles, but also that the dictatorship of the Church was for them stronger than their convictions.

On the 16th of March it is Laurier himself who alleviates the tension in the House. This sell-out par-excellence declares in a speech (entirely in English), that Riel "at his worst was a subject fit for an asylum; at his best he was a religious and political maniac." He adds a prediction that Mercier will commit political suicide in trying to form a national party. He chastizes the government for not heeding the "Métis' complaints." He suggests that the government should have shown clemency and not vengeance in Riel's case.

Immediately the English see in Laurier the successor to Cartier, the lay Negro-King indispensable for the continued domination of the Canayens. He has only 10 years to wait to become Prime Minister.

As for Honoré Mercier, he continues to promote the national movement, so well in fact that in 1887 his *Parti National* came to power in Quebec. He becomes Prime Minister of Quebec.

In 1867, Pierre Chauveau and his Conservatives had formed the provincial government. All the laws they passed had no other purpose than to help the Church and private enterprise take over new lands. By

1887, 60 percent of the province's budget ($1,535,536) is derived from federal subsidies.

In 1873, Ouimet's Conservative government had resigned following the Tanneries Scandal: speculators had slipped hush-money to some cabinet ministers to get the government to buy lands in the Montreal region at prices twenty-five times the market value. The Conservatives, however, were brought back to power with Boucherville as Prime Minister, thanks to the Clergy who went so far as to threaten to refuse the sacraments to those who dared vote Liberal.

In 1875, Boucherville, obedient to the same bishops who had supported him, abolished the Ministry of Public Instruction (ministry of education). Education was henceforward to be entirely in the hand of the Council of Public Instruction, founded in 1869 and divided into two committees, Catholic and Protestant. The Protestant Committee was to be responsible for the English Protestant schools, and was at liberty to set up its school system as it pleased. The Catholic Committee was composed of all the bishops of Quebec and an equal number of laymen nominated by the government. So this new law put virtually all of Canayen education into the hand of the Clergy.

In 1878 Chapleau, another Conservative, became Prime Minister of Quebec. His major accomplishment was to sell the Quebec-Montreal-Ottawa and Western Railway for 7 million dollars. It had cost the province 12 million. He also got involved in a few other frauds with a speculator named Senecal, and was succeeded in 1882 by the moderate conservative Mousseau, who in turn was replaced in 1884 by an *Ultramontain* conservative John Ross.

So much for the activities of the Quebec government until the arrival of Mercier. In short, until then, the government had been clearly an instrument in the interests of the Church and the speculators.

Is anything to change with Mercier, the man who had the audacity to call himself Riel's brother in his speech of November 22nd? Will this former provincial Liberal, now leader of the *Parti National*, really do something different? As a matter of fact, nothing is going to change. The corruption continues and the Church extends its power.

In 1854, the seigneurial system had been modified. Two thirds of the seigneuries were by then in the hands of the English merchants, who pressured the government into buying them at a high price and then selling the lands back to the *habitants* at prices higher still. But even though some of the *habitants* could now claim to be owners of the means of production in this one economic sector, production remained entirely at the mercy of a market completely controlled by the Canadian bourgeoisie. Western grains, for example, could be brought in to flood the Quebec market.

In this way the Canayen farmer was forced to orient himself towards the dairy industry. But here again he had no important outlets; very often he simply withdrew from the market, content to produce enough merely for subsistence. Some small mixed farming, a little grain cultivation, a little cattle-raising, some vegetable, eggs, and milk production are all that is necessary to feed his family, with a little surplus to be able to buy those necessities he cannot produce.

In the other economic sectors the Canayen is a worker—in the forests, in factories, on the docks and in ship-yards. The workers' conditions are so bad and the workers so discontented that in 1884 Macdonald establishes a Royal Commission of Enquiry into the relations between capital and labour. Among other things the report reveals: fines imposed on workers that are often higher than their weekly salary; the unbelievably high number of workers who can neither read nor write; the exploitation of children eight years of age; a working day 14 hours long; children sent to the factory prison known as the "black hole" as a disciplinary measure; instant dismissal without previous notice; total lack of job security; unsanitary and overcrowded housing.

Macdonald of course hides the report in the back of a drawer, since the employers would hardly welcome having to change these conditions of the working class. Macdonald and the government are in the service of the employers, and if they dared pass laws favouring the working class they would soon be thrown out by their bosses.

What does Mercier do about all this? He creates the Ministry of Agriculture and Colonization. He leads it himself, with the parish-priest Labelle as Deputy Minister.

He builds a railway to Lac St. Jean, lengthens the Montreal line from St. Felix-de-Valois to St. Gabriel de Brandon, and gives parents of 12 children or more 100 acres of land. He speaks a lot about the autonomy of the provinces and about the necessity for Quebec to assert itself as a province of the French and Catholic nation.

In short he does precious little, except to persuade the people to clear land that won't yield, to perpetuate the myth of the Canayen vocation of farming, and to exploit the national sentiment of the people in order to stay in power.

What does he do with the Manitoba school question? The same thing, nothing.

In any case, he is to be defeated before the question is resolved. After a triumphant tour of Europe, where he is decorated by the President of the French Republic, by the Belgian king and by Pope Leo XIII who makes him a papal count, he comes home to a scandal in his administration. Contractors for the construction of the Baie-des-Chaleurs railway, it seems, had paid no less than $100,000 to the Liberal treasurer, Ernest Pacaud.

So in the 1892 elections, the *Parti National*, built on Riel's scaffold, falls into the most abject political corruption. Pacaud and Mercier stand trial soon after. Arthur Buies, one of the more honest journalists of the time, writes in *La Patrie:* "Mercier had in his hands the most brilliant opportunity that has ever been given to a Canadian statesman; he had a whole people behind him and a glorious role to play; his vanity, his egotism, and his absolute lack of moral sense has lost him everything."

The Conservatives come back to power in Quebec. Taillon is Prime Minister, then Flynn.

But what has been happening meanwhile in Manitoba in 1890?

The Manitoba Constitution, established in 1870, provided for a denominational school system, a Catholic section for the Canayens, and a Protestant section for the others. In 1870 the Canayens made up one half of the population. By 1890 they are only one third. In this position of strength, Greenway's Liberal Manitoba government is able to move to abolish the Catholic section. Hereafter only English schools are to receive state subsidies. If the Canayens and the Canayen Métis want French schools so much, let them pay for them out of their own pockets. We can see that the same Anglo-Saxon imperialism that assassinated Riel continues its work of annihilation of all traces of Canayen or Métis culture in the West.

The Manitoba Canayens appeal to Macdonald to disallow this provincial act under Article 93 in the Constitution, which is supposed to protect minority groups' school rights. Macdonald of course refuses, and advises them to appeal to the courts. The Supreme Court passes the buck to the Privy Council in London, which declares that the province has the right to adopt such an act but that the federal government can pass a remedial act if it wants to.

It is therefore up to the federal government to defend the rights of the Canayens of Manitoba. Macdonald's death in 1891 results in a government shake-up that gives the Liberal Party, with Laurier now at the helm, the opportunity to exploit the Manitoba Schools Question in order to win elections. In the English provinces Laurier wins support with the line that he has no intention of meddling in the affairs of provincial governments. But in Quebec he promises to do something to settle the question.

In 1896, the Liberals win the majority of seats in the federal elections. Laurier becomes Prime Minister, thanks to the Québécois who vote three to one in his favour. In the other provinces the Liberals make a fairly good showing.

Why this Liberal support in Quebec? What other choice did the Québécois have? If they do not vote Liberal, they must vote Conservative. Conservative means Macdonald's party, the party that forced them to swallow Confederation, that assassinated Riel, that had hardly come out in support of the Manitoba Canayens. In addition "Conservative" means the Church and its continuing domination. The Canayen, instructed by the bishops that to vote Liberal is a "mortal sin," nevertheless voted against the Church and against the party in power. He voted for Laurier who was Canayen in origin, and who was at least opposed to Riel's hanging.

As soon as Laurier takes over, he moves to settle the Manitoba School Question. He negotiates with Greenway, the Liberal Prime Minister of Manitoba. And here is the Greenway-Laurier Compromise: the Manitoba school system is to remain neutral—that is, English Protestant. However, in some cases, a teacher can teach the religion of his choice and teach in either French or English in a school where there is a high percentage of Canayens. With a bit of patience the English will soon see the Canayens disappear from Manitoba. The Canayens of Manitoba know full well that Laurier sold them out.

Nor are the Canayens in Quebec satisfied. Still, Laurier can afford to lose a few supporters in Quebec, in view of his widespread popularity in that province. What interests him is not to protect the Canayens against English domination, but to govern a country "from sea to sea" in the name of Her British Majesty Queen Victoria.

12

Confederation, 1870–1896: The End of the Macdonaldian Constitution and the Return to Duality*

W. L. Morton

WHEN THE NATIONAL IDEAL faltered amid economic distress, politicians and lawyers, argues Professor Morton, "created out of an imperial system remade for national purposes, a federal system of co-ordinate sovereignties based on popular sovereignty." "The Macdonaldian concept of Confederation was rejected as though the British Empire had never existed, and as though the American Civil War had never been fought."

In this article is expressed, perhaps in the strongest language anywhere, the argument that the admirable constitutional system of the Fathers was destroyed by localism, particularism, sectarianism, and lack of courage and replaced by a rigid and legalistic classical federalism which even the Americans had rejected in 1865. But while the Grits and Laurier remain destructive, neither Macdonald nor Cartier escapes major responsibility for the defeat. In the New Brunswick school question of the early seventies, the chief architects of union, for obvious and perhaps legitimate short-run political reasons, failed to display the courage necessary to maintain the system on its intended course. From the failure in New Brunswick to protect French-speaking minorities outside Quebec, Professor Morton can trace the growing tendency of the French of Quebec to fall back on the fortress of their province and to champion the doctrine of provincial rights developed in Ontario.

* *Journal of Canadian Studies*, I (May, 1966), pp. 11–24.

The article reinforces what Peter Waite has asserted in *The Life and Times of Confederation* (Toronto, 1964), that while there was great popular newspaper debate about Confederation, there was very little popular understanding either of federalism or of the imperial nature of the Quebec-Westminster scheme. What did exist was a growing commitment to local majoritarianism.

I

THE MACDONALDIAN CONCEPT of the constitution was a compromise between what Macdonald, the British governors, and the Colonial Office had favoured, a legislative union under one government and one Parliament, and what was in fact necessary.[1] That, as all but the most unrealistic admitted, was some acceptance of the federal principle.

Once this need was accepted, however, American example became relevant. And American example during the years of Confederation and the Civil War was that a central government insufficiently strong led to disruption and civil war. Any federation of British North America must therefore have a strong central government.[2]

A federation so like a legislative union Macdonald could accept, for he could hope that the same forces, the needs of defence and development, which had produced a confederation would continue to strengthen the central power. Cardwell, the colonial secretary, could accept it with good conscience as the best arrangement possible for the setting up of a practically independent state at a time when England proposed to withdraw from the St. Lawrence valley. The defenders of local powers, if they did not reject it, as Prince Edward Island did, could give reluctant assent because at least the principle was admitted of the existence in one system of both central and local powers. Like Macdonald, they too could hope

---

[1] By the Macdonaldian constitution is meant a constitution preponderantly national in powers and interest, in which the national interests were safeguarded by disallowance, and in minority educational rights by the national power of remedial action under Section 93 of the B.N.A. Act.

By duality is meant political action by English Canada and French Canada as groups, or blocs. Such action happened most strikingly in the Canadian Union from 1841 to 1866; it has recurred to a large degree in Canada since 1896, and particularly since 1917.

'Dual' political action has, of course, never been absolute, nor has it ever been institutionalized, even in the Canadian Union. It is a tendency in the Canadian political system, in the writer's opinion, much to be regretted and definitely to be opposed in any form.

[2] This development may be supposed to explain why the plan of union was first usually called a "federation," and after the Westminster Conference of 1866 a "confederation," i.e. in its proper, but not historical sense, of a strongly centralized federation. This is presumably the meaning of the assertion in the preamble of the B.N.A. *Act* of 1867, that the provinces were to be "federally united."

for the future development of the constitution being favourable to their views.

The Confederation of 1870, then, was an extremely intricate and subtly poised combination of powers. Like the American Constitution after 1865, it rested on the explicit subordination of local powers to central, of the state, and of the province, to the nation. Unlike the American, which enjoyed the enormous advantage of having had the fundamentals on which it rested clarified by revolution, it did not rest on the principle of popular sovereignty. On the contrary, it rested on the traditional concept of allegiance to the Crown in which was vested the right and power to govern. The monarchical and imperial constitution of the United Kingdom was to be used for national ends in the Dominion of Canada. Yet, since the Crown was that of a constitutional and parliamentary monarchy, Confederation combined the legal authority of the Crown with the democratic power of the people. The Crown was meant to be, then, the centralizing element in the Confederation, and its principal government, the central one, was given all the great powers of government, with the former imperial powers to disallow provincial legislation, and to appoint provincial governors who were to correspond with Ottawa alone. To this was added the general power to legislate for "the peace, order, and good government of Canada." As if to stress its supremacy, the central legislature was given the power to tax "by any mode or system of taxation."

In contrast, the powers given to the provinces were merely local and private in nature; the powers of taxation were limited to the little used direct taxation of the day. The provinces were not, in fact, expected to be self-supporting as they were not thought sovereign even in their spheres of exclusive jurisdiction. They were subordinate governments in both appearance and in fact. They had no great tasks to perform and were given no great powers.

Thus Confederation in its Macdonaldian conception was a strongly centralized government which made no more provision for local government than was necessary to obtain assent to Confederation from the colonial legislatures. The old colonies and new provinces were not, it is true, to be municipalities, but neither were they to be states. They were, perhaps, to be provinces like those of the New Zealand constitution of 1852, or even bodies like the English counties after 1888. Such subordination, it was hoped, would prove acceptable in the general expansion and prosperity which, it was also hoped, Confederation would bring.

The former was a hope, but it would be unjust to infer that it was a delusive hope. Macdonald, Galt, Cartier, Brown—all who accepted the Quebec Resolutions and even more those who, unlike Brown, accepted the Westminster Resolutions, knew how delicate were the compromises, how thin the paper over the cracks, of this constitution, at once traditional and innovating. One delicate subject was education, for example, which in Canada as in the United Kingdom meant religion also. An attempt had been made at Westminster to extend the Canadian compromise of separate schools to the whole Dominion in Section 93 of the *B.N.A. Act.* But the section did not make the Catholic schools of the other provinces separate; it guaranteed them only if they were established "by law" at the time of union, or established thereafter.

Another such subject was language, and the only language at issue then was French, which was necessarily involved with both religion and education. By the *B.N.A. Act* it was recognized only in the Province of Quebec, and the federal Parliament and courts. But denominational schools carried with them teaching in French as a matter of usage, and were thus a matter of language as well as religion in the Acadian districts of New Brunswick, the French settlements of Ontario, and later in Manitoba.

Confederation had the effect of creating the belief that the French province of Quebec had secured self-government in local and cultural matters, and that elsewhere the Roman Catholic religion and the French language were secured by the guarantee of separate schools in Section 93 of the *B.N.A. Act* of 1867.

That belief had, after all, been laid down by Cartier, who had declared emphatically: "Under this system of federation which places in the hands of the Central Government all matters of general interest, and to whom questions of race will be indifferent, religious or national rights will not be ignored."[3] The duality of French and English in United Canada was at once politically absorbed and culturally guaranteed in Confederation. It was the shattering of this delusion that by 1896 had made Quebec adhere to provincial rights secured by a federal system of coordinate powers and reject a national guarantee of cultural rights secured by the central government.[4]

And finally there was the matter, undefined but powerful, of local democracy. Two of the provinces, Nova Scotia and New Brunswick, were former self-governing colonies now diminished in power and stature and made subordinate to a government in majority Canadian. And Quebec had accepted a minority position in Confederation in return for local self-government at home. How could the question of the extent and powers of provincial government fail to arise?

For the moment, however, the Hercules who had carried Confedera-

---

[3] A. D. Decelles, *Cartier* (*Makers of Canada, 1926*), Vol. V, p. 75.

[4] Two other factors greatly affected the development of the constitution after 1867. One was the fact, referred to in debate from time to time, that all the men active in carrying Confederation entered Dominion politics, or were given non-political office at or after 1867. Oliver Mowat significantly was the great exception. Thus provincial politicians were young men who had of necessity to make the most of their provincial positions.
The other factor, too little noted, was the ending of dual representation in all provinces by 1874. The practice was in many ways a continuation of the Union. After 1874 two separate kinds of politicians developed, the national and the provincial.

tion seemed to have silenced these Hydra heads beneath the rock of the new Confederation. There they hoped they they would remain securely buried, but they were not at all unaware that the heads were likely all to prove immortal.

II

Such were the basic elements of Confederation—a union that was imperial rather than federal, one that deliberately avoided American example, that required the most exquisite observance of practical religious toleration, that committed the national Parliament to the maintenance of separate schools; a union that left local matters, including education, and the language of instruction, to provincial jurisdiction.

That union meant, moreover, for Canada, division; for the other British North American colonies, diminished powers and subordination; for the united colonies expansion as the Dominion of Canada. Expansion was to reveal, however, that there was a French element outside Quebec: the *métis* of Red River. That fact was to introduce in another province of the Dominion the principle of ethnic duality, the duality that had been recognized in Quebec, and guaranteed by the national government, although on doubtful legal grounds and by implication with respect to language, in New Brunswick and Nova Scotia.

It was better, in the circumstances, to treat with Riel in the winter of 1869–70 than to fight with him in the summer of 1870. Out of those very tortuous and hurried negotiations came that curious result, the *Manitoba Act*. By that measure the Dominion acquired a new province, one not very much wanted by anyone and kept almost ludicrously small. It was only small territorially, however; in principle it was enormous, for it was in fact a little Quebec on Red River. It was bilingual; it had a dual system of confessional schools; it possessed a legislative council, like Quebec and unlike Ontario. It might even have adopted, had its legislature chosen, the Quebec civil code as its civil law. Thus the principle of duality, restricted to Quebec in old Canada, had reappeared in the West in the first province created by the Dominion.[5]

III

The *Manitoba Act* and the establishment of duality in the West did not affect the constitution of Confederation, except with respect to representation and that only temporarily. The West as far as the Rockies had merely been opened to settlement by both of the Canadian cultures. One

---

[5] The same nationally sanctioned duality was extended to the Territories by Parliament in 1875, and developed by the Council of the North-West Territories before 1890.

other event did, however, like a puff of wind through curtains, reveal all the possibilities of constitutional change. That event was the *New Brunswick School Act* of 1871. It did so because it brought into the open one of the concealed contradictions of the *B.N.A. Act* of 1867. United Canada had developed two systems of public schools, schools supported by local taxes and open to all children up to the eighth grade. Each section had developed its own system, Quebec a denominational system of Catholic and Protestant schools, Ontario one of public schools with provision for separate schools. As long as the Union continued, the confessional minority of each section was in effect guaranteed by the confessional majority of the other. With Confederation each would pass under the jurisdiction of a majority to be given control of education in each of the two provinces. The question of how to preserve the former guarantee nearly wrecked the Confederation scheme in the last session of the Parliament of the old province of Canada. In consequence a guarantee of minority educational rights as they existed at the Union, or as they might be created thereafter, was devised, to become Section 93 of the *B.N.A. Act*. And at the Westminster Conference of 1866, as a result of the powerful lobbying of Archbishop Thomas Connolly of Halifax, who had done so much to carry Confederation in the Maritimes, the guarantee was extended to cover minority educational rights in all provinces of the Union. At the insistence of Alexander Galt, the representative of the Quebec Protestants, however, the right was qualified with the words, "by law." There can be no doubt, legally speaking, that this term defeated Connolly's purpose, as he himself thought, although Hector Langevin all too optimistically did not.[6]

The *New Brunswick School Act* of 1871 disrupted the situation glossed over by the *B.N.A. Act* of 1867 by established a system of tax-supported free and non-sectarian schools. Henceforth there were to be no grants made and no taxes paid to schools in which there was denominational teaching. As a result what the Roman Catholics of New Brunswick had in practice, state-supported denominational schools, were abolished despite the supposed guarantee of the *B.N.A. Act*. Moreover, as so often in Canada, the matter was not merely one of denominational teaching. Many of the Catholics of New Brunswick were Irish by nationality. But many were Acadian French. Their schools were therefore not only denominational; they were also French in language. Now education was to be non-sectarian, in English, and from textbooks prescribed by the province.

The *Act* therefore precipitated a contest which was, by implication at least, one of major constitutional significance. Certainly, it was of the first importance politically. Politics in Quebec revolved around the question for four years, and nothing in his last years gave more concern to Cartier. The province by Section 92 of the *B.N.A. Act* had control of education in

---

[6] W. L. Morton, *The Critical Years* (Toronto, 1965), p. 208.

the province. But a religious minority under Section 93 was guaranteed the possession of any right it had by law at the time of union (or that it might acquire thereafter). What rights, then, had the Roman Catholic minority of New Brunswick as against the new school act?

The answer came quickly when they requested the central government to disallow the measure under the powers given by the *B.N.A. Act*. The Minister of Justice, Prime Minister Sir John Macdonald, found that the act was within the competence of the provincial legislature, as Roman Catholics had lost no rights they had by law at the Union, or had acquired since.[7] There was no reason for disallowance, or for remedial action under Section 93. The opinion was to be upheld by the law officers of the United Kingdom and by the Judicial Committee.

For four years, however, a struggle against this decision was kept up by John Costigan, Irish Catholic member for Gloucester, a county of New Brunswick which was at least half Acadian. Costigan was supported by Timothy Anglin, also an Irish Catholic, and the member for Victoria, which was in the majority Acadian.[8] Even more significant was the steady and concerted support which they received from French Catholic members from Quebec. The nature of the support reveals how the school question, always nominally religious, was also usually, as in this instance, linguistic and cultural as well.

It was not the only support they received, of course; some came from English Protestants, and not only from Quebec. The question was in fact one of general interest as well as one of strong concern to Roman Catholics. It was so because it opened, in one of the most sensitive regions of Canadian life, the question of just what kind of constitution Canada had. And the debates on the question in the federal parliament raised all the issues that were settled by 1896, sectarian belief, local interest, Grit democracy.[9]

IV

The debates in Parliament began when in the spring of 1872 Auguste Renaud, the only Acadian member of the House of Commons, moved for the correspondence on the *New Brunswick School Act*. Macdonald defended his action in recommending that the act should not be disallowed. "It was known to everyone," he declared, "that the question of

---

[7] *Canada, Sessional Papers, 1872*, Vol. 7, No. 36, Macdonald's Report, Jan. 20, 1872.

[8] H. G. Thorburn, *Politics in New Brunswick* (Toronto, 1961), p. 38.

[9] By Grit democracy is meant the Canadian version of democratic thought which was occupied with ending privilege and effecting popular sovereignty in Western Europe and North America in the nineteenth century. Most were, of course, members of the Liberal party, but the Conservative party was affected by this prevalent mode of political thought. The term is used without partisan implication.

education had threatened Confederation at its very inception, and a proposition that education should be left to the General Legislature of the Dominion would have been enough to secure the repudiation of Confederation by the people of Lower Canada." The only grounds for disallowance, he said, were unconstitutionality or the detriment of the general interests of the Dominion. Neither ground existed in the present case. The federal power could not on other grounds be used to over-ride the powers given to the provinces, as was the control of education. "The constitution which had hitherto worked so easily and so well, could not survive the wrench that would be given if the Dominion Government assumed to dictate the policy or question the action of the Legislatures of the different Provinces on the subjects reserved by the *B.N.A. Act* to those Legislatures."[10]

This stand by the chief maker of the *B.N.A. Act* is surprising. It is to be explained by the fact that he had made his bargain with those who had insisted on a federation rather than a legislative union. By keeping that bargain he would help that growth of a sense of national union and general interest on which he counted. To use the central power in a clear case of provincial jurisdiction would hinder the growth for which he hoped. Cartier fully supported Macdonald. The Catholics of New Brunswick must get redress by political action within the province. But J. H. Bellerose, a Quebec member and an ultramontanist, protested that it was understood when the *Confederation Act* was passed that the rights of minorities in matters of education would be preserved.[11] The issue of the use of national power to defend minority rights against a provincial majority was clearly drawn.

The trouble was that in law there were no minority educational rights in New Brunswick. The next move by its opponents was a motion by Costigan requesting the government to disallow the *Act*, which was still possible as a month remained of the year following the passage of an *Act* during which disallowance was possible. The motion provoked an even stronger statement of the government's position from Cartier. The effect of disallowance, he asserted, would be to place the fate of the Roman Catholics of Canada in the hands of the Protestant majority. "The question of education rested entirely with the Local Legislature . . ." This he had insisted on when Confederation was formed; only existing legal rights were to be guaranteed. Again came a protest from a Quebec member, this time from the Rouge Leader, A. . Dorion, who justly pointed out that ". . . the spirit of the Act of Confederation was to maintain all rights enjoyed at the time of the Union . . .", whether embodied in law or not.[12]

---

[10] *Canada, Debates, 1872*, III, pp. 199–201.

[11] *Ibid.*, pp. 201–202.

[12] *Ibid.*, pp. 704–708.

The debate waned to an anti-climax when J. H. Gray of St. John, moved in amendment that the *School Act* was constitutional, and P. J. O. Chauveau of Quebec in sub-amendment that the Queen be requested to use her influence on the government of New Brunswick.[13] The debate yielded little further light. Joly of Quebec, in support of the motion, declared in pregnant terms that "There might be national unity, but religious unity was impossible."[14] The amendment and sub-amendment were defeated, and then on May 29, an amendment by C. C. Colby of Quebec was carried. It was only an expression of regret by the House at a seeming injustice caused by the *Act*. More to the point was Alexander Mackenzie's motion, accepted with relief by the government, that the Dominion aid an appeal to the law officers of the United Kingdom and to the Judicial Committee of the Privy Council.[15]

The *New Brunswick School Act* had thus revealed the flaw in the *B.N.A. Act*, always known to those like Cartier, Langevin and Galt, that it had guaranteed no right in separate schools not established by provincial law. It had put Macdonald, the great centralizer of 1867, in the position of an unyielding defender of provincial powers. The deathless heads of sectarian belief and local rights were still writhing under the stones of the *B.N.A. Act*.

In 1873 the question arose once more with a motion by Honoré Mercier for correspondence following the resolution of 1872, and by an amendment to the motion to go into supply by Costigan, in which he asked for disallowance of the now amended *New Brunswick School Act.* Macdonald in debate said frankly that he regretted that the Quebec system had not been extended to New Brunswick. He himself had favoured a legislative union for Confederation, but a federal one had proved necessary, and must now be maintained as such. For ". . . the moment there was any attempt to coerce New Brunswick all hope for the Catholic minority was gone." To Macdonald thus speaking as the future Laurier, L. F. R. Masson replied that the Dominion Government must stand in the same over-riding relation to the local government as the imperial did to the Dominion. The *Act* should therefore be disallowed. He spoke as a supporter of Riel and the *Manitoba Act* in which the federal power had been used to create a denominational school system. It is interesting, and not wholly ironical, to see a Quebec ultramontanist demanding that the federal government be imperial and paramount. The ultramontanes were down to 1896 prepared to invoke the federal power to maintain the educational rights of minorities. Masson, however, failed to carry the support of his fellow French Canadians. Hector Langevin, for example, urged an appeal to the Privy Council, Dorion to the powers of

---

[13] *Ibid.*, pp. 760–764.

[14] *Ibid.*, p. 900.

[15] *Ibid.*, pp. 899, 907, 909.

remedial legislation in Section 93 of the *B.N.A. Act.* Each relied on the use of established procedures, without an explicit assertion of paramountcy by the central government. Then, despite Smith of Westmoreland's claim that New Brunswick was within its rights, and must not be interfered with, or Confederation would be a sham, Costigan's amendment was carried, Macdonald voting with the nays against most of his Quebec supporters.[16]

The law officers of the United Kingdom had already upheld Macdonald's opinion of the inadvisability of disallowance, and now did so again on this second reference. The appeal to the Judicial Committee, which was paid for by the central government, in turn upheld the validity of the *New Brunswick Act.*[17] The debates of 1874 are therefore silent on the subject except for a motion by Costigan for an address to the Imperial Government for an amendment to do what had been intended in 1867, he alleged, to provide for separate schools in New Brunswick. He, however, withdrew this logical, but daring, motion.[18]

Nevertheless in 1875 he made the motion again, and by doing so precipitated the most revealing of the debates on the underlying question of the nature and extent of central and local, federal and provincial powers, in Canada.[19] Appleby of Carleton strongly opposed the motion as an indefensible invasion of provincial powers. These, he declared, were absolute and could not be over-ridden. "He would lay down this principle that the Local Legislatures of this country on all subjects which came within their exclusive power, had equally with the Parliament of Canada, the quality of omnipotence."[20] Here was the language of the Judicial Committee in Liquidators of the Maritime Bank vs. the Receiver-General of New Brunswick in 1892, the declaration that the provinces were as sovereign in the exercise of their exclusive powers as the Dominion, or the Imperial governments, were in theirs.[21]

It was also the language of Edward Palmer in the debates of the Quebec Conference. Something of the sources of such thought was indicated by the member for Welland, W. A. Thomson, economist and author. "His political creed had always been Popular Sovereignty. He had given a good deal of study to the history of the United States during the last thirty or forty years, and that had led him to the belief that the only safety for the perpetuation of the institution of the United States was

[16] Canadian Library Association Microfilms, *Debates of Canadian House of Commons,* May 14, 1873, pp. 188–190.

[17] W. E. Hodgins, *Reports of Ministers of Justice and Orders in Council Upon the Subject of Dominion and Provincial Legislation* (Ottawa, 1896), pp. 693–94.

[18] C.L.A., *Debates, 1874,* May 18, 1874.

[19] *Canada, Debates, 1875,* I, p. 555.

[20] *Ibid.,* p. 564.

[21] E. R. Cameron, *The Canadian Constitution* (Winnipeg, 1915), p. 418.

state sovereignty." This view the unreconstructed Mr. Thomson had upheld during the formation of Confederation, and still did.[22]

Cranky and a trifle archaic Thomson's views might be, but in substance they were held by most speakers. A. L. Palmer of St. John declared that, "The harmony of this Dominion, and the future working of the constitution depended on the strict observance of the powers conferred on each legislative body. . . ."[23] And Mackenzie Bowell, one day to be prime minister in similar circumstances, opposed the motion on the ground that it would be improper for the House of Commons to do anything to interfere with the powers of the provincial legislature.[24] As Macdonald had already, he would have to reverse his views when faced with the conflict of local, general and sectarian interests of Canadian politics.

Costigan's motion was of course defeated; it was probably meant to embarrass the Liberals in the northern counties of New Brunswick by forcing a statement of their views on what were to be called "provincial rights." Amended to ask only to request the Queen to use her influence in New Brunswick, it was carried to no purpose.[25] The *New Brunswick School Act* had continued in operation, enforced on one occasion in early 1875 by the use of the militia.[26] Prompted perhaps by that outburst and its repression, the government and the Roman Catholic Church reached in the same year a *modus vivendi* with respect to the question of the teaching of religion in the schools. With respect to the use of French in the schools, however, nothing was formally attempted until 1928, when even then the matter had to be dropped because of objection from English and Protestant opinion.[27]

The New Brunswick School Question had ceased to be a national political issue in a mere four years. Yet it was of first importance in the development of the Macdonaldian concept of the constitution. It had seen in the early years of its formation a seeming repudiation of the national character of that constitution by both Macdonald and Cartier. Those two astute politicians would not have taken that stand unless they both felt bound by the compromise between national and local interests on which Confederation rested, and by the threat of a conflict of national and provincial interests which in the circumstances would harm the cause of the national constitution. Cartier in particular was troubled by the question in Quebec. It was in many ways the chief issue in that province in the general election of 1872, and a powerful factor in Cartier's personal

---

[22] *Canada, Debates, 1875,* I, p. 576.

[23] *Ibid.,* p. 579.

[24] *Ibid.,* p. 616.

[25] *Ibid.,* pp. 611 and 634.

[26] James Hannay, *History of New Brunswick,* (St. John, 1909), II, p. 320.

[27] Thorburn, *Politics in New Brunswick,* pp. 33 and 38.

defeat in Montreal East. In Quebec indeed the question began that cleavage between Cartier's Bleus and clerical conservatism that was to aid the growth of the Rouge party, and prepare the cornerstone in Quebec of the dominance of the Liberal party in power in Canada after 1896. Most of all it forced on Quebec the choice between reliance on the national government for defence of minority rights in education, carrying with them in practice the use of the French language in French districts, or a reliance on the self-government of Quebec to preserve the French language and Roman Catholic schools in that province, if need be alone. In short, the trend towards provincial rights and the return to the institutionalized duality of the period of the *Act of Union* had begun.

V

Nothing so clear-cut was of course apparent in 1875. All the School Question had done was to make it clear how difficult it was to provide a general government, based on the principles of constitutional monarchy in a democracy, for communities as diverse within and among themselves as were those of Canada. The difficulty was now to be further illustrated by the history of temperance legislation in Canada between 1878 and 1896.

In 1878 the *Scott Act* became law for the whole Dominion. It thus extended legislation hitherto confined to Ontario to all the other provinces. It also bestowed the powers of local option on counties and cities, that is, on larger units than had the *Dunkin Act*. Finally, it tried to distinguish between the retail sale of liquor, which could be forbidden and the wholesale distribution of liquor which remained lawful for export and sale in those parts of the country not under local option: it refrained, of course, from trenching upon the provincial power to license taverns, etc., for the raising of a revenue. The *Act*, like Confederation itself, was a masterpiece of legal ingenuity. Its provisions were to come into operation only by a vote in a county or a city. Yet it was a Dominion statute based on the power to legislate for the peace, order and good government of Canada, and to regulate trade and commerce. A vast federal creation, it floated like a cloud castle over the country, but came to earth only in those parts of the land where a majority of the inhabitants called for it. Here perhaps was a piece of legislation which would, unlike the *B.N.A. Act* of 1867 in the instance of the *New Brunswick School Act*, uphold the exercise of a local democracy in the general interests of the Dominion.

At first it seemed that it might be so. Then in a bare three years, a gentleman of the name of Charles Russell of the city of Fredericton, New Brunswick, was fined in magistrate's court for selling intoxicating liquors contrary to the second part of the *Canada Temperance Act*. The Supreme Court of New Brunswick, and the Supreme Court of Canada had upheld the magistrate. Mr. Russell, presumably a publican of some wealth, and clearly a man of some determination, then carried his case to the Judicial Committee. That distinguished body, still the highest court of appeal for Canadian civil cases, also upheld the constitutionality of the *Temperance Act,* in perhaps the most famous of its Canadian decisions, *Russell vs. Regina,* 1882.[28] The power of the federal parliament to legislate in the general interest of the Dominion was vindicated and the Macdonaldian constitution was confirmed and reached the height of its growth.

VI

It was very natural to put the utmost interpretation on the decision in *Russell vs. Regina* in 1882. The whole Macdonaldian concept of Confederation was in full flower. The depression of the 1870's was behind, and prosperity had returned. The government of Mackenzie, prudent and penurious, had been defeated in 1878. The National Policy with the protective tariff of 1879 had freed Canadian industry from the fear of American and British dumping, and indeed of competition. The policy of building the Pacific Railway piecemeal as a public work and as the revenue of the country permitted, had been replaced by construction as a whole with all possible speed by a private company with government aid. The railway had linked Fort William with Winnipeg, and from the prairies and the Pacific was driving westward and eastward towards a junction in the Rockies. Even immigration was growing, as British farmers, at long last feeling the consequences of the abolition of the Corn Law, moved onto the fertile lands of the prairies. The development of the vast territories so recently united was going forward under Dominion powers and with federal support.

The new sweep of federal power and national prosperity had not, however, caused the provinces to wither away, or ended the strength of local sentiment in Canadian democracy. The next decade was to hear and see asserted in Canada and in London the new doctrine of "provincial rights."[29] The former colonies had not been abolished, or recreated, by Confederation. They had been united in Confederation, with diminished powers, but still with the essentials of responsible government, the Crown, the cabinet, and the legislature. There had come into being a tribe of provincial politicians who had not known Joseph and who sought, both for the sake of personal advancement and to serve their communities, to defend and add to provincial powers. And they were aided fortuitously by a curious paralleling of events. These were the

---

[28] Cameron, *The Canadian Constitution,* pp. 310–22.

[29] The term seems not to have been used in the 1870's, but was widely used in the 1880's. Its usage indicates how both the Grit democracy of Canada and the justices of the Judicial Committee had come to interpret the Canadian constitution, framed to be as little like that of the United States as possible, in terms relevant to that document.

return of depression in 1883, and the wish of the Judicial Committee to clarify the *B.N.A. Act* so as to make it a federal document as clear in federal principle as that of the United States. To this odd coupling of bad times and bad law, Judah B. Benjamin, late Attorney-General of the Confederate States of America and practising law in his London exile, was a macabre hedge priest. They were to be aided also by certain repercussions of the building of the Pacific Railway and the onset of depression in the West, the Saskatchewan Rebellion and the chartering of railways by the Province of Manitoba in defiance of the charter of the Canadian Pacific Railway.

The new trend towards provincial rights and the "federalisation" of the *B.N.A. Act* began innocently enough with the conviction by Magistrate G. T. Denison of a tavern keeper, Mr. Archibald G. Hodge, for having added a billiard room and table to the St. James Hotel on York Street, Toronto. The basis of the conviction was the *Ontario Licensing Act* of 1877. Hodge appealed on the ground that that Act was beyond the powers of the province. The appeal was refused in the Queen's Bench of Ontario, but upheld by the Ontario Court of Appeal. It was also upheld by the Judicial Committee of the Privy Council. *Russell vs. Regina*, it declared, was founded on the federal powers of Section 91, but these did not diminish or impair those of the provinces in Section 92. Nor were the provincial legislatures to be limited in the use of their powers. They had . . . "authority as plenary and as ample within the limits prescribed by Section 92 as the Imperial Parliament in the amplitude of its power possessed and could bestow. Within these limits of subjects and areas," the judgment continues, "the local legislature is supreme, and has the same authority as has the Imperial Parliament, or the Parliament of the Dominion, would have had under the circumstances . . ."[30] One can only hope that Mr. Appleby read this majestic confirmation of his oratory of 1872.

On Mr. Hodge's billiard table, then, the Macdonaldian concept of Confederation was baulked. The case was the point of turning away from the belief that in Parliament lay a general power which might in the national interest be used to legislate for the whole Dominion. From that point it was, legally speaking, only a step to the case of *Liquidators of the Maritime Bank vs. the Receiver-General of New Brunswick* of 1892. In that the Judicial Committee declared: "The object of the *B.N.A. Act* was neither to weld the provinces into one, nor to subordinate the provincial governments to a central one, but to create a federal government in which they should all be represented, entrusted with the exclusive administration of affairs in which they had a common interest, each province retaining its independence and autonomy." They, moreover, possessed, "powers, not of administration only, but of legislation, in the

---

[30] Cameron, *The Canadian Constitution*, p. 346.

strictest sense of that word; and within the limits of Section 92 of the *Act of 1867,* these powers are exclusive and supreme."[31] The provinces, then, possessed powers not subordinate to, but co-ordinate with those of the Dominion, powers as sovereign in their spheres as it was in its own.

Any embarrassment that *Russell vs. Regina* might create was removed in the Local Prohibition Case of 1896. The Lords of the Privy Council neatly removed it from practical consideration by holding that the *Canada Prohibition Act* of 1886[32] rested only on the peace, order and good government clause of Section 91 and not on the power to regulate trade and commerce, thus reducing the former to the character of an emergency power.[33] The Macdonaldian concept of Confederation was ended in the law courts; and the premonitions of the *New Brunswick School Act* debates were firm law. And the judicial verdict was echoed in the political debates that marked the ending, also in 1896, of the controversy over the *Manitoba School Act* of 1890.[34]

VII

That controversy reached its climax in the great debate, which became a filibuster, on Tupper's motion of March 3, 1896 for the second reading of the Remedial Bill to right the wrongs suffered by the Roman Catholics of Manitoba. Most of what was said had already been uttered in debate since 1892, especially in the debates of the session of 1893. Much was repetitious and political by-play within the debate itself. The real interest at the time lay in the forthcoming election. The main interest now lies in the statements of the Liberal opposition which spelled out the political and constitutional theory which parallelled and confirmed the judicial interpretation of the constitution consummated by the Judicial Committee in the Local Prohibition Case of the same year.

The Liberal voices may be cited as the clearest spoken examples of the constitutional position that the Manitoba School Question had brought to a head. One was the silver voice of Laurier, whose understanding of the constitution was as comprehensive as Macdonald's, although antithetic to it. The other was the ponderous voice of David Mills, the school inspector-lawyer expert of his party on constitutional matters. Laurier, having on March 3 moved in amendment that the Bill be given the six month's hoist, dealt with the awkward and undoubted power of the Dominion Parliament to pass remedial legislation, when a religious minority had demonstrated it had a grievance to remedy in matters of education. The power

---

[31] *Ibid.,* p. 419.

[32] Successor to the Scott Act.

[33] Cameron, *The Canadian Constitution,* pp. 492–94.

[34] The best account of the politics of these years is J. T. Saywell's *Introduction to the Canadian Journal of Lady Aberdeen, 1893–1898* (Toronto, Champlain Society, 1960).

of disallowance, he said, was based on the Imperial power of vetoing and supervising colonial legislation. "This," he went on, "may be easily understood because colonies are dependencies. But the relations between the Dominion and the provinces are not the same. Between these there is no superiority and no inferiority; all are equal, with this exception, that the Dominion Parliament is invested with larger powers, that is, powers of a more extended and more important character than the local legislature." This, of course, is the doctrine of co-ordinate powers, with which there could be no paramountcy. But why should there be two sets of co-ordinate powers, why should provincial rights be as sovereign as federal powers? Laurier's answer is both curious and illuminating, because in making it he slipped from the legal to the political. "Indeed," he went on at once, "it must be accepted, and accepted as a truism, that under popular government the majority must rule,"[35] must rule, that is, in its exclusive jurisdiction in a federal system. This was Grit democracy speaking the language of the electoral mandate, not that of parliamentary authority.

It is not necessary to follow Laurier to his conclusion that the overriding powers of the constitution had been an error, and that now "the power of interference . . . must be applied in such a way as not to provoke irritation . . ."[36]

It is sufficient to note that, except with its explicit powers, the federal government and Parliament were powerless in the face of a provincial majority; a national majority in matters not explicitly federal had ceased to exist, except, one must suppose, in emergency.

Thus was the Laurierian constitution proclaimed, the constitution as it was to be down to 1926.

The nails were now to be driven into the coffin of the Macdonaldian constitution by David Mills. Heavy, humourless and honest, Mills was the intellectual embodiment of that strain of Grit ideology which, held at bay by Macdonald at Confederation, by the creeks and inlets of provincial life had come flooding in during the post-Confederation generation. Facing on March 18 the same question as Laurier, how were the undoubted remedial powers of Parliament to be exercised, he was much more forthright and more profound. In using those powers, he warned, Parliament was not to treat the local legislatures as inferiors or with contempt. "They are bound," he affirmed, "to deal with the local legislature and government in this matter precisely as one state would deal with another. The whole of this proceeding from beginning to end is diplomatic in character, and there is a mode of procedure marked out in the law and each step must be taken in its turn"[37]—not necessarily a diplomatic procedure, one is bound to remark.

---

[35] *Canada, Debates, 1896*, I, p. 2741.
[36] *Ibid.*, p. 2742.
[37] *Canada, Debates, 1896*, II, p. 3821.

The massive Mills, however, ploughed on in his course like the Victorian ironclad he was. Of rigid intellectual honesty, he declined to take Laurier's course on the soft turf of political democracy; he struck to the granite path of the law. "The Federal Parliament and the Federal Administration," he asserted unequivocally, "have their rights, duties and responsibilities under the constitution. These have been bestowed for general and for special purposes, for the peace, order and good government of Canada, and are not less entitled to be respected than those which, by the same instrument, are conferred on the provinces."

Mills spoke as a declared federalist, and did not intend the seeming condescension implied when he placed federal powers on the same level as provincial powers. But having given the federal powers their due, he had also to define those of the provinces. This, with the same unbending honesty, he did in terms of "provincial rights." "What," he asked, "is meant by the doctrine of provincial rights in its true constitutional sense? Not rights beyond the law, but rights in conformity to the law, fairly and properly interpreted. It is this—that within the sphere of government and legislation assigned to the exclusive jurisdiction of the province the principle of parliamentary government shall be preserved, and the responsibility of the provincial ministry to the legislature, and of the legislature to the electorate of the province, shall not be interfered with. Within its own exclusive sphere it shall be sovereign. This is what I understand by provincial rights, and it is a constitutional doctrine of great importance in our federal system, for upon this doctrine rests the security of the provincial legislatures and government against federal encroachments."[38]

This was the end of the Macdonaldian constitution, the calm assertion that a national majority might not "encroach upon" or "coerce" a provincial government in its exclusive jurisdiction. It was the end of Macdonald's hope that in the growth of Confederation a national spirit might develop which would give the national government and parliament the practical power, and when not power, then the influence, to legislate when called in the national interest to do so by public opinion, for the peace, order and good government of Canada. It is of no avail now to protest that provincial rights may be minority, or national, wrongs. It was of no avail then to use weasel words with Tupper, and claim that Mills had substantiated the position of the government and justified remedial action as the remaining exception in an otherwise federal system.[39] Mills had ponderously capped the work of King of New Brunswick, Mowat of Ontario, and Greenway of Manitoba; of the Judicial Committee and Judah B. Benjamin, and affirmed that the constitution of Canada was all but a purely federal one in law, and practically should be applied as though it were.

---

[38] *Ibid.*, pp. 3833–34.
[39] *Ibid.*, p. 3879.

VIII

Why such an outcome? And why did the two different and separate currents of political conflict and judicial interpretation which ran through this period move to the same conclusion of co-ordinate sovereignties in a federal system? Why did Macdonald's concept of a central government exercising all the great powers of government and a judicious para- mountcy in all matters of national concern fail to become the dominant idea of the Canadian Confederation?

It is suggested in answer here that there were two chief reasons, one a failure of Macdonald conservatism, one a success of Grit democracy. The former was that the peace, order and good government clause was at once too sweeping and too imprecise to serve as the basis for a central, national government in all matters not strictly local and exclusive to the provinces, except in the most fortunate of economic and national circum- stances. The Macdonaldian constitution rested on the hope that territorial expansion and national prosperity would allow a central government by Parliament to become a national agent to which the provinces would be habitually and willingly subordinate. The frictions caused by national expansion and the failure to achieve national prosperity before 1896 led to a process of political conflict and judicial refinement in which the lawyers created, out of an imperial system remade for national purposes, a federal system of co-ordinate sovereignties based on popular sover- eignty.

The triumph of Grit democracy was aided by the same factors of economic distress and the failure of the national ideal to flourish. Yet it was a powerful force in itself, and as such bound to affect the develop- ment of the constitution. By a process going back to the use of the historic county franchise and the grant of the vote to Roman Catholics in Canada in 1791 and in Nova Scotia in 1823, Canadian democracy was from the first widely extended, and representation in the colonial legisla- tures was widely popular. The democratic element in Canadian politics was always stronger than any other, including allegiance to the Crown. Under Grit influence after 1867 it was led to see the constitution as something based on popular will in both central and local jurisdiction, and that those jurisdictions were therefore equal and co-ordinate. Under Grit leadership in the provinces also Canadian democracy failed to become national; it remained what it had always tended to be, sectarian and local. And the lawyers, by recognizing the Crown in the provinces, gave a constitutional halo to the democratic image. Even the Crown became local, and failed to achieve the exclusive national role which Macdonald had hoped for it.

This (the monarchical idea) was the Canadian equivalent of the American "We the people" and "the supreme law" of the land. It carried with it the principle of centrality and paramountcy. But the monarchy in Canada was an idea and an ideal, at bottom the lawyer's abstraction of the Crown, a convention and a legal fiction. American democracy was a warm and living thing, and it was to make the American constitution such. But Canadian democracy, no less real than American, was not to be led to make the Confederation of 1867 a real and living thing as a monarchial form of government popularly inspired. Led by Grit democracy operating in the soreness of hard times, it was to insist on local independence and provincial rights. And in these circumstances the lawyers, set the intriguing problem of monarchial sovereignty operating in a federal system, used the fiction of the Crown to dissect the living organism of 1867 into two sets of co-ordinate sovereignties, equal in their various exclusive jurisdictions.

Thus the idea of centrality and paramountcy was reduced to that of a mere emergency power. A national majority could not operate in Canada except within the limits of the listed powers of Section 91, or in wartime.

Such was the curious outcome of the Macdonaldian attempt to use the constitution of the Empire for national ends. It is even difficult now, particularly in the light of his own stand on the *New Brunswick School Act,* to see how he could have hoped that it might succeed. Yet, if one recalls the circumstances of Confederation, and of Canada in the Empire and America at the time of Confederation, one can see that the shapers of the Canadian constitution had little choice except to use British institutions and conventions, and to accept the moral of the American Civil War, that states rights could lead to the disruption of a federal system. The explanation of the outcome of the replacement of the Macdonaldian constitution with its provision for an overriding national interest, by the Laurierian constitution of the co-ordinate powers of a Canadian federal system, is to be found in the failure of expansion and economic growth to give the new constitution a full tide for its launching, in the natural affinity of Grit democracy for local interests and provincial rights, and in the divisibility of the Crown among legislatures enjoying responsible government. Economic depression, Grit doctrinairism, and judicial legalism, had undone the hopes of 1867.

That explanation may explain; it does not justify. The destruction of the Macdonaldian constitution was surely a failure by Canadian politicians and British lawyers to grasp what had happened in the 1860's, that Britain in withdrawing her military power from North America had left behind a new state governed by British parliamentary institutions and not an American federal system, and that in the Civil War the American federal system had been destroyed and replaced by one essentially national. The Macdonaldian concept of Confederation was rejected as though the British Empire had never existed, and as though the American Civil War had never been fought.

The result was to make Quebec rely, not on national guarantees but on provincial rights, to safeguard the concern of French Canadians with religion and language. The duality of the Canadian Union, submerged and diffused in Confederation, re-appeared anew, armed with provincial powers, ingrowing and separatist in temper and in Quebec committed to a reliance on one party which has ever since thrust into Canadian politics the possibility of an English "backlash." And by a supreme irony the province, the interests of which would have benefited most by the carrying of remedial action, gave the Liberal party in the election of 1896 the victory which it failed to gain in English Canada. Quebec voted for provincial rights in a federal system by a majority of thirty-three; English Canada gave the Conservatives a majority of three over the Liberals, on the face of it for remedial action and justice to minorities in a national federation.[40]

The result was that the Quebec reliance on provincial rights, itself the outcome of the failure before 1896 to maintain the Macdonaldian hope of a national spirit making a reserve paramountcy of the national government possible, was the revival of the duality of French and English which had brought the Canadian Union to deadlock before 1864. Instead of a national guarantee, imperfect but practical, of the mutual rights of Catholics and Protestants, French and English, the provincial rights of the Province of Quebec became the guardian of the French in Canada. This prepared the way for a duality of French and English in Canada reminiscent of that in the United States before 1864. The redefining of the *B.N.A. Act* into a federal system of co-ordinate central and provincial powers prepared the way for separatism and the demand for special status, or even independence, for Quebec.

---

[40] The Liberals had a majority of thirty-three in Quebec; the Conservatives a plurality in the other provinces as a whole, a majority of seventy-two to sixty-nine. Seven other candidates were elected in those provinces.

I am indebted to Mr. Lovell Clark, whose work of the 1890's changes the usual account of that decade, for pointing out the above.

13

Nova Scotia Regional
Protest, 1867–1967*†

G. A. Rawlyk

"MERE POLITICAL RHETORIC, however paranoid," argues George Rawlyk, "was and is no adequate substitute for POWER POLITICS." Yet repeatedly, Nova Scotians and many other Maritimers seem content to express their disenchantment "in words rather than in effective action." In this highly revisionist and thoughtful article, the author emphasizes class and psychological factors in explaining the nature of recurring regional protest. Professor Rawlyk argues that on several occasions "the Nova Scotia economic, social and political establishment" has channelled "the deep-rooted and sometimes violent frustrations of ordinary farmers, fishermen and workers against Ottawa rather than against Halifax." Confederation and "Upper Canadians" are the scapegoats which make it easier for Maritimers to ignore their own internal social inequalities.

Although many traditional historians might reject this interpretation, the thesis places the author in the vanguard of the new wave of social and intellectual historians. His argument seems easiest to sustain when it relates to the way the Conservative party in the mid-1920s, when previously almost moribund, helped destroy the Farmer-Labour movement and secured office for itself. Recently, there seems to be hints of the Rawlyk thesis in the politics of New Brunswick and in the way much of the Prince Edward Island elite reacted critically to the federally directed development plan which seemed bound to challenge the social status quo.

---

* *Queen's Quarterly*, LXXV (Spring, 1968), pp. 105–123.

† This paper was presented at the Canadian Historical Association Centennial Seminar, at University of Victoria, Victoria, B.C. on Aug. 22, 1967.

I N LATE JUNE, 1967, I returned to Nova Scotia from the "fleshpots of Upper Canada." Within a few days of my arrival, I seriously wondered whether Nova Scotia's major Centennial project had been the revival of the "repeal movement" and the concomitant growth in intensity of anti-"Upper Canadian" sentiment. Almost the first thing I heard on the radio was an impassioned attack on the Federal Government by a former Halifax Conservative M.P. He denounced Ottawa for spending millions of dollars to provide ice-breaker service for various St. Lawrence ports, thereby assuring the further decay of Halifax as an ocean port. He also questioned the spending of vast sums of federal money on further improvements on the Welland Canal while Nova Scotia continued to be an economic backwater of despair. He concluded his emotional address by declaring that the time had come for all true Nova Scotians to take the initiative and save their own province from the indifferent if not hostile Ottawa Liberal administration. The banner of "Repeal" had apparently been raised once again in Joseph Howe's province and Sir Charles Tupper once again was without question spinning wildly in his grave!

The following day, before I had time to recover fully from the virulence of the radio broadcast, I heard this strange fragment of conversation in Halifax. "I did not know how he would use the material—so I was particularly careful—you know he might have been an Upper Canadian." At that moment I expected all available Nova Scotians to burst out singing their own version of the old Newfoundland anti-Confederate folk song:

> Would you barter the rights that your fathers have won,
> No! Let them descend from father to son,
> For a few thousand dollars Canadian gold,
> Don't let it be said that our birthright was sold.
> Nova Scotia's face turns to Britain
> Her back to the Gulf
> Come near at your peril
> Canadian wolf!

Any "Canadian wolf" should realize that since 1867 two important ingredients in Nova Scotia regionalism have been an often profound dislike of Upper Canada and "Upper Canadians" and also a basic distrust of Confederation itself. Often these two attitudes have blurred into one another and have been further strengthened by the widespread parochialism and clan spirit of the population.

Nova Scotia's distrust of Confederation can be seen in numerous statements made by a host of provincial patriots. Most of these declarations have two important characteristics in common—First, Confederation is considered to be directly responsible for the economic decline of Nova Scotia since 1867. Second, it is contended that "Repeal" or "Secession" would bring back the never-to-be-forgotten glorious "Golden Age" of the Reciprocity period of 1854–1866. H. W. Corning, M.L.A. for Yarmouth, enunciated these classic arguments on April 21, 1923 at the beginning of the "Maritime Rights Movement":

> Restore our province as an independent, self-governing British dominion, make us once more free and independent in the matter of trade and commerce, competent to protect ourselves sanely and wisely from the products of Ontario and Quebec as well as other lands, then there would undoubtedly be a great revival in business and local manufacturing in this province. Instead of decreasing, as at present, our population would increase. In a comparatively short time, in my opinion, we would have a million people in Nova Scotia. Farming would become remunerative. Manufacturing, commerce and foreign trade would quickly and actively develop. Enterprise would flourish. Distributing houses, banks and other institutions would quickly spring up. (Halifax *Herald*, April 23, 1923.)

It may be argued that the anti-"Upper Canadian" and anti-Confederation attitudes have combined to produce what may be called the "Paranoid Style in Nova Scotia Regionalism." Such a "Paranoid Style," to use Professor Richard Hofstadter's term,[1] is not unique to the Atlantic province. The "Paranoid Style" approach could also be used to examine regionalism in other areas of Canada as well as Canadian attitudes towards the United States.

The "Paranoid Style" approach to Nova Scotia regionalism has numerous fascinating research possibilities. Like Professor Hofstadter, I would argue that when I refer to the "Paranoid Style" I am using the term in a rather vague unclinical manner. In the Nova Scotia context, the spokesman of the regional "Paranoid Style," men such as Joseph Howe before "Better Terms," William Annand, H. W. Corning in the 1920s, Edmund Morris, the former Halifax M.P. in the 1960s, felt that the hostile and almost conspiratorial world of "Upper Canada" was directed specifically against their beloved Nova Scotia. Their extreme political rhetoric reveals a great deal about the nature of their regional protest movements.

Confederation was seen by the "Paranoid Style" spokesman as a blatant example of the vicious power of a hostile enemy. It was argued that the British North America Act had brought to a sudden end the material and cultural growth of Nova Scotia. Almost overnight Nova Scotia was transformed into an economic, political, social and cultural backwater. The province was carefully bypassed by the flood of immi-

---

[1] Richard Hofstadter, *The Paranoid Style in American Politics* (New York, 1965).

grants to Canada; old industries left the province because of the advantages of "Upper Canada" and the new industries never came. Young Nova Scotians were compelled to emigrate and old Nova Scotians grew increasingly bitter and disillusioned subjects. They usually remained sullen and quiet until those periods of extreme, economic crises when the embers of their discontent and suspicion were fanned into the flames of regional protest by the propagandists of the "Paranoid Style."

Of course, there was some truth in the charges made against Ottawa by the proponents of Nova Scotia "Rights." Until the time of Diefenbaker, Nova Scotia's special problems were seldom dealt with in a constructive manner by the federal authorities in spite of numerous persuasive submissions made by various provincial administrations. A few palliatives were made available when the cry from Nova Scotia became too shrill but few fundamental issues were dealt with. There is and there was therefore some justification for the "Paranoid Style." But this political rhetoric, which came in waves of decreasing intensity after Confederation, was also an attempt to explain away the province's unfortunate lack of adequate natural resources in the post-Confederation period as well as the end of Nova Scotia's "Golden Age"—the age of "Wooden Ships and Iron Men." Moreover, and of some consequence, the "Paranoid Style" was effectively used by the Nova Scotia economic, social and political establishment to channel the deep-rooted and sometimes violent frustrations of the ordinary farmers, fishermen and workers against Ottawa rather than against Halifax. In periods of economic crises, as in 1868–1869, 1885–1886, 1922–1925, movements emphasizing provincial rights have been organized and "Upper Canadian interests" singled out for blame and abuse. In some respects, therefore, the "Paranoid Style" of Nova Scotia regionalism has played a key role in preserving the *status quo* in the province.

An examination of the three major outbursts of Nova Scotian regionalism—that of the immediate post-Confederation period, that of 1886 and that of 1922–1925 should throw further light on the development of the "Paranoid Style." But, of course, this concept in itself, it must be stressed, does not explain these outbursts. Nova Scotia regional protest should be seen in its proper geographical and historical context. Only then, can perceptive generalizations be made.

Nova Scotia is like a giant disfigured foot kicking out towards Newfoundland. Nova Scotia is only 21,068 square miles in area. Most of the soil is of low fertility and the province has not been blessed with an abundance of natural resources. No point in Nova Scotia is more than fifty miles from the sea—the province's most important natural resource. In many respects it has been the sea that has given Nova Scotia its special character and it has been the sea that has played a significant role in conditioning the province's historical development. As D. C. Harvey observed in 1934, the Atlantic Ocean was:

. . . the first heritage of the Maritimes and their first contribution to the Dominion. It was seen in the primary interest of Europeans in our fisheries, which coloured all our early history; in the privateering industry of the Napoleonic wars and the War of 1812; in the struggle with the United States for control of the West Indian trade; in the shipbuilding industry which dominated our golden age; and it still lives in countless families whose homes contain muniments of ships and men who roamed the seven seas and brought home mementoes of their distant voyages. It lives today in the heart of many a retired sea-captain in the Canadian West who contemplates ruefully the "prairie schooner" and swaps stories in the Cutty Sark Club in Winnipeg. Its power in transforming the lives of men may be studied with profit in the story of Lunenburg, Nova Scotia, where a community of land-loving immigrants from Hanover have in less than two centuries become the finest deep-sea fishermen in the North Atlantic.[2]

Unfortunately D. C. Harvey never developed his argument regarding the "transforming power" of the sea on Nova Scotians. In certain respects, the Atlantic can be considered Nova Scotia's frontier. One does not have to be a maritime disciple of Frederick Jackson Turner to pursue the fascinating possibilities of such a thesis. Surely the life at sea, whether as a fisherman or as a deckhand, encouraged the development of the so-called frontier traits. Furthermore, the Atlantic provided an escape-valve for those disenchanted with the *status quo*. It was also of great consequence in the psychological sense. It was always there—*if needed*. It always promised excitement and possible wealth. It added much therefore, to the myth of potential abundance—a myth that was destined to play havoc with any radical political or economic movement in the province.

The influence of the "maritime frontier" on the historical development of Nova Scotia should not be underestimated. Until well into the 19th century Naval power politics in the North Atlantic affected Nova Scotia. Moreover, sea communications tended to strengthen the area's ties with Great Britain on the one hand, and New England on the other.

From the founding of Acadia in the first decade of the 17th century until the Confederation period, it was Nova Scotia's misfortune to be ground between the millstones of contending imperial forces in North America. Until the end of the French and Indian War, Nova Scotia had been sandwiched between the imperial thrusts of France and Britain. During the period from the outbreak of the American Revolution until Confederation, it can be argued that the Americans appropriated the earlier British thrust while the Anglo-Canadians took upon themselves the old French imperial thrust into the continent. However, during most of these two periods, it should be noted, British naval power was supreme in the North Atlantic and this fact was destined to be more

---

[2] D. C. Harvey, "The Heritage of the Maritimes," *Dalhousie Review*, XIV (April, 1934), 29.

important than any other in determining Nova Scotia's response to hostilities.

In time of war, the inhabitants of the region, often torn between contending loyalties as well as being aware of military and economic realities, chose to walk the knife-edge of neutrality. It is noteworthy that the vast majority of Acadians, when France was at war with Britain, were neutral. This was certainly the case during King William's War, 1689–1697, Queen Anne's War, 1702–1713, King George's War, 1744–1748, and the French and Indian War, 1754–1763. Not knowing which side would eventually win and eager to make a profit from both sides if necessary, the shrewd and pragmatic Acadians found in neutrality a perfect answer to their perplexing problem. The Acadian answer would be the one given by the "Neutral Yankees of Nova Scotia" during the American Revolution. Most of them, it seems certain, if they had been completely free would have joined the Revolutionaries. But the isolation of the Yankees and British seapower persuaded them to choose neutrality. During the War of 1812, the Nova Scotians—Scots, Acadians, Pre-Loyalists and Loyalists—once again adopted virtually a neutral stance. Of course, Nova Scotian privateers were active but their activities can be regarded as business rather than as military operations. There was no fighting in the colony whose merchants eagerly provided both sides in the dispute with badly needed supplies. A kind of Nova Scotia pragmatism had developed by the War of 1812. Matters of principle would almost always take second place to military and economic realities—this was particularly the case with Nova Scotia's ruling élite.

If the sea is regarded as the most important single formative force in the pre-Confederation history of Nova Scotia, the influence of New England is probably the second. From the early seventeenth century, New England exerted a powerful influence on Nova Scotia. Certainly until the revolutionary period, the latter area, was the northeastern frontier of New England; it was "New England's Outpost." Even after the Revolution had shattered permanently the British American colonial empire, there were still surprisingly strong economic, social, religious and cultural ties between Nova Scotia and New England. In the post-Revolutionary period, many Nova Scotians, descendants of Pre-Loyalists and Loyalists, were not absolutely certain that choosing to remain part of the British Empire had been a wise decision. These people apparently had serious second thoughts when they unfavourably contrasted the slow economic growth of Nova Scotia with the dynamism of nineteenth century industrial and commercial America. The ease with which Nova Scotians could compare their society with that in the United States helped to raise many embarrassing questions. Because of the various close ties to New England, it is not surprising that for a significant number of Nova Scotia residents what New England offered was much more attractive than anything offered by "Upper Canada." This same point of view would also exert some influence in the post-Confederation period, especially in the latter part of the 19th century.

The British connection can be considered the third formative force in the historical development of pre-Confederation Nova Scotia. After the American Revolution, the Loyalist migration, reinforced by economic, strategic and constitutional considerations, drew Nova Scotia closer to Britain. The increasingly strong ties with Britain effectively neutralized the New England impact in Nova Scotia.

The fourth force in the evolution of pre-Confederation Nova Scotia and by far the weakest, was "Upper Canada." Events occurring there did not go unnoticed in Nova Scotia and, as J. S. Martell has demonstrated, by 1867 "Intercolonial Communications," had "provided the facilities for closer relations between the Canadians and their fellow colonists down by the sea."[3]

The interplay of these four major formative forces has to be examined in order to place historical events, not only in pre-Confederation Nova Scotia in their proper perspective, but also events since 1867. The interplay of the influences of New England, Britain and "Upper Canada" in Nova Scotia should provide the basis for any examination, however superficial, of Nova Scotia regionalism after Confederation.

JOSEPH HOWE AND REPEAL:

As Professor J. Murray Beck has observed, there were two major qualities that apparently determined Howe's conduct and generally shaped his career. There was a "restless, agitating uncertainty" and also a "reverential, almost mystical attitude towards the British connection."[4] In addition, Howe possessed an unusual grasp of Nova Scotia public opinion and his opposition to Confederation, for example, reflected the general mood of his province.

He opposed Confederation vigorously for three main reasons. He felt that Confederation was not in the best interests of his concept of the New British Empire. Second, it was not in the best interests of his native province. And third, the people of Nova Scotia had not been consulted. That Howe did not want to play "second-fiddle" to Tupper was of little actual consequence in moulding Howe's thinking concerning Confederation.

Howe's attitudes were succinctly expressed in a letter to Sir John C. D. Hay, written in November, 1866:

I am a dear lover of Old England, and to save her would blow Nova Scotia into the air . . . With an enormous amount of shipping at sea Nova Scotia

---

[3] J. S. Martell, "Intercolonial Communications, 1840–1867," *Canadian Historical Association Report*, 1938, 61.

[4] J. M. Beck, *Joseph Howe: Voice of Nova Scotia* (Toronto, 1964), 12.

must belong to a great sea power. When England throws her off, her destiny is inevitable and nobody with the eye of a statesman in his head can suppose that she will choose Ottawa for a capital when she has lost London and can have New York . . . We go in for "the Empire one and indivisible" but when the old ship is broken up we are not such fools as to trust our lives in a crazy craft in which we are certain to be drowned.[5]

The gist of Howe's argument is not difficult to follow. He sincerely believed that Nova Scotia's economic and political future was dependent upon closer ties with the Mother Country. He also considered Nova Scotia to be superior in most respects to "Upper Canada" and he did not want to be associated with "a nation with a helot race within its bosom."[6]

Howe was also aware of the attractions of closer ties with the United States. He once complained that "Placed between two mighty nations, we sometimes feel that we belong to neither."[7] This may help to explain why Howe was compelled to work so hard at being more British than the British. Subconsciously, it seems that he sometimes questioned the decision of his father to become a Loyalist. Howe was fully aware of the "swelling surges of republicanism"[8] as they affected himself and Nova Scotia and he did everything in his power to become an "Imperial Zealot."

Nova Scotia's attitude towards Confederation was accurately expressed in the provincial and federal elections of 1867. In the former, 36 out of 38 anti-Confederates were elected and the latter 18 out of 19. It would be distorting historical facts to contend that Howe was solely responsible for the strength of the anti-Confederation movement which probably reached its zenith in 1868. There were at least four important forces which appear to have converged in 1868 to bring about the intense anti-Confederation movement.

First, Confederation ushered into the province a serious economic recession. A good example of the import of the recession can be seen in the total trade figures of Nova Scotia. In 1865, the trade was worth $23,212,355, but in 1868 it was only worth $13,655,147. (*Yarmouth Herald*, Nov. 11, 1869.) In such a period of economic crisis and adjustment there was bound to be considerable discontent. Something had to be blamed and Confederation became a kind of scape-goat.

Second, the old business élite, especially those people in Halifax closely tied to the old commercial system, were hard hit by the changes

---

[5] Public Archives of Canada, J.H.P. IX 199–210, Howe to Sir John Hay, Nov. 12, 1866.

[6] J. A. Chisholm, The Speeches and Public Letters of Joseph Howe (Halifax, 1909) II, 26, Howe to Moffatt, May 8, 1849.

[7] Quoted by R. A. Maclean in "Joseph Howe and British-American Union," (Unpublished Ph.D. thesis, University of Toronto), 1966, 99.

[8] Chisholm, *op. cit.* I, 610, Howe to Lord John Russell, 1846.

Confederation introduced. These men had invested a great deal in the old system and they naturally resisted the necessary major readjustment in their thinking and policies.

Third, there was a widespread feeling, especially among the old business élite, that the Mother Country has sacrificed Nova Scotia interests on the altar of political expediency. Because of their previous dependence on Britain and because of the strong emotional ties, the change in British policy precipitated a violent reaction in Nova Scotia. Like the St. Lawrence merchants during the temporary aberration of the Annexation Manifesto period, many Nova Scotians—"the leading bankers and merchants, the wealthiest farmers, and the most independent gentlemen in the province"[9] felt that they had been betrayed by the Mother Country and like children made aware for the first time of an adulterous parent they were bitterly disillusioned.

Fourth, and this was particularly the case in the southern part of the province, pro-New England sentiment became increasingly important. Such sentiment had been effectively neutralized by the Anglophile tendencies in Nova Scotia development until the "betrayal of 1867."

It is clear that Joseph Howe did not create the profound anti-Confederation sentiment in Nova Scotia. He unsuccessfully attempted to harness it and to use it to obtain repeal from the British authorities. But when he realized that the British would not grant repeal he decided instead to seek "better terms" for Nova Scotia. When Howe entered John A. Macdonald's Cabinet on January 30, 1869, the repeal movement received a fatal blow. Conceived in frustration and economic discontent, it had a relatively short life in Nova Scotia and when signs of an economic upswing appeared in 1869 the movement withered.

Why did Howe leave the movement? He simply realized that repeal was impossible if Nova Scotia hoped to remain a part of the British Empire. He did not want annexation and reacted violently to the proponents of such a view in the repeal movement. He could not advocate warfare against his beloved Britain and he was also fully aware of British military power and the hopelessness of the cry of the Digby *Bluenose:* "The remedy lies in our own legislation, but most of all in our stout hearts and strong arms. The only power that will ever repeal the Stamp Act of '67 is the power that repealed the Stamp Act of '76." (Digby *Bluenose,* March 4, 1868.)

From 1867 to 1869, repeal had a great deal of emotional appeal in Nova Scotia. The practical problems involved in actually bringing it about may have added to this emotional appeal, Independence was the only solution and independence was impossible when British military power and American indifference were taken into account. Howe clearly

---

[9] Public Archives of Nova Scotia, C.O. 217, Archbishop MacDonnell to Cardwell, Feb. 16, 1865.

saw the cul-de-sac before him and jumped off the "repeal wagon" just before it ground to a halt.

W. S. FIELDING AND "SECESSION" 1885–1886

The "better terms" agreement negotiated by Howe provided only minor concessions and did not adequately deal with the fundamental objections Nova Scotia had concerning Confederation. The "better terms" were deliberately and narrowly financial in nature; but they gave Howe and other anti-Confederates some valid justification—or so they rationalized—for accepting what was in fact, inevitable. The anti-Confederation feeling in Nova Scotia, however, lingered on in Nova Scotia reappearing as a political force usually during periods of economic stress. As Professor R. A. Maclean has contended: "Had the economic resources of the provinces been more viable and marketable, such attitudes would have weakened sooner than they did."[10]

More than anything else, the secession movement of 1885–6 was the product of the acute financial embarrassment of the government of Nova Scotia in the 1870s and early 1880s. As early as 1878 the Conservative Holmes-Thompson administration felt compelled to adopt a policy of retrenchment, made necessary in part, by the expiration of the "better terms" agreement of 1869 and also by an economic recession. Apparently John A. Macdonald underestimated the extent and significance of Nova Scotia's grievances and in the provincial election of 1882 the Liberals swept into power with 24 out of 38 seats.

Almost immediately, the Liberals began to stress provincial rights and they continued to make political capital by attacking the indifferent if not hostile Ottawa authorities. Macdonald's National Policy received most of the Liberal salvos. The tariff was blamed for most of the province's woes as was western expansion "to keep up that conglomeration of rocks (British Columbia) and Digger Indians." (Halifax *Morning Chronicle,* April 22, 1886.)

On February 24, 1885, the Liberal M.L.A., James A. Fraser gave notice of a motion respecting the separation of Nova Scotia from Canada, and the establishment of a Maritime Union. On March 12, Fraser finally moved his resolution by declaring that:

Since the financial and commercial condition of the Province was in a very unsatisfactory state, and there was no prospect of improvement while it remained part of Canada, the interests of the people of Nova Scotia, New Brunswick, and Prince Edward Island, would be advanced by withdrawing from the Canadian Federation and forming a Maritime Union.[11]

---

[10] Maclean, *op. cit.,* 480.

[11] P. R. Blakeley, "Party Government in Nova Scotia, 1878–1897" (Unpublished M.A. thesis, Dalhousie University, 1945), 94.

If the other Atlantic Provinces refused to accept the scheme, Nova Scotia was to return to the status of an independent province of Great Britain.

On March 25, W. S. Fielding, the close-lipped Liberal Premier, moved an amendment which reflected government policy:

That if the Government and Parliament of Canada fail to make provision, during the present session of said Parliament, to place the Province of Nova Scotia in a better financial position in the union, this House affirms that it will be necessary to consider the advisability of taking steps to secure a severance of the political connection between the province and the Dominion of Canada.[12]

Fielding was endeavouring to pressure the Federal Government into providing more financial aid to Nova Scotia but he had little actual bargaining power. Secession was impossible within the framework of the British Empire and only a few Nova Scotians wanted annexation—and most Americans did not! But threat of secession was part of the political game in the federal system, and Fielding realized that in tapping the almost limitless reservoir of hostility to "Upper Canada" and Confederation he could not lose politically in Nova Scotia. The threat of secession had already become a part of the political ritual.

In the Speech from the Throne in 1886, Fielding had to admit that Macdonald had called his bluff by declaring that the Dominion had made a final settlement of the province's financial objections to the British North America Act in 1869. No further concessions would be made!

This refusal aroused a storm of protest both in the Legislature and throughout the province. Fielding endeavoured to take advantage of this wave of discontent; he was also eager to control it effectively in order to strengthen his political position. On May 8, 1886, he therefore moved his famous "repeal resolution":

. . . That if it be found impossible, after negotiations . . . to secure the co-operation of the respective Governments of the sister provinces in withdrawing from the Confederation and entering instead into a Maritime Union, then this Legislature deems it absolutely necessary that Nova Scotia, in order that its railways and other public works and services may be extended and maintained . . . its industries properly fostered; its commerce invigorated and expanded; and its financial interests placed upon a sound basis, such as was the case previous to Confederation, should ask permission from the Imperial Parliament to withdraw from the Union of Canada and return to the status of a Province of Great Britain with full control over all fiscal laws and tariff regulations within the Province, such as prevailed to Confederation.[13]

The debate lasted only one day since Fielding wished to go to the people as quickly as possible for their endorsation of his policy.

In general, there were three main issues in the provincial election of

---

. [12] Quoted by Blakeley, *op. cit.*, 94.

[13] *Journal* of Nova Scotia Assembly, 1886, 147–9.

1886—repeal, the progressive administration of the Fielding government and both provincial and federal railway policy. It would be a serious mistake to argue that "repeal" was the only issue. Most Nova Scotians must have realized that "repeal" was a constitutional impossibility. Certainly most Liberal politicians were aware of this fact. But the "Paranoid Style" served a useful purpose as an emotional outlet for many frustrated Nova Scotians. The secession threat was little more than political blackmail. In the past, John A. Macdonald had often been willing to purchase support or quell discontent when the cries of protest became too shrill for his sensitive ears. It was a well known fact that all provinces had their grievances and it was also realized that they also had their price!

The election results pleased Fielding;—the Liberals increased their number of seats to twenty-nine, the Conservatives dropped to eight and there was one Independent. Conservative strength was restricted to northeastern Nova Scotia where the industrial areas were bound by the advantages of the National Policy to the Dominion. The residents of this region were convinced that repeal and closer ties with the United States would probably destroy their struggling steel industry and lower the price they could receive for their coal. Two commercial systems were therefore in conflict and in 1886 it appeared that the advocates of the "Golden Age" were still in the ascendancy provincially. The election also was an opportunity for patriotic Nova Scotians to reassert their intense love and pride in their province. A vote for Fielding was a vote for Nova Scotia; a vote for the Tories was a vote for "treason."

Fielding now had more than an adequate mandate for his policy of repeal. But he refused to do anything until the 1887 federal election. His point of view was expressed in the *Novascotian* on February 19, 1887.

Without a decisive and overwhelming vote now for repeal, the great victory of last summer will amount to nothing. Every man who voted for repeal then is bound by every obligation that can have influence upon an intelligent, consistent, and patriotic citizen, to repeat it now, and not only that, but to exercise all legitimate influences to persuade his neighbour to do the same. . . . Let the victory of February 22nd (1887) be a perfect Waterloo for Tupper and his fellow conspirators. (*Novascotian*, Feb. 19, 1887.)

On February 22nd the "conspirators" won 14 seats and the Liberals 7, the same as in 1882. Apparently, the support for Repeal had lost some of its fervor between the two elections. Fielding's procrastinations fooled few people. Furthermore, on the whole, the Liberals ran their best candidates provincially while the Conservatives ran theirs federally. This might help to explain the shift in voting behaviour.

The results of the federal election gave Fielding the excuse he so desperately needed. He maintained in Nova Scotia House:

I have felt, since the February election, that the hands of the government were tied . . . . I am persuaded that our true policy is to tell the people of

Nova Scotia that they had the matter in their own hands, that they had a glorious opportunity of asserting their desires on this question, and of placing themselves in a fair position to secure the accomplishment of those desires, that they lost that opportunity, and that, until they are prepared to take up the question again with greater firmness, and repair the damages of the February election, this repeal movement can have no reasonable hope of success.[14]

Repeal had failed in 1886–1887, because it was never really a viable political issue. It was of course an emotional election issue but only in the sense of being the vehicle of anti-Upper Canadian and anti-Confederation feeling. Once some Nova Scotians got this venom out of their systems they were content to accept the *status quo*. Their ties were gradually being strengthened with "Upper Canada" and they had no other future but that as a "Maritime outpost of Upper Canada."

MARITIME RIGHTS AND THE HALIFAX HERALD

In 1920, the Nova Scotia Conservative Party was humiliated at the polls and was replaced as the Official Opposition in the Legislature by the new Farmer-Labour movement. In the 1920 provincial election, the Conservatives won three seats, Farmer-Labour, eleven, and the Liberals twenty-nine. For the first time in Nova Scotia's history fundamental socio-economic reforms were being advocated by the Official Opposition.

The post-war recession, agricultural and labour discontent, the disorganization of the Conservative Party had all helped to give rise to the Farmer-Labour movement. But even before the election, the farmers and industrial workers were at each other's throats. The movement began to disintegrate soon after the election and this disintegration was accelerated by the sudden revival of Nova Scotia regionalism as expressed by the desperate Conservative Party.

The Conservatives realized that if they hoped to continue as a viable force in provincial politics they would have to absorb the protest movement that had brought forward the Farmer-Labour movement. Furthermore, there were many substantial Nova Scotians who were disturbed by the reforms advocated by the new political movement and they wished to check its further growth. They wanted to continue to operate under the old accepted ground rules.

Internal disintegration of the Farmer-Labour movement, the dynamic Conservative re-organization activity, and the clever use of the "Maritime Rights" issue all played key roles in the gradual rebuilding of the provincial Conservative Party. In the "Maritime Rights" movement, leading Conservatives, particularly those associated with the Halifax *Herald,* saw *the* emotional issue to ensure not only the survival of their party, but also eventual electoral success.

---

[14] Nova Scotia *Debates,* 1887, 254–255.

Although the serious post-War depression would have made life difficult for any party in power, it was the ringing cry of "Maritime Rights" that rallied the discontented to the banner of the new-look Conservatives against both federal and provincial Liberals. Despite the election of the so-called "solid sixteen" Liberal M.P.'s from Nova Scotia, MacKenzie King neglected the province. He tended to take Nova Scotia for granted.

The birth of the "Maritime Rights" movement in Nova Scotia occurred publicly on the editorial page of the Halifax *Herald* on July 27, 1922:

We want to say that it is time for the people of the Maritime Provinces to put shoulder to shoulder and fight for their rights. And cease not until those right(s) are acquired. We have the lesson of the Western Members of Parliament who stand like a rock and compelled the government to DELIVER THE GOODS. Our "Solid Sixteen" marched up the hill and then marched down again.

What did they bring home to Nova Scotia? Frothy assurances and fulsome promises are the only things they offer the people. We have had enough of these. Now we want action and practical rational results . . . be no longer humbugged by claptrap.

W. H. Dennis owner of the *Herald* and H. S. Congdon, editor of the Dartmouth *Patriot* were the vociferous propagandists of "Maritime Rights" in Nova Scotia and they worked hand-in-glove with the Maritime Board of Trade—an organization intimately involved with the rise of the new "protest movement" in all three Maritime provinces. The important speech made by H. W. Corning, House-leader of the Conservatives, on April 19, 1923, outlining the case for Nova Scotia "Rights" was prepared by Dennis, Congdon and others. This address was used by the Conservatives to show that "Maritime Rights" had become the cornerstone of their party policy. It was a calculated gamble and it apparently worked.

The effectiveness of "Maritime Rights" as an election issue was demonstrated in a federal by-election in Halifax late in 1923. The Conservatives, who emphasized "Maritime Rights" to the exclusion of any other issue, won an unexpected victory. This victory acted as a catalyst in the reorganization of the provincial Conservatives and gave them a badly needed psychological lift. Always swift to adjust to changing public opinion, the Liberals soon became ardent advocates as well of "Maritime Rights." The Liberals maintained that the tariff was responsible for Nova Scotia's woes thus endeavouring to force the Conservatives to support protection against free trade. The Conservatives refused to fall into the trap but instead wisely discussed "Maritime Rights" in a vague and emotional manner. The issue of "Maritime Rights" played a significant role in the 1925 provincial election, when the Conservatives won 40 seats—60% of the vote and the Liberals only 3 seats and 36% of the vote and in the federal elections of 1925 when the Conservatives almost annihilated the federal Liberals.

In the Conservative Party Platform of 1925 are to be found three planks dealing with "Nova Scotia Rights":

(8) Promotion and maintenance of Nova Scotian rights and equalities in national enterprises and undertakings. . . .

(13) Removal of economic injustice and disabilities under which the province is found to be labouring and in the event of failure to obtain redress, to submit the question directly to the people of the province, to obtain the will of the electors in regard to the injustices complained of, and in particular to mandate and empower the Provincial Administration to petition and request the Dominion Government to modify or relax its arrangements on the subject of taxation, trade, and the fisheries which may be found to prejudice the business and industrial interests of the people and province of Nova Scotia.

(14) If, after such action, the Federal authorities will not meet our fair demands with respect to freight rates, trade adjustments and the fisheries, then we must carry our case to the British Government for such amendments of the British North America Act as may be necessary to ensure the welfare and existence of the people of the province.[15]

No mention was made of the words repeal or secession. The Tories simply demanded certain financial concessions in spite of the ritualistic shibboleths of regional protest. The rhetoric of Nova Scotia "rights" was good political propaganda and if successful could be carefully put away until the next election. Emotional demands did not require action—only votes!

The cap could always be dusted off, and the cup polished and rich Mr. Ottawa approached for a little "conscience money." Full equalization could be demanded by some Nova Scotia politicians in the 1960s but most Nova Scotians could not understand so they would not listen. They were satisfied with small mercies—a post office here, a wharf there.

In the Canadian federal system each section, in theory at least, is supposed to have its interests looked after by its representative in Ottawa. But as Professor Beck has observed:

This raises the question whether Nova Scotian members of Parliament have been more concerned with maintaining party solidarity than with safeguarding provincial interests While the western Canadian Provinces have undoubtedly found it to their advantage to return third-party representation in strength, the Maritimes have rarely deviated from old-party lines to the extent of more than a single member, and the political leaders at Ottawa have had no difficulty in keeping them in line by what might be alleged to be little more than temporary sops.[16]

Mere political rhetoric, however paranoid, was and is no adequate substitute for POWER POLITICS. Nova Scotia may be experiencing the

---

[15] Quoted by E. R. Forbes, "The Rise and Fall of the Conservative Party in the Provincial Politics of Nova Scotia 1922–33," (Unpublished M.A. thesis, Dalhousie University, 1967), 205–206.

[16] M. Beck, *The Government of Nova Scotia* (Toronto, 1957), 338–339.

"Stanfield Revolution" but most citizens are content with federal "sops." In the last federal election the party that enthusiastically advocated full equalization grants to Nova Scotia received less than nine percent of the popular vote and no seats. "Upper Canada" is still often blamed by Nova Scotians for their plight, but they nevertheless seem content to have their disenchantment expressed in words rather than in effective action. Is there any other choice for a dependent, "colonial" society?

part III

*Late-Victorian
Canada and Her
External Interests*

14

Loyalty*†

Goldwin Smith

IN THE LONG HISTORY of Canadian letters, Goldwin Smith must rank as *the* most controversial figure. A writer of lucid prose, he was the outspoken champion of laissez-faire liberalism and the Manchester school of free trade economics. Born in England, he rose to become Regius Professor of Modern History at Oxford, emigrated to Cornell, and eventually settled in Toronto in 1871. He was attracted for a time to the Canada First movement (see Gagan article) and was throughout a prolific and vitriolic pamphleteer on many Canadian issues.

The following are excerpts from Smith's three lectures to the Young Men's Liberal Club in Toronto following the heated election campaign of 1891. During this campaign Smith had supported the "Unrestricted Reciprocity" program of the Liberal Party under Laurier. Because Smith's views in favour of eventual continental union were well known he drew the fire of the opposition on himself and the Liberal Party. He was accused of being party to a conspiracy to destroy the imperial ties to Britain. It was against this alledged "disloyalty" of Smith and others that Sir John Macdonald made his famous electoral plea: "A British subject I was born—A British subject I will die. With my utmost effort, with my latest breath, will I oppose the 'veiled treason' which attempts, by sordid means and mercenary proffers, to lure our people from their allegiance."

In the light of the current debate over economic relations with the United States, it is important to go back to see the controversies of 1891 and the arguments of an emphatic champion of continental union.

* From *Loyalty, Aristocracy, and Jingoism* (Toronto, 1891), pp. 9–34, 94–102.
† Delivered before the Young Men's Liberal Club, Toronto, February 2nd, 1891.

Y OU HAVE DONE me the honour, Gentlemen of the Liberal Club, to desire that I should read to you an address on the subject of "Loyalty." I gladly respond to your request. But you will allow me to address you on this occasion as liberal-minded men, not as Liberals in the party sense of the term. I have been asked, as I am with you in this struggle, why I do not join your party? I reply that I am with you and with anyone in a struggle such as that on which you are now entering against Commercial Monopoly and Government by Corruption, and hope with other citizens to do my best in the day of battle; but when I am invited to join a party my answer must be that I have always steadfastly set my face towards national government, and that I and others, if there are any who think as I do, are more likely to be useful by being true to our own principle, and saying what there is to be said for it, than by compromising it in order to take a more active part in politics. Then I am not sure about my qualification for admission. A Liberal in England I was held to be, and even a thorough-going Liberal, though I always had a rooted abhorrence of violence and revolution. But I am not sure that I should pass muster with your organization. I am a Liberal of the Old School, one of those who wish Government to mind its own business, who desire that at last man should have a chance of self-development, and who are no more inclined to submit to the tyranny of majorities calling themselves the State, than to the tyranny of kings. Perhaps the best reason of all is that at my time of life it is too late to put on new harness, and a man can only go on his own way supporting what he thinks right and opposing what he thinks wrong. With those who are fighting against Monopoly and Corruption no good citizen can hesitate to take part.

But to the question. It is not wonderful that you wish just now to get all the information you can about loyalty. The air is full of loud professions of it, and still louder denunciations of disloyalty. The suspicion of disloyalty evidently entails serious consequences, extending in certain contingencies to being sabred by some loyal warrior on the street. What is, perhaps, of more practical importance is that the cry, by its effect on nervous persons, is likely to prevent the fair consideration of questions vital to the welfare of our people.

There certainly is something peculiar about this virtue. There is a species of it, at all events, which very happily coincides with self-interest. The loyal are sometimes like the Puritan Saints, who deemed it their religious duty to inherit the earth. Conquerors and oppressors, for instance, always call submission loyalty and patriotism treason. Again, loyalty seems, unlike other virtues, to find a home in breasts in which no other virtue can dwell. No men ever were louder or probably more sincere in their professions of it than were Scroggs and Jeffreys at the time when they were judicially murdering Russell and Sydney or going on a Bloody Assize. The carpet-baggers who governed and swindled the South after the Civil War, in like manner, overflowed wi'' '' d whenever they had been detected in some gross act of corr e defence was that they were always "truly loil." On the othe n some breasts where other virtues, political as well as social, i- ably dwell in full measure, we find this virtue strangely absent. In the British Empire loyalty seems to have the peculiarity of being eminently colonial. It is like the reverence for the Papacy, the intensity of which was always found to vary in direct proportion to the distance from Rome. At the Plimsoll banquet the other night, after we had listened to the usual declamations on this theme, a speaker remarked that Mr. Plimsoll might know he was not in England, but in Canada, when he heard so much about loyalty, of which nobody boasted in England. This remark was true as well as neat. In England you never heard a word said on the subject. Everybody takes it for granted that you are not in a plot to overturn the dynasty. Suppose a lady were to go about in society assuring everybody that her hair and teeth were her own, that her complexion was not paint, and that the lines of her figure were those laid down by nature, would she not be apt to create the suspicion which she was so anxious to avert?

What is the original signification of the word? *Loyauté* means respect for law and fidelity to obligation. Shakespeare uses it for fidelity to the marriage vow, to filial duty, to friendship, as well as for fidelity to the king. Milton makes Comus offer the lady the shelter of a "loyal" cottage, that is, a cottage true to the law of hospitality. The term especially denoted fidelity to those feudal obligations which were the organic law of the time. Those obligations were reciprocal; it was not only the vassal that owed duty to the lord; the lord also owed duty to the vassal. If the lord did not perform his duty, the vassal renounced his allegiance by a regular form, called defiance. De Montfort and the patriot barons thus formally renounced their allegiance to Henry III. Divine Right was not the creed of those days, nor was there any blind and spaniel-like devotion to the person of the king. The feudalists were rough but they were not fools; if they had been they could not have founded European society and the British Constitution. Edward I., the greatest of all feudal monarchs, was no fetich, but a noble man living in free and frank intercourse with his peers, foremost in battle and adventure, claiming loyalty by a right truly divine. It is not till we come to the Tudor despotism that the fetichism begins. Before Henry VIII., a bloated monster of selfishness and vice, steeped in uxoricide and judicial murder, his slaves grovel in the dust. They compare him to the sun in its glory and almost to God. Adulation well-nigh equally extravagant is paid to his daughter, though in this case the baseness is redeemed by the generous illusion which saw the nation impersonated in its queen. Shakespeare, however, you will see, though thoroughly monarchical, is never slavish. But it is with the Stuarts that Divine Right appears as the courtiers' creed, and that loyalty arrogates the character of a distinct virtue. Bishops tell James I. when he insults the Puritans that he speaks by the inspiration of God, and divines preach before Charles I. the doctrine that there can be no such thing as justice between the king and the subject, any more than between God and the creature. Now it is that the hearts of all who support Stuart despotism, in the words of the Cavalier song, are "crowned with loyal fires." We respect the tradition of the Cavaliers as we respect any tradition of gallantry and misfortune. Some of those men really sacrificed estate and life for what they sincerely believed to be the right, though there was also a large element of what Carlyle calls "truculent flunkeyism." But nobody in England would think of bowing his head to the descendants of the Cavaliers or letting them settle the destinies of the Nation. The grass has grown over the graves of Edgehill and Naseby, as it must grow at last over all graves. The other day, when on a visit to England, I found myself in the house of a friend who represented one of the Cavalier families. The relics of Charles the First's standard-bearer at Edgehill hung on the walls, but the family were leading Liberals. However, it was under the Restoration, and especially at the evil close of Charles the Second's reign, that the Loyalists became a regular party supporting royal usurpation and judicial murder, and being well paid for their devotion. North, himself a strong Tory, describes that party of the men that went about drinking and huzzaing. One of the loudest of them was Chief Justice Scroggs, of whom North says, "that he was of a mean extract, having been a butcher's son, who wrought himself into business in the law," that he was "a great voluptuary, being a companion of the High Court rakes," and "had a true libertine principle." "Scroggs," North tells us, "was preferred for professing loyalty, but Oates, coming forward with a swinging popularity, he took in and ranted on that side most impetuously." The same men, under the same romantic designation, combined to support the tyranny of James II. and to help him in cutting the throat of national liberty. But when James II. laid his hand upon the rich possessions of the Church, the other side of loyalism was seen. We can understand the King's surprise and partly sympathize with his disgust. However, loyalism soon recovered itself, and after calling in William of Orange to deliver it, it began to show its fidelity to principle by plotting against his Government and life. Presently it proceeded to signalize itself by betraying the nation at Utrecht, and afterwards by a series of half-tipsy intrigues and pot-valiant swaggerings in the interest of the "King over the Water." A more despicable party than the English Jacobites, who seemed to themselves and in a sense were, the very pink of loyalty, never appeared on the scene of history. It is needless to say how loyalism repaired its golden fires under George III., how passionate was its devotion to the person of that excellent monarch, especially when he was out of his mind, and what services it rendered to the country by bringing on the American war and vetoing Catholic Emancipation. Places, pensions, bishoprics, deaneries, and sinecures without number, were its reward.

In Canada loyalty was at its zenith under the "Family Compact." But again it showed its peculiar character as a virtue. So long as the Crown was on its side, gave it all the patronage and emoluments, and protected it against reform, it was passionately devoted to the Crown and the mother country. But when with the growth of the Reform movement in England the Crown changed its policy, a change came over the spirit of Colonial loyalism also. When two Family Compact officials were dismissed for opposing the Liberal policy of the Government, Loyalist organs began to proclaim that their attachment to the Empire had received a fatal shock and that they would have to turn their eyes elsewhere. Afterwards we know what an exhibition of loyalty ensued upon the passage of the Rebellion Losses bill. The principle of the Loyalists upon that occasion, it must be owned, was severely tried; but it did not prove equal to the trial. Flinging rotten eggs and stones at the Governor-General was a singular display of devotion to the Crown. We need not insinuate that on that account loyalty was insincere. The African believes in his idol though he whips it for not giving him what he wants.

In the days of old the idol of loyalty was, at all events, a substance, not a shadow, as it still is in countries really under monarchical government, and in which the people look up like children, for the maintenance of order and almost for their daily bread to their paternal king. But how is it with us? Sunday after Sunday we solemnly pray to God that Her Majesty and Her Majesty's representative may be enabled to govern us well. Let Her Majesty or Her Majesty's representative presume to do a single act against the wishes of the Tory Prime Minister; let eith⟨...⟩n veto a single job or bribe, and we know what would be t⟨...⟩ Yet we profess to believe that God is not to be mocked. This p⟨...⟩devotion to an empty name is, however, not without its substantial use. By loud protestations of loyalty to the Crown, which he knows will never cost him anything, a man absolves himself from loyalty to the commonwealth. He feels himself perfectly at liberty to cabal and conspire as much as he pleases against the public good in his own interest, or in that of some exclusive order or sectional combination, because he is loyal to a Crown divested of all its power, and to the name of a connection with the mother country which he has practically reduced to a mere shadow. I do not mean to speak disrespectfully of any feeling which is genuine however out of date, but there are not a few cases, in which loyalty to the Crown is a fine name for disloyalty to the country and loyalty to British connection is a fine name for disloyalty to Canada.

The loyalty cry is now being raised, in default of any economical argument, to deter the country from accepting the benefits of Reciprocity and to scare it into acquiescence in a policy of which commercial atrophy and the exodus are the visible and inevitable results. Here we see with what curious exactness a Loyalist's virtue follows the lines of his own interest through all their twistings and windings. To exclude British goods by protective duties is perfectly loyal. It is perfectly loyal to wage what in fact is a tariff war against the mother country. But to discriminate against the mother country is disloyal in the highest degree. The very thought of it is enough to almost throw a loyal man into convulsions. Yet discrimination would have no disloyal object. It would be not against England in particular but against all countries alike. It would evince no change of feeling towards the mother country, or towards the political connection. It would not take a penny from the revenue of the crown or a particle from its power or dignity. It would hardly take away anything from the commercial wealth of the British people. The enhanced value of their Canadian investments which would result from free trade would probably make up to them for the loss which a few exporting houses would sustain. But the same measure would expose the protected manufacturers of Canada to Continental competition. Therefore he who proposes it is a traitor.

The commercial unity of the Empire is at an end. It was formally declared to be at an end when an Australian colony claimed the right to lay protective duties on British goods, and the question having been considered by the Home Government was decided in favour of the claim. Great Britain has withdrawn all commercial privileges from the colonies, and by the same act she has conceded to them the liberty of doing the best they can commercially for themselves, each according to the circumstances of its own case. The commercial circumstances of Canada are those of a country placed alongside a great neighbour who is under the protective system, and whose policy it is impossible for her in regulating her own to ignore, as it is to ignore the physical features of her continent. The commercial unity of the Empire having been, I repeat, dissolved by the act of the mother country herself, which deprived the colonies of their privileges, there can be nothing disloyal in recognizing the necessities of our own case. Offer us free trade with the whole world, the mother country included, and there are some of us who will gladly accept it. Will the loyal men of the Red Parlour do the same?

We are disloyal, it is said, because we propose to enter into a tariff arrangement with the United States, and by entering into a tariff arrangement with the United States we should compromise the fiscal independence of the country. Of course you cannot make a treaty without surrendering to that extent, and so long as the treaty lasts, your independence of action. But if the treaty is fair, where is the dishonour? Was there any dishonour in the Elgin Treaty? Was there any dishonour in the commercial treaty made by England with France? It is idle to think that in commercial matters we can be entirely independent of the United

States. We must be beholden to them for our principal winter ports. We must trust to their comity for the transmission of our goods in bond. Our railway system is bound up with theirs. What we call our great national road, the road which was to be the pledge of our eternal separation from them, not only has branches running into their territory, but actually passes with its trunk line through the State of Maine. If there is any ⟨...⟩ in this matter it would appear to be in maintaining a fiscal ⟨...⟩ch is constantly driving the flower of our population over the ⟨...⟩ ⟨...⟩aves Canada from annexation by annexing the Canadians.

Does anyone want to be told what is really disloyal? It is disloyal to assemble the representatives of a particular commercial interest before the elections and virtually sell to them the policy of the country. It is disloyal to seek by corrupt means the support of particular nationalities, churches, political orders, or sectional interests of any kind, against the broad interest of the community. It is disloyal to sap the independence of provinces and reduce them to servile pensioners in the Central Government, by systematically bribing them with "better terms" and federal grants. It is disloyal to use the appointments to a branch of the national legislature as inducements to partisans to spend money in elections. It is disloyal to use public works, which ought to be undertaken only for the general good, for the purpose of bribing particular constituencies. It is disloyal to make concessions to public contractors which are to be repaid by contributions to an election fund. It is disloyal to corrupt the public press, and thus to poison the wells of public instruction and public sentiment. It is disloyal to tamper with the article of the Constitution respecting the time of general elections by thimblerigging dissolutions brought on to snap a national verdict. It is disloyal to vitiate the national verdict by gerrymandering. It is disloyal to surrender the national veto on provincial legislation, the very palladium of nationality, out of fear of the Jesuit vote. All corruption is disloyalty. All sectionalism is disloyalty. All but pure, straightforward and honourable conduct in the management of public affairs is disloyalty. If it is not disloyalty to a Crown on a cushion, it is disloyalty to the Commonwealth.

"Loyalty" still has a meaning though the feudal relation between lord and vassal has passed away. It means thorough-going and self-sacrificing devotion to a principle, a cause, or the community. All that is contrary to such devotion or tends to its disparagement is still disloyal.

The question of our political relations is not now before us. We are dealing with the commercial question alone. But suppose the political question were before us, would there be any disloyalty in dealing with it frankly and honestly? I say frankly and honestly. There is disloyalty in any sort of intrigue. But who has intrigued? According to the Government organs the country is a nest of conspirators. Everybody who goes to Washington goes for the purpose of conspiracy, as though real conspirators would not have the sense to keep their names out of the hotel book. I have myself been charged in the Government organ with going to Washington to sell the country. I go to Washington every Spring with my wife on our regular Southern trip, and at no other time; mainly for the purpose of seeing personal friends, the chief of whom was the late Mr. Bancroft. I have been charged by the same organ with being a party to bringing American money into the country for the purpose of influencing the elections, the evidence being that my friend Mr. Hallam, to whom I never said a syllable on the subject of political relations, had proposed to raise a fund for the diffusion of knowledge about the traiff question.[1] An attempt was at last made to connect me with what was alleged to be a treasonable publication by means of a document purporting to my instructions to my printers. The document was stated to have been stolen from the printing office by a person employed there, an act which, to burning loyalty, seemed loyal. But it was proved by me conclusively to be a fabrication.

Treason is a crime. If anybody has been guilty of it bring him to justice. But it is time that people should know that to charge your fellow-citizens, men in as good standing as yourself, with treason and with trying to sell the country, without any proof of the fact, is a social offence. He who, for the purpose of his own ambition or gain, falsely divides the community on such lines, is himself guilty of the most pernicious treason.

There has just been a meeting of Imperial Federationists, of whose aspiration I desire to speak with all respect. The object of Imperial Federationists is to make a great change in our political relations. They seek to reverse the process of decentralization which, apparently, in obedience to the dictate of nature, has been going on for so many years, to take from Canada a part of her self-government, and to place her again under the authority of a central power. They fancy, indeed, that they can have an Imperial Federation without detracting from colonial self-government. But how could this be when each of the colonies would be subject certainly to military assessments, and probably to fiscal control; for it is hardly possible to imagine a federation with a multiplicity of tariffs, some of them hostile to others, as those of protectionist colonies now are to the mother country? What the plan of the Imperial Federationists is, remains a mystery. They tell us not to ask them for a cut-and-dried scheme. We do not ask for a scheme either cut or dried, but only for one that shall be intelligible and a possible subject of discussion. Readjustment of postage-rates is not confederation. However, it lies not in their mouths to say that a proposal of change must be disloyal. If they are at liberty to advocate centralization, "Canada First" was equally at liberty to advocate independence. "Canada First," in its day, was denounced as disloyal. I well recollect when you were told that to speak of

---

[1] It has since appeared that the very persons who brought this charge themselves did not scruple to take toll of an American firm for a political purpose.

Canada as a nation was treason. We have now got beyond that point, I suppose, since adherence to the National Policy is now the height of loyalty. If there is any question of loyalty in the matter, it might be thought that they were the most loyal who desired for their country a higher position than that of perpetual dependence. Whether their aspirations were feasible is another question. They hardly took into account the French difficulty, nor did they or perhaps anybody at that time distinctly see what effect the enormous extension of disjointed territory toward the West would have on the geographical unity of the nation. But their aspiration was high; they were responding in fact to the appeal which the authors of Confederation themselves had made to the heart of the country, and never was the name of loyalty more traduced than when they were called disloyal.

There are men living, high in public life and in the Conservative ranks, who signed a manifesto in favour, I do not say of Annexation, which is a false and hateful term, but of political union with the United States. Nothing is more irrational or ungenerous than to taunt people with opinions which they once honestly held and have since not less honestly renounced. It is not for any such purpose that I refer to the Montreal manifesto. But such a manifesto could not have been signed by such men if the question were not one which might be entertained without disloyalty, provided always that those who entertain it remain firm, pending its solution, in their dutiful allegiance to their own country. For my own part, being not a politician, but a student, and restrained by no exigencies of statecraft, I never conceal my opinion. I have always deplored the schism which divided our race a century ago. I hold that there was wrong on both sides, and not less on the side of the American Revolutionists than on that of the British Government. I hope and steadfastly believe that some day the schism will be healed, that there will be a moral reunion, which alone is possible, of the American colonies of Great Britain with their mother country, and a complete reunion, with the hearty sanction of the mother country, of the whole race upon this continent. Great Britain will in time see that she has no real interest here but amity and trade. The unity of the race, and the immense advantages of a settlement which would shut out war from this continent and make it an economical whole, will prevail, I feel convinced, in the end over evil memories and the efforts of those who cherish them. That the consummation will come in my time is unlikely, though a Government of monopoly and corruption is driving it on apace. At all events, I have no more personal interest in it than in any astronomical event. Nor would I wish to see it hastened by any means which would impair its perfect spontaneity. On the other hand, nobody who believes in ultimate union can wish to see the earnings of the people wasted in desperate efforts to perpetuate separation. A hundred millions of public money or money's worth, at least, have been spent on this great national road by which the triumph of the Separatist policy was to be secured forever. Not a Yankee was to have a cent in the enterprise or to have anything to do with it, and the road was to run entirely over our own territory, not touching the accursed Yankee soil. The road has been built partly with Yankee money; it had for some time an eminent Yankee politician for its vice-president; it has now a Yankee for its president; it runs through the Yankee State of Maine, and connects our system with the Yankee system at more points than one. It is, in fact, half a Yankee road. So much for the wisdom and hopefulness of a fight against Nature.

Whether Commercial Union would accelerate political union or retard it, who can say? The Elgin Treaty manifestly put off political union by removing discontent. But railway union and social union and the fusion of the populations by the exodus, all manifestly tend to political union. Who thinks it disloyal to contribute to these? If a man makes himself prominent in cultivating loyal antipathy to Americans, you are as likely as not to find that he is in the service of an American railroad company and helping, honourably enough, to send Canadians to the States. The other day I was myself reviled in the most unmeasured language for my supposed American proclivities. Soon afterwards I heard that my assailant had accepted a call as a minister to the other side of the line.

On this continent, not in Europe; in the New World, not in the Old; the lot of Canada and of Canadians is cast. This fixes our general destiny, whatever special arrangements of a political kind the future may have in store. This sets the m   *4*   r aspirations and traces the line of our public duty. This dete   r us what is genuine loyalty. That course of action which lead   happy development of man on our own continent is for us loyal. To say that loyalty consists in keeping this community always in dependence on a community three thousand miles off and condemning it to be without a life of its own, is to set loyalty at fatal odds not only with nature but with genuine sentiment. Nature assigns us not only the more practicable but the nobler part.

It is irrational to rail against British aristocracy. British aristocracy is an historical institution; it had its day of usefulness in its own country; and perhaps in its own country, if it faces the crisis gallantly, it may do some good still. But it can do no good here. It can breed and does breed nothing here but false ambition, flunkeyism, title-hunting, and sycophantic professions. It draws away the hearts of wealthy and ambitious Canadians from their own country to Downing Street and Mayfair. Let it retire to its own land. To sacrifice Canada to its policy and make her a perpetual engine in its hands for preventing the triumph of democracy on this continent is to put her to service which loyalty to her and to humanity as well as good sense abhors. Let British aristocracy, I repeat, do the best it can and live as long as it can in Great Britain; it has no business here. It is said, I believe truly, though it was not reported at the time, that when the Mulock Resolution was put, one very eminent member of the Opposition uttered some manly words and went out of the House. He carried true loyalty with him and left something that was not loyal or true behind. Let British aristocracy withdraw with grace from a world for which it has done nothing, and which has never belonged to it. The Governor-Generalship surely would not be a great loss to it. How can any man of mark or spirit wish to play the part of a figure-head, or, worse still, by the exercise of his mock prerogative to help in loading the dice for a gambling politician?

There might be danger and there might be disloyalty in touching this question if there were on the part of Americans any disposition to aggression. But there is none. If the Americans meditated annexation by force, why did they not attack us when they had a vast and victorious army? If they meditate annexation by pressure, why do they allow us bonding privileges and the use of their winter ports? The McKinley Bill was eagerly hailed by Separatists here as an act of American hostility. Its object was simply to rivet and extend protection, at the same time catching the farmer's vote, for which politicians fish there with the same bait with which Sir John Macdonald fishes here. Of course as there are paper tigers on our side of the line, there are tail-twisters on the other side. One of the most valiant of them, in the person of Senator Ingalls, has just bitten the dust. The tail-twisters have as much influence there as the paper tigers have here, and no more. These suspicions when unjustified are undignified. They expose us to ridicule, while they prevent us from seeing in its true light and settling wisely the great question of our own future.

Those who say that the country is suffering from a bad fiscal policy and from the corruption of government are branded as disloyal. They are charged with decrying Canada by telling this unpleasant truth. Truth, pleasant or unpleasant, can never be disloyal. But let the accusers look back to their own record before 1878, when the opposite party was in power. What pictures of national distress and ruin were then painted! What pessimism was uttered and penned! What jeremiads rung in our ears! Soup kitchens, some thought, were opened not so much for the relief of distress as to present in the most vivid and harrowing manner the state to which Liberal policy had reduced the people. Is it the rising flood of prosperity that is sending so many Canadians over the line? It was disloyal to say that railway monopoly was keeping back the North-west. What do they say about that now?

Is it loyal to turn our Public Schools into seedplots of international enmity by implanting hatred of the Americans in the breasts of children? The Public Schools are maintained by all for the benefit of all, and it is an abuse of trust to use them for party purposes. Nor does it seem very chivalrous to be inveigling children instead of appealing to men. Celebrations of victories gained in byegone quarrels over people who are now your friends are perhaps not the sort of things to which the bravest are the most prone. Wellington and the men who had fought with him at

Waterloo used to dine toget 5 at day. This was very well, especially as those victorious vete: ot crow or bluster. But it forms no
precedent for boastful dem _____as by us, who did not fight at
Queenston Heights or Lundy's Lane. And when this war spirit is got up,
whom are we to fight? The one million of Canadians and their half-
million of children now settled on the other side of the line? All the
British immigrants who have been pouring into the United States during
the last generation? Literally when we take away from the population of
Canada the French and other nationalities, there would be as many men
of British blood on the enemy's side as on ours. "Bombard New York!"
said a Canadian of my acquaintance; "why, my four sons live there!"

Is it loyal to threaten us with settling questions on horseback, in other
words, with military coercion? The English people would not endure
such threats from the commanders of the army which won the Alma and
Inkerman. I heard one of these tirades read out at a Commerical Union
meeting by a tall farmer, who when he had done said, "Now we want no
nonsense"—where-at a number of other tall farmers with deep voices
cried, "Hear! hear!" There is force enough, let us hope, in the country to
vindicate its own freedom of deliberation and its power of self-disposal.
The only effect of menaces such as are sometimes heard will be to make
our people more deaf than ever to the appeals of British Imperialists who
exhort us to maintain a standing army as a safeguard for our independence. Our independence is safe enough from any hostile aggression, and
our liberty is safer in our own hands than in those of warriors who
propose to decide political questions for us on horseback.

I trust that in dealing with American history, I have not failed to do
justice to the United Empire Loyalists. I have classed their devotion with
the character of Washington, and the fortitude of his soldiers at Valley
Forge as the three heroic features of the American Revolution. But there
must be a limit to the claim of their descendants to dictate Canadian
opinion. The children of the U. E. Loyalists are now a small minority of
our population and probably by this time, the exodus having been always
going on, there are almost as many of them on the other side of the line,
as there are on this side. Nor was every U. E. Loyalist exile a martyr to
his allegiance. Not a few owed their loss of country to acts committed by
them during a revolutionary war, for which they would have justly
suffered had they remained at home. Hence Lord Cornwallis, when com-
manding in Ireland, could compare the behaviour of the ferocious
yeomanry there to that of the American Loyalists. Richard Lippincott, for
example, from whom one of the U. E. Loyalist families traces its descent
and derives its claim to consideration, was forced to fly, not on account of
his loyalty, but as the murderer of Huddy, a Whig prisoner of war committed to his hands. Not Washington only, but the British Commanders,
Sir Henry Clinton and Sir Guy Carleton, expressed the strongest indignation at the crime. Washington, failing to get Lippincott into his hands,

selected by lot for retaliation Captain Asgill of the guards, who was saved from execution only by French intervention on his behalf.[2] A pedigree traced to such a Loyalist as this, can hardly entitle any family to special homage, much less to the privilege of indulging in insolence towards its fellow citizens.

Loyalists appeal to the memories of those who fought and fell at Queenston Heights and Lundy's Lane. We also appeal to those memories. Honour to the brave who gave their lives for Canada! As they did their duty to their country then by defending her against unjust invasion, they would now, if they were alive, be doing their duty to her by helping to rescue her from monopoly and corruption. Honour, once more, to the truly brave! Let us build their monuments by all means. We are all as ready as any Loyalist to contribute, if only we may be allowed, to make the memorial, like the joint monument to Wolfe and Montcalm at Que   ble and chivalrous tribute to heroism, not an ignoble record of a   feud, and to grave on it words expressive not of perpetual enmity, but of the reconciliation of our race.

Let us be true to the country, keep her interest above all other interests, personal, partisan, or sectional, in our hearts; be ready to make all sacrifices to it which a reasonable patriotism demands; be straightforward and aboveboard in all our dealings with public questions, and never, out of fear of unpopularity or abuse, shrink from the honest expression of opinion and the courageous advocacy of whatever we conscientiously believe to be good for the community. So long as we do this, depend upon it, we are loyal. . . .

Under the policy which at present prevails, we are constantly sending into the United States the flower of Canadian youth. Do these men become base and hateful, when they cross the line? The two sections of English-speaking people are in a state of social fusion: that is the fact; and with fusion assimilation must come. Some men seem to fancy that they can make themselves English gentlemen by parading contempt for Yankees. Let them indulge the fancy and be happy. But the truth is that if you were taken with your eyes bandaged from Canadian to American society, you would hardly be conscious of the change. One cannot help thinking, when some of our Jingoes are reviling the Yankee, that if we were to quarrel with the United States for the difference between them and the Yankee, it will be the smallest bone of contention that ever set two nations by the ears.

All these imaginary or conventional antipathies, whether political, or social, are apt to betray their unreality as soon as the touchstone of interest is applied. How many Jingoes are there who would refuse a good berth on the other side of the line? Some of the most violent abuse of the

---

[2] See Sabine's *Loyalists of the American Revolution*, II., 18. Sabine, though an American, is thoroughly just and sympathetic.

Continental Policy and party here comes from Canadian Jingoes settled in the United States. Yet these patriots have not scrupled where their own interest was concerned to embrace a policy eminently Continental.

Our book-stores and libraries are full of American literature. Our magazine literature is chiefly American. Not only our intellectual tastes but moral and social character will be in some danger if we are always imbibing the effusions of depravity and baseness.

It is not likely, gentlemen, that I shall ever again address you or any other audience on the subject of Canadian politics. A political student when to the best of his power he has laid a question in all its bearings before the community has done all that it pertains to him to do and must leave the rest to the practical politician. Besides, the sand in my hourglass is low, and before it quite runs out, there are a few things gathered during a student's life which I should like, if I can, to put in shape. I see it is said again that nothing which I write can take hold because I have never shared the national aspirations. There are plenty of other reasons why what I write should not take hold, but as I showed in my first lecture, it is not true that I have never shared the national aspirations. Aspirations for perpetual dependence and colonial peerages with which some bosoms seem to swell, I have not shared; national aspirations I have. If you had time to waste in looking back to the old files of the two great party organs of former days, you will find frequent amenities bestowed on me for sympathizing with what was then called "Canada First." I was singled out for attack, because to attack a newcomer was much safer than to attack some who, though much more prominent, had followings and connections here. As I have said before, I never belonged to the Canada First Association. Membership of a political organization would hardly have become one who had only just settled in this country. But I did very heartily sympathize with the desire of making Canada a nation, which was the vision of my lamented friend Mr. W. A. Foster and the generous youth of Canada at that day; and I gave the movement such assistance as I could with my pen. The movement, however, at that time failed, its flag was suddenly allowed to fall: the star which had risen in the East and which it had followed ceased to shine. Then I, like others, had to review the situation. A community could not become a nation or acquire the national attributes of force, spirit, and dignity without independence. So far the hearts of Canada First had pointed true. But otherwise, was their vision capable of realization? There can be no use in pursuing what is not practicable, however noble or however fondly cherished our idea may be. Was there any real hope of blending into a nation these Provinces, geographically so disjointed, and so destitute of any bond of commercial union among themselves, while each of them separately is so powerfully attracted by commercial interest to the great English-speaking community on the South of it? Was there any real hope of fusing French with British Canada, or if they could not be fused, of bringing about a national union between them? These questions cannot be settled by our wishes or decided on horseback. I found myself compelled to answer both of them in the negative. From that time it has been my conviction that the end would be a return of the whole English-speaking race upon this continent to the union which the American Revolution broke, that to prepare for this was the task of Canadian statesmanship, and that to spend millions upon millions in vainly struggling to avert it was to waste the earnings of our people. All that has happened since has confirmed me in this belief. The difficulty of holding the Confederation together and keeping it apart from the rest of the continent, otherwise than by corruption, has seemed to me half to excuse the system of Sir John Macdonald, calamitous as the consequences of that system have been not only to the finances and the material prosperity, but to the character of our people. Nor, noble as may be the dream of a separate nationality, does it appear to me that our lot will be mean if we are destined to play our full part in the development of civilization on this broad continent, which we hope is to be the scene of an improved and a happier humanity. Let us have hearts for the romantic and heroic past; let us have hearts also for the grand realities of life. There would surely be nothing shameful in a compact like that by which Scotland united her illustrious fortunes with the illustrious fortunes of her partner in Great Britain. There can never be a reason why we should break with our history or discard anything that is valuable in our traditions and, it may be, in our special character as colonists of Britain, who have preserved the tie. In a vast Federal Union there will always be many mansions for character, and Ontario as well as Massachusetts or Virginia may keep her own. To help in making Ontario keep her own character in the literary sphere and in building up her intellectual life, has been my Jingoism, Jingoism of a very mild type it must be owned. Of course I understand and respect: not only do I understand and respect, but I heartily share reluctance to leave the side of the mother country. But we should not in any real sense leave her side by mere political separation: probably we should draw back to her side this English-speaking continent, which it is the tendency of political complications to estrange. To be run politically by a backstairs clique in Downing Street, or by operators in the London railway share market, is not to be at the side of the mother country. England sways us far more by her books than through her Governors. The interest of the British people is one with that of the Canadian people, as the British people begin to see. Their consent to any changes is, by me at least, always supposed. Of the Imperial Federationists I never said a harsh word. I sincerely respect their aspirations. But there are at least three parties among them, that of the Parliamentary Federationists, that of the War Federationists, and that of the Commercial Federationists, each of them at variance with the others, while, after twenty years of eloquent exposition, not one of them has yet ventured on any practical step for the fulfilment of its idea. Let them put the question to one legislature, Imperial or Colonial, and let us see what the answer will be.

I know too well that these opinions are distasteful to many. They are distasteful perhaps to many of my present audience whose thoughts and efforts point a different way. That they are gross and unsentimental, because union with our Continent would bring an increase of the material prosperity to our people, I cannot admit. Political and military sentiment are excellent in their way and within reasonable limits, but there is a sentiment also attached to material wellbeing; it is the sentiment which waits on well-rewarded industry and has its seat in happy and smiling homes. What is the object of all our political arrangements if it is not to give us happiness in our homes? Empire which is not happiness, even though it may be world-wide, is not greatness. However, be my opinions right or wrong, my convictions have been deliberately formed and are sincere. A political student is neither bound nor excused by the exigencies of statecraft. He can serve the community only by speaking, to the best of his power, the truth and the whole truth.

While I, gentlemen, am leaving the scene, you are entering on public life. I would with my parting words conjure you at all events to look facts steadily in the face, and make up your mind one way or the other. You can afford to drift no longer. Whether your highest aim be to live and die British subjects, or to live and die members of an Imperial Federation, or to live and die Canadian freemen and citizens of this Continent, firmly embrace the policy which will lead you to that mark. Your people will not be content always to have poorer chances and to be worse off than their neighbours. They are beginning to signify this in more ways than one, above all by the melancholy token of the Exodus. Both Lord Durham and Lord Elgin told you that it would be so. Both of them said that commercial reciprocity and equality with the United States were indispensable. Blindness to the future often styles itself practical wisdom, but the title is usurped and in no case more usurped than in ours. The Census tells us, with a clear, sad voice, what, if we take no thought for the future, the future is likely to be. For the few who profit by the system there may be large fortunes and baronial mansions in England, where they will win titles and social consequence by making Canada move, or pretending to make her move, in conformity with the interest of an aristocratic party in Great Britain. For the people at large there will be the inevitable fate of a country kept by artificial separation and restriction below the level of its Continent in commercial prosperity and in the rewards held out to industry. There will be a perpetual exodus of the flower of our population to the more prosperous and hopeful field; Manitoba and the North-West excluded from the commercial pale of their Continent and barred against the inflow of its migratory population, will continue to lag in the Census and in the records of material prosperity behind the neighbouring States.

This loss of our active spirits will be attended with a political deadness, such as we already see accompanying commercial depression in those maritime provinces with which under an evil star Ontario has become politically bound up. With the neediness of the constituencies venality and servility will increase, and the grip of corruption will thus become stronger than ever. So things may go on for a long time, the very impoverishment and depletion which the system causes being the evil securities for its continuance. But at last the inevitable will come. It will come, and when it does come it will not be that equal and honourable Union of which alone a patriotic Canadian can bear to think; it will be Annexation indeed.

15

The Protestant Protective Association of Canada: An Example of Religious Extremism in Ontario in the 1890s

James T. Watt

IN THE LATE 19TH CENTURY, religion acted as a divisive factor, separating Canadians and disrupting the fragile national unity of the young Dominion. The two Riel Rebellions, the Jesuit Estates Bill, and the Manitoba Schools crisis all tended to promote militant Protestant feelings on one side of the Ottawa and equally intense Catholic feelings on the other. The early 1890s were years of recession in Canada that tended to promote tension and the search for a scapegoat to explain the country's ills. Some focussed their frustration on the alleged "Popish" conspiracy to subvert the political institutions of the country. These passions were intensified by the Ultramontane movement within French-speaking Catholicism and equally militant ultra-Protestant societies such as the Equal Rights Association and the Orange Order.

This paper analyses the rise and influence of another of these movements, The Protestant Protective Association, which developed in western Ontario early in the 1890s. Mr. Watt brings out clearly the political and social significance of the movement and illustrates vividly the religious and ethnic tensions of Victorian Canada. In considering the nativist elements in the P.P.A., comparison can be made with similar concepts and ideas in the Gagan article on Canada First and the Page article on the Imperial Idea.

T HE 1880s AND 1890s were decades of deep national disunity. Early hopes for the creation of a new Canadian nationality based upon cultural diversity seemed dashed by the political, religious, cultural, and economic bickering. In reaction to what many nationalists believed was the refusal of French Canadians and Roman Catholics to join in the creation of a broad Canadian nationality,[1] the twin theses of anti-Catholicism and Anglo-Saxon racialism, long incipient in Canadian life, burst forth in a flurry of nativistic hostility against the two minorities, both of which seemed to be frustrating the ideal of a homogeneous nation founded on a common language and cultural background, and a general pride in the so-called Anglo-Saxon race. Nativism was the animosity towards a minority group with foreign overtones which, therefore, presented an internal threat to the very life of the nation.

In Canada anti-Catholic nativism found expression in a defensive nationalism, reacting against Catholic allegiance to the Pope. Hence, anti-Catholic nativism exploded to the surface with the enactment of the Jesuits Estates Act of 1889, in which the Quebec Government endowed what many considered was a politico-religious organization, and an enemy of civil and religious liberty, with public funds; to fervid Protestants the endowment of the incarnation of "popish intrigue" was serious enough, but to call in the Pope, as the bill did, to be the final arbiter of the money, threatened the supremacy of the beloved Queen. Manitoba's abolition of the official use of the French language as well as the dual system of denominational schools, inflamed the racial and religious war brought on by the Jesuits Estates Act. The secular school system of Manitoba became a patriotic symbol to ultra-Protestants who saw the demand for disallowance of the act as the efforts of the Ultramontane elements of the Roman Catholic church to extend their influence in the West.

These deep political, cultural, and religious divisions were accompanied by an increasing economic polarization of Canadian society as a wealthy business class grew up behind a protective tariff, creating further cleavages within the two major ethnic groups. Adding further to this economic malaise was the advent of a serious depression during the early 1890s. It is under such conditions that irrationalism comes to have a strong appeal.

The Protestant Protective Association, or P.P.A. as it was commonly called, was a secret, oath-bound, anti-Catholic organization which infil-

---

[1] See David P. Gagan, "The Relevance of 'Canada First,' " Reading 6, for examples of this intolerance.

trated Canada from the United States in the early 1890s. Although originally an American organization[2] it quickly acquired some Canadian characteristics. For six years the P.P.A. carried on a secret campaign to protect the British institutions of Canada against what it regarded as the insidious threat of a foreign power—the Roman Catholic Church. It battled against the Catholic conspiracy by boycotting Catholic-owned businesses and by attempting to drive Catholics out of political life. The P.P.A. rose suddenly to national prominence as a result of its activities in Ontario. It ran candidates in municipal, provincial, and federal elections to the consternation of the national political leaders. Its power seemed so ominous that one Ontario journal predicted civil war or the break up of Confederation if its growth continued.[3] For the historian, however, the importance of the movement lies not in its electoral activities but as an insight into the spirit of an age dominated by religious questions and religious passions.

Anti-Catholic nativism blossomed during the opening years of the 1890s as discontent caused by unemployment and rising prices, and a bewilderment about the deep divisions in the country, caused men to rally against all "foreign elements," of which Roman Catholics and French Canadians were the most prominent, in order to rebuild national unity. With the bonds of this unity strained to the breaking point, the Protestant Protective Association offered a way of championing national homogeneity because it pleaded for a reawakened patriotism and supported the values of nationalism in an explicit way.

Although the P.P.A. was an ultrapatriotic Canadian organization, ironically its birth had taken place in the United States. The centre of power of the American Protective Association, the parent of the P.P.A., was located in the American Midwest, and particularly in Michigan, where William J. Traynor had introduced the association to that state. Traynor's background explains the circumstances behind the entry of the nativistic society into Canada. A Canadian who had been born in Brantford in 1845, Traynor left Ontario and moved to Detroit where, after various publishing ventures, he became publisher of the *Patriotic American,* an organ for anti-Catholicism which supported any organization which offered a hope of defeating "Romanism."[4] Traynor's connections with Canada provided him with a special interest in extending anti-Catholicism into Ontario. As a high-ranking Orangeman,[5] the Detroit publisher must have been acquainted with prominent Orangemen in the Windsor area.

---

[2] For an interesting summary of the American organization see D. L. Kinzer, *An Episode in Anti-Catholicism: The American Protective Association,* Seattle, 1964.

[3] *The Week,* 26 May 1893.

[4] D. L. Kinzer, "The American Protective Association: A Study of Anti-Catholicism," unpublished Ph.D. thesis, University of Washington, 1954, pp. 198–9.

[5] D. L. Kinzer, *An Episode in Anti-Catholicism: The American Protective Association* (Seattle: University of Washington Press, 1964), pp. 92–3.

Probably late in 1891 a branch of the American organization was formed in Windsor as Council No. 1 of the Protestant Protective Association.[6] The chief founder of the Canadian council and its first Grand President, was John H. McConnell, who had served the Protestant cause in the Windsor area through the Orange Order.[7] The P.P.A.'s most prominent member was Oscar E. Fleming, a distinguished Windsor lawyer and the son of a prominent Essex County family. Knowledge of the organization became widespread in Essex County after Fleming, partly on the strength of P.P.A. support, was elected mayor of Windsor in 1892.[8]

In the beginning the P.P.A. was merely a branch of the American organization;[9] thus, the ritual and general principles of the society were taken almost unaltered from the A.P.A.[10] In essence the P.P.A. operated as a secret, ultrapatriotic, nonpartisan organization committed to act against any political party which attempted to win office by catering to the Roman Catholic hierarchy. The P.P.A. did not interfere in any election where the supposed concessions to the Roman church were not an issue; where the alleged "solid Catholic vote" was not a factor, members were free to vote as ordinary citizens. But in every federal, provincial, municipal, or school board election contested between a supposed pro-Catholic candidate and a Protestant candidate, the P.P.A. was to form a solid vote to offset the Catholic influence.

The membership was theoretically supreme in the government of the society; however, the actual power resided with the Grand Executive, consisting of the Grand President, Grand Vice President, Grand Treasurer, Grand Secretary, and Grand Chaplain. Authority descended from this main body to the divisional council, which represented individual lodges, to the local lodge itself.[11]

To achieve membership in the P.P.A., the candidate appeared before

---

[6] The date of the founding of the first P.P.A. lodge in Windsor is in doubt. In an interview with the Grand President, the Rev. J. C. Madill, the *Globe* of Jan. 31, 1894 quoted him as saying it had been in existence at that time for more than two years. The *Sarnia Observer* asserted on Jan. 4, 1894 that the P.P.A. had been in existence in Windsor for three years. Its introduction would have occurred some time late in 1891.

[7] In a speech given on July 12, 1894, at a joint meeting of Orange, A.P.A., and P.P.A. organizations, McConnell boasted publicly that he had "started" the P.P.A. With other members of the P.P.A. present, it is likely that he would have been repudiated if his statement had not been true. This speech was reported in the *Sarnia Observer*, July 20, 1894 and the *Globe*, July 13, 1894.

[8] *Globe*, Dec. 12, 1893.

[9] "The P.P.A. Suit," Toronto *Mail and Empire*, April 7, 1897. In March, 1897, William Harding entered a suit against Grand Secretary Jackson Little to receive payment for lodge paraphernalia supplied to the society.

[10] Public Archives of Canada (P.A.C.), *The P.P.A. in Ontario, History and Principles of the Organization* (n.p., n.d.).

[11] "A Powerful Order," the P.P.A. Convention, Hamilton, 1894, *Mail*, Jan. 25, 1894.

the chaplain of the local council and, with hand on heart, swore never to permit a Roman Catholic to become a member of the society; not to aid the Catholic Church or any of its institutions in any way; not to employ a Catholic when a Protestant was available; to shun controversy with a Catholic on the subject of the society; and, more significantly, to refuse to vote for, or approve the nomination of, a Catholic for public office.[12] The P.P.A. theorized that Roman Catholics were unfit to hold a public or military position, considering them a "subversive" element which owed its first allegiance not to the government of Canada but to "a foreign ecclesiastical potentate." In owing allegiance to the head of the church, who was in effect a foreign ruler, the P.P.A. held that a Roman Catholic became an alien. According to the citizenship laws of the time the society would allow him the right to hold property and therefore be liable to taxation.[13]

With the swearing of this oath, the blindfold was removed, symbolically returning the new member from "mental darkness" so that he made the final vow in full possession of all his senses. With his right hand on the emblem of the Catholic Church, a cross, and his left hand on the "Book of Faith," the Bible, he repeated:

I hereby denounce Roman Catholicism. I hereby denounce the Pope sitting at Rome or elsewhere; I denounce his priests and emissaries and the diabolical work of the Roman Catholic Church, and hereby pledge myself to the cause of Protestantism to the end that there be no interference with the discharge of the duties of citizenship and I solemnly bind myself to protect with all the means in my power, the good name of the order and its members, so help me God, Amen.[14]

In the spring of 1893 a statement of the principles of the P.P.A., representing the political platform of the order, was published in pamphlet form ostensibly to overcome "false misrepresentations":

One—Nationality is not a bar to membership. We ask no man where he was born.

Two—We attack no man's religion, so long as he does not attempt to make his religion an element of political power.

Three—We regard all religio-political organizations as the enemies of civil and religious liberty.

Four—We unite to protect our country and its free institutions against the secret, intolerant and aggressive efforts that are being persistently set forth by a certain religio-political organization to control the Government of the Dominion of Canada, and its provinces, and to destroy our blood bought civil and religious liberty.

Five—We are in favour of preserving constitutional liberty and maintaining the Dominion of Canada.

---

12 "P.P.A. Principles, Proceedings of the Grand Board, Change of Oaths," *Globe*, Feb. 23, 1894.

13 *The P.P.A. in Ontario, History and Principles.*

14 *Ibid.*

Six—We believe in maintaining and extending one general unsectarian free school system and we oppose all attempts to supplant it by sectarian institutions.

Seven—We believe in laws taxing all church property, with the exception of buildings actually used for public worship.

Eight—We believe it perilous to appoint or to elect to civil, political or military offices in this country men who owe allegiance to any foreign king, potentate or ecclesiastical power, or men, whose religion demands that in a conflict between the State and Church, the Church should prevail.

Nine—We believe in establishing such immigration laws as will protect our citizens and labourers from cheap, pauper and criminal labour, which through the instrumentality of European propagandist societies and in this country by the aid of strikes and the subtle influence of priests, are rapidly supplanting our free and educated citizens in every line of industry.

Ten—We believe that there should be an educational qualification to the elective franchise that will require every Canadian citizen to be Canadianized.

Eleven—We believe in putting into office, honest and true patriots, who are best qualified to fill the position regardless of political parties.

Twelve—We believe in the public inspection of all convents, nunneries, monasteries, orphanages, asylums and similar institutions which are in receipt of public subsidies.

Thirteen—We are opposed to any sectarian organization or community engaging in industrial or manufacturing enterprises or pursuits, to the detriment of legitimate capital and labour.

Fourteen—We are opposed to all attempts local or national to use public funds for any sectarian purpose.

Fifteen—We mean to be governed by these principles in our future political action.

Sixteen—Our mission is to awaken Canadians from their lethargy and indifference. "Eternal vigilance is the price of liberty," yet the Protestants of this Dominion have ceased to be vigilant and in conscious strength are either intently chasing the almighty dollar, or quietly dozing while we swiftly drift toward a more tremendous and terrible crisis than this country has yet known.[15]

A comparison of the initiation oaths with the statement of principles reveals that the P.P.A. endeavoured to tone down its public statements, probably to appeal to as broad a segment of the population as possible. To individuals within the shrouded ranks of the society, however, the P.P.A. was anti-Catholic not only in politics but in personal relations.

During the first two years of its existence in Canada the P.P.A. grew steadily, taking root in most of the larger towns in southwestern Ontario. Branches of the dying Equal Rights Association provided a ready-made network of councils, while its members, still aroused by the alleged Catholic conspiracy, likely provided a major source of P.P.A. membership

---

[15] *Catholic Register,* March 30, 1893.

in the early years. From the organization's beach-head in Windsor, where three councils were established, the P.P.A. invaded Sarnia in Lambton County, where Council No. 4 was organized,[16] and then Parkhill in Middlesex, an area which, along with Lambton, became the western stronghold of the organization under the leadership of Dr. Thomas Ovens.[17] Henry Macklin, one of London's most respected and vigorous citizens, helped to organize councils. From this area of the province the P.P.A. quickly made its way eastward to Toronto where Jackson Little, a druggist who served three terms as Grand Secretary, helped to organize councils early in 1892.[18] During this early period two men who became the society's most prominent adherents were elected to public office— E. T. Essery, the P.P.A.'s most effective platform speaker, was elected mayor of London in December 1892,[19] and George Sterling Ryerson, the ablest member of the P.P.A., won the provincial by-election in East Toronto on February 28, 1892.[20] Thus by late 1892 the association had shown surprising political strength in several areas of the province.

Even with these political successes, the P.P.A. was not widely known in 1892. The *Mail,* a newspaper in sympathy with the ultra-Protestant cause, for instance, does not allude to it until as late as December 19, 1892, when it mentioned an interview with a P.P.A member.[21] A. H. U. Colquhoun, an editor of the Toronto *Empire,* a prominent Conservative M.P.P. who later became Premier of Ontario, wrote to his friend Sir James Whitney, prominent Conservative M.P.P., asking him "if you have heard anything down your way of the P.P.A. . . . in my view of profound political import."[22] Although there is no evidence of a reply, the rapid organization of the P.P.A. during the latter part of 1892 makes it likely that Whitney had heard of the new association.

The society surged onto national scene when Sir John Thompson, a Roman Catholic, became Prime Minister on the retirement of Sir John Abbott, November 25, 1892. That a convert from Methodism to Roman Catholicism should ascend to the highest elective office in the country aroused the suspicion and fears of staunch Protestants. The assumption that Thompson, when Minister of Justice, participated in a Roman Catholic conspiracy gained wide acceptance because of his advice to the cabinet on the decision not to disallow the Jesuits Estates Act.[23] The first wave of Protestant extremism stormed against Thompson himself, con-

[16] Ontario Department of Public Records and Archives (P.A.O.), Wallace Papers, newspaper clipping sent by Robert Birmingham to Clarke Wallace, April 16, 1895.

[17] Hamilton *Spectator,* Jan. 5, 1894.

[18] London *Free Press,* March 7, 1893.

[19] *Ibid.,* Jan. 2, 1894.

[20] Ryerson, an opthamalogist, was the son of the Rev. George Ryerson and a nephew of Egerton Ryerson. The *Ryerson Family Scrapbook* (privately held), p. 35.

[21] The *Mail,* Dec. 19, 1892.

[22] P.A.O., Whitney Papers, A. H. U. Colquhoun to Whitney, Dec. 10, 1892.

[23] *Globe,* Jan. 21, 1893.

demning his so-called desertion of Methodism. Dr. George Douglas, Principal of Wesleyan Theological College in Montreal, gave credence to the fear of a Catholic conspiracy by calling Thompson "a clerical creature" and a "lay Jesuit in the Government."[24] In view of the alleged danger to Canadian institutions by a government leader believed to be in league with the Jesuits, many ultra-Protestants sought refuge in the Protestant Protective Association to counter the influence of Rome.

The growth of the P.P.A. during 1893, however, resulted from the fact that many Orangemen became disenchanted and flocked to the P.P.A. when two of their most prestigious officers, Grand Master Clarke Wallace and past Grand Master Mackenzie Bowell, accepted cabinet posts under Thompson, apparently sacrificing the principles of the Orange Order for political office. This dissatisfaction intensified when the ultra-Protestant members of the order were effectively muzzled by the approval of a resolution prepared by Wallace and other members of the pro-Conservative Orange executive that forbade the publication of resolutions passed by local lodges criticizing the conduct of Grand Officers.[25] For one disgruntled member, the Order had become "nothing more than a Tammany society for the Conservative party" and for this reason "thousands of Orangemen are joining the Protestant Protective Association."[26]

During 1893 the P.P.A. did grow rapidly, solidifying its hold on southwestern Ontario while spreading eastward to Peterborough and Belleville and north to Simcoe County and the Muskoka region. In March 1893 the London *Free Press* remarked on "the phenomenal growth of the P.P.A.," estimating its membership at fifteen hundred to two thousand in that city.[27] Toronto bested that total with three thousand members enrolled in twenty lodges.[28] In Belleville the total P.P.A. strength was estimated at one hundred and twenty-five.[29] In Simcoe County the secret society spread to almost all the communities of any importance in the region. As early as December 1893 the Orillia *Packet* estimated P.P.A. membership at two hundred persons,[30] while in smaller centres such as Coldwater,[31] Hawkestone,[32] Severn Bridge,[33] Shanty Bay,[34] and Graven-

[24] J. C. Hopkins, *Life and Work of the Right Honourable Sir John Thompson* (Toronto: United Publishing House, 1895), p. 296.

[25] "The Meeting of the Orange Grand Lodge of Sault Ste. Marie," London *Free Press*, Aug. 4, 1893.

[26] Letter to the editor, *Mail*, Oct. 16, 1893.

[27] London *Free Press*, March 11, 1893.

[28] *Mail*, Jan. 27, 1893.

[29] P.A.C., McCarthy Papers, W. G. Fee to McCarthy, Feb. 5, 1894.

[30] The Orillia *Packet*, Dec. 22, 1893.

[31] *Ibid.*, Feb. 2, 1894.

[32] *Ibid.*

[33] *Ibid.*, March 30, 1894.

[34] The *Northern Advance*, Nov. 9, 1893.

hurst in Muskoka,[35] membership numbered from eighteen to sixty during the early part of 1894. Yet the P.P.A. membership figures cannot be taken at face value, since these statistics were inexact and usually exaggerated. The rapid growth of the organization in Canada was reflected by the fact that it was sometime during 1893 that the P.P.A. severed its ties with the parent body in the United States.[36]

The P.P.A. councils were established by several methods. In some instances members of the Grand Executive were organizers, establishing lodges where and when they could; paid organizers also travelled throughout the province lecturing and assigning charters. Probably the most successful agents were the self-styled "ex-nuns" and "ex-priests" who travelled from town to town presenting anti-Catholic propaganda with a personal touch. Without a doubt the work of Mrs. Margaret Lisle Shepherd, described by the *Catholic Register* as "the foundress of the P.P.A. in Canada" was by far the most successful.[37] An immigrant from Britain, she had arrived in the United States in 1887 and became associated with the A.P.A. In 1892 she travelled to Canada where she began her series of lectures which took her to most parts of Ontario where she helped to inspire the formation of numerous P.P.A. lodges.[38] C. W. Sawers of Peterborough described Mrs. Shepherd as "an exceedingly crafty woman," who, during a meeting in that town, had packed the Opera House and "stirred up the people almost to a fighting state." According to Sawers, Mrs. Shepherd had succeeded in her objective and "that association (the P.P.A.) had already a very large membership not only here but in other parts of the country."[39] As to the effect of the lecturing of P.P.A. organizers, the *Catholic Register* gives vivid testimony:

In every small town and city, neighbours, hitherto friendly . . . are engaged in controversial bickerings. . . . Thus an incipient war of creeds is being waged in almost every district. A new lecturer from Boston or Chicago is imported almost every month to add fire to the flames.[40]

This intensification of anti-Catholic nativism also attested to the increase in the number of P.P.A. councils, evidence of which increasingly appeared in the contemporary press. From spring of 1893, editorials and articles appeared in Liberal newspapers such as the *Globe,* the Sarnia *Observer,* and the Hamilton *Evening Times,* as well as in Catholic

[35] The Orillia *Packet,* Oct. 27, 1893.

[36] University of Toronto Archives, *The P.P.A. in Ontario, being Extracts from the Letters and Speeches of J. D. Edgar,* M.P., (n.p., n.d.).

[37] *Catholic Register* (Toronto), April 27, 1893.

[38] M. J. Brady, *A Fraud Unmasked: the Career of Mrs. Margaret L. Shepherd* (Woodstock, Ontario, 1893).

[39] P.A.O., Wallace Papers, C. W. Sawers to Wallace, Nov. 21, 1893.

[40] *Catholic Register,* May 4, 1893.

weeklies, attacking the principles and membership of the P.P.A. In many cases a vitriolic exchange occurred between these newspapers and the extreme Protestant journals such as the *Mail*, the Hamilton *Spectator*, the Forest *Standard*, and the London *Free Press*, all of which took up the P.P.A. cause. The rival *Globe* and the *Mail* were probably the most active in debating the worth of the P.P.A.

The Liberal *Globe*, edited by John Willison, was particularly interested in exposing the P.P.A. because Sir Oliver Mowat's Liberal government was the target of many of the P.P.A.'s darts. The ousting of Catholics from public office, the *Globe* argued in one of its first attacks, "would only serve to intensify the evil against which the association is striving to contend."[41] With the Mowat government approching an election, the attacks of the *Globe* grew more shrill. Although the movement had probably gained "the support of well-meaning people," nevertheless, the *Globe* asserted, after "very little reflection" no man who supported Confederation could "conscientiously give his adhesion to a set of principles" which intended the exclusion of Catholics from office.[42] The *Globe*'s attacks on the P.P.A. were answered through the editorial columns of the *Mail*, where numerous letters from P.P.A. adherents were published attacking the *Globe* as the "mouthpiece" of Mowat's Liberal administration, a government which ultra-Protestants accused of being linked to the "Romish hierarchy." One letter printed in November condemned the Liberal party in Ontario as "the tool of the priests," declaring that the P.P.A. was founded "to stop this political dealing with the Catholic vote."[43] Another described how the Catholic Church supposedly was able to control the government through the Catholic vote, which could turn "a minority into a majority purely for its own aggrandizement."[44] This propaganda warfare, carried on by the anti-Catholic society, was heightened by the appearance of a P.P.A. leafllet entitled *Facts for Protestant Electors*, which purported to prove, by the use of false statistics, the subserviency to the Catholic hierarchy of both federal and provincial governments, as was shown by the disproportionate number of Catholics in the civil service both in Ottawa and Toronto and by the amount of public funds granted to Catholic charities.[45] This document touched off a further controversy as newspapers in centres throughout Ontario published figures on the number of Catholics and Protestants employed by civic and municipal authorities.

The nomination of a P.P.A. candidate for the provincial by-election in East Lambton provoked a declaration of war from the Liberal party,

41 *Globe*, March 27, 1893.

42 *Ibid.*, Spet. 30, 1893.

43 Letter to the editor, *Mail*, Nov. 25, 1893.

44 *Ibid.*, Dec. 13, 1893.

45 *Facts for Protestant Electors*, excerpts quoted in the *Globe*, Nov. 15, 1893.

which placed its campaign under the direction of J. D. Edgar, a prominent federal Liberal and close associate of Laurier. At the annual meeting of the Toronto Reform Association held in Toronto on November 21, 1893, Edgar condemned the existence of "a new weapon" being used "to stab Sir Oliver Mowat" and denounced the P.P.A. members as "emissaries of bigotry and hate."[46] As part of his campaign against the P.P.A. Edgar wrote several letters to newspapers attempting to allay fears of an unholy alliance between the Catholic hierarchy and the Ontario government and pointing out as well the dangers of a militant Protestantism sweeping the nation. Edgar's letters to the press involved him in a debate with William O'Brien, Conservative M.P. from Muskoka and a follower of D'Alton McCarthy. O'Brien maintained that Edgar's attacks on the P.P.A. were not motivated by principles of tolerance but by political partisanship. To O'Brien's way of thinking the Church was "the scourge of humanity," which kept its people in ignorance, and with the aid of politicians like Edgar was forcing its system on the province of Manitoba and the North West. If the Roman Catholic Church would confine itself to its spiritual functions, and not trade for votes, O'Brien concluded, there would be no need for the P.P.A.[47]

By the autumn of 1893 the Protestant Protective Association had achieved a place of influence. With an organization in most counties of southern Ontario and into some parts of Manitoba and English-speaking Quebec, it was prepared to test its political strength. The P.P.A.'s upset victory in the Ontario by-election of East Lambton and its spectacular success in municipal elections rocked the country and disturbed the national conscience. The *Globe* interpreted the election of P. D. McCallum, the P.P.A. candidate in East Lambton, as not only a setback for Mowat's government, but also a rejection of liberalism in its historic sense.[48] The French language press was also quick to denounce the anti-Catholic society, *Le Monde* partly attributing its formation to a reaction against the Ultramontane party.[49] On the other hand, among English language dailies both the *Mail* and the *Herald* of Hamilton hailed the P.P.A. victory as an important new force in politics.[50] By January 3, 1894 members of the P.P.A. had also been elected to the office of mayor in Brantford, London, Hamilton, Chatham, Kincardine, and Petrolia.[51] The

---

46 *The P.P.A. in Ontario, Extracts from Edgar's Letters.*

47 Letter of William O'Brien to J. D. Edgar printed in the *Mail*, Dec. 13, 1893.

48 Editorial on the East Lambton by-election, *Globe*, Dec. 4, 1893.

49 *Le Monde*, quoted in the *Globe*, Dec. 5, 1893.

50 "A New Political Force," The *Mail*, Dec. 4, 1893; the *Herald*, Hamilton, quoted in the *Spectator*, Hamilton, Scrapbook of Clippings for the *Spectator* and other Hamilton newspapers, Hamilton Public Library, pp. 130–33.

51 *Globe*, Jan. 2, 1894. London *Free Press*, Jan. 2, 1894. Hamilton *Spectator*, Jan. 2, 1894. P.A.C., McCarthy Papers, W. G. Fee to McCarthy, Feb. 5, 1894. N. Robertson, *History of the County of Bruce* (Toronto, 1906), p. 459. *Sarnia Observer*, Jan. 12, 1894.

Montreal *Witness* probably reflected the feelings of many Canadians when it declared:

Wherever they [the P.P.A.] have run candidates of their own or wherever they have taken a special interest, they have carried the day by large majorities. Indeed it is the strength of the majorities which is most significant . . . the general strength of the Association in Ontario is a thing which must be taken into serious account.[52]

As future events were to prove the P.P.A. had reached the peak of its success. Confined to Ontario at first, its notoriety had by early 1894 spread throughout the country, subsequently earning the denunciation of two of the most prominent Canadians of the day, Lord Aberdeen and Wilfrid Laurier. Fearful of ethnic and religious strife in Canada, Laurier had approved of Edgar's speeches and public letters attacking the P.P.A.,[53] and in a speech delivered in Quebec City on January 4, 1894, the federal Liberal leader made a plea for civil and religious freedom. Laurier viewed the theory advanced by the P.P.A. that Catholics could not be good citizens because they owed their first allegiance to the Pope was "positively false." To substantiate his statement he quoted a letter of Cardinal Newman to the Duke of Norfolk which pointed out that while the Pope possessed supreme jurisdiction in spiritual matters, he claimed none in temporal matters.[54] Speaking at the Toronto Board of Trade, Lord Aberdeen did not mention the P.P.A. by name, but spoke on a loftier plane, hoping that Ontario would take the lead in "promoting the broad, tolerant and sympathetic spirit" which he termed "the true and necessary result . . . of civilization . . . and especially of true Christianity." He hoped that nothing would emerge in Ontario that would militate against that "tolerant spirit" which comprised "the best kind of patriotism."[55]

Such viceregal pleas had some effect. Those within the P.P.A. who wished for a moderation of oaths, revealed themselves at the Grand Convention of late January 1894; they demonstrated that the more moderate members had been influenced by the torrent of criticism. The P.P.A.'s third annual meeting convened in the Y.M.C.A. Hall in Hamilton in order to celebrate the victories and to prepare for its expansion in the coming year. The onus was on delegates to formulate policies which would strengthen the organization and increase their power in national politics. Speaking before a group the *Mail* described as "well-to-do solid traders, a number of lawyers and goodly number of intelligent mechanics,"[56]

---

[52] Montreal *Witness,* quoted in the *Mail,* Jan. 4, 1894.

[53] P.A.C., Laurier Papers, Edgar to Laurier, Dec. 25, 1893.

[54] Speech of Laurier at Quebec City, Jan. 4, 1894, quoted in J. S. Willison, *Sir Wilfrid Laurier and the Liberal Party* (2 vols., London, 1903), II, pp. 368–9.

[55] Speech of Lord Aberdeen delivered at the banquet of the Toronto Board of Trade, quoted in the *Catholic Register,* Jan. 11, 1894.

[56] "A Powerful Order," the *Mail,* Jan. 24, 1894.

Grand Secretary Jackson Little announced that the membership had increased from ten thousand to 49,799 organized in 439 councils throughout the country.[57] Beneath the surface, however, lurked differences of opinion which could not be stifled. Those members who had been disturbed by the storm of press criticism concerning the intolerance of the culmination oath whereby a member swore not to employ a Roman Catholic voted to delete it. Many of these moderates believed that the existence of the P.P.A. was justified only if it opposed the political influence of the Roman Catholic Church. Their wishes were not heeded. On the urging of the newly elected Grand President James Cross Madill the ritual was changed so that an initiate swore that he would not keep company with Catholics, a revision which was just as severe as the deleted clause. Another contentious revision of the ritual pledged members to "stand by the principles of this association and . . . loyally support the legal nominee of the order if such there be." In opposition it was argued that under this oath members would be compelled to vote for the nominee of a divisional council, and therefore the action of a few would control the votes of three or four thousand. Both these changes promoted dissension within the P.P.A. which eventually contributed greatly to the destruction of the society.[58]

Soon after the convention it became evident that Grand President Madill's leadership caused discord. One observer in Orangeville had predicted accurately that a Mowat victory in the Ontario election would destroy the P.P.A.'s influence and added: "Ever since the mayoralty contest here they are on the decline in this locality and also generally since they could get no better leader than Rev. Mr. Madill."[59] This dissatisfaction with the leadership of the P.P.A was increased by the provincial election results in June, 1894. The P.P.A. had concentrated all of its energies for two years in attempting to unseat the Mowat government and their failure, despite the election of fourteen P.P.A. members, was bound to depress the rank and file, particularly after the myth of invincibility which had developed after its early political successes. Hence, members complained of "the bungling and mismanagement at headquarters" and singled out Madill as "not large enough calibre to preside over an association of such large proportions as the P.P.A."[60]

The first major defection from the front ranks of the P.P.A. came in November, 1894, after the publication of an interview with Grand Treasurer E. J. McRoberts, the chairman of the London Board of Educa-

[57] "The P.P.A. Convention," *Globe*, Jan. 25, 1894.

[58] "The Complete Ritual, Initiation, Service and Oaths of the P.P.A. as Amended by the Convention of 1894," *Globe*, Nov. 27, 1895. Cf. "Proceedings of the Grand Council, Change of Oaths," *Globe*, Feb. 23, 1894.

[59] Wallace Papers, J. S. Leighton to R. S. White, M.P., Feb. 13, 1894.

[60] Letter to the Editor, *Mail*, July 17, 1894.

tion, in which he brought out into the open the resentment of the dictatorial control held by Madill over the affairs of the P.P.A. Like many other disenchanted members, McRoberts had been alienated at the January convention. He blamed Madill and his clique for introducing "doctrines" which were designed to ostracize individual Roman Catholics. "There is a tendency towards disruption," he declared, "unless a big change is made in the administration."[61] The results of the municipal election of late 1894 seemed to prove the validity of McRobert's prediction. In an editorial the Sarnia *Observer*, a Liberal journal, commented perhaps too hastily, on the declining fortunes of the P.P.A.:

Taken generally throughout the Province the P.P.A. experienced a set-back in the municipal elections. In Brantford, a city that was controlled by the members of that order last year, not one has been left to tell the tale. London wiped out the last trace of it when it left ex-Alderman Coo (prominent P.P.A. member, W. C. Coo) at the foot of the polls, and elected a Liberal Mayor, and even Toronto came within a few votes of electing a Liberal Mayor.[62]

The difficulties and divisions within the P.P.A. were carefully disguised from the public during its 1895 convention held in Toronto in late January. The Grand Executive attempted, through a carefully edited press release, to appear as a harmonious and expanding society. According to this release, the P.P.A. revealed a membership of 100,000 in 908 councils located in every province with the exception of Prince Edward Island. The almost total turnover of officers, however, indicated that all was not well within the shrouded ranks of the society. Of the previous members of the Grand Executive only Grand Secretary Jackson Little was reelected. The Grand Presidency went to Edward S. Busby of Southampton, a former Conservative.[63] Busby's connection with the dynamic D'Alton McCarthy, the powerful leader of the extreme Protestant wing of the Conservative party who was attempting to organize an independent political organization called the McCarthyite League, made the new Grand President an important asset to the P.P.A. and was probably a strong factor in his victory: if McCarthy could be brought into the P.P.A. fold the problem of leadership and respectability would be solved and the diminishing fortune of the P.P.A. might be recouped.

A rapprochement was achieved between the P.P.A. and D'Alton McCarthy during the federal election of 1896. This arrangement, however, was based on terms which benefited the McCarthyite League more than the P.P.A. The document which laid down the plan of attack for the

---

[61] "A P.P.A. Bombshell," *Mail*, Nov. 21, 1894. Cf. London *Free Press*, Nov. 22, 1894.

[62] "The P.P.A. in the Municipal Elections of 1894," Sarnia *Observer*, Jan. 11, 1895.

[63] "The P.P.A. Convention, 1895," *Mail and Empire*, Jan. 26, 1895. Cf. *Globe*, Jan. 23, 1895.

P.P.A. in the election asserted that McCarthy had met with the Grand Executive and had promised to support the P.P.A. platform. Thus, the Committee on Elections naively urged the nomination of joint candidates "wherever practicable."[64] McCarthy had no intention, however, of truly allying with the P.P.A.; an official alliance would serve only to alienate support for his League by associating it with what to many was a disreputable organization.[65] Consequently, McCarthy denied the idea that his organization and the P.P.A. had officially merged by stating in a letter to the *Globe* that he had "nothing whatever to do with" the Circular,[66] although he made it clear that he would welcome the voting support of the secret society providing no strings were attached.[67] His candidates probably received this support.[68]

Despite the P.P.A.'s support of McCarthyite candidates, the election results proved that the vaunted power of the society had almost vanished. Third party candidates of all stripes received a popular vote of 63,000 or 15 percent of the total vote.[69] Only two McCarthyites, including Dalton McCarthy and one member of the P.P.A., were elected, and the latter's victory could not really be attributed to the strength of the organization.[70] The bandwagon years had ended. No longer did the P.P.A. appeal as a mysterious society whose power could manipulate party candidates. The complete collapse of the P.P.A. was graphically revealed in a letter from Grand Treasurer T. M. Ovens to Protestant

---

[64] P.P.A. Circular 226, *Globe*, May 3, 1895.

[65] A letter from the organizer of the McCarthyite League, W. G. Fee, to McCarthy reveals the policy of the League in regard to the P.P.A. Fee wrote that it "will never do to allow the association (i.e. the P.P.A.) to control our work. . . . There is no reason why, by judicious management, that they should do so. We must not play second fiddle to (any) society or organization. With the close of the Local Election in June (the Ontario provincial election of 1894) they will cease to be an officious factor and will fall into line and support us from principles." McCarthy Papers, W. G. Fee to McCarthy, Feb. 17, 1894.

[66] McCarthy's letter to the *Globe*, May 4, 1895.

[67] Fee recommended to McCarthy that copies of McCarthy's speech attacking the use of the French language in Canada be sent to every P.P.A. lodge. McCarthy Papers, W. G. Fee to McCarthy, Aug. 1, 1894.

[68] While McCarthy received P.P.A. support, he also made an arrangement with the Patrons of Industry and the Liberals whereby a number of constituencies in southern Ontario were divided up to avoid splitting the anti-Conservative vote. The revelation of this agreement was made by the disgruntled Patron Grand Secretary, L. A. Welch, who objected to the supposed nonpartisan farmers' organization entering into such an alliance. Welch sent several letters between himself and Grand President C. A. Mallory, which traced the history of the negotiations, to the press. The *Mail and Empire*, June 6, 1896. For other details of the arrangement, see McCarthy Papers, W. G. Fee to McCarthy, July 4, 1896, and Laurier Papers, R. Cartwright to Laurier, Oct. 22, 1894.

[69] E. P. Dean, "How Canada has voted," *Canadian Historical Review*, XXX, 1949, p. 734.

[70] Laurier Papers, P. H. McKenzie to Laurier, July 10, 1896. In this letter McKenzie, the defeated Liberal candidate, suggested that John Tolmie, the P.P.A. winner, also had an endorsement from the Patrons of Industry as well as some support from the Liberal and Conservative organizations.

champion Clarke Wallace suggesting the formation of a new, secret, ritualistic, anti-Catholic association. This new society, according to Ovens, would have none of the weaknesses of the P.P.A. He hoped that its finances would allow the proposed new society to "keep an organizer on the road"; furthermore, by gaining "control of the Conservative Party we would, of course, have the Conservative press by the throat," thus solving the problem of hostile treatment from the press. The other major weakness, the lack of a nationally prominent and able leader, would be solved for the new society by Clarke Wallace, "the Hero of the hour," whom the organization would make "Premier of Canada."[71] Ovens' appeal to Wallace went unheeded. Now reduced to the core of what had once been a well-supported movement, the P.P.A. stumbled on for two more years in relative obscurity.

In the period following 1896 the political atmosphere in Canada altered due to the relative absence of divisive religious disputes and the consequent weakening of the abrasive strains of anti-Catholic nativism. With the final settlement of the Manitoba School Issue and the abandonment of the Ontario Conservative party's "No Popery" campaign,[72] the idea of a Catholic conspiracy seemed less real. The most important factor in allaying fears of Catholic domination, however, was probably the resignation of Premier Oliver Mowat, who accepted the Ministry of Justice in Laurier's new Liberal government. His record of a generous consideration of Catholic interests had won for the Liberal party the support of Ontario Catholics, as well as the resentment of militant Protestants who had interpreted his cooperation as the sign of an unholy alliance with the "Romish hierarchy." No such tie of personal loyalty bound Catholics to Mowat's successor, A. S. Hardy. At the same time Canadians could now concentrate on the burgeoning prosperity that developed during the early years of the Laurier regime.

Without the sustaining conditions of religious strife and racial tension, the Protestant Protective Association could not survive. The P.P.A. revealed its near moribund state in a disastrous court case during the spring of 1896, when some of its members became involved in a lawsuit centring on the responsibility for debts incurred by the organization. This section grew out of an agreement made by John McConnell and J. C. Madill, and Grand Secretary Jackson Little whereby William Harding, a member of P.P.A. Council No. 2 in Sandwich, agreed to supply sets of lodge paraphernalia—a pair of scales, flags, two gavels, and a crucifix—to the P.P.A.; apparently two hundred sets were purchased for a total of $1,500. As Harding had received only $900 he sued Little for the amount outstanding. Little's counsel, former P.P.A. stalwart O. E. Fleming, claimed that the former Grand Secretary was not personally responsible because he was merely carrying out the orders of the Grand Executive.

71 Wallace Papers, Ovens to Wallace, July 15, 1896.
72 P.A.O., Whitney Papers, G. F. Marter to Whitney, Dec. 7, 1894.

The judge, however, ruled in favour of Harding, who was awarded a judgment of $400.[73] Little lost his subsequent appeal, and the action was dismissed without costs.[74] The small amount of press coverage given to the P.P.A. during the trial shows that it no longer caught the interest of the public. The *Catholic Register,* the only journal to comment editorially on the trial, reflected public reaction to the exposure of the P.P.A.: "The P.P.A. dragon is burned. . . . But the post-mortem explanation that took place in the law-courts over the cost of regalia showed that the dragon was stuffed almost from the beginning. . . ."[75]

Although there were periodic press references to the dissolution of the association, there is evidence that the Grand Executive, led by Grand President Busby, continued to exist at least until the court case in 1897.[76] After that time the society dropped from view and very few references to it appeared in the press. The indirect cause for the dissolution of the Grand Executive was probably the revealing evidence of the court case; the direct cause was the appointment of its leader, E. S. Busby, to the Canada Customs Service, an appointment which took him out of the country to Boston and later to the Yukon.[77]

The only trace of the old P.P.A. organization in the provincial election campaign of 1898 appeared in Lambton County where A. F. Gurd and P. D. McCallum, the incumbent P.P.A. members, ran under the banner of the so-called Independence party; however, both defeated by Liberals.[78] Of the original fourteen M.P.P.'s previously elected as supporters of the P.P.A. only five were reelected, all as Conservatives. Referring to the defeat of the two Lambton M.P.P.'s, the *Sarnia Observer* noted that the area had "dealt a death blow to the P.P.A. . . . the disgrace of the surrender of the Lambtons to the fanaticism of that unrespectable (organization) has been wiped out and Lambton can once again raise its head in pride. . . ."[79] It was an appropriate obituary for the Protestant Protective Association, which had shot into national prominence after its first major political victory in that same Lambton County. So ended the Protestant Protective Association in that same county where it achieved its first outstanding political triumphs. As an organization it did not have a lengthy career but it illustrated graphically the passionate religious convictions of many Canadians in the Victorian era.

---

[73] For the P.P.A. trial, see the *Sarnia Observer,* March 26, April 9, 1897; Hamilton *Spectator,* April 10; *Mail and Empire,* April 7, 1897.

[74] *Globe,* Nov. 6, 1897; *Sarnia Observer,* Nov. 2, 1897.

[75] *Catholic Register,* Jan. 6, 1898.

[76] Whitney Papers, A. E. Belcher to Whitney, April 3, 1897.

[77] H. W. Morgan, ed., *The Canadian Men and Women of the Time* (Toronto, 1912), p. 180.

[78] *Sarnia Observer,* Jan. 28, 1898.

[79] *Ibid.,* March 4, 1898.

16

The Conservative Party in the 1890's*

Lovell C. Clark

"It was not the ecclesiastical leaders which Quebec repudiated in 1896," argues Lovell Clark, "but its former Ontario partners." In so arguing Professor Clark has established a position for himself in revisionist historiography, as more and more scholars have come to dismiss the old and liberally comforting Whig view that in the deeply significant election of 1896 French Canadians chose Laurier, one of their own, over the admonitions of their Church. Clark points out that about half of the Conservative candidates in Ontario in fact openly opposed their party's official stand favouring remedial legislation on behalf of the supporters of Roman Catholic schools in Manitoba. The Conservative party of Ontario, he asserts, had in fact succumbed to "militant Protestantism and Anglo-Saxon racialism." The majority of French Canadians thus teamed up with the pragmatic Liberalism of Oliver Mowat.

But Lovell Clark, along with many other younger scholars, also asserts that at the basis of Confederation, as far as the Province of Canada was concerned, lay a limited, extra-legal entente between the two cultures to cooperate together on many national projects, the chief of which was to build a bicultural society in the vast common patrimony which was to be acquired in the North-West. He thereby places himself in the opposite camp from Donald Creighton and the Laurentian school. Clark argues that the Ontario Conservative party, always threatened by its Orange wing, fell prey to it and that the new political alignment under Laurier and Mowat that resulted was not based on Confederation's cultural dualism.

Furthermore, Lovell Clark attempts to redeem Sir Charles Tupper

---

* *The Canadian Historical Association Report* (1961), pp. 58–74.

from the aspersions cast on him by the meddlesome Lady Aberdeen and by Professor John Saywell and other scholars. The result is a lively and important article.

T HIS ARTICLE is an attempt to describe what happened to the Conservative Party in the eighteen-nineties, and, in particular, to offer an explanation for its defeat in the general elections of 1896 that differs somewhat from the explanations commonly put forward. The attempt rests upon a thesis that the Confederation of 1867 was a compact, not in the usual sense of an agreement between separate provincial governments, for this can scarcely be sustained, but in the sense of an agreement betwen two cultures to put their racial and religious differences aside in provincial compartments, and to cooperate on the national plane on certain projects of mutual benefit. Chief among these projects was the acquisition of a vast empire in the west and north. It was part of the compact also that French-speaking and English-speaking Canadians would have an equal right of way throughout the whole of this new domain. The Manitoba Act of 1870 and the North-West Territorial Act of 1875, providing for separate schools and the official status of French as well as English, are sufficient proof of this fact.

The Conservative Party, which had been the first to recognize that Canadian political life rested upon a cultural dualism, was the progenitor of this compact, and under the leadership of Macdonald and Cartier was the faithful guardian of its observance. In the eighteen-nineties, however, the Ontario wing of the Party lost sight of the historic alliance between a tolerant Ontario Toryism and a conservative Quebec, upon which the Liberal-Conservative Party (to give it its full name) was based. More specifically, the Ontario wing of the Party fell prey to what can only be described as militant Protestantism and aggressive Anglo-Saxon racialism, which destroyed the alliance. A new political alignment on the part of Quebec was the result.

It may be objected that the eclipse of the Conservative Party in the eighteen-nineties can be explained without recourse to such a thesis. There were the successive leadership crises following the death of Sir John A. Macdonald; the depressed economic conditions of the first half of the decade; the series of scandals which erupted during 1891 and the years immediately following; and, finally, the troublesome Manitoba school question which plagued the Conservative Government from 1890 onwards. The way in which the Party handled the problem of leadership and the school question illustrates the thesis of this paper. The other two issues—depressed economic conditions and the scandals—do not appear to have had an important bearing on the fate of the Party in 1896.

II

The depression prevailing in the world generally, with consequent low market prices and financial stringency, together with the "exodus" of population to the United States, have tended to obscure the fact that Canada continued to make substantial economic progress during the first half of the eighteen-nineties. Precise figures are lacking, but there is every indication that foreign capital continued to flow into Canada during at least the first four years of the decade,[1] and that, if anything, net capital formation was greater in 1890 than it was in 1900.[2] There was also a healthy growth of secondary industry and of commerce under the aegis of the "National Policy." In short, the policies of Macdonald Conservatism were helping to create the requisite conditions for what a contemporary economist has termed the "take-off period," in which economic growth becomes self-sustaining.[3]

Moreover, it is not generally realized that Canada fared much better during the depression of the eighteen-nineties than the United States and many other countries. Even Liberal journals were constrained to admit on occasion that Canada had experienced far less real distress and had had a remarkable immunity from the financial disasters, and the farm and labour discontent, which had occurred in the United States and elsewhere.[4] It is true that Canadian industry, which was just emerging from a small-shop system to large-scale factory production, was not yet able to absorb fully the labour which was drifting from the farms to the urban areas, and thence to the United States, where opportunities for employment were more varied. The Liberals made much of this "exodus" of population to the United States, but the Conservatives could justifiably contend that reducing or ending protection of Canadian industry would not stop the emigration. It would only deprive Canadians of the opportunity of finding employment in Canadian factories.[5]

The Liberal trade policy of the early eighteen-nineties was both disastrous and illogical—disastrous because it resulted in the Party being tarred with the brush of disloyalty and annexationism; illogical because

---

[1] Jacob Viner, *Canada's Balance of International Indebtedness, 1900–1913* (Harvard, 1924), p. 37.

[2] O. J. Firestone, *Canada's Economic Development, 1867–1953* (London, 1958), p. 112.

[3] W. W. Rostow, *The Stages of Economic Growth* (Cambridge, 1960).

[4] *The Globe*, January 1, 1893.

[5] It is not generally realized that the years of heaviest emigration have been the ones of heaviest immigration as well. Moreover, that throughout much of Canadian history there has been an "exodus." For example, emigration exceeded immigration during 26 of the 33 years from 1867 to 1899 inclusive. See Firestone, *op. cit.*, pp. 240–1.

their policy of "unrestricted reciprocity" with the United States, even supposing it could have been obtained (which is highly doubtful), raised almost insuperable revenue problems in a pioneer country where governmental expenditures to assist economic development were a necessity. The Liberals also remained curiously oblivious to the possibilities of the British market. Canadian exports to Britain continued to greatly outstrip those to the United States until by 1898, the year of greatest disparity, exports to Britain amounted to approximately 68% of the total, while those to the United States were approximately 28%. Liberal obsessions about the "sixty million market" and "the continent to which we belong" were thus being dispelled by the course of economic events. There can be little doubt that the policies of the Conservative Party on tariffs and trade were sound ones which met with the approbation of the Canadian public.

Nor do the scandals seem to have had the adverse effect on the Conservative Party's fortunes that one might have expected. The Public Works scandal, which destroyed Sir Hector Langevin in 1891, was followed by another involving Sir Adolphe Caron and other Conservatives in 1892, and by the "Curran bridge" scandal at Lachine in 1893. Sir John Thompson showed no disposition to be lenient in probing these scandals to the bottom, and his relentless prosecution of some of the malefactors may have helped to assuage any public indignation.[6] One prominent Liberal M.P., William Mulock, confided to Laurier that: "Notwithstanding the slips Sir John made, politics are cleaner for his having been premier."[7] At all events, the Government seemed to survive the scandals without serious loss of public support.

The best evidence that neither the "hard times" nor the scandals seriously affected the Conservative Party's fortunes is the fact that the Party continued to win by-election after by-election in the years following 1891, until by the time of the Parliamentary session of 1895 its majority of thirty-one had increased to sixty-three. The Conservatives sustained a few losses during the succeeding year, but their majority was still fifty-eight on the eve of the general elections of 1896. In summary, out of eighty-four by-elections between the general elections of 1891 and those of 1896, the Conservatives won sixty-two, the Liberals twenty-one, and Independents one.[8] It is clear that the electoral upset of 1896 has to be explained with reference to factors other than those of depressed economic conditions and scandals.

---

[6] Whether there was any, or much, public indignation is of course difficult to determine. Thomas McGreevy, whom Thompson had sent to goal for his part in one of the scandals, was elected for Quebec West in a by-election in 1895 (!)

[7] Public Archives of Canada (P.A.C.), Laurier Papers, 8, Mulock to Laurier, December 14, 1894.

[8] See N. Omer Côté (ed.), *Political Appointments, Parliaments and the Judicial Bench in the Dominion of Canada, 1867–1885* (Ottawa, 1896), pp. 285–294; and *Supplement, 1896–1903* (Ottawa, 1903), pp. 526–528.

III

The successive leadership crises following 1891 were much more important. At the time of Macdonald's death the Party had two extremely able men available in Sir Charles Tupper, the High Commissioner to London, and Sir John Thompson, the Minister of Justice. Tupper declined the pleas of prominent Party members that he accept the leadership, and urged his son, Charles Hibbert Tupper, Minister of Marine and Fisheries, to give his "hearty support" to Thompson.[9] One Party member said that at least three-fourths of the Conservative rank and file in the House of Commons had wanted Tupper for leader. "But small men did not want a *big* leader."[10] That Tupper would have responded to a Party "draft" seems evident from his letter in reply to a flattering one from Dr. George M. Grant, Principal of Queen's University:

> I confess I thought I had some reason to fear that I would be called upon to lead the Party after Sir John Macdonald's death, but was greatly relieved by that responsibility not being placed upon me . . . . I am sure after what I have done for my Party you would not consider it my duty to re-enter Parliament and compel, as I doubt not I could, jealous and ungrateful men who owe their official existence to my efforts to accept my leadership. Besides if I am right in the impression that unrestricted reciprocity with its annexation tendency is dead I am not justified in thus shortening my life.[11]

Sir Charles Tupper obviously did not believe in hiding his light under a bushel (a fault which mars his *Recollections*), but this does not alter the fact that he was a capable and aggressive leader. Dr. Grant felt that the Party had made a great mistake and would have to send for him yet.

Having passed over Tupper, whose capabilities even political foes conceded, why did the Party also pass over the other outstanding man, Sir John Thompson? The explanation of the Party's failure to press the leadership upon Thompson is simple, if sad. Thompson was a Roman Catholic convert from Methodism, and in the swelling tide of militant Protestantism (or secularism, masquerading as such[12]), which seemed to

---

[9] P.A.C., Tupper Papers, 23 (Journal), May 31, June 3, 1891.

[10] *Ibid.*, 9, Donald Macmaster to Tupper, August 14, 1891. (Macmaster's italics). The "small men" were the members of the Cabinet.

[11] *Ibid.*, 7, Tupper to Principal Grant, October 20, 1891.

[12] See John S. Ewart, "Isms in the Schools," *The Canadian Magazine*, July, 1893, pp. 356–366. Ewart makes the interesting suggestion that the main enemy to Roman Catholic schools was not militant Protestantism, but secularism; that it was "the sceptics . . . (not merely those so avowed, but that very much larger class that is practically unbelieving, although still pronouncing the shibboleths) that are the most determined in their hostility to the Catholic religion being taught in the Catholic schools." Ewart may well be right in seeing a disguised secularism behind this "militant Protestantism." The confusion arises from the fact that the proponents of 'national schools' insisted, at the same time, upon religious teaching in the schools.

be engulfing much of English-speaking Canada at that time, such a leader was deemed to be unacceptable, especially in Ontario, where the Orange Order was strong. One prominent Ontario Orangeman, Sam Hughes, who was always proffering Thompson advice, wrote him that "many of our best men" felt that "Sir John is the right man but it is a d—— pity he is a pervert."[13]

When the Governor-General recognized Thompson's manifest merits by calling upon him to form a government, Thompson declined, bowing instead to the "sectarian climate" of the times. "A modest, unassuming man . . . who at the same time leaves an unmistakable impression of ability," as Lady Aberdeen had written,[14] Thompson did not press his claims upon the Party. "I will never forget the unselfish way in which you have sacrificed yourself for the Party," wrote David Creighton, Managing Director of *The Empire*, official Party organ in Ontario. "I believe it was unnecessary, for as I told you, we could have carried things through with you as Premier, even though such men as Dr. Douglas exhibited bigotry, for you would soon live down any prejudice."[15] Nevertheless, Lady Macdonald confided some time later that:

> Sir John Thompson was right to refuse the Headship of the Government. There would have been, I am sure, a stampede of Ontario supporters. It is not so much his religion, as the fact of being a pervert—but he is a tower of strength in his post & really our very best debater.[16]

In the light of such considerations the Conservative Party passed over its two most obvious candidates for the leadership and settled upon Senator J. J. C. Abbott. Seventy years old and in ailing health he had already contemplated retirement, and, moreover, did not want the post. As he himself said at the time, "I am here [as Prime Minister] very much because I am not particularly obnoxious to anybody. . . . Something like the principle on which it is reported some men are selected as candidates for the Presidency of the United States . . . that they are harmless and have not made any enemies."[17]

Abbott was thus a "stop-gap" Prime Minister until such time as the Party could bring itself to accept its first Roman Catholic leader. When,

---

This religious teaching was to be "free from denominational bias." It is arguable that what most of these people were aiming at was simply ethical and moral training, and that the "religious" teaching which they envisaged for the schools was so diluted as to be scarcely religious, let alone Christian.

[13] *P.A.C.*, Thompson Papers, 135, Hughes to Thompson, August 15, 1891.

[14] *Ibid.*, M.G. 27; I; B5; Vol. 6 (Lady Aberdeen's Diary), Sept. 29, 1890.

[15] *Ibid.*, Thompson Papers, 130, Creighton to Thompson, June 17, 1891. Rev. Dr. Douglas, Principal of the Wesleyan Theological College, Montreal, had made scurrilous attacks upon Thompson, denouncing him as a "Jesuit," an appellation he did not intend as a compliment.

[16] *Ibid.*, Tupper Papers, 17, Lady Macdonald to Tupper, November 4, 1891.

[17] *Debates of the Senate*, 1891, pp. 97–98.

nearly a year and a half later, the Party reluctantly accepted Thompson's leadership, it was with the tacit understanding that he associate himself with a prominent Protestant leader from Ontario. It had been strongly urged by many Party members in Ontario that William Ralph Meredith, Provincial Conservative leader, should be brought into the Cabinet, while a smaller number also favoured the inclusion of Dalton McCarthy, Conservative M.P. for North Simcoe. Since Meredith had been "riding the Protestant horse" in the Provincial elections of 1886 and 1890, while McCarthy had been conducting a crusade against the French language and separate schools in Manitoba and the North-West Territories, it was an ominous sign that so many Conservatives should wish to see them in the Cabinet.

Despite his misgivings, Thompson made an attempt to bring Meredith into the Ministry. What stopped the appointment was the opposition of the redoubtable Dr. James Vincent Cleary, Roman Catholic Archbishop of Kingston, who considered Meredith an unpardonable bigot because of his constant attacks upon the Roman Catholic separate schools of Ontario.[18] Thompson thereupon abandoned the attempt to secure Meredith, and settled instead upon Nathaniel Clarke Wallace, M.P. for West York, and Grand Master of the Orange Lodge of British America since 1887.

As one of the "Noble Thirteen" (or "Devil's Dozen"), who had broken Party ranks in 1889 to vote for disallowance of the Jesuit Estates Act, Wallace was expected to fulfill the role of a "Protestant Champion" to balance the Roman Catholic Prime Minister. In fact, however, Wallace proved to be a serious source of weakness. His chief aim was to vie with Dalton McCarthy and the Protestant Protective Association in arousing racial and religious bigotry. More than one member of the Ministry, and many people outside it complained to Thompson about this.[19]

Sir John Thompson was Prime Minister when Protestant extremism and Anglo-Saxon racialism seemed to be irrepressibly obtruding upon the national scene. Confronted with the assault on Roman Catholic separate schools and the French language in both Manitoba and the North-West Territories, Thompson bent over backwards to avoid even the appearance of favouring his co-religionists. It is arguable that in the process he did them less than justice. At the very time when he was being cruelly

---

18 *P.A.C.*, Thompson Papers, 141, Bishop John Cameron to Thompson, November 17, 1891; *ibid.*, 143, James G. Moylan to Thompson, December 20, 1891. Bishop Cameron, Moylan, and others interceded with Cleary at Thompson's request to no avail.

19 *P.A.C.*, Thompson Papers, 179, J. J. Curran (Solicitor-General) to Thompson, March 22, 1893; *ibid.*, 223, Senator Sir Frank Smith (Minister without Portfolio) to Thompson, October 24, 1894. Curran felt that Wallace did not have "the art of making his Yahoos cheer without putting his foot in it," and said that the Government had gone too far in the direction of catering to the *ultra* Protestants; while Smith complained that Wallace was giving the public the impression that the Ministry was composed of "P.P.A. men."

attacked as a "Papist" and a "Jesuit," not to be trusted, by the Protestant Protective Association, and by such men as Rev. Dr. Douglas (Principal of the Wesleyan Theological College, Montreal) and Rev. Dr. Carman (Superintendent of the Methodist Church), Thompson was also being assailed by J. Israel Tarte (Liberal M.P. for L'Islet) as ". . . the instrument of fanatical Protestants and consequently our worst enemy."[20] The first charge was completely unfounded and purely malicious, but the Tarte verdict had a measure of truth. It was the extreme Protestant wing of the Conservative Party in Ontario to which Thompson had surrendered, and which occasioned all his difficulties.

Sir John Thompson's tenure of the leadership was too brief to leave its impress, or to demonstrate whether he could have rallied his Party. Although he lacked the genial personality of Macdonald, and the dynamic nature of Tupper, Thompson was a man of formidable intellect and unquestionable integrity, and a worthy predecessor to Canada's two other Roman Catholic Prime Ministers. It was tragic irony for any Roman Catholic to be Prime Minister at a time when racial and religious bitterness was rending his country and Party. For Thompson, with his agonizing concern to be impartial, it was also a pitiable dilemma.

With Thompson's premature death at the age of 50 in December, 1894, the Conservative Party was faced with its third leadership crisis in as many years. With Macdonald, Abbott, and now Thompson gone, and no other men of remotely equivalent stature in the Cabinet, the choice pointed unmistakably to Sir Charles Tupper, the High Commissioner to London. Despite his seventy-three years, Tupper towered above all his Conservative colleagues in political astuteness, and in the vigour and breadth of his conceptions. That he was not called upon to lead the Government is traceable to two factors: first, the knot of jealous and feuding individuals in the Cabinet, who in pursuit of their own ambitions disregarded the undoubted wishes of the rank and file members of the Party in the House of Commons and the country generally; and second, but by no means less significant, the fact that the office of Governor-General was ". . . held by a man so little fitted for its responsibilities as the Earl of Aberdeen. . . ."[21]

The Earl of Aberdeen had succeeded Lord Stanley as Governor-General of Canada in September, 1893. Both he and his wife, Isabel, had been actively engaged in British Liberal politics and carried their partisanship into Canadian politics. It was not merely that the Countess revealed a marked preference for Laurier and the Liberal Party in her Diary. Such partiality might well have been excused, especially in view of Laurier's personal charm, had it not been manifested on a number of

[20] *The Empire*, August 18, 20, 22, 1894.

[21] Maurice Pope (ed.), *Public Servant: The Memoirs of Sir Joseph Pope* (Toronto, 1960), p. 104.

occasions which proved crucial to the future of the Conservative Party. The partisanship was bad enough, but the Aberdeens had, in addition, a violent and unreasoning dislike of Sir Charles Tupper, whom they were determined to keep from the leadership at all costs. Sir Charles, who admittedly was not an impartial witness, later described Aberdeen as ". . . a weak and incapable Governor under the controll [sic.] of an ambitious and meddlesome woman. . . ."[22] That Aberdeen was an amiable mediocrity, dominated by an able and aggressive woman (to paraphrase Tupper), seems beyond question. The occasions on which the Governor-General's wife was permitted to discuss affairs of state, not only with members of the Conservative Party outside the Cabinet, but with members of the Opposition as well, were too numerous to allow any other conclusion.[23]

The influence of the Aberdeens, on the occasion of Thompson's death, is clear from the Countess' Diary. In discussion with her husband, the two of them decided against George Eulas Foster, the Minister of Finance, as a successor to Thompson. They went on to consider two other possibilities in the Cabinet:

And Mr. Haggart, who is the strongest man is admittedly a Bohemian & also idle—he would probably not serve under Mr. Foster nor Mr. Foster under him. Mr. Mackenzie-Bowell [sic.] himself is 75, rather fussy & decidedly common-place, also an Orangeman . . . but he is good and straight man & he has great ideas about the drawing together of the colonies & the Empire, as was evidenced by all the trouble he took about getting up that Conference.[24]

On the same day the Countess went to console Lady Thompson, who, despite her grief, was able to talk of political matters. In the course of conversation, reference was made to ". . . that old fox Sir Charles Tupper, who has been manoeuvring so finely through all this. He was in truth a bitter enemy of Sir John's & gave him much trouble, & constantly tried to trip him up, to step in his shoes & to make difficulties so as to pave the way either for him or his son." Lady Thompson said that if Tupper were called upon by the Governor-General to head the Government she would consider it an insult to her husband's memory. "I was able to reassure her as to H.E.'s [His Excellency's] intentions about this," Lady Aberdeen wrote in her Diary. "Never if he could help it should Sir Charles be again in Canadian politics. He is another of those who are able mysteriously to provide largely for his sons & daughters."

This fixed determination of the Governor-General to exclude the most

---

[22] *P.A.C.*, Tupper Papers, 18, Tupper to Moberly Bell (of the London *Times*), June 7, 1897.

[23] For one example, see the episode related by Sir Joseph Pope in Maurice Pope (ed.), *op. cit.*, p. 113.

[24] *P.A.C.*, Lady Aberdeen's Diary, December 12, 1894. Bowell, incidentally, was not yet seventy-one.

able Conservative from the leadership had fatal consequences for the Party. Quite aside from the impropriety of such an attitude, and particularly of allowing his wife to divulge it to an outsider, the allegations that Sir Charles Tupper had "been manoeuvring so finely through all this," and that he was "in truth a bitter enemy of Sir John's," seeking to step into his shoes, were completely without foundation. So far from seeking the leadership at the time of Macdonald's death, Sir Charles had rejected the overtures made to him by various Party members and had urged his son to give his "hearty support" to Thompson.[25] If he were "in truth a bitter enemy of Sir John's," then the numerous letters which he wrote to his son, avowing his friendship for Thompson, were a form of deceit one would scarcely expect to find between two so devoted members of a family.[26] If Lady Thompson had in fact expressed such a view of Tupper as the Countess attributes to her, it must be assumed that she was reflecting her late husband's attitude as well. In that event Thompson had been imposed upon by false friends, for the evidence does not bear out the charge.

Moreover, on the occasion of Thompson's death, Sir Charles Tupper revealed no burning desire to "step in his shoes," despite the urging of very influential supporters, including Sir William Van Horne, Richard B. Angus, Sir Donald A. Smith, and Thomas Skinner.[27] Tupper showed no inclination to accede to these pleas, although once again, as at the time of Macdonald's death, he probably would have accepted a clear mandate from the Party that he assume the leadership. Only a few days previously, his doctor had advised him that his heart was "seriously affected," and had forbidden him to accompany Sir John Thompson's body to Halifax on H.M.S. *Blenheim,* or indeed to go as far as Portsmouth.[28] Tupper did say "yes" to his son's appeal that he at least agree to enter the Government, but wrote that ". . . I felt I was signing my own death warrant. I was inexpressibly relieved when the reprieve came."[29]

Such is the evidence of the "old fox" conspiring to depose Sir John Thompson during his Prime Ministership and to clamber into his place

---

[25] A fact which Professor John T. Saywell neglects to mention in his Introduction to *The Canadian Journal of Lady Aberdeen, 1893–1898* (Toronto, 1960). Instead, Professor Saywell prefers to say that Tupper "scoffed" at the idea of giving up the office of High Commissioner in order to succeed Macdonald, "while listing all the reasons which led him to fear that he might expect to be summoned!" (p. xli).

[26] For one example, see *P.A.C.,* Tupper Papers, 17, Tupper to Sir Charles Hibbert Tupper, November 28, 1893.

[27] *Ibid.,* 9, Thomas Skinner to Tupper, December 14, 1894. Skinner, long time financial adviser to the Canadian Government in London, mentioned the ". . . present interesting and supreme crisis in Newfoundland" as one of the reasons why it was desirable to have "an experienced and large-minded statesman" at the head of the Canadian Government.

[28] *Ibid.,* 23 (Journal), December 15, 1894.

[29] *Ibid.,* 18, Tupper to Sir Charles Hibbert Tupper, January 7, 1895.

upon his death. It was with such misconceptions and prejudices regarding Sir Charles Tupper that the Earl of Aberdeen called upon the "fussy & decidedly commonplace" Mackenzie Bowell to form a Government.

The only mystery remaining in connection with Bowell's assumption of power is the willingness of the other members of the Cabinet to accept so tamely a leader whom they obviously regarded as their inferior. Bowell did not succeed in forming his Ministry until December 21st, so that there were eight days in which the Ministers could have refused to cooperate with him and presumably have compelled the Governor-General to make a more satisfactory selection. An explanation for this, although an incredible one, is contained in a Diary entry by the Countess some months later. During a conversation with Sir Charles Hibbert Tupper, Lady Aberdeen complained (on the behalf of her husband of course) about Bowell's "weakness & consequent shiftiness." Tupper told her that the late Sir John Thompson had concluded that Bowell was not fit for Cabinet office and had determined to retire him. Why then had he been Acting-Prime Minister during Thompson's absence in England? Simply because he was the senior Privy Councillor, Tupper replied. Tupper went on to say that when Lady Aberdeen's husband had been appointed Governor-General, Sir John Thompson and other Conservative leaders had feared that he would be very partisan and would do his best to put the Liberals in power. This was why the Cabinet Ministers had accepted Bowell as Prime Minister. They had been meeting one night and discussing how to keep Bowell from the leadership, when a telegram or newspaper item came to their attention stating that one of the Governor-General's aides had been seen with Laurier. "We all turned in like sheep into the fold at the very rumour. We thought it quite on the cards that H. E. would say, 'Well, you have had nearly a week—you evidently cannot form a Government. I will send for someone who can.' "[30]

That the Ministers thought it possible that Lord Aberdeen would have the effrontery to attempt a *coup d'état*, by calling on the Leader of the Opposition Party, which was in a minority of over sixty in the House of Commons at the time, was a tribute either to their naiveté or to the strength of their belief in Aberdeen's partisanship and poor judgment. However improbable the explanation, none other presents itself. The Governor-General and his wife were violently prejudiced against Sir Charles Tupper, the obvious selection, and were determined to exclude him. At the same time, the nucleus of jealous and largely mediocre men in the Cabinet, who doubtlessly did not want a "*big* leader," as Donald Macmaster had commented in 1891, were sufficiently frightened of Aberdeen's partisanship that they acquiesced in a choice which they

---

[30] *P.A.C.*, Lady Aberdeen's Diary, July 18, 1895. Cited in J. T. Saywell, "The Crown and the Politicians: The Canadian Succession Question," *The Canadian Historical Review*, December, 1956.

knew to be disastrous. That it was indeed disastrous is best conveyed in the words of Sir Joseph Pope:

All the chiefs had disappeared with the exception of Sir Charles Tupper, who on Thompson's death should have been summoned without delay, but who for some inexplicable reason was passed over by Lord Aberdeen in favour of Mr. Mackenzie Bowell, a worthy, loyal man, but one as little qualified to be Prime Minister of Canada as Lord Aberdeen was to be Governor-General. Then followed days which I never recall without a blush, days of weak and incompetent administration by a cabinet presided over by a man whose sudden and unlooked-for elevation had visibly turned his head, a ministry without unity or cohesion of any kind, a prey to internal dissensions until they became a spectacle to the world, to angels, and to men.[31]

Under Bowell's leadership the Government staggered from crisis to crisis, until by the time of the Cabinet revolt of January, 1896, Sir Richard Cartwright could exclaim with his usual caustic eloquence:

Sir, as I understand it, we are in the presence of the Royal Ottawa Low Comedy Troupe. . . . What we have been listening to, after all, has been a series of rehearsals. We had number 1 rehearsal . . . a sort of undress rehearsal, as we may call it, in July, when three persons went out, and one of them, being a person of some honour and self-respect, stayed out. Then we have lately had what I may call a full dress rehearsal, when seven members went out, and practically seven came back, because the mere substitution of junior for senior, or senior for junior, really hardly affects the situation, as no one will more frankly admit than the hon. member for Pictou [Sir Charles Hibbert Tupper]. Now these hon. gentlemen being pretty nearly letter perfect, we can have the real performance, which will not long be delayed, when all go out and none come back.[32]

On the occasion of the Cabinet revolt the Aberdeens once again succeeded in keeping Sir Charles Tupper from the Prime Ministership.[33] It was not until April 27, 1896, barely two months before the general elections, that the Governor-General reluctantly called Tupper to the post which should have been his long before. It was well past the eleventh hour. As Laurier said of Tupper years later:

Indeed, it has always been a mystery to me and to those who sat on this side of the House that Sir Charles Tupper was not sent for when the old

---

[31] Maurice Pope (ed.), *op. cit.,* p. 104.

[32] *Debates of the House of Commons,* 1896, Vol. I, p. 75.

[33] *P.A.C.,* Lady Aberdeen's Diary, January 12, 1896. The Aberdeens urged Bowell to reconstruct his Cabinet, rather than to resign as he twice tried to do. It is clear from the Diary that Aberdeen had resolved to call upon Laurier if Bowell failed in his attempt at reconstruction. Professor Saywell seeks to justify Aberdeen (in this resolve) by pointing to the sorry record of the Bowell Administration. (*op. cit.,* p. lxiii) He tends to overlook the fact that it was the Governor-General who had foisted Bowell on the Party and kept him there, despite the attempts of many Conservatives to secure Tupper as leader.

chieftain died. He was sent for at last, but then it was too late. The battle was already lost and notwithstanding the vigour and brilliancy with which he threw himself into the battle, he could not redeem the fortunes of his Party.[34]

Such is the sorry record of the leadership crises which plagued the Conservative Party in the years immediately following Macdonald's death. Sir John Thompson had been kept from the leadership for a time, owing to the Protestant prejudices of the Ontario wing of the Party; and Sir Charles Tupper, who should have succeeded upon the death of Thompson, was excluded until the last moment by the prejudices and partisanship of the Governor-General. This last was of course an historical accident, but the first indicated a deep-seated malaise within the Party itself. This became evident with the advent of the Manitoba school question.

IV

The Protestant bigotry and Anglo-Saxon racialism, which Thompson had bent over backwards to placate and which Bowell was utterly incapable of stemming, continued to erode the Conservative Party, finally shattering it over the issue of Manitoba schools. The school question is much too complex to receive adequate discussion here, but certain points should be made about it.

The first is that the "credit" for starting the agitation in Manitoba in 1889, against separate schools and against French as an official language, belongs almost entirely to Dalton McCarthy and the Equal Rights Association. It has been asserted that there was agitation in the Province prior to McCarthy's arrival, and indeed that the Provincial Government's policy on the school question had been announced before McCarthy's speech at Portage la Prairie on August 5th. This is not so.[35] On the contrary, the evidence suggests that the "triumph" belonged to McCarthy and the "Equal Righters" alone. The motives of Premier Greenway and Attorney-General Joseph Martin in capitalizing on McCarthy's inflammatory appeals to bigotry are, of course, another matter.

It was later alleged by the Provincial Government of Manitoba, as well as by many polemicists on the subject, that the separate schools had been

---

[34] *Debates of the House of Commons*, 1916, Vol. I, p. 586.

[35] Canada, *Sessional Paper 20B*, 1895, pp. 105–6. This contains an account of John S. Ewart's personal confrontation with McCarthy, early in 1895, on this very point. That the Provincial Government had not in fact announced a decision to abolish the separate school system before August 5th, is evident from an editorial in the *Manitoba Free Press* of August 19th, which observed that ". . . it is not yet clear that the Provincial Government has resolved to assail the separate school system. . . ." That the *Free Press* did not consider the agitation to be of local origin is equally obvious from the same editorial, which protested against ". . . Manitoba being made the battleground of Ontario fanatics, who dare not propose the abolition of separate schools in their own province."

inefficient, and that illiteracy was rife among the Roman Catholic populace. These charges were afterthoughts. Since the Provincial Government appointed the personnel of the Board of Education, as well as the superintendents of both the Protestant and Roman Catholic schools, and, moreover, was free to prescribe such secular standards as it saw fit, the responsibility for any inefficiency was clear. In fact, however, Martin thanked the former Board of Education for the "great good" which it had accomplished. "The Government's action," he said, "had not been determined because they are dissatisfied with the manner in which the affairs of the Department are conducted under the system, but because they are dissatisfied with the system itself."[36] Some years later, Senator Bernier said in a Senate debate:

Never, before the Manitoba Government had announced its policy on this matter in 1889, never was any remark made to us about the alleged inefficiency of our schools; never was any suggestion thrown out to us; never was any blame cast upon us; never was a hint given us as to any drawback that was supposed to exist, or as to any improvement that could have been desired.[37]

Another point of interest in the Manitoba school question is the mishandling of the case of the Roman Catholic minority by Sir John Thompson. When the Supreme Court of Canada had unanimously ruled in favour of the minority, and the case was about to be appealed to the Judicial Committee of the Privy Council in England, Archbishop Taché urged Thompson to secure Edward Blake as counsel, along with John S. Ewart, who had acted for the Roman Catholic minority thus far. On three occasions Taché entreated Thompson to engage Blake, pointing out that this was Ewart's desire also.[38]

Thompson had a strong prejudice against Blake, however, and declined to engage him, counting instead upon securing a noted English lawyer, Sir Horace Davey. Thompson assumed that the Dominion Government's firm of English solicitors, Bompas, Bischoff and Company, had a general retainer on Sir Horace Davey which would give the Government first claim upon his services. This proved incorrect, however, for the technical reason that the name of neither the Crown nor the Dominion Government appeared in the title of the Barrett case.

In the end, Sir Horace Davey was retained for the Province of Manitoba, assisted by Dalton McCarthy and Isaac Campbell, a Winnipeg lawyer. The Roman Catholic minority was represented by Sir Richard Webster, assisted by Samuel H. Blake and John S. Ewart. Sir Richard

---

[36] *The Manitoba Free Press*, March 5, 1890, reporting the second reading of the Public Schools Act.

[37] *Debates of the Senate*, 1895, p. 395.

[38] *P.A.C., Thompson Papers*, 140, Taché to Thompson, November 10, 1891; 144, same to same, December 29, 1891; 151, same to same, March 21, 1892.

Webster (later Lord Alverstone) had been displaced as Attorney-General of England as a result of the defeat, at this very time, of the Conservative Government of Lord Salisbury. Webster handled the case of the Roman Catholic minority very poorly, perhaps because his time may have been taken up with the general elections and the ensuing change of government in Britain. According to one source, John S. Ewart expressed the opinion that if the Roman Catholic minority had been represented by Sir Horace Davey, it would have won its case, but that Webster ". . . didn't look at the brief, knew nothing of the case and blundered from start to finish so that Sam Blake could say nothing without contradicting his senior."[39] Taché, who had tried in vain to persuade Thompson to engage Edward Blake, subsequently wrote that ". . . le Gouvernement ne sut pas et ne voulut pas confier cette cause à ceux qui auraient pu la défendre avec le plus grand avantage, et elle fut perdue."[40]

A final point of interest, for the purposes of this paper, concerns the position taken by the Conservative Party on the Manitoba school question prior to and during the general election campaign of 1896. The Conservative Party is commonly represented as having campaigned on a platform which included remedial legislation to restore the rights of the Roman Catholic minority of Manitoba. In the elections the Conservatives lost heavily to the Liberals in Quebec, but gained the largest number of seats elsewhere in Canada,[41] and great surprise has been expressed at the behaviour of French Canada in thus repudiating a Party which was ostensibly seeking to aid the Roman Catholic minority of Manitoba. The usual explanation is that offered by Sir Mackenzie Bowell at the time:

> I have not yet recovered from surprise and astonishment at the returns from Quebec. What does it mean? Have the people in that province thrown off the influence of the Church, or did the desire for a French Premier counter-balance all other considerations? I am somewhat inclined to the latter opinion, race having had more influence with the people than creed.[42]

This view that nationalism triumphed over religion has been echoed by many writers on the election results of 1896. Undoubtedly the desire of many French-speaking Canadians to see one of their compatriots become Prime Minister was a factor, especially since Laurier had engaging personal qualities and was gaining popularity among both French and

---

[39] *P.A.C.*, Thompson Papers, 160, N. C. Wallace to R. S. White, August 6, 1892. (Enclosed in White to Thompson, August 8, 1892). Wallace is quoting what he heard while in Winnipeg.

[40] *Ibid.*, 203,Tach é to J. A. Ouimet, March 14, 1894.

[41] The standing in Quebec was: Conservatives—16, Liberals—49. Outside of Quebec it was: Conservatives—72; Liberals—69; Independents—7 (4 McCarthyites, 3 Patrons). See James G. Foley, *Résumé of General Elections and By-Elections, 1896–1916* (Ottawa, 1916), p. 16.

[42] *P.A.C.*, Tupper Papers, 10, Bowell to Tupper 30, 1896.

English. As an explanation of Quebec's behaviour it is not without some validity, but it is not a sufficient or necessary explanation. At best it requires drastic qualifications.

These qualifications concern the behaviour of the Ontario wing of the Conservative Party. From the very beginning of the school controversy, while the Federal leaders of the Party were moving in the direction of redress of the Roman Catholic grievance in Manitoba, the Ontario members were solemnly warning that the Party in their Province would not tolerate such a course. In the various Parliamentary debates on the school question, the Ontario members made it painfully evident that regardless of the outcome of the second court case (Brophy and Others vs. the Attorney-General of Manitoba), they were opposed to any remedy for the Roman Catholic minority. On one occasion, when it appeared that Bowell might proceed with remedial legislation in the summer of 1895, he was confronted with a "round-robin" signed by a cabal of forty Ontario Conservatives, led by no less a person than the Party "Whip" in the House of Commons.[43]

Nor did this attitude change when the Conservative Government at Ottawa, after long delay and internal dissensions, finally committed the Party to remedial legislation. In the election campaign which preceded June 23, 1896, nearly half of the Conservative candidates in Ontario pledged themselves to vote against remedial legislation, and many of the others gave it only nominal support or else sought to avoid the issue in their campaign speeches.[44]

Moreover, Sir Charles Tupper was apparently obliged to sanction this behaviour of the Party's candidates in Ontario. In letters to local Conservative organizations, he wrote concerning the nominee that ". . . notwithstanding his opposition to the Government on the second reading of the Remedial Bill, he is a tried and true supporter of our general policy, and as such I should be glad to see him succeed at the coming elections."[45] Typical is his letter to E. B. Osler, prominent Toronto lawyer and Conservative candidate in one of the Toronto ridings:

> I was very glad to learn also that you promptly refused to submit to the dictation of the McCarthyites who required you, I understand, to oppose the Government on everything if they brought in a measure to restore the privileges of the Roman Catholic minority in Manitoba which had been taken away from them. I think they should be quite satisfied with your pledge to vote against remedial legislation which is certainly all that they have a right to demand.[46]

---

[43] *Debates of the House of Commons*, 1895, pp. 4196, 4242. The Party "Whip" was George Taylor, M.P. for South Leeds.

[44] Conservative candidates ran in 88 of Ontario's 92 constituencies. Of these, 48 were listed by *La Presse* (3 juin, 1896) as supporters of remedial legislation of the 56 Conservative M.P.'s from Ontario on the eve of the election, 43 sought reelection. Of these, 23 were supporters of remedial legislation.

[45] *P.A.C.*, Tupper Papers, 10, Tupper to Andrew Elliott, April 11, 1896.

[46] *Ibid.*, Tupper to Osler, May 19, 1896.

There is no question of Sir Charles Tupper's sincerity in supporting remedial legislation, but the same cannot be said for some of his principal lieutenants from English Canada. *La Presse* of Montreal, which had the largest circulation of any newspaper in Canada at the time, lauded Tupper for his forthright and courageous declarations on the school question during the campaign, but complained on more than one occasion about the insincerity of some of his Cabinet colleagues, in particular Foster, Haggart, Montague, and Prior. It charged these Ministers with evading the issue of remedial legislation in their speeches, and suspected them of conspiring to eliminate it from the Party's programme. *La Presse* questioned the sincerity of "our Ontario allies," and observed that only a small number of the Conservative candidates in Ontario were prepared to do justice to the Roman Catholic minority of Manitoba, and had the courage to say so.[47]

Thus the commonly accepted view that the Conservative Party campaigned on the behalf of remedial legislation in 1896, is, so far as Ontario is concerned, simply untrue. Whatever the sincerity of Tupper and some of his colleagues, and whatever the pledges made elsewhere, the Party did not stand upon any such plank in Ontario.

In the light of this, the electoral result in Quebec is not at all surprising. The Equal Rights Association and the Protestant Protective Association had cast their spell of bigotry upon the Conservative Party in Ontario. Dalton McCarthy, Clarke Wallace, William R. Meredith, and many other prominent Ontario Conservatives; the Toronto *Mail,* The Toronto *World,* and, to a lesser extent, *The Empire;* all had "fed at the P.P.A. trough."[48] The fortunes of the Liberal-Conservative Party rested upon a tolerant Ontario Toryism in alliance with a conservative Quebec, and the first of these no longer existed. Quebec voted against the Conservative Party in 1896 because of the evident bigotry and the manifest insincerity of the Ontario Conservatives.

The fact that the Roman Catholic Bishops issued a *Mandement* on the subject of Manitoba schools prior to the elections of 1896, has made some Protestant observers quick to see in Quebec's vote on that occasion a check to what they are pleased to term the "aggressiveness" of the hierarchy. The fact is, however, that the *Mandement* was very moderate

---

[47] *La Presse,* 27, 29, 30 mai; 20 juin, 1896.

[48] *The Mail,* owned principally by Charles Riordon and his brother-in-law, Christopher Bunting, long time Conservative, had been the official Party organ in Toronto until 1886, when its anti-Catholic tirades caused Sir John A. Macdonald to withdraw the Government's support, apparently on the representations of Archbishop Cleary. (*P.A.C.,* Thompson Papers, 199 Archdeacon Kelly to Thompson, February 6, 1894.)

The World, violently anti-Catholic and anti-French, was owned by William Findlay Maclean, Conservative M.P. for East York.

The Empire had on occasion done admirable work in combating the bigotry of McCarthy and the *P.P.A.,* but it had stultified these efforts by its support of Meredith in the Provincial campaigns.

in tone (much more so than the pronouncements of Protestant Church councils at the time), and did not operate in favour of the Conservative candidates because their Liberal opponents could (and did) pledge themselves to abide by it. It was not its ecclesiastical leaders which Quebec repudiated in 1896, but its former Ontario partners.

This becomes all the more apparent when one remembers the performance of the Conservative Party of Ontario under the leadership of William R. Meredith, in the Provincial elections of 1886, 1890, and 1894. By his continual attacks on the separate school system, and on the use of French in the schools of eastern Ontario, Meredith had earned the Conservative Party a reputation for bigotry and intolerance. By contrast, the Liberal Government of Sir Oliver Mowat, which had successfully resisted these attacks, emerged as a genuinely tolerant one and a suitable partner for Quebec in a political re-alignment. J. Israel Tarte, the master strategist who helped to guide Laurier and the Liberal Party to victory in 1896, saw this clearly. Writing to Laurier early in 1894, just after Sir John Thompson had refused to disallow the North-West Territories' School Ordinance,[49] Tarte had envisaged the political possibilities as follows:

Si j'étais les ministres français, je tiendrais ferme comme un roc. Sir John Thompson serait obliger de céder. Ses collègues tories d'Ontario se sépareraient de lui—plusieurs d'entre eux, au moins—et nous verrions la répétition de ce qui s'est fait à la Confédération. C'est à dire qu'il se formerait un parti, appuyé sur le Bas Canada et sur le parti Mowat dans Ontario. Le programme de ce parti serait le respect de toutes les races et de toutes les ententes, ou conventions qui ont été la base de la Confédération. Nous écraserions McCarthy et L'Association Protestante. Nous reduirions à l'impuissance le toryisme pour quinze ou vingt ans.[50]

In subsequent letters to Laurier, Tarte reiterated this theme of an alliance between Quebec and the Mowat party of Ontario.

Si vous commandiez à cinquante députés de la province de Québec, vous seriez bien maître de la situation, n'est-ce pas?

Si les évêques avaient du sens politique, ils vous feraient cette majorité, sans bruit.

Je publierai, jeudi, sur le «Cultivateur», un article disant que le temps est venu pour les conservateurs de cette province de rompre avec leurs alliés d'Ontario.[51]

In 1896 French Canada did precisely what Tarte urged. In view of the behaviour of the Ontario Conservatives during the preceding few years, the re-alignment presents no mystery.

---

[49] This Ordinance (No. 22), of December, 1892, seemed to imperil Roman Catholic separate schools.

[50] *P.A.C.*, Laurier Papers, 8, Tarte to Laurier, January 30, 1894.

[51] *Ibid.*, same to same, February 5, 1894.

The militant Protestantism and Anglo-Saxon racialism, to which the Conservative Party succumbed in the eighteen-nineties, remained to plague it long afterwards. In the meantime, the events in Manitoba and the North-West Territories had broken the compact of 1867, and profoundly altered the nature of the Canadian Confederation. The hope of the "Founding Fathers" that French-speaking and English-speaking Canadians would share the new western domain on equal terms was shattered. Henceforth French Canada could feel sure of its cultural rights only within the confines of the Province of Quebec.

17

Laurier and Imperialism*

H. Blair Neatby

In the historiography of imperialism the basic differences
of opinion between French and English Canada have always been evident. But one of the questions which muddies the waters was the curious
ambivalence on imperial issues of Sir Wilfrid Laurier, the French-
speaking Prime Minister. He was opposed to imperial federation but he
often gave eloquent public endorsement to the ideals of the British
Empire. His biographers from Skelton to the present have not explained
this seeming inconsistency. Here Blair Neatby of Carleton University
attempts to explain Laurier's approach in terms of his rational appreciation of the British principles of liberty and justice which he saw reflected
in the empire. Thus a French-speaking Prime Minister could preside over
the sending of Canadian troops to South Africa because he saw the
British effort there as an attempt to uphold these liberal principles.
Laurier, also, felt that these principles of tolerance and political justice
were important for Canadian unity.

In addition to being an explanation of Laurier's imperial ideas, this
article, helps to illustrate his political philosophy which he termed "liberalism." This essay was an outgrowth of the author's excellent Ph.D.
study of "Laurier and a Liberal Quebec" for the University of Toronto,
now being published in the Carleton Series.

A discussion of any aspect of Sir Wilfrid Laurier's career must begin
with the recognition that Laurier believed that the relationship between
the English-Canadian and the French-Canadian societies was the central
problem in Canadian politics. As he wrote to a friend in 1904: "My object

---

* *Canadian Historical Association Report* (1955), pp. 24–32.

is to consolidate Confederation, and to bring our people long estranged from each other, gradually to become a nation. This is the supreme issue. Everything else is subordinate to that idea."[1] It was inevitable that Laurier should focus his attention on the problem of racial harmony within Confederation. As a member of the minority group, and as a leader of a political party which depended upon political support from both racial groups, he was constantly conscious of the need to devise a political policy acceptable to both groups. Even before Laurier became Prime Minister, the Riel crisis and the Manitoba Schools Question had sharply divided Canadians. Thus, when in office, Laurier instinctively considered political problems in terms of avoiding friction between English- and French-Canadians. One such political problem, of direct concern to us, was the question of Canada's relation to the Empire. English-Canadians and French-Canadians differed in their attitude to the Empire, and Laurier had to bear in mind these different attitudes.

To English-Canadians, imperialism was an attitude or a sentiment. Imperialism in Canada had no connection with Marxist imperialism, the "last stage of monopoly capitalism." Monopoly capitalism was not unknown in Canada, but for it Canadians had invented the phrase "National Policy." Nor was Canadian imperialism closely associated with the mission of "bearing the white man's burden." Canadians were too concerned with establishing themselves in North America to become involved in carrying their civilization to others. In Canada, imperialism had a meaning of its own. Broadly speaking, it meant the consciousness of belonging to the British Empire; in practice it meant a devotion to England, the heart of the Empire.

This affection for England took various forms. The most articulate form of Canadian imperialism was based on the assumption of racial superiority; the belief that Anglo-Saxons were destined for world leadership. This vision of a militant Anglo-Saxondom appealed to some English-Canadians, to whom a united Anglo-Saxon Empire seemed preferable to the relative obscurity of an isolated colony. Thus in 1892 Sir George Parkin published a book entitled *Imperial Federation*, significantly subtitled "The Problem of National Unity."[2] Parkin argued that there was already an imperial unity based on the common racial origins of British subjects at home and in the colonies. It was natural for men like Parkin to look forward to/a political union which would reflect this racial unity. Such extreme Canadian imperialists merit attention because they were a vocal group, and to many French-Canadians at least, seemed representative of all Canadian imperialists.

Racial imperialism was not typical of English-Canadians. More com-

---

[1] Public Archives of Canada, Laurier Papers, 92017, W.L. to W. Gregory, 11 Nov., 1904.

[2] Sir George Parkin, *Imperial Federation* (London, 1892).

mon was the imperialism of those bound to the old country by less clearly formulated sentiments. Many Canadians were British emigrants, or sons of British emigrants, who felt a natural affection for their Motherland. Others were nurtured on the traditions of the United Empire Loyalists and so developed a loyalty to Great Britain which was often firmly founded on family or social pride. Added to this was the appeal of patriotic English literature, and especially English poetry, at a time when such literature had no domestic Canadian rival. However intangible and undefined such sentiments may have been, they were ever-present factors to be reckoned with in Canadian politics, as both Macdonald and Laurier knew.

But there was yet another form of Canadian imperialism; another way in which Canadians were conscious of belonging to the Empire and of being indebted to England. And this form is especially relevant because Sir Wilfrid Laurier was such an imperialist. This was the imperialism based on a respect for the principles, and especially the political principles, which Great Britain seemed to represent. To such imperialists, pride in the Empire was based on the belief that the British Empire was the bulwark of liberty and justice in the world. This might be described as intellectual imperialism rather than racial or emotional imperialism. Being a reasoned rather than an emotional attachment to England, it was the most moderate form of imperialism, but it was nonetheless significant.

In French-Canadians, Canadian imperialism evoked much different responses. Appeals to the unity of the Anglo-Saxon race could arouse nothing but repulsion. Indeed, the counterpart of the racial imperialists among French-Canadians was that group of extreme *nationalistes* who looked forward to the creation of a French-Canadian nation in North America.[3] Similarly, the sentimental attachment felt by English-Canadians for the Mother Country was duplicated among French-Canadians by a love for the land of their birth. And the political attitude of French-Canadians was to a large extent determined by their desire for survival as a racial, linguistic and cultural group. Any form of political unity for the Empire would so reduce their influence as to endanger this survival. Many French-Canadians respected and appreciated an Empire in which Canada had been granted self-government, and in which the minority in Canada were given certain guarantees of language, religion and law. Yet even here, their concern was with the preservation of what they considered to be their rights. In view of the Riel episode and the Manitoba Schools Question, it seemed unlikely that their rights would be extended. Thus French-Canadians in general were suspicious of any form of imperialism. Any changes in Canada stemming from devotion to England were not likely to improve their chances of survival.

Sir Wilfrid Laurier had stronger imperialist sentiments than many of

---

[3] See *Québec, La Verité*, 1 June, 1905, for statement by J. P. Tardivel.

his compatriots. Naturally, he too lacked the strong emotional attachment to Great Britain based on the concept of Anglo-Saxon superiority, as well as the sentimental attachment to Great Britain as the Motherland. But Laurier did have a sincere respect for the British political system, and for British political ideals, and even for British society. This respect for Britain is apparent at the outset of Laurier's career. His attitude as a young politician may be illustrated by his famous speech on political liberalism in 1877.

This speech was delivered at a time when the Liberal Party in Quebec was threatened with extinction. The Roman Catholic clergy had virtually identified the Party with the Catholic-liberal movement in Europe, the movement within the Roman Catholic church by which some men had hoped to reach a compromise between the church and the liberal democratic ideas of the mid-nineteenth century, but which had been condemned by the Syllabus of Errors in 1864. And the episcopacy of the Province had openly declared its intention to intervene in politics whenever the sin of Catholic-liberalism was apparent.[4]

Laurier's speech was a reply to the charge of Catholic-liberalism. He of course found it necessary to deny that the Liberal Party still adhered to the anti-clerical policy of social revolution advocated by the *Rouges* in the past. But of more significance was his attempt to distinguish between Catholic-liberalism and political liberalism. His argument was surprising, in view of the continental origin of the problem and the background of the man himself. It must be remembered that the radicalism of the *Rouges* had been transplanted to Quebec from France, that the extreme clericalism in Quebec had its counterpart in France, and that such compromises as the separation of church and state had their advocates in France. And discussing this problem was Laurier, a young French-Canadian lawyer, educated at L'Assomption College, articled to a French-Canadian law firm in Montreal, practising law in a small French-Canadian town, entering politics at an early age; all this was typical of an ambitious French-Canadian of the period. And yet Laurier did not turn to the history of French Canada to defend his political philosophy, he did not claim to be following in the footsteps of Lafontaine or Cartier. Nor did this French-Canadian turn to French sources to support his arguments; he included no quotations from Montalembert or Lacordaire in spite of the fact that these men had written on the similar problem in France. Instead, this French-Canadian included in his speech two lengthy quotations from Macaulay and supplemented them with three verses from Tennyson.[5] Macaulay and Tennyson are not cosmopolitan

---

[4] *Mandements, lettres pastorales, circulaires et autres documents publiés dans le diocèse de Montréal* (Montreal, 1887), VII, 211.

[5] U. Barthe, ed., *Wilfrid Laurier on the Platform, 1871–1890* (Quebec, 1890), pp. 51–80.

literary figures; among historians and poets they seem peculiarly English in their beliefs and prejudices. It is significant that Laurier should turn to them when analyzing the political philosophy of the Liberal Party in Quebec. Even at the beginning of his career he instinctively turned to Great Britain as the source of his political ideas.

In this speech Laurier made it clear that to him, English liberalism represented the principles of liberty and political justice. "Liberty as it has been practised in France has nothing very attractive about it. The French have had the name of liberty, but they have not yet had liberty itself."[6] Laurier attributed political liberty in Canada "to the liberal institutions by which we are governed, institutions which we owe to our forefathers and the wisdom of the mothercountry."[7] In this speech he refers to the achievements of Fox, O'Connell, Grey and Russell to illustrate this political liberty and justice. Twenty years later, on the death of Gladstone, he selected as Gladstone's supreme quality, "his intense humanity, his paramount sense of right, his abhorrence of injustice, wrong and oppression wherever to be found. . . ."[8] Always, Laurier found in English politicians the political principles to which he himself subscribed.

Laurier found much to admire in nineteenth century English liberalism because he too was a nineteenth century liberal in his views on economics, society and politics. A firm believer in the right of private property, he could even express regret that Canada had no constitutional counterpart of the American "due process of the law" clause. "I have often thought it would be well to introduce such an amendment to our own constitution. The provisions of the American constitution protecting the sacredness of contract have been a source of incalculable strength to the union."[9] Laurier even considered that he was a free-trader. The exigencies of Canadian politics or, less cynically, the necessity for a diversified Canadian economy, explained the Liberal tariff policy after 1896, but this did not represent a change in Laurier's economic philosophy. Even in 1909 he could describe himself as "a free-trader sound in theory, but somewhat deficient in practice."[10]

It is worth noting that this emphasis on individual rights did not mean that Laurier was an ardent democrat in the equalitarian sense. Again he found much to attract him even in the social structure of English politics. In 1877 he extolled the peers of England who had sacrificed their privileges for the benefit of their fellow beings.[11] In 1909,

6 *Ibid.*, p. 73.

7 *Ibid.*, p. 78.

8 Canada, House of Commons, *Debates,* 26 May, 1898, p. 6118.

9 Laurier Papers, 161567, W.L. to W. Nesbitt, 3 Nov. 1909.

10 Laurier Papers, 159367, photostat of inscription in book, 1 Sep., 1909.

11 Barthe, ed., *Laurier on the Platform,* p. 65.

during the Parliament Bill controversy, Laurier wrote in almost nostalgic vein about the decline of the English aristocracy. "I am sorry that the aristocracy did not rise to the occasion. The old order of things must give way. It made England very great, but has served its time and must be replaced by the new force which is coming to the front everywhere: democracy."[12] These are the sentiments of a man who himself had the charm, the dignity and the reserve of a *grand seigneur*. Thus Laurier's respect for British political traditions went beyond intellectual appreciation, and even involved a sentimental admiration for the political role of the old Whig aristocracy.

But of greater significance to Laurier was the political aspect of the English liberal philosophy. Laurier's predilections were political rather than economic. And the liberal emphasis on individual rights in the political sphere had a natural appeal to a French-Canadian Liberal. The answer to clerical interference in the 1870's was to be found in the individual liberty of the elector. In 1886, Laurier could defend the Métis of western Canada on political grounds, and so avoid appeals based on race or religion. The French-Canadian emphasis on provincial rights and, later, on minority rights was also a natural development of this liberalism. The French-Canadian minority in Canada was dependent upon the tolerance and the sense of justice of the English-Canadian majority, and these were the very qualities emphasized by liberal philosophy. Nor is it irrelevant that in the early years of his political life, Laurier found himself closely associated with Edward Blake. In spite of the differences in religious and social background and even in temperament, Blake and Laurier were liberals of the same mould. And Blake, more than any other English-Canadian of the period, seemed able to apply these English liberal standards of tolerance and political justice to French-Canadians at a time when racial intolerance was so prevalent. This friendship must have confirmed Laurier's belief that English political principles could provide a solution for the problem of racial harmony in Canada. It was this respect for British political traditions which helps to explain Laurier's attitude to imperial problems in later years.

Laurier's liberal philosophy could not make him an Imperial Federationist. Imperial federation—or any other scheme of imperial centralization—was out of the question for a French-Canadian or for any politician interested in racial harmony in Canada. But also, the principle of individual liberty in imperial relations meant local autonomy. Laurier believed that it was the recognition of the political rights of the separate colonies which had made the survival of the Empire possible. Thus he regarded imperial federation as the negation of the principles upon which the Empire rested. To him it was such a visionary scheme that it bore no relation to practical politics.

---

[12] Laurier Papers, 164110, W.L. to J. Sutherland, 25 Dec., 1909.

In his early years, Laurier even assumed that separation, not centralization, was to be the fate of the Empire. He expected local autonomy gradually to be transformed into independence. But Laurier had no intention of hastening the process. Until English-Canadians and French-Canadians alike could accept independence, he was willing to suppress his view in the interest of racial harmony.[13] And in later years he more willingly accepted Canada's position within the Empire. Separation could be avoided by the preservation of autonomy in the future. It might be argued that this concept of the Empire was no more than the idea of independence in disguise. It seems a paradox to talk of countries being autonomous, and yet being part of an Empire, and it might appear that Laurier had resolved the paradox by accepting colonial bonds only when those bonds became meaningless. But this conclusion cannot be justified. Instead, to Laurier the Empire had a fundamental unity. To Laurier, the imperial connection was based on the rather intangible bonds of a common political heritage and common political ideals; yet these intangible bonds had concrete results when imperial problems arose at the turn of the century. The British Empire could have vitality even without contractual obligations.

Laurier's respect for British political traditions was an essential part of his policy during the Boer War. From the beginning he was convinced that the crisis in the Transvaal was of no concern to Canada. He informed the press that the Canadian militia could not be sent off to South Africa because the war was not being fought for the defence of Canada and that, in any case, nothing could be done until Parliament was summoned to provide the money.[14] But these were only pretexts. Like Sir John A. Macdonald in 1885, Laurier did not believe it was his responsibility to help "Chamberlain and Co." out of a hole. But when it became obvious that English-Canadians believed that the Boer War was of direct concern to them, Laurier had to reconsider his decision. Again he was faced with an issue upon which the two racial groups in Canada disagreed; again he sought a compromise which would at least be acceptable to both groups. The Canadian Government decided to recruit, equip and transport volunteers to South Africa, with the Imperial Government assuming all subsequent expenses.

It seems clear that the decision to send troops, although necessary because of the danger of racial division, was possible for Laurier only because he believed that the Boer War was a just war. With his interest in political liberty and justice, it was natural for Laurier to sympathize with the British subjects in the Transvaal. Months before the war began, he had privately expressed to Governor General Minto his strong sym-

[13] Public Archives of Canada, Lemieux Papers, I, Laurier to R. Lemieux, 1 Dec., 1892.

[14] *Toronto Globe,* 4 Oct., 1899.

pathy for them.[15] To a more cynical correspondent, he could state that, "To me it is clearly and manifestly a war for religious liberty, political equality and civil rights."[16] In Parliament he went so far as to state that he believed "there never was a juster war on the part of England."[17] Since he believed this, the decision to send troops could be determined by a consideration of Canadian interests. Once he recognized that public feeling among English-Canadians was strongly in favor of participation, Laurier was free to accept participation in the interests of national unity. His confidence in the honorable motives of British statesmen had made his decision an easier one.

To illustrate the importance of Laurier's confidence in the British sense of justice it is instructive to contrast his attitude with that of Henri Bourassa. Bourassa agreed wholeheartedly with Laurier's original decision to keep out of the war. But when Laurier changed his mind, Bourassa felt constrained to oppose his leader. Bourassa could not credit British statesmen with such honorable motives as the desire to defend political liberty. Instead, Bourassa saw the war as the result of commercial imperialism; the natural result of the decline of British industrial supremacy.[18] Thus to Laurier the war was an isolated incident; to Bourassa it was the first of many such imperial wars. And so to Laurier, participation would eliminate a cause of friction between the two races in Canada; whereas to Bourassa, participation would set a precedent for future participation in imperial wars. Thus the disagreement between Laurier and Bourassa as to the British motives helps to account for the disagreement with respect to participation. If Laurier had not been an intellectual imperialist, with confidence in the justice of British diplomacy, it would have been difficult for him to accept participation in any form.

The same attitude can be seen in connection with Laurier's naval policy in 1910. Again Laurier would have preferred to avoid the question. At the Colonial Conference of 1902 he had refused to consider a direct contribution to the British Navy, explaining that his Government was "contemplating the establishment of a local naval force."[19] In 1909 his Government was still contemplating. In that year, however, the German naval threat in Europe and the imperial sentiment roused by it in Canada ended the procrastination. The Naval Service Act of 1910 authorized a Canadian Navy, a navy which could only be placed on active service when the Governor in Council decided that a state of emergency had

---

[15] Public Archives of Canada, Minto Papers, XX, 98, 2 May, 1899.

[16] Laurier Papers, 40865, W.L. to L. Gabriel, 6 Jan., 1900.

[17] Canada, House of Commons, *Debates*, 13 Mar., 1900, p. 1842.

[18] H. Bourassa, *Great Britain and Canada* (Montreal, 1902), p. 27.

[19] *Colonial Conference*, 1902, *Minutes of Proceedings and Papers* (London, 1902), p. 74.

arisen; but a navy which could be placed at the disposal of the British Admiralty if the Canadian Government considered it advisable.

In this connection, the crucial point is whether Laurier expected this navy to become part of the British Navy in time of war. It seems clear that, in the event of a major war, he did. We may safely ignore his phrase, "When Great Britain is at war, Canada is at war,"[20] since this was only a legal dictum and gave no guarantee of active participation in such a war. And yet, in spite of Laurier's well known aversion to the "vortex of European militarism," he could agree with the more aggressive Canadian imperialists that British naval supremacy was desirable. And in a speech delivered in Montreal Laurier went even further and stated that Canada should support Great Britain when this naval supremacy was threatened.

Nous ne sommes obligés de prendre part à aucune guerre, mais cependant je déclare que, s'il y avait des guerres—je ne veux pas Messieurs, d'équivoque sur ce point,—je suis ici pour défendre la politique que nous préconisons, s'il y avait une guerre dans laquelle la suprématie navale de l'Empire serait mise en péril, je serais d'opinion moi-même,—et je ne veux pas que d'autres en soient blâmés, parce que j'en prends la responsabilité—*je crois que nous devions aider l'Angleterre de toutes nos forces.* [21]

To understand fully the significance of this statement, it should be remembered that this speech was delivered in October, 1910, during the Drummond-Arthabaska by-election campaign, and was in fact Laurier's campaign speech. At this time Laurier was being denounced by Bourassa and the *nationalistes* as an imperialist. Under these circumstances it is inconceivable that Laurier would have made such a provocative statement if he had not been sincere. Even though it was his policy, that he could make this statement at such a time suggests that Laurier had a quality considered rare among Canadian politicians, that he had the courage of his convictions.

Again the contrast between the attitude of Laurier and Bourassa illustrates how Laurier's respect for the political principles which Great Britain represented, made possible the acceptance of an imperial role for the Canadian Navy. Bourassa still suspected the motives of the British leaders, and so believed that Laurier's policy would involve Canada in wars provoked by the Chamberlains and the Rhodes in England.[22] And so Bourassa could argue that the British Navy was no concern of Canada's; that Canada's only potential enemy was the United States, and that against the United States the British Navy would be of no protec-

---

[20] Canada, House of Commons, *Debates,* 12 Jan., 1910, p. 1735.

[21] A. D. DeCelles, ed., *Discours de Sir Wilfrid Laurier,* 1889–1911, (Montreal, 1920), p. 192, editor's italics.

[22] H. Bourassa, *Le Projet de loi navale* (Montreal, 1910), p. 9.

tion.[23] But implicit in Laurier's policy was the assumption that Great Britain was the bastion of political liberty in the world, and that in a major war the British Navy would be defending the principle of political liberty rather than furthering British commercial interests. Hence Laurier was willing to commit Canada to the defence of British naval supremacy because the navy was a defence of British political principles in Canada too.

Laurier's attitude during the war of 1914–1918 is consistent with this point of view. In the special session of 1914, he reaffirmed his confidence in the motives of the British authorities by describing the war as being fought for freedom, for democracy, for civilization.[24] In 1916, to the suggestion that the war was luring Canada towards imperial federation, Laurier replied that "looking at it from the broader aspect, the triumph of Germany would be the triumph of Imperialism ten times aggravated by German *Kultur*."[25] And even in 1917, when the war was increasing racial tensions in Canada to an alarming degree, Laurier was still able to argue that the various suggestions of a negotiated peace could not be accepted because such a settlement could not secure the principles for which the allies were fighting.[26] Had Laurier been an isolationist, he would surely have favored peace on almost any terms in 1917 in order to avert the conscription crisis. Even Laurier's attitude towards conscription was not inconsistent with this point of view. To Laurier, unity in Canada was still of paramount importance. He rightly believed that conscription would divide the country. Since conscription was unacceptable to the French-Canadians under any circumstances, it would be the negation of British political traditions to coerce them. The necessity of Canadian participation in the war was never questioned, but it should not be at the cost of sacrificing the political principles upon which the "consolidation of Confederation" depended.

Thus our conclusion must be that Laurier was a moderate imperialist. On one occasion he wrote: "I have stated again and again that I was neither an Imperialist nor an anti-Imperialist: I am . . . a Canadian first, last and always."[27] But as a Canadian, vitally concerned with racial harmony in Canada, Laurier found in British liberal traditions the political principles upon which he believed the successful union of the two races could be achieved. To him, the Empire, and more specifically Great Britain, came to represent the bulwark of political liberty. For this reason he could and did oppose any schemes of imperial federation, since such centralization challenged the political liberty of the component parts of

---

[23] *Ibid.*, p. 22.

[24] Canada, House of Commons, *Debates*, 19 Aug., 1914, p. 9.

[25] Laurier Papers, 192951, W.L. to J. Walsh, 31 Aug., 1916.

[26] Laurier Papers, 194414, W.L. to W. Edwards, 11 Jan., 1917.

[27] Laurier Papers, 196799, W.L. to F. Carrel, 24 Aug., 1917.

the Empire. But he was willing to condone Canadian participation in the Boer War because he saw it as a war to enforce political justice, and he was willing to rally to the defence of Great Britain in time of danger because he believed Great Britain would be defending the very political principles upon which the consolidation of Confederation depended. To this extent, Laurier was an imperialist.

18

The Canadian Response to the "Imperial" Idea during the Boer War Years* †

Robert J. D. Page

THIS ARTICLE attempts to break new ground in several directions with regard to the analysis of imperialism in Canada. Up to now the great emphasis has been on political and military matters in the tradition of O. D. Skelton. In this article Mr. Page attempts to switch away from this traditional approach to assess the movement in terms of the social, economic, and intellectual factors which influenced and promoted its rise.‡ The author, also, considers the importance of religion and especially the missionary impulse in the imperial response. He sees a number of moral concepts of Victorian Canada that were deeply involved. Then in looking at Canadian novels and poetry of the period he detects strong elements of Anglo-Saxon racial pride and an adolescent form of English-Canadian nationalism. Finally he considers the role of economics in promoting imperial enthusiasm. Although Canadian action was not determined by economic motives, it certainly was strengthened by them. Businessmen were in search of imperial contracts and politicians of the means for developing Canada. The philosophy of the National Policy was not unrelated to imperial zeal.

---

* *Journal of Canadian Studies* (February, 1970), pp. 33–49.

† This is a revised version of the original article.

‡ See also Carl Berger, *The Sense of Power* (Toronto, 1970), which appeared after this article.

A s CANADA approached the twentieth century there was no single topic which moved Canadians as powerfully and as emotionally as "The Empire." In the Dominion, as elsewhere in the western world, the enthusiasm for and the romantic rhetoric of empire peaked towards the end of the last decade of the nineteenth century; but its influence and the myths it created carried on to bedevil Canadian politics and weaken the fragile unity of the young nation. For English-speaking Canadians the empire engendered a fierce pride which came out in their novels and poetry, their politics and economics, their approach to education and religion. It was, in fact, the embodiment of so much that was enshrined in the ideals of an age. It brought together in a single focus so many of the elements of Victorian society in Canada.

Past Canadian historiography of the imperial movement has suffered from an overly heavy political emphasis, almost excluding its relationship to society in general. Those who interpret this movement in such narrowly political terms see only the visible tip of the iceberg, not its deep underlying base in society itself. It is only here that we find the explanation for much of the fanaticism of the enthusiasts and the reasons for its almost universal acceptance throughout English-speaking Canada. What follows is a first step to open and provoke discussion. I propose to look at imperialism in religious, moral, economic, and intellectual terms as background to its political implications as a divisive factor for Canada during this period.

The expression of Canadian attitudes to the empire in the period prior to 1897 gave few warnings of the exuberance of feeling to come. For the average Canadian there were periodic indications of loyalty but little action and surprisingly little public enthusiasm for anything external to Canada. Britain seemed to have lost interest in the colonies, absorbed in the "little England" philosophy. In economic matters the Dominion had turned sharply nationalist and protectionist in the late 1870's, away even further from the free trade economic doctrines of Victorian Britain. Generally the first thirty years of Confederation was a period of poor economic conditions: even the National Policy proved more appealing politically than stimulating economically. Canadians looked inward, fully engrossed with their internal problems. English and French bickered bitterly and emotionally over the two Riel rebellions and Roman Catholic separate schools in Manitoba. Although this bitterness existed, it in no way related to Canada's position within the empire. Sir John Macdonald's attitude was broadly representative of his countrymen; he gave many expressions of unbounded loyalty to the British connection on the public platform but he was always careful to ensure that nothing was done to strengthen those existing ties. He opposed sending troops to the Sudan at the time of Gordon's encirclement in 1884 and later gave explicit instructions to his ministers to avoid implicating the government in any way in the Imperial Federation movement. When the Colonial Conference of 1887 was called Macdonald sent two minor officials to represent Canada. Generally Macdonald confined his imperial enthusiasm to election rhetoric, such as his 1891 cry that "a British subject I was born, a British subject I will die." For political reasons he tried to portray the Liberals as attempting to sever the relationship with Britain. He emerged, therefore, as a champion of the *status quo* rather than of imperial federation.

In the late 1890's all this changed, with a great explosion of public feeling for the empire. In this process both internal and external factors were involved. The political thought and literature of mother Britain provided an important part of the intellectual diet of Canadians. The works of Dilke, Seeley, Henty, and Kipling were all read avidly by young English Canadians, especially those of an idealistic nature. Kipling in particular had a profound impression on that generation, for he emphasized not only the glories of empire but also its responsibilities; he had the effect on that generation that the folk and protest songs have had on this, and his influence was that much greater because in this respect there was no generation gap to divide young and old. Imperial zeal became the medium for youthful idealism; it became the means whereby youth hoped to improve their world through the spread of British political ideas and institutions. It was, also, closely tied to the intense religious commitment of that generation.

For most Canadians religion constituted the most vital ingredient in late nineteenth century society. Victorian idealism tended to centre around a number of religious and semi-religious movements all aiming for a better world; temperance and imperialism were the most prominent in the late 1890's. Religious passions and prejudices had been kept at a fever pitch since Confederation by the Protestant-Catholic feuds mentioned earlier. By the 1890's, however, the Protestant denominations were experiencing unprecedented zeal for overseas missions. In Canada this interest in Protestantism and imperial enthusiasm came together under the missionary banner. It provided the main ingredient in the Canadian conception of the "white man's burden," which in turn was the English Canadian rationalization for interest and involvement in Africa and Asia.

The desire to bring "Christian civilization" to the heathen and illiterate masses was a much broader concept than merely a spiritual one—it included medical help, education, political efficiency and stability, and trade. None the less its greatest single component—and the one which gave it such an overtone of sanctity and invincibility—was the missionary impulse. Canada throbbed with a sense of Christian expansionism which was exhibited in the religious literature, the periodic mission Sundays, and huge multi-denominational mission conferences such as those held in Toronto in 1902 and 1909 with thousands of delegates attending.[1]

The proud, almost boastful, slogan of these groups was "to evangelize the world in this generation" and many of the strongest supporters of this movement were laymen, not clergy. To the 3800 delegates to the national missionary congress of 1909 the chairman, Newton Wesley Rowell, the aspiring young Methodist and Liberal politician and imperialist, defined Canadian goals with precision. She must convert all within her borders and 40 million in non-Christian lands. This was to be accomplished by sending out 1600 missionaries at an annual cost of $3.2 million. Rowell felt they must recapture the spirit of the crusades in carrying the gospel to the heathen.[2] J. W. Flavelle, a leading Canadian industrialist, was another of the featured speakers at the conference.

The close links between the missionary and the imperial movements were stressed by the representative of the Student Volunteer Movement:

Every issue under discussion at this Congress is an imperial one. And in our various communities and congregations what we shall seek to maintain and develop will be the imperial vision, the imperial ambition, the imperial interest, and let us lay it down as fundamental that this cannot be done unless they are intelligent regarding imperial affairs.

Rowell made a similar point when he linked the work of the Canadian missionaries and that of the great British proconsuls in the field.[3]

The mission theme produced a vast array of popular literature in Canada, the United States, and Britain.[4] The tales of the African martyrs evoked a wide popular response. The works on David Livingstone were of greatest interest. However, even those dealing with lesser figures in the pantheon of African martyrs sold very well in Canada. In 1902 one life of Mackay of Uganda published in Toronto was in its eleventh edition in eleven years[5] and a total of 45,000 copies had sold or been distributed. The sermon literature of the period—a source often overlooked by historians—was filled with imperial themes. Even newspaper comment reflected the fervent idealism of society in general. The Toronto *Globe* emphasized:

These journeyings, martyrdoms, voluntary surrender of self and all the human heart holds dear for the sake of sharing with remote and unsympathetic peoples

---

[1] The two greatest conferences were the Student Volunteer Movement (1902) and the Laymen's Missionary Movement (1909).

[2] N. W. Rowell *Canada's Missionary Congress* (Toronto, 1909), pp. 45–47.

[3] Ibid., pp. 218– and 36.

[4] See *World Wide Evangelism: The Urgent Business of the Church,* The Report of the fourth International Convention of the Student Volunteer Movement, Toronto, 1902, appendix, "Bibliography of Missionary Literature."

[5] "J.W.H.," *The Story of the Life of Mackay of Uganda* (Toronto, 1902).

the Christian ideal and life, from the brightest and most reassuring chapter in the story of man.[6]

Here for the *Globe* as for many Canadians lay the great hope for the future of the world. Their concept of world progress rested on the twin pillars of missions and imperialism. The spread of Christianity and British control and institutions would give the world with a new golden age of peace and development. As one clerical leader as late as the 1920's would claim: "The *Pax Britannica* has helped the on-coming of the *Pax Christi.*"[7]

One of the simplest and most direct ways in which empire supported church missions was in the matter of physical protection. Churchmen were alarmed by the very serious antagonism amongst indigenous religious or tribal organizations which the missionaries aroused by their proselytizing. For instance, in China (where European colonial control had not developed), 150 European missionaries and thousands of their converts were murdered by the rampaging Boxers during the disturbances of 1900.[8] These losses were a serious setback to the mission work in China and seemed to be an object lesson of the need for European control in these areas. Many churchmen saw the close links between the churches and imperialism as important and beneficial for the state. By involving itself, the church could act as a conscience to purify the actions of the state.[9] In London this argument found support in the mission lobby for the welfare of native peoples throughout the empire. On many occasions, this lobby acted as a progressive influence in championing the rights of Africans, Maoris, and others.

In Canada, however, such positive or humanitarian goals seldom appeared in the church's formal efforts to encourage imperial activity. There were no public subscriptions for the relief of the great famine in India, but churchmen did try to marshall opinion in other areas of policy. Formal petitions were sent to the Colonial Office in London on questions such as the South African War when the Protestant churches reflected and possibly promoted the militancy of English Canada. One such petition was from the Protestant Ministerial Association of Montreal, comprising the Anglicans, the two branches of the Presbyterians, the Methodists, the Congregationalists, and the Baptists. The appeal was directed to Joseph Chamberlain, the Colonial Secretary, in October 1899 just after hostilities had commenced in South Africa. The petitioners extolled the strong stand taken by Chamberlain and the Salisbury Government in dealing with the Boers in "the cause of righteousness, justice,

---

[6] The Toronto *Globe*, 25 March, 1899.

[7] J. N. Ogilvie, *Our Empire's Debt to Missions* (London, 1923), pp. 258.

[8] Ibid., pp. 256–260.

[9] Bishop of Stepney, "The Empire and the Church," in C. S. Goldman *The Empire and the Century* (London, 1906), pp. 166ff.

and humanity"; British supremacy was the only route to lasting peace in South Africa. The Association denounced the Transvaal for bringing on the war "with all its inevitable horrors"; they also emphasized the benefit which the war had brought about by demonstrating imperial unity and "brilliant energy of irrepressible imperial service." The clerics felt deeply involved in these questions not only as individuals but also as "preachers of the gospel of peace."[10] At a time when religion was still such a key factor in society the clergy played an important role in moulding public opinion.

Even the Methodists, who had shown pacifist tendencies in the mid- and late-nineteenth century, demonstrated no reservations during the Boer War. At their quadrennial conference in 1902 they supported Chamberlain's war effort because it had been waged "not for greed or conquest, but for freedom, for just and honest government."[11] In English Canada the close links between imperial and Christian expansion blinded many potential critics and destroyed their powers of objective analysis on imperial questions. British imperialism in Africa and Asia became merely an applied form of Christianity, the secular arm for the expansion of Christ's word. This combination gave imperialism much of its intensity of purpose, its unquestioned acceptance in principle and its inevitability in practice. In many eyes it was all part of the divine plan.

It would be wrong, however, to portray all the clerics of Canada as vociferous imperialists; the Roman Catholic clergy of French Canada were the opposite. As one parish priest from the pioneer Lac St. Jean region wrote to Laurier:

Pour l'amour de Dieu faites tout ce qui est possible pour no pas aider Chamberlain dans son injuste guerre contre le Transvaal.[12]

This strident cry of protest was probably representative of the passionate isolationism of so many French Canadians on imperial military questions.

Goldwin Smith, ever a critic of imperialism, summed up the links between the churches and imperialism in the following terms: ". . . the Protestant churches for the most part sought popularity by pandering to the passions for war, the Catholic church so far at least as I saw, abstained and remained neutral."[13] One can question whether the Protestant churches "sought popularity" by pandering to the war spirit, but their support for the imperial movement was unfaltering through the years at the turn of the century. With their deep commitment to missions at the time, their interest in and support for imperial expansion is under-

---

[10] The Protestant Ministerial Association of Montreal to Joseph Chamberlain, 25 October 1899. Co 42/869/479. Public Record Office, London.

[11] J. M. Bliss, "The Methodist Church and World War I," *CHR*, XLIX (1968), pp. 213–214.

[12] Père Trembly, St. Félicien, à Laurier, 10 octobre 1899. Laurier Papers, *PAC*.

[13] Goldwin Smith to Henri Bourassa, 4 December 1902. Gregory Papers, Douglas Library, Queen's University.

standable. When every "Mission Sunday" was an indirect means of promoting imperial enthusiasm, the churches played a crucial role in the development of this enthusiasm in Canada and in giving it overtones of sacred purpose.

In addition to the Protestant churches there were many other groups which showed an almost unanimous commitment to imperial ideas; one of the most interesting was the intellectual community as it then existed. Although this question has yet to be explored comprehensively, a number of tentative conclusions emerge clearly. Of the English-speaking intellectual community only Goldwin Smith, that voluble relic of Gladstonian "Little Englandism," opposed the general enthusiasm within the country; many of the writers, poets, historians, and university professors actively promoted the campaign in spite of the anti-imperial activities of some British and American intellectuals. Among university students the only opposition appeared at French language institutions; universities such as McGill and Queen's had wild demonstrations demanding a strong and militaristic stance for Canada. The Principals of both these universities, William Peterson (McGill) and George Monro Grant (Queen's), were outspoken imperial exponents. The reasoning of many of these intellectuals provides a crucial and interesting insight into the nature of the Canadian response. It deserves serious consideration, for it shows how deeply Canadians felt about imperialism. This feeling arose not merely from blind emotion and passion but from their concept of their past history, their hopes for the future, and their idea of world progress. Some of these intellectuals were not prominent public figures but the popular press often picked up their ideas and gave them wide circulation.

Of the many poets, historians, and novelists who supported the imperial creed, one of the most interesting was Sir Charles G. D. Roberts, who had some claim to being all three. Born in New Brunswick of Loyalist stock, Roberts was influenced in high school by one of his teachers, George R. Parkin. After teaching school himself, in 1883 he became the first editor of *The Week*, a literary journal founded by Goldwin Smith; his tenure was short, however, for he clashed politically with Smith over the founder's annexationist views. Between 1885 and 1895 he taught English and Economics at King's College, Windsor, Nova Scotia, while producing the poetry which established his reputation. During the crucial decade 1897–1907 he spent most of his time writing in the United States, but this did not cool his ardour in any way for Canada and her imperial destiny.

In 1897 Roberts published his *History of Canada*, which combined in a romantic and eloquent fashion the two basic themes of English Canadian patriotism—national pride and imperial enthusiasm. In 1895 he had claimed "a good Canadian Nationalist must be a good Imperialist."[14] a theme, which he stressed in subsequent writing. In his *History* he por-

---

[14] E. M. Pomeroy, *Sir Charles G. D. Roberts* (Toronto, 1943), p. 70.

trayed imperial federation as the logical, almost inevitable culmination of Canada's historic evolution from the "disruption of 1776," through the War of 1812, and beyond. Independence he interpreted as "selfish in its aims," while federation would appeal "to a higher and broader patriotism." He then elaborated on the great paradox of imperial consolidation—federalism and autonomy.

It is possible to conceive of a form of Imperial Federation which would so guard the autonomy of each federating nation and so strictly limit the powers of the central government as to satisfy even those who desire absolute independence. The practical independence enjoyed under such a federation would be secured by the force of the whole empire.

Here Roberts was stressing something fundamental to his contemporaries' understanding of imperial federation. It was a basis whereby the federating nations would relinquish no local autonomy. Roberts avoided any implication of colonial status. The Federating nations would combine to assume responsibility in certain areas still controlled by Britain—such as foreign relations—and the new federal organization would then control these. This very limited concept of imperial federation contrasted sharply with the meaning of the phrase when used by Joseph Chamberlain or others in Britain who hoped to achieve a centralized political structure.

Charles Roberts was concerned, also, about the criticism that any scheme of federation was impracticable because of the distances involved. He rejected this position because of the rapid and continuing improvements in transportation and communications; moreover he added the further simplistic explanation that "it is the fashion of our race to overcome difficulties." Without federation Canadians would not achieve "full political manhood." Roberts, like Sir George Bourinot and other Canadian observers, never produced any detailed scheme of federation. They expected that, like so many other aspects of the British constitution it would slowly and imperceptably evolve.

Roberts' work also reflected the romantic element in imperial writing in Canada. He concluded his analysis of Canadian history with this vision of the Canadian role in imperial destiny:

It would build up such a power as would secure the peace of the world. It would gain for our race such a glory beside which the most dazzling pages of earth's history would grow pale. It is a less daring dream than that which Canada brought to pass when she united the shores of three oceans under the sway of one poor and scattered colony. It is Canada who has taught feeble provinces how to federate, how to form a mighty commonwealth while remaining within the empire. It may be her beneficient mission, also, to lead the way toward the realization of the vaster and more glorious dream.

In Roberts' view the power of a federal empire would ensure world peace; beneath the protective shield of Pax Britannica mankind would enter a new age of peace, stability, and civilization. To many Canadians this was their "idea of progress," their blueprint for human betterment.

This excerpt demonstrates another characteristic of much of Canadian writing at the time—the combined emphasis on the glories of the race and the youthful form of Dominion nationalism. For the young aspiring Canadian the imperial vision provided the opportunity for the achievement of something great, something on a world scale in which Canada could play an important, possibly a crucial role. Public explanations by press and politicians for sending troops to South Africa appealed to the young Canadian searching for a national role on the world stage. The empire offered influence and power to a degree that no small nation on her own could hope to achieve.[15]

Many other Canadian writers promoted such imperial ideas. Sir George Bourinot, Chief Clerk of the House of Commons, George Monro Grant, Principal of Queen's University, George Parkin, Headmaster of Upper Canada College, and George T. Denison, Toronto magistrate and militia officer, were all literate exponents of the imperial creed. Thanks to the work of Carl Berger[16] we have an interesting and clear appreciation of Bourinot's historical works which were appearing at the same time as Roberts' *History*.[17] Bourinot's approach to history reflected closely the nature of his constitutional studies. He interpreted the superiority of the Canadian pattern of constitutional development to the American as a consequence of Canada's British traditions and principles. This hypothesis provided him with a rational basis for his imperial zeal. Like Roberts, he pictured the ultimate culmination of these forces as some form of imperial federation, but he shrank from advancing any detailed plan. Imperial ideas were obvious from the lessons inherent in Canadian history and experience, something internal and precious to the nature of Canadian society. They were not something resulting from external movements and pressures. Bourinot believed that world development moved inevitably to increasingly larger political units. There is a certainty of federation in his works that few can appreciate today.

Another of the intellectual figures who had an influential role in the promotion of the imperial ethic was George Monro Grant, the dapper little cleric and controversial Principal of Queen's University. Grant's importance lay in his pamphlets, his letters to editors, and his personal contacts with many prominent people. He knew both Macdonald and Laurier, was a key figure in the Imperial Federation League in Canada,

---

[15] C. G. D. Roberts, *A History of Canada* (Toronto, 1897), pp. 438–441, revised editions of this appeared in 1898, 1903, and 1909. The influence of this work may be judged by its use in Ontario High Schools as late as 1928.

[16] Carl C. Berger, "Race and Liberty: The Historical Ideas of Sir John George Bourinot," *CHAR* 1965.

[17] *The Story of Canada*, 1897, and *Canada Under British Rule*, 1900.

and was an important religious leader who served once as moderator of the Presbyterian church. Like Bourinot and Roberts he combined national and imperial fervour, which he blended at times with an intense religious commitment. Nationality, he emphasized, was "an ultimate God-ordained fact," and the constitutional evolution of the country was "the very body which the inner life has gathered around it from the past and the present." His commitment to the empire was not based upon any abstract political theory or in any belief that Britain had done much for Canada; he bitterly denounced the lack of support by British diplomats for Canadian interests. But he believed passionately in the purity of British national ideals. In the social, political, and religious spheres they were superior to those of any other nation, and especially those of the American Republic.

Grant's imperial ideas were all the more interesting because his support for Britain was by no means automatic. On the South African problem he corresponded with J. H. Hofmeyr, one of the leading Cape Afrikaners; after the Jameson Raid he expressed publicly his sympathy for the Boer position, because the activities of Rhodes seemed to involve a rejection of what he envisaged as the imperial ideal. However, he switched to supporting Chamberlain's position in October 1899 when the Boer ultimatum to Britain led to hostilities. Now he even pressed Laurier for Canada to send troops. As a nation in the empire, he felt Canada should accept all her responsibilities; he urged his fellow clerics to speak out in favour of a greater national military contribution.[18] For Grant and for many other Canadians, sending troops to South Africa was a visible demonstration to the world of Canada's coming of age, and their achievements, such as at the Battle of Paardeberg, were a matter of great national pride.

Although a leading figure in the Imperial Federation League, Grant had no clearer conception of federation than any of his fellows.

For my part I do not look for any startling constitutional change or any paper scheme for re-organizing the Empire. This is not the way of the British. They build after the fashion of insects that construct coral reefs. . . . They do the duty of today, and that becomes precedent, and so "freedom slowly broadens down," based not on theories but on necessities.[19]

In a way similar to Bourinot's, Grant regarded imperial fervour as a logical growth from the "freedom" of responsible government, but with much less emphasis on race as a factor in Canadian development.

---

18 Grant to Salem Bland, 1 April 1902. Quoted p. 418 Grant and Hamilton, *George Monro Grant* (Toronto, 1905).

19 G. M. Grant, "Introduction" to T. G. Marquis *Canada's Sons on Kopje and Veldt* (Toronto, 1900), p. 6. See also following pamphlets by Grant: *Imperial federation* (Winnipeg, 1890), *Advantages of Imperial Federation* (Toronto, 1891).

Another influential exponent of the imperial ethic in Canada was George R. Parkin, Principal of Upper Canada College and later organizing secretary of the Rhodes Trust at Oxford. In 1892 Parkin wrote an important little volume entitled *Imperial Federation* which was widely read in Canada and throughout the empire. This book is filled with so much of the presumption of the imperial age—the superiority of the Anglo-Saxon race and the Christian religion—that it merits attention. Following the lead of American and British writers of the day, he used Darwinian terminology to explain his racial and political conclusions. The development of the race and its political ideas had been "a steady process of evolution" covering, hundreds of years. He described it in organic terms:

The glory of the British political system is often said to lie in the fact that it is a growth; that it has adapted itself and is capable of continuous adaptation, to the necessities of national development.

But behind the events of history lay a "race characteristic." "A special capacity for political organization may, without race vanity, be claimed for Anglo-Saxon people." Parkin viewed the world situation as a struggle for survival between nations and races, and it would be survival of the fittest. In his view, the fittest were the Anglo-Saxons, but the empire should be consolidated to ensure the result. Parkin did not present this picture merely to emphasize the brute power and the political glory of the Anglo-Saxons but to challenge their sense of responsibility. He stressed: "To the Christian, the moralist, the philanthropist, no inspiration could be greater" than to realize that this growing strength and energy of the empire might be harnessed for the "world's good." The empire stood as no other in history "on that borderland where civilization confronts barbarism." Not even classical Rome could claim a parallel range of influence.[20]

Parkin's "racial" analysis of the contemporary world included commentary on his French-speaking compatriots. In his view French Canadians were a great hindrance to the modern development of Canada. "One has no hesitation in discussing frankly this question of race inertia in Quebec. The most clear-sighted men of the province admit and deplore it." Les Québeçois were "a simple and docile" people if left to themselves, but they were capable of being stirred to sudden "unreasoning" fury by their clerical and lay leaders. Parkin hoped the latter would lead them from "narrow, bigoted, and isolated" ways. He noted in passing that Laurier was "free from some of the most inveterate preju-

---

[20] G. R. Parkin, *Imperial Federation* (London, 1892), pp. 1–4, 46–48. The term "race" had a very broad meaning in the 1890's and included what we would call ethnic divisions. For instance André Siegfried in his book *The Race Question in Canada* analyses the English-French split.

dices of his compatriots."[21] Though never stated, the underlying assumption seemed to be that only through anglicization could French-speaking Canadians overcome their racial and cultural inferiority.

Naturally such writings were anathema to French Canada, and newspapers such as *La Patrie* were quick to respond. Their suspicions were, also, aroused by the activities of men who were influential in the imperial federation movement. D'Alton McCarthy, well known for his anti-French, anti-Catholic tirades on the Manitoba Schools issue, was President of the Imperial Federation League in Canada. Thus, although this imperial organization had nothing whatever to do with anti-French projects, the actions of some of the leading members in other fields tainted the whole movement in the eyes of French Canadians. In addition the underlying assumptions of the imperial movement with its great emphasis on Canada as a "British" nation seemed to threaten "la survivance,"[22] and imperial issues clearly demonstrated the weakness of French-speaking M.P.'s when faced with an aroused English majority in Ottawa. As the crisis over the sending of contingents to the Boer War showed, even a French-speaking premier could not stem that determined flood. Thus the interpretative writings of Roberts, Grant, and Parkin illustrate some of the intellectual ingredients as well as the passion which Canadians experienced for their "empire."

Canadian novels and novelists also reflected a commitment to the imperial ideal. Gilbert Parker in his writing and in his speeches during his trips back to Canada often gave eloquent expression to them. But probably the most interesting and revealing novel was *The Imperialist* by Sarah Jeannette Duncan. Born and educated in Brantford, Ontario, she made this town the setting for her work published in 1904. It contains realistic social analysis of "small town" Ontario and of its reaction to the imperial idea. *The Imperialist* suggests the key role of politics and religion—the two passions and distractions for most Canadians during the Victorian years. From this novel it is apparent that the author was an ardent imperial supporter; but this alone does not explain the strength or the interest in the work. In Duncan's eyes the imperial movement became the embodiment of many aspects of society and a reflection of the *mores* of Victorian Canada.

Lorne Murchison, the central figure of *The Imperialist*, is an able young politician and a fervent exponent of the new imperialism. Typical of some Canadians of the time, however, he is far more concerned with imperialism as a force for moulding Canadian development than as a means of British expansion in Africa or Asia. He exhibits clearly his

---

[21] G. R. Parkin, *The Great Dominion* (London, 1895), pp. 135–144. Similar views were expressed by the poet Wilfred Campbell. (See Carl Klinck, *Wilfred Campbell*, p. 190.)

[22] *La Presse* (Montreal), 23 septembre, 1901.

determination to see Canada develop as a *British* nation with a strict social and political morality. Prior to a trip to London he attempts to explain his feelings:

We're all right out here, but we're young and thin and weedy. They did not grow so fast in England, to begin with, and now they're rich with character and strong with conduct and hoary with ideals. I've been reading up the history of our political relations with England. It's astonishing what we've stuck to her through, but you can't help seeing why—it's for the moral advantage. Way down at the bottom, that's what it is. We have the sense to want all we can get of that sort of thing. They've developed the finest human product there is, the cleanest the most disinterested, and we want to keep up the relationship—it's important.

To Murchison this was the crucial ingredient in the Canadian fervour rather than imperial defence protection.[23] Murchison's zeal approached that of a religious mystic while his emphasis on moral superiority suited the moral tone of Victorian society in Canada.[24]

Murchison's commitment to British ideals, however, did not blunt his criticism of aspects of British society which he felt warranted it. Because imperial influences must be reciprocal, he saw a positive role for Canada as a conscience and a refining influence on Britain. Without class lines and with a superior educational system, Canada could inspire the motherland especially in economic matters. Murchison explained some Canadian feelings of superiority to an English friend. "Industrial energy is deserting this country; and you have no large movement, no counter advance, to make against the increasing forces that are driving this way from over there—nothing to oppose to assault (sic). England is in a state of siege, and doesn't seem to know it." With the new American and German competition, the resources and energy of the new Dominions must be utilized to revive the British economy and make it truly imperial. To the young Murchison, Chamberlain's economic schemes seemed to be the realistic answer for the future of Canada and the empire.[25] Considerable Canadian self-interest and national pride was involved; with the newly opened west, an expanded overseas market had to be found. Canadians were certain they had a bright and prosperous future ahead of them and they were fiercely proud of the contribution which they could make to the development of the empire as the greatest economic, politi-

---

[23] S. J. Duncan, *The Imperialist* (New Canadian Library Edition), 1961, pp. 93–124.

[24] The emphasis here is very similar to the "moral genius" of the Anglo-Saxon race, a theme of Wilfred Campbell, the poet. See C. Klinck, *Wilfred Campbell* (Toronto, 1942), 212.

[25] In this novel many of the politicians of the day appear under fictitious names; Chamberlain is Wallingham.

cal, and moral force in the world. Such an imperial partnership would at the same time ensure the development of Canada.

Canadian historians and novelists were not alone in the literary world in promoting the imperial posture of the day. Following the lead of Kipling and of the poet laureate, Alfred Austin, Canadian verse of the late 1890's reflected the imperial theme. As a medium it provided much wider horizons for the romantic vision. Wilfred Campbell produced a volume on *Sagas of Vaster Britain;* Bliss Carman, an "Ode on the Coronation of King Edward VII"; Rev. J. D. Borthwick edited a 208 page anthology of *Poems and Songs of the South African War* published by the Montreal *Gazette;* William Henry Drummond wrote ringing militaristic verse of the Kipling pattern. Some of this was verse and little was poetry but its value to the historian rests in its contemporaneity rather than its aesthetics. It was the strident cry of protest of an adolescent nation expressing its hopes, its fears, its triumphs, and its frustrations. Poetry to a far greater extent than the novel or historical works reflected the shrill, strident, almost ugly emotionalism of the era. In the events of this decade poets found ample scope for their imagery: the pomp and splendour of Queen Victoria's Diamond Jubilee, the bloodshed on the South African veld, the potential economic greatness of Canada within the empire, the white man's burden, and "Pretoria Day" (the wildest twenty-four hours that Toronto ever experienced).

During this period some elements in Canadian society acquired a militaristic flavor which was not to leave it completely for half a century; no where was this reflected better than in its poetry. Rev. Duncan Anderson in his "Transvaal Ho" captured some of the passion of the moment:

> Sons of a clime where freedom reigns,
> And brethren breathe alike God's air;
> Go! Break forever serfdom's chains,
> And hunt each hell hound from his lair.[26]

In the same volume Wilfred Campbell contributed his famous "Our Pit of 'The Thin Red Line,' " written before a similar poem by the poet laureate. Campbell here shows his deep personal pride in Canada's South African contingent and his uncompromising hostility to any "traitor" not supporting fully this national expression of Canada's position in the empire. Some of the more dramatic efforts of other poets were little short of bloodthirsty jingoism.

> To arms, To arms, for mother land and strike the deadly blow!
> Let crimson blood wash hill and dale, and stain the ocean's flow![27]

---

[26] J. D. Borthwick, *Poems and Songs of the South African War* (Montreal, 1901), pp. 36–46.

[27] Ibid.

What the Boers had done to provoke such vengeance was never explained, but the war fever of 1899–1902 intensified the imperial fervour of English Canadians and helped to make the whole business repugnant to sensitive young French Canadians such as Henri Bourassa.

In common with the prose, poetry reflected the contemporary concept of "race." As Wilfred Campbell liked to stress:

> But stronger far yet is the race-tie,
> The kinships that kindle and bind,
> And evermore true to the breed and the thew
> Are the sons of the world-old kind.[28]

He perceived a "divine purpose" in racial evolution and his terminology showed the influence of Darwin, British neo-Hegelian thought, and Victorian ethics. In his view the development of British civilization had been controlled by "the spirit of the people," which guided them through the "evolution" from barbarism to refinement in a pattern "more ethical" than that of any other race. Anglo-Saxons had a responsibility to ensure the continuance of this process through "race piety." For him, French Canada was accordingly "useless, despotic, intolerant, and ultra-conservative in her body politic and her social ideas."[29]

For Campbell there was really no escaping from the imperial question. Canada lived in a world of competing imperial systems and movements. Canadians had to choose which of the imperial systems they wished to be drawn into, and for most Canadians the British was the only choice.[30] Such a belief involved a firm rejection of the isolationism which Bourassa, Tarte, and other French Canadians stressed. For many Canadians isolationism as national policy was not only cowardly but irrelevant, because Canada would never be left alone in peace and isolation to pursue her own way.

There was a basic commitment by English-speaking intellectuals to the imperial creed. Here they were no different from most of their compatriots outside Quebec, and they contributed to the estrangement of that province with some of the same vehemence as the popular press and the anti-French demagogues. But the question remains: when academics in the United States and Britain were opposing imperialism, why did their Canadian counterparts subscribe so fervently to the creed? The final answer awaits further studies, but the phenomenon would appear to be an indication of how deeply some of these ideas were rooted in Canadian society and it would indicate that many of these academics reflected, consciously or unconsciously, these social values or ideals. The intellectual community in English Canada was as yet a rather conservative unchallenging group.

---

[28] From "The Children," published in Ottawa *Evening Journal*, 26 September, 1903.

[29] C. Klinck, *Wilfred Campbell*, pp. 190–213.

[30] Ibid.

Another aspect of the imperialist creed which has received very little consideration within the Canadian context involves economics. Although the Hobson-Lenin thesis[31] has had a profound impact on the interpretation of American and British movements, Canadian historians have yet to consider its relevance to the Dominion in spite of the close ties between the Laurier Government and the business community and the large number of industrial and commercial leaders who were vociferous in their imperial enthusiasm.[32]

In the early efforts of the Imperial Federation League in Canada, trade matters were the primary focus of their campaign for support. As early as April 1888, the President of the League called for reciprocal trade preferences between Canada and Great Britain[33] and this very issue immediately created differences and tension, for some free trade elements supporting the parent League in Britain. By the end of the last decade of the century, imperial trade preferences were the most popular and the most significant aspect of the imperial policy evolved by the Laurier Government.

Canadian willingness to embark upon a scheme of unilateral trade preferences was supported and abetted by the words and actions of Joseph Chamberlain, the Colonial Secretary. The latter delivered his first major speech on imperial economics to the Canada Club in London in March 1896. Chamberlain called for an imperial zollverein (free trade within the empire and an external tariff). Although this was not as far as the Canadians would have liked him to go, it was a serious departure from free trade principles which his English critics were quick to seize upon. His proposal was impossible to implement at the time; the British could not abandon free trade, nor the colonies protection. But the proposal was an encouragement to the Canadians who had shown at the Ottawa conference of 1894 and afterwards a strong interest in preferential trade. The speech was taken by the Canadian premier as an indication of potential British willingness to compromise free trade and consider a preferential trade system.[34]

In the election campaign of 1896 both Canadian parties promised imperial preferential tariffs—the Conservatives by raising the tariffs on foreign imports and the Liberals by reducing them on empire trade.[35]

---

[31] J. A. Hobson (British economic analyst) and V. I. Lenin (Soviet leader). Imperialism was merely a means of economic exploitation and in Lenin's view the last stage of capitalism.

[32] See the deliberations of the Canadian Manufacturers' Association and the various Boards of Trade in Canadian Annual Review.

[33] Canada, House of Commons, *Debates*, 1888, Col. 1069 (April 30), speech by D'Alton McCarthy.

[34] The Manchester *Guardian*, 26 March 1896, and *PAC*, Tupper Papers, Vol. II, Sir Charles Tupper to Sir Howard Vincent, 19 May, 1896.

[35] The *Globe* (Toronto), 17 June, 1896, and *The Mail and Empire* (Toronto), 13 June, 1896.

This election campaign, usually remembered only for the Manitoba Schools' issue, brought the first discussion of imperial fiscal ideas, and these were embodied a year later in the Fielding tariff, before "imperialism" had become a household word.

Another area of practical economics which provoked Canadian interest comprised a series of projects for imperial trade and communications. Subsidized fast steamship lines, all "Red" telegraph systems, imperial penny postage, were all schemes which were either initiated by the Canadians or strongly supported by them. They were also interesting examples of inter-colonial cooperation and of crown intervention into areas previously left to private enterprise. For any Canadian Government of the day these imperial ventures had great significance. With protectionist forces firmly in control of the United States Congress, the projects were an appealing means of expanding the Canadian share of the British market. When Sydney Fisher, Laurier's Minister of Agriculture, announced the new cold storage service for perishable farm exports to the United Kingdom in January 1897, he forecast that this would be merely the beginning of a whole new era in imperial trade across the North Atlantic.

When Laurier came to introduce the revolutionary imperial preferential tariff in 1897,[36] it was not from some imperial visionary that he received the idea in its final form, but from George Bertram, a leading industrialist from Toronto.[37] Such a policy would be totally consistent with a policy of protection because it was American imports which Canadian manufacturers feared. At the same time it provided obvious political fodder in the year of Queen Victoria's Diamond Jubilee for those wishing an imperial gesture or tariff reform to fulfil the party's policy of the early 1890's.

The imperial trade posture of the Laurier Government had a number of important repercussions. In the summer of 1897 Laurier was the great popular favourite at the Jubilee celebrations in London, and Joseph Chamberlain interceded with British authorities to help to eliminate problems faced by the Canadian Government. Kipling wrote his famous "Our Lady of the Snows" to celebrate the new Canadian tariff and its imperial implications—surely the only time in history that fiscal policy has provoked the poet's muse. The new recognition for Laurier and Canada was not confined merely to outward show. Even the London money market reacted with new interest and new confidence to Canadian issues—an important trend for Canadian development. In the fall of 1897 the Dominion Government floated successfully a 2½% loan, being the

---

[36] Immediate reduction of one eighth to become one fourth as of 1 July, 1898, to all countries giving "favourable" terms to Canadian goods. Britain with free trade was the only country which Laurier intended should qualify.

[37] *PAC*, Laurier Papers, Bertram to Laurier, 22 March, 1897.

first colonial government to attempt such a low rate of interest. Fielding credited their success to the favourable publicity which Canada had received for her imperial role in the summer of 1897.[38]

In 1897–1898 the preferential tariff was widened from a strictly British to an imperial one with the extension of the lower rates to goods from the British West Indies, India and New South Wales. These changes promoted a steadily widening conception of what the empire would mean for Canadian trade. Although Britain remained the great imperial market, there was new interest in Australasia, India, South Africa, and the other colonial areas.

The closing years of the nineteenth century were important ones for imperial military activity. Expeditions were sent to West Africa, the Sudan, and China while a major war was fought in South Africa. All these efforts required supplies, and the Canadians wanted to share in the lucrative contracts involved. In September 1898 Lord Strathcona, the Canadian High Commissioner resident in London, asked to be notified of future tenders for supplying the War Office or the Admiralty so that Canadians might bid. The Colonial Office passed the request on to the two departments without comment or recommendation. The Canadians were particularly interested in diverting contracts from the United States and other foreign countries into their own hands.[39]

With the outbreak of the Boer War in October 1899 the size and number of imperial contracts increased rapidly. Within a few days of the Boer ultimatum Fitzpatrick, the Canadian Solicitor General, was urging Laurier to get forage contracts from the imperial authorities. This he argued would be a "grand political coup," which would secure a number of doubtful Quebec constituencies for the coming election. Canadian companies were quick to protest when newspaper reports indicated that British contracts were going to American firms. Laurier's pressure on Chamberlain brought a number of contracts to Canadian companies for supplying food, saddlery, forage, horses, waggons, huts, and uniforms to the War Office for South Africa, and to the India Office which was responsible for the British contingent to the Boxer rebellion in China. The forage contracts to South Africa for one year alone amounted to $2.50 million and the Laurier Administration made prominent use of these contracts in the election of 1900 to illustrate the material benefits harvested by Laurier from the imperial relationship.[40]

Unfortunately some of the consignments shipped from Canada were

[38] *PAC*, Laurier Papers, Fielding to Laurier, 23 October, 1897.

[39] PRO CO42/860 Strathcona to Colonial Office 23 September, 1898. The Man, *Free Press*, 8 October, 1897, and Toronto *Globe* 11 January, 1899.

[40] *PAC* Laurier Papers, Fitzpatrick to Laurier, 14 October, 1899; Massey-Harris Co. to Laurier, 27 December 1899; Toronto *Globe* 1 September 1900, and 12 June 1901; Laurier Papers, page 49896.

not of high quality. The 30,000 uniforms (complete with great coats) ordered for the Peking expedition were shipped deliberately before the imperial inspector resident in Canada could see them; on their arrival they were judged unsatisfactory. Many of the Canadian food shipments were condemned on arrival in South Africa. Of the 17 consignments in one group only four received favourable enough reports to be classed "fit for issue." Some of the 187,000 tons of hay bought through the Canadian High Commissioner in London was of exceedingly low quality, and a good deal of the rest deteriorated badly *en route*. One War Office inspector complained that Canadian hay was "the worst I have seen in this campaign."[41]

Profiting from this trade, many Canadian companies hoped it might continue after the conclusion of the Boer War. The Canadian Manufacturers Association pressed Laurier to propose a resolution at the Colonial Conference of 1902 calling for empire preference on imperial contracts. With Australian support a resolution was passed covering War Office and Admiralty contracts. In the following months weak steps were taken to implement this policy, and some contracts for reconstruction work in South Africa were received in Canada.[42]

As the periodic debates in the House of Commons showed, Canadians were never fully satisfied with the extent to which they participated in these contracts. In June 1903 the Conservative leader, Robert Borden, was sharply critical of the government because Britain was still buying some cattle for South African reconstruction from American sources. The Canadians seemed to expect these contracts as an imperial right rather than as a result of lower prices and higher quality. It would appear that the War Office had some well founded hesitation in awarding these contracts to Canada; poor performance aroused legitimate suspicion of Canadian political practices. The Canadian civil service was still in its infancy in making proper control and inspection of government contracts. Nevertheless the Canadians did supply a considerable quantity of goods for the South African War and reconstruction, and this was considered a new and potentially important role for Canada in imperial affairs. Canadians were glad to participate in these "practical" and material benefits of empire.[43]

Even an emotional imperialist such as George T. Denison of Toronto resorted to economic arguments to support his case. He argued that the settlement of the Canadian west would be retarded without preferential

[41] *PAC*, Minto Papers, Vol. 26, Foster-Minto Corr. 1900; *PRO*, CO42/886–895 Col. Off.—War Office Correspondence.

[42] *PAC*, Laurier Papers, Canadian Manufacturers Assoc. to Laurier, 30 June 1902. *PRO*, CO885/8 Misc. 144 pp. 144–157.

[43] Canada, House of Commons, *Debates*, 1903, 54154 (25 June), *PRO* CO42/876 Minto to Chamberlain, *secret*, 15 December, 1901.

entry into the British market, and that it was in Britain's interest to promote Canadian production because Canada would be the only certain, major supplier in the event of war. Denison even attempted to pressure Lord Salisbury into accepting his views, and Chamberlain received similar letters from other Canadian political figures.[44] Chamberlain was prepared to support most of these economic schemes in the hope that they would lead the colonies into accepting closer imperial ties, a hope he clung to despite steadily decreasing prospects of success.

For the Laurier Administration the political value of its imperial economic policy increased after 1897. With the outbreak of the Boer War in October 1899, the whole field of imperial relations entered a new and more difficult period for Laurier and his associates. To retain support in English-speaking Canada, the government had to present an imperial posture. Yet to maintain its hold on French Canada it had to appear as an opponent of imperial military commitments. The common denominators acceptable to both groups were imperial preference and other economic projects. French Canadian suspicions were minimal here, provided Canadian autonomy was not jeopardized. Prior to the election of 1900 Laurier increased the preferential tariff to 33⅓% and the Liberals fought the campaign in English-speaking Canada with an emphatic imperial program emphasizing their economic policy. The Conservatives, with less to lose in Quebec, did not have to take as great care with questions of military commitments.

Laurier's imperial preferential trade program was not accomplished without repercussions in Canadian trade with other countries. The Germans in particular were annoyed by the Canadian initiative, even though their trade with Canada was insignificant. They feared that the idea would spread, that new tariff barriers would be erected, and that it would be more difficult to sell everywhere in the empire, including Britain. In mid-1898 the German Empire specifically excluded Canada from "most-favoured-nation" tariff status, the only section of the empire to be so classed. British protests to Germany only brought the demand that Canada abandon her preferential tariff and the stern warning that any similar action by other British colonies would bring similar German retaliation. As long as Britain remained committed to free trade, she had no basis to threaten retaliation. Britain's weak bargaining position infuriated Chamberlain, who was very sensitive to the Canadian demands for action. The affair provided a further example to him of how free trade was a direct impediment to meeting colonial wishes and strengthening the empire. In 1903 Canada struck back at Germany with a special 33⅓% import surtax. Thus the imperial preferential scheme embarked on with such innocence by Laurier in 1897 created the first major dispute for

---

[44] Salisbury Papers, Christ Church, Oxford. Salisbury-Denison correspondence; Chamberlain Papers, University of Birmingham, JC 9/2/1m.

Canada with a European power and a tariff war with the German Empire resulted, and would persist for a decade. It also pushed Chamberlain towards tariff reform as a means of rousing imperial sentiment in the colonies, and indirectly prompted his resignation when he failed to get his program through the British cabinet.

At least for a few Canadians, economic motives and material considerations thus helped to promote imperial enthusiasm. There is little evidence to support the application of the extreme Hobson-Lenin thesis in Canada, but economic factors deserve more consideration in the analysis of the imperial movement than they have received thus far from Canadian historians.

One of the most recent explanations for the rise of Canadian imperial enthusiasm was that put forward by Norman Penlington, who saw anti-Americanism as the decisive factor. He stressed that, "The compulsive power of Canadian jingoism in 1899 was stimulated primarily by, and expressed through, anti-Americanism." The whole imperial unity movement from the Pacific cable to the sending of troops to South Africa was a result of this feeling.[45] Certainly no one would deny that anti-American feelings existed in Canadian society through this period. However, one must isolate the factors peculiar to the late 1890's which explain the rise of imperial passions at that particular time. Penlington's thesis would be sound if the upsurge of imperial feeling coincided with a period of relatively strong anti-Americanism. But the evidence hardly justifies the conclusion.

The high points of anti-American feeling were the winter of 1895–1896 (the Venezuela Boundary Dispute) and 1903 (the Alaskan Boundary Tribunal and decision). The former coincided with an Imperial crisis in South Africa, the Jameson Raid, yet there was no demand by Canadians for action, as there would be in 1899. Also, in 1898, when imperial enthusiasm was mounting steadily, there would be a noticeable slackening of anti-American feeling in Canada. The Dominion warmly applauded the imperial efforts of the United States in the Spanish-American War, and later in the year a Joint High Commission was set up to negotiate a solution of all outstanding issues between the two countries. Thus while imperial feelings were mounting to a climax in 1899–1900, there were not unusually strong anti-American feelings in Canada. It was only after the assassination of McKinley and the succession of Teddy Roosevelt (with his bellicose approach to the Alaskan question) that anti-American feelings once again became so pronounced, but by 1903 imperial passions were already beginning to wane.

One element in the Canadian populace by its very nature tended to promote the imperial military virtues discussed earlier in connection with Canadian poetry. The members and former members of the Canadian

---

[45] N. Penlington, *Canada and Imperialism* (Toronto, 1965), pp. vii and 213.

militia welcomed "imperialism," for they saw in it a chance for excitement, glory, medals, and promotions through Canadian involvement. They were an outspoken group, with political connections in both parties in the House of Commons. They helped to inject imperial ideas into public discussion and promoted them with zeal through the press and the political parties. The horrors of war had long been removed from the Canadian experience and colonial campaigns of the late nineteenth century usually resulted in only very light casualties. The enthusiastic attitude of the militia to war was very close to that of the athlete to sport. This military group had read with a growing sense of frustration about the glorious deeds of Kitchener's forces in the Sudan, and about Teddy Roosevelt's charge up San Juan hill; they yearned for active service. As there was virtually no opportunity for military service in Canada, they sought to involve Canada in imperial campaigns. Led by the Honourable Frederick Borden on one side of the House and Sam Hughes on the other, they were a potent factor in fomenting public enthusiasm for sending troops to South Africa.

The popular press of English Canada was another agent for promoting imperial enthusiasm, and unlike the press of Australia, it was virtually unanimous in its support.[46] Conservative and Liberal papers competed to show which party more truly and ardently represented the interests of the empire.[47] On the outbreak of war the papers played a leading role in increasing the intensity of feeling in the English-speaking areas and in forcing a reluctant federal government to send contingents. In so doing they utilized some of the worst techniques of "Yellow Journalism." One prominent Ontario daily gave great emphasis to a story that the Boers had dynamited a train carrying 300 British refugee women and children fleeing from the Rand. Such a tale, with no foundation in fact, could leave few fellow Britons in Canada unmoved. With an agent of the Imperial South African Association (a front for the Rhodes mining interests) actively spreading "information" in Canada on the true nature of the Boer Republics, one can understand the reasons for such a distorted picture of the South African situation in the Canadian press. A few Ontario newspapers saved some of their fire for denouncing French Canada and her press on the issue. Papers such as *The Mail and Empire* and *The News* of Toronto and the Hamilton *Spectator* had no reluctance in accusing the French Canadian press of fomenting disloyalty to Canada and the empire; the counterblows from *La Patrie* opened a lengthy running battle which deepened the ethnic split.

This "war of words" in the popular press was a reflection of passions

---

[46] The sole exceptions known to the author were the two papers owned by Goldwin Smith: *The Farmer's Sun* and the Bobcaygeon *Independent*.

[47] For analysis of the press see R. J. D. Page, *The Impact of the Boer War on the Canadian General Election of 1900 in Ontario* (unpublished M.A. thesis), Queen's University, 1964.

which went deep into the social fabric of the country. In March 1900 there was serious rioting in Montreal. The disturbances were initiated by McGill students who in celebrating the relief of Ladysmith, besieged the offices of *La Patrie, Le Journal,* and *La Presse* and then moved on to stage a provocative demonstration at the branch of Laval University in Montreal. French-speaking students met it with a counter-demonstration. Soon the groups were no longer confined to students but included rival masses flaunting the Union Jack or the Tricolor; fighting took place with the police. At length the militia was called out, and two or three days were required before full order was restored. Sensational reports of the riot were carried nation-wide by the press; the Ottawa *Free Press* called it "The War in Montreal"; one Conservative member of Parliament blamed it on "paid emissaries of the Transvaal Republic" and on the provocative words of *La Patrie* which was doing President Kruger's work for him in Canada.[48]

Unfortunately for the domestic unity of Canada, anti-imperialism was almost solely confined to French Canada. At first the basis of the French-Canadian opposition to imperial commitments was essentially isolationist. Whether the war was just or unjust was immaterial; Canada had no business getting involved. She needed all her resources of men and money for her own development. It was a dangerous precedent for the future, for it might involve an endless stream of futile colonial wars. French-speaking Canadians were suspicious of the militarism which they saw in the English-Canadian attitude to the empire, and they feared where it would lead the whole country. As the war proceeded in South Africa, violently criticial European reports of British policy were published in Quebec, and the opposition to the war took on a more anti-imperialist and in a few instances an anti-British tone. For most French Canadians the events in Africa were of little importance to Canada, but they felt that imperial enthusiasm was drawing English Canadians away from their loyalty to Canada. English Canadians seemed to them to have two loyalties; one here, and one in Britain. French Canadians had always assumed that loyalty to Canada was the greater, but following the events of the Boer War they had grave doubts. Without the ties of blood, they had no hope of understanding the emotional response of English Canada.

The political importance of this ethnic split cannot be minimized. To a sensitive and proud young French Canadian like Henri Bourassa the whole experience was profoundly disturbing. Not only were contingents sent, but they were sent by a Liberal Government headed by a French Canadian supposedly espousing the principles of Gladstone. Bourassa soon realized what majority democracy meant and how impotent the French Canadians were on any issue where the English and French were split.

---

[48] The Ottawa *Free Press*, 3 March 1900, and Canada, House of Commons, *Debates*, 5 March 1900.

The English majority ruled and French-speaking members could be hissed down as "disloyal" in the House of Commons for expressing dissent. The South African crisis and succeeding events early in the twentieth century led to a weakening of French Canadian commitment to a federal state and to its great linch pin, federal parties composed of both ethnic groups. During this period a rupture of the "national" parties was possible when dissentient Tory and Liberal elements threatened to form a French Canadian nationalist party. The novelist Jules-Paul Tardivel went all the way to separatism. With Laurier's careful handling of the situation the new party did not materialize, but it remained lurking in the wings for 1911 and 1917.

Outside of the French-speaking areas one of the great strengths of the imperial idea in Canada was its very ambiguity. It could mean so many things to many people—merchants, politicians, militia, or missionaries. In the Canadian context the term tended to be divorced from reality because Canadians were not supporting their own generals and administrators in the field; therefore they were not as concerned about the criticisms of any individual. In Canadian eyes individuals might fail but the ideals of empire remained unchallenged. In Africa the British Government had to convert abstract idealism into concrete government policy, but on most questions the Canadian Government and people could remain relatively aloof, in the position of the interested although ignorant spectator. For instance, in spite of Canada's participation, the issues involved in the Boer War were never seriously discussed in Canada. It was easier and more comforting for Canadians to remain divorced from reality in their emotional rhetoric overflowing with Victorian moral values. The result, however exhilarating, was far from a satisfactory or a realistic approach to the matter. In English Canada, the empire was a matter of faith like belief in God.

The late nineties marked the first years of real economic prosperity that Canada had experienced since Confederation. Immigration soared and there arose new feeling of self-confidence. Canadians who had been sceptical of their future now came forth with fantastic predictions of prospective wealth and population. Within half a century Canada would expand to 50 million people and become a new world power. As the United States had expanded and developed in the nineteenth century, so Canada would in the twentieth. J. A. Hobson, the British critic of imperialism, compared public feeling in the two countries: "To visit Canada just now is a bracing experience for the torpid Briton. For Canada is conscious, vocally, uproariously conscious, that her day has come . . . the poor relation has come into her fortune, a single decade has swept away all her diffidence, and has replaced it by a spirit of boundless confidence and booming enterprise."[49] Canadians seemed certain that

---

[49] J. A. Hobson, *Canada To-Day* (London, 1906), pp. 3–4.

they were on the road to founding a powerful and influential "British" nation which would become the keystone of the empire.

The reaction of English-speaking Canada to the sending of contingents provided a further illustration of this point. As the many speeches of the day indicated, Canadian troops were going to fight for the empire but they were also fighting as a demonstration of Canada's new strength and aspirations. As the first contingents sailed from her shores, their progress and achievements were followed with pride. When Lord Roberts congratulated the Canadians for their "most dashing advance" in forcing the surrender of General Cronje and the Boer force at the Battle of Paardeberg, there was great pride and jubilation in Canada. The Dominion seemed to have become a factor of military significance in the empire. Laurier illustrated this exaggerated feeling of importance when he commented on the news of Paardeberg in the House of Commons: "is there a man whose bosom did not swell with pride . . . the pride of the consciousness that that day the fact had been revealed to the world that a new power had arisen in the west."[50]

The Colonial Conferences of 1897 and 1902 showed the enthusiasm of the Canadians and also their negative attitude to any of the responsibilities involved in maintaining the imperial structure. Joseph Chamberlain assumed that one was an indication of the acceptance of the other. He and others in England failed to see that Canada wanted to use and to glory in the empire not to assume major imperial obligations. In their desire for glory and an entrance to the world stage through the medium of the empire, Canadians saw an opportunity for the Dominion to achieve a new status. Ironically the British leaders helped to stimulate this attitude by the flattery and attention that was given to Laurier and to other leading Canadians on occasions like the Diamond Jubilee. At a time when American chauvinism found its outlet in Cuba and the Philippines, Canadians reacted by stressing Canada's important role as a power within the empire.

The Boer War was the great high water mark for imperial zeal in Canada. The contingents crisis of 1899 and the general election of 1900 acted as catalysts in bringing the intensity of feeling to a fever pitch. But the Boer War brought with it the seeds for the weakening of imperial sentiment. The final two years of fighting were almost solely confined to the brutality and frustrations of guerilla warfare. The British forces were involved in many acts, such as the operation of concentration camps and the burning of farms, which were hardly consistent with the rhetoric of the idealists. Imperial feeling carried on after 1902, but it never regained that certainty of sacred purpose of 1899. The mounting criticism from British liberal and radical circles in the latter stages of the war made many Canadians more restrained in their enthusiasm and slightly more

---

[50] Canada, House of Commons, *Debates*, 13 March 1900, Col. 1848.

realistic in their attitude to international affairs. Imperial sentiment remained, but without the wild excesses of the Boer War.

The ultimately significant effect of Canadian imperial zeal was not that it had stimulated elements of nationalism, but rather that it perpetuated and intensified the split between the two developing nationalisms in Canada. Lacking a revolutionary tradition, Canada was faced with the problem of producing unifying bridges which would join the national attitudes and aspirations of the two language and cultural groups. The excesses and prejudices involved in the imperialist patriotism of English-speaking Canada postponed the possibility of building those bridges and widened the gap that they had to span. Although the nationalism of English Canada developed out of enthusiasm for empire—and that of French Canada in opposition to the imperial creed—they still had other interests in common. In the bitter aftermath of the Boer War, however, these common interests, were lost from view.

19

The Interest of the Central Canadian Press, Particularly the Toronto Press, in the Autonomy Bills, 1905

Edward McCartney

To SOME EXTENT at least, Laurier had won power in 1896 because of his stand for classical federalism and provincial rights. He had opposed federal coercion of Manitoba even to restore what he regarded as legitimate educational rights for his French-speaking co-religionists in that province. Then in 1905, on the grounds of justice and his understanding of the Confederation "compromise," Laurier defended the right of the Canadian parliament to ensure the survival and perhaps even the restoration of certain educational rights for the same minority in the about-to-be-created provinces of Saskatchewan and Alberta. Federal responsibility and authority with regard to the constitutions of new provinces were quite different, Laurier argued, from federal interference with existing provinces.

In this article, Mr. McCartney shows how the Central Canadian press, especially the Toronto dailies, reacted to Laurier's intentions during the period before Sir Clifford Sifton's famous resignation. He argues that while all of the Toronto dailies, including the two Liberal ones, were upset by Laurier's moves, the more vehement Protestant organs frequently used the jargon of federalism, provincial rights, and popular sovereignty to mask rather unconvincingly their violent semi-racist, anti-Catholic, and anti-French convictions. In these papers there certainly was no comprehension let alone endorsation of the idea of two cultures permanently cohabiting the same transcontinental domain.

This paper is a slightly modified version of Chapter II of Edward

McCartney's masters' thesis, "Provincial Rights, Separate Schools, Minority Privileges: The Attitude of the Toronto Dailies on the Autonomy Bills, 1905," Trent University, 1967. Elsewhere in the thesis he further elaborates his point by showing the hollowness of those self-proclaimed champions of provincial rights who virtually ignored the real restriction on Prairie self-government, the restriction which most agitated the Westerners themselves, their lack of control over their own natural resources, especially crown land.

ANGLO-SAXONISM and militant Protestantism reappeared in federal politics in February 1905. For the remainder of that year, the federal bills creating the new provinces of Alberta and Saskatchewan out of the Northwest Territories registered a series of blows against the delicate harmony existing between the two major language and religious groups in Canada. The issue, which exhumed the old conflicts, was the federal government's provision in the Autonomy Bills to guarantee to the Catholic minority, which was primarily French-speaking, a limited separate school system. The separate school clause, Clause 16 of the Autonomy Bills, became the foundation of Orange-Conservative and Grit-Liberal resentment against the Laurier government, Roman Catholics, and French Canadians.

Prime Minister Sir Wilfrid Laurier, in his addresses to the House of Commons and in his private correspondence, requested critics to imbibe the spirit of toleration and compromise by which he claimed the Fathers of Confederation in 1867 had overcome prejudices and parochialism. He believed that subsections one and three of Section 93 of the British North America Act, by intent and interpretation, extended the federal government's legal and even moral right to provide educational guarantees for the religious minority in territorial areas about to be made into provinces. The English-language press of Ontario advised the federal government to abandon any attempt to uphold separate school privileges for the minority and to permit the new provincial governments to draft their own educational clauses. The newspapers, in short, demanded that the federal government refrain from interfering in a problem clearly within the provincial sphere of jurisdiction and maintain the right of a provincial majority to settle matters affecting its interests. It was assumed by the press that the local majority would favour a public school system but would probably grant minimal concessions to the Roman Catholic minority.

The daily press of Protestant Toronto reflected the complex party and local aspirations of Ontario. Indeed, the Toronto journals apparently considered themselves the spokesmen for Ontario, and with some condescension they examined and set forth the reasons for the crisis. The more ultra-Protestant dailies charged that the Liberal government was abetting with the Roman Catholic hierarchy in the interests of the French-Catholic minority in the N.W.T. As a consequence, the demand in these papers for provincial rights and local majoritarianism served as a cover for their appeals to English-Protestant prejudices against French Catholicism. For them, the constitutional arguments were merely tactics by which they could indicate the menace of Catholicism in political affairs and the threat that denominational schools would continue the existence of the unassimilated French Canadian.

As early as 1903, John S. Willison, editor of the Tornoto *News* (independent) and biographer of his friend Laurier, had anticipated difficulties in the negotiations for provincial autonomy between the ministers of the federal government and leaders in the Territorial Assembly. In November 1903, the *News* had editorialized on the prospects of autonomy for the western territories. The area was ready for provincial status, but the federal government had hesitated to take up the issue. Such indecision, the *News* announced, resulted from the government's awareness of pressure which the Roman Catholic hierarchy of Quebec would exert in order to make separate schools an inviolable legacy in the provincial constitutions. The preoccupation of the hierarchy with the separate school system in the West could not be tolerated. Indeed, the *News* considered it imperative to restrict separate school privileges to the Eastern provinces and not to extend those rights to the West:

We in the original Provinces . . . entered into the pact whereby the dual language system was established and the Church was given its hold on the school system. We had grave and urgent reasons for paying the price—a price we still must regard the concession, for it is open to question whether the official use of French and the Ecclesiastical turn given to the education of part of the people has benefited even those who demanded it. Absolutely no reason exists for transplanting that concession to the West. The West belongs to the people of the West, and to no one else. They must solve these questions in their own way, which may or may not be our way. Eastern Canada must not try to interfere in their development.[1]

Fundamentally, the *News* wished the Roman Catholic hierarchy, based in Quebec, to renounce interest in school claims for the external French Catholic minority. The school question forecast a contentious period in establishing the constitutions of Alberta and Saskatchewan.

The Roman Catholic hierarchy, in the personage of Monsignior Sbaretti, papal ablegate to Canada, had made its sentiments known to the federal government as Willison's *News* had cannily foreseen. On March 1,

---

[1] Toronto *News*, November 7, 1903. Other editorials appearing on October 23, 31 and November 3 had advocated autonomy but had not brought forth the separate school issue.

1904, Sbaretti wrote Laurier about the Honourable R. W. Scott's visit to him. Senator Scott, Secretary of State in Laurier's Cabinet and a noted Catholic layman who had been the author of the Upper Canada Separate Schools Act of 1863, had informed the delegate of the government's intention of including a clause to guarantee separate schools for Catholics in the Northwest. Sbaretti wished Laurier to confirm these proposals so that the delegate could communicate Laurier's assurances as leader of the party and head of the government to Rome.[2] Laurier complied with this request in a lengthy letter on March 7. His promise of guarantees to the Catholic minority was based upon "the letter and spirit of the constitution under which the Canadian Confederation was brought into existence." In any province where separate schools existed at the Confederation the provincial legislature under Section 93 of the British North America Act could not abolish or curtail the minority's "absolute right" to separate schools. Such a provision introduced in 1867 for the welfare of the minority would "apply with equal force for the benefit of the minority in any new province that may be formed. . . ." The conditions, Laurier stated, did prevail in the Northwest:

When these territories in 1875 were organized and endowed with the first rudiments of a civilized administration, the system of separate schools existing in some of the other provinces, was therein introduced by positive enactment of the law. The system has grown up, keeping pace with the development of the territories. . . .

My opinion is very clear, that when the territories are admitted as a province, the minority should not be placed in a worse condition than it is today; that its schools ought to receive the same degree of protection as is granted to the minority in Ontario and Quebec where separate schools existed at the first establishment of Confederation, and that the act of admission of the territories into confederation should especially provide that system of separate schools now in existence shall be secured and [put] beyond the power of the provincial legislature as provided by section 93 of the Constitution, either to abolish or even prejudicially affect such schools. . . .[3]

Laurier thus indicated that he would not dodge the issue of separate schools if it arose in granting provincial autonomy. On the other hand, when it appeared, his Clause 16 did not acknowledge that the school system had evolved at the expense of the minority over thirty years but seemed to open the possibility of reestablishing and guaranteeing in full the separate school provisions of the Act of 1875. His argument to retain separate schools was constitutionally correct despite what the *News* and other journals might argue. Even his moderate opponents later crucified

---

[2] *Public Archives of Canada (PAC)*, Laurier Papers, Mgr. Sbaretti to Laurier, March 1, 1904.

[3] *Ibid.*, Laurier to Sbaretti, March 7, 1904. See also *Debates*, February 21, 1905, pp. 1451–52.

him for his oversight, whether or not intentional, in not clarifying what school situation the Bill was guaranteeing.

In the late spring of 1904 the *News* under Willison's direction once more referred to the relation between provincial autonomy and separate schools. No one in the older Canadas, the *News* intoned, wished to interfere with the existing territorial school system in the quest for western provincial autonomy. The paper did, however, reject any feature of the provincial constitution, which the federal government might favour, limiting "the control of the new Provinces over the question of education." The *News*, in other words, upheld the principle of broad provincial, majoritarian rights: the new provinces should not be handicapped in any way from modifying their educational system in the interests of an English-Protestant majority. The Catholic ultramontanists, the *News* editorial concluded, should, therefore, be forewarned from pushing the federal government into forcing the new provinces to preserve sectarian schools.[4]

The outburst of editorial activity by the *News* against separate school guarantees in new provincial constitutions evoked a series of letters between Laurier and Willison. Laurier chided his friend for awakening the antipathies of the "now dormant separate school question." He conceded that the question would arise, but he did not wish it to open with public opinion hostile to it because the school matter would "come in a very different form from what it was in 1896. . . ." Laurier warned Willison that he would fight extremists; his policy was "clear" in his own mind, and he would uphold the British North America Act. Then in a placating tone, he asked Willison to remember that Confederation had been a compromise for which men like George Brown had made giant personal sacrifices. The work of Confederation was not complete. He requested Willison to embody the spirit of 1867 when the government undertook to finish the Confederation scheme.[5]

Thrusting sharply to the core of the problem, Willison outlined for Laurier his views on allowing the western governments to control their own educational affairs. "If the question is not raised before the country," Willison argued, "the matter will probably be quietly settled between the two parties and put through without discussion." The alternative suggested by Willison was a frank statement from the federal government that "the federal authorities would not attempt to impose a school policy upon the new Territories [*sic*]."[6] The nature of the school question, Laurier replied, prevented any calm consideration of its merits. The issue, which Willison had already unveiled in the *News*, could only unleash the full fury of unreasoning invective against the French-Catholic minority.

---

4 *News*, June 2, 1904. See also editorials of May 4, 13 and 26, 1904.

5 *PAC*, Willison Papers, Laurier to Willison, June 7, 1904.

6 *Ibid.*, Willison to Laurier, June 9, 1904.

In blunt tones Laurier threw down the gauntlet to Willison and other men of his convictions:

I will ask no quarter from you or from anyone, if, when the time does come to face & solve that old question, I do not solve it according to your conception of right. The fight has absolutely no terror for me, but I would rather discuss the question before a calm & dispassionate audience.[7]

The Laurier-Willison correspondence of June 1904 foreshadowed the crisis between the two men when the Autonomy Bills were before Parliament. In June 1904, the journalist and politician, however, hastily apologized to one another in succeeding letters for their frank words about the school question.[8] Their break would not occur prematurely; nevertheless, the factors necessary to sunder their friendship existed.[9]

An opportunity to put the issue of autonomy for the N.W.T. before the public seemed available in the general elections of 1904. The federal government instead stressed the significance of the second transcontinental railway and of tariffs. Laurier merely revealed his government's intention to grant provincial status to the N.W.T. after the federal election. But as a platform of either the Liberal or Conservative party in the election campaign, provincial autonomy received scant attention.[10] This official silence did not prevent Willison's *News* from galvanizing discussion of autonomy and separate schools. A report in mid-October from a Quebec correspondent of the *News* alluded to some *entente cordiale* arranged between Laurier and the Roman Catholic hierarchy about separate schools in the West. The details of the negotiations were not complete; an accidental disclosure of the terms, the correspondent hinted, would make Liberal electoral victory doubtful.[11] To these innuendoes,

---

[7] *Ibid.*, Laurier to Willison, June 11, 1904.

[8] Laurier Papers, Willison to Laurier, June 14, 1904; Willison Papers, Laurier to Willison, June 14, 1904.

[9] Laurier and Willison had had previous disagreements over government policy. An earlier dispute had occurred at Laurier's announcement of plans for a second transcontinental railway. Rather than construct a new Quebec-Moncton branch as proposed by Laurier, Willison preferred linking the Intercolonial Railway with the Canada Atlantic Railway, the latter railway to be purchased by the federal government. Willison, moreover, had favoured government construction of the transcontinental; Laurier, however, refused to see the public burdened with a large debt as had developed with the Intercolonial Railway. These differences they had discussed in their correspondence without the acerbity that took place over separate schools in the Northwest. See Laurier Papers, Willison to Laurier, January 27, 1904 and Willison Papers, Laurier to Willison, January 22, 29 and June 11, 1904.

[10] In his study of the *News* under Willison's directorship, J. G. Harris suggests that the Conservative party did not take up Willison's agitation on the autonomy question because Conservatives "could not gain Quebec from Laurier no matter what course they followed." J. G. Harris, "A Study of the Politics of *The News* under the Editorship of Sir John S. Willison," unpublished M.A. Thesis, University of Toronto, 1952, p. 40.

[11] *News*, October 7, 1904.

the *Star* (Liberal) devoted a scathing editorial. It was "indecent" to infer that Laurier had come to some arrangement with the Roman Catholic hierarchy about separate schools. Many voters, the *Star* pointed out, forgot that the Conservative party in 1896 had negotiated with the hierarchy in an attempt to coerce Manitoba. The provincial Conservative party of Ontario, moreover, had "baited" the province's Roman Catholic minority until they discovered that Sir Oliver Mowat, the Liberal Premier of Ontario until 1896, protected the Catholic minority, held the Catholic vote, and kept winning provincial elections. Thereupon, the provincial Conservative party "turned a neat handspring and landed in the camp of toleration." The new course, however, did not rest easily with some Conservative adherents. By comparison, the Liberal party had always been the party of toleration and local autonomy. Those principles, the *Star* commented, "forbid the suspicion that Sir Wilfrid has entered into any compact to coerce any section of the population. . . ."[12] The *Star* in February 1905 might have recalled these statements about Laurier and the Liberal party with a pang of conscience. In November 1904 the evidence, so presented by the *Star,* indicated another Conservative effort to rustle English-Protestant voters by a religious cry. But Willison was not dissuaded from raising the issue of separate schools and provincial rights.

A keen analyst of political affairs, he cautioned voters against the dangers in idolizing a popular leader. "Personal magnetism" should not sway responsible, clear-headed parliamentarians from looking objectively at the measures advocated by their leaders. The grant of provincial autonomy in the Northwest would require impartiality. The politicians not only would be working for their own political fortunes but would also be planning for the interests of a western population, present and future. "Any attempt to bind them [the new provincial legislatures] unjustly to give them less than the power and freedom to which they are entitled, will be a legacy of discord and difficulty for the future." To prevent any misuse of power, frequent party conventions should be held to judge a political leader's actions, the *News'* editorial proposed. In addition, the lowest party supporter could broadcast his opinion to the not "infallible" leaders and could make his leaders responsible to the wishes of the party.[13]

A later editorial revealed dissatisfaction with the idea of maintaining silence on the autonomy issue during the campaign. Because "the question is not only whether autonomy shall be granted, but how and in what

12 Toronto *Star,* October 17, 1904.

13 *News,* October 17, 1904. Elsewhere Willison was to attack "the remarkable notion that loyalty to a party leader is so sacred an obligation as loyalty to King and country." J. S. Willison, "Journalism and Public Life in Canada," *Canadian Magazine,* vol. 25, no. 6 (October, 1905), pp. 555, 556.

measure," the voters should impress their reaction upon a political party and should send representatives to Ottawa responsive to their point of view. Arguing for what amounted to popular sovereignty rather than provincial rights, Willison wished M.P.'s to demand the paramountcy of the provincial government in legislating for education. With provincial control over the school system realized, the local English-Protestant majority could curtail separate school provisions in the future. In Willison's opinion, the Roman Catholic proposal for denominational schools,

. . . is a question that has arisen in old Canada, in Ontario, in New Brunswick, in Nova Scotia, in Manitoba. In these cases it has been argued . . . that Separate Schools were guaranteed by the constitution, that the present generation is bound by promises and agreements made long ago. We have now to deal with a new question; not whether a promise or agreement shall be fulfilled, but whether it shall be made. We have the power to give these new Provinces their start in life unfettered by restrictions. . . .

There will surely be no injustice in this course. It will not bind the new Provinces either to accept or to reject separate schools. They will be allowed to deal with the matter from time to time as new conditions and circumstances arise. The millions whose coming Sir William Laurier foreshadowed will know their own business better than the politicians of this generation, and better than outsiders in this or any generation.

. . . It is argued that a majority of the people of the Territories may do injustice to a minority unless restrained by the constitution. This argument, carried to its logical conclusion, is an argument against popular government. Majorities may . . . be unjust and tyrannical in this or in any other matter, but government by majority is the only form of popular government that is workable. With all its faults it is better than government by minority. It is better that several millions of people in the territories shall have their way in the future, than that they should be fettered by a handful of politicians at Ottawa today. . . .[14]

Willison's peroration that western citizens would do better than "a handful of politicians at Ottawa" in settling the school system to everyone's satisfaction indicated a scepticism about the behaviour of certain federal politicians. He probably assumed that federal politicians who were remote in interest and place from the western problems might be more amenable to minority exhortations for guarantees than a majority cognizant of the area's aspirations.

Early in January 1905, the *Globe* (Liberal) reported that F. W. G. Haultain, Ontario-born Premier of the Northwest Territories, and G. H. V. Bulyea, Territorial Commissioner of Public Works, at Ottawa to conduct interviews with federal ministers about provincial autonomy.[15] Conferences took place intermittently between January 5 and February 20, 1905. By analysing the draft bill in order to discover what was dis-

---

[14] *News*, October 19, 1904. Refer also to editorials on October 14 and 26, 1904.
[15] Toronto *Globe*, January 5, 1905.

cussed in the meetings, one observer has stated that "the draft bill contained no direct reference to education, and it appears to have played little part in the negotiations between the two governments."[16] Indeed, Haultain later charged that Laurier did not show his educational proposals to either of the Northwest delegates until noon of the day he introduced the Autonomy Bills into the House of Commons. A private letter of Bulyea's to Laurier, on February 1, 1905, however, indicates that certainly Bulyea was aware of the proposed school arrangements. In his letter, Bulyea expressed his regret at "complications" arising in the talks on the autonomy legislation. He believed that if his suggestions of leaving the school system as it presently operated under "Legislative Control" had been accepted, "there would have been no serious agitation or objection so far as people there are concerned." A Liberal in federal politics, Bulyea, who became the first Lieutenant-Governor of Alberta, thought that the proposed arrangement might not satisfy the "ultra-Protestant" or "ultra provincial rights man" but would win the support of Liberals to the extent of guaranteeing "two Liberal local governments at the first election and . . . the same proportion of federal seats at the next Election. . . ."[17]

The Roman Catholic hierarchy did have an active concern in watching the proceedings at Ottawa. In addition to the secular interests represented by Haultain and Bulyea at Ottawa, certain respected Roman Catholic clerical leaders from the Northwest visited Ottawa and Montreal at this time. Professor Lingard has written that, since "the Roman Catholic element in the North-west, with its prestige of pioneer work, its schools and convents, was very influential," the federal ministers could not ignore their presence and opinions.[18] Sbaretti and Laurier, moreover, kept one another informed of developments by correspondence. The papal delegate offered advice on wording in order to fortify the rights of the minority to separate schools. Laurier acknowledged Sbaretti's comments but did not feel obliged to accept them.[19] Laurier must have realized the peculiarity and the precariousness of his position in dealing with a problem fundamental to his native co-religionists. But, it would have been disastrous to the French in particular and to the peace of the country as a whole if he had put himself too plainly on the side of the hierarchy against the wishes of the Protestant majority in the Northwest.

Laurier's dilemma mirrored the deeper political-religious division, which the Toronto newspapers only partially understood but dramatically voiced, between French-Catholics and English-Protestants in

---

16 C. C. Lingard, *Territorial Government in Canada,* Toronto, 1945, p. 130.

17 Laurier Papers.

18 Lingard, p. 139.

19 Laurier Papers, Sbaretti to Laurier, January 21, February 7, 11 and 15, 1905 and reply February 16, 1905.

Canada. In 1907, André Siegfried, a French traveller and student of
political and social affairs, brought out perceptively the problem between
the two groups in his statement:

The anti-Catholic feeling is much stronger in Canada than in England, partly
because in the Dominion the Church of Rome is so much stronger and more
menacing, partly because the religious conflict is intensified by the conflict of
race.

Being in a majority and masters of the country by the right of conquest, the
Protestants naturally wish to maintain their ascendancy. In their efforts to this
end they are uncompromising. In a hundred different ways they keep on working for it, noting anxiously and resenting the slightest advances of their rivals
in the councils of state. Thus they have become used to looking at the life of
the State from a denominational instead of from a neutral or secular point of
view. Herein is to be seen a profound cause of the bitter and determined nature
of political conflicts in Canada.[20]

To protect the religion and way of life of the French-Canadian Catholic, Roman Catholic prelates of Quebec understood that they had to
influence federal politicians from Quebec. The English-Protestant, on the
other hand, considered it essential for his politicians to remain united
against any designs of the French-Catholic and his Church. In 1877,
Charles Lindsey, son-in-law of the patriot-rebel, Willian Lyon Mackenzie, had foreseen a continuous struggle between English-Protestants
and French-Catholics over the principle of the separation of Church and
State. Since 1763, he wrote, the Catholic Church of Quebec had become
more ultramontane in spirit, and ultramontane Catholics believed in the
subordination of the secular power of the state to the temporal power of
the church. This fact meant subservience to the Pope because the Pope
was the Church.[21] To check this hateful tendency of civil subordination
to ecclesiastical authorities, English-Protestants battled viciously any
threat by the Church to win concessions for its adherents through pressure on the federal government. During the autonomy debate, the
Toronto newspapers would unconsciously emphasize that theme.

As the date for presenting the Autonomy Bills to Parliament drew
inexorably closer, the Toronto dailies devoted more attention to autonomy. An article reported from Calgary, N.W.T., to the *World* (independent) spoke of a "furious turmoil" that must result there if the Autonomy
Bills guaranteed separate schools to the minority. Ontarians who had
taken up residence in the West had little sympathy for separate schools.[22]
Refuting somewhat the vigorous statements of the *World,* an editorial
of the *News* nevertheless reminded the federal government of its duty to

---

[20] André Siegfried, *Race Question in Canada,* London, 1907, pp. 59–60.

[21] C. Lindsey, *Rome in Canada,* Toronto, 1877, pp. 21, 40–41.

[22] Toronto *World,* February 1, 1905.

uphold provincial rights, to "let the inhabitants . . . establish their own school system" and to allow them to change it at will.[23]

Laurier, moreover, could scarcely have been mollified by the gentle regrets of the editor of the *Globe* (Liberal) that the paper could only champion the proposal of "leaving the Provinces free to deal with their educational problems."[24] Although the *Globe* would not make "a campaign on the question" of provincial rights, Laurier would be without the services of this key propaganda voice in Ontario during the crucial first stages of the debate. Little assurance, furthermore, came from Atkinson's *Star* to comfort the Prime Minister. Whether separate school provisions would be included in the new constitutions or left out, the decision, the *Star* naively explained, belonged to the authorities in Regina—the city in which the Northwest Legislative Assembly met. In the pragmatic but English-Protestant opinion of this Liberal daily, the minority's privilege of denominational schools seemed of little consequence:

If the people of the North-West want separate schools abolished, or if they desire to have no clause in their constitution providing for them, they have no right to look to Ontario to do the shouting and the agitating. The constitution will be theirs, the schools are theirs, and the question is now theirs. If they have a grievance, they will say so, and if they do not get excited, our people need not. On the other hand, if the people of the West are determined not to have anything in their constitution influencing them either way in this matter, there is not the least doubt that the public opinion of Ontario will be strongly with them. The people of this Province who do not believe in Separate Schools would in that case be with them, as also would be those who believe in the Provincial right of self-government and genuine home rule. But no question of Provincial rights can be raised by any Province except the one interested.[25]

The "banns of unholy marriage between Church and State" had occurred in the promulgation of the Autonomy Bills, the independent Toronto *Telegram* charged on February 22. "Evil days for Canada" and "perpetual privileges" for the Roman Catholic hierarchy in the Northwest would result from Clause 16. The iniquitous Laurier measure uncovered a "bishop-bossed Parliament of Canada" and repudiated the former Liberal principle of separation of Church and State.[26] The *Globe* solemnly declared that whatever the intention of Clause 16 might be, the real issue was simply: "Is it right or wise for the Dominion Parliament to attempt to make the maintenance of separate schools a permanent constitutional obligation on the new western Provinces?"[27] The federal govern-

---

[23] *News*, February 2, 1905. Other editorials on separate schools and freedom for the West were printed on February 3, 4, 10, 11, 13 and 17, 1905.

[24] Laurier Papers, Reverend Macdonald to Laurier, February 2, 1905.

[25] *Star*, February 14, 1905.

[26] Toronto *Telegram*, February 22, 1905.

[27] *Globe*, February 22, 1905.

ment had the authority to apply educational provisions in a Territory, but it had no right to legislate for the educational policy of the new provinces. Section 93 of the B.N.A. Act referred to the original confederating provinces of 1867 and not to any new province erected out of the Territories.[28] The federal parliament should leave school policy totally for the inhabitants of the new provinces to settle amicably and justly for themselves. Indeed, it was probable that the people would incorporate the present school system; and, "such privileges once granted, could not be withdrawn without creating a grievance, for which, under the Constitutional Act, the Dominion Parliament may pass remedial legislation."[29]

The *Mail and Empire* (Conservative) saw no reason why Laurier should impose a "drastic" coercive policy upon the West unless he had "less confidence" in the capacity of the western people to be fair. With power in their own hands, the majority might advance generous treatment to the minority. Such a provincial undertaking was preferable to a "binding" arrangement imposed by the federal government. Like the *Globe,* the *Mail and Empire* found the government's effort to make Section 93 the norm in the new provinces, as well as in Ontario and Quebec, unacceptable.[30] In a measure affecting the status of majorities and minorities, the *Star* contemplated, a settlement for one group would be a concession at the expense of the other group. As for separate schools, the editorial pointed out:

It is possible for the Federal authority when framing a constitution to provide that people of a peculiar religious belief shall have the right to support with their taxes a separate school friendly to their faith. It is not possible for the Federal authority to frame a constitution composing such restraints on Public schools as will guarantee that they cannot be made offensive to minority beliefs.

The minority, according to the *Star,* was not unhappy with the present school system. It feared what might happen to its separate schools if the province controlled education without federal restraint and a new Protestant majority lobbied for sacrificing separate schools. Clause 16, the Liberal daily inferred, would satisfy minority presentiments by continuing the present, workable and favorable separate school set-up.[31]

Now that the school clauses were before the public, Willison repeated his demands in the *News* that the federal government should uphold his brand of provincial rights.[32] The privilege guaranteed by Section 93 of

---

[28] *Ibid.,* February 24, 1905.

[29] *Ibid.,* February 25, 1905.

[30] Toronto *Mail and Empire,* February 24, 1905.

[31] *Star,* February 23, 1905.

[32] *News,* February 25, 1905. See also Willison's address to the Canadian Club, "Northwest Autonomy and the School Question," *Proceedings of the Canadian Club,* Toronto, vol. II, 1904–1905, February 27, 1905, pp. 97–107.

the B.N.A. Act "was intended to apply only to 'both Canadas'. . . ."[33]
The *World* commented that Laurier was forcing separate schools on the
"English West" because he had "a solid Quebec behind him in this
attack." The issue was provincial rights; Laurier had acted "unconstitutionally," had "treated two great free English-speaking communities . . .
as wards" and had "insulted the public school system. . . ." But, "If he
ever thinks either he or his party or Quebec can shackle the west they will
run up against an early and a rude awakening."[34]

At the beginning of the controversy in February 1905, the newspapers
tackled the Autonomy Bills upon the questions of provincial rights and
separate schools. There was no realization until early March that Clause
16 might reverse the trend away from duality that the school system had
been taking in the Northwest. In the interval other Ontario characteristics
were expressed in the press. The *News* regarded Robert Borden, the
leader of the Conservative Opposition and head of a party which had a
majority of the Ontario representatives in the House of Commons, as the
natural chieftain of an Ontario bloc to offset the political bloc from
Quebec. By not straddling the issue of provincial rights, the Conservative
party could achieve greater political gain in Ontario at the expense of the
Liberal party. A united English-Protestant group from Ontario could
help Laurier fend off the entreaties of the French-Catholic body from
Quebec for enlarged separate school rights.[35] The difference, the *Mail
and Empire* prophesied, between the entrance of Alberta and Saskatchewan with constitutional restrictions upon their provincial powers and the
union of 1867 in which Ontario and Quebec had voluntarily submitted to
restraints on their educational power could lead to future turmoil on the
separate school question. The quarrel could no longer be settled locally in
the courts. Because of Section 93 local minority disputes would be
brought into the federal arena.[36]

Opposition toward the school clauses could take an activist turn. The
Globe published an article on a meeting of the Lord Erne Lodge, No. 40,
Loyal True Blue Association, where a resolution had been passed expressing the Lodge's objection to the federal government's Clause 16. The
members believed,

. . . such outrageous attempts of the Romish hierarchy to fasten its religious
educational system on our Canadian Provinces will hasten the time when there
will arise in Ontario a determined demand for the revision of the B.N.A. Act
with a view to the elimination of the detestable section 93 of that act.[37]

---

33 *Ibid.*, February 23, 1905.
34 *World*, February 25, 1905.
35 *News*, February 18, 1905.
36 *Mail and Empire*, February 25, 1905.
37 *Globe*, February 25, 1905.

In an interview, Colonel Sam Hughes, an English-Protestant M.P. from Lindsay, Ontario, explained that there would be a "rebellion" in the Northwest if the government persisted in passing its "tyrannical piece of legislation" so reminiscent of the "dark ages."[38] A certain group of Ontario citizens, therefore, saw the separate school clauses as a Roman Catholic plot and were anxious to put the papists in their place. Since Laurier had extolled the benefits of separate over public schools in his address on February 21,[39] the *News* countered that the opponents of separate schools had as much right to attack denominational education as "the parent of ignorance and tyranny" and "a menace to individual liberty, to liberty of thought, and to the growth of the human intellect."[40] The modern, progressive world found separate school education out-moded. The tremendous technological and material advance of the United States was "due largely to its national school system."[41] Canadian progress depended upon national schools to give a solid education for all children and to assimilate the youngsters of foreign parents into the Anglo-Saxon civilization.

Vituperative criticism dripped from the pages of certain Toronto dailies. Journals in other Ontario centres responded to the controversy in a manner revealing either mild support for provincial rights and public schools or partisan loyalty to the government's course of action. The Ottawa *Journal* (independent) plumped for provincial sovereignty and national schools. Denominational schools, the *Journal* argued, worked against a concept of the national policy; they might cause "a weakening of the possible general efficiency and unifying effects of the [public] schools and so of the fibre of the nation."[42] A competitor of the *Journal* in Ottawa, the *Free Press* (Liberal), carried ecstatic editorials applauding Laurier's feat in drafting a clause embodying the school system estab-lished in the N.W.T.[43] A better editorial in the *Free Press* attacked the principle of provincial rights as "casuistical and founded upon a mis-apprehension of the foundations of our institutions." The question of provincial rights failed to take into consideration the "rights of minor-ities," and "ignores the fact that [,] the sovereignty of the territories being invested in the Dominion of Canada [,] it is for the Parliament of Canada to decide upon what terms autonomy shall be granted under the provisions of the British North America Act. . . ."[44] Similarly, the Ham-ilton *Times* (Liberal) agreed that whatever one might think about the

---

38 *News,* February 25, 1905.

39 *Debates,* February 21, 1905, pp. 1458–1459.

40 *News,* February 38, 1905.

41 *Ibid.,* March 1, 1905.

42 Ottawa *Journal,* February 20, 1905.

43 Ottawa *Free Press,* February 20 and 22, 1905.

44 *Ibid.,* February 27, 1905.

benefits of a national school system it was essential to preserve the separate school rights of the minority enacted in the Act of 1875 and guaranteed in Section 93 sub-section 1 of the B.N.A. Act.[45] To the moral question posed by the *Times*—whether it would be legal or just to deprive the minority of their thirty-year old school privileges—the London *Advertiser* (Liberal) had replied editorially that: "It was clearly the belief of Parliament, when a constitution was granted the Northwest Territories in 1875, that separate schools had been guaranteed to the minority for all time." The western separate school system, the *Advertiser* pointed out to its readers, only differed from western public schools by having a noncompulsory half-hour religious instruction at the end of the school day.[46] Even the Conservative London *Free Press* thought it ridiculous to initiate an unwelcome uproar in Ontario over separate schools in the Northwest if the westerners were satisfied with Clause 16. The *Free Press* observed that the western inhabitants, presumably the English-Protestant settlers, still had the opportunity to decide,

whether their social welfare and commercial progress can go hand-in-hand with denominational schools or would be clogged by a divided system of education. . . .[47]

Unlike their journalistic colleagues in Toronto, the editors of the English-language dailies of Montreal did not immerse their papers very deeply in the swirling waters of separate schools and provincial rights. The language in the Montreal dailies, even in opposition to Laurier's Clause 16, was not as sarcastic, or as colourful, as that of the Toronto press. The *Herald* (Liberal) thought the main issue revolved about Laurier's interpretation and reading of the B.N.A. Act rather than the merits or demerits of separate schools. At Confederation a compromise had been worked out with respect to the school systems of Ontario and Quebec; this compromise (Section 93) was intended to extend to new provinces joining the Confederation. By the Act of 1875 the Liberal Mackenzie government had allowed the establishment of separate schools in the N.W.T. In designing Clause 16, Laurier had thought it necessary to retain the separate school privileges for Saskatchewan and Alberta. This move, the *Herald* in a curious conclusion added, showed "that the dead hand of past Parliaments stretches over the present one. . . ." In spite of a preference for national schools, the *Herald* believed that it, as well as other newspapers, would have to adopt Laurier's virtue of toleration in accepting Clause 16.[48] Reasonableness and compromise, the *Star* (independent) intoned, should be the prerequisite for studying the school

---

[45] Hamilton *Times,* February 24, 1905.

[46] London *Advertiser,* February 22, 1905.

[47] London *Free Press,* February 24, 1905.

[48] Montreal *Herald,* February 22, 1905.

question.[49] But the oldest Conservative newspaper, the *Gazette,* expressed dismay at the Liberal policy of upholding separate school rights, especially when the anti-Remedial Bill agitation of 1896 hung in the Liberal party's closet. The *Gazette* said that, despite the government's claim under the B.N.A. Act to maintain minority privileges, it would have been more judicious for the local inhabitants of the territories through their legislatures to draft the school clauses.[50] The *Gazette's* argument rested upon an assumption that there was little evidence to indicate a western movement to end the separate school privileges.[51]

In the opinion of the editors of the French language dailies, *La Patrie* and *La Presse,* the federal government did have an obligation to continue minority guarantees in Alberta and Saskatchewan. *La Patrie* (independent) argued that Laurier, despite revived ethnic and religious cries, had included Clause 16 in the Autonomy Bills. As for separate schools, "c'est une garantie à laquelle les catholiques ont droit et que leur accorde expressément l'acte de la Confédération." The objectives of 1867 had been justice and toleration. Within Quebec the French-Catholic majority had treated the English-Protestant minority respectfully. Yet Ontarians seemed determined on the goal of "domination" and chose as their lesson: "Rien pour les Catholiques, tout pour les protestants. . . ."[52] *La Press* (independent), the largest circulating daily in Canada, also condemned the lack of generosity of Ontarians. The paper regarded the Ontario storm over separate schools as an illustration of the hypocritical Protestant idea of free conscience. Catholic dogma emphasized the duty of religious teaching in the schools—a belief that men of other faiths should recognize. The theory that Catholics advocated denominational schools as a means to aggrandize the power of the Church rather than to spread the faith was preposterous. Separate schools posed no threat to public schools; Catholics demanded their own schools in order to limit the dangers of a completely materialistic view of life being taught to children. The paper, furthermore, rejected the notion raised by Haultain and other Protestants that Ontario and Quebec had voluntarily agreed to

[49] Montreal *Star,* February 22, 1905. The *Star*—in contrast to other Montreal newspapers—devoted more space to a discussion of the Autonomy Bills, presented articles illustrative of the attitude prevailing in various Ontario dailies, interviewed certain Westerners for their opinions and reprinted western newspaper coverage of the debate. At important moments the *Star* gave full page spread to reports; however, all these comments were found not on the front page but in the inside pages. Unlike the Toronto newspapers, the *Star* contributed very few editorials to the debate.

[50] Montreal *Gazette,* February 23, 1905.

[51] Lingard has mentioned that less concern was displayed in the West about education than was generated in the East. Even after Sifton disclosed the discrepancies in Clause 16, westerners apparently were content to continue the school system but not to extend denominational privileges. Lingard, pp. 172–173.

[52] *La Patrie* (Montréal), février 25, 1905.

separate schools in 1867 but that the federal government imposed unconditionally such schools on the new provinces. In the new provinces, the French-Catholic minority had a certain advantage. Under the B.N.A. Act, to make concrete the allegations of *La Presse*, the federal government had the power to create new provinces and to act as the protector of minority rights. The English-Protestant majority, if it were in control of education at the provincial level of government in Alberta and Saskatchewan, might at present refrain from interfering with separate schools. Yet in the future, with a new influx of anti-separate school settlers, the provincial governments, as had happened in Manitoba, might revoke the Catholic privileges to separate schools so that new cultural and religious dissensions could result. Since the Protestant minority in Quebec had secured religious safeguards, the Catholic majority of Quebec believed that privileges should be extended to the Catholic minority groups by Protestant majorities in other provinces.[53]

Laurier's fear of an unhappy reception to a federal guarantee for separate schools was not unfounded. A "calm" and "dispassionate" audience did not exist when he spoke on the Autonomy Bills before the House on February 21. The prospect of separate schools in Alberta and Saskatchewan had sparked such newspapers as the *News* to proclaim the sanctity of provincial rights and the ability of the English-Protestant majority in the new provincial legislatures to decide the question of separate schools. Once English-Protestants understood that Clause 16 embodied federal guarantees to separate schools, the press, representative of their views, asked why the government would not allow the provincial bodies to control education untrammelled by federal restrictions. Thereupon, the French-language dailies of Montreal responded by claiming that the Confederation compromise included minority guarantees not only in Ontario and Quebec but in other provinces as they were created. In February 1905, the real interest was the problem of provincial rights, a phrase which permitted some Toronto papers to discuss separate schools and to resurrect the Roman Catholic bogey.

---

[53] *La Presse* (Montréal), mars 1, 1905. It should be noted that this editorial was the sole editorial contributed by this French language daily in the early days of debate.

20

The Alaskan Boundary Dispute*

F. W. Gibson

THE ALASKAN BOUNDARY dispute was probably one of the most bitter diplomatic battles in the long history of Canadian-American relations. For both countries, the boundary became an intense internal political issue with partisan political pressures reinforcing the normal nationalistic instincts and prejudices. The discovery of gold acted as a further stimulus to foment greed within each country and to intensify public opinion. When Teddy Roosevelt succeeded McKinley as President, the temperature of the dispute was raised. However, the Canadians could have resolved the dispute earlier had they accepted McKinley's offer. At a time when Canada was going through its first assertive period of self-confidence, the dispute took on a certain symbolic significance for Canadian pride. When Canadians failed to achieve their goals the dispute became a source of bitterness in their attitudes to the United States and a source of frustration with Britain, regarding control of Canadian external affairs.

F. W. Gibson of Queen's University undertook a very extensive and thorough treatment of the subject for his M.A. thesis and this article was the product of that research. It remains the best analytical summary of the dispute.

THE ALASKAN boundary dispute arose between Canada and the United States over the boundary of the long strip of territory dangling down the British Columbian coast from Alaska and known as the Alaskan Panhandle. The dispute was one of interpretation of the terms of a treaty

---

* *Canadian Historical Association Report* (1945), pp. 25–40.

signed by the representatives of Russia and Great Britain on February 28, 1825. The United States by its purchase of Alaska in 1867 succeeded to the Russian rights of territory under the treaty of 1825 and Canada by the entrance of British Columbia into the Canadian union in 1871 acquired British rights of territory under that treaty.

The line of demarcation was described in Articles 3 and 4 of the treaty as follows:

Commencing from the southernmost point of the island called Prince of Wales Island, which point lies in the parallel of 54 degrees north latitude, and between the 131st and 133rd degree of west longitude (Meridian of Greenwich), the said line shall ascend to the north along the channel called Portland Channel, as far as the point of the continent where it strikes the 56th degree of north latitude; from this last-mentioned point, the line of demarcation shall follow the summit of the mountains situated parallel to the coast, as far as the point of intersection of the 141st degree of west longitude (of the same meridian); and finally from the said point of intersection the said meridian line of the 141st degree, in its prolongation as far as the Frozen ocean, shall form the limit between the Russian and British possessions on the continent of America to the North-west.

IV. With reference to the line of demarcation laid down in the preceding article, it is understood:

First. That the island called Prince of Wales Island shall belong wholly to Russia.

Second. That whenever the summit of the mountains which extend in a direction parallel to the coast, from the 56th degree of north latitude to the point of intersection of the 141st degree of west longitude, shall prove to be at the distance of more than 10 marine leagues from the coast, the limit between the British possessions and the line of the coast which is to belong to Russia, as above mentioned, shall be formed by a line parallel to the windings of the coast, and which shall never exceed the distance of 10 marine leagues therefrom.

The treaty of 1825 established a line of demarcation between Russian and British possessions in an area that was remote from Europe and a subject of interest at that time only to a few fur-traders and explorers. When the treaty was signed knowledge of the geographical features of the area was limited to surveys of the coastal waters made by navigators and consequently the definition of the inland boundary lacked precision.

The ambiguities of the treaty were revealed as the activities of traders and prospectors slowly laid bare the topography of the Panhandle. It gradually became clear that the area contained no well-defined range of mountains and was in fact a sea of mountains.[1] A series of boundary incidents on the Stikine River and on Lynn Canal made it evident by 1885 that the description of the boundary contained in the treaty of 1825

---

[1] *Proceedings of the Alaskan Boundary Tribunal* (7 vols., Washington, 1904), III, pt. II, 323–4, W. H. Dall to G. M. Dawson, April 24, 1884. (*Proceedings of the Alaskan Boundary Tribunal* hereinafter cited as *A.B.T.*)

was not strictly applicable to the ground traversed.[2] By 1888 there emerged a clear-cut difference of opinion between Canadians and Americans on the meaning of the boundary provisions that were to be applied. Conversations held in Washington in February of that year between Dr. G. M. Dawson, Director of the Geological Survey of Canada, and Mr. W. H. Dall of the United States Coast and Geodetic Survey revealed that the officials of both countries who were most immediately concerned with the location of the boundary held widely different interpretations of the boundary terms of the treaty of 1825.[3] Dr. Dawson believed that the treaty contemplated a boundary drawn along the summit of the mountains arising immediately from the shore of the sea and that in any case the line should be drawn without reference to the numerous inlets which pierce the coast. Mr. Dall held that Russia had sought and obtained by the treaty an unbroken coastal strip and that the boundary line must be drawn from the heads of the inlets. The Dall-Dawson conversations were, however, purely unofficial and the differences of opinion which they disclosed were not translated into official policy on the part of either government for another decade.

Although the exact location of specific points of the Alaskan boundary occasioned intermittent controversy between the governments of Great Britain and the United States, during the second half of the nineteenth century, the location of the boundary as a whole and the meaning of the boundary terms of the treaty of 1825 were not made subjects of vigorous governmental disputes until the end of the century. In 1896 gold was discovered in the valley of the Klondike River. The subsequent rush of goldseekers through the Alaskan Panhandle into the Canadian Yukon created serious problems of law enforcement for the Canadian authorities. Their difficulties were increased by the fact that the Canadian government could not send any militia or police to the Yukon except through the Alaskan Panhandle and with the consent of the United States government. Canadian leaders were soon alive to the need for an all-Canadian route and the government brought forward a plan to have a railway built from a point on the headwaters of the Stikine River to Dawson City which would provide direct communication between British Columbia and the Yukon.[4]

The defeat of the Yukon Railway Bill at the hands of the Senate concentrated attention on the alternative possibility of obtaining for

---

[2] *A.B.T.*, III, pt. II, 324–30. Secretary Bayard to E. J. Phelps, November 20, 1885.

[3] *A.B.T.*, IV, pt. II, 94–113, Mr. Dall to Secretary Bayard, February 13 and December 11, 1888, with accompanying memoranda; *A.B.T.*, III, pt. II, 338–43, Dr. Dawson to Sir Charles Tupper, February 7 and 11, 1888.

[4] A full account of the circumstances surrounding the Yukon railway project may be found in John W. Dafoe's *Clifford Sifton in Relation to His Times* (Toronto, 1931), chap. VI.

Canada a port on Lynn Canal, the main entry from the sea to the gold-fields. Dyea and Skagway, the two principal ports at the head of Lynn Canal were in American hands. Mr. Clifford Sifton, Canadian Minister of the Interior, speaking in the House of Commons on February 15, 1898, admitted that the United States had been "in undisputed possession of them for some time past" but supported Canadian claim to ownership of the summits of White and Chilkat passes behind the two ports.[5]

Several months later, Mr. Sifton wrote to Sir Wilfrid Laurier who was then attending the Quebec sessions of the Joint High Commission and urged the Prime Minister to bargain with the American delegates for a port on Lynn Canal.[6] He regarded the acquisition of such a port as essential to the development of Canadian trade with the Yukon and although he had no hope that this could be achieved by submitting the Alaskan boundary dispute to an arbitral commission he thought a bargain might be arranged if the question of a Canadian port were linked with an offer by Canada to relax her rights in the matter of pelagic sealing.

Pending final settlement of the issue the British and American governments agreed in May, 1898, to establish a provisional boundary on the summit of the watershed at the head of Lynn Canal.[7] The whole question was then placed on the agenda of the Joint High Commission appointed to settle certain issues outstanding between Canada and the United States. Lord Salisbury in his instructions to the British and Canadian members of the Commission, indicated that the British government had been prompted to press for an early settlement of the question for two special reasons: first, the influx of miners through the Panhandle into the Yukon had created the need of a Customs frontier on the coastal inlets; second, the whole Panhandle was believed to be auriferous and the discovery of large quantities of gold in the disputed territory would give rise to serious difficulties.[8]

With its inclusion in the agenda of the Joint High Commission the Alaskan boundary dispute entered upon a new and more exciting phase. The problem of locating the boundary had hitherto engaged the attention only of a few government officials and local interests and it had therefore been largely confined to a few quiet backwaters of Anglo-American relations. Now, however, the flood of miners into the Klondike had swept the Alaskan boundary question into the mainstream of the relations between the British Empire and the United States. It thus became impossible to treat the dispute as an isolated problem to be dealt with solely on its own

---

[5] *Canada: House of Commons, Debates, 1898*, February 11, 1898, I, 407.

[6] Dafoe, *Clifford Sifton*, 171, Clifford Sifton to Sir Wilfrid Laurier, October, 1898.

[7] *A.B.T.*, III, pt. II, 376, memorandum prepared by Sir Julian Pauncefote, April 18, 1898; *ibid.*, 377, Secretary Day to Sir Julian Pauncefote, May 9, 1898.

[8] *Ibid.*, 384–6, Lord Salisbury to the High Commissioners, July 19, 1898.

merits. A solution *in vacuo* was no longer possible; settlement of the question would be determined by the general climate of Anglo-American relations and would affect and be affected by other issues disturbing those relations.

In the closing years of the nineteenth century Anglo-American relations were growing warmer under pressure.[9] The spectre of a Europe dividing into two great armed camps both of which looked with envious eyes upon the fruits of British imperial activity, convinced many British statesmen of the inadequacies of a policy of "splendid isolation" and of the need to seek outside support in keeping open the sea-lanes which knit together the widely scattered British Empire. But if the gradual disintegration of the concert of Europe and the rising might of Germany did, as Henry Adams claimed it did, "frighten England into America's arms,"[10] those arms were no longer reluctant to receive British attentions.

With the passing of the frontier as a safety valve in American life, Americans came to have a new appreciation of the value of an overseas as distinct from a continental empire. The United States emerged from the Spanish-American War an imperial power whose colonial responsibilities in the Caribbean and the far Pacific made it difficult for her to maintain her old position of aloofness from world affairs. At the same time she discovered that her departure from isolation at the expense of Spain had aroused the disapproval of the nations of Europe with the exception of Great Britain. British friendliness was appreciated by American statesmen and a common interest in the White Man's Burden drew the two nations together so that it appeared to at least one Washington diplomatist that "the old pirate and the young pirate are joining forces for moral support." If these foundations of an Anglo-American *rapprochement* were to be extended and strengthened it was necessary to remove all sources of serious friction from the relations of the two countries. In the light of this necessity, the issues outstanding in Anglo-American diplomacy acquired a new and urgent significance.

The Joint High Commission had been appointed to deal with a number of these issues arising out of the field of Canadian-American relations. Foremost among those remaining within the larger sphere of Anglo-American relations was that of a canal across the Isthmus of Panama.

The growing desire of the United States for an Isthmian canal received a tremendous stimulus from the Spanish-American War. The general lack of sympathy abroad for the American cause and the need to safeguard their latest territorial acquisitions convinced many Americans of the need

---

[9] A full account of this development may be found in Lionel M. Gelber, *The Rise of Anglo-American Friendship: A Study in World Politics 1898–1906* (London, 1938), chaps. I, II, and *passim*.

[10] Henry Adams, *The Education of Henry Adams* (Boston, 1918), 363.

for a canal which would make possible the rapid concentration of American naval forces in the Atlantic or Pacific Oceans. Such a canal could be built only with the abrogation of the Clayton-Bulwer Treaty of 1850. By its terms Great Britain and the United States had agreed that neither was to build a canal through Central America without the consent of the other. Great Britain had held firmly to her rights under the treaty and had insisted that those rights did not admit the United States to exclusive control of an Isthmian canal.[11] But the demonstrations of British friendliness during the war with Spain made the end of the war appear to be a propitious time for the United States government to propose revision of the treaty. Lord Salisbury received the proposal very favourably and agreed in principle that an Isthmian canal could be built under the sole protection of the United States government. But he was not prepared to consent to this modification of British rights without compensation. The American proposal was made at a time when the British and American members of the Joint High Commission stood in sharp disagreement on the subject of the Alaskan boundary. Lord Salisbury, seeking a lever with which to move the American commissioners from their position on that question, argued that British concessions on the Isthmian canal question should be made a *quid pro quo* for American concessions on the Alaskan boundary.[12]

Disagreement on this question had arisen early in the meetings of the Joint High Commission. It had been referred to a committee composed of Lord Herschell, Sir Wilfrid Laurier, Senator Fairbanks, and General Foster and the committee had divided on national lines with respect to the true interpretation of the treaty of 1825.[13] When it became clear that further argument would not shake the confidence of either side in the strength of its case several attempts were made to reach a compromise settlement. The most promising of these was a proposal by the British commissioners that the line should be drawn so as to give the United States the whole of the territory bordering on Lynn Canal except Pyramid Harbour and a strip of land from that port to the boundary line, thus securing for Canada access to the Yukon by the Dalton Trail.[14] The

---

[11] R. B. Mowat, *The Diplomatic Relations of Great Britain and the United States* (London, 1925), 226–31.

[12] Allan Nevins, *Henry White: Thirty Years of American Diplomacy* (New York, 1930), 145, Henry White to Secretary Hay, December 23, 1898; Gelber, *Rise of Anglo-American Friendship*, 42 ff.

[13] The record of the attempts made by the Joint High Commission to settle the dispute is to be found in *Foreign Office Correspondence Respecting the Proceedings of the Joint Commission for the Settlement of Questions Pending Between the United States and Canada* (hereinafter cited as F.O. *Correspondence* etc.).

[14] F. O. *Correspondence* etc., 156 ff., "Draft Article Respecting the Alaska Boundary," given by the British commissioners to Senator Fairbanks, February 2, 1898.

remainder of the boundary was to be drawn "in the main conformable to the contention of the United States."[15]

In response to the suggestion by President McKinley that British consent to revision of the Clayton-Bulwer Treaty hung in the balance, the American commissioners were prepared to receive the British proposal favourably. Although they objected to several of its terms, it appeared for a time that the details would be adjusted and the compromise plan accepted. But the scheme was halted just short of fulfilment. Willingness to compromise on the part of the American commissioners had been induced largely by pressure from abroad; it was now to appear in response to pressure at home. When news of the proposed surrender of Pyramid Harbour leaked out, American shipowners on the Pacific coast, fearing that the existence of a Canadian port on the Yukon would endanger their monopoly of the carrying trade with the Yukon, lodged a strong protest with the United States government.[16] President McKinley was standing for re-election in the following year and his commissioners therefore withdrew their acceptance of the compromise plan.

With their failure to agree either on the meaning of the treaty of 1825 or on a compromise settlement the commissioners fell back on an attempt to find an acceptable method of resolving the dispute by arbitration. Once again their efforts met with no success. The American commissioners insisted on an even-numbered tribunal and the British held out for an odd-numbered tribunal along the lines of the Venezuela Boundary Commission.

Failure to resolve the Alaskan boundary question brought the Joint High Commission to an impasse and prevented final settlement of the other issues before it. The Commission therefore adjourned, and as it never reconvened, the Alaskan boundary was thrown back into the ordinary channels of diplomacy.

In the months that followed the adjournment of the Joint High Commission it proved difficult to inject new life into the Alaskan boundary negotiations which had run such an exhausting course in the sessions of the Commission. The newly-born Anglo-American *rapprochement* had received a setback and tempers were wearing thin in both North American capitals.[17]

But Secretary Hay was determined that no obstacle should be allowed to hinder the development of friendlier relations between the United

---

[15] John W. Foster, "The Alaskan Boundary" (*National Geographic Magazine*, X, 455).

[16] Charles C. Tansill, *Canadian-American Relations 1875–1911* (New Haven, 1943), 180, American Ship-owners to Senator George C. Perkins, February 2, 1800.

[17] Gelber, *Rise of Anglo-American Friendship*, 46; John Buchan, *The Earl of Minto* (London, 1924), 168; the Earl of Minto to Arthur Elliott, August, 1899; W. R. Thayer, *John Hay* (Boston, 1916) II, 205–6, Secretary Hay to Ambassador Choate, April 28, 1899.

States and Great Britain and he patiently gathered up the scattered threads of diplomacy for another attempt to solve the troublesome boundary question. His resolution was fortified by rumours of impending disorders on the unsettled frontier and by the knowledge that upon the success of his efforts depended the fate of the revised Clayton-Bulwer Treaty.

In April, 1899, Hay renewed the proposal made by the American members of the Joint High Commission to refer the question to an even-numbered tribunal of arbitration.[18] The British government repeated its objection that this plan contained the possibility of deadlock and again recommended that the dispute be settled along the lines insisted upon by the United States in the Venezuela boundary dispute, that is, by an odd-numbered tribunal. Secretary Hay now felt that this offer was "about as good a one as we can get" and he was disposed to accept it until the Canadian government attempted to attach to it a clause providing that Pyramid Harbour should be given to Canada irrespective of the decision of the tribunal.[19] Hay regarded this condition as utterly inadmissible and the British offer was rejected.[20]

In July the British government once again put forward the plan of an odd-numbered tribunal but this time accompanied it with an alternative proposal very similar to one which had been discussed in the meetings of the Joint High Commission. It was now proposed that the United States grant to Canada a perpetual lease of half a square mile of territory at a suitable point on Lynn Canal with the right to construct and maintain exclusive control over a railway from the concession to the Canadian border.[21] Secretary Hay was delighted. He believed that the lease arrangement would decide the whole question in favour of the United States because "the very act of granting a lease implies unquestionable possession."[22] President McKinley and his Cabinet agreed that it was a "reasonable solution" provided that the details could be arranged so as to protect American shipping interests and safeguard American sovereignty over the area to be leased. But Senator Davis, Chairman of the Senate Foreign Relations Committee, was firmly of the opinion that the lease arrangement would not command the two-thirds majority necessary for

---

[18] Tansill, *Canadian-American Relations*, 190, Secretary Hay to Ambassador Choate, April 19, 1899.

[19] Tyler Dennett, *John Hay* (New York, 1933), 229; Secretary Hay to Ambassador Choate, May 1, 1899; *A.B.T.*, IV, pt. II, 125; Lord Salisbury to Ambassador Choate, May 17, 1899; Tansill, *Canadian-American Relations*, 192.

[20] Thayer, *John Hay*, 206–7, Secretary Hay to Ambassador Choate, June 15, 1899.

[21] Tansill, *Canadian-American Relations*, 107, Ambassador Choate to Secretary Hay, July 18, 1899.

[22] A. L. P. Dennis, *Adventures in American Diplomacy* (New York, 1928), 149–50, Secretary Hay to Senator C. K. Davis, August 4, 1899.

its ratification by the Senate and on his advice the British suggestion was dropped.[23]

The abandonment of the lease arrangement temporarily exhausted the resources of Anglo-American statesmanship with respect to the Alaskan boundary. In October a provisional boundary was arranged for the area at the head of Lynn Canal[24] but further progress towards the establishment of a permanent boundary could not be made until the operation of forces external to the dispute should alter the bargaining strength of the parties thereto.

In the autumn of 1899 forces were set in motion that were to break the deadlock. The Boer War broke out on October 10. The nations of Europe, never displeased to hear of discord within the Brisith Empire, responded to the news of early British disasters in a manner strongly reminiscent of Kaiser Wilhelm's telegram of 1896. To Great Britain, strongly resentful of being compelled to play Goliath to President Kruger's David, the benevolent neutrality of the United States stood out in bright contrast to the strongly disapproving attitude of the nations of Europe. As the splendour of British isolation faded rapidly amid the encircling gloom of European hostility, the British government learned to place a rising premium on the value of American friendship. British statesmen grew increasingly sensitive to the advantages of removing all obstacles to the development of that friendship. Of the issues outstanding between the two nations, the unsolved riddle of the Isthmian canal remained the most important. The canal problem could be solved by obtaining British consent to the abrogation of the Clayton-Bulwer Treaty. In the negotiations which had taken place on that subject since December, 1898, the British government had shown a persistent disposition to make revision of the treaty conditional upon a settlement of the Alaskan boundary question. Failure to provide for a final settlement of that question had brought to a standstill negotiations upon the canal treaty. Into these negotiations new life was forcibly injected by the introduction into Congress in January, 1900, of a bill empowering the United States government to "excavate, construct and protect" an Isthmian canal. Secretary Hay condemned the Canal Bill as a violation of the Clayton-Bulwer Treaty but he took advantage of the situation to urge upon Lord Salisbury the desirability of forestalling the Bill by immediate joint revision of the treaty.[25] Lord Salisbury was convinced of the need of doing everything possible to cultivate American friendship but he realized that if he yielded unconditionally to American demands for revision of the Clayton-Bulwer Treaty he would thereby

---

[23] Tansill, *Canadian-American Relations,* 200, Senator C. K. Davis to Secretary Hay, July 31, 1899.

[24] The text of the *modus vivendi* of October 20, 1899, will be found in *Foreign Relations of the United States,* 1899, pp. 330–1.

[25] Thayer, *John Hay,* 222–3, Secretary Hay to Ambassador Choate, January 15, 1900.

surrender Canada's most important bargaining counter in the Alaskan boundary negotiations.[26] It was particularly difficult for him to make this surrender at a time when Canada's assistance in an imperial war gave her additional claims to consideration by the mother country. But his desire for Anglo-American solidarity finally overbore there reservations and he appealed to the Canadian government to give its consent to a new canal treaty.[27] This consent the Canadian government gave, though reluctantly, and the Hay-Pauncefote Treaty was signed on February 5, 1900. The new treaty was ratified by the Senate only after three amendments were added which materially altered its character. Great Britain refused to accept the amended treaty but a new treaty was concluded on November 18, 1901, and it proved acceptable both to the British government and to the American Senate.

The settlement of the Isthmian canal question had profound effects on the diplomatic strength of Great Britain and the United States in their relations to one another. Great Britain emerged from the settlement with strong claims to American gratitude but with the loss of a powerful bargaining counter in her relations with the United States. The finality of the settlement ensured to the United States greater independence in her future relations with Great Britain. Upon the settlement of the Alaskan boundary question, the State Department with its international position no longer exposed to attack on the Panama flank could now bring to bear its diplomatic big guns. But the Foreign Office, to whose position the canal question had been a diplomatic outwork, found that its surrender weakened the resistance that could be offered to attack at other points along the line of empire.

Already in May, 1901, Secretary Hay had renewed his proposal to submit the dispute to arbitration by an even-numbered tribunal.[28] The Canadian government was still disinclined to accept such an arrangement and replied in November with a suggestion that the dispute be referred to a tribunal with two neutral arbitrators.[29] But in the meantime the assassination of President McKinley in September had brought Theodore Roosevelt and his "incalculable impetuosity" into the White House. Mr. Roosevelt was convinced that the Canadian case did not "have a leg to stand on" and that it was "dangerously close to blackmail."[30] He was

[26] Tansill, *Canadian-American Relations*, 215, Ambassador Choate to Secretary Hay, January 27, 1900.

[27] Mowat, *Diplomatic Relations of Britain and United States*, 279–80, Joseph Chamberlain to the Earl of Minto, January 30, 1900.

[28] *Canada Sessional Paper No. 46a*, 3–4 Edward VII, A. 1904, 31–4, "Draft Arbitration Convention," communicated unofficially by Mr. Hay and forwarded by Lord Pauncefote, May 10, 1901.

[29] *Ibid.*, 35–7, the Earl of Minto to Mr. Joseph Chamberlain, November 6, 1901.

[30] T. A Bailey, "Theodore Roosevelt and the Alaska Boundary Settlement" (*Canadian Historical Review*, XVIII, 124), President Roosevelt to J. St. Loe Strachey, July 18, 1902.

vigorously opposed to any arbitration of the dispute and the negotiations in search of an acceptable method of arbitration were therefore discontinued. But two years later, incidents in the gold-fields made him change his mind.

Roosevelt's first inclination was to "let sleeping dogs lie" but rumours of disorder in the Klondike and at the head of Lynn Canal prompted him in May, 1902, to dispatch troops to south-eastern Alaska for police purposes.[31] The presence of American troops on the boundary aroused grave misgivings on the part of the British and Canadian governments and at the end of June Lord Lansdowne urged Ambassador Choate to discuss the whole question with Sir Wilfrid Laurier who was then in London.[32] Both Choate and Henry White had conversations with Sir Wilfrid and found him anxious for a prompt settlement of the dispute and ready to accept the American proposal for arbitration by an even-numbered tribunal.[33] The arbitration convention was signed on January 24, 1903.[34] By its terms the Alaskan boundary dispute was to be referred for settlement to a tribunal consisting of "six impartial jurists of repute, who shall consider judicially the questions submitted to them, each of whom shall first subscribe on oath that he will impartially consider the arguments and evidence presented to the tribunal, and will decide thereupon according to his own true judgment." Three members of the tribunal were to be appointed by the President of the United States and three by His Britannic Majesty. All questions considered by the tribunal were to be decided by "a majority of all the members" and the decision of the tribunal was to be final. The tribunal was to consider and decide seven questions relating to the meaning of Articles iii, iv, and v of the Anglo-Russian treaty of 1825 and it was also to consider any acts of the several governments before or after the treaties of 1825 and 1867 which throw light on the original understanding of the parties as to the limits of their respective territorial jurisdictions under these treaties.

Senator Henry Cabot Lodge was able to secure prompt ratification of the treaty by the American Senate on February 11, 1903, after he had disclosed in confidence to his fellow Senators the names of the men whom the President intended to appoint to the tribunal and thereby satisfied their demand that no one should be appointed who would yield on the American claim.[35] On February 14 the British government was informed

---

[31] Dennis, *Adventures in American Diplomacy*, 143, President Roosevelt to Ambassador Choate, January, 1902; Philip C. Jessup, *Elihu Root* (New York, 1938), I, 391–2, George B. Cortelyon to Secretary Root, March 27, 1902.

[32] Tansill, *Canadian-American Relations*, 224, D. J. Hill to Ambassador Choate, telegram, June 30, 1902.

[33] Nevins, *Henry White*, 192–3, Henry White to Secretary Hay, June 28, 1902; Dennett, *John Hay*, 457–9, Ambassador Choate to Secretary Hay, July 5, 1903.

[34] The text of the treaty may be found in *A.B.T.*, II, 1–6.

[35] "Memoir of H. C. Lodge" (*Transactions of the Massachusetts Historical Society*, April, 1925) as quoted by James White, "Harry Cabot Lodge and the Alaska Boundary Award" (*Canadian Historical Review*, December 1, 1925, 334).

that President Roosevelt would appoint to the tribunal Secretary of War Root, Senator Lodge of Massachusetts, and Senator George Turner of Washington.[36] By no reasonable interpretation of the terms of reference could these gentlemen properly be described as "impartial jurists of repute." Root was a cabinet member of the government of one of the parties to the dispute; Lodge had repeatedly expressed himself as hostile to the Canadian claims;[37] and Turner represented in the Senate that state which was most interested in securing a full confirmation of the American claims. The character of these appointments was a breach of faith and of contract on the part of the United States government. It was determined partly by the need to nominate persons acceptable to the Senate and partly by the President's conception of the nature and purpose of the tribunal. Mr. Roosevelt did not regard the tribunal set up under the treaty of January, 1903, as an arbitral tribunal in the sense in which that term was usually employed in international law.[38] He had flatly refused to expose what he felt were the irrefutable claims of the United States to any possibility of compromise at the hands of a tribunal with a neutral umpire. He had consented to refer the dispute to an even-numbered tribunal from which the United States need not fear an adverse decision and he had done so in order to facilitate a favourable settlement of the dispute by providing the British government with a means of escape from what he believed to be an untenable position. It is therefore not surprising that he should have nominated to the tribunal three experienced politicians on whom he could rely to uphold unflinchingly the American case.

The Canadian government lodged a strong protest with the British government and Sir Wilfrid Laurier made a personal appeal to Secretary Hay urging the unsuitability of the American appointments.[39] But Sir Michael Herbert, British Ambassador to Washington asserted that the President had "got his back up" and advised that it would be useless to protest.[40] The British government therefore made no formal protest against the appointments and ratified the treaty.

On March 7 the British government on the recommendation of the Canadian government appointed to the tribunal Lord Alverstone, the

---

[36] *A.B.T.*, V, pt. IV, 21, Sir Michael Herbert to Lord Lansdowne, February 14, 1903.

[37] See, for example, Senator Lodge in a speech to the electors of Northampton, Massachusetts, October 16, 1902, as quoted by *Manitoba Free Press*, February 24, 1903.

[38] T. A. Bailey, "Theodore Roosevelt and the Alaska Boundary Settlement," (*Canadian Historical Review*, XVIII, June, 1937, 124–5), President Roosevelt to F. W. Holls, February 3, 1903.

[39] Dafoe, *Clifford Sifton*, 220, the Earl of Minto to the Earl of Onslow, February 19, 1903; *A.B.T.*, V, pt. IV, 22, same to same, February 21, 1903; Dennett, *John Hay*, 357–8, Sir Wilfrid Laurier to Secretary Hay, February 24, 1903.

[40] Lord Newton, *Lord Lansdowne* (London, 1929), 262–3, Sir Michael Herbert to Lord Lansdowne, February 21, 1903.

Lord Chief Justice of England, Mr. Justice Armour of the Supreme Court of Canada, and Sir Louis Jetté, Lieutenant-Governor of Quebec and formerly puisné judge of the Superior Court of Quebec. On the death of Mr. Justice Armour in July, Mr. A. B. Aylesworth, a leader of the Ontario Bar who was in England at the time, was appointed in his stead.

Throughout the spring and summer of 1903 while the British and American cases were being prepared for presentation to the tribunal in the autumn, President Roosevelt took particular care that no one who could possibly influence the decision of the tribunal should remain unaware of his attitude toward the dispute. In letters to each of the American commissioners, to Mr. Justice Holmes, and to Henry White the President made it perfectly clear that he considered the American case to be impregnable, that he regarded the tribunal solely as a device to enable the British government to escape gracefully from an impossible position, and that if the tribunal failed to decide in favour of the American contention he intended to ignore its decision and run the line, by force if necessary, in accordance with the American contention.[41] In view of the general climate of Anglo-American relations the leaders of the British government to whom the letters to Holmes, Lodge, and White were shown, could not fail to respond to such vigorous brandishment of the big stick.

The tribunal sat in London and heard the arguments of counsel from September 15 to October 8. During those days "the undercurrents of diplomacy," as Henry White described them,[42] moved to shape the decision of the tribunal as they had molded its structure and composition. Whenever Lord Alverstone showed signs of differing from his American colleagues that fact was reported to the White House and President Roosevelt resorted to the familiar device of diplomatic pressure. Through the offices of Ambassador Choate, Henry White, and Senator Lodge the President did his best to persuade A. J. Balfour that failure of the tribunal to reach a decision would have very serious effects on Anglo-American relations because in the event of a deadlock he would not consent to arbitration of the dispute but would treat the disputed territory as American soil.[43] The evidence shows that on at least two occa-

---

[41] Jessup, *Elihu Root*, I, 395, President Roosevelt to Messrs. Root, Lodge, and Turner, March 25, 1903; James White, "Henry Cabot Lodge," 340–1, President Roosevelt to Senator Lodge, July 16, 1903 and August 16, 1903; J. B. Bishop, *Theodore Roosevelt and His Times Shown in His Own Letters* (New York, 1920), I, 259–61, President Roosevelt to Mr. Justice Holmes, July 25, 1903; Nevins, *Henry White*, 199, President Roosevelt to Henry White, September 26, 1903.

[42] Nevins, *Henry White*, 200–1, Henry White to Secretary Hay, October 20, 1903.

[43] *Ibid.*, 199–200, President Roosevelt to Henry White, September 26, 1903, and Henry White to Secretary Hay, October 20, 1903; "Memoir of H. C. Lodge" as quoted by James White, "Henry Cabot Lodge," 335; Tansill, *Canadian-American Relations*, 258–9, Ambassador Choate to Secretary Hay, October 20, 1903.

sions the British Prime Minister in conversation informed Lord Alverstone of the President's attitude.[44] This is not to suggest that Lord
Alverstone's findings were wholly or even principally the product of
diplomatic pressure; but it is to say that it would have been extremely
difficult for any man appointed as the English member of the tribunal,
knowing the character of the American appointments and aware of the
operation of political forces behind the judicial façade, to persuade
himself that the method of settlement being employed was entirely
judicial (in the strict sense) and that he must remain uninfluenced by
considerations of expediency as distinct from considerations of law.

The tribunal was asked to answer seven questions. The most important
was the fifth; it asked whether it was the intention of the treaty of 1825
that Russia should receive a continuous strip of coast, not exceeding the
marine leagues in width, separating the British possessions from the bays,
ports, inlets, havens, and waters of the ocean, and extending from a point
on the fifty-sixth degree of north latitude to a point where the boundary
should intersect the one hundred and forty-first degree of west longitude.
This was the crux of the whole dispute and the evidence to support the
American contention on this question was very strong if not conclusive.

The United States requested the tribunal to answer the fifth question
in the affirmative and fortified its request by a detailed analysis of the
negotiations leading up to the treaty of 1825.[45] American counsel contended that Russia's chief interest had been to protect the monopoly of
the Russian American Company to the fur trade of the north-west coast
and to prevent the founding of any foreign fur-trading establishments on
the islands or inland waters of the coast north of 55° latitude north. It
was for this reason that the Russian government had issued the ukase of
1821 prohibiting foreign vessels from approaching within one hundred
Italian miles of the coast of the continent and it was for this reason that
the Russian government strove in the negotiations to erect a territorial
barrier between her coastal possessions and the inland dominions of
Great Britain. American counsel argued convincingly that these purposes
Russia achieved in the treaty of 1825.

The United States held that the central aim of Great Britain had been
to preserve the free navigation of the high seas and therefore to secure
the renunciation of the extravagant Russian claims to maritime jurisdiction contained in the ukase of 1821. As a secondary objective Britain had
sought to confine Russian territory to the west of the Rocky Mountains
and as far north as possible on the coast in order to secure a large area
for the future operations of the Hudson's Bay Company and an uninter-

---

[44] Nevins, *Henry White*, 200, Henry White to Secretary Hay, October 20, 1903;
Tansill, *Canadian-American Relations*, 258–9, Ambassador Choate to Secretary Hay,
October 20, 1903.

[45] *A.B.T.*, I, pt. II, 29–65 and IV, pt. I, 40 *ff.*

rupted outlet for its furs to the Pacific. By the treaty of 1825 Britain had obtained the renunciation by Russia of her maritime pretensions and prevented the extension of Russian territory as far east as the Rocky Mountains, but had failed to push the southern boundary of the Russian strip any farther north than 55°. American counsel argued very powerfully that Great Britain had failed to obtain any rights with respect to the Russian *lisière* other than the right in perpetuity to navigate the rivers and streams which crossed its eastern boundary and the right for ten years to frequent the interior seas, gulfs, havens, and creeks along the coast of the *lisière*.

British counsel were unable to combat this argument effectively[46] and the tribunal upheld the American contention by a majority of four to two, Lord Alverstone siding with the American commissioners. Although the Commission went on to draw a mountain boundary line that was a compromise between the British and American contentions there can be little doubt that there was ample evidence to sustain the majority in favour of an unbroken coastal strip belonging to the United States. It was with respect to the answer which the majority gave to the comparatively unimportant second question that the award of the tribunal betrayed most clearly the influence of political forces.

The second question asked: "What channel is Portland Channel?" Great Britain contended very strongly that Portland Channel was that body of water discovered and named by Vancouver and running to the north of four islands, Pearse, Wales, Sitklan, and Kaunaghunut.[47] The United States argued that Portland Channel was the body of water running to the south of the four islands.[48] During the proceedings Lord Alverstone had informed his Canadian colleagues that on this question he considered the British case irrefutable and had intimated that he would prepare an opinion to this effect which they might sign. On October 12 he had read to the tribunal a memorandum embodying the views of the three British commissioners on the subject of Portland Channel.[49] His Canadian colleagues were therefore astounded when at the meeting of the tribunal on October 17, Lord Alverstone voted with the American commissioners that Portland Channel after passing to the north of Pearse and Wales Islands flows between Wales and Sitklan and enters the sea to the south of Sitklan and Kaunaghunut. The majority decision on this question was manifestly a compromise since the four islands had been treated as an entity throughout the proceedings by British and American

---

[46] *A.B.T.*, III, pt. I, 73–6; *A.B.T.*, IV, pt. I, 31–42; *A.B.T.*, IV, pt. II, 26–55; *A.B.T.*, V, pt. I, 65–99; *A.B.T.*, V, pt. II, 35–43.

[47] *A.B.T.*, III, pt. I, 51–69; *A.B.T.*, III, pt. II, 196–208; *A.B.T.*, IV, pt. II, 15–20; *A.B.T.*, IV, pt. III, 18–22; *A.B.T.*, V, pt. II, 12–18.

[48] *A.B.T.*, IV, pt. I, 8–17, 25–6; *A.B.T.*, V, pt. I, 39–45.

[49] Dafoe, *Clifford Sifton*, 230.

counsel alike. To the American commissioners Lord Alverstone's *volte-face* was no surprise. Determined to push their country's claims to the limit they had, at the last moment, insisted that unless a division were made of the Portland Channel islands they would refuse to sign the award.[50] The Chief Justice, fearful of the consequences of deadlock, and believing that the islands were of no value to Canada bowed to the American demands and altered his previous view stated on October 12.[51] The majority decision on this question derives its importance not from the loss to Canada of two islands of no economic and questionable strategic value but from the fact that the patently non-judicial character of that decision cast the whole award into disrepute and made it possible to impugn the judicial character of the answers to other and more important questions before the tribunal.

The majority finding of the question of Portland Channel offended the judicial sensibilities of the two Canadian commissioners who appear to have been unaware of the possibility that their own thorough-going support of their country's case might have been affected by the non-judicial atmosphere which surrounded the labours of the tribunal. Sir Louis Jetté and Mr. Aylesworth refused to sign the award of the tribunal on the ground that it was not a judicial finding. They filed dissenting judgments both of which upheld the British position in its entirety and attacked the majority award on the question of the islands as "a mere compromise dividing the field between two contestants."[52] They also issued a joint statement to the *Times* explaining to the people of Canada the character of the award and their reasons for not signing it.[53]

Lord Alverstone held aloof from the public controversy that followed the award, but in the privacy of correspondence with Sir Wilfrid Laurier, Mr. Aylesworth, Sir Louis Jetté, and Mr. Clifford Sifton, he revealed that he was deeply offended by their expressions of want of confidence in his decision. The record of the correspondence that passed among these gentlemen reveals a striking contrast between the position taken by the Canadians who flatly denounced Lord Alverstone's decision on the ground that it was not a judicial finding and the position taken by Lord Alverstone who stoutly maintained that his decision was founded solely on judicial considerations.[54] This seeming incompatibility of view is

---

[50] *Ibid.*, 232.

[51] For a comparison of Lord Alverstone's first opinion and his final judgment see John S. Ewart, "The Alaska Boundary" in *The Kingdom of Canada and Other Essays* (Toronto, 1908), 322 *ff.*

[52] *A.B.T.*, I, pt. I, 86 *ff.*

[53] The *Times*, October 21, 1903.

[54] Lord Alverstone to A. B. Aylesworth, October 21, 1903 and October 26, 1903; A. B. Aylesworth to Lord Alverstone, November 3, 1903, November 9, 1903, and November 11, 1903; Lord Alverstone to Clifford Sifton, October, 1903; *Memorandum* of Lord Alverstone, October 24, 1903. These documents are to be found in the Sifton MS.

partly to be explained by the fact that the Canadians attached a very different meaning to the word "judicial" from that given to it by Lord Alverstone. They restricted the term "judicial" to those considerations directly related to the interpretation of the law as embodied in the treaty of 1825. Lord Alverstone used the term in a much wider sense which enabled him to give weight to considerations such as the unfortunate consequences of deadlock in the tribunal and the value of the Portland Channel Islands to the parties.

Lord Alverstone's more liberal interpretation of the term "judicial" reflected his view of the nature of the tribunal and of the functions he was called upon to perform in it. The peculiar structure and composition of the tribunal restricted the range of its possible results to two inescapable alternatives, an American victory or deadlock. In the choice between these alternatives the judgment of Lord Alverstone would almost inevitably be decisive. Under these circumstances he conceived his position to be not that of one judge among six but that of an umpire appointed to adjust the claims of two conflicting groups. The tribunal itself he regarded not as one of arbitration but as "an attempt to solve by mutual discussion and friendly consideration questions which might have become the subject of discord between the two nations concerned."[55] Lord Alverstone, holding this broad view of the nature and purpose of the tribunal did not feel bound in his deliberations to consider only the evidence presented to him in the written arguments and the arguments of counsel. Throughout the proceedings he was particularly sensitive to the consideration that the failure of the tribunal to reach an agreement would be an international calamity.[56] Believing that his first duty was to secure an award he attempted to double in the roles of diplomat and judge. His performance of this exacting dual role exhibited dignity and perseverance but lacked the delicacy and insight needed to harmonize its desperate parts into a consistent pattern. He came naturally into close relations with the American commissioners without whose consent an award was impossible. Toward his Canadian colleagues Lord Alverstone maintained an attitude of grave courtesy but he seriously blundered, as a mediator if not as a judge, in failing to enter into close collaboration with them and especially in neglecting to inform them privately of his change of opinion on the question of Portland Channel. In the atmosphere of the tribunal, charged with suspicion, the Canadian commissioners were only too ready to regard any such omission as evidence of a willingness on the part of the Chief Justice to be guided by considerations of policy rather than of law. To that want of complete frankness on the part of Lord Alverstone may be traced much of the bitterness of the Canadian commissioners and

---

[55] Taken from a speech made by Lord Alverstone at a dinner at the Mansion House, as reported in the *Times*, October 14, 1903.

[56] A. B. Aylesworth to Lord Alverstone, November 3, 1903, Sifton MS.

no small measure of the acerbity of their accusations which inflamed Canadian opinion against the whole award.

The record of Canadian-American relations had led many Canadians to see annexationist designs in every positive assertion of American territorial claims along the Canadian border and had persuaded them that, in any dispute between Canada and the United States, Great Britain was likely to surrender Canadian interests on the altar of Anglo-American friendship. From the beginning Canadians had been profoundly sceptical of the arrangements for the settlement of the Alaskan boundary dispute and the award of the tribunal realized their worst fears.[57] The refusal of the Canadian commissioners to sign the award, their issuance of separate decisions, and their condemnation of the majority decision in the statement to the *Times* unleashed in Canada a storm of protest which one historian has described as "vigorous, wide-spread and sustained beyond anything in the country's annals."[58] Canadian indignation was aroused not so much by the details of the award as by the methods which were believed to have been employed in reaching it.[59] Canadians vent their anger to a lesser degree upon the United States for having violated the treaty in its appointments to the tribunal and to a greater degree upon Great Britain for having offered such feeble resistance to American aggressiveness.[60] The circumstances surrounding the settlement of the dispute produced serious dissatisfaction with Canada's position in the British Empire.[61] Those circumstances did not reveal any clear and desirable alternative to existing imperial relationships but they convinced many Canadians that those relationships were no longer adequate and should be changed in ways which would give Canadians greater control over their own affairs and in this way they helped to create an atmosphere favourable to the reception of new ideas concerning Canada's relation to the mother country.

The influence of political forces on the structure, membership, and

---

[57] Toronto *Telegram*, January 25, 1903; *Manitoba Free Press*, January 25, 1903; Victoria *Daily Colonist*, February 26, 1903; Toronto *Globe*, February 19, 1903 and February 21, 1903; Ottawa *Citizen*, February 19, 1903; Halifax *Herald*, February 25, 1903; London *Morning Post*, September 3, 1903.

[58] O. D. Skelton, *The Life and Letters of Sir Wilfrid Laurier* (London, 1922), II, 153.

[59] Gelber, *Rise of Anglo-American Friendship*, 162; H. L. Keenleyside, *Canada and the United States; Some Aspects of the History of the Republic and the Dominion* (New York, 1929), 227; P. E. Corbett, *The Settlement of Canadian-American Disputes* (Toronto, 1937), 22.

[60] H. F. Angus (ed.), *Canada and Her Great Neighbour; Sociological Surveys of Opinions and Attitudes in Canada Concerning the United States* (Toronto, 1938), 78; Montreal *Gazette*, October 21, 1903; Toronto *World*, October 19, 1903; Ottawa *Journal*, October 21, 1903; *Manitoba Free Press*, October 21, 1903; London *Daily Mail*, October 20, 1903, and October 26, 1903.

[61] Sir Wilfrid Laurier, *Canada, House of Commons Debates*, October 23, 1903; Toronto *Globe*, October 26, 1903; Monteal *La Presse*, October 26, 1903.

award of the Alaskan Boundary Tribunal indicates clearly the limitations of arbitration as a method of settling international disputes. The Alaskan boundary dispute was not susceptible of judicial or quasi-judicial settlement because one of the parties was unwilling to have the dispute taken out of international politics and settled by judicial as distinct from political criteria. Once it is admitted that considerations of policy were bound to have a most important place in the settlement of the dispute it is difficult to see how a result could have been reached materially at variance with that which was the decision of the Alaskan Boundary Tribunal. The essential facts were that the United States had a very strong case, that a settlement was becoming increasingly urgent, that President Roosevelt was determined to have a settlement wholly favourable to the United States, and that in the existing state of international relations no British government could afford to uphold Canadian claims to the extent of jeopardizing Anglo-American understanding. Concessions had to be made on the British side and the substitution of Canadian weakness for British desire for American friendship in the equation of the settlement would not have altered the result in Canada's favour. British diplomacy created an atmosphere of friendly relations and facilitated the adjustment of an awkward and irritating dispute which, if it had not been settled, might have produced a breach in the Anglo-American *rapprochement* and impeded co-operation of the English-speaking peoples in the Great War. In the development of Anglo-American solidarity Canada had a far greater stake than that which she was called upon to surrender in the settlement of the Alaskan boundary dispute.

Yet in 1903 Canadians believed that they were being asked to make all the sacrifices for the cause of Anglo-American amity. An uncritical assumption that Canada had the stronger case, together with a refusal to recognize that in imperial diplomacy the interests of the whole must take precedence over those of the part, and that in international politics disputes are settled in accordance with the views of the stronger party, all lay at the source of a wave of Canadian indignation which vented itself upon British supineness and American bullying. This indignation gave a tremendous stimulus to the movement for full self-government which later became formalized in new relations among the members of the British Commonwealth of Nations. Her sense of nationality quickened by what she regarded as ill-treatment at the hands of two great English-speaking powers, Canada moved out of the colonial era into a period of conscious aspiration for national status.

part IV

Early 20th Century Canada

21

Clerics, Politicians, and the Bilingual Schools Issue in Ontario, 1910–1917*

Margaret Prang

ENGLISH-SPEAKING Canadians have long seen the Conscription issue as the great, cataclysmic crisis which divided the two Canadian cultures during World War I, and indeed it was that issue on which the ominous election of 1917 was fought. But French Canada had been emotionally aroused much earlier by the "Prussians of Ontario" in their attempt to restrict, some said eventually to eliminate, the use of French by Franco-Ontarians in the schools. In this article Margaret Prang shows that "the vast majority of the people of Ontario rejected entirely the concept of cultural duality."

In studying the article the reader is warned to distinguish carefully between the argument over French as a language of instruction and the argument which finally dominated the issue and centred around the word "hitherto," that of the role of French as a subject of study in certain elementary schools.

Professor Prang, a keen student of the career of Norman Rowell, the Ontario Liberal leader, shows how both Ontario parties were infected with anti-French Canadianism, the Conservatives with their powerful Orange element, ironically this time provincially allied to the Irish Catholics, and the Liberals with their old Presbytarian Grit and evangelical Methodist elements. Although the militancy was stronger in the Conservative party, Laurier could appeal in vain before his Ontario partisans to the tolerant tradition of Oliver Mowat. The result was a fascinating and significant debate, which Miss Prang explains, between Rowell and

---

* *Canadian Historical Review*, XLI (December, 1960), pp. 281–307.

Laurier on the meaning of Mowat's federalism, which each man claimed to follow. What course of action if any does a provincial minority which feels persecuted have against a permanent provincial majority which denies what that minority and its confères in Quebec regard as the essential compromise of Confederation? The debate foretold the disruption of the Liberal party and the temporary formation by the national cultural majority of a "Union" government. These events seem to strengthen Professor Michel Brunet's assertion that federalism is really an unstable and authoritarian form of government rather than Lord Acton's assertion that federalism is liberal and the highest and most tolerant form of government known to free man.

THE CONSERVATIVE VICTORY in the Ontario election of 1905 brought to power a party which had gone on record fifteen years earlier as opposing the use of any language but English in the schools of the province. During their years in opposition the Conservatives had made few criticisms of the regulations of 1890 which provided that French and German might be taught in districts where parents desired instruction in one of these languages, as long as English remained the language of general instruction. But a Conservative cabinet which included several Orangemen and a party which had a militant Orange wing might be expected to take a more active interest in the question. The most vigilant guardians of French-Canadian interests were now apprehensive.

They soon found cause for concern on February 25, 1906, when English-speaking separate school ratepayers in Ottawa passed a resolution calling for an end to the unified administration of the separate schools of the city, established only three years earlier, and a return to separate control of the finances and administration of the schools attended by the children of the two groups.[1] For the present, the English-speaking Catholics, who had recently become a minority in Ottawa, made no progress with their demands; however, at the end of 1909 they were cheered by the announcement that Father Michael Fallon, who had been a leading figure in the language controversy at the University of Ottawa and who had subsequently spent several years in "exile" in the United States, was to return to Ontario as Bishop of London.

Bishop Fallon had been consecrated only some six months when much of the French-Canadian press began to accuse him of attempting to

---

[1] C. B. Sissons, *Bilingual Schools in Canada* (Toronto, 1917), 72. For a concise outline of the language question in Ontario from pre-Confederation days see *Report of the Royal Commission on Education in Ontario,* 1950 (Toronto: The King's Printer), chap. XVI.

Anglicize the schools of his diocese by reducing or abolishing the teaching of French; Fallon denied that he wished to exterminate French from the schools but asserted that he favoured full obedience to a law which countenanced bilingual, but not French, schools.[2] Although determined to maintain the primacy of English in the schools, Bishop Fallon was anxious lest the school question explode in such a way as to make separate schools and the French language synonymous in the minds of the Protestant majority in the province. This catastrophe might well be precipitated by the majority's growing awareness of the rapid increase in the French-speaking population in Northern Ontario and the counties just west of the Ottawa River.

At the moment, separate school supporters could have no complaints against the Whitney government; early in 1910 the government began to draft plans for a redistribution of funds to the elementary schools, under which the separate schools would receive larger grants.[3] The proposed change naturally had the support of the bishops of the province,[4] and the English-speaking majority among their number hoped that agitation over the language question would not provoke hostility against separate schools in general so that the government would refuse to proceed with the redistribution. As a consequence of these fears the formation of the French-Canadian Education Association of Ontario in January, 1910, with its demand for "equal rights" for the French language in Ontario, created much tension between the French and English bishops.[5] Within two months of the Association's formation the fears of the English group proved justified when Premier Whitney informed the archbishops of the province that because of recent public agitation about the language question the government was unable to proceed with the plan for a redistribution of school funds.[6]

In the spring of 1910 when Bishop Fallon paid his first official visit to Sarnia, he invited the local member of the Legislature, W. J. Hanna, who was also Provincial Secretary, to call on him; to Hanna the bishop complained that in some schools in the county of Essex, which lay within his diocese, there were large numbers of pupils who were unable to speak English. The immediate cause of Fallon's alarm was the assertion by an English-speaking school inspector in Essex that he had received instructions from the Department of Education to cease inspecting certain bilingual schools, and his belief that a French-speaking inspector would

[2] *Canadian Annual Review*, 1910, 421.

[3] University of Toronto Library. "Correspondence between the Ontario Department of Education and the Roman Catholic Authorities concerning the Bi-lingual School Issue," John Seath to Sir William Meredith, Feb. 17, 1910.

[4] *Ibid.*, G. F. Shepley to Sir William Meredith, March 10, 1910.

[5] *Ibid.*, memorandum of Bishop Fallon for the bishops of Ontario, Jan. 24, 1917.

[6] *Ibid.*, copy of Whitney to the archbishops of Ontario, March 9, 1910.

be appointed in his place; further, Fallon had heard that the department was prepared to accept some Quebec teaching certificates in the Ottawa area. In short, it appeared to Fallon that the government was about to succumb to French-Canadian agitation; if his information proved correct he was prepared to wage total war against the government; meanwhile, he would do all he could to discourage the perpetuation of bilingual schools in his own diocese. Hanna, who seems to have been somewhat surprised and mystified by the intensity of Fallon's feelings, assured him that he was misinformed as to the government's intentions; then he sent a written account of the interview to Premier Whitney and to the Minister of Education, Dr. R. A. Pyne.[7] For the present Fallon made no public denunciation of what he understood to be government policy.

In mid-August the activities of the French-Canadian Education Association were the subject of heated discussions at a meeting of the bishops of the ecclesiastical provinces of Kingston and Toronto most of whom now believed that the whole position of separate schools was seriously threatened; they delegated Fallon to wait on Premier Whitney to request that there be no yielding by the government to the demands of the bilingualists; Fallon came away well satisfied that the premier had accepted his argument.[8] A month later the Twentieth Eucharistic Congress, the first such assembly held in North America, met in Montreal. This added to Protestant apprehensions (already aroused by the struggle over the application of the *Ne Temere* decree in Quebec) that the influence of the Roman Catholic hierarchy in Canada might be growing. The Eucharistic Congress did add fuel to the bilingual controversy when Archbishop Bourne of Westminster issued his unexpected call to the Canadian church to identify itself thoroughly with the English language if it would fully serve the Roman Catholic mission in Canada. This provoked an impromptu and impassioned reply from Henri Bourassa which immediately enhanced the nationalist leader's public influence and served notice on the rest of Canada that the fight for the French language throughout the Dominion would not be abandoned.[9]

It was against this background that G. Howard Ferguson, spokesman for the ultra-Protestant wing of the Ontario Conservatives, introduced in the Ontario Legislature in the spring of 1911 a motion asserting that "no language other than English should be used as a medium of instruction" in any school in Ontario.[10] For reasons which were probably not uncon-

---

[7] W. J. Hanna to R. A. Pyne, May 23, 1910, printed in full in Sissons, *Bilingual Schools,* 73–9.

[8] Correspondence . . . concerning the Bi-lingual School Issue," Fallon to Pyne, Jan. 2, 1912.

[9] Robert Rumilly, *Henri Bourassa* (Montreal, 1953), chap. xviii, gives a colourful account of this episode and its effect in Quebec.

[10] *Journals of the Legislative Assembly of Ontario,* March 22, 1911, 260.

nected with the current efforts of the federal Conservative party to form the alliance with the Quebec Nationalists which was to prove so fruitful in the election later that year, Ferguson soon withdrew this resolution. He then introduced a modified resolution which declared that English should be "the language of instruction and of all communication with the pupils in the public and separate schools . . . except where, in the opinion of the department, it is impracticable by reason of the pupils not understanding English." This resolution received the unanimous support of both parties.[11]

In mid-October the unauthorized publication of W. J. Hanna's letter of eighteen months ago describing his interview with Fallon[12] caused the controversy to flare up again. The bishop exonerated Hanna from responsibility for publishing the letter, although he said that the document as published did not entirely accord with his own recollection of his conversation with Hanna; in particular, he asserted that the reference to a meeting of the bishops of Ontario had no basis in fact.[13] It appeared that Fallon was not averse to seeing the bilingual issue brought into the arena of full public debate; once this had happened his first contribution was a denunciation of the attempt of the Department of Education to carry on the study of both languages simultaneously, an approach which he believed pedagogically unsound, resulting in inadequate training in both languages and "encourag[ing] incompetency, giv[ing] a prize to hypocrisy, and breed[ing] ignorance."[14] Within a few days the government announced that Dr. F. W. Merchant, an official of the Ontario Department of Education had been appointed to investigate conditions in the bilingual schools.

With the question thus removed at least partially from politics for the moment, Whitney suddenly called an election for December 11. But the issue inevitably became an important one in the campaign although the newly elected leader of the Liberal party, N. W. Rowell, did not go out of his way to make it so, contenting himself in his initial address to the electors with a promise of "adequate training schools, a sufficient supply of competent teachers . . . to ensure under proper regulations that the pupils in every school . . . shall receive a thorough English education."[15] Rather, it was certain prominent members of the Conservative

[11] *Ibid.* This resolution was simply a confirmation of the existing law, Statutes of Ontario, 59 Vic. c. 70, s. 76.

[12] See note 7. The secretary of the French-speaking Minister of Public Works, Dr. J. O. Reaume, lost his position on charges that he had released the private letter for publication to a Quebec paper: Sissons, *Bilingual Schools,* 73.

[13] In two other documents Fallon says that the meeting was held. "Correspondence . . . concerning the Bi-lingual School Issue," Fallon to Pyne, Jan. 2, 1912 and memorandum of Bishop Fallon for the bishops of Ontario, Jan. 24, 1917.

[14] *Globe,* Oct. 18, 1911.

[15] Public Archives of Canada, Rowell Papers, *Address to the Electors by N. W. Rowell* (Ontario Reform Association, 1911).

party and the Conservative papers, the Toronto *Telegram* and the *News,* who seemed most determined to keep the issue alive with their promises that they would oppose the teaching of any French in the schools.[16] But the Liberal *Toronto Daily Star* also helped to keep the issue before the public by publishing the results of investigations by two of its own reporters which showed that there were some areas of the province where French was used exclusively and that standards were generally low in the bilingual schools.[17]

As the election battle developed, it became increasingly clear that the language question cut across party lines. In the government ranks, the Attorney-General, J. J. Foy, a Roman Catholic of Irish origin representing the riding of Toronto South, declared for nothing but English,[18] thus allying himself with Bishop Fallon, Howard Ferguson, and the Orange Order. Foy's statement created anxiety among some Conservative politicians who predicted losses for the party in the coming election unless Premier Whitney publicly refuted Foy.[19] The statement of the Minister of Public Works, Dr. J. O. Reaume, a few days later, that, as a French-speaking Canadian he could confidently support Whitney's view that all children should learn English and might be allowed to use French in the early grades[20] was apparently intended to undo any damage that might have been wrought by Foy.

Although the Liberals tried to use this display of cabinet dissension to show that the Conservatives had no policy, there was slight advantage in doing so, since they also exhibited a variety of convictions on the subject. While the recently retired Liberal leader, A. G. MacKay, member for the strongly Orange riding of Grey North, argued for no language but English,[21] Rowell told a North Bay audience that "the state has no right to say that these same children should grow up without further knowledge of the language which they first lisped at their mothers' knees."[22] Rowell's emphasis was somewhat less positive in the riding he was personally contesting, North Oxford; there, he stated that there was no excuse for schools where only French was taught and called on Whitney to declare whether he stood with Mr. Foy or Dr. Reaume.[23]

There were only two Ontario ridings, Prescott and Russell, in which French-Canadians were in the majority, but there were fourteen others in

16 *Canadian Annual Review,* 1911, 473.

17 *Toronto Daily Star,* especially issues of Nov. 20 and 22, 1911.

18 *Globe,* Nov. 21, 1911.

19 Ontario Archives, Whitney Papers, Andrew Broder to Whitney, Nov. 23, 1911; A. A. Aubin to Whitney, Nov. 28, 1911.

20 *Globe,* Nov. 30, 1911.

21 *Ibid.,* Dec. 1, 1911.

22 *Ibid.,* Nov. 30, 1911.

23 *Weekly Sun* (Toronto), Dec. 6, 1911.

which they constituted 10 per cent or more of the population and possibly another six in which they might be decisive in a very close contest,[24] most of these were at present held by the Conservatives. When the election results came in two of the five seats gained by the Liberals were in ridings where the French-speaking vote was probably significant.[25]

In the first session of the new legislature, Rowell lost no time in raising the bilingual issue; in his first speech he observed that although the premier had said during the campaign that such schools did not exist in Ontario the public accounts provided for the salaries of three "inspectors of bilingual schools." Whitney refused to make any statement, pending the report of Dr. Merchant, but called attention to the resolution which had been approved unanimously in the previous session requiring English in all schools except where the students did not yet understand the language.[26] Rowell's further efforts to obtain a more specific statement of government policy were met by the well-founded charges of Napoleon Champagne, Conservative member for Ottawa East, that the Liberal leader was thoroughly equivocal in his own statements. Champagne declared that while Rowell had said that nobody should deprive a French-speaking child of his mother tongue, he had never spelled out just what this should mean for school policy. Rowell's reply can scarcely have satisfied Champagne; it asserted that the leader of the Opposition was under no necessity to declare a precise policy, and called attention again to the contradictory statements made by Conservative politicians in various parts of the province. In contrast, declared Rowell, the Liberal policy was consistent; every child must have "a thorough education in English . . . but we have no right to say any child shall be ignorant of its mother tongue."[27]

Toward the end of the session the controversy entered a new phase when the Merchant Report[28] was presented to the legislature on March 6. The report confirmed the charges of the critics of the bilingual schools; Dr. Merchant found that in 80 per cent of the separate schools in eastern Ontario and in 90 per cent of the rural public and separate schools in the northern districts French was used in teaching all subjects except English, which was treated merely as one subject among others on the curriculum. The professional qualifications of most of the teachers in these schools were minimal and some had so slight a knowledge of English as to be doubtful teachers of the language. Thus, it was revealed that while

---

[24] The author's calculation, based on figures in *Census of Canada, 1911.*

[25] Party standings after the election were Conservatives, 83; Liberals, 22; Independent, 1; the Conservatives and Liberals each had three French-speaking members.

[26] *Globe,* Feb. 9, 1912.

[27] *Ibid.,* Feb. 21, 1912.

[28] F. W. Merchant, *Report on the Condition of English-French Schools in the Province of Ontario* (Toronto: King's Printer, 1912).

there were some schools which might properly be called bilingual there were many more which were really French. Moreover, attendance at these schools was often poor and many children left school very early to go to work, equipped with an inadequate education in any language. Although Dr. Merchant admitted that the bilingual schools laboured under a difficulty not faced by others—the necessity of helping students to master a second language, English, in a short period of time—he could only conclude that "the English-French schools are, on the whole, lacking in efficiency."

Several attempts by the Liberals to secure an immediate debate on the report were rebuffed by government promises of a debate in due course. Finally, half an hour before prorogation, Whitney announced a school policy. The proposal provided for additional inspection of schools to assure testing of progress and enforcement of the regulations; henceforth, government grants to schools would be contingent on the employment of teachers able to instruct in English; no text books other than those authorized by the Department of Education were to be used; and, although French might be used as the language of instruction on the recommendation of the supervising inspector, this would not normally be continued beyond the first two years of school. Rowell asked whether the new policy meant that the regulations of the Mowat government, providing that French and German might be used fairly extensively in addition to English in specified areas, would be rescinded, and was told that they would not be withdrawn for the present. The opposition leader interpreted this to mean that, in practice, the use of French as a language of instruction was to continue pretty much as before; for this he thought there was "much to be said." Rowell also supported Dr. Merchant's recommendation that French be made a subject of study in public schools throughout the province, as it was in the high schools.[29] Thus, "Sir James had performed the sword dance awkwardly enough, but apparently without cutting his feet. Mr. Rowell had pirouetted on eggs without cracking a shell."[30]

A few days later Rowell devoted most of an address at a Liberal rally in Toronto to the bilingual question. He accused the government of insincerity and cowardice and charged that the facts revealed in the Merchant Report had been known to the Department of Education for several years. He doubted whether the new provisions for inspection were adequate, but added that if the government pursued its announced policy the whole character of the bilingual schools would be improved.[31]

---

[29] *Globe,* April 15, 1912.

[30] *World,* Toronto, April 15, 1912.

[31] *Globe,* April 20, 1912. The essential unity of the two parties on this issue is obviously due primarily to the dominantly English-speaking and Protestant character of Ontario, but in considering the reluctance of the opposition to criticize government

The Liberal leader had, in effect, served notice that the government need fear no serious criticism from his party; there was now an essentially bipartisan policy on the bilingual schools.

The opponents of bilingual education felt confirmed in their views when the official census of 1911 was published. The census provided statistical proof that the racial division in Ontario in the second decade of the twentieth century was very different from what it had been in the days when Mowat had applied more generously regulations which were very similar to those announced by Whitney. Between 1881 and 1911 Ontario's population had increased from 1,926,922 to 2,523,274, a gain of nearly 600,000; in the same period the French-speaking population had increased from 102,743 to 202,442.[32] However, this latter figure was generally believed to be very conservative; the ecclesiastical census of the province in 1909 had reported 247,000 French-Canadians,[33] and the figure usually quoted by the politicians in 1911 was 250,000. Thus, in the preceding thirty-five years the French-Canadians had accounted for about 25 per cent of the total increase; where they had composed 5 per cent of the population in the 1880's they were now about 10 per cent. English-speaking alarmists found in the census support for such assertions as the one made, during the recent campaign by the Toronto *Star*, that in another twenty-five years Northern Ontario would have a population of two million, of whom 75 per cent would be exclusively French-speaking.[34] The prediction was hysterical, but it fed the fears of the majority in Protestant Ontario for whom religion and language could not be separated; anyone could see that the bilingual schools were nearly all Roman Catholic separate schools. Nobody understood the possible implications of this identification more clearly than the Irish Catholic bishops.

Whitney's policy was formalized on June 15, 1912, when the Department of Education published a new circular of instructions on the bilingual schools, soon popularly known as "Regulation 17."[35] Ten days later

---

policy it must be noted that at this time the Liberal party had a very powerful Protestant "directorate." Its leader, N. W. Rowell, was one of the most prominent Methodist laymen in the province; in the summer of 1912 a group of Toronto Liberals organized a fund to provide the leader with secretarial assistance and to place a party organizer in the field. This group included A. E. Ames, E. R. Wood, J. H. Gundy, W. E. Rundle, Col. F. H. Deacon, all leading financiers, and J. E. Atkinson, publisher of the *Toronto Star* and J. F. Mackay, business manager of the *Globe*. With the exception of Mackay, who was a Presbyterian, all of these men were active supporters of the Methodist church, and it is evident that they were frequently consulted on party policy.

[32] *Census of Canada, 1911.*

[33] *Canadian Annual Review*, 1911, 471.

[34] *Toronto Daily Star*, Nov. 30, 1911.

[35] The most controversial parts of Regulation 17 were in Section 3: "(1) Where necessary in the case of French-speaking pupils, French may be used as the language of instruction and communication; but such use of French shall not be continued beyond Form I, excepting during the school year of 1912–13, when it may also be

in Quebec City the first French Language Congress held in North America pronounced itself firmly in favour of the extension of fully bilingual schools to every province where there were numbers of French Canadians.[36] This aspiration was supported on the platform of the Congress by a member of Whitney's cabinet, Dr. Reaume.[37] Before the opening of the new school term the government issued a further order, "Regulation 18." It ruled that any school which failed to comply with Regulation 17 would forfeit support from public funds and that its teachers would be liable to suspension or cancellation of their certificates.[38] These measures received enthusiastic endorsement by the Irish Catholic clergy of the province who urged Whitney to stand firm in his clear distinction between separate and bilingual schools.[39] At the same time Conservative politicians in Ottawa and Quebec were alarmed at the damage which they believed Whitney's policy would do to the party's prospects in Quebec.[40] Prime Minister Borden commented on "the very great outcry in the Province of Quebec" and requested Whitney to give "a reliable and correct statement of the regulations and the reasons why the same were promulgated . . . to some of our friends in Quebec . . . because misapprehension as to the course your government has pursued is likely to do mischief."[41] Whitney's reply was merely a digest of the Merchant Report. He asserted that the new regulations were designed simply to enforce a policy which had been in effect for many years but which, of late, had not been properly administered; no injustice was being done to anyone and he was confident that the majority of French-Canadian parents in Ontario wanted their children to learn English and

---

used as the language of instruction and communication in the case of pupils beyond Form I who, owing to previous defective training, are unable to speak and understand the English language. (2) In the case of French-speaking pupils who are unable to speak the English language well enough for the purposes of instruction and communication, the following provision is hereby made: (a) As soon as the pupil enters the school he shall begin the study and use of the English language (b) As soon as the pupil has acquired sufficient facility in the use of the English language he shall take up in that language the course of study as prescribed for the Public and Separate Schools." The regulation is published in full in Sissons, *Bilingual Schools*, Appendix 2; also in *Report of the Minister of Education, 1912* (Toronto: King's Printer, 1913), 211–13.

[36] Robert Rumilly, *Historie de la Province de Québec* (32 vols., Montreal, 1940–60), XVII, chap. IV

[37] *Globe*, June 25, 1912.

[38] *Report of the Minister of Education, 1912*, 213–15.

[39] Whitney Papers, Bishop D. J. Scollard to Whitney, Oct. 21, 1912; Bishop W.A. Macdonell to Whitney, Nov. 13, 1912; Very Rev. A. E. Burke, president of the Catholic Church Extension Society, to Whitney, Nov. 14, 1912.

[40] *Ibid.*, Thomas Chapais to Whitney, Oct. 10, 1912; L. P. Pelletier to Whitney, Oct. 21, 1912.

[41] *Ibid.*, Borden to Whitney, Oct. 16, 1912.

were satisfied that this would not rob them of their French language and heritage.[42]

Opposition within the province came to a focus at the end of the year when a large delegation representing nearly all the French-speaking school districts waited on Whitney to demand the withdrawal of Regulation 17. The delegates argued that the ruling was not only unjust and illiberal but also *ultra vires* because it was contrary to the earlier Regulation 12 which still permitted both French and German in some schools. In defending his policy the premier asked "where in any country . . . an hour a day was allowed in each class for the study of one subject" as was allowed for French in Ontario. He found that nobody could mention so generous a provision elsewhere.[43] He then assured the protesters that every inspector would report at the end of the current school year on the effects of the instructions now being followed and might recommend changes, but he allowed none of his audience to entertain the slightest hope that a third type of school, "the racial school," would be tolerated.[44] Many Irish Catholics were now confident that the whole issue was settled and that little more would be heard of it.[45]

Certainly the Liberal party in Ontario, having once given tacit approval to Regulation 17, showed no disposition to discuss the subject. In spite of earlier appeals from some English-speaking Catholic Liberals that the federal Liberal party should publicly disavow the activities of Senator Belcourt and other Liberals in the French-Canadian Education Association of Ontario,[46] Laurier had thus far made no public comment. When Laurier appeared on the platform in Toronto in October, 1912, with Rowell, Sir Allen Aylesworth, and Sir George Ross, who had been Minister of Education under Mowat, there was no reference to the language question. Throughout the autumn Rowell and other Ontario Liberals kept clear of the issue in their prepared addresses. When he was asked a direct question, Rowell's answer was always that he favoured an adequate English education for every child; beyond that he would not go. Laurier's public advice to French-Canadians in Ontario "to speak French at home and English on the street"[47] was understood in some

[42] *Ibid.*, Whitney to Thomas Chapais, Oct. 16, 1912; Whitney to Borden, Oct. 17, 1912; Whitney to L. P. Pelletier, Oct. 22, 1912.

[43] *Ibid.*, Whitney to Archbishop C. H. Gauthier, Dec. 28, 1912.

[44] *Globe*, Dec. 28, 1912.

[45] Whitney Papers, Fallon to Whitney, Dec. 28, 1912; Michael O'Brien, inspector of separate schools, Peterborough, to Whitney, Dec. 28, 1912; Whitney to S. M. Genest, Jan. 9, 1913.

[46] P.A.C., Laurier Papers, Fallon to Charles Murphy, June 3, 1911; Murphy to Laurier, June 19, 1911.

[47] *Ottawa Journal*, Nov. 20, 1912.

Conservative circles at least to mean that federal Liberal leaders had no serious objections to Ontario's policy.[48]

During the 1913 session of the legislature the only reference to the bilingual issue came from two French-speaking Liberals, Z. Mageau and Gustave Evanturel of the constituencies of Sturgeon Falls and Prescott. They demanded the publication of letters from Bishop Fallon to members of the government since 1910, and, charging that Dr. Reaume's continued presence in the cabinet constituted a betrayal of his race, they called for his resignation. No English-speaking Liberals supported their two colleagues, the government refused to be drawn into battle,[49] and to the evident relief of both parties the session ended without any major discussion.

In the following August the government issued Regulation 17 in a slightly revised form. The Chief Inspector was given power to permit the use of French as the language of communication beyond the first two years of study where he deemed it necessary, and to allow the study of French for more than one hour a day in certain schools, provided he was satisfied that this would not retard the pupils' progress in learning English.[50] Thus, while the objective of the policy remained unchanged, the rules could be applied more leniently at the discretion of the Department of Education. Although the Minister of Education denied charges that this represented a partial retreat from the original policy,[51] the government was chastised by the Conservative *Mail and Empire* for its weakness.[52]

Meanwhile, during the autumn of 1913 meetings of the Saint-Jean-Baptiste Societies in Quebec were better attended than they had been in many years and the dominant theme was always the fate of the beleaguered brethren in Ontario. The fifth annual convention of the French-Canadian Education Association enjoyed the largest registration yet, and during its sessions unremitting war against Regulation 17 was again declared. A few weeks later Henri Bourassa carried his campaign against the regulation into Ontario itself where he delivered a number of addresses.[53] In Ottawa, Roman Catholics who sent their children to public schools to ensure that they were taught in English were threatened with refusal of the sacraments,[54] while the provincial government announced

[48] Whitney Papers, J. A. Ellis to Whitney, Nov. 27, 1912; Whitney to Ellis, Nov. 29, 1912.

[49] *Globe*, Feb. 8 and March 4, 1913.

[50] *Report of the Minister of Education, 1913* (Toronto: King's Printer, 1914), 318–20.

[51] *Globe*, Sept. 19, 1913.

[52] *Mail and Empire*, Sept. 19, 1913.

[53] For an account of French-Canadian reaction to Regulation 17 see Rumilly, *Histoire*, XVII–XXII, *passim*.

[54] *Mail and Empire*, Sept. 1, 1913.

that the Ottawa Separate School Board would receive no public funds, since it had refused to submit reports on its affairs or to admit inspectors during the past year.[55]

During a by-election in Peel when the Provincial Treasurer, I. B. Lucas, challenged the Liberal leader to state his school policy in concrete terms, Rowell was forced into breaking his silence. After noting that the French Canadians were playing an important part in the development of the province and now constituted one-tenth of the population, Rowell chastised the government for the neglect which had produced the conditions revealed in the Merchant Report, rehearsed the conflicting statements of cabinet members on the bilingual issue, and asserted that it was little wonder, in view of Whitney's promises to stand by the original rules, that the Conservative press and the Orange Lodges felt betrayed by the revised Regulation 17; on the other hand, the French Canadians also felt that they were the victims of bad faith. Once more, in contrast to the government's vacillation, the Liberal policy was firm: "What we are concerned about is that they [the pupils] should master English and not that they should be ignorant of French. The problem in its working out is largely one of teachers and administration." There was still no direct comment on Regulation 17 or its revised form.[56]

In the 1914 session of the legislature both parties again ignored the bilingual question. When the ailing Whitney suddenly called an election for June, 1914, the Liberals tried to keep their "abolish-the-bar" programme as the central issue, and to avoid the language question; but the Conservatives, while campaigning primarily on their record in promoting the economic development of the province in the last nine years, seemed less anxious to by-pass it.[57] In any case, in view of the great public interest in recent events in Ottawa, it could scarcely be ignored completely. There, the English and French members of the Separate School Board were at loggerheads over the latter's refusal to enforce Regulation 17. When the French-speaking section sought a city by-law allowing it to issue debentures to raise money for new schools to be operated independently of the Department of Education's language rulings, the English minority obtained a court injunction preventing this move and called on the government to enforce Regulation 17 or to withdraw it. On the eve of the election the Supreme Court of Ontario was beginning hearings on the validity of the injunction.

During the campaign the government renewed its pledges of full enforcement of Regulation 17, while the Liberals continued to assert that

---

[55] *Ibid.,* Oct. 24, 1913.

[56] Rowell Papers, MS of address, Oct. 27, 1913.

[57] Rowell told Laurier later that in this election the government had used the bilingual question to divert attention from "abolish-the-bar." Laurier Papers, Rowell to Laurier, April 15, 1916.

there could be no objection to the study of French in the schools as long as children learned English but declined to say what they would do with Regulation 17 if elected. W. R. Plewman, who had recently resigned as editor of the Orange paper, the *Sentinel*, because of the Conservative "betrayal" in revising Regulation 17, urged the election of the Liberals as the means of safeguarding the English language.[58] At the same time the Ottawa paper, *Le Droit*, founded in 1913 for the specific purpose of defending French interests in Ontario, advised its readers to support the Liberals as the guardians of the French language.[59]

At the end of June the Conservatives were swept back into power with a slightly larger popular vote than they had received in 1911, but the Liberals gained six seats including three of the six newly created seats and two previously held by French-speaking Conservatives: one of these was Essex North, where Dr. Reaume was defeated, the other Ottawa East. In the new legislature there were thus six French-speaking members, five Liberals and one Conservative, as compared with three of each in the previous House.

The day after the Ontario provincial election the Ottawa Separate School Board closed all its schools, asserting that since it had been deprived of some of its provincial grants it could not pay its teachers. The chairman of the Board soon admitted that the purpose of this action was to force the Department of Education to consent to the Board's employment of twenty-three Christian Brothers whose teaching certificates were not valid in Ontario. Thus, with the opening of the school term in September, 1914, some 8,000 Ottawa students were without teachers. The Ontario Supreme Court ordered the Board to reopen the schools and to employ only qualified teachers. This court ruling was the signal for renewed protests from French-Canadian leaders. In Montreal on December 21 party ties were forgotten as Nationalists Henri Bourassa and Armand Lavergne, the Conservative Senator Landry, and Liberal Senators Dandurand and Belcourt appeared on the platform with Archbishop Bruchési and other church dignitaries to launch a campaign to raise funds for "les blessés d'Ontario."[60] Early in January, 1915, Cardinal Bégin published a letter to Archbishop Bruchési defending the inalienable right of every race to its own language and affirming the "noble duty of the French and Catholic province of Quebec to assist with all its influence and all its resources those who suffer and struggle until full justice shall be rendered them."[61] Within a week the Quebec legislature had adopted unanimously a resolution deploring the controversy and

---

[58] *Canadian Annual Review*, 1914, 448.

[59] *Ibid.*, 454.

[60] Rumilly, *Histoire*, XIX, 104.

[61] *Globe*, Jan. 9, 1915.

asserting that the legislators of Ontario were deficient in their understanding and application of traditional British principles.[62]

The increasingly active participation of the Quebec clergy in the
protest movement naturally confirmed Ontario Protestants in their conviction that extension of the French language inevitably meant extension
of the power of the Roman Catholic Church. However, Father Michael
Whalen of Ottawa soon gave a demonstration that his church did not
possess the monolithic character usually ascribed to it by Protestants. He
published an open letter to Cardinal Bégin blaming the racial war on *Le
Droit* and on extremists in both political and clerical circles:

> We can easily explain why continuous reckless raiding on the schools of the
> province, to make them French, was regarded by the Protestant majority as a
> carefully planned campaign by the Quebec hierarchy to acquire on Ontario soil
> dominion in civil affairs. We deny that the French-Canadian raiders on the
> school system of Ontario have a right to declare, in the name of the Catholic
> Church, a religious war on the Government of this province. We protest against
> their dragging religion into their language agitation; we protest against their
> identifying their cause with that of the Separate Schools; we reprobate their
> methods as un-Catholic. We assert that only the united Catholic Hierarchy of
> Ontario has a right to declare a Province-wide religious war against a law or
> regulation of the Ontario government. The United hierarchy has not done so.[63]

After revealing in the 1915 session of the legislature that 190 bilingual
schools had ceased to be eligible for grants of public funds during the
past year because of their failure to conform to the language regulations,[64] the government secured passage of a bill empowering it to set up
a commission to take over the duties of the Ottawa Separate School
Board if that body continued to defy the Department of Education.
During the debate on this measure most of the English-speaking Liberals
refrained from taking any part, but they voted for the bill.[65] Toward the
end of the school term the government announced that it was paying the
overdue salaries of qualified teachers in the inspected English separate
schools of Ottawa directly to the teachers in order to keep these schools
open.[66] Shortly after this, the Ottawa Board's appeal against the earlier
court order to reopen the schools was rejected.[67] A week later an Order-
in-Council placed the Ottawa separate schools under the jurisdiction of a
three-member commission, and in the autumn of 1915 the Supreme Court
of Ontario sustained the validity of Regulation 17. Chief Justice Sir
William Meredith said he could find no support whatever for the view

---

[62] *Ibid.*, Jan. 15, 1915.
[63] *Mail and Empire*, Feb. 14, 1915.
[64] *Globe*, March 26, 1915.
[65] *Ibid.*, April 2, 1915.
[66] *Ibid.*, June 4, 1915.
[67] 32 Ont. L.R. 245.

that the French language was guaranteed either by constitutional or natural right.[68] With every round won by the Ontario government, French-Canadian resistance stiffened.

The issue was now complicated by open expressions of English-Canadian suspicions that French Canada was providing considerably less than its share of army recruits, and by French-Canadian retorts that when justice was done in Ontario it would be time to talk about the war in Europe. At the third biennial congress of the French-Canadian Educational Association of Canada Bishop Latulippe of Temiskaming claimed that his recent presentation of the claims of the Franco-Ontarians had received the entire support of the Pope. Encouraging reports were also presented showing the receipt of funds from even the remotest Quebec villages for the war on the Ontario front.[69] Two weeks later the Quebec legislature bolstered this cause by passing a bill allowing local Catholic school commissions to contribute officially to the fund.[70]

The Quebec legislature's action was greeted with much strong language, especially from the Conservative press of Ontario, and the Liberal *Globe*, in the strongest editorial it had yet published on the subject, now asserted that Regulation 17 was fully justified and denounced much of the French-Canadian press for its unfounded contention that the French language in Ontario had a legal status which must be defended.[71] For the first time Laurier was brought into sharp conflict on this issue with the leaders of Ontario Liberalism. Laurier accused the *Globe*'s editor, Stewart Lyon, of deserting traditional Liberal policy; what was needed was an enforcement of the Mowat policy, which would rightly rule out the existence of exclusively French schools, but would allow for the learning of French as well as English by those who wished to do so. "Instead of this, Regulation 17 . . . practically wipes out the teaching of French. . . . This is a very serious matter . . . which must be considered immediately if I am to remain in the position which I now occupy."[72] At the same time Rowell complained to Laurier about the intervention of Quebec in the affairs of Ontario through its authorization of "a fund to carry on bilingual agitation in Ontario," and declared that it was essential that he make a statement in the legislature making clear the position of the Ontario Liberal party—that "the question is one which must be settled by the people of Ontario alone." As it was now five years since the Merchant investigation he would propose a new one to see how Regulation 17 had worked out in practice, and whether in fact any French-Canadian children were being deprived of a knowledge of

---

[68] 34 Ont. L.R. 335.

[69] Rumilly, *Histoire*, XXI, 45.

[70] *Ibid.*, 48–52.

[71] *Globe*, Feb. 26, 1916.

[72] Laurier Papers, Laurier to Stewart Lyon, Feb. 29, 1916.

French. He suggested that a three-member commission composed of the Roman Catholic Archbishop, Neil McNeil of Toronto, a representative of the Ontario French-Canadians, and some independent person of the prestige of President Falconer of the University of Toronto should examine present conditions and make recommendations for future policy. Any suggestions Laurier could make about further steps which Rowell might take to improve relations between Ontario and Quebec would be heard gladly, as long as Laurier remembered Rowell's basic position:

> I cannot depart from the position I have always taken . . . that it is the duty of the state to see that every child in the Province receives a good English education and that consistent with this requirement, where the parents of the children desire that the children should also study the French language, there should be no objection to their doing so. The practical difficulty is to ensure the first without appearing unduly to interfere with the second, and the difficulty is greatly increased by the extravagant and entirely unwarranted claim put forth by the Nationalists with reference to the right to use the French language in this province.[73]

Laurier said he agreed with Rowell's general statement of policy, but added: "I would express it, however, more strongly than you do, and I would substitute for the words, 'there should be no objection to their doing so,' that 'the law should provide that they may do so.'" He welcomed Rowell's proposed commission, thought Archbishop McNeil an excellent choice, and as the French-Canadian suggested Bishop Latulippe whose extreme views represented a position which must be considered. Laurier thought Rowell's interpretation of the recent action of the Quebec legislature was probably unfounded, but said he would look into it: "I would be much surprised if a man of Gouin's prudence had allowed the passing of a law to carry on bilingual agitation . . . but what I believe is that the Legislature has authorized municipalities to assist French children in Ontario in obtaining a French education in addition to the English education." Laurier found the Ontario Department of Education "much confused not only in their ideas but in their language," but after studying the rulings he believed he understood their meaning:

> . . . the French language can be taught with certain restrictions in all schools where it was taught in the month of August, 1913, but is not to be taught in any other school, that is to say, that henceforth the Orange doctrine is to prevail—that the English language only is to be taught in the schools. That seems to me absolutely tyrannical.[74]

The extent of anxiety among Quebec Liberals about the meaning of the term "hitherto" in the regulation was further revealed when Stewart

---

[73] *Ibid.*, Rowell to Laurier, Feb. 29, 1916.

[74] *Ibid.*, Laurier to Rowell, March 1, 1916. This letter is printed in O. D. Skelton, *Life and Letters of Sir Wilfrid Laurier* (2 vols., Toronto, 1922), II, 475.

Lyon held consultations with Laurier, Senator Dandurand, and Rodolphe Lemieux; they interpreted it as prohibiting French entirely in new schools established after August, 1913.[75] Lyon was commissioned to find out what it meant in Rowell's mind. He received an answer which implied that their understanding was probably correct:

> He is inclined to take the view that it does not limit the teaching of French after the first form or the second form at the option of the inspectors in a greater degree than the Legislature intended. An amendment, however, except as part of a general settlement, could not be put through the Legislature at the present time. Howard Ferguson and the extreme Orange element feel that there is Party advantage for them in insisting upon greater restrictions in the teaching of French, just as Bourassa, Lavergne and the extreme partisans on the other side feel that there is advantage for them in insisting upon the recognition of French as an official language in the Province of Ontario.[76]

Meanwhile, Rowell's conversations with Archbishop McNeil, who was now making overtures to the Franco-Ontarian bishops to ascertain their terms for a settlement, left him with the conviction that "if McNeil once went into the case his shrewd common sense and absence of bias . . . would be an important factor in settling the dispute." However, he was less hopeful that Premier Hearst would respond to his plan for a fresh investigation of the bilingual schools unless considerable pressure were brought to bear upon him by federal Conservatives.[77] Yet some modification of Conservative policy seemed possible for Laurier was waited upon by an unofficial emissary from Hearst and Borden with the information that the Ontario government was disposed to make a compromise with the Ottawa Separate School Board and agree that if the schools were reopened the government would pay the teachers. Regulation 17 would then remain in abeyance until its validity was determined by the Judicial Committee of the Privy Council. However, said the Conservative spokesman, Hearst was afraid to go ahead with this compromise for fear of attack from the Liberals. Laurier's assurance that Rowell would "consider the matter fairly and even sympathetically"[78] was met by the Ontario leader's willingness to discuss the matter, although he made no comment on the general nature of the proposed compromise.[79] There is no evi-

---

[75] The disputed word appeared in Section 4: "In schools where French has hitherto been a subject of study, the Public or the Separate School Board . . . may provide, under the following conditions, for instruction in French Reading, Grammar, and Composition in Forms I to IV . . . in addition to the subjects prescribed for the Public and Separate Schools." The regulation clearly allows the interpretation given it by Laurier. However, in expanding the discretionary powers of the department, the revised form of 1913, allowed the minister to designate certain schools so that they would come under the old Regulation 12. See Sissons, *Bilingual Schools*, 108–12.

[76] Laurier Papers, Lyon to Laurier, March 6, 1916.

[77] *Ibid.*

[78] *Ibid.*, Laurier to Rowell, March 4, 1916.

[79] *Ibid.*, Rowell to Laurier, March 7, 1916.

dence that any overtures were actually made to Rowell, and it must be concluded either that the Ferguson wing of the party refused to have anything to do with a compromise, or that apprehension about the Liberal reaction to such a plan remained sufficiently strong to prevent the move.

The case for a truce was shortly put forward very strongly by representatives of the Montreal Chamber of Commerce who conferred in Toronto with politicians and business leaders of both parties with a view to securing a relaxation in the enforcement of Regulation 17 until the end of the war or the Privy Council decision on its status. This move was dictated by a mixture of patriotism and commercial interest since Montreal firms owned by English-speaking Canadians were finding their goods boycotted by their French-Canadian customers and many Toronto firms had been told by Quebec clients that until Ontario did justice to the French language they would place no further orders.[80]

Within a week of the Montrealers' trip Rowell introduced in the legislature his plan for a three-man commission to examine the operation of Regulation 17 during the past five years. At the same time he reaffirmed Ontario's absolute right to control education without outside interference. The government, speaking through the Acting Minister of Education, Howard Ferguson, claimed that it understood the situation well enough without setting up another commission and nothing came of Rowell's proposal. He can scarcely have expected any other result; the delay occasioned by another investigation might have reduced tension within the federal Liberal party and made life easier for certain Montreal and Toronto business interests, but it would undoubtedly have been interpreted by many Ontarians, probably by a majority, as capitulation to Quebec. Given this public temper there was no political necessity for the Ontario government to give even the appearance of being willing to reconsider its policy; indeed, all the political arguments pointed in the opposite direction. By the same token the assurance that the government would reject a further commission made it safe for the Liberals to propose one without too much political risk to themselves; and possibly the gesture would be worth something in relations with the Quebec Liberals in the federal party. In short, there could be no disagreement with the comment of one of Laurier's closest friends in Ontario who declared that public opinion was almost entirely in favour of the strict enforcement of Regulation 17 and would "oppose and slaughter any man or any party who talks of granting greater privileges to the French."[81]

While Ontario maintained this near unanimity there were pressures within both federal parties to take a positive stand in the controversy.

---

[80] *Ibid.*, M. K. Cowan to Laurier, April 12, 1916.

[81] *Ibid.*, Laurier to M. K. Cowan, April 11, 1916. This letter is printed in Skelton, *Laurier*, II, 472–3. The phrase quoted was originally Cowan's.

Borden refused the request of the three Quebec members of his cabinet that the Dominion government refer the whole question of the status of the French language in Canada to the Privy Council,[82] on the ground that under Section 133 of the B.N.A. Act the issue was already settled.[83] Borden also rejected Senator Landry's suggestion that a government supporter should sponsor a motion of censure of Ontario's policy in the House of Commons,[84] as well as the more desperate remedy sought in a petition signed by Landry, Cardinal Bégin, and most of the French-Canadian bishops—federal disallowance of Regulation 17.[85] As far as short-term political strategy was concerned it was easy enough for Borden to resist these demands. The presence of the three Quebec members in his cabinet was a token only, for the Conservative-Nationalist alliance had begun to collapse long before the war and was now in total eclipse; the Conservatives had little to lose in Quebec.

Inevitably the conflicts within the federal Liberal party were much more severe. In the face of persistent rumours that a Liberal member of the House of Commons would endorse some form of interference in Ontario's affairs Bishop Fallon warned that any such move would be "nationally dangerous" and "politically dishonest,"[86] while Rowell told Laurier that it would seriously inflame public opinion in Ontario.[87] But Laurier's reply to the latter implied that the decision to raise the question in parliament had already been taken and asserted that "if the party cannot stand up for the principles advocated, maintained and fought for by Mowat and Blake . . . it is more than time for me to step down and out."[88] In the lengthy private debate on the Mowat tradition which these comments provoked Laurier and Rowell agreed that provincial rights and justice for minorities were paramount but they were far from agreement on the current application of these principles. Rowell contended that "the minority in each province must depend upon the sense of justice and fair play of the majority to secure any redress of grievances . . . and any action . . . by the Federal Parliament would . . . be looked upon as an interference with the free action of the province in settling its own

---

82 P.A.C., Bordon Papers, OC302, T. C. Casgrain, P. E. Blondin, and E. L. Patenaude to Borden, April 20, 1916.

83 *Ibid.*, Borden to T. C. Casgrain, P. E. Blondin, and E. L. Patenaude, April 24, 1916.

84 Rumilly, *Histoire,* XXI, 112.

85 *Ibid.*, 86–8.

86 P.A.C., Murphy Papers, Fallon to Charles Murphy, April 14, 1916. Murphy, who was, at least by his own account, Laurier's most vigorous and faithful political manager in Ontario, had earlier boasted that he had been able, by astute behind-the-scenes organizing "to secure practically the unanimous support of the English-speaking Catholics for the Liberal party." Laurier Papers, Murphy to Laurier, June 19, 1911.

87 Laurier Papers, Rowell to Laurier, April 15, 1916.

88 *Ibid.*, Laurier to Rowell, April 18, 1916.

problems."[89] Laurier agreed with Rowell's belief that, in order to divert attention from the government's incompetence in handling the war effort, the Conservatives were exploiting the racial issue which they themselves had done so much to create by nourishing the Nationalist movement, yet he could not break the force of the Nationalists as long as the Ontario minority was treated unjustly and the toleration practised by Mowat was denied. Laurier rejected disallowance, but he asked, "does the idea of provincial rights go to the extent that it will not receive the complaint of a minority?"; there was ample precedent for the federal parliament if it wanted to make representations to a provincial legislature.[90] But Rowell maintained his objection to comment of any kind from the Dominion parliament: "Of course, it is the duty of any Government to consider all complaints presented to it; but complaints by residents of this province are one thing; resolutions or other proceedings by the Federal Parliament are of an entirely different character."[91] Laurier could only conclude that he and Rowell "had reached a line of cleavage . . . final and beyond redemption."[92]

Ernest Lapointe's resolution of May 10 in the House of Commons[93] threatened to make the rift between the Ontario Liberals and the federal leadership complete. In support of the resolution, Laurier delivered one of his last great addresses in the Commons, with its impassioned appeal not to "constitutional arguments . . . or the cold letter of any positive law . . . but to the sober reasoning and judgment of my fellow-countrymen of all origins." This alone, he felt, could persuade the people of Ontario to take a fresh look at Regulation 17 and prevent Canadians of both races from allowing the language question to poison their thinking about the nation's participation in the war.[94] In opposing the resolution Borden argued that there was no proof that Regulation 17 worked an injustice on French Canadians in Ontario and quoted the Laurier of 1896 on federal intervention in educational affairs.[95] When the vote was called five Conservatives, all from Quebec, supported the Lapointe resolution.

---

[89] *Ibid.*, Rowell to Laurier, April 26, 1916; see also Rowell Papers, Rowell to Laurier, May 9, 1916.

[90] Rowell Papers, Laurier to Rowell, April 28, 1916; see also Laurier to Rowell, May 11, 1916.

[91] *Ibid.*, Rowell to Laurier, May 9, 1911.

[92] Laurier Papers, Laurier to Rowell, May 11, 1916. This letter is printed in Skelton, *Laurier*, II, 477.

[93] Canada. *House of Commons Debates*, May 10, 1916, 3676. The resolution moved "That this House . . . while fully respecting the principle of provincial rights and the necessity of every child being given a thorough English education, respectfully suggest to the Legislative Assembly [of Ontario] the wisdom of making it clear that the privilege of the children of French parentage of being taught in their mother tongue be not interfered with."

[94] *Ibid.*, 3697–3709.

[95] *Ibid.*, 3690–6.

All the Liberals from Quebec and the Maritimes voted for it, while all eleven Western Liberals opposed; most of the Ontario men were strongly disposed to vote against it too, but in the end they supported it out of personal loyalty to "the Old Man" who had indicated that he could only resign if the Ontario group went against him.[96]

While the *Globe* castigated the federal party leaders for allowing the introduction of the Lapointe resolution, Rowell, after paying tribute to the tone of Laurier's address in the House, once more denied the constitutionality and the political wisdom of the resolution; the Ontario Liberal party was convinced that just as Mowat had resisted the plea that the Ontario legislature should support an appeal for the disallowance of the Jesuit Estates Act, so the Quebec liberals should follow the same course now that the situation was reversed. The circumstances were not precisely the same, Rowell admitted; the Lapointe resolution was not a request for disallowance, yet it was more than a personal appeal from a member or group in the House and, in principle, involved "a certain supervisory relation on the part of the Federal Government of Provincial Legislation," and it could do no good, either for relations between Ontario and Quebec, or for the minority in Ontario:

> If, upon a question so vital as the province's control over her own educational affairs, the Liberal party in this province should surrender its views to the views of the party leaders at Ottawa, it would not only be doing what I believe to be wrong to the Province, but it would be committing political suicide. Surely we should not be expected to do this.[97]

Bishop Fallon was also distressed by the Lapointe resolution, and especially by the fact that the leading Irish Catholic member from Ontario, Charles Murphy, had supported Laurier and Lapointe:

> Your public approval of . . . the Lapointe resolution lends your countenance to the baseless and mischievous statement that the French Canadians are an oppressed minority in Ontario. . . . politically, educationally, and religiously, the French Canadians in Ontario have far more . . . than they can [justly] . . . claim. It seems to me that I have heard you say as much.
>
> There is, however, an aspect of your public attitude on this question which calls for the plainest rebuke. I speak as a member of another minority—the unfortunate Irish Catholics. In Quebec, in the Maritime provinces, in Ontario and throughout the whole Northwest, tens of thousands of the men and women of the race to which you and I belong have been lost to the Faith—and that is my only concern—through the callous neglect, the quiet persecution, and the continuous opposition of that same minority of which you now make yourself the champion. You need not travel beyond your own city for undoubted evidence of the truth of my statement. You will not wonder then that many of us are in amazement at the stand you have taken and ask ourselves what is to become of

[96] Skelton, *Laurier*, II, 484.

[97] Rowell Papers, Rowell to Laurier, May 19, 1916.

us between the upper millstone of French-Canadian nationalism and the lower millstone of Protestant bigotry.[98]

Faced with the strong possibility of a serious break with the Ontario Liberals, Laurier made plans to go to Toronto immediately after prorogation "in a last attempt to clear up what is becoming an intolerable situation."[99] He was armed with evidence that his understanding of the term "hitherto" in Regulation 17 was well founded—evidence in the form of copies of letters from the Department of Education to the Windsor School Board prohibiting the use of French in a new school in "a place where French has been the language of many for more than two hundred years."[100] Laurier's visit to Toronto convinced him that matters were not quite as desperate as he had supposed, although they were serious enough. If the Irish could be restrained something might be salvaged from the party's disunity in that quarter,[101] since the party as a whole did not feel as violently on the bilingual issue as his Toronto informants had led him to believe. "The resolution will have no effect in any part of the province, if our friends have the courage to maintain that it is right. This, however, will not be done in Toronto, and all the damage we will suffer will come from that direction,"[102] and in particular from the Toronto Liberal press.[103]

For a time, after their discussions with Laurier, Toronto Liberals ceased to make a public issue of the bilingual question. Beyond a few relatively unimpassioned assertions of Ontario's right to control her own affairs neither the *Globe* nor the *Star* had much to say on the subject for some weeks. Early in June when one hundred and fifty leading Liberals from all parts of the province met to consider party policy "there was not a solitary word on bilingual troubles."[104] An uneasy truce was maintained until the early autumn of 1916 when Laurier took exception to a *Star* editorial which had asserted that the sole purpose of Regulation 17 was to ensure that every child received an English education.[105]

This is not the policy which has again and again been put forward in the *Orange Sentinel* and in the *Toronto News,* and which is being carried out insiduously but effectively by the introduction of the word "hitherto" in the fourth paragraph of Regulation 17. No amount of quibbling by Mr. Ferguson has been able to explain this away.[106]

---

[98] Murphy Papers, Fallon to Murphy, May 16, 1916.

[99] Laurier Papers, Laurier to Rowell, May 16, 1916.

[100] *Ibid.,* Laurier to Stewart Lyon, May 13, 1916.

[101] *Ibid.,* Laurier to Rodolphe Lemieux, May 26, 1916.

[102] *Ibid.,* Laurier to W. M. German, May 27, 1916.

[103] *Ibid.,* Laurier to E. M. Macdonald, May 27, 1916.

[104] *Ibid.,* P. C. Larkin to Laurier, June 7, 1916.

[105] *Toronto Daily Star,* Sept. 15, 1916.

[106] Laurier Papers, Laurier to J. E. Atkinson, Sept. 20, 1916.

The editor of the *Star*, Joseph Atkinson, who was well able to speak for the inner circles of Toronto Liberalism, asserted that the total exclusion of French was not the intention of any responsible persons known to him; it was, he claimed, the extreme statements of the Orangemen which had given the French Canadians the impression that the real aim was more rigorous. Whatever the theoretical interpretation of the word "hitherto," the regulation must be judged on the basis of its enforcement; he knew of at least two schools where permission to give instruction in French had been granted since the adoption of the regulation, and he believed that the department was disposed to interpret the ruling generously.[107]

During this "era of good feeling" the first project of the Bonne Entente movement was carried out when about fifty prominent Ontario citizens visited Quebec in early October. Although participation was by no means confined to Liberals, they were the leading spirits in both provinces and the idea had been conceived by a correspondent of the *Toronto Star*, Arthur Hawkes, a journalist much admired by Laurier. The scheme must be understood, at least in part, as an attempt to save the Liberal party from the destruction with which it was threatened by the widening abyss between the two races created by the bilingual issue and the war, and as a design to restore the trade position of English-speaking manufacturers in Montreal. The Ontario pilgrims to Quebec had not long returned when there occurred two events which did more to bank the fires of the language controversy than any truce among party leaders or cordial speeches at Bonne Entente dinners.[108]

The first of these was the publication of the papal encyclical, *Commisso divinitus*, the Vatican's answer to the many representations received from both Irish and French Catholics over the past six years. Pope Benedict XV deplored the enmity and rivalry which had allowed even priests to take an unseemly part in a controversy which threatened the peace and unity of the Canadian church, counselled moderation by all, and said that the bishops most directly concerned must decide on the specific questions at issue. But, the Pope cautioned:

Let the Catholics of the Dominion remember that the one thing of supreme importance above all others is to have Catholic schools, and not to imperil their existence. . . . However, these two requirements are to be met, namely, a

---

107 *Ibid.*, Atkinson to Laurier, Sept. 20, 1916. The Deputy Minister of Education would have agreed with Atkinson's comments on his department's policy. "The French language was in no sense proscribed by it. On the contrary, what is considered a generous provision for the use of French . . . was made. . . . A number of French schools have adopted it. No complaint from them has reached the Department that in the working out of the law French is proscribed or neglected. The law has been, and will be enforced in a reasonable and considerate spirit." Dr. A. H. U. Colquhoun to Lt.-Gov. J. S. Hendrie, Feb. 17, 1916, in "Correspondence . . . concerning the Bilingual School Issue."

108 Rumilly, *Histoire*, XXI, 180.

thorough knowledge of English and an equitable teaching of French for French-Canadian children.[109]

Although a minority of the Quebec press asserted that the Nationalist cause had been vindicated, clearly there was little reason for thinking so. This was well illustrated by the silence of Bourassa and *Le Devoir* on the encyclical and the rather vague approval given it by most of the French-speaking papers.[110] On the other hand, Bishop Fallon was pleased with the Pope's letter but anxious lest the French-Canadian bishops find it possible to place upon the call to moderation an interpretation other than his own; he therefore prepared a lengthy memorandum for a meeting of the Ontario bishops called by Cardinal Bégin to consider the apostolic letter.[111] Fallon asserted that one of the worst features of the bilingual controversy was the fact that it had undermined a great source of respect for the Roman Catholic Church—its support of lawful authority and a conservative society. The papal encyclical had restored that respect, as witness the absence of a single hostile word about it in the English-Canadian press. How great then was the responsibility of the bishops to refrain from any action "that would in the public mind be judged as sympathetic with the dying agitation" which had previously done so much "to jeopardize our entire Catholic school system in Ontario." After a detailed analysis of "the preposterous demands" of the French-Canadian Education Association and its defiance of the moderate course which he had advocated for so long amid so much misunderstanding (and which was now vindicated by His Holiness), Fallon declared that "never before had the French language legally enjoyed such privileges as it does under this much-maligned Regulation 17"; previously, it had depended solely on the good faith of the government but now it had legal protection to the end of the second form.

When the Ontario episcopate met, the three French-speaking members failed to accept Fallon's interpretation of the papal letter,[112] although this fact was not evident in the pastoral letter read in all Ontario churches ten days later. The letter enjoined obedience to "the just laws and regulations enacted from time to time by the civil authorities," asserted that much of the earlier unrest was due to doubt about the meaning of the school regulations, and expressed confidence that the discretionary powers given to the Minister of Education would be used liberally.[113]

A week after the publication of the papal encyclical the waters were

---

[109] *Globe*, Oct. 27, 1916. The encyclical is also printed in full in Sissons, *Bilingual Schools*, Appendix 3.

[110] Rumilly, *Histoire*, XXI, 188–192.

[111] "Correspondence . . . concerning the Bi-lingual Schools," memorandum of Bishop Fallon for the bishops of Ontario, January 24, 1917.

[112] Rumilly, *Histoire*, XXII, 25.

[113] *Globe*, Feb. 5, 1917.

calmed further by the Privy Council decision in the two cases referred from the Ontario courts. Although the legislation establishing the Ottawa School Commission was ruled *ultra vires*,[114] Regulation 17 was declared *intra vires*,[115] and the government of Ontario had thus won the essential point. Although their Lordships regretted that the regulation was "couched in obscure language" so that it was "not easy to ascertain its true effect," they found that it was only denominational and not language privileges which were guaranteed under the B.N.A. Act and the Department of Education was free to make any ruling concerning the teaching of French.

While the question hung fire as to whether Quebec and the Ontario minority would accept these ecclesiastical and constitutional defeats gracefully, a Bonne Entente group from Quebec paid a return visit to Toronto and Hamilton when Hearst, Rowell, and Gouin vied with one another in supporting the war effort and national unity.[116] But Senator Landry and the members of the French-Canadian Education Association were not devotees of the Bonne Entente. The day after the reading of the pastoral letter of the Ontario bishops Landry urged a fight to the finish against Regulation 17,[117] and the Orange Order soon replied with the threat of a campaign for total abolition of separate schools if the bilingual agitation were revived.[118]

The Ontario government had still to find some way of enforcing Regulation 17, notably in Ottawa. Thus the issue reappeared in the Legislature in the winter of 1917 with the introduction of a bill to appoint another commission to take over the duties of the Ottawa Separate School Board if it persisted in its resistance. The government apparently believed that the bill was sufficiently different from the earlier measure to pass the scrutiny of the courts. Although Rowell doubted the constitutionality of the new bill, and said so publicly,[119] he and his party, except for the five French-speaking members, did not oppose it. Rowell explained this apparent inconsistency to Laurier:

We cannot put ourselves in the position of appearing to excuse non-compliance with the law.

Many of our members think the bill . . . is deliberately introduced with the view to laying a trap for us, and that if we opposed it they would go through all the country in their campaign trying to link us up with the opposition of the Ottawa School Board to the regulation. We cannot permit them to put us in this position.[120]

---

[114] *Ottawa Separate Schools Trustees* v. *Ottawa* [1917], A.C. 76.

[115] *Ottawa Separate Schools Trustees* v. *Mackell* [1917], A.C. 62.

[116] *Canadian Annual Review*, 1917, 476.

[117] *Globe*, Feb. 6, 1917.

[118] *Ibid.*, March 15, 1917.

[119] *Ibid.*, March 31, 1917.

[120] Laurier Papers, Rowell to Laurier, March 29, 1917.

A further bill empowering the Ontario government to collect from the city of Ottawa the $300,000 spent during the time it had operated the Ottawa separate schools under the recent commission, now declared illegal, was greeted with a mild protest from Rowell on constitutional grounds, but all the English-speaking Liberals voted for it.[121] Once more Laurier was disgusted with the Ontario Liberal party.[122]

While these two bills were before the legislature the dispute between the English and French wings in the church continued, although no longer before the public gaze, and Cardinal Bégin was impelled to send two envoys to the Vatican for further advice. Thus, by mid-summer of 1917, feeling over the bilingual schools was still acute among Roman Catholics, at least among the bishops, and Senator Landry talked of possible bloodshed and even of schism.[123] On the other hand, the English-speaking Protestants, being supported now by the Privy Council decision and drawing more comfort from the recent papal encyclical than the leaders of the French-Canadian Education Association, were calmer than they had been in some years. Within the two provincial parties there was only one slight breach in the wall of resistance to any alteration in Regulation 17–the five French-speaking Liberals were at odds with the rest of their party, but they were too few to be significant. The Conservatives rightly believed that the Liberals were never seriously tempted to question the basic premise of Regulation 17[124]–that English was *the* language of the province and all must learn it. The vast majority of the people of Ontario rejected entirely the concept of cultural duality.

In their private and public discussions Laurier and Rowell separated the bilingual schools issue from their disagreement over coalition with the Conservatives, which Rowell began to urge upon Laurier early in 1917, and from the conscription issue which eventually brought the two leaders to the parting of the ways. But extremists in both Ontario and Quebec made no such distinction. Bourassa and the Nationalists declared frequently that the defeat of "the Prussians of Ontario" had a prior claim over the war in Europe. On the other side, the essentially bipartisan policy of the provincial parties on the bilingual problem reinforced the traditional disposition of most Ontarians to display a united front against French Canada. The necessity of "making the French Canadians do their duty" was a prominent feature of Unionist publicity in Ontario during the conscription election of 1917. Although it is impossible to isolate this from other factors in the campaign, the emotions already aroused by the language struggle help to explain the victory of Union government candidates in all but eight of Ontario's eighty-two seats.

---

[121] *Globe,* April 4, 1917.

[122] Laurier Papers, Laurier to Rowell, April 4, 1917.

[123] Rumilly, *Histoire,* XXII, 45.

[124] Borden, Henry, ed., *Robert Laird Borden: His Memoirs* (2 vols., Toronto, 1938), II, 588.

22

The Economics of the Drink Question*

F. S. Spence

In the period between 1890 and 1920 prohibition excited Canadians as few internal issues of history ever have. Among Protestants, especially Methodists, Presbyterians, and Baptists, prohibition became a panacea for so many social ills, including crime, insanity, and slums. The "Demon Rum" allegedly brutalized society and destroyed personal morality. The temperance societies grew out of the Victorian ethical and evangelical idealism which abounded in Canada. But there was nothing temperate about the fanatical crusade they mounted. With fiery rhetoric they promised to end political corruption and increase the economic efficiency of the country. Alcohol, they argued, weakened the commitment to the work ethic which was fundamental to the type of society Canadians wished to build.

Some of the drinking habits of Victorian Canada were a product of the earlier frontier when men drank to get drunk, to escape from the brutal routine of the mining camp, the lumber crew, or the clearing of land. However, as Canadian society became more "respectable" in the latter decades of the 19th century, drinking came to be viewed with less and less tolerance in middle-class circles and those aspiring to them. Women first entered the political arena through organizations such as the Women's Christian Temperance Union. Temperance was another issue which separated French and English Canadians because the former followed the wine tradition of Europe. Temperance tended to divert reform sentiment from the economic and social problems of urbanization and industrialization. The campaign also took a nativist twist when European immigrants were blamed for some of the drinking excesses.

---

* *The Campaign Manual 1912* (Toronto, 1912).

Temperance societies existed in British North America from the 1820s. As the century proceeded they tended to change their program from voluntary abstinence to a program of compulsory prohibition. In 1878 the federal Scott Act was passed which provided a local option and a patchwork of wet and dry areas developed. Early in the 1890s provincial plebiscites were held in Manitoba, Ontario, Prince Edward Island, and Nova Scotia. All registered majorities for prohibition, but governments were reluctant to act. Petitions then flooded in to Ottawa, and a royal commission investigated the subject between 1892 and 1894. Finally in 1898 Laurier held a federal plebiscite with every province but Quebec endorsing the proposal. As only 43 percent of the electorate voted, Laurier refused to act. After 1900 the movement centred on activities in the provincial arena, reaching its peak during World War I. By 1919 every province had established some form of prohibition. However, the great expectations of the movement for a moral utopia were never achieved; its support waned in the 1920s and Canada returned to a local option approach.

Here we have a long excerpt from the 1912 campaign manual for prohibition that illustrates clearly many of the above points.

I T IS WELL KNOWN that the drink habit and the drink traffic, working together, are responsible for much waste of wealth, and this waste not only involves the impoverishment of the liquor consumers, but the impoverishment of the country as a whole.

When attention is called to the great expenditure on strong drink it is sometimes said in reply that this amount of money is not destroyed, that it remains and circulates, and, therefore, if some are made poorer by the expenditure, others are made richer and the aggregate wealth of the community is not lessened.

It takes no deep knowledge of economics to demolish this absurdity. The liquor consumers have toiled for the production of the wealth which their money represents, or someone else has toiled for them. If they pay that money for clothing, food, furniture, fuel or other necessities or luxuries, they receive value for their toil. The producers of these articles have the money, the purchasers have the goods, and the community possesses the wealth represented by both, or double the amount which the purchasers have invested.

If, on the other hand, the money is spent in drinking, while the liquor vendors may have the amount of money named, the liquor consumers have absolutely nothing to show for their investment, and there is in the possession of consumers and dealers on the whole only one-half the wealth that existed when the money was otherwise invested.

What applies to the country at large applies also to a municipality. The money spent at the bar by the people of a municipality leaves the local community that much poorer. Money cannot be spent on strong drink without being as really wasted, as absolutely destroyed, as if that amount of money or goods were buried in the bottom of the sea, or as if the money were spent in purchasing articles of value and committing them to the flames.

The actual spending of money in intoxicating liquor is not the only waste of wealth chargeable to the drink system. There is serious loss of wealth production, through idleness of men who are out of employment because of the drinking habits of themselves of others. There is serious loss through the curtailment of the lives of citizens who, had they lived, might have been factors in the country's wealth production. There is loss through the practical destruction, in liquor manufacture, of large quantities of grain that would otherwise be among our surplus food products for export. There is loss through misdirection of the labor employed in this destruction. There is loss through the lessening of the market for products of all industries through the impoverishment of consumers. There is loss through the expenditure imposed upon the community in the custody and care of those who are morally, mentally and physically degraded through intemperance.

The business which causes all this waste is used by governmental institutions as a convenient method of raising revenue, because of the facilities it gives for imposing extra taxation on the consumers of drink. These consumers contribute to the direct loss that goes on, and also are required to make special and large contributions for public purposes.

These and some other aspects of the relation of the drink system to the individual and community wealth and poverty, will be presented in the following series of articles that will be found more suggestive than exhaustive by those who have time to study this important question.

1. Canada's Drink Bill

The total quantities of intoxicating beverages of different kinds entered for consumption in Canada, for the year ending March 31st, 1911, is set out in the following table, compiled from the Government blue books, in which the various items are found:

	Gallons
Canadian Spirits	4,146,425
Imported Spirits	2,591,956
Canadian Malt Liquors	41,750,863
Imported Malt Liquors	1,193,155
Imported Wines	833,339
Total	50,515,765

The application of these estimates to the quantities already quoted will give the following table as the expenditure on intoxicating liquors in the Dominion of Canada for the year:

Canadian Spirits	$24,878,712.00
Imported Spirits	20,735,648.00
Canadian Malt Liquors	29,225,604.10
Imported Malt Liquors	2,386,310.00
Imported Wines	4,166,695.00
Total	$81,392,969.10

The official government estimate made by the Inland Revenue Department of the quantity of liquor taken for consumption during the year, gives the following as the average for every thousand persons:

	Gallons
Spirits	859
Beer	5,434
Wine	104
Total	6,397

If the total expenditure for drink as above stated is divided by the figures for the population of Canada, as shown by the census taken on June 1st, 1911, it will be found that the actual per capita expenditure for intoxicating liquor was $11.30.

2. Drink Caused Idleness

The interference of the drinking habit with the country's wealth production is very great. The Royal Commission examined a great many employers of labor, and the general testimony of these men was that much time is lost by drinking employees, and that work is frequently interfered with, sometimes seriously by the absence or incapacity of drinking men.

The loss to the country is, of course, not at all represented by the mere loss of time by men who are regularly employed. The country loses through drink because of the prevention of the production of wealth on account of the persons in jails, in hospitals, in asylums out of employment or in any way idle when intemperance has caused the idleness.

It is also worthy of note, having been stated to the Commission by a number of witnesses, that the working of a gang of men in a factory or any set of persons who work to a certain extent dependent upon each other, is much interfered with by the absence of some or even of one.

This is more and more the case as industrial development progresses, as machinery is being more generally used, and work more and more sub-divided. In a highly-organized manufacturing industry, any interference with one part of the work affects the operation of the whole. So, not only those who drink lose time and possibly earnings, but their fellow-employees who do not drink are also losers, and the industry which employs them suffers interference and loss.

There is also an important depreciation of wage-earning capacity on the part of men who habitually drink. They are less qualified for the performance of good work, and what they do is in both quality and quantity inferior to the work of men of sober habits.

The total loss in these various ways aggregates a very large percentage of the otherwise available working power of the community. There is some difficulty in estimating exactly how far this loss extends. The matter was inquired into some years ago by an English Parliamentary committee, the report of which contains the following statements:

> The loss of productive labor in every department of occupation, is to the extent of at least one day in six throughout the kingdom (as testified by witnesses engaged in various manufacturing operations), by which the wealth of the country created, as it is, chiefly by labor, is retarded or suppressed to the extent of one million of every six that is produced, to say nothing of the constant derangement, imperfection and destruction in every agricultural and manufacturing process, occasioned by the intemperance and consequent unskilfulness, inattention and neglect of those affected by intoxication, and producing great injury in our domestic and foreign trade.

Canada suffers less in this way than do Old World countries. The people are more sober. Still the waste is very great. The Hon. Geo. E. Foster and the Hon. Geo. W. Ross both estimated that one-tenth the producing power of the country is destroyed by intemperance. If we fix it still lower, and say, to be safe, that only one-twelfth our working power is lost through intemperance, we shall have a basis from which a calculation may be made.

According to the estimate that the liquor traffic destroys one-twelfth of our country's wealth-producing power, the amount stated is only eleven-twelfths of what it would be if the liquor habit and the liquor traffic did not interfere with our workers and their work, and our country through loss of liquor-destroyed working power is kept poorer each year by $66,017,429.

3. Misdirected Labor

As far as enriching the country is concerned, the labor of the men engaged in the liquor business is absolutely thrown away.

The cabinet-maker takes some of the wood that is the raw material of his industry, and turns it into an article of furniture. He has added to the aggregate of the country's wealth the difference between the value of the material and the product.

A storekeeper takes the finished article of furniture, exhibits it for sale, delivers it at the home of its customer where it is of even more value than it was when the cabinet-maker had finished his work. The customer is better off in his ownership of the furniture than he was with the money which it represented.

The storekeeper and the cabinet-maker have added to their possessions the profits of the business done, and for years to come the whole community will be richer by the difference between the value of the raw material in the cabinet-maker's shop and the furniture in the customer's home.

We might illustrate the working out of the same principle in any line of industry. The supply of the community's needs means the benefiting of supplier and supplied, and the community enjoys the results of the work performed.

Now take the liquor makers and the liquor-sellers. Here is the grain fitted to furnish sustenance, and supply strength to man and beast. The liquor-maker destroys every particle of its value to the community, and turns it into a curse instead of a blessing. The liquor-seller stands behind his bar and hands out to his customers the distiller's product. When the whiskey is drunk, and the whole transaction is completed, we can examine the results. The customer has nothing. There is no sustenance or strength or property anywhere to represent the material taken for the liquor industry. The consumer's money is divided between the maker and the dealer and the government, but there is no furniture in the customer's home. He is poorer by the full amount that has been transferred to other parties.

The liquor business adds nothing to the sum of the commonwealth's common wealth. It may result in injured health, shortened lives, disease, poverty, insanity, remorse, or crime, but it has had no material result except the enrichment of some at the expense of others. The work of the liquor-maker and seller is worse than wasted as far as any wealth-producing effect is concerned.

Had the business energy, the judgment, the foresight, the physical power, the capital, and the time of these men been invested in almost any other occupation, they would have added to the country's wealth. As it is they are mere parasites, living on a community to which they give nothing in return. Were it not for this liquor system we would be better off by all that the capital and qualifications of the liquor-traffickers would have done for us if employed in some other way.

Rev. Joseph McLeod, D.D., a member of the Dominion Royal Commission on the liquor traffic, estimated that a man was worth to the country $596 a year. That is, that every worker besides providing for his own maintenance, made at least this addition to the wealth possessed by himself and his fellow-citizens. Let us take an estimate even more conservative still, and count an average man as worth only $500 a year to the country in which he works. Now, according to the Dominion census of manufacturing industries, we had in the year 1905, 3,692 persons employed in production of strong drink. We had in the country at large not less than 5,000 more whose time was given up to the selling of liquor. Let it be assumed that through reduction of the number of liquor selling places there are now only 4,000, still we have 8,692 men worse than idle, who, but for the liquor traffic, would have been helping to make our country better off and according to the estimate already made, would each have added at least $500 to the country's wealth. We lose every year the value of the labor of the men engaged in the liquor business, a total loss of not less than $3,846,000.

But the loss is even greater. We have calculated that an average man's work produced at least enough to maintain himself besides the additional $500. There was no result from the liquor men's labor with which to maintain them. Their very living had to be taken out of the people who were foolish enough to spend their money for strong drink. Adding to the aggregate loss to the wealth of the country the maintenance of those 7,692 non-producers, at $300 each, increases the waste by $2,307,600. These totals combined give us an aggregate of $6,153,600, which is lost to the country every year by misdirection of the labor of men who ought to be profitable citizens.

4. Drink Caused Mortality

It is not practicable to ascertain accurately the extent to which the drink habit shortens life. Official reports of the causes of death are not of much help in solving this problem. Deaths are charged to diseases of many kinds, which diseases frequently grow out of intemperate habits.

The carelessness that leads to fatal accidents is often the result of the dulling by drink of the keenness of men's mental faculties.

Drink-caused poverty is the parent of a great mortality.

Recent investigations and deliverances by eminent medical men have given us knowledge of the fact that tuberculosis frequently finds its origin in drinking practices and facilities, and that its progress is accelerated by the same causes.

This applies to many other vital disturbances and weaknesses, which are not directly attributed to strong drink.

In Great Britain and the United States extensive investigations have been made to ascertain how far the death rate of the community was affected by indulgence in strong drink. One method adopted was an inquiry among a large number of physicians as to how many of the deaths for which they gave certificates were traceable directly or indirectly to the drinking habits of the deceased or someone else.

In England, Dr. Norman Kerr undertook such an inquiry "with the avowed object of demonstrating and exposing the falsity of the perpetual teetotal assertion that sixty thousand drunkards die every year in the United Kingdom." His conclusions were that the statement which he started to disprove fell short of fully expressing the magnitude of the evil it represented. Dr. Sir Benjamin Ward Richardson, after a careful inquiry, was convinced that ten per cent. of all the deaths in Great Britain come earlier than they would were it not for the drinking habit.

A widespread and thorough investigation made in the United States in the year 1890 among physicians chosen with the assistance of the editors of leading medical magazines led to the conclusion stated in the New Voice that "the total per cent. of mortality from drink would appear to approximate in the United States the per cent. calculated by Dr. Richardson for England and Wales." It certainly has not fallen off since.

In Canada, as a rule, the people drink less than in Great Britain and the United States, yet scarcely a day passes without some newspaper story of some terrible fatality directly attributed to strong drink. It is well known that diseases of many organs are caused or accelerated by intemperance. Everyone can think of some life which he is certain has been shortened because of the liquor evil, though no one would say it ended in a drink-caused death. We are probably well within the mark if we estimate the number of deaths from drink in Canada is being one-half the proportion calculated for Great Britain and the United States. This means that five per cent. of our mortality may be said to be the result of this evil.

The population of Canada in 1901 was 5,371, 315, and in 1911 was 7,204,527, an increase of 34.12 per cent. The number of deaths reported for the former year in the census of 1901 was 81,201. Assuming that the death rate was still the same, there would be an increase of the total annual deaths to say 108,900.

Five per cent. of this number would be 5,445, and this is certainly a very low estimate of the number of lives that are cut short in Canada every year by strong drink.

Many of the persons whose lives are thus shortened would otherwise have been useful citizens for many years. If the untimely death of each one of them meant a loss on the average of ten years of participation in the activities of this young and progressive community, then our country was last year deprived because of this loss of the services of 54,450 persons who were in untimely graves, instead of being useful citizens, enjoying life and helping to build up the nation's prosperity.

A calculation made in the preceding article of this series gives as the result of one year of a citizen's life and work, an addition to the country's wealth of $500 beyond what was necessary for his own maintenance.

The liquor traffic robs this country annually through shortening the lives of citizens, of not less than 54,450 times $500. Our annual financial loss from the liquor traffic, through this loss of life alone, aggregates $27,225,000.

5. The Waste of Grain

Canada is a grain-growing country. Every year it produces vast quantities of wheat and other cereals more than the people of the country need. These products are shipped to other lands, and their value is represented by the products of other lands which our country is made able to buy. Every surplus bushel of Canadian grain is a national asset, an increase in the accumulating wealth of this prospering country.

In the year ending March 31st, 1911, the quantity of barley turned into malt for the production of beer and spirits was 125,546,514 pounds. In addition to a part of this malt the distillers used the following:

	Pounds
Corn	52,080.594
Rye	11,320,088
Molasses	18,531,379

besides smaller quantities of wheat, barley, oats and other materials. If we take all the grain thus disposed of, we shall find it totalling more than 5,500,000 bushels, and worth at average market prices more than $4,000,000.

A good deal of the distillery-used grain was imported. It was mainly American corn, but money for which Canadians worked hard had to be sent to purchase it. Nearly all the grain used in the making of malt was Canadian product. It is true that some of the spirits produced was exported, but the quantity was small, and the value of the material used in manufacturing it would not equal the value of other material used in the manufacture of strong drink for consumption in Canada in addition to the grain above specified.

Here we have the wasteful destruction of grain that might have been exported, and a consequent lessening of the wealth of the country to the extent stated. Someone will say: "The farmers were paid for their grain." That is true, but the grain was destroyed, and the liquor consumers had to be impoverished to produce the price which the grain grower received. If all the grain in the country were insured, and all burned up, the farmers would be paid for their grain, but the country would still be the loser. There can be no waste or destruction without loss, and in this case, as shown, the loss is fully $4,000,000.

6. Outlay Made Necessary by Drinking

The public expenditure incurred through intemperance is very great. It is universally admitted that much of the disease, insanity, idiocy, and other misfortunes which go to increase the dependent classes, is due to the liquor habit, and that a very large proportion of the pauperism and crime of the country is attributable directly or indirectly to the same cause.

The support of our great charities is, to a large extent, voluntary. Private benevolence supports homes, refuges, hospitals, and various other institutions for the maintenance of the destitute and other afflicted persons. There is no way of ascertaining what amount of money is expended in this way.

We can, however, obtain an approximate idea of the amount appropriated from public funds for such purposes as those indicated. Even here we are hampered by the fact that full returns are available only for some of the provinces, and to a certain extent we are driven to the plan elsewhere also adopted, of taking Ontario as a standard and deducting Dominion expenditures pro rata from the expenditures that we know are made in that Province.

The expenditure of the province of Ontario, which comes under the heading, "Administration of Justice," is estimated for the fiscal year ending in 1912, at $747,922.83. This of course does not include certain salaries and expenses of judges, paid by the Dominion Government. Only a part of it is outlay of which the liquor traffic is the cause.

If we omit all the appropriations for superior courts, and the courts devoted specially to civil business, taking into consideration only the money paid out on account of administration of justice in Counties and Unorganized Districts, Provincial Police, Crown Counsel, Prosecutions, and Criminal Investigations, we will have left an amount of $533,947.

The amount estimated to be paid by the province for the maintenance of asylums and prisons, including the Central Prison and the Mercer Reformatory, was $1,383,507. This is merely the account for maintenance, and does not include anything for expenditure on buildings or equipment, or for interest on the large amount of money invested, and it makes no allowance for the amount received for patients in the asylums, and the profit made by the Central Prison industries.

The Government's appropriation for hospitals and charities, not including the cost of industrial schools and other outlay for work among neglected children, amounts to $420,388.

According to a report issued by the Provincial Government for the year

1908, the municipalities of Ontario expended in that year on administration of justice, maintenance of gaols, reformatories, hospitals, asylums, and poorhouses, and for police expenses, a total of $2,450,231.

The foregoing items of a year's outlay in the Province of Ontario for public services that are to some extent made necessary by intemperance, may be summarized as follows:

Provincial Asylums and Prisons	$1,383,507
Administration of Justice	533,947
Hospitals and Charities	420,388
Municipal Expenditure for Similar Purposes	2,450,231
Total	$4,788,073

The population of Ontario is in round figures 34.13 per cent. of the population of the Dominion. It is possible that the expenditure in other provinces may be less proportionately than in this. There may be more expense in the administration of justice in certain sparsely populated territories, notably in the northwest, where the mounted police are maintained by the Dominion Parliament. If, however, we take thirty-five per cent. as the proportion paid by Ontario of the aggregate provincial expenditures of all the provinces, we arrive at the conclusion that the annual national public expenditure for the support of our neglected, helpless, insane and criminal classes, totals $13,680,208.

To this expenditure made by provincial and municipal authorities, there must be added, as part of the cost of crime, destitution and insanity, the expenditure by the Dominion upon penitentiaries which it maintains, and which, after deducting the revenue derived by the government from prison industries, amounted in the year 1910 to $494,363, bringing the total outlay for these purposes up to the enormous sum of $14,174,571.

How much of this vast expenditure ought to be attributed to the liquor traffic and the liquor habit?

The Hon. Sir Oliver Mowat, late Lieutenant-Governor of the Province of Ontario, was a man of cautious and conservative temperament, as well as of wide experience and close observation. He stated in the Ontario Legislature, when he was leader of the Provincial Government, that in his opinion, not less than three-fourths of the poverty, vice, disease and crime which afflicted the country was chargeable to the evil of intemperance. Let us be even more moderate in our reckoning than was Sir Oliver Mowat. Let us estimate that only one-half of the vast public outlay which we have detailed, results from the drinking habits of our people. Even then we have to face the formidable fact that in addition to all the suffering, the sorrow, the shame, and the sin that intemperance inflicts upon our fair Dominion, one year's cost of caring for those upon whom the liquor curse has fallen, which must be paid out of public funds, amounts to over $7,087,285.

7. The Liquor Revenue

A large public revenue is derived from the liquor traffic. About twenty or twenty-five per cent. of the amount paid by the consumers for intoxicating liquors is appropriated for public purposes. The amount thus collected by the Dominion Government is easily ascertained. It is difficult to arrive at an accurate conclusion concerning the amounts received by provincial and municipal bodies, as the duties levied and the returns made are not so uniform and complete as in the case of the Dominion. The following statement will give a good idea of the whole situation.

Total Revenue

Taking, then, the actual revenue collected by the Dominion, and the probably excessive estimate of revenue collected locally, we find the total contribution of the liquor traffic in Canada to the public funds to be as follows:

National Revenue	$16,443,407
Local Revenue	2,899,517
Total	$19,342,924

8. It Does Not Pay

In the foregoing statements are set out details of some of the losses to the country, and some of the losses to individuals, which are the result of the liquor traffic and the liquor habit. It may be well to sum up these items so as to ascertain what they represent in the way of aggregated loss.

The amount actually paid for drink by consumers, has been shown on a conservative basis to be at least $81,392,969. This is total loss. It may be said that it is spent for articles of consumption, just as in the case of other beverages. There is this difference,—that in this case the purchased commodities immediately disappear, without giving any benefit to the consumers. Science and experience have demonstrated the invariable uselessness, and the very frequent injury, of drinking practices. The money is paid for a product of investment and labor, which product is immediately totally destroyed, just as if a house or crop were burned, or destroyed by an earthquake. The community is poorer by the value of the property that has disappeared, that is, what is received for the money unwisely paid for it.

The loss to the country through the idleness of men who are kept from work through their own drinking or the drinking of others, has been shown to be at least $66,017,429.

Not fewer than 5,445 citizens have their lives cut short every year because of intemperance. Nearly all of these, if they had lived, would have been a part of the work-producing power of the country. It has been shown that a worker is worth at least $500 to the community, and if the average shortening of the lives of the four thousand be taken at ten years each, our country is impoverished every year through drink-caused deaths to the amount of $27,225,000.

These amounts have to be added as total loss to the amount paid for drink. Had the idleness and death not taken place, all the wealth production set out would have been added to the country's wealth production, and the country as a whole and some individual citizens are poorer to the extent set out.

It has been shown that the destruction in the manufacture of liquor of grain that might have been exported or otherwise used for the enrichment of the country, involves a national loss of $4,000,000.

This, however, is a loss of a different character. It is paid for out of the money spent for strong drink, and therefore cannot be added to the aggregate national impoverishment twice. The same is true of the item representing misdirected labor, which also has been paid for by the liquor purchasers.

It is true in a sense that both the grain and the labor, if not employed in liquor-making, would have been represented by some surplus form of products which would have been available for export, and resulted in the bringing into this country of other wealth in exchange or money to represent it; but this more desirable exchange would not have altered the position of the producers, who are already paid for their product by the purchasers of the liquor. We cannot address these items unto our total bill of loss.

It is altogether different with the next item in our calculations, as a result of the drinking of the liquor for which the purchasers paid. The taxpayers were called upon to pay over large amounts for police courts, jails, and the like. It has been shown that this expenditure amounts to at least $7,087,285.

This is only a part of the expenditure for this purpose. It is the part contributed in taxes. Outside of this, individual citizens are continually paying large sums voluntarily towards hospitals, homes, and other institutions, which they would not have to pay, were it not for the liquor traffic. The amount herein set out is only the amount which the people are compelled to contribute.

It is clear, then, that really the only salvage from the money paid by the liquor purchasers is the amount which is taken out as revenue by the government authorities, and which they would have to collect from the people in some other way, if they had not collected it from them as part of the price of the liquor.

Putting the various foregoing expenditures in the form of a table, and setting out against it the total revenue which the liquor traffic contributes in every way to meet this vast expenditure, we obtain the following results:

COST OF THE LIQUOR TRAFFIC

Paid for liquor	$ 81,392,969
Labor lost	66,017,429
Loss by deaths	27,225,000
Cost of intemperance	7,087,285
	$181,722,683

RECEIPTS FROM THE LIQUOR TRAFFIC

Aggregate of Dominion Provincial and Municipal Revenues	$ 19,342,924
NET LOSS	162,379,759
	$181,722,683

Readers who have carefully studied the foregoing calculations will admit their moderation. The charges against the liquor traffic have been as small as could be justified by any fair argument, and in the amount counted as paid by consumers no allowance has been made for the great extent to which liquors have been diluted by vendors, and sold below their full strength. The expense to which the country is put by the liquor traffic is very much greater on the whole than what is represented by the public outlay and loss which the foregoing table sets out. It is well within the mark to say that the liquor habit costs our country much more than $180,000,000 per year.

CRIME AND DRUNKENNESS IN CANADA

It is true that during recent years there has been a rapid and regrettable increase in drunkenness and other crime in nearly every part of the Dominion of Canada. From the last published Government Criminal Returns, the following table is compiled, showing (1)the total number of convictions for all offences, including drunkenness, and (2) the total convictions for drunkenness alone:

Year	All Convictions	Convictions for Drunkenness
1898	 38,206	 11,259
1899	 38,710	 11,090
1900	 41,653	 12,215
1901	 42,148	 12,727
1902	 43,536	 13,324
1903	 50,404	 16,532
1904	 54,946	 18,895
1905	 62,450	 21,621
1906	 70,903	 25,110
1907	 79,170	 29,802
1908	 88,633	 31,089
1909	 89,951	 31,105
1910	 102,903	 34,068

The population has also increased during these years, but not at all in the same ratio as has the criminal record. The population, according to the census, in the year 1901 was 5,371,315, and in the year 1911, was 7,204,527.

Canada is a comparatively sober country. Its per capita consumption of intoxicating liquor is less than one-third that of the United States, and only about one-fifth that of England. A good deal of its territory is under prohibitory law, and the people, as a whole, are progressive, and have a reputation for sobriety and morality. What is the explanation of the increase in drunkenness and crime?

As compared with even the United States, Canada is a new country. For many years the provinces which are now federated in the Dominion, were separate colonies on the eastern and western seaboards, and along the southern frontier of the great territory which occupies nearly half a continent. Even after Confederation the Dominion in 1868 had an area of only 662,148 square miles. The territory over which the Dominion Parliament now exercises jurisdiction has an area of 3,729,665 square miles.

It required some time for the machinery of the federation of the original colonies and the subsequent addition of other areas to be adjusted to its work, and to develop effectiveness. Even in the matter of compiling statistics, time was needed to secure efficiency, and the records for early years were very defective. Recent returns are more accurate than those before obtained, and official statements come nearer to being a correct record of actual conditions. The thoroughness of law enforcement has also increased, so that for example the illicit manufacture of strong drink has been thoroughly suppressed, and crime, in general, now rarely escapes official recognition and action. No doubt, this change has had some influence in increasing the official figures of drink consumed, and crime punished. Their effect upon the record of the last ten years has, however, been very slight.

The three main factors or causes in the increased drinking and criminal record of Canada are: (1) A very large immigration; (2) unusual prosperity; (3) the concentration of population in large cities.

As is well known, there is now entering Canada a very large stream of the overflow of European population. England's per capita consumption of strong drink is over thirty gallons. Canada's is less than seven. It is easy to see that immigration tends to change the Canadian figures. Other European immigrants have grown up under conditions and customs in regard to strong drink very much like those of Great Britain. The rapid increase of Canadian population in this way tends to increase the record of both drinking and drunkenness. With an increase in drinking and drunkenness there always comes an increase in crime.

Police Court records register very fairly any change in the general material prosperity of the community. When men are well off, they develop luxurious habits. With a certain class of the population, increased earning power means increased drunkenness. Men who have money to pay police court fines put in more convictions than men who are compelled to serve terms of imprisonment which are imposed as alternative penalties. Here again, the increased drinking and drunkenness which comes with increasing prosperity are always accompanied by an increase in violations of law and order. So-called "good times" bring a history of bad conduct.

Improvements in agricultural machinery and the growing demand for manufactured articles have had the effect of concentrating a greater number of people in cities and large towns. The urban population of Canada has increased much more rapidly than the rural population, notwithstanding the vast agricultural possibilities which the country presents. Furthermore, the better class of immigration goes out on the land where drinking facilities and temptations are scarce, and the towns fill up with new-comers of a less desirable class. There is always more drinking and crime in congested centres than in sparsely-populated districts. Some Canadian cities are having a phenomenally rapid growth.

Certain industries, such as mining, attract a population that is not only large and congested, but made up to a certain extent of reckless people associating under conditions that do not promote order and morality.

There is another factor in Canadian conditions which tends to enlarge the criminal record. It is the stern and continuous operation of the machinery for the detection and punishment of offences against law and order. A high record of convictions may mean a high record of effective law enforcement. Therefore, comparisons between the criminal records of different countries are not of much value unless at the same time consideration is given to the thoroughness or laxity of law administration in the places compared.

The relations of the liquor traffic to crime is strikingly shown in the fact that, generally speaking, those Canadian provinces in which prohibition is most extensive have the lowest criminal record. There is one province, Prince Edward Island, under a prohibitory law throughout. The province of Nova Scotia comes next in the extent to which it has been brought under prohibition, by the Local Option plan. Then comes New Brunswick, and so on. In the following tables the provinces are arranged proportionately to the extent to which prohibition prevails in them, beginning with the province entirely under prohibition, and going down to those in which there is the least prohibition territory and the laxest liquor law, Local Option not being in force over any important area in any of the last-named three, and peculiar conditions making law enforcement probably least thorough in British Columbia.

The Criminal Statistics report for the year 1908 contains statements of the number of convictions for all offences, proportionately to the population, and these statements give us the following results:

ALL CONVICTIONS PER 1,000 OF THE POPULATION

Prince Edward Island	2.90
Nova Scotia	11.01
New Brunswick	8.71
Quebec	10.45
Ontario	15.61
Manitoba	20.42
Saskatchewan	13.32
Alberta	22.74
British Columbia	23.83

CONVICTIONS FOR DRUNKENNESS, PER 1,000

Prince Edward Island	1.82
Nova Scotia	6.00
New Brunswick	5.56
Quebec	3.85
Ontario	4.22
Manitoba	8.62
Saskatchewan	3.38
Alberta	7.39
British Columbia	10.51

If the figures in the first of these tables are arranged so as to show the number of persons in each province proportionate to each conviction made for any offence, the result is as follows:

ONE CONVICTION FOR

	People
Prince Edward Island	345
Nova Scotia	91
New Brunswick	115
Quebec	96
Ontario	64
Manitoba	49
Saskatchewan	75
Alberta	44
British Columbia	42

Even in considering these tables, it must be remembered that the factors of concentrated and new population, have their influence. Prince Edward Island is an agricultural province with a stationary population. British Columbia is a province with large mining industries, growing cities, and increasing population. These conditions in the other provinces vary nearly in the proportion in which the list is arranged. The figures are for the year 1908, before the Nova Scotia Temperance Act was passed.

Taking Canada as a whole, prohibition sentiment is growing, and the territory and population under prohibition is rapidly increasing. Because of immigration and concentration in urban centres, the population under license is still increasing more rapidly than the population under prohibition. As the prohibition area spreads, the relative proportions of increase will change and ultimately become reversed; but it is possible that for some time Canada may still present the apparent anomaly of development of prohibition sentiment and law, along with an increase in liquor consumption and crime. Yet the progress towards the general adoption of the prohibition plan is certain and rapid.

Ontario's Jail Record

Sir Oliver Mowat was an able statesman, a keen observer, comprehensive in his grasp of facts and cautious in his statements. He said that 75 per cent. of the crime committed is attributable to intemperance.

In the light of this strong but not unreasonable statement, the following figures ought to be carefully studied. They set out the aggregate number of commitments to the jails of the province of Ontario for the ten years ending on Sept. 30th, 1910:

```
Men, over 16 years of age ............    95,910
Boys, under 16 years of age ..........     1,445
Women, over 16 years of age .........    12,673
Girls, under 16 years of age ...........      159
Total   .........................   110,187
Total women  ....................    12,832
Total children  ...................     1,604
```

This gives an average, in a civilized Christian community, of 10,000 men and women every year, who are so degraded and dangerous that they have to be restrained between stone walls and behind iron bars as if they were wild beasts. The high privilege of personal liberty must be taken from them for the safety of the public; while the governing authority raises money for public purposes, including the maintenance of philanthropic institutions, by licensing the business that has caused 75 per cent. of the crime which is dealt with so severely.

APPENDIX—THE PLEBISCITE FIGURES

Frequent inquiries are received concerning the votes polled in the various plebiscites that have already been taken. The actual results obtained are set out in the subjoined tables. In the plebiscite for the Province of Ontario, taken on Jan. 3, 1894, the votes polled were as follows:

	Men	Women	Total
For Prohibition	180,087	12,402	192,489
Against Prohibition	108,494	2,226	110,720
Total votes polled	288,581	14,628	303,209
Majority for Prohibition	71,593	10,176	81,769

Other Provincial plebiscites were taken on the dates and with the results set out in the following statement:

Province	Date of Voting	Votes cast for Prohibition	Votes cast ag'st Prohibition	Majority for Prohibition
Manitoba	July 23rd, 1892	19,637	7,115	12,522
Prince Edward I.	Dec. 14th, 1893	10,616	3,390	7,226
Nova Scotia	Mar. 16th, 1894	43,756	12,355	31,401

The Dominion plebiscite was taken on September 29th, 1898, and the votes polled gave the following results:

	For Prohibition	Against	Majority For	Majority Against
Ontario	154,498	115,284	39,214	......
Quebec	28,436	122,760	......	94,324
Nova Scotia	34,678	5,370	29,308	......
New Brunswick	26,919	9,575	17,344	......
Prince Edward Island	9,461	1,146	8,315	......
Manitoba	12,419	2,978	9,441	......
British Columbia	5,731	4,756	975	......
North-West Territories	6,238	2,824	3,414	......
Total	278,380	264,693	108,011	94,324

On the fourth day of December, 1902, a vote of the Legislative Assembly electors of the Province of Ontario was taken upon the question of the approval of the Liquor Act, 1902, which was a thorough-going measure of Provincial prohibition. The result of that vote was as follows:

Votes for the Liquor Act, 1902 199,749
Votes Against the Liquor Act, 1902 103,548

Majority for the Act 96,201

23

The Ideas of Henri Bourassa*†

M. P. O'Connell

WHEREAS the earlier articles by Neatby and Page centred on Laurier and English Canadian attitudes to the imperial questions, this one analyses the political and social ideas of the leading French Canadian nationalist, Henri Bourassa. Bourassa was famous for his opposition to the sending of Canadian troops to South Africa in 1899, to the Laurier Naval Bill, and to conscription in 1917. He founded *Le Devoir* as a crusading newspaper for the nationalist cause in 1910. As a journalist, orator, and political activist he was a key figure in the evolution of French-Canadian nationalism in the 20th century.

Bourassa developed a wide ranging political philosophy which was both conservative and nationalist and even in certain ways progressive. His thinking was a reaction to a group of factors: the new imperialism which he felt threatened the very existence of Canada, the rapid settlement of the Canadian West largely by European settlers who knew nothing of the cultural duality of Canada, and urbanization and industrialization which could change the moral values fundamental to French-Canadian society. Although Robert Rumilly has written a biography of Bourassa (*Henri Bourassa, La Via Publique d'un grand Canadien.*), this article remains the clearest statement of Bourassa's overall position. The social aspects of this article have recently been seriously challenged. See Joseph Levitt, "Henri Bourassa and Modern Industrial Society, 1900–1914," *Canadian Historical Review*, 1969, pp. 37–50, and *Henri Bourassa and the Golden Calf* (Ottawa, 1969).

---

* *Canadian Journal of Economics and Political Science*, XIX (August, 1953), pp. 361–376.

† This paper was presented at the annual meeting of the Canadian Political Science Association in London, June 4, 1953.

THE PURPOSE of this paper is to sketch briefly some aspects of Bourassa's political and social thought and to indicate in particular a few of the influences shaping his complex mentality. With the historical detail of his public career, and of the Nationalist movement which he led in the first two decades of this century, the paper is not directly concerned. Nor is any attempt made to reach a final estimate of his influence or significance in Canadian politics.

The difficulties in examining Bourassa's ideas are many and arise not only from his radical temperament and tendency to over-statement. They spring also from his great sensitivity to the intellectual and emotional currents of his day which found expression in innumberable pamphlets, speeches, and editorials in his newspaper of ideas and combat, *Le Devoir*, founded in 1910. Difficulties are implicit in the complicated nature of the task he sought to perform. For he set out, at the turn of the century, and with a sense of the opening of a new era in the historic development of the French-Canadian people, to re-examine every aspect of his people's situation; political, social, economic, moral, religious, and intellectual. He proposed to expound principles basic to their social thought and action in a new set of circumstances.

Three main elements in the new era were of special concern. First was the impact upon Canada of the new imperialism, opening up prospects of direct involvement in imperial wars in an age of mounting imperial rivalries, and threatening, moreover, so he believed, to undermine toleration of cultural and ethnic difference in Canada. A second major change in circumstance was the rapid development after 1900 of the Canadian West on the basis of a large immigrant population of diverse peoples, posing grave difficulties to the achievement of the ideal of a dual nationality throughout Canada. Finally, he became much concerned with the deeper significance to French-Canadian nationality of the whole complex of adaptations—ideological, moral, economic, and social—being made in response to the coming of North American urban industrialism to the province of Quebec.

In attempts to influence the adjustments of Canadians to this pattern of change the Nationalist movement was born. It was without formal organization other than the "Ligue nationalistie," begun in Montreal in 1903 and centred around a dozen young intellectuals, notably journalists, of whom Bourassa was unchallenged leader.[1] Through newspapers and mass rallies, and in the actions of a few independents in Parliament,

---

[1] Among the founders of the League were Olivar Asselin, Omer Héroux, and Armand Lavergne.

particularly Bourassa and Lavergne, the Nationalists sought a following and a body of opinion independent of the two political parties. Their movement was entirely conservative in spirit, governed by an ideal of hierarchy and balance, and offered as a force making for stability of conditions. It emphasized traditional social order and institutions of authority and control, especially the Roman Catholic Church.[2] It never became a political party, although the Nationalists engaged in heated electoral campaigns in favour of one party or the other. Bourassa himself could not have been a party leader for he would too readily have sacrificed party interest or power for a principle.

The Nationalist movement was designed to slow the pace of industrial change while making secure the position of the small propertied classes, and enrolling the new urban working classes in national and Catholic labour unions, thus integrating them with the general purpose of social unity and ethnic survival. It was designed, secondly, to fight imperialism and to foster the maximum independence of Canada compatible with remaining under the Crown. A main object of the movement's anti-imperialism, which was its characteristic feature and upon which it developed its maximum political force, was to orient Canada's defence policy in the direction of neutrality in wars of the Empire that were not fought strictly for the defence of Canada. Finally, the Nationalist movement was founded upon the advocacy of an Anglo-French nation extending throughout Canada, and requiring the spread of Franco-Catholic groups into the English-speaking provinces with the provision therein of Catholic education and a general bilingualism.

In all their endeavours in imperial affairs, dual nationality, and problems of social order, the Nationalists stressed the broad Canadian character of their interest and outlook. The direction of their thought was stated by Bourassa in 1904 in an exchange of views with Jules Paul Tardivel, whom he believed, though with little justification, an important precursor of Canadian nationalism.[3] Tardivel represented at the end of the nineteenth century a narrowly French, Catholic, and separatist nationalism, looking towards the creation of a French state in north-eastern North America, and suggesting, in the meantime, a Catholic political party similar to those in some countries of Europe. With this nationalism Bourassa had nothing in common although he was undoubtedly influenced by Tardivel's uncompromising spirit, his attacks upon the party

---

[2] See for example, *Le Devoir*, Sept. 3, 1910, "French-Canadians have experienced such profound changes through the force of arms and accidents of history in their national situation, their political constitution and social state, that they have, so to speak, clung fast to the Papacy as the most stable of institutions governing men."

[3] See the article by Bourassa on the tenth anniversary of Tardivel's death in *Le Devoir*, April 26, 1915, "If I seek the origins of some of my ideas I have no difficulty in finding them in the articles of Tardivel, and even more perhaps in our too infrequent conversations."

spirit of the clergy, and his appeal for a form of political action above party lines. In his newspaper, *La Vérité*, Tardivel wrote: "Our national-ism is French-Canadian nationalism. . . . The patriotism we wish to see flourish is French-Canadian patriotism. . . . For us, the homeland, while not precisely the province of Quebec, is French Canada. The nation we wish to see founded at the hour set by divine providence is the French-Canadian nation."[4] To which Bourassa replied in *Le Nationaliste*, the weekly newspaper recently launched by Asselin and others to promote the new Nationalism:

Our nationalism is a Canadian nationalism founded on the duality of races and the distinctive traditions which that duality implies. We work for the develop-ment of a Canadian patriotism which is in our view the best guarantee of the coexistence of the two races and of the mutual respect they owe each other. . . . The homeland for us is the whole of Canada, that is to say, a federation of distinct races and autonomous provinces. The nation we wish to see develop is the Canadian nation composed of French and English Canadians . . . sepa-rated by language and religion and legal arrangements . . . but united in a sentiment of fraternity and devotion to a common homeland.[5]

To the three elements in this concept of nationalism, that is, cultural dualism, provincial autonomy, and the idea of the whole of Canada as the nation, was added the idea of national independence under the British Crown—an independence to be made effective and concrete in a distinctive Canadian foreign policy, and by this he meant a foreign policy free from all taint of military or sentimental imperialism. No longer tenable was the nineteenth century passive colonialism summed up in the formula "No annexation, no separation from Great Britain, let us remain as we are." What was needed in the new era was an expansive, yet selfish concept of the national interest that must appeal to both nationalities. Central to this concept was a policy of peace abroad and of integral dualism, or justice and liberty, at home.

I

Diverse and sharply contrasting forces shaped Bourassa's mentality with strains evident in his temperament and politics. "In the prime of my youth," he said, "I was entirely and uncompromisingly ultramontane

---

[4] *La Vérité*, April 2, 1904. See also *ibid.*, April 15, 1905, ". . . perhaps we may be permitted to suggest a solution to the problem, that is, to repartition the Dominion on a new basis, subdividing it into two or more confederations." See also Tardivel's *Pour la Patrie* (Montreal, 1895).

[5] *Le Nationaliste*, April 3, 1904. Both citations may be read in Abbé Arthur Maheux, "Le Nationalisme canadien-francais au l'aurore du XXᵉ siècle," Canadian Historical Association, *Annual Report*, 1945, 68–9. See also Olivar Asselin, *A Quebec View of Canadian Nationalism: An Essay by a Dyed in the Wool French Canadian, on the Best Means of Assuring the Greatness of the Canadian Fatherland* (Montreal, 1909), a pamphlet of 61 pages dedicated to "The Great English Race."

Catholic and passionate Rouge"[6]—a combination of such opposite poles of Quebec politics as to draw from Laurier the remark, "Bourassa is a Castor-Rouge, a monster; I have never known another."[7] He tossed between vigorous partisanship and assertive independence of views. The Riel affair of 1885 first awoke his political passions. He was then seventeen years of age and completing his formal education. In 1887 he campaigned for Mercier and his Parti National, but soon left him, finding the provincial Rouges "insufferable with vanity." Two years later, at the age of twenty-one he was mayor of Montebello where he had gone to manage lands inherited from the Papineau seigniory and to be a farmer.[8] Here, on the border of Ontario and Quebec between Ottawa and Montreal, he launched himself into a political career. So Rouge and emotionally implicated were his politics, that in the Ottawa county council in 1891 he obstructed the passage of a resolution of condolence upon the death of Macdonald. "We had no business," he said, "expressing sympathy for the man who let Riel hang." Towards the end of his career, however, he was describing Macdonald as the "only truly national statesman" that Canada had possessed.

He turned to federal politics, to Laurier and to the Liberal party—the party, he said, of "ideals and justice," opposed to the big interests and favourable to the farmers. In 1892 he purchased a small newspaper, *L'Interprète*, bringing it to Montebello where he published it for two years in vigorous partisanship. Tory doctrine, he told his readers in the polemical style that never left him, was simply: "Grind the people down with taxes, bleed them white for the maintenance of the British Empire, and in compensation England will from time to time choose some good Tory and send him here and there to conclude treaties in which Canadian interests will generally be sacrificed to the interests of England. The people cry famine: It does not matter, Toryism is satisfied, the Empire is united, Britannia rules."[9]

---

[6] *Le Devoir, ses origines, sa naissance, son esprit* (Montreal, 1930), 3. See also some comments on Bourassa's early politics by his father in Napoléon Bourassa, *Lettres d'un artiste canadien*, col. Mlle Adine Bourassa (Bruges, 1929). "Imagine the multiple horrors of your aunt! She thought she had raised a chicken but finds an eagle under her wings. . . . He is everywhere in action, neither sleeping nor staying at home, running from one assembly to another, speaking tariff, free trade, reciprocity, misery of the people, etc., etc." (p. 368). See pages 456–7 for the advice to conduct his politics "without ill-will to Laurier, and inspiring and holding the confidence of moderate English opinion in the manner of Lafontaine."

[7] *Le Devoir*, Oct. 14, 1943, in the first of ten souvenir addresses.

[8] Some details are in *Le Devoir*, Oct. 14, 1943, and in Abbé Michel Chamberland, *Histoire de Montebello* (Montreal, 1929), *passim*.

[9] *L'Interprète*, Oct. 12, 1893. The newspaper was sold in 1894 and reappeared on the Ontario side of the Ottawa River at Clarence Creek as *Le Ralliement*. Bourassa continued to contribute articles, particularly in support of the Laurier-Greenway school settlement in Manitoba. See the issue of February 20, 1896. "We have always said, and say again, that Mr. Laurier could achieve a better and more effective result by his conciliatory attitude than the Government could ever achieve by its sterile

When the area surrounding the former seigniory was created the constituency of Labelle (1892), Bourassa became the Liberal party candidate. He refused party financial support and made public declarations of his freedom from party discipline. Elected in the Liberal victory of 1896, he represented this constituency in Parliament for twenty-one years divided into two periods: the first extending to 1907 during which time he separated from his party to develop the Nationalist movement; and the second period from 1925 until 1935, in which year he was defeated in general elections and retired from public life. For four years (1908–12), during the most critical period of Nationalist agitations, he was a member of the Quebec legislature where he supported the small Conservative Opposition against the Liberal Government of Lomer Gouin.

The Catholic cast of his mind was formed by early training especially under his aunt, Exilda Papineau, who taught him "to love the Bible, Pius IX, and Msgr. Bourget": Pius IX, who had turned the Church against European liberalism after 1848, and Msgr. Bourget, the patriot bishop of Montreal, who had led the attacks on the Rouges, on Papineau, and on others, as on the Institut canadien, and who best exemplified the uniting of patriotism with ultramontane Catholicism and hostility to liberal democracy. He read much as a youth in the library of his uncle Médard Bourassa, curé at Montebello, and an ardent Castor, that is, ultra Conservative in politics. The religious and political background of his family, however, was unorthodox, and such as to accentuate his own individuality. His grandfather, Louis Joseph Papineau, was an agnostic who attended High Mass in his capacity as seignior at Montebello. He had been, as is well known, foremost political leader of his people for twenty years preceding the Rebellion of 1837, and had brought to Canada, from his exile in the France of the 1840's, republican, democratic, and liberal ideas which became the inspiration of a radical wing of the Rouge party. Though little influenced by Papineau's ideas, Bourassa had the same passion for struggles, aristocratic ideal of leadership, and incapacity to conceal his thoughts.[10] Unorthodox thought and activity were evident also in his uncle, Amédée Papineau, who in 1893 made public profession of his conversion to the Presbyterian faith, "the most rational," as he said, of all creeds, and at the same time tried, without success, to interest Bourassa in a movement of annexation to the United States.[11]

Many of his mentors as a youth were spokesmen of minority opinion in reaction to the prevailing currents of their day. His opinions on the rela-

---

blusterings." See also the issues of May 23, 1895, January 23, 1896. The author wishes to express his thanks to Mr. Rosario Gauthier of Papineauville for the opportunity of reading a collection of these two newspapers.

[10] See *Le Devoir*, Oct. 14, 1943; *House of Commons Debates*, March 13, 1900, p. 1830.

[11] See Chamberland, *Histoire de Montebello*, 258; *Le Devoir*, Oct. 8, 1910.

tions of church and state were taken from the conservative historian, de Maistre, foe of the Enlightenment and passionate advocate of patriotism fused with religion. His favourite newspapers were Tardivel's *La Vérité* of Quebec, and Trudel's *L'Etendard* of Montreal, both devoted to the conservative Castors and to the ultramontane bishops who had much harried the Rouges. For his model, Bourassa chose Louis Veuillot, leading Catholic polemicist in nineteenth-century France, champion of Catholic schools, and exponent of supra-party patriotism.[12] From Veuillot and others he absorbed into his mentality that inflexibility of spirit and utter commitment to the Catholic ideal which distinguishes his public career. He saw his life as an apostolate. His politics were an extension of his Catholicism, which, when joined to his ardent nationalist sentiment, tended to displace his liberalism.

Ultamontanism, however, restrained Bourassa's nationalism by emphasis on an international church and the subordination of all things to religion. He was too rational in a Catholic sense to be racialist. He never emphasized the nation to the neglect of other values. Indeed, his order of precedence was the Church, family, society, Canada, and French Canada.[13] Yet he found no real conflict between religion and his nationalism. Ultramontane Catholicism appeared moreover as special protection to French-Canadian nationality as he made evident in stating that the Church, "because Catholic, must not, and can never be in America or elsewhere an instrument of assimilation for the advancement of one race, or a factor of unification and of political hegemony in the service of the British Empire, or the American democracy."[14]

Emphasis upon religion introduced a factor of resignation into his international outlook. This derived in part from a notion that Europe for three centuries had been slowly destroying itself and lapsing into a new barbarism from which it would be redeemed again only by a return to the Church. Protestantism, Jacobinism, and Bolshevism had been three attempts at suicide. The decline of the West was further hastened by the grinding action upon each other of great irrational forces, namely, Pan-Germanism, Pan-Latinism, Pan-Slavism, and Pan-Anglo-Saxonism. What

---

[12] See *La Paix romaine* (Montreal, 1929); *Le Devoir*, Oct. 14, 1943.

[13] Though the restraining influence of religion was always present it was more apparent after his audiences with the Pope in 1922 and 1926. He was always prepared to submit to ecclesiastical discipline. See *Le Ralliement*, Jan. 28, Feb. 6, 1897; *Religion, langue, nationalité* (1910); *La Presse catholique et nationale* (1921). He condemned such extremist nationalism as that of Maurras and the *Action française*. See *Le Devoir*, Nov. 24, 26, 1923. See *Le Devoir, ses origines* . . .: "Since then [1926] I became persuaded that light comes from Rome, not only in the order of truths of faith and morals . . . but even in the solution of political and social problems . . . and in logical consequences. . . . I took the resolution to obey the Pope and follow his counsels, even when his directions or advice might run counter to my ideas or those of my friends, political associates, or of my compatriots."

[14] *La Langue, gardienne de la foi* (Montreal, 1918), 8.

the world needed, he thought, was "certitude in belief" and an "infallible moral guide."[15] The Church was the last rampart of collapsing social and international order. These views and attitudes were factors in his advocacy of neutrality for Canada in case of European or imperial wars.

Religion, finally, introduced a mystic element in Bourassa's nationalism, best shown in two pamphlets, *La Langue, gardienne de la foi* (1918) and *Le Canada apostolique* (1919). In these writings Catholicism and nationalism are united in the concept of a special mission for the French-Canadian people in North America. The idea of a special mission was, of course, not new with Bourassa. It had been given a strong impulse and religious connotation by Msgr. Lafleche of Three Rivers half a century earlier and had been a recurrent theme ever since.[16] As Bourassa stated it, French-Canadians prolong in North America the Christian and civilizing mission claimed by Catholic France in Europe. They are the bearers of superior cultural goods, performing their task under conditions of great difficulty in a sea of Anglo-Saxonism. They and the Franco-Americans constitute "the only important peoples of French race and language outside Europe." Added to this concept of uniqueness, which fostered nationalist sentiment, was the religious idea of the race of an extension of ecclesiastical order.[17] In this idea also was a feeling for permanence or duration over time. A characteristic feature of the feeling concept, furthermore, was that the mission was fulfilled, not least, for the benefit of others, for the Church, the entire race, for the whole of America; that is, the national aim was wider than the ethnic group itself. And this, in turn, was important for the concept of dual nationality as the basis of the Canadian nation.

II

Upon Bourassa's social conservatism and profound Catholicism was grafted a liberal political creed drawn from the English tradition, and represented mainly by the radical nineteenth-century school of Little Englanders. He much admired the British constitution and the civil and political liberties under which it grew. He wanted none of the excessive individualism and the levelling philosophies of the French tradition. The "English spirit of progress and stability," he declared, was "one of the

---

[15] See *L'Infaillibilité doctrinale du pape, fondement de son autorité sociale* (Montreal, 1920); *Le Pape, arbitre de la paix* (Montreal, 1918); *Le Devoir*, Nov. 24, 26, 1923, "Patriotisme, nationalisme, imperialisme."

[16] See Jeán-C. Bonenfant and Jean-C. Falardeau, "Cultural and Political Implications of French-Canadian Nationalism," Canadian Historical Association, *Annual Report*, 1946, 62.

[17] See *La Langue . . .*, 42, 49; *Le Canada apostolique*, 17, 164, and *passim; Hier, aujourd'hui, demain* (1916), 122; *Le Devoir*, May 13, 1919.

greatest moral, political and social assets of Canada."[18] The English middle classes, especially that politically conscious section holding itself free from party ties, he described as the "most sane, independent, enlightened, and most truly patriotic in the world."[19] The want of such a class in Canada made difficult a "truly national politics." It was clear that the Nationalist movement was meant to supply some of this deficiency.

The Little Englanders were the heart of his liberal England. They would not unwillingly have seen the Empire dissolve; or at least grow, in Burke's phrase, by "salutary neglect." In their name he appealed for the rights of small nationalities, international arbitration, and peace, and against militarism and imperialism. Typical was his profession of faith in the House of Commons in 1900: "I am a Liberal of the British School. I am a disciple of Burke, Fox, Bright, Gladstone and of the other Little Englanders who made Great Britain and her possessions what they are. . . . A Liberal I was born, and a Liberal I will die."[20]

But the influence of the Little Englanders he well knew was eclipsed in the last quarter of the century by the new expansive and centralizing imperialism, not without its jingoist and racialist elements. And significant for his future politics were his conclusions after a trip to Great Britain in 1901 to sound out the depth of the imperialist current: "A new chapter is opened in the history of our country which alters the situation so favourable to us of sixty years ago. . . . The champions of our liberties are no more; their disciples, reduced to impotency, have been succeeded in the British cabinet by adherents of a new school of thought, the direct descendants of the very men who had planned our enslavement. To sum up, I tell you in the language of our neighbours: 'Eternal vigilance is the price of liberty.' "[21]

This weakening of liberal imperialism in England was paralleled, he contended, by a related decline in the liberal nationalism of Macdonald and Blake. "Of sole devotion to Canadian interests," he protested, "we hear no more."[22] It thus became a primary function of the new Nationalists to resume the "selfish Little England and Little Canada" traditions of the nineteenth century.

---

[18] *House of Commons Debates*, Jan. 12, 1926, pp. 78, 79. "I would far rather secede from Great Britain and remain British in spirit, than remain and go on as we are, British in name, but Yankeefied in spirit, morals, and habits, and becoming more so from day to day."

[19] *Le Devoir*, Aug. 11, 1910; *Great Britain and Canada: Topics of the Day* (Montreal, 1902), 44.

[20] *House of Commons Debates*, March 13, 1900, p. 1828.

[21] *Great Britain and Canada*, 19.

[22] *Ibid.*, 5: "The only point of real dispute between both parties is which of the two will eat the biggest piece of jingo pie." See also *Le Devoir*, April 23, 1917: "The leaders of the two parties have for a long time been the instruments of British imperialism and of English high finance. Their differences of attitude for almost twenty-five years have been superficial." Also *Le Canada, nation libre?* (Montreal, 1926), 9: "Since his death, the old nationalist spirit which guided Sir John and all those who surrounded him has disappeared."

Bourassa's liberalism was weakened by lack of faith in democracy. "We Nationalists," he declared in 1921, "are not devotees of democracy," and this expressed a long-standing attitude.[23] Charges made familiar by conservative critics of democracy, of parties, elections, and universal franchise, were all repeated. Democracy led to a weakening of the principle of authority and to the collapse of hierarchy in values and functions. In practice at least, it was "synonomous with deception and instability." At bottom it was "the right of majorities to oppress minorities." Intense party spirit corrupted public morality, and, in the experience of French Canadians, had led to concessions undermining their national rights and safety. He both affirmed and denied that political parties were necessary for the working of a parliamentary régime, at one time characterizing the two-party system as a "modern excrescence of British parliamentary institutions."[24] During the war he protested that everything happening in Canada testified to the "failure and illusion of parliamentarism and the cynical dupery of the party régime."[25] The parliamentary system he described in 1919 as "anti-social, dissolvant, and injurious in itself."[26] Liberal democracies he thought unlikely to solve the "social problem," particularly the antagonism of social classes. Class warfare which he believed in the offing, particularly for the Anglo-Saxon nations, would finally put an end to the "worm-eaten edifice" of parliamentary democracy. Liberal democracy seemed of declining interest to the middle classes crushed between the upper and nether millstones of plutocracy and proletariat in a society tending to oscillate between capitalist tyranny and socialist despotism. And he repeated the familiar anti-democratic doctrine that both fascism and communism grew logically out of liberal democracy.[27]

Finally, in this radical critique of democracy, there was an undercurrent of hostility to British parliamentary democracy related to the belief both that it operated best in a Protestant environment, and that it was integral with a civilization steeped in soul-destroying materialism. Liberalism, he once declared, was for many Catholics a "morbid state of the mind."[28] Protestantism he was close to associating with tendencies to

---

[23] See *Le Devoir*, Oct. 20, 1921; Dec. 4, 1919; April 25, 1917; Aug. 15, 1917. *La Langue . . .*, 9.

[24] See *House of Commons Debates*, March 14, 1928, p. 1334; *Le Nationaliste*, March 27, 1904; *Le 5ᵉ Anniversaire du Devoir* (Montreal, 1915), 70. It was a "profound error" to believe political parties essential to the parliamentary régime.

[25] *Conscription* (1917), 38.

[26] *Le Devoir*, Dec. 10, 1919: "It has brought us to deify men. . . . At the same time there operated among us a confusion between authority and the men who exercised it. . . . The Protestant environment has atrophied the Catholic social sense. . . . We acquired the habit of neutrality and laicism."

[27] See *Impressions d'Europe* (Montreal, 1938), 26; *La Propriété, ses bornes, ses abus* (Montreal, 1925), 27.

[28] *L'Infaillibilité doctrinale du pape*, 73.

social anarchy. Thus, on a note of pessimism in 1918, he asked: "Whither tends the régime of British 'liberty and democracy,' fully imbued with a deliquescent Protestantism already bordering on atheism, if not to a weakening of every principle of authority, to the laxity of the family tie, to the negation of social duty, to individual egoism, to class hatred, to the unbridled cult of physical well-being, to a thirst for wealth, in a word, to Paganism? Yes, and to a paganism without gods and poetry, to the animal paganism of a soulless humanity."[29]

Notwithstanding this general critique of parliamentary democracy, flowing in part from the irritations of Canadian politics, and from the belief that the system too much supported the forces of change, Bourassa had few proposals for reform. He showed much sympathy for the exponents of group representation from Western Canada in the mid-twenties.[30] But he did not think, as they did, of economic class organization as the basis of the group system, calling rather for a "free" representation of such vague categories as provinces, races, classes, currents of opinion, and diverse interests. He did not propose coalition cabinets, although they would seem to be an integral part of any developed group system. He did, however, suggest a fixed term to the life of Parliament to protect it against dissolution by the executive. He favoured also the adoption of the rule that governments not resign upon the defeat of their measures in the House, but only upon an explicit vote of want of confidence. But none of these constitutional proposals did he advocate with any persistence. They reflect only the general direction of his radicalism towards the break-up of the party system into an undefined group system. In particular, it may be noted, he never effected a union between the group ideas in government and the general syndicalism he was supporting in economic life. Nor did he want an authoritarian state. In effect, his was a radicalism, in this field as in others, which was not prepared to go beyond a certain point. It served to discharge irritations and anxieties but it left behind a volume of anti-democratic thought upon which others could draw.

His lack of sympathy with democratic principles was further revealed in views upon the franchise, which he would reserve for the male population only. Female suffrage he opposed as an "insanity," and this reflected a general attitude towards the changing status of women. Upon one occasion also he suggested a 4-to-1 preponderance in favour of rural

[29] *Le Pape, arbitre de la paix*, 20. See also, *Femmes-hommes ou hommes et femmes?* (Montreal, 1925), 42: "From the moment that the ideal state of society is found in the electoral and parliamentary system, and that the pivot and end of social order is found in the human individual . . . then one ends logically in the Protestant, rationalist, and individualist conception."

[30] *House of Commons Debates*, Jan. 12, 1926, p. 83; Feb. 2, 1926, pp. 646–7; March 14, 1926, pp. 13–35; Feb. 14, 1927, p. 289; June 15, 1926, p. 4506; Jan. 22, 1935, pp. 104–6.

representation in Parliament, mainly in the interests of stability. Excluded from the franchise should be persons dependent upon the state, such as recipients of soldiers' pensions and the unemployed on relief. Voting should be the function of "useful citizens," those who contributed to the building up of the country, who paid taxes in support of its government. "If we want to save democracy," he said in 1935, "we must put it [the franchise] in the hands of the people who have democracy at stake."[31]

Bourassa's liberalism was further modified by advocacy of plebiscites in determining the popular will on important and specific national policies. He was close to believing that, if held within reasonable bounds, plebiscitary consultation was "more conformable to the true principles of social order than the electoral and parliamentary régime."[32] This leaning towards a plebiscitary democracy was based on a number of supports: on a theory of popular sovereignty as opposed to parliamentary sovereignty; on a belief in the rightness of the popular instinct and will if approached more directly than through party and electoral agitation; and apparently also on a compact theory of Confederation which would require explicit consent either of the provinces or of the "two founding races" (it is not certain which) before constitutional change took place. It was clear that, by constitutional change, Bourassa had in mind not only formal amendment but also major policy decisions, as, for example, the decision to participate in the South African War, or to build a Canadian navy which would be "imperial in time of war," or to impose conscription for overseas service.[33] These, in fact, were the occasions on which the Nationalists demanded plebiscites, although there is nothing in Bourassa's principle which prevents its general extension. That he hoped to achieve a veto on these occasions was, of course, evident, and made even more so by the extent of the favourable majority required. Upon one occasion (1900) a majority was demanded in every province, and at other times (1910 and 1917) the favourable vote was set at a majority of the total electorate, unpolled votes to count in the negative.[34]

These various proposals of group representation and related changes, a restricted franchise, and the use of plebiscites were advanced with the

[31] See *House of Commons Debates*, March, 1898, p. 2704; Feb. 19, 1935, p. 987; *Femmes-hommes ou hommes et femmes?*, 24–5; *Le Devoir*, Feb. 23, Nov. 9, 1923.

[32] *Conscription*, 41; See also *Le Devoir*, Nov. 11, 1911; *ibid.*, Jan. 2, 1918: "I do not say that the plebiscite or the referendum is an ideal mode of government or even of popular consultation. I limit myself to saying it is better, and above all more sincere, than the kind of consultation that can be had on a concrete question, by a parliamentary election."

[33] See *Le Devoir*, Jan. 13, 1910; Oct. 23, 1911: "Parliament has not received from the people the moral right to engage us in a new policy whose ultimate consequences will necessarily affect the autonomy of Canada, its world-wide relations, the security of its commerce and industry, the resources of its people, and the lives of its sons."

[34] See *House of Commons Debates*, March 13, 1900, p. 1821; July 28, 1899, p. 8891; *Le Devoir*, Feb. 18, 1910; June 1, 8, 9, 1911; *Conscription*, 29.

intention of securing the responsibility of government to Parliament and of Parliament to the people. That they would achieve these objectives is altogether doubtful for reasons that need no elaboration here; among them, and especially with respect to group representation and the plebiscite, a weakening of prestige and sense of responsibility on the part of Parliament, and a corresponding increase in power and irresponsibility on the part of the executive.

An economic radicalism based on Catholic social doctrines became prominent in Bourassa's nationalism in the first decade of the century. It rested on the belief stated in 1908 that the economic struggle would be the critical one for French Canadians in the twentieth century.[35] His economic policy pointed towards a liberal collectivism, although he himself depended more on a return to Christian principles than on increasing the role of the state in economic life. It was a radicalism striking out in all directions, against international finance, international unionism, "abusive capitalism," and "detestable state socialism." It reflected the point of view of the smaller propertied classes for whom he made himself spokesman; that class composed of farmers, small traders, small industrialists, small capitalists, and *rentiers*. This class he always thought the key to social solidarity and the basis of security for French Canadians as a people. He considered them also to be latent revolutionaries if not protected from big business and big unionism.

His position was the familiar one of rejecting both the economic liberalism of the doctrinaire Manchester tradition, and the socialist solution—two systems seen as equally destructive of private property and individual liberty. The property régime of modern capitalism rested, he said, upon a "false theory of absolute property right" inspired by a desire for unlimited accumulation and unchecked by social obligation.[36] This radical critique of economic liberalism paralleled his denunciations of liberal democracy, but went no further than an attempt to make more secure a private property economy and to have it serve social ends.

In 1907 and 1908, when preparing to enter the provincial legislature, he urged labour legislation patterned on that of Catholic Belgium, and with a view to creating a Labour Council (Chambre syndicale) in which representatives of labour unions and employers' syndicates would meet continuously for collective bargaining.[37] The role of the state would be confined to creating a legal framework for the joint labour-capital administration of industries, and to protecting general interests. At the same time in the House of Commons, he declared himself in favor of compulsory arbitration of industrial disputes but recognized that the public was

---

[35] See *Le Nationaliste*, Oct. 11, 1908.

[36] See *La Propriété, ses bornes, ses abus*, 8–10, 20.

[37] See *La Patrie*, Aug. 14, Sept. 3, 1907; *Le Nationaliste*, May 31, 1908.

not yet ready for that step.[38] After visits to Belgium in 1910 and 1914 he became a strong advocate of Catholic and national labour unions, and of a general syndicalist organization among employers, craftsmen, and consumers, as also of co-operatives in production and credit.[39]

He favoured also an extension of the public sector of the economy in basic utilities such as railways and telephones and in important resources such as hydro-electric power. But he doubted the wisdom of state operation of such enterprises in a country afflicted, as he put it, with the electoral and parliamentary system.[40] Reluctance to see state activity increase in social welfare schemes reflected his dependence upon the Church and voluntary associations, and sprang from an ideal of a society composed of relatively self-sufficient families. It was important to avoid undermining the "social sense" of the people by such schemes as non-contributory old age pensions, and to avoid taking money from one class to give to another.[41] During the depression of the thirties he called upon the state to "bring about a better distribution of wealth," to "curb the power of finance," to bring fiscal relief to small and medium enterprises and heads of families, to reduce relief expenditures and war veterans' pensions, and to institute a policy of small public works scattered throughout the country.[42] In all these proposals and attitudes the basic viewpoint of his social class was evident, and not untouched by a class egotism deplored in others.

Religious and ethnic considerations influenced his economic analysis. Thus in 1921 he warned that the "inordinate passion for business" was for French Canadians "the most active agent of Anglo-Saxon and Protestant conquest." Not in "les grandes affaires" should French Canadians seek freedom from the "economic dictatorship" of trusts, combines, and high finance, but in a "multiplicity of small patrimonies and the social improvement of small capital." Such economic wealth, he said, alone merited the blessings of God, and only towards it must an "intelligent

[38] *House of Commons Debates,* 1906–7, vol. I, pp. 1177–81.

[39] See *Le Devoir,* Aug. 1, 8, 12, 14, 15, 1914, "Les Syndicats chrétiens de Belgique," written while in Europe, and pointing to the chaotic social scene in England in contrast to the general stability of the relatively egalitarian socio-economic structure in Belgium. See also *Religion, langue, nationalité,* for an appeal to follow the path laid out by Pope Leo XIII, the "Pope of the Workers." See also *Syndicats, nationaux ou internationaux* (Montreal, 1919), *passim.*

[40] See *Syndicats, nationaux ou internationaux,* 25.

[41] See *House of Commons Debates,* March 26, 1926, p. 952; also Feb. 14, 1935, pp. 850–7, for remarks on the dangers inherent in the Unemployment Insurance Bill of that year. See also *Une Mauvaise Loi, l'assistance publique* (Montreal, 1921), 1–2, 22, in which an Act of the Quebec legislature providing for assistance and regulation of certain charitable works was held to "accelerate family and social disorganization" and to be a certain step toward "detestable state socialism."

[42] *House of Commons Debates,* Jan. 30, 1934, pp. 108–9; March 20, 1934, pp. 1645–61; Feb. 2, 1938, p. 1724; April 15, 1931, p. 626.

and noble Catholic people" aspire.[43] His economic radicalism thus tended to be converted into a petit-bourgeois nationalism supported by religious sanctions.

III

A concept of Canadian nationality was basic to Bourassa's nationalism. It was designed to provide security and expansion for French-Canadian nationality throughout Canada, and to equate this with a broad national interest. Its essence was an integral dualism, which he hoped to see taken up by all Canadians, not simply as something to be endured, but as a positive goal giving the nation its unique character. Indeed, for Bourassa, the fundamental condition for having a Canadian nation at all in North America was that cultural and ethnic dualism be extended everywhere and in a concrete manner.

His idea of a "broad Canadian nationality" thus repudiates the concept of a "Quebec reservation"; that is, the view of 1867 that Quebec would be the French province and that the other provinces would be English in character. For him integral dualism meant the spread of French-speaking settlements, as distinct communities, as "little provinces of Quebec," into the English-speaking provinces and the surrounding of them, as he said in 1905, with an "atmosphere preservative of their native character and original qualities."[44] To settle French Canadians in the West would make that country "homogeneous"; that is, give it a "double mentality" without which a Canadian nation would with difficulty emerge. French-speaking groups in the West would serve to "unify" the country and to stand as the only permanent barrier to absorption—mental, economic, and social—by the United States.[45]

Essential to this design of dualism were separate schools for Catholic education and a system of bilingual instruction, together with related arrangements, such as the general use of French in business and government. French Catholics, in effect, must find as minorities and not as individual citizens the "same liberty that the Anglo-Protestant minority finds in the province of Quebec."

That his ideal was not shared in his time by the majority of English-speaking Canadians was made evident in the school and language disputes in the North-West and in Ontario, notably in 1905, 1912, and

---

[43] See *La Presse catholique et nationale*, 35–8, 52–5; *Le Devoir*, Nov. 16, 1918.

[44] See *Les Ecoles du Nord-Ouest* (Montreal, 1905), 2; *La Langue française et l'avenir de notre race* (Montreal, 1913); *Les Devoir*, July 28, 1913.

[45] See *La Langue française au Canada: ses droits, sa nécessité, ses avantages* (Montreal, 1915), 45; *Le Devoir*, July 6, 7, 1915; also *French and English: Frictions and Misunderstandings* (Montreal, 1914).

1913–16. Many repudiated state-supported denominational schools both on liberal principles and because of their own sentiment of nationalism. Nor did judicial interpretation of the British North America Act support Bourassa's case that the constitution was being "flagrantly violated" by the actions of legislatures and Parliament in these disputes. In appeals to natural justice, history, and the national interest his case was stronger. But it depended ultimately on the quality of the relations between majority and minority in order that both formal and informal steps might be taken towards the ends he had in mind. This Bourassa quite realized. But the immediate effect of his Nationalist campaigns was to strain further the relations between the two language groups, making difficult the practical problem of government, the finding of workable compromises in view of existing differences. He has presented, however, a concept of Canadian nationality which may well be the only one compatible with social peace in a mixed community. Certainly it is the only one to which French-speaking Canadians could subscribe, and on the bilingual issue, at least, it ought to find increasing support among English-speaking Canadians.

Bourassa's conception of Canada's future status was that of an independent nation under the Crown. He repeatedly asserted that he sought no more than Macdonald's ideal of a Kingdom of Canada, but he had none of Macdonald's attachment to the Empire. He wanted no separation but more liberty. He was less insistent than was John S. Ewart in his advocacy of independence, being content with a slow evolution, nor did he follow Ewart into republicanism. Independence, he believed by 1916, would bring the two nationalities closer together in Canada, making easier the settlement of their differences. He thought the constitution as safe in Ottawa as it was in London; and by 1927, at least, he proposed the dropping of appeals to the Judicial Committee of the Privy Council, and the amendment of the constitution entirely by Canadians.[46]

Independence he equated with neutrality, and this, in turn, with a belief in the military security of Canada regardless of the fate of the Empire. If independent, he stated in 1914, Canada would enjoy "perfect security" and would find her chances of becoming involved in war "enormously reduced."[47] Reliance on geographic isolation from Europe and on the Monroe Doctrine reinforced a pacifist outlook. In 1928, for example, he announced that he had reached the "deep-seated conviction" that Canada should maximize her guarantees of peace by disarming "totally and absolutely against the world"; and in 1935 he stated in the Commons, "Let us proclaim to the world that we are disarming as the

---

[46] See *Hier, aujourd'hui, demain*, 131; *House of Commons Debates*, March 9, 1927, p. 1048.
[47] *Le Devoir*, Sept. 8, 1914.

best means of defending Canada." Canada, of all world countries, he
believed, could do this with least danger to herself.[48]

His policy of neutrality in British wars and his general pacifist outlook,
when coupled with the dependence which he advised upon American
military power, could lead only to a new colonialism with respect to the
United States. Indeed, Bourassa seemed to have accepted American
leadership in foreign policy as inevitable and as the determining influence
upon Canadian policy.[49] In 1935, for example, he suggested in the House
that Canada make it clear to the Americans that she stood loyally by
Great Britain, "so long as Britain stands for peace," but that she tell the
British that if "England chooses war and the United States decides for
peace, then we also shall decide for peace."[50] What counterbalance to
American influence he sought was not in the Commonwealth, for that
implied involvement in European wars, but rather in the Pan-American
Union, membership in which he suggested as early as 1916.[51]

Bourassa's attitude towards Canada's participation in World War I
evolved from qualified acceptance in 1914 to bitter opposition within a
year. One month after the outbreak of war he had written: "Canada, an
Anglo-French nation bound to England and to France by a thousand
ethnic, social, intellectual and economic ties, has a vital interest in the
maintenance of the prestige, power and world-wide action of France and
England."[52] And he went on to conclude that although bound by no
legal obligations or question of national defence it was none the less
Canada's "national duty to contribute in the measure of her resources and
by means of an appropriate action to the triumph, and above all, to the
endurance of the combined efforts of France and England." In a pamphlet published early in 1915 he reaffirmed his belief that to promote all
efforts rendering Canada's war effort more effective was "not only legitimate," it was an "imperious duty."[53]

---

[48] *House of Commons Debates*, Feb. 7, 1928, p. 239; June 4, 1929, p. 3237; April
1, 1935, p. 2289. See *ibid.*, May 23, 1928, p. 3340: "The geographical position of
Canada is such that there is less risk for Canada in standing squarely for a peace and
disarmament policy than there is, not merely for any other British country, but for any
other country on earth . . . more practical results are to be derived, not by mere
verbal assertion . . . but by proving in fact that what we say we mean; that we
disarm, first because we do not believe in war, and second, because we do believe that
the position which Canada occupies enables us to take that stand." See also *The
Possible Role of Canada in International Arbitration* (Montreal, 1913).

[49] See *Hier, aujourd'hui, demain*, 165, 168.

[50] *House of Commons Debates*, April 1, 1935, p. 2286.

[51] *Hier, aujourd'hui, demain*, 168–170; *House of Commons Debates*, March 29,
1927, p. 1692; Feb. 19, 1929, p. 274; April 1, 1935, p. 2289; *Great Britain and
Canada*, 47.

[52] *Le Devoir*, Sept. 8, 1914.

[53] *The Duty of Canada at the Present Hour: An Address Meant to be Delivered at
Ottawa in November and December, 1914, but Twice Suppressed in the Name of
"Loyalty and Patriotism"* (Montreal, 1915), 44.

This was a considerable concession on the part of the Nationalist leader who had been asserting ever since the Boer War that military contributions from the colonies to Great Britain were the essence of British imperialism.[54] He sought to justify his attitude of approval by insisting that Canada participate "as a nation" or even as "a human community"; that she think of her "relations with the world at large"; that is, that she intervene on other than imperial grounds.

He soon became convinced, however, by the statements of public leaders, and by what he called the "excessive" extent of the war effort which accorded ill with the limited character of Canada's responsibilities, that the war was being turned into a vast imperial revolution with conscription as its inevitable accompaniment. Thus in 1916, he stated: "The participation of Canada and the other autonomous possessions of Great Britain in the European War marks the striking triumph of British imperialism."[55] And at the end of the war he was insisting that, although antagonisms had been certain to occur, "the only way to have reduced the dangers would have been to maintain Canada's participation within reasonable bounds, and especially to have made it exclusively national.[56]

The complex anti-war propaganda which he developed after 1914 reflected both lack of confidence in the nationalism of English-speaking Canadians and a distorted view of British imperialism. He became obsessed with the presence of a new "Pan-Anglo-Saxonism" intent upon mastering the world by its wealth and military might, with disastrous consequences for Christianity, for small nationalities, and for social peace. The new spirit in the Empire, if triumphant in Canada, he said, would lead to the "complete Anglification of all non-English Canadians." By 1916 he had begun to link the new imperialism with the restrictions recently placed upon bilingual education in Ontario. "Our vanguard regiments," he protested, "are the French groups in the other provinces"; the front line of defence, he said, is not in Flanders, it is at Ottawa.[57] And to a correspondent in Paris, he wrote, "The enemy, the permanent enemy is Anglo-Saxonism."[58] Such views and attitudes made brittle his

---

[54] See *Great Britain and Canada*, 4: "MILITARY CONTRIBUTIONS FROM THE COLONIES TO GREAT BRITAIN in men and treasure, but mainly in men, constitute British Imperialism."

[55] *Le Devoir et la guerre: le conflit des races* (Montreal, 1916), 15.

[56] *Le Devoir*, Jan. 3, 1918. See also *Le Devoir*, April 23, 1917: "The Canadian Government and Parliament without violating any principle or tradition and while reserving all future eventualities could have decreed the participation of Canada as a nation for the defence of higher interests threatened by the Germanic coalition. Our governors did not see fit to do that. . . . They have persisted in stamping our intervention with the marks of British imperialism. . . . It is for the Empire we fight."

[57] *Le Devoir et la guerre: le conflit des races*, 12.

[58] *Le Devoir*, June 17, 1916. See *La Prochaine Guerre imperiale, en serons-nous?* (Montreal, 1920), p. 21: "The triumph of world-wide Anglo-Saxonism—English or American—would give the last and fatal blow to the religious, social, and political order established by the victory of Christianity over Paganism."

Canadian nationalism and highly unstable the terms on which he sought an accord between the two nationalities.

Towards conscription Bourassa maintained an unbending opposition, but within the context of limited liability governing Canada's share in the war. Indeed, he has made statements which appear to say that granted agreement on the principle of total war in the interests of Canada, then conscription was a logical and proper policy. Thus, in 1917, he wrote: "I am not an irreducible foe of conscription. Upon several occasions I have expressed the opinion that a systematic measure of conscription would be better in all respects than the absurd, odious, and detestable method of enrolment so falsely called 'voluntary.' . . . Selective conscription is beyond contradiction the only rational mode of assuring the maximum of military efficiency and economic activity."[59] He himself was never brought to the belief that the defence of Canada was deeply involved in the defence of the Empire or of the European power balances that from time to time were destroyed and rebuilt by war. The formula of true patriotism had become for him in 1917: "No conscription, no enlistments: Canada has done enough."[60]

IV

Bourassa's radical nationalism was essentially a continuation of the defensive reactions of French Canadians in the preceding century. More weight and new meaning, however, were given to the demand for equality, and a new concern was shown for a social and economic organization basic to a free cultural development. The dangers he stressed were already familiar: a tendency to passivity, or the acceptance of corroding compromises to conciliate the majority, and the pervading threat of Anglo-Saxonism, now assuming new proportions in imperialism and industrialism. Safety lay in a firmer stand on crucial issues affecting the nationality, in emphasis on the spiritual qualities of the national life, and in a gradual development of the older order based on rural society, familial traditions, small economic enterprise, and an intellectual formation suited to a French and Catholic mentality. He addressed his appeal mainly to the *élite*, seeking to unite them above party lines. Social solidarity was uppermost in his mind and a prime impetus to his nationalism. Concern for continuity led to emphasis on morality, religion, and traditions.

Running throughout his radicalism was constant stress on the need for equilibrium or balance over time, and this checked latent tendencies to extremes. His concept of equilibrium, however, was static in nature and

---

[59] *L'Intervention americaine* (1917), 45. See also *Hier, aujourd'hui, demain*, 105–7; and *Conscription*, 12, 17. Also *Le Devoir*, March 27, 1917 in which Bourassa noted that if Canada's fate were indeed bound up with that of Britain, then the government had the duty of raising the requisite number of soldiers by conscription should voluntary methods fail.

[60] *Conscription*, 17. *Le Devoir*, June 28, 1917.

related to a mechanical dialectic of opposing forces; for example, imperialism and nationalism, rural and urban society, individualism and communism, with extensions in religion, nationality, and other fields. The function of statesmanship was to achieve a balance among opposing forces and this meant conscious reactions, in one direction or the other, against disturbing changes.

Restraints upon his nationalism arose from many sources: from religion, from a desire to achieve a common life with English-speaking Canadians, a willingness to remain under the British Crown, and a recognition of necessary and intimate ties with the United States. Increasing Canadian autonomy in external affairs and the mild character of British imperialism meant that a violent nationalist movement would find little support anywhere in Canada. A tendency to pacifism in international affairs further checked nationalist sentiment. Similarly, economic prosperity in Canada during the period of Bourassa's nationalism denied the movement a basis in social distress.

Henri Bourassa was one of the most controversial figures in Canadian politics. Much for which he strove in the way of independence has since been realized. But he was mistaken to associate this independence with a narrow concept of responsibility in world affairs. Progress towards his ideal of dualism has not been negligible and he himself recognized this in the later twenties. He was among the most intellectual of Canadians in public life. He did much to lead his compatriots to a fresh and enlarged view of their national position. His ideas were an expression of his Canadianism.

24

Conscription, 1917:
A Brief for the Defence*

A. M. Willms

OF ALL THE CRISES in Confederation from 1867 to the present, probably 1917 was the most serious. For the only time in Canadian history the federal political parties seemed to split along English-French lines. The English-speaking Liberals joined the Conservatives to form the Union Government and were faced by the Laurier Liberals, a mere handful of them English-speaking. The issue was tragically clear; English Canada was passionately for conscription and French Canada was opposed. There have been few elections in Canadian history which have been so bitter and few events where the ethnic wounds have taken so long to heal.

Because it was such a divisive issue, the government which brought in conscription has tended to be strongly criticized by Canadian historians. If the facts were as clear as they are sometimes presented, one could certainly question Borden's decision to push through conscription. As a reaction to the prevailing anti-conscription view of historians, A. M. Willms has written this brief for the defence in an attempt to place the whole question in a little more balanced perspective and to make the actions of Borden and his government a little more understandable.

THE REACTION of French Canada to conscription has been treated in some detail by Professor Mason Wade[1] and Miss Elizabeth Armstrong[2] but the story of its effect on the Liberal party and on the election of 1917

---

* *Canadian Historical Review*, XXXVII (December, 1956), pp. 338–351.

[1] *The French Canadians 1760–1945* (Toronto, 1955).

[2] *The Crisis of Quebec 1914–1918* (New York, 1937).

has not yet been fully told. Recently the papers of several leading men in this political drama have been made available to historians and they inspire further study of these events. The papers of Sir Wilfrid Laurier trace like a fascinating novel the collapse of the strong Liberal party around its tragic, white-plumed hero. They blame the catastrophe on the political machinations of the Government and contend that conscription was neither necessary nor successful, but that it caused a serious rift between Quebec and the rest of Canada. Thus the Laurier Papers tend to confirm the story of conscription as it has been accepted by Canadian historians. But there are other versions of this story in such collections as the Borden Papers, the Rowell Papers, and the Dafoe Papers. In fact the cumulative effect of new materials is to show that not only was conscription militarily necessary—that Canada's contribution to the fighting lagged behind that of her principal allies and sister Dominions until conscription was employed—but also that the success of conscription was not achieved at the cost of a national tragedy.

One fact that constantly obtrudes on the reader of the new collections is the remarkable political success of conscription. This raises the suspicion that the Military Service Bill was introduced by the Government as a political expedient. There is no absolute evidence to prove or disprove this suggestion, but it deserves fuller examination.

Whenever the members of the federal Conservative party assessed their political stock during the winter of 1916 to 1917 they felt very uncomfortable. The extended life of Parliament was running out and the Government was unpopular with the public. The Liberal party on the other hand was, or appeared to be, strong and confident. The Conservatives were in trouble. Of seven provincial elections held between August, 1915, and June, 1917, they lost seven. In three provinces Conservative governments were ousted and in all the other elections the Conservatives held fewer seats after the voting than they had before. In Manitoba and British Columbia the elections were utter routs. In the latter province the Liberals had started the year 1916 with no seats in the provincial legislature and finished with 37 out of 47, and in Manitoba the Conservatives lost 22 seats, giving the Liberals an over-all majority of 32 seats. While provincial elections do not always reflect the standing of federal parties, these were unusually heavy portents. Of the New Brunswick election Dafoe wrote: "The result in New Brunswick must have been very discouraging to them, as that was in fact a trial of strength between the Dominion parties";[3] while a leading federal Liberal admitted modestly: "Our successes in the provincial arenas are due solely to the mistakes, corruption and incompetence of our opponents. . . ."[4]

Federal by-elections are another measure of government popularity. The paucity of by-elections in this period constitutes an admission of

---

[3] Public Archives of Canada, Dafoe Papers, Dafoe to Sifton, Feb. 27, 1917.

[4] P.A.C., Laurier Papers, E. M. Macdonald to Laurier, Sept. 28, 1916.

Government weakness; for, while the Conservative party retained its seats in the three ridings that were opened, the Government dared not issue writs in the other twenty constituencies which became vacant between March, 1915, and July, 1917.

There were reasons for the Government's unpopularity. Its weakness and ineptness appeared quite obviously in the Ross Rifle *débâcle*. Wartime patronage and profiteering was not proven by a royal commission or in a court of law, but the Liberal members of Parliament were not alone in believing the repeated accusations and in blaming the laxity of the Government. The cost of living was rising very sharply with the wartime economic boom and the benefits of higher prices did not accrue to all the population. The parliamentary Opposition felt that Messrs. Mackenzie and Mann should not be reimbursed for a railway taken over by the Government when at the point of bankruptcy. Sir George Foster feared this might make electioneering material,[5] while of the Quebec and Saguenay Railway purchase he wrote: "The Quebec and Saguenay mess goes through—an unsavory and absolutely indefensible job—put through by the Prime Minister in pursuance of arrangements made with Forget and the Bank of Commerce nearly three years ago."[6]

The extraordinary personality of Sam Hughes constituted both an internal weakness within the Government and an election handicap. This was almost unanimously admitted on both sides, while the adverse report of Judge Galt on Hon. Robert Rogers' connections with government contracts in Manitoba was honey to the Opposition bears. Of these two ministers Foster asserted: "Both have been loads to carry—neither should have been made minister—for both the party has paid and will pay dearly."[7] The increasing failure of recruiting and the dismal flop of two substitute measures, national service and the semi-active militia, served to increase a general lack of confidence. The Prime Minister was accused of weakness, inaction, and vacillation; "a well meaning incompetent"[8] Dafoe dubbed him, while a member of the cabinet repeatedly denounced his policy of "drift—corroding drift."[9]

The Conservative who looked at the political scene would then turn anxiously to the calendar. The life of Parliament would expire on October 7, 1917, and the belligerent Opposition were not likely to grant another extension. With six months left, Dafoe predicted: "Their defeat when they appeal to the people appears inevitable, unless some new factor enters into the contest and gives them a good battle cry."[10]

---

[5] P.A.C., Foster Papers, Diary, Aug. 16, 1917.

[6] *Ibid.*, May 16, 1916.

[7] *Ibid.*, Aug. 17, 1917.

[8] Dafoe Papers, Dafoe to G. M. Wrong, Dec. 12, 1916.

[9] Foster Papers, Diary, Oct. 8, 1915.

[10] Dafoe Papers, Dafoe to Laurier, April 26, 1917.

The miracle happened. Six months later, a new factor gave Borden and his party not only a great battle cry but a large majority in the election. The Liberal Opposition so strong in January was pitifully weak in December, its leader had offered to resign, and a majority of its outstanding members had left the party or refused it their support. Strong provincial or local Liberal organizations had melted away or deserted intact to the enemy. In 1916 the Liberal party in Saskatchewan had a well-oiled party machine. Its engineer, Hon. J. A. Calder, boasted: ". . . our people are but awaiting the fray. The general federal election cannot be brought on too soon to please our people."[11] A year later, almost to the day, a lone Saskatchewan Liberal appeal for help: "So far as organization goes Calder is the whole thing and his going . . . has left us high and dry."[12] "We are in a bad way here."[13]

In New Brunswick "Fighting Frank" Carvell, the most promising of the young Liberals and a recent nominee to succeed Laurier, took his political army over to the Government. In Nova Scotia the astute provincial Premier—Prime Minister five years longer than Mackenzie King—had considered an offer to enter the Union cabinet and had promised to back Government candidates in his province. Laurier lamented his lost follower "whose judgment is so clear and whose sagacity was never at fault."[14] Fielding, the old veteran, the crown prince of the Liberal party, was bewailed in biblical language.[15] In Ontario the provincial Liberal leader was one of the first to join the Borden cabinet, and more ill news soon reached Laurier: "Yesterday it was Pardee and today it will be Graham. Graham and Pardee as dear to me as my own brothers."[16] In Alberta and Manitoba the leading Liberals also deserted, and in Alberta the two remaining Liberal leaders, Oliver and Cross, were by this time bitter foes. In British Columbia the Liberal Premier made overtures to the federal Government. The two great Liberal newspapers followed the traitors, setting an example that was emulated by all but three of the Liberal papers west of the Ottawa River.[17]

This great tribulation was brought on the Liberal party by the announcement of the Government's Military Service bill. It pulled the Borden Government out of the mire and set it on its feet. It split both of the old parties and made Union Government possible. It won the election of 1917 for Borden and company. There were, of course, other factors

---

[11] Laurier Papers, Calder to Laurier, Nov. 8, 1916.

[12] *Ibid.*, Knowles to Laurier, Nov. 6, 1917.

[13] *Ibid.*, Nov. 24, 1917.

[14] *Ibid.*, Laurier to E. M. Macdonald, Nov. 19, 1917.

[15] H. S. Ferns and B. Ostry, *The Age of Mackenzie King* (London, 1955), 231.

[16] Laurier Papers, Laurier to A. B. Aylesworth, June 22, 1917.

[17] *Edmonton Bulletin, Peterboro Times, London Advertiser:* Laurier Papers, Laurier to R. R. Cromarty, Nov. 23, 1917.

that contributed to the Government's revival. The ditching of Sam
Hughes and Bob Rogers, the last-minute adoption of a mild form of
income tax, the slight boosting of an inadequate profits tax; the appointment of a vigorous food controller, though with but limited powers, the
admission of wheat and flour tariff-free into the United States, and the
fixing of wheat prices at over two dollars a bushel, all helped. The nefarious War Times Election Act also increased the votes for the Government
and denied votes to the Opposition. But conscription was the big issue; it
acted as a solvent on Liberal party bonds while it brought together an
amazing array of political talent in the Union Government. It was the
dominant issue before the electors at the polls. In all the provinces of
Canada this issue was sentimentalized and exaggerated; it was screamed
from the hustings and thundered from the pulpits. Those against it were
"cowards and traitors" and those for were "autocrats worse than the
Kaiser." Unquestionably, then, conscription proved a wonderful political
expedient. But was it nothing more?

A crisis existed. Canada was fighting a war. She was fighting not for
England and not for France but for Canada. She was not only defending
the principles of right, of justice, and of democracy, but she was also
defending Canada's right to these principles. Laurier said of the Canadian soldiers: "They have left their avocations to do battle for a cause
which they deem, and rightly deem the cause of freedom . . . to save
civilization from the unbridled lust of conquest and domination."[18]
Whether Canada was expecting an imminent invasion was immaterial,
for, as Foster pointed out, "It makes very little difference if we do not win
this war whether the Hun today is three thousand miles away from
Canada or only half a mile beyond our coasts. In either case if the Hun
wins the ultimate result would be the same."[19] Rowell outlined the basic
military strategy involved: "Surely the time has come when we can all
recognize that Canada is being defended in Flanders and in France just
as truly and much more effectively than she could be defended on the
banks of the St. Lawrence."[20]

There is no doubt that the war in 1917 was balancing finely, too finely,
in the scales of the future. In the spring of 1917 Russia's vast manpower
resources were becoming useless while the fighting potential of the
United States could not be mustered immediately. Italy was not always
holding her own against Austria, and in the French armies there were
mutinies. Even in Britain there was defeatism and some despair as the
early over-optimism gave way to dark pessimism. The submarine was
wrecking havoc in the Atlantic, while the mighty British navy was vainly
casting about for adequate counter measures. Bloody fighting had taken

---

[18] *Canada, House of Commons Debates,* 1917, III, 2392.
[19] *Ibid.,* 2408.
[20] Laurier Papers, Rowell to Laurier, May 29, 1917.

place in 1916 with but small advances by either side, and leaders on both sides were coming to realize that victory must entail further great sacrifices and possibly prolonged and increasing hardships.

With this crisis at hand, was Canada doing all in her power to help defeat Germany? There were many Canadians who contended that Canada had sent overseas as many men as her economy could possibly spare. There were those who claimed that Canada had done enough. Canada had indeed contributed a substantial share to the allied effort; but she had done less than others. In the contribution of manpower she lagged far behind Great Britain and France, and she had done less than the other Dominions. Straight comparisons, especially with the older countries, are not really valid but the ratios are striking. According to Hon. N. W. Rowell, to equal Australia's effort Canada should have had overseas at the end of January, 1917, 500,000 men; to compare with New Zealand her quota was 450,000, and with South Africa, over 400,000. In actual fact there were 284,000 Canadians in England and France. France and Great Britain had respectively four and three times as many men in the forces in proportion to their population. These figures are difficult to verify. By the end of the war the ratios had changed, but this was mostly because of Canada's great effort in 1918 under the pressure of conscription. But never at any time was Canada suffering seriously from lack of manpower. Her booming economy was one indication. Rowell claimed that "Canada has profited the most and suffered the least from this war of any of the nations of the empire."[21] Individuals were making great sacrifices, but the nation was not, either in manpower or in national wealth.[22]

It is impossible to compare accurately the economy of Canada in the First and Second World Wars. Both periods were eras of great expansion, but the contribution in manpower in the Second World War was proportionately greater. With an increase in population of 50 per cent, her commitment in manpower increased over 60 per cent. Even this greater contribution, however, did not seriously impair Canada's vital industries.

Canada had sent 312,000 men overseas by the end of April, 1917, and in France she was maintaining four divisions with supporting units, a total of more than 125,000 men. The Canadian Government had hoped to send a fifth division to France, but the decreasing enlistment at home prohibited this. To keep the four divisions up to strength, an estimated 10,000 men were required every month as reinforcements.[23] The figures of actual reinforcements available are hard to find and can be deduced

---

[21] Quotation and figures from P.A.C., Rowell Papers, Rowell to Laurier, July 11, 1917.

[22] E. L. Bogart, *Direct and Indirect Costs of the Great World War* (London, 1920).

[23] P.A.C., Borden Papers, OC 499, p. 53524.

only approximately, yet it would seem that at the end of April Canada had reinforcements for approximately six months, under normal circumstances. There were, however, some complications with regard to existing reinforcements. Losses were heaviest in the infantry, but the men available were not all infantrymen. The voluntary enlistment of infantry in the first four months of 1917 was so low that normal wastage in Canada left very few men for overseas. Thus April and May produced a gross total of 3,000 infantry recruits who still had to be trained, with a percentage of wastage resulting. In these same two months Canadian battle casualties in France were 20,045. Approximately 10,000 of these casualties, or about 80 per cent of the wounded, could be expected to return to the trenches eventually, but the loss of men still exceeded the gain by over 7,000. Normal infantry reinforcement requirements were 7,800 per month.[24] At the rate of the 1917 spring enlistment it would take more than four months' enlistment to make up one normal month's loss—and enlistment had not yet reached its lowest point. These were the figures as they appeared at the time conscription was introduced. In actual fact the existing reinforcements together with the reduced voluntary enlistments were adequate for a year; a year that had, however, much lighter casualties than were expected.

In the meantime the High Command was presenting to the Imperial War Cabinet its urgent requirement for more troops. Borden, Perley, and Kemp, the ministers most closely connected with Canadian military decisions, saw what a strenuous effort the other allies were putting forth; they saw the great need for men at the front but they could not, under the circumstances, commit Canada to the sending of a fifth division. Instead they set themselves the goal of enlisting another 100,000 men. Whether these men could be used to fill out the fifth division or whether they would have to be used entirely in reinforcing the four divisions would depend on military factors and on the speed of enlistment. The need was great and the men were available. How could they be best mobilized?

It would appear that by the spring of 1917 the Canadian Government had exhausted the potentialities of voluntary recruiting. In the first three years of war the Government and the Militia Department had made many mistakes, some of them gross errors in tact and common sense. The greatest offender was the Minister of Militia, but the rest of the cabinet and especially the Prime Minister must share the blame. They had antagonized over-sensitive Quebec; they had authorized the recruiting of units and then broken them up; they had commissioned too many officers and lacked the courage to put them to work or discharge them; they had failed to recruit wealth as they recruited manpower and they had not stopped profiteering or patronage. By 1917 many of these mistakes had

---

[24] Figures are from *House of Commons Debates*, 1917, II, 1816; III, 2892; also Borden Papers, OC 332, pp. 39112, 39121, 39128, OC 494.

become obvious even to the Government, but the damage was done. The trend of enlistment showed a fairly steady downward curve from about 30,000 a month in January, 1916, to under 5,000 a month in April 1917.[25] Measures had to be adopted to check this trend. Drastic solutions were suggested and tried. A semi-active militia force was to replace all soldiers in Canada who were willing to go overseas; a board of national service directors was appointed to advise the Government and local authorities on recruiting matters and stimulate enlistment in all parts of Canada. An Order in Council was passed prohibiting all male persons between the ages of 18 and 45 from leaving Canada subject to regulations. An income tax was introduced and profit taxes were slightly increased. The formation of a French-Canadian brigade was given serious consideration—two years too late. Major-General Lessard and Colonel Blondin were sent to work up a recruiting campaign in Quebec, while members of the cabinet toured other parts of Canada in the interests of recruiting. Distinguished French veterans were sent from France to help the campaign in Quebec; and the help of the Catholic clergy from France was offered and accepted. But enlistments dropped to 3,000 in August, 1917. This was not enough to keep even two divisions in the field. The obvious answer to this manpower problem was conscription. Almost every country was using it and using it effectively. Selective conscription they found to be more efficient and more just than voluntary recruiting.

It would appear, then, that the consequent Military Service Act could have played a dual role in the Government's plans; it did help to win an election and it was also required as a most necessary spur to the war effort. Probably both of these roles were incentives to its adoption, but it is quite evident that the political potential of this move, if it was actually recognized, was vastly underrated. In fact, when the Conservatives introduced the Military Service Bill they were not at all certain that it would get the support of the majority of the country. They were afraid to trust it to a referendum, for they saw what had happened in Australia. The restrictive franchise laws are probably the best indication of the Government's lack of confidence in conscription as a vote-getter. Of course, once the election campaign was well under way there was little doubt on either side as to popular opinion. Outside the province of Quebec 20 anti-conscription and 150 pro-conscription members were elected to the House of Commons; the popular vote outside Quebec was 509,940 against the Government out of 1,501,719 votes cast.[26]

Conscription was not introduced specifically to win an election; for at

---

[25] Enlistment figures have been compiled from several excerpts from *House of Commons Debates*, notably 1917, III, 2202, 2892. A full set of enlistment statistics month by month is available in the War Service Records Office of the Department of Veterans Affairs.

[26] *Canadian Annual Review*, 1917, 643.

the time of its introduction a wartime election was no certainty. Many Conservatives were vigorously urging Borden to have the life of Parliament further extended. The British government was approached through Perley to see if an extension would be granted on an address of Parliament passed by a mere party majority, and the answer was favourable.[27] Moreover, Sir Robert certainly did not see compulsory recruitment as a political stepping-stone, for having introduced the measure, he offered to resign in favour of anyone who could form a coalition government. In fact, there were men who apparently sacrificed all their political achievements in backing this measure, men such as Fielding and Graham. On the other hand, it seems no less apparent that the Borden Government did not envisage the long-term effects of conscription on the fortunes of the Conservative party. In any case one might doubt that such a realization would have swayed them from this measure. Assuredly, men on both sides of the question were most sincere.

There seems to be no proof, in short, that the leaders of the Conservative party saw conscription as a political expedient, while there is some evidence to show that the Military Service Act was introduced with fear as to its political effect. It is difficult to believe, however, that the Government was so far out of touch with popular feeling that it introduced the Act without at least a strong hope that the measure would improve the political outlook.

Quite apart from its possible implications for the Conservative party the passing of conscription seemed to be fraught with serious consequences to the country. Apparently the most serious danger was that conscription would cause a grave rift between Quebec and the rest of Canada. Conscription was opposed by a large group in Canada. Their argument that the Government had mismanaged recruiting and other military matters was undoubtedly sound, but this would not help to rectify the current serious crisis. They also maintained that conscription would split the country and that a divided country could not put forward as great an effort as a united country. This was one of the most prevalent but also one of the weakest arguments, for the country was in fact no longer united and it would become severely rent whether conscription was introduced or no. The English-speaking provinces were growing ever more furious and indignant at Quebec, while Quebec became more bitter. Dark threats were uttered as to how Quebec would react to conscription, yet there was no guarantee that inflamed feelings in the other provinces might not also boil over. Borden wrote to Archbishop Bruchési:

> Believe me, I have given much anxious thought to the consequences which you apprehend as probable or even inevitable upon the enactment of the proposed legislation. . . . But I fear your Grace may not be well informed as to

[27] P.A.C., Perley Papers, 228, 229.

the strength of feeling which exists in practically every province outside of Quebec on this question. . . . If the measure were abandoned or if no such measure had been introduced and the present Government should persist in attempting to carry on the affairs of the country in the face of so intense and vehement a feeling, disorders as grave perhaps even graver than those which your Grace apprehends would be extremely probable if not inevitable.[28]

There is a good deal to support this statement. Dafoe, for instance, a normally level-headed man, showed his intensity of feeling in a letter to Thomas Coté:

Do you not know my dear Coté, that in Australia, 14 percent of the whole population enlisted voluntarily? On that basis there would be in the Canadian armies today about 150,000 French Canadians in place of 15,000 or 20,000 at the outside. When you have done half as much as Australia it will be time for you to talk.

The trouble between the English and French Canadians has become acute, because French Canadians have refused to play their part in this war—being the only known race of white men to quit. They try to excuse themselves by alleging that they have domestic grievances which should first be righted. The excuse, if true, would be contemptible. In the face of an emergency like this domestic questions have to stand.

Do not flatter yourself with the idea that the English Canadians are disturbed by your attitude of injured innocence or your threats of reprisals. You can do precisely as you please; and we shall do whatever may be necessary. When we demonstrate, as we shall, that a solid Quebec is without power, there may be a return to reason along the banks of the St. Lawrence.[29]

One of the most moderate of the English magazines, *Saturday Night*, a pro-Laurier publication almost to the last, burst out in its turn: "Any measure taken by the Government whereby the various Provinces can be forced to give their per capita proportion toward the Army and to other war activities, would not only silence this nest of traitors by giving them some real work to do, but it would have the unqualified approval of Canadians from Halifax to Vancouver."[30] Or again: "There is no doubt in the world that a conspiracy exists against it [Military Service Act] in the French portions of the Province of Quebec. It is certainly not the intention of English Canada to stand idly by and see itself bled of men in order that the Quebec shirker may sidestep his responsibilities. If this maladministration of a law of the land is allowed to continue, the Government may just as well understand now as later that English Canada does not propose to put up with it."[31]

---

[28] Borden Papers, Memoir Notes, 2119.

[29] Dafoe Papers, J. W. Dafoe to Thos. Coté, Jan. 1, 1918.

[30] Saturday Night, May 19, 1917.

[31] *Ibid.*, Dec. 1, 1917; also June 9, 1917, Jan. 26, 1918, April 13, 1918, Aug. 11, 1917, Sept. 8, 1917.

Other papers were considerably more rabid;[32] while a high ranking soldier wrote from overseas: "It seems to me that the issue of conscription now before the people will clear the air generally. If it is not decided by peaceful means I should think one day guns will have to decide that too."[33]

Nor was Borden idly prating when he spoke of the hardened veterans of Ypres, the Somme, Vimy Ridge, and Courcelette: "If what are left of 400,000 such men come back to Canada with fierce resentment in their hearts, conscious that they have been deserted and betrayed, how shall we meet them when they ask the reason? I am not so much concerned for the day when this Bill becomes law, as for the day when these men return if it is rejected."[34] How these men felt can be seen in the way they cast their ballots in December, 1917. There was only one issue for the soldier in that election and the result was almost 12 to 1 in favour of conscription.[35] Anyone who has spoken to veterans of the First World War could hardly doubt their feelings on this subject. That they could act in unison to demonstrate their purpose they showed in 1919 in Witley and Rhyll Camps. And there they were only venting minor grievances.

Despite the variety of evidence, the intensity of feeling among English-speaking Canadians on conscription has been generally disregarded by historians. One reason for this is that the English-speaking provinces were not united on the desirability of conscription whereas Quebec showed a solid front against it. Another reason is that until the election campaign of 1917 leadership was lacking for the pro-conscription forces; but then it emerged in great strength.

Most historians also seem to have accepted the thesis that conscription was a failure, that it did not produce worthwhile results. But this is not true. The Military Service Act was passed to enlist men as required; the first requirement was repeatedly announced as being from 50,000 to 100,000 men, and the Act itself provided that "unless further authorized by Parliament the reinforcements provided under this Act shall not exceed one hundred thousand men." Conscription produced that number. The figures from different sources vary from less than 80,000 to over 170,000. The one generally accepted is 83,355 but this figure is generally conceded to be that of the number of draftees actually "on parade." This fails to take into account several categories of men who had also been raised. They were the men discharged, those whose medical category was lowered after enlistment, those on compassionate or harvest leave, and those who had enlisted in the Imperial forces. Except for harvest leave

---

[32] E. H. Armstrong, *The Crisis of Quebec*, 207–8.

[33] Rowell Papers, J. M. Macdonnell to Rowell, June 14, 1917.

[34] *House of Commons Debates*, 1917, III.

[35] Soldier votes were 215,849 for Union Government, 18,522 against: *Canadian Annual Review*, 1917, 643.

these were the types of casualties quite common to the C.E.F. before the Military Service Act, and therefore in comparing the results of conscription with those of voluntary recruitment most of them should be included. The most detailed figures available appear in the report of the Director of the Military Service Branch to his Minister in 1919.[36] They are as follows:

Made available for military service by M.S.A.	179,933
Not processed by Nov. 11	26,225
Defaulters	24,139
"Placed in uniform" by the M.S.A.	129,569
Of these 7,673 enlisted in Imperial forces	

The total enlistment of Canadians in the First World War is constantly quoted as 619,636. This total was arrived at by counting personnel documents or attestation papers. Out of this total 121,896 must be credited to the Military Service Act, for whether men were on leave or discharged their attestation papers remained on file. In other words:

$$\frac{\text{M.S.A.}}{\text{total enlistment}} = \frac{121,896}{619,636}$$

Reduce one figure and you must reduce the other. Neither the figure 121,896 nor 129,569 shows the effective result of conscription. Owing to circumstances only a fraction of these numbers had any influence on the outcome of the war, but what these figures represent is the total of Canadian attestations under the Act and the total of Canadian plus Imperial attestations. The figures released by the Department of National Defence are invariably lower than this: thus in the departmental memoranda of 1918 and 1919 the figure 83,355 is insisted on, with the stipulation that this does not include those discharged or on leave without pay. The total enlistments according to these memoranda is 549,339 and not 619,636.[37] The latter figure is vouched for by the machine card operators who checked these totals for the Department of Veterans Affairs. A fairly detailed study of the Military Service Act by the Historical Section of the Department of National Defence uses the figures as quoted from the Report of the Director of the Military Service Act.[38]

In any case, the monthly enlistment was raised from 4,500 in December, 1917, to over 19,000 in January, 1918, while the average enlistment for the first eight months of 1918, until the war had been virtually won, was over 18,000 a month, whereas the average monthly enlistment during

---

[36] *Canada, Sessional Papers,* no. 246, 1919, "The Report of the Director of the Military Service Act to the Minister of Justice."

[37] *Memoranda Respecting Work of the Department of Militia and Defence,* nos. 5 and 6, 1918 and 1919.

[38] *Memo and Statistics,* compiled by Historical Section of Department of National Defence, Nov., 1944.

1917 had been less than 6,000. The total enlistment in the C.E.F., both draftees and volunteers, for the period the Act was in force to the end of the war was 156,018.[39] Plainly, the Military Service Act was not a failure and it was not ineffective, even though the administration of it was inefficient.

In this last respect, it proposed to fulfil its original purpose of enlisting 100,000 men by calling up selected groups as they were required. The Act divided the manhood of Canada into six classes. Class 1, to be called first, included single men age 20 to 34; these were over 400,000 in number. But the exemptions were too generous and too vague: "if it is in the national interest" was the phrase used in the Act to justify exemption. Well might an Opposition member exclaim: "By this act all may be called, and by this act all may be exempted."[40] The exemption clause was manipulated somewhat obviously for election purposes. On December 3, 1917, ten days before the election, the Government exempted all farmers from compulsory enlistment. This gave the farmers an idle winter; but then in the middle of April, when the farmers were beginning their spring work, all exemptions for the ages 20 to 22 were cancelled. Moreover, while the Act became law on August 29, 1917, the first men were not called until October 13, and they were not called to report until January, 1918. Undoubtedly there must be administrative lapses, but this particular lapse was not entirely in tone with the Government's grim picture of the existing crisis.

The Military Service Act, however, was to produce manpower not only for immediate reinforcements but also for the big allied effort which was envisaged, and which like the Normandy invasion of 1944 turned out to be not as costly as forecast. Accordingly, as late as September, 1918, Borden warned Lloyd George about the commitment of these reserves: "Having regard to policy practically settled before my departure as to conserving troops for decisive offensive next year I conclude that different policy has been adopted. . . . Is there any apprehension that enemy is holding powerful reserves of highly trained troops for counter attack at opportune moment. . . ."[41] The allies expected to make their big push in 1919. Fortunately the enemy broke sooner, and under the skilful leadership of Foch the allies exploited the break-through most successfully. This early victory was not foreseen by even the most sanguine in 1917 or 1918. Under these circumstances only 47,509[42] draftees were sent overseas. There are no figures to show how many of them served at the front.

Conscription in 1917–18 was one of the big issues of Canadian political

---

[39] Month-by-month enlistment statistics at War Service Records, DVA, Ottawa.

[40] *House of Commons Debates*, 1917, IV, 3207.

[41] Perley Papers, Borden to Lloyd George, Sept. 7, 1918.

[42] *Canadian Annual Review*, 1919, 24.

life, and it continues to reappear at intervals, its advocates parading its economy, its efficiency, and its justice. But the politician shudders at its appearance and quickly turns his back. If he were induced to discuss it, he would probably admit that in the First World War conscription proved a very successful short-term political device, though its success was not foreseen. He would also have to admit that Canada's war effort, especially in manpower, compared unfavorably with that of the other major allies and with the efforts of the other Dominions; that voluntary recruiting for various reasons was dead while conscription was undoubtedly the most sensible as well as the most expedient substitute; and that Canada was fighting a war which would certainly have been lost in the spring of 1918 if other countries had followed Canada's tardy example. He probably would require some convincing that conscription did little to aggravate an existing schism; that it aired a festering issue and perhaps prevented a more serious breach. And he would then conclude: "Let's forget it. It's bad business."

25

Critic or Entertainer: Leacock and the Growth of Materialism*

Frank W. Watt

The social scientist and especially the student of political economy is compelled to make his peace with satire or humour. The callous vulgarity which characterizes the humour of the medical profession is paralleled by cynicism in the social scientist.

H. A. INNIS.
Stephen Butler Leacock (1869–1944).

IN THE LAST DECADE scholars of Canadian literature and history have begun the task of assessing the importance of indigenous literature for the development of Canada and Canadian society. In this article F. W. Watt tries to judge an issue on which past critics have differed widely. Some have interpreted Leacock's humour as just plain fun while others have seen it as social criticism.

Leacock was born in 1869 in England but as a child he was brought to the Lake Simcoe area of southern Ontario. After an education at Upper Canada College and the University of Toronto he taught at Upper Canada College until 1898 when he left to do graduate work at the University of Chicago. Here he met Thorstein Veblen and other thinkers of the progressive era. In 1903 he was appointed lecturer in Economics and Political Science at McGill and he remained with that department until his retirement in 1936. Most of Leacock's humour appeared in the period between 1910 and 1940 when Canada was undergoing profound economic and social change. For further details of his life see R. L. Curry, *Stephen Leacock: Humourist and Humanist;* eight of his works have been republished in paperback in the New Canadian Library series.

* *Canadian Literature* (Summer, 1960), pp. 33–42.

At the turn of the century Canadian society was undergoing changes so drastic as to constitute a social revolution. The agrarian and industrial "boom" following the opening of the West brought the Canadian economy its first great period of material expansion, returned the social order to a state of flux, stimulated the speculative spirit and the accumulation of wealth, and encouraged a mood of political and commercial optimism. It was an era to which Canadian writers for the first time applied the term "materialistic." This is the era that gave birth to Stephen Leacock, Professor of Political Economy and Humorist, and, to an extent scarcely yet realized, stamped his work with its imprint.

It is the *Arcadian Adventures,* with its destructive satirical portrayal of a rampant plutocracy, that marks an extreme of social consciousness and the closest approach to sustained social criticism in Leacock's work. Nowhere else is it quite so simple a matter to see the objects of his condemnation and his standards of judgment; and nowhere else, at the same time, is the element of kindliness (which, as we shall see, he considered a necessary part of the highest form of humour) spread so thinly. Leacock's portrayal of the ethos of the plutocracy centres on the Mausoleum Club: "The Mausoleum Club stands on the quietest corner of the best residential street in the City. It is a Grecian building of white stone. About it are great elm trees with birds—the most expensive kind of birds—singing in the branches." The conjunction of childlike pastoral purity and simplicity and the artificial powers and splendours of the wealthy is an incongruity Leacock allows mainly to speak for itself:

The sunlight flickers through the elm trees, illuminating expensive nursemaids wheeling valuable children in little perambulators . . . Here you may see a little toddling princess in a rabbit suit who owns fifty distilleries in her own right. There, in a lacquered perambulator, sails past a little hooded head that controls from its cradle an entire New Jersey corporation. The United States is suing her as she sits, in a vain attempt to make her dissolve herself into con-stituent companies . . . You may meet in the flickered sunlight any number of little princes and princesses far more real than the poor survivals of Europe. Incalculable infants wave their fifty dollar ivory rattles in an inarticulate greet-ing to one another . . . And through it all the sunlight falls through the elm-trees, and the birds sing and motors hum, so that the whole world seen from the boulevard of Plutoria Avenue is the very pleasantest place imaginable.

The princes of the Old World and those of the New, the hum of the motors and the singing of the birds, small innocent children and giant soul-less capital enterprises, fifty dollar ivory rattles and elm-trees in the sunlight, all together in the same idyllic scene form an active complex of incongruities. In the next paragraph the complexity gives way momentarily to a direct and harsh contrast:

If you were to mount to the roof of the Mausoleum Club itself on Plutoria Avenue you could almost see the slums from there. But why should you? And on the other hand, if you never went up on the roof, but only dined inside among the palm-trees, you would never know that the slums existed—which is much better.

It is significant that Leacock was typically less concerned with such overt contrasts between the palaces of the rich and the hovels of the poor than with incongruities within the life of the wealthy. He sought to explode that life's myths and belittle its attractions, rather than to attack its villainies. The wealthy exploiter in Leacock's portrayal attains none of the grandeur of evil. Thus, that "wizard of finance," Mr. Tomlinson, emerges from the darkness of his backwoods farm into the highest circles of plutocratic achievement despite his earnest attempts to avoid the greatness thrust upon him. Mere ignorance of the mysteries of finance fails him, and even his most determined violations of common sense business practice cannot make him the poor man he involuntarily left behind him. The cult of money-making is debased to the level of its newest idol, a simple, ignorant farmer whose allegedly gold-bearing farm has transformed him into *"Monsieur Tomlinson, nouveau capitaine de la haute finance en Amerique,"* as Paris called him, an unhappy man whose fortune grows no matter how he tries to lose it. The qualifications of the members of the Mausoleum Club appear in a changed light in their mistaken admiration for Mr. Tomlinson; they remain neither admirable, dangerous or evil, but merely objects of scepticism and ridicule.

In similar fashion when the spectre of labour unrest appears in Leacock's Arcadia, it is merely an opportunity for the wealthy to display their ludicrous self-centredness and inconsistency. "Just imagine, my dear," says one rich lady to another, "my chauffeur, when I was in Colorado, actually threatened to leave me merely because I wanted to reduce his wages. I think it's these wretched labour unions." The "wretched labour unions" threatened the very heart of Arcadia, the Mausoleum Club, by a strike of the catering staff at a moment which proved embarrassing for Mr. Fyshe, the successful financier: "Luxury!" he was exclaiming at the beginning of the sumptuous dinner scene set to trap the (non-existent) fortunes of the Duke of Dulham, "Luxury! . . . It is the curse of the age. The appalling growth of luxury, the piling up of money, the ease with which huge fortunes are made . . . these are the things that are going to ruin us." Mr. Fyshe's propensity for social revolutionary doctrine, however, did not survive the test:

"Eh? What?" said Mr. Fyshe.
The head waiter, his features stricken with inward agony, whispered again.

"The infernal, damn scoundrels!" said Mr. Fyshe, starting back in his chair. "On strike! In this Club! It's an outrage!"

But the *Arcadian Adventures*, even though its thesis is modest and uncontentious, makes Stephen Leacock appear more of a socially purposeful satirist than he really was. His work as a whole is not contained within the level of that severe, obvious and well deserved criticism of the vices and follies of the over-privileged which is characteristic of the *Arcadian Adventures*. Nor is there more justification elsewhere for an attempt to define Leacock as a writer with serious interests in radical reform. On the contrary, Leacock looked upon himself as a humorist (that being for him the term of wider range) rather than a satirist, and freely confessed himself to be a Tory in politics. Like Lucullus Fyshe, Leacock could have claimed himself to be, on the basis of the *Arcadian Adventures*, something of a "revolutionary socialist." But in *The Unsolved Riddle of Social Justice* (1920), his most elaborate and explicit discussion of the politics and economics of contemporary society, he denied himself this possibility once and for all: the book is primarily a critique of radical idealism, an attack on the socialist answer to the "riddle of social justice." In 1907 Thorstein Veblen, whom Leacock had known during their post-graduate days at the University of Chicago, indicated his awareness of the fact that socialism for many serious exponents of radical ideas had passed out of the Utopian phase. "The socialism that inspires hope and fears today," Veblen wrote, "is the school of Marx. No one is seriously apprehensive of any other so-called socialistic movement, and no one is seriously concerned to criticise or refute the doctrines set forth by any other school of socialists."[1] Leacock himself ostensibly did not agree with or did not know this argument of his brilliant acquaintance. *The Unsolved Riddle* is concerned with refuting socialism as it is described in Edward Bellamy's *Looking Backward;* and in the fact that it repeats the task undertaken in Canada by Goldwin Smith a generation before, it suggests the course of thought (or lack of it) on such matters undergone by certain portions of the Canadian intelligentsia during these years. "The scheme of society outlined in 'Looking Backward'," Leacock asserted, without alluding to other socialist writings, "may be examined as the most attractive and the most consistent outline of a socialist state that has, within the knowledge of the present writer, been put forward . . . No better starting point for the criticism of collectivist theories can be found than in a view of the basis on which is supposed to rest the halcyon life of Mr. Bellamy's charming commonwealth." "Nor was ever," he claimed, "a better presentation made of the essential program of socialism." Without undue difficulty Leacock succeeded in knocking down this idealist of a former era. Socialism, he

---

[1] I. Kipnis, *The American Socialist Movement*, p. 4.

concluded his analysis, would function admirably in a community of saints, but for ordinary human beings it would be unworkable. "With perfect citizens any government is good," he argued (apparently he was no more aware than the theorist he was criticizing that the public and private virtues, the motives of the individual and the organization of social relations, are never in a simple causal relationship). "In a population of angels a socialistic commonwealth would work to perfection. But until we have the angels we must keep the commonwealth waiting." The movement towards socialism, he warned, using the apocalyptic image that runs through the book, will lead "over the edge of the abyss beyond which is chaos."

Not only did Stephen Leacock differ with socialism, as he saw it, in regard to solving the problem of social justice, but, as one would expect, he differed in his analysis of the conditions which gave rise to socialism. He saw the same kind of inequalities and incongruities in the materialistic society of 1920 as did the radicals:

Few persons can attain adult life without being profoundly impressed by the appalling inequalities of our human lot. Riches and poverty jostle one another upon our streets. The tattered outcast dozes on his bench while the chariot of the wealthy is drawn by. The palace is the neighbour of the slum. We are, in modern life, so used to this that we no longer see it.

But Leacock's emphasis was different. While socialists were crying out against the suffering of the underprivileged, Leacock counselled against what he assured the reader was a kind of sentimentality which might lead to unfortunate social consequences:

An acquired indifference to the ills of others is the price at which we live. A certain dole of sympathy, a casual mite of personal relief is the mere drop that any one of us alone can cast into the vast ocean of human misery. Beyond that we must harden ourselves lest we too perish.

We make fast the doors of our lighted houses against the indigent and the hungry. What else can we do? If we shelter *one* what is that? And if we try to shelter all, we ourselves are shelterless.

For Leacock the root of social evils lay not at all in the nature of the political or economic system, but entirely in the nature of man. Thus, the war of 1914–18 for Leacock was a demoralizing force because it gave cause for an outbreak of the old Adam: "A world that has known five years of fighting has lost its taste for the honest drudgery of work. Cincinnatus will not go back to his plow, or, at the best, stands sullenly between his plow-handles arguing for a higher wage." But Leacock's most important difference with the socialists was in regard to the concept of freedom. Leacock, in the tradition of nineteenth century Liberalism, maintained that in his society the individual, whatever his hardships, was a free agent; the socialists were arguing that political freedom was meaningless in the face of economic slavery. Leacock wrote:

Yet all [men in our society] are free. This is the distinguishing mark of them as children of our era. They may work or stop. There is no compulsion from without. No man is a slave. Each has his 'natural liberty', and each in his degree, great or small, receives his allotted reward.

But although Leacock was conservative in his rejection of the blue-print state, and in his refusal to "sentimentalize" the lower levels of society, his awareness of the vices of modern industrial civilization did not allow him easily to become an uncritical spokesman for reactionary Toryism. In the *Unsolved Riddle,* while condemning socialism, he also condemned the nineteenth century doctrine of laissez-faire individualism. Fifteen years later in the midst of the Great Depression, his was a somewhat chastened and reformed individualism: "I believe," he wrote, "that the only possible basis for organized society is that of every man for himself—for himself and those near and dear to him. But on this basis must be put in operation a much more efficient and much more just social mechanism."

There was something remarkably anachronistic about Leacock's failure (though himself an economist) to understand those economic factors of the modern world which were making freedom and individualism in any simple sense impossible. In 1936 he complained:

I cannot bear to think that the old independent farming is to go: that the breezy call of incense breathing morn is to be replaced by the time-clock of a regimented, socialized, super-mechanized land-factory. We must keep the farmers. If they cannot regulate the "how much" of their production, let them, as they used to, raise all they damn can, and then fire it around everywhere—pelt one another with new-mown hay and sugar beets. But don't lets lose them.

If such gaiety and gusto seem a little remote from the actual conditions of farming and marketing in the mid-thirties, on the other hand Leacock had no illusions about rural life as such, despite such parables of its virtues triumphing over the decadence of the city as that of Mr. Tomlinson, "wizard of finance." Having been raised on an Ontario farm "during the hard times of Canadian farming," Leacock could claim as he did in the Preface to *Sunshine Sketches of a Little Town* that he had seen "enough of farming to speak exuberantly in political addresses of the joy of early rising and the deep sleep, both of body and intellect, that is induced by honest toil."

Leacock has been described (by Desmond Pacey) as a "country squire" upholding the "eighteenth century values: common sense, benevolence, moderation, good taste,"[2] but he apparently believed there was nothing in his own age which approximated or even partially embodied these values. The mild eighteenth century satire of Addison and Steele, certainly, was based on the kind of positive faith in man and in

---

[2] *Creative Writing in Canada,* p. 101.

society which Leacock frequently and explicitly renounced. Leacock's attitude was more akin to that of cynicism, the cynicism of Diogenes, for example, of whom it has been said:

He would deface all the coinage current in the world. Every conventional stamp was false. The men stamped as generals and kings; the things stamped as honour and wisdom and happiness and riches; all were base metal with lying superscription.

Leacock's extensive dissertation, *Humor, Its Theory and Technique* (1935), reveals more about the author than perhaps any other of his works. Especially it throws light on the basic attitudes which led Leacock to squander his talents in a mass of books turned out for the Christmas book-trade, to use his humour sparingly as a weapon or a tool of criticism, and by and large to accept the social *status quo* despite his criticism of it, rather than to try to alter it. In that work there is, indeed, praise for the two "greatest" humorists, Charles Dickens and Mark Twain, because each in his own way "sought as a part of his work to uplift the world with laughter." There is also condemnation for those modern writers who merely aimed at pleasing the masses, the "ten-cent crowd":

Please the public! That's the trouble today . . . with everything that is written to be printed or acted, everything drawn, sung, or depicted. Nothing can appear unless there is money in it . . . It is the ten-cent crowd that are needed if profits are to be made, not the plutocrats. Hence has been set up in our time an unconscious tyranny of the lower class. The snobbishness of the term may pass without apology in view of the truth of the fact . . . It is the wishes and likings of the mass which largely dictate what the rest of us shall see and hear.

But these remarks cannot be taken as support for a kind of humour which is devoted to immediate social or moral purposes. On the contrary, Leacock has just as little use for that type: "Much of our humour now—dare one say, especially in America?—is over-rapid, snarling, and ill-tempered. It is used to 'show things up', a vehicle of denunciation, not of pleasure." The satirical aspect of humour must always mind itself lest it become simply "mockery, a thing debased and degraded from what it might have been." Somewhere in the course of history, "mere vindictiveness parted company with humor, and became its hideous counterpart, mockery," but still "too much of the humor of all ages, and far too much of our own, partakes of it."

The highest humour, then, is such that it will uplift the world but nevertheless avoid denunciation and mockery. Leacock apparently sees this type in the portrayal of Mr. Pickwick, for example, who "walks through life conveying with him the contrast between life as it might be and life as it is." Humour of this kind depends on a clearly understood and firmly held pattern of values, manners, and presuppositions. The difficulty arises when one attempts to infer such a pattern from Leacock's own works. *Sunshine Sketches* holds out the best promise of such a pattern, and readers have professed to find it there. Leacock's Preface offered the lead, touching as it does at its conclusion tenderly on the "land of hope and sunshine where little towns spread their square streets and their trim maple trees beside placid lakes almost within echo of the primeval forest," and asserting the "affection" at the basis of its portrayal. Mariposa, the most peaceful and the most foolish of small towns, stands as an unconscious critique of the big city ways it tries to ape. Yet Mariposa itself does not contain a pattern or even hints of the good life, unless we choose to pitch our understanding at the level of the beguiling narrator. There is nothing admirable, nothing fine, nothing dignified, nothing sacred in Leacock's portrayal of the little town: all its coinage is defaced. The only virtues are its sunshine and its littleness, its failure to achieve the larger vices of modern industrial urbanism, hard as it tries to do so.

One is tempted to say that Mariposa's curiously nostalgic appeal lies not in its positive attractions but in its success in transforming great evils into small, its rendering innocuous if not innocent the worst aspects of our modern world. Much of Leacock's writing answers to the same formula. "In retrospect," Leacock claimed in his book on humour, "all our little activities are but as nothing, all that we do has in it a touch of the pathetic, and even our sins and wickedness and crime are easily pardoned in the realization of their futility." It is by this perspective that *Sunshine Sketches* charms the reader, by making the "real" pleasantly innocent, not by comparing it with the "ideal," the "might have been." We are perhaps to understand that humour "uplifts" the reader by bringing him to this Olympian height of contemplation. In Leacock's philosophy the ideal is illusory. On occasion he himself may have looked back longingly at "the wholesome days of the eighties or nineties," or at the simple life of the farmer, but at other times he repudiated such attempts to escape the present:

Each age sees the ones that preceded it through a mellow haze of retrospect; each looks back to the good old days of our fore-fathers . . . Each of us in life is a prisoner. We are set and bound in our confined lot. Outside, somewhere, is infinity. We seek to reach into it and the pictured past seems to afford us an outlet of escape.

But in the end, "Escape is barred."

Humour as Leacock conceived it lay at the heart of his philosophy, in fact *was* his philosophy:

. . . humor in its highest meaning and its furthest reach . . . does not depend on verbal incongruities, or on tricks of sight and hearing. It finds its basis in the incongruity of life itself, the contrast between the fretting cares and the petty sorrows of the day and the long mystery of the tomorrow. Here laughter and tears become one, and humor becomes the contemplation and interpretation of our life. In this aspect the thought of the nineteenth century far excelled all that had preceded it. The very wistfulness of its new ignorance—contrasted with the barren certainty of bygone dogma—lends it something pathetic.

The allusion to nineteenth century agnosticism is by no means irrelevant. It is the doubt about man's ultimate significance that provides the basis for humour at its highest, for the universe itself is a kind of "joke" in which the trivial and futile aspirations of mankind are the crowning incongruity. Humour

. . . represents an outlook upon life, a retrospect as it were, in which the fever and the fret of our earthly lot is contrasted with its shortcomings, its lost illusions and its inevitable end. The fiercest anger cools; the bitterest of hate sleeps in the churchyard and over it all there spread Time's ivy and Time's roses, preserving nothing but what is fair to look upon.

Presumably the best joke of all, conducive to the most tears and the most laughter combined, will be the apocalypse as Leacock describes it:

Thus does life, if we look at it from sufficient distance, dissolve itself into 'humor'. Seen through an indefinite vista it ends in a smile. In this, if what the scientist tells us is true, it only offers a parallel to what must ultimately happen to the physical universe in which it exists . . . At some inconceivable distance in time . . . the universe ends, finishes; there is nothing left of it but nothingness. With it goes out in extinction all that was thought of as matter, and with that all the framework of time and space that held it, and the conscious life that matched it. All ends with a cancellation of forces and comes to nothing; and our universe ends thus with one vast, silent unappreciated joke.

For Stephen Leacock as cynic there was no "might have been" except in a wistful and illusory nostalgia, and even here his sense of the follies and shortcomings of men would not allow him to be blinded. It was easier for him, with his belief in the futility of man's petty actions to take his role of artist lightly, to observe the evils of his society without bitterness or indignation, accepting and defending the world as he found it, and to turn his irreverent humour on every aspect of experience and upon all manner of people and things. But perhaps after all he was less like Diogenes, who also credited the world with no virtue, yet who asked its princes nothing in return but that they "stand a little out of his light," than like that other cynic, Teles, who taught the doctrine of self-love and received money from the hands of rich patrons with words like these: "You give liberally and I take valiantly from you, neither grovelling nor demeaning myself basely nor grumbling." For Stephen Leacock was a part of the prospering materialistic civilization of which he wrote; he was sometimes its critic, but always its entertainer.

part V

The Inter-War Years

26

Meighen and the Montreal Tycoons: Railway Policy in the Election of 1921*

W. R. Graham

"GOUIN is the tool of the C.P.R.," wrote a confident to Arthur Meighen about the Quebec Liberal chieftain, and "he represents corporation Quebec; you must remain representative of progressive Canada." With regard to railway policy, argues Roger Graham, Arthur Meighen tried to do just that, although in the end he lost every seat in Quebec. Professor Graham is the author of the three-volume biography of Arthur Meighen. Before this monumental work on the great Conservative chieftain appeared, this article foretold some of its forthcoming flavour. Appearing at the dawn of Diefenbaker era, here was a piece of revisionist scholarship not at all defensive. Indeed, Meighen emerges as the responsible progressive, while the Gouin-Lemieux Quebec Liberals are seen as hopelessly kept men of the C.P.R.–Bank of Montreal–Montreal *Star* complex, *rois nègres* André Laurendeau would have called them. The Montreal moguls, led by the "inscrutable" Lord Atholstan, are portrayed as unscrupulous plotters who hardly stopped short of planning a bloodless *coup d'état* to advance their corporate interests and destroy the emerging Canadian National Railway system.

I⊤ IS PART of the folk lore of Canadian politics that the Conservative party, under whatever name and whatever leader, has been peculiarly susceptible to the will and influence of Big Business. This tendency to

* *Canadian Historical Association Report* (1957), pp. 71–85.

identify the party as the political arm of an economically dominant minority goes back to the heyday of high Toryism before responsible government. It is to be found in the dear, dead Clear Grit days beyond Confederation and it crops up frequently on this side of that great divide. It has resulted in the prevalence of a rather Macaulay-like view of the party struggle which gives the Reform-Liberal tradition an affectation of virtue, as representative of popular rights and interests, and the Tory-Conservative tradition the appearance of a perpetual last ditch stand on behalf of special interests against the gradual but irresistible progress of democracy. One finds this view expressed by a long line of distinguished Reformers and Liberals, such as William Lyon Mackenzie, George Brown, Sir Richard Cartwright and William Lyon Mackenzie King, each of whom contributed variations on the basic theme. It is not, of course, the purpose of this paper to discuss the development of the theme throughout Canadian history but one general observation may, perhaps, be permitted: that what had been in the day of Mackenzie a set of substantially true opinions about the enemy had become a century later nothing more than a collection of demagogic shibboleths, sanctified by incessant ritualistic repetition. After all, times do change and political parties with them, and there was as much difference between the realities of the eighteen-twenties and 'thirties and those of the nineteen-twenties and 'thirties as there was between the incisive utterance of "The Firebrand" and the shapeless verbosity of his grandson.

Mr. King, with his habit of moralizing, was prone to treat the party battle as a monumental struggle between the forces of good and evil. He seems to have thought of himself as filling his grandfather's shoes in carrying on the fight against the powers of darkness and to have regarded all his Conservative opponents, but chiefly Arthur Meighen, the most dangerous because the most able, as the spiritual descendants of those arrogant and autocratic men against whom his rebellious ancestor had so valiantly contended. Thus, in King's view, Mr. Meighen, like the Tories of old, in addition to being a subservient colonial, a bigoted enemy of French Canada and a subverter of Parliament, was the creature of that powerful group of oligarchs whose ambition to dominate the state threatened the very foundations of Canadian democracy. Speaking in the budget debate in the 1921 session of Parliament, he put this opinion in the following words, which may incidentally help to explain why Meighen once referred to the "essential humour" of King's addresses[1]:

. . . we have come to have in Canada, on the one hand, a Prime Minister and a ministry to whom usurpation of office and the exercise of autocratic methods in Government belong as a sort of natural right, and, on the other, a small circle, a sort of little oligarchy of interwoven financial, manufacturing, transportation and distributing interests, prepared in return for a continuation

---

[1] Canada, Parliament, House of Commons, *Debates*, 1921, I, 26.

of favour and special privilege, to use their wealth and influence to keep the Administration in power, and thereby constituting in a very true sense the real though invisible Government of this country.

We have, in other words, political power united with plutocracy in a bond of self-interest, the former the visible symbol of authority, the latter the governing and directing force in the State. We have a Government, democratic in form, but autocratic in behaviour, and back of that Government, and vastly superior to it in many respects, we have the privileged coterie of wealthy and influential men, . . . who are not satisfied with sharing in the control of industry and the State, but wish to dominate both. They are for the time being able to exercise this domination at their own free will, for the Administration owes its existence to their dictation and its continuance in office to the powerful influence which in a multitude of directions, they are able to exert. There is the real situation with which this country is, faced at the present time. That is the danger to Canada at the moment . . . that we have on the one side the selfish groups united together working for their joint ambitions and, on the other, the great body of the people left to look after themselves.[2]

It is generally admitted that the city of Montreal has been for some time a financial, manufacturing, transportation and distributing centre of some importance and that the business class of that city has had, on occasion, both political ambition and political influence. Arthur Meighen, like all his predecessors, and no doubt like Mr. King, was naturally anxious to enlist that influence on the side of himself and his party. In this he was, by and large, unsuccessful; true *rapport* with St. James Street eluded him. Indeed, some of the leading personages of that thoroughfare did all they could to embarrass him in order to force his resignation as Conservative leader and replace him with someone more to their liking. Their failure to support him, together with the bitter hostility of French Canada, which was unscrupulously fostered by the Liberals of Quebec, created in that province the most important and bafflingly complex political problem he had to face between 1920 and 1926.

In the forefront of the anti-Meighen movement conducted by some of the tycoons of Montreal was Hugh Graham, Baron Atholstan, a man whose career cries out for investigation—by someone with a knowledge of abnormal psychology. Immensely rich and successful, he was the owner of several newspapers, chiefly *The Family Herald and Weekly Star* and *The Montreal Daily Star* which Graham and his father had established shortly after Confederation. In 1920 the former had the largest circulation of any Canadian publication and among the daily newspapers the latter was second only to *La Presse*. *The Montreal Daily Star* under Graham's guidance was given to tub-thumping campaigns and bizarre crusades which made the other main English language paper in the city, *The Gazette*, seem by contrast even more sedate and respectable than it was. Graham had obtained (some might say extorted) a knighthood in

---

[2] *Ibid.*, IV, 3603.

1908 through the good offices of Sir Wilfred Laurier and a peerage in 1917 on the recommendation of Sir Robert Borden. The latter, writing in his diary, sized up *The Star's* owner as, "a singular mixture of cunning and stupidity. His great weakness lies in his belief that he can hoodwink others. . . . Evidently he is consumed with immense desire for peerage. Speaks of it as a bauble hardly worthy of his acceptance."[3]

The first (and last) Baron Atholstan was noted for his large philanthropies and petty conspiracies. During the South African War he had insured the lives of Canadian soldiers to the extent of $1,000,000. To celebrate the marriage of his daughter and only child in 1925 he donated $250,000 to charity and gave his employees double pay for the week. He took a special interest in the problem of disease, providing $100,000 for cancer cure research and the same amount for the establishment of the Montreal Anti-Tuberculosis and Public Health League. Many other worthy institutions and well-intentioned groups profited from his generosity, from McGill University to the Society for the Prevention of Cruelty to Children.

But the Atholstan was more than a benefactor of mankind. Obviously he aspired to play a dominating role in politics from behind the scenes as a puppet-master manipulating the politicians. He was, Meighen has said of him, "a political intriguer in a class by himself,"[4] a "circuitous, gum-shoe sort of person"[5] who "could turn a corner so fast you could hear his shirt tails snap."[6] He "had a passion for being inscrutable. He wanted to be sought after and he wanted to be feared."[7] And, it may be added, he wanted someone other than Arthur Meighen to lead the Conservative party. To that end his conspiratorial talents and the news and editorial columns of *The Star* were pretty consistently devoted between 1920 and 1926.

In this desire Atholstan was by no means alone among the Montreal magnates, though he seems to have played a more or less lone hand and certainly employed methods uniquely devious and unscrupulous in seeking to attain it. *The Gazette,* perhaps in lesser measure and undoubtedly in a less sensational manner, was also hostile to Meighen, presumably reflecting the views of much of the city's business community and in particular those of the C.P.R.-Bank of Montreal group, whose mouthpiece, it has been rumoured, *The Gazette* was. As for the leading members of that group themselves it is difficult to document their part in

---

[3] Sir Robert Borden, *Diary*, May 4, 1916. The *Diary* is in the possession of Mr. Henry Borden, Q.C. of Toronto. I am indebted to him for permission to read it.

[4] Arthur Meighen to the writer, February 12, 1952.

[5] Same to same, July 30, 1952.

[6] A remark attributed to Meighen by various persons in conversation with the writer.

[7] Meighen to the writer, October 14, 1952.

these matters. Circumstantial evidence there is aplenty but as their deliberations were no doubt carried on verbally and in private the record is obscure. It would be interesting, for example, to know just what part, if any, E. W. Beatty played in the Montreal politicking of the 1920's, which was so largely inspired by dislike of railway nationalization. We are told by Beatty's biographer that, "as President of the C. P. R. we see him opposed to nationalization while as a patriotic Canadian he wished every success to this new railway venture."[8] But from the same source one gets the impression that Beatty believed that what was good for the C. P. R. was good for Canada and there is no doubt that he thought the existence and completion of a publicly owned system bad for the C. P. R. Meighen is of the opinion that Beatty was not personally implicated in any scheme to oust him from the leadership, as a necessary first step towards modifying or terminating the policy of public ownership. However, more than once he received warnings, especially prior to the election of 1921, that the influence of the C. P. R. organization was being brought to bear against the Conservative party.

Meighen's unpopularity among the bigger "big wigs" of Montreal, most of whom by instinct and the traditions of their class were inclined to support his party in national affairs, seems to have been caused chiefly by the fact that he was, in their sight, most unsound on the railway question. This was a subject which loomed so large in the thinking of some of them as to amount almost to an obsession and they apparently thought that Meighen had to be put out of the way before the problem of the railways could be solved to their satisfaction. To these men anyone more radical than Warren G. Harding was a dangerous revolutionary and no one had been so prominently active as Meighen in framing, explaining and defending the various measures giving effect to a policy which *The Star* described as, "that discredited and ruinous fantasy of the most demented form of Socialism, viz.:—Government ownership of railways."[9]

Related to the Montrealers' dislike to public ownership was their suspicion that the Conservative party under Meighen's leadership, as under Borden's, was too much under the influence of financial interests in Toronto, represented mainly by the Canadian Bank of Commerce and the National Trust Company. This alleged influence was personified best by two men prominent in public life—Sir Joseph Flavelle and Sir Thomas White. Flavelle was President of the trust company and a Director of the bank. White, before he joined the Borden Government in 1911, had been General Manager of the National Trust and after his retirement from politics in 1919 became a Director of that company and Vice-President of the Bank of Commerce. It was felt in Montreal that this Toronto group, which included besides Flavelle and White such others as Sir Edmund

<hr>

[8] D. H. Miller-Barstow, *Beatty of the C. P. R.*, (Toronto, 1951), p. 35.

[9] *The Montreal Daily Star*, December 7, 1921.

Walker, Z. A. Lash and E. R. Wood, had been instrumental in forcing Borden and his colleagues to embark upon the treacherous sea of public ownership by acquiring the Canadian Northern Railway in 1917, and that that step had been taken to save the Canadian Bank of Commerce from disaster. The continuing influence of these men was to be seen in the appointment in 1920 of White as the member representing the Government of Canada on the Grand Trunk Arbitration Board and in the choice of Flavelle as Chairman of the Grand Trunk Railway in 1921, pending its amalgamation with the other Government lines. As some incidents of the 1921 campaign were to show, Meighen, in the eyes of St. James Street, was too much under the baneful domination of Toronto, a charge that could be used to good political advantage in Quebec.

There were other counts against him as well. For one thing, as *The Gazette* explained, "Quebec will not have Mr. Meighen." The alleged crimes and enormities committed against French Canada during the war had been and would continue to be attributed to him by the Liberals of Quebec, who delighted in depicting him as a slavish colonial eager to sacrifice Canadian blood and treasure in Britain's wars. It was fruitless, *The Gazette* contended, to argue that the charges made against him were untrue; the important fact was that they were believed to be true by the mass of French Canadian voters. It was idle to hope that the Conservatives could effectively combat the kind of propaganda used against them as long as Meighen remained in command of the party. Until there was a change of leadership the party might as well write the province of Quebec off as virtually a dead loss.[10] In this connection it is fair to remark that neither *The Gazette* nor *The Star* made any effort to refute the absurd calumnies about Meighen which were spread broadcast throughout Quebec. Sometimes they reported them in their news columns but never did they devote editorial space to exposing the cynical mendacity that typified Liberal campaign methods in that province. In fact there were relatively few Conservatives in Quebec who had the will or the courage to defend Meighen; it was not the popular thing to do.

Meighen, then, was looked upon in Montreal as a hopeless political liability as far as Quebec was concerned. At the same time, paradoxically, to some people in the city he was suspect as being too lukewarm where the mother country and the imperial connection were concerned. For example, *The Star* was highly critical of his stand on the Anglo-Japanese Alliance at the Imperial Conference of 1921.[11] Lord Atholstan was an imperialist of extraordinary emotional fervour and before the conference convened his newspaper waged an intensive editorial campaign in favour

[10] *The Gazette,* Montreal, September 22, 1926.

[11] On this subject see J. Bartlett Brebner, "Canada, the Anglo-Japanese Alliance and the Washington Conference," *Political Science Quarterly,* L (1), March, 1935, 45–58.

of renewing the alliance. Meighen, however, argued skillfully and successfully against renewal and *The Star* made no attempt to hide its displeasure. The Prime Minister, it remarked disgustedly, "had a chance to
show . . . that a Conservative leader regards it as a duty and a privilege
to co-operate with the British Empire in policies which its responsible
officials think essential to Imperial safety." Instead he had sided with the
United States against the United Kingdom, Australia and New Zealand;
he had failed in his duty and refused the privilege.[12]

These were some of the reasons why Meighen was looked askance at
by the moguls of Montreal. Anxious for their support and yet not willing
to give ground where his policies and convictions were at stake, his
strategy was to appeal to them and to Quebec generally on what in his
opinion was the great issue of the day—the tariff. Pointing to the tariff
resolution of the 1919 Liberal convention, he sought to strengthen his
support within his own party and also to detach Liberal protectionists
from their allegiance to Mackenzie King by contending that a government headed by the latter would sell out to the Progressives and lower
the tariff in a bid for Western support. Had he succeeded in convincing
Quebec of this danger it is conceivable that railways, conscription and the
Empire might have become less dominating political factors in that
province than they were. But his argument made little impression in
Quebec where the 1919 platform was not taken very seriously and where
it was widely held that a province with sixty-five seats in the House of
Commons had the best possible guarantee that its economic interests
would not be endangered. Even when the King Government did reduce
the duties on agricultural implements in 1924 the Conservatives were
unable to benefit greatly from the resulting division in Liberal ranks,
since to the mass of voters in Quebec the iniquities of conscription were
made to seem more terrible and the danger of war with Turkey more
imminent than any threat to the protective system. Furthermore,
Meighen was handicapped in trying to arouse the businessmen of Montreal to join with him to preserve protection by the fact that Sir Lomer
Gouin became, first, a Liberal candidate in the 1921 election, and then a
member of the King ministry which that election put into office. Gouin, as
The Gazette pointed out, had "the respect, the confidence of all classes in
Quebec" and was "solid and steady and sane in matters political."[13]
Certainly he enjoyed the trust of the business class, a great many of
whose Conservative members had supported him during his fifteen years
as Quebec's Premier. They looked upon him as one of their own, as his
election in 1920 to the Boards of Directors of the Bank of Montreal and
the Royal Trust Company indicated. They were confident that any
Government of which he was a member would pursue a safe and sound

---

[12] *Star*, December 7, 1921.

[13] *Canadian Annual Review of Public Affairs*, 1921, p. 483.

course with respect to the tariff. Consequently, until Gouin's resignation shortly before the tariff-reducing budget of 1924 was brought down, Meighen found it difficult indeed to attract to his protectionist banner that element in Montreal, whether Liberal or Conservative, for whom the maintenance of the National Policy was at once an economic and an emotional necessity.

The tariff, then, in the opinion of the businessmen of Montreal was not really an issue, at least until 1924. The overriding fact in their minds was that the Conservative party, with Meighen in the forefront, had needlessly and to its eternal shame led the country down the garden path towards the public ownership of certain railways; the overriding necessity was to rescue the country from the consequences of that ill-conceived and disastrous policy. If this could be done through the Conservative party by inducing a change of heart in its leader or by wringing some concessions from him, well and good; if not, other means would have to be found. In September, 1921, shortly after the dissolution of Parliament, Lord Atholstan tried a gambit of characteristic effrontery, evidently in the hope of bringing Meighen around. His Lordship's journalistic and financial support was important to the Conservatives of Quebec. This he knew and they were willing to admit. He was, of course, in a position to dictate the terms on which such support might be offered and in 1921 the terms included a willingness on Meighen's part to give ground on railways. Atholstan scribbled in pencil on a scrap of paper the draft of a letter which he intended the Prime Minister should send out over his signature, addressed to Senator George G. Foster and A. J. Brown, both prominent Montreal lawyers with extensive business connections, and to Atholstan himself. The draft letter reads as follows:

In any matter subject to my control or my influence directly or indirectly in respect of the Railway problem I will take you into consultation and will associate with you one other probably Sir Robert Borden and myself and thoroughly thrash out all possible plans for the relief of the country of as much of the annual deficits as possible and what any three of us agree upon as the best solution will have my earnest support under all circumstances. In the meantime I ask you to give earnest study to the question from the standpoint of the country's interest. In addressing the public I will say it is too soon to condemn pub[lic] ownership but if the deficits continue something must be done and it may be very drastic.[14]

For Meighen to have sent out such a letter would have made him Atholstan's captive and subject to blackmail. The letter was not sent and the public reference to the railway matter suggested by Atholstan was not made. Early in October, replying to a letter from Brown containing the same suggestion that the Government should consult with Foster, Athol-

---

[14] Arthur Meighen Papers, Public Archives of Canada, draft of letter in Lord Atholstan's handwriting, September 17, 1921.

stan and him, the Prime Minister expressed his willingness to do so but added, "It is understood, of course, the Government must take into consideration the views of, and consult with its supporters in Parliament. . . ."[15] Since their views, like Meighen's own, were averse to the changes so much desired in Montreal, it must have been evident to Atholstan and his friends that nothing was to be gained by trying to work through the Conservative party as then constituted and led.

When Atholstan spoke in his draft letter of "possible plans for the relief of the country," he no doubt had in mind a proposal set forth in a memorandum submitted to Meighen in the previous April by Lord Shaughnessy, President of the C. P. R. until 1918 and still one of its Directors, a proposal which found much favour in Montreal. In a letter accompanying the memorandum Shaughnessy stated, "To my mind the railway question involving, as it does, such an enormous draft on the annual revenue of the country with no prospect of any improvement in the near future is the most momentous problem before our country at this time." The memorandum, he pointed out, "merely brings up to date on very much the same lines a similar paper that I prepared about the end of 1917, and sent to Sir Robert Borden. He feared, I imagine, that as my plan would apparently create a Canadian Pacific monopoly in transportation it would not be acceptable to the country." Shaughnessy admitted that some people would again find in his suggestions "a selfish desire on the part of the Canadian Pacific to control the railway situation. The Canadian Pacific bogey has served its turn on every occasion in the past thirty-five years, when schemes were being promoted with disregard of the cost to the country."[16]

Shaughnessy's proposal in brief was that the Grand Trunk, the nationalization of which had provoked a particularly violent protest in Montreal, should be returned to its former owners and relieved of all obligations with respect to the Grand Trunk Pacific, so that it might stand on its own feet. The railway properties of the C. P. R. should be separated from its other assets and added to the Government Railways. This consolidated railway system should be administered and operated on behalf of the Canadian people by the existing C. P. R. management for a term of years approaching perpetuity. The shareholders of the C. P. R. would be compensated by the Government of Canada contracting to pay, "in perpetuity, a fixed annual dividend on the share capital, to be supplemented by a further payment when the whole property was yielding a specified return."[17] These changes, it was argued, would result in very large economies in railway operation.

It is difficult to believe that Shaughnessy seriously thought his plan

[15] *Ibid.*, Meighen to A. J. Brown, K.C., October 3, 1921.

[16] *Ibid.*, Shaughnessy to Meighen, April 6, 1921.

[17] *Canadian Annual Review*, 1921, pp. 410–11.

had any hope of acceptance by Meighen, who was more intimately connected with the policy attacked in the memorandum than anyone else in public life. Two cardinal principles inherent in that policy were that a railway monopoly must be avoided and that in a system of public ownership public control was essential. Such control should not involve political interference in the day to day management of the lines but it must involve ultimate political authority over an enterprise in which public funds were so heavily invested. Both these principles were violated by the Shaughnessy plan and on that account, if on no other, it was unacceptable to Meighen. He acknowledged the letter and memorandum verbally[18] but did not send a written reply. However, his opinion of the scheme was expressed in a letter to a friend in Ontario.

You will see on reading Lord Shaughnessy's memorandum that it is not a suggestion for the Government to acquire the C. P. R., it is a suggestion embodying the transfer of the National Railways to the C. P. R., the management of the railways by the Company, the Government paying the deficit whatever it is, and guaranteeing the C. P. R. shareholders their dividends, but having nothing to say as to who should constitute the management or as to what obligations are incurred. I do not find the approval very general but there are a certain number who would approve of almost anything if it comes from a source they favour. I have every respect for Lord Shaughnessy but he has been a long time with the C. P. R.[19]

If Meighen was not prepared to give serious consideration to the plan, some other politicians were. In fact, so it seemed to the press barons and financiers of Montreal, the Quebec Liberals were more alive to the gravity of the railway problem than the Prime Minister and, in their vigorous and consistent opposition to nationalization, had adopted a more correct and more truly Conservative stand than the Conservative party itself. Sir Lomer Gouin, for instance, was an outspoken critic of public ownership and on his influence, chiefly, the Montrealers pinned their hopes for a new policy. In a campaign speech at the end of October Gouin declared, "The Railway question is of paramount importance now. Unless it is settled there will be a national tragedy. . . . Our roads show immense deficits while privately owned roads over the same territory can declare dividends . . . and so long as we run nationally-owned roads so long will our debt increase. The problem must be settled, no matter who wins. If the Meighen policy continues we will certainly have a national disaster."[20] Of the same view was Rodolphe Lemieux, who stated explicitly, ". . . only one solution has been proposed, and that is the one given by the most competent man on this continent, Lord Shaughnessy. I prefer

---

[18] See Meighen Papers, Shaughnessy to Meighen, April 20, 1921.

[19] *Ibid.*, Meighen to J. C. Hodgins, April 27, 1921.

[20] *Canadian Annual Review,* 1921, p. 484.

a monopoly to bankruptcy."[21] Walter J. Mitchell, Quebec's Provincial Treasurer until he became a candidate for a House of Commons seat in 1921, was equally critical of the course that had been followed and many other Liberal candidates in Quebec came out against public ownership.

This was undoubtedly a source of embarrassment to Mackenzie King in the rest of the country and he was moved to state that Lemieux, in endorsing the Shaughnessy plan, had been speaking only for himself.[22] This inspired a scathing editorial in *The Star*, which referred contemptuously to the "Boy Leader," who owed his position to the Quebec Liberals and who would lose it if he got too far out of step with them.[23] Indeed, in Montreal Gouin, rather than King, seems to have been looked upon as the real leader of the Liberal party and the man whom the forthcoming election would place in a dominating position at Ottawa. The expectation was that no one of the three parties would have a majority in the new House of Commons. *The Star* explained that the formation of a Government would have to be preceded by "negotiations" in which Gouin would presumably be the key figure,[24] and *The Gazette* predicted that his control of the large Quebec representation would "enable him to command the situation."[25] In fact a major re-alignment of political forces would have to take place so that Liberals and Conservatives of sound business judgment and common sense could combine to save the nation from financial ruin. C. H. Cahan, in declining to oppose W. S. Fielding in Halifax, probably spoke the mind of the Montreal business class when he said, ". . . the financial and economic problems, which so sorely beset us, will undoubtedly necessitate entirely new political alignments; thoughtful and experienced minds of both the old political parties must break from former party affiliations and cooperate to preserve the solvency of the country."[26]

An inkling of what the Montreal oligarchs apparently had in view in the way of new political alignments may be gained from a memorandum prepared for Meighen's information by his old friend and fellow Manitoban, Senator W. H. Sharpe, in August. Reporting on opinion as to whether there should be an election that autumn or the following spring, Sharpe wrote:

. . . the Bank of Montreal and the C. P. R., and many of our friends in Montreal are in favour of an election this fall, and they claim if you have an election this fall and come back with 75 or 80 members you can make a deal with Quebec members who during the election will be solid against us. I have

21 *Ibid.*, p. 482.
22 *Ibid.*, p. 490.
23 *Star*, October 17, 1921.
24 *Ibid.*, November 24, 1921.
25 *Canadian Annual Review*, 1921, p. 484.
26 *Ibid.*, p. 489.

met friends of the Hon. Mr. J. L. Parent, who stands very close to Sir Lomer, and at my request, they have had several meetings and decided to meet you and have an understanding before an election is called.

Also you should certainly have a meeting with Mr. Beatty and the President of the Bank of Montreal, for they control Sir Lomer and a large number of the members from Quebec, and I am told Sir Lomer will come into the Government with you after the election.[27]

Sharpe did not go on to specify the terms of the projected "deal" but it is probably safe to assume that they would include a revision of railway policy, perhaps along the lines of the Shaughnessy plan. This Meighen would be expected to concede in return for an alliance with the Liberal protectionists and the voting strength in the House which their accession would bring. In some respects this must have been an enticing prospect for Meighen. Quebec was by far his party's most serious weak spot and it would be helpful indeed to be able to count on Gouin's undoubted influence there. Furthermore, as such a reorientation of political groups would probably bring the low tariff Liberals and the Progressives together against the combined protectionist elements, the tariff could more easily be made the chief national issue as Meighen thought it should be. On the other hand there were serious disadvantages to be considered. For one thing, a coalition with Gouin would antagonize French Canadian Conservatives who had been fighting him on the provincial level for years. For another, it might alarm and alienate Conservatives in other provinces. Some of them had had enough of coalitions since 1917 and desired to see traditional party alignments restored as fully as possible. Many of them, too, were inclined to fear the influence of Quebec, not only of French Canada but as well that of the great business interests alleged to be behind Gouin. Furthermore, Conservative opinion outside Quebec was on the whole favourably disposed to the railway policy then in force. Finally, a bargain with Gouin, if it involved a new departure with respect to railways, would necessitate a repudiation by Meighen of a major policy of the Borden Government. As a member of that Government, of which he felt his own to be a continuation, he assumed responsibility for all its actions and was prepared neither to revise nor to repent them.

On balance these disadvantages of a union with the Gouin Liberals outweighed any advantages it might bring, and the understanding which Sharpe had envisaged failed to materialize. In any case once Sir Lomer had thrown down the gauntlet by declaring that, "If the Meighen policy continues we will certainly have a national disaster," Meighen could not unite with him except at the cost of disowning everything he had done in the field of railway affairs. Instead he did the only thing he could do—

---

[27] Meighen Papers, Memorandum, August 2, 1921. It is unsigned but bears the notation, "Memorandum to be returned to Senator Sharpe."

strike back at Gouin. Thus transportation was added to conscription as one of the main issues in the campaign of 1921 in Quebec and Meighen was forced to give up his last hope of keeping the tariff question to the fore there.

Among his supporters were some who argued that it would be good strategy to make railway policy the chief issue in the rest of the country as well, in order to exploit the general popular approval of public ownership. Since the attempt to detach the Liberal protectionists of Quebec from their party had failed, why not try to take advantage of the widespread fear that Gouin's influence might bring about the destruction of the National Railways in the event of the Liberals forming a Government? One of those who propounded this idea was Tom Blacklock, then Ottawa correspondent for *The Gazette,* a close friend of Meighen and a shrewd political observer. About a fortnight before the election Blacklock sent to the Prime Minister an interesting analysis of the situation along with some urgent advice.

I have always been convinced [he wrote in part] that the great issue was the consolidation and preservation of the National Railway System . . . . It is indisputable that the future of the National Railway System is menaced by Sir Lomer Gouin's support—the Canadian Pacific Railway and allied Montreal corporate interests. Eight provinces favor the retention of the National Railway System but those eight provinces are not voting on this issue while the great province of Quebec is being mobilized to attack and destroy that system. . . .

The Canadian Pacific is using its whole power and prestige against you. Right here in Ottawa every non-union C. P. R. employee is against you, and in Montreal the C. P. R. organization is in compact with your enemies. Why should we hesitate to force them into the open and make the co-ordination and preservation of the National Railways the supreme issue? The C. P. R. cannot do more against you than they have done and will do.

A Meighen-Gouin coalition would mean your political ruin. Opposition is much preferable to office with the suspicion that would be attached to such coalition. Gouin is the tool of the C. P. R.; would return the Grand Trunk to former owners; would destroy the National Railway System; is opposed to your imperialism, and the enemy of organized labour. Can you afford such association? Such a coalition could only be accomplished at a price—the fulfillment of the desire of the C. P. R., and everybody knows of that desire. A coalition would be a betrayal of the Quebec Conservatives to their bitterest enemy Gouin, and the terms of the pact, a betrayal of the Nationalization advocates throughout the Dominion. . . .

I firmly believe you must make the issue—Canada vs. C. P. R. You may not win but you would make impossible a Liberal-Farmer coalition; make possible a bonne Entente between Conservatives and Farmers; and would preserve the National Railway System by exposing the C. P. R. conspiracy . . . . Do not become a party to any scheme that means either co-operation or coalition with Gouin. He represents corporation Quebec; you must remain representative of progressive Canada.[28]

28 *Ibid.,* Blacklock to Meighen, November 21, 1921.

To this rather gamy missive Meighen replied, "In pointing out the direction to me, I think you are right as to just what words should be used now. There is room for no other opinion."[29] But he must have had in mind another bit of advice he had received a day or two earlier from one more cautious than Blacklock and an equally keen student of matters political—James A. Calder. ". . . hit Gouin &c hard on the railway question without dragging in the C. P. R. if this is possible," Calder wrote. "I know it is difficult and that if C. P. R. passes the word along the result may be disastrous. Personally I would take the chance if it is well handled."[30]

To make the issue "Canada vs C. P. R." or to "hit Gouin &c hard without dragging in the C. P. R."—that was the question. The decision had to be made a few days later. On November 25th C. Grant MacNeil, Dominion Secretary of the Great War Veterans' Association, who had recently discussed the whole matter with the Prime Minister,[31] sent identical telegrams to him, Mackenzie King, T. A. Crerar, Sir Lomer Gouin, E. W. Beatty and Sir Vincent Meredith, President of the Bank of Montreal. They were asked to comment on the following charges:

. . . it is alleged that an alliance has been formed under the leadership of Sir Lomer Gouin between the Quebec Liberal party interests, the Canadian Pacific Railway interests, the Bank of Montreal interests and Wall Street interests to accomplish through traitors in all parties:

1. Confusion in the public mind on election issues to minimize the possibility of a party majority on December sixth, thus enabling manipulation for Government through coalition.

2. The betrayal and downfall of Hon. Mackenzie King as leader of the Liberal party to enable accession to that post of Sir Lomer Gouin supported by Hon. W. J. Mitchell and a Quebec bloc.

3. The betrayal of the Right Hon. Arthur Meighen from within his party for the purpose of enforcing agreement to coalition with Sir Lomer Gouin on the terms dictated by the latter, failing which the elimination of Mr. Meighen.

4. The corruption of the "key men" in the Progressive Party to undermine confidence in the integrity of its leaders.

5. The formation of a coalition Government which would acquiesce in the return of the Grand Trunk Railway to its former owners and the ultimate disposal to American Railway interests as well as the looting of the Canadian National Railways to the point where transfer to private corporation control would be welcomed by the tax-payers.[32]

The other recipients of the telegram denied all knowledge of any such conspiracy but Meighen answered:

29 *Ibid.*, Meighen to Blacklock, November 22, 1921.
30 *Ibid.*, Calder to Meighen, November 20, 1921, confidential.
31 *Ibid.*, MacNeil to Meighen, November 25, 1921, telegram, personal.
32 *Ibid.*, Same to same, November 25, 1921, telegram.

There is ample evidence that first two parties referred to Sir Lomer Gouin and leading Quebec Liberals, are determined on transfer or disintegration of present National Railway system. Proposals of Lord Shaughnessy on same subject have been expressed in memorandum now public. Beyond that I do not know views others referred to.

Whether downfall of Hon. Mackenzie King as leader is sought on behalf of Sir Lomer Gouin, backed by a Quebec bloc, is for them to say.

Personally I have been loyally and splendidly supported by all Parliamentary followers and candidates for Parliament in our behalf and judging from every indication am being now supported by the great mass of the people. The policies stated in your message to be subject of attack after election are policies established and put into effect by the present Government. I have defended them through many sessions against every assault. By those policies I stand and no combination or manoeuvre will turn me from my course.[33]

Apparently this attack on Gouin and Meighen's unequivocal delcaration of adherence to established railway policy was too much for Lord Atholstan. On November 30th *The Star* became openly hostile to the Government in a manner that provided a sensational climax to the campaign. Until then its stand on the approaching election had been somewhat ambiguous. It had expressed its contempt for King and for much of that remarkably variable platform on which he was campaigning. On the other hand it had refused to endorse the Conservative party, its leader or its candidates. Rather it had urged the voters to support candidates who believed in protection and "economy," the latter probably being in *The Star's* vocabulary a euphemism for the Shaughnessy plan. What Atholstan obviously desired was the election of a large *bloc* of Quebec members of the Gouin-Lemieux-Mitchell variety but until the end of November his newspaper refrained from openly attacking the Meighen Government. Meighen's reply to the MacNeil telegram presumably provoked the extraordinary roorback which *The Star* used in the closing days of the campaign to ensure the defeat of Conservative candidates in Quebec and in Montreal more particularly.

In its issue of November 30th *The Star* gave front page prominence to what purported to be a despatch from its Ottawa correspondent. This was headed:

STARTLING RUMOR!
REVOLUTIONARY RAILWAY CHANGES SAID
TO BE CONTEMPLATED
Measures Calculated to Tie the Hands of the
New Government

The "despatch" stated, "on authority that would be recognized as unimpeachable that the Railway Board contemplate making immediate and important

---

[33] *Ibid.*, Meighen to MacNeil, November 26, 1921, telegram.

changes in the staffs of the Government railways. The report is that Montreal
. . . is to be deprived of many of its best railway men; and it is suspected that
Sir Joseph Flavelle may be behind the new policy."[34]

In succeeding issues these assertions were repeated and amplified,
leaving the impression that the plot was to remove the head office of the
Grand Trunk from Montreal to Toronto preparatory to making the latter
city the headquarters of the consolidated National Railway system which
would be formed when the Grand Trunk was united with the other
publicly owned lines. A similar rumour had been spread in Montreal the
preceding summer and *The Gazette* at that time had angrily declared it
to be the settled policy of the Government and Sir Joseph Flavelle to
make Toronto the capital of the National Railways.[35] But the rumor had
been laid when Flavelle wrote a categorical denial to *The Gazette.*[36]

With the revival of the charge by *The Star* the Liberals in Quebec
were quick to catch their cue. The party's publicity committee took full
page newspaper advertisements to proclaim, "Montreal Threatened. Destruction of One of Its Greatest Assets."[37] Sir Lomer Gouin asserted that
a vote for the Government would be a vote for the removal of the
National Railway headquarters from the city and the loss of 50,000 of its
population.[38] Herbert Marler, a candidate in Montreal, declared at a
public meeting, no doubt to great applause, that he would not tolerate
the withdrawal of railway headquarters from his city.[39] It seemed
evident, as J. A. Stewart, the Minister of Railways put it, that the purpose
of *The Star's* allegations "was to provide new material for Gouin and
other Quebec speakers."[40]

Both Meighen and Flavelle denied absolutely that there was any truth
whatsoever in the "startling rumor" and the former demanded that he be
shown the proofs which *The Star* claimed were available. A week after
the defeat of his Government Meighen went down to Montreal with
Stewart. On the train they happened to meet Flavelle who joined the
party. The three were met at the Ritz-Carlton Hotel by Lord Atholstan
and A. R. Carman, Editor of *The Star,* and were driven to the office of
Howard G. Kelley, President of the Grand Trunk. What ensued can best
be told in Meighen's own version which he wrote to Calder:

Today I was down to Montreal to see the "proofs." Jack Stewart went with
me, also Sir Joseph Flavelle happened to be on the train, and I took him up as
well. We were met at the Ritz by Lord Atholstan, Carman, the Editor, and a

[34] *Star*, November 30, 1921.
[35] *Gazette*, July 28, 1921.
[36] Meighen Papers, Flavelle to the editor, *The Gazette*, August 8, 1921, copy.
[37] *Gazette* and *Star*, December 3, 1921.
[38] *Star*, December 2, 1921.
[39] *Ibid.*, December 5, 1921.
[40] Meighen Papers, Stewart to Meighen, December 2, 1921, telegram.

witness, I suppose he was, by the name of Rowat. They took us to Kelley's office and the scene there was really absurd beyond words. Kelley and Carman cut a sorry figure and looked the part. They asked me what questions I had to ask and I said "None; I was there to be presented with those proofs." After a lot of stupid stammering Kelley pulled out a key and got a sealed envelope from a vault containing letters that I had already seen and that referred only to the retirement of a few officials. Not a word even contemplating or suggesting the removal of one man out of Montreal. I took a record of them, told them there was no evidence there that would impress a child out of the cradle. Kelley admitted there had never been a suggestion to move anybody from Montreal. Lord Atholstan was quite debonnair but the others looked the part of convicted humbugs. I had the satisfaction of telling them that the entire episode was the most despicable conduct I had ever known in my life. This they took without rebuke as well as other sentences of an equally flattering character.[41]

The letters referred to had passed between Flavelle and Kelley and concerned the pending retirement of four Grand Trunk Vice-Presidents, who Flavelle proposed should not be replaced in the interest of economy and in view of the approaching amalgamation of all Government railways.[42] Nothing in them, as Meighen told Carman, "bore the remotest relation to the allegations, which by way of super-structure your newspaper built up through successive issues just prior to the election, upon the slender and purposely fashioned foundation of an Ottawa 'despatch.' . . . Indeed nothing referred to in the correspondence affected Montreal as a City, any more than it affected Honolulu."[43] In this opinion *The Gazette* concurred.[44] Its proprietors had little love for Meighen and still less for his railway policy but they did operate a newspaper and not a sheet whose news columns could be brazenly prostituted for an immediate political advantage.

The Star, in commenting on the disastrous defeat of the Conservatives, summed it up by saying, "This time the railway interests distrusted and feared them. This time, British sentiment was not enlisted in their favor. This time there was no reason why industry should dread a Liberal victory with Sir Lomer Gouin and his stalwart Protectionists at headquarters. . . . The cure is to get back to Conservative principles."[45] A few weeks later it had decided that the Conservative party had not been defeated because, "THERE WAS NO CONSERVATIVE PARTY IN THE LAST CAMPAIGN . . . . only by giving proof of its sincerity of purpose can . . . a party win respect and only under leaders of discern-

---

[41] *Ibid.,* Meighen to Calder, December 13, 1921.

[42] The entire correspondence and a laboured defence of *The Star's* conduct in the affair was printed in its issue of December 14, 1921.

[43] Meighen Papers, Meighen to Carman, December 15, 1921.

[44] *Gazette,* December 15, 1921.

[45] *Star,* December 7, 1921.

ment, faith and ability can it command success."[46] In the opinion of the Montreal tycoons Meighen, for all his transcendent ability as a parliamentarian, was not such a leader and in the interests of party and nation he must be made to give way for someone who was. As he settled down to play the new role of Opposition leader he was soon to learn that his troubles in Montreal had only begun.

----

[46] *Ibid.*, January 4, 1922.

27

H. H. Stevens and
R. B. Bennett, 1930–1934*

J. R. H. Wilbur

IN 1930 Mackenzie King was defeated at the polls and R. B. Bennett and the Conservatives were swept into office partly as a protest against King's inactivity in combatting the depression. These years and the conditions they witnessed had a profound impact on all Canadians from the Atlantic to the Pacific. The bitter frustrations forced many to reconsider the effectiveness of traditional approaches to political problems. Massive unemployment and the long bread lines spawned the C.C.F. and many more radical movements. There seemed to be a complete collapse of the traditional economic system and the practices of many large companies were a matter of great suspicion. These frustrationing problems had their effect on some members of the existing Conservative party who were distressed with the inability of the government to act effectively.

This article by J. R. H. Wilbur traces the relations between Premier Bennett and one of his senior cabinet colleagues, H. H. Stevens, Minister of Trade and Commerce. This is the first of two articles on Stevens and Bennett; the second is "H. H. Stevens and Reconstruction," *Canadian Historical Review*, 1964. Mr. Wilbur, formerly in the History Department at the University of New Brunswick, is now a freelance writer and broadcaster. He is continuing his writing on this period. His work has provided us with important insights into the nature of the Bennett response to the depression.

---

* *Canadian Historical Review*, XLIII (March, 1962), pp. 1–16.

WHEN THE CONSERVATIVE CABINET of R. B. Bennett was sworn in on August 10, 1930, one of its more experienced parliamentarians was the Minister of Trade and Commerce, H. H. Stevens. He had held cabinet posts in the two Meighen administrations of 1921 and 1926, and had played a leading role in the customs scandal of 1926 and the subsequent investigation. For nineteen years Stevens had been the Conservative member from Vancouver, and he was a logical choice to represent his province in the new government. At least Bennett must have thought so, for when Stevens suffered his first defeat in the 1930 election, Bennett soon found him a vacancy in East Kootenay.

During the first three years of the Bennett administration, Stevens appeared to be a loyal if unspectacular minister, but in 1934 he became something less than loyal, and an embarrassment both to Bennett and to several other cabinet ministers closely connected with large financial and business institutions. In January of that year, and again in October, Stevens tendered his resignation; the first one was quietly ignored, but the second was accepted amid a storm of publicity and rumour that did not die until after the Conservative defeat in 1935.

Stevens' defection from the cabinet and later from the Conservative party was not merely the action of a disgruntled politician. Nor should his final resignation be considered only in the light of Stevens' future political career, for it came at a time when Bennett desperately needed an issue to appeal to the depression-ridden voters. By launching the Price Spreads Inquiry of 1934, Stevens had provided the issue as well as much favourable publicity—favourable to the general public if not to the "powerful eastern urban interests" which had long been the backbone of the Conservative party.[1] Stevens' resignation split the party into two camps, and his departure, coupled with Bennett's indecision about his own retirement, did much to send the Conservatives into the political doldrums. For this reason, a closer study of Stevens' role in the Bennett government warrants more than passing academic interest.

When Bennett went out of his way to get Stevens into his cabinet, he must have felt sure of his man. He might well have. He had met Stevens in 1911 when both men began their parliamentary careers and they had also worked together in 1927 on the parliamentary inquiry into the customs scandal. However, although we have no evidence of it, Bennett

---

[1] According to Escott Reid, "the new government group was dominated by eastern, urban, creditor and capitalist interests to a greater degree than any previous government." See "Canadian Political Parties: A Study of the Economic and Racial Basis of Conservatism and Liberalism in 1930," *University of Toronto Studies in History and Economics: Contributions to Canadian Economics,* VI, 1933, 20.

may have had one slight misgiving about Harry Stevens. In October, 1929, Stevens had written to Bennett, now the party leader, indicating his intention of quitting politics at the end of the current session. He felt that his personal affairs had deteriorated after eighteen consecutive years in Ottawa, and he was determined to make his fortune.[2] In a second letter, a week later, Stevens gave another reason for his decision: certain other Conservative members, "whom we count along the front rank, while possessed of abundant wealth themselves, do not hesitate to cast aspersions upon me because I was unable to match them, dollar for dollar, in personal wealth."[3] He added that "none of them apparently have given me any credit for the sacrifices of my personal affairs in the interests of public duty."

Bennett replied that he understood and appreciated the situation. "I passed through it once myself, and instead of going into public life, I undertook to accumulate a competence."[4] Several others, soon to be Stevens' colleagues in the cabinet, had followed paths similar to Bennett's. They, too, had substantial competences. Sir George Perley, the senior cabinet minister in terms of service, had married the daughter of the Montreal financier, Sir Thomas White, and was himself a bank director and a railway executive. Arthur Meighen, the former Conservative leader, who remained in the cabinet until his Senate appointment in 1932, was closely connected with Toronto financial interests. Edgar Rhodes, who had resigned as premier of Nova Scotia to become the Minister first of Fisheries and later of Finance, was from a wealthy business family. The Minister of National Revenue, E. B. Ryckman, had retired as director of several Toronto companies before entering the cabinet. The Secretary of State, C. H. Cahan, was a St. James Street lawyer long associated with power projects and other major ventures. (One report has it that Cahan was "backed" by Lord Atholstan, owner of the *Montreal Star*,[5] a man once described by Meighen as "a political intriguer in a class by himself."[6]) As for Bennett, he had controlling interests in the E. B. Eddy Company just across the Ottawa river from the Parliament building that gave him a special entrée into eastern business circles. Only two of the senior cabinet ministers had no apparent connection with Ontario or Quebec commerce—Stevens and Dr. R. J. Manion of Port Arthur, the Minister of Railways and Canals. Any federal

---

[2] Public Archives of Canada, Stevens Papers, vol. 12, S. to R. B. Bennett, Oct. 31, 1929.

[3] *Ibid.*, Nov. 7, 1929.

[4] *Ibid.*, Bennett to S., Nov. 9, 1929.

[5] This is according to Harold Daly of Ottawa, a prominent Conservative supporter and one of the organizers of the 1930 election campaign.

[6] Quoted in W. R. Graham, "Meighen and the Montreal Tycoons: Railway Policy in the Election of 1921," Canadian Historical Association, *Report*, 1957, 73.

cabinet has its share of successful businessmen, but they seemed to be even more prominent in the Bennett administration.

Perley and Cahan were probably among those "casting aspersions" at Stevens in 1929. Their relations with him would hardly improve with the close contact of cabinet meetings, held against the backdrop of a deepening depression. This sensitiveness of Stevens toward more successful businessmen and the wealth they represented should be borne in mind as we turn to a brief study of his role as Minister of Trade and Commerce.

Many times during the first three years, it must have seemed to Stevens that Bennett had left him little to do. Furthermore, Stevens soon learned that he was not to speak out of turn. In October, 1930, after Bennett had completely dominated a special session of Parliament called to discuss unemployment, the official Canadian delegation left for London and the Imperial Conference. Stevens, one of three cabinet ministers accompanying Bennett, was the only one who did not head a committee. Shortly after they returned home, Stevens left to spend the Christmas vacation in Vancouver and to mend some political fences. After addressing a meeting at Fernie, he wired Bennett about the possibility of extending the freight rate subvention to railway coal used east of Kenora "as formerly considered by you. Would strongly urge this as useful solution to Crowsnest district problem."[7] Bennett was not pleased with this suggestion. "You have placed us all in a difficult and embarrassing position. Please leave Vancouver Christmas night. . . . Cabinet greatly distressed." More probably was said when Stevens got back to Ottawa, but there the matter ended. Stevens seemed to have learned his lesson.

During the next few months, he often went out of his way to answer opposition charges that Bennett was a one-man government. In May, 1931, Fernand Rinfret, one of the Liberal spokesmen, noted that a member of the Department of Trade and Commerce who had recently returned from a trade mission to China had reported directly to the prime minister. "I hope that in addition to [holding the Finance and External Affairs portfolios Bennett] has not taken a slice out of [Stevens'] department because I think he will prove to be a good minister, as good as may come from the ranks of his party."[8] Stevens was quick to reply: "I do not know of anyone I would rather have cooperating with me . . . than the present Prime Minister." Nevertheless, when it came to important trade legislation, Bennett rather than his minister usually did introduce it and answer Opposition questions. In fact, just a few moments before Rinfret's remarks, Bennett had introduced the Tariff Appointment Act to establish a Tariff Board. It was the same story in July, 1931, when Bennett introduced the Australian Trade Agreement. Several times throughout the

[7] Bonar Law–Bennett Library, University of New Brunswick, Bennett Papers, vol. 121, Stevens to R. B. B., Dec. 22, 1930.

[8] Canada, House of Commons, *Debates*, May 14, 1931, II, 1618.

session, Liberal members had asked Stevens if he knew when this agreement would be signed, but he had never given a definite answer. The Canadian trade picture was deteriorating so rapidly during the first two years of the Conservative administration that one might have expected the Prime Minister to play the dominant role in trade matters; still, the few items of good news might have been left for Stevens to announce.

In April, 1932, Stevens praised the conversion loan outlined in the budget, saying that it would mean "a progressive saving in interest of . . . ultimately around five or six million dollars a year. This is an achievement. It was successful largely because of the foresight and skill with which it was handled by the leader of this government."[9] Turning to his own field, Stevens declared that the solution to trade problems must be found in the co-operation of the nations of the world, and until that co-operation was achieved, Canada should "buy British."

Bennett expanded on this theme in July when he welcomed the delegates to the Imperial Economic Conference. Stevens' main role at this much heralded gathering was to chair the committee studying monetary and financial questions. This was one of the most important committees and for our purposes, it is significant to note that the Canadian point of view not only on this subject but on the depression generally was given by Bennett as Canadian spokesman before that committee. The Imperial Economic Conference was anything but a success, for it emphasized the wide gap between the economic policies of the United Kingdom and some of her dominions, especially Canada. It also brought reports of dissension among the Canadians themselves. Stevens was not involved. The rumours centred around C. H. Cahan, the Secretary of State. According to Professor A. R. M. Lower, Cahan threatened to resign when it appeared that Canada might make tariff concessions to help Britain's sick cotton industry. It was no secret that Cahan was closely associated with Montreal businessmen, many of whom were intimately connected with Canada's textile industry. "It is a fair deduction," writes Lower, "that the men behind the cotton mills, traditionally Conservatives, were reading the riot act to the Secretary of State."[10] Cahan did not resign, but the reports, however accurate, are worth remembering, for there seems to be a sequel that directly involved Stevens, Cahan, and the textile interests.

For the remainder of 1932 and well into 1933, Stevens was one of the most active public speakers for the Government. It seemed as if he had been given the main speaking chores while Bennett hunted for a solution to the depression in international conferences and meetings with heads of state. In April, 1933, Bennett went to Washington to discuss trade problems with the new American president, Franklin Roosevelt; he was accompanied only by his private secretary, R. K. Finlayson. Late in June,

---

[9] *Ibid.*, April 11, 1932, II, 1903.
[10] A. R. M. Lower, *Colony to Nation* (Toronto, 1947), 509–10.

Bennett was away again, this time to attend the World Economic Conference in London, and he returned overseas that same summer to sign the World Wheat Agreement.

At home, Stevens watched the Canadian economy slow to a crawl and heard first-hand accounts of local and national economic problems. In May, 1933, the House of Commons Select Standing Committee on Agriculture and Colonization tabled a report of its investigation into milk production and distribution and particularly into the spread of milk prices. The report noted that, unlike most other industries, the dairy firms were still making good profits while the milk producers "were not receiving an equitable share."[11] This prompted Stevens to suggest that it would be possible "without interfering with private rights, to direct and supervise the manufacture of our dairy products so that all our exportable surplus will be turned into by-products for the foreign markets."[12] Stevens did not want the Government to take over the dairy industry, but thought that "reasonable supervision should be provided." No reply was made in writing, probably because the Prime Minister was due to leave in a few days for London.

As autumn approached, Stevens began to hear of new economic hardships. On September 1, 1933, he and James Walsh, managing director of the Canadian Manufacturers' Association, drove to Lake Couchiching where Stevens had a speaking engagement. Walsh gave him a stark picture of "over two hundred small manufacturers being driven into bankruptcy by certain practices" of the buyers of large department and chain store organizations. "He appealed to me as Minister of Trade and Commerce to do something."[13] Stevens passed on this information to Bennett who decided that it was a provincial matter. A few days later, Stevens heard of sweatshop conditions in the clothing industry. His informant was Percy Sparks, a former Ottawa clothier and an important witness in the customs investigation of 1927. Once again, Stevens wrote to the Prime Minister, suggesting that "the fair wage officer of the labour department might be asked to investigate the conditions in some of those factories now working on government contracts."[14] Bennett did not make a written reply.

Late in October, Stevens got a closer look at the plight of Canadian farmers when he spoke at Winnipeg. As Minister of Trade and Commerce, he might have been expected to extol the virtues of the recent World Wheat Agreement. Stevens made only a brief reference to it, perhaps because he was aware that his audience included wheat farmers

[11] Canada, House of Commons, *Journals,* 1932–3, LXXI, 562.

[12] Stevens Papers, vol. 12, S. to Bennett, May 25, 1933.

[13] *Ibid.,* S. in recorded interview with Dr. W. K. Lamb, Dominion Archivist, held in Ottawa, July 25, 1955. Copy of interview in special volume, 153.

[14] *Ibid.,* vol. 12, S. to Bennett, Sept. 6, 1933.

who had seen prices drop from 78 cents a bushel in 1928 to 29 cents in 1932. And the western livestock farmer was faring no better, for the worst drought in thirty years had ruined most of the potential grazing land. In his speech, Stevens acknowledged all this in the dry terms of an accountant: "The trouble with agriculture is the existence of a very low level of commodity prices and a very high weight of debt obligations."[15] Higher prices for beef, butter, and eggs would, in Stevens' opinion, help to offset the low wheat prices. He concluded that "if private enterprise fails to find a solution, then the government may have to step in," even though the Government was not "the best qualified party to determine prices, in view of the constitutional restrictions." He thought a better solution would be to have the private producers get together and raise livestock prices themselves.

Among the many letters Stevens received after this speech was one from a Manitoba farmer, who enclosed an official receipt from the Winnipeg Stockyards for the sale of eleven head of pure-bred Shorthorns. It read: "$103.92 less shipping charges of 39.90, giving a net return of $64.02 or $5.82 per head."[16] Stevens' secretary added this comment: "Good dope on spread of poultry and cattle." A Vancouver man thought that it was "amazing to read in your speech" that the interest rate must be cut on mortgages "while Mr. Bennett, in his address to the Women's Canadian Club in Ottawa the same day, stated that he was for a sound dollar and that Canada will pay what she owes. This shows that there is a difference of opinion in the cabinet."[17]

Differences there probably were, but the Prime Minister saw nothing radical or dangerous in Stevens' public remarks over the past months. Just before leaving for the Christmas holidays, he asked Stevens to replace him in Toronto as the speaker at the national convention of Canadian boot and shoe manufacturers.

Several hundred delegates were present at the Royal York Hotel to hear Stevens speak on January 15, 1934, and a local radio hook-up gave him a much wider audience. From his opening remarks, it was clear that he planned to discuss more than the boot and shoe industry. Stevens accused the large retailers, especially the department and chain stores, of misusing their tremendous buying power by forcing manufacturers to give them major price concessions or lose the business.[18] This, in turn, resulted in sweatshop conditions among the workers. He declared his belief in private property rights and individual initiative but said: "I am getting to the point where I see that there must be action taken of some kind." He urged businessmen "to face the evils that have developed like a

15 *Winnipeg Free Press*, Oct. 20, 1933.
16 Stevens Papers, vol. 29, W. B. Cornack to S., Nov. 7, 1933.
17 *Ibid.*, W. Dick to S., Nov. 16, 1933.
18 Toronto *Globe*, Jan. 16, 1934.

canker. I warn them that unless they are destroyed, they will destroy the system." Without naming any firm, Stevens then gave examples of the pressure of the mass buyer on individual manufacturers and especially on the workers in the clothing trade. He blamed the large packing firms for paying farmers as little as 1½ cents a pound for beef which retailed at 19 cents. He was not against large businesses, but "I do object to such powerful organizations being used for the purpose of crushing or eliminating their individual competitors. . . ."

According to the *Globe's* account, "Those militant declarations came with machine-gun precision, but increasing salvos of applause met them with regimental accuracy and the entire gathering stood to its feet like one man as the speaker concluded." The reporter's military terminology was to prove prophetic, for Harry Stevens had fired the "opening gun" in his battle against big business.

His adversaries were quick to reply. Stevens' speech was headlined in next morning's *Globe*, but the story began not with his statements but with denials from R. Y. Eaton, president of the T. Eaton Company, and from C. L. Burton, president of the Robert Simpson Company. They wanted Stevens "to name the concerns misusing their power" and said that his allegations did not apply to their firms. In a third statement, also on page one, the chairman of the Ontario Minimum Wage Board denied having any knowledge of the charges of sweatshop conditions. To find out what Stevens had actually said, the *Globe's* readers had to turn to page fourteen. Reaction to Stevens' speech was not confined to newspaper denials. Even before he left his hotel to return to Ottawa, he had received a call from an Eaton company official. As Stevens explained it, "he took strong exception to my remarks and demanded the names of persons to whom I referred."[19] Stevens refused this request, but added that he was prepared "when the proper time comes" to give ample evidence.

On January 17, the Prime Minister returned to Ottawa from Calgary and was immediately confronted with a delegation from the T. Eaton Company, voicing strong complaints against Stevens. When the two met the next day, Bennett told Stevens that from the press reports he thought that the speech "went further in formulating policy, without reference to the head of the government or his colleagues than a minister should go under sound constitutional practices."[20] He requested Stevens to "desist from further utterances of this kind." Stevens refused and the next day sent Bennett his resignation from the cabinet.

In a long letter of explanation, Stevens said that the Toronto speech

---

[19] Stevens Papers, vol. 71, S. to Bennett, Jan. 19, 1934.

[20] *Ibid.*, vol. 31, Bennett to S., Oct. 27, 1934. This letter, written after Stevens' second and final resignation, contained Bennett's account of their conversation on Jan. 18, 1934.

had been the direct result of three delegations he had received two or three days before. One, representing the small millers, had given him "startling information regarding the effect of the ownership of chain bakeries by the large flour mills upon the smaller millers and independent retail bakers."[21] The second group had told him about sweatshop conditions existing in the clothing industry, while the third, representing the smaller meat packers, had referred "to the overpowering control and interests" the larger packers had in the livestock exchanges. "So impressed was I that I felt the time had arrived when I was bound to urge the attention of the businessmen of this country of the imperative necessity of resisting such unethical and unfair methods."

As explained by Stevens, it was all a matter of coincidence. He would have given a routine speech, similar to many he had delivered over the past three years, had it not been for these three delegations arriving just before the speech deadline. On the other hand, how can we explain this letter Stevens received from Warren K. Cook, a prominent Toronto clothing manufacturer, written two days after the Toronto speech? "You may remember that I predicted it would have a definite reaction so far as you were concerned personally and I cannot tell you in a letter the remarks I have heard from many sources. . . . Percy [Sparks] will tell you some of our various plans to heap coals on the fire."[22] This suggests that the speech had been carefully planned as the first step in a definite campaign. Stevens may have been taking a calculated risk that his resignation would not be accepted. After all, he had been the faithful cabinet minister for three long years, praising Bennett at every turn and echoing the Government cry that the depression would soon end. One speech out of line might well be forgiven.

It was. Bennett treated the resignation as if it had not been written, and what is more, agreed that the charges raised in the Toronto speech should be investigated. Stevens wanted a Royal Commission presided over by a judge, but Bennett decided to establish a Select Committee of the House of Commons with Stevens as its chairman. Two weeks later, the Prime Minister introduced a motion which would establish a Select Committee of eleven members "to inquire into and investigate the causes of the large spread between the prices received for commodities" and the prices paid by the consumer.[23] It would also study the system of distribution of farm and other natural products, as well as manufactured goods; examine labour conditions in industry, department and chain stores; look into relations between the flour-milling industry and the bakeries; and finally investigate livestock marketing.

Had Stevens succeeded in forcing Bennett to make this close study of

---

[21] *Ibid.*, vol. 71, S. to R. B. Bennett, Jan. 19, 1934.

[22] *Ibid.*, vol. 101, Warren K. Cook to S., Jan. 17, 1934.

[23] Canada, House of Commons, *Debates*, Feb. 2, 1934, I, 188.

private industry? Bennett was not the sort of person to yield under pressure, especially when applied by a member of his own cabinet. From his point of view, there were definite political advantages in having Stevens head such an investigation. It would indicate to the voters, as election time drew nearer, that the Conservatives were concerned about the welfare of the small businessman, the farmer, and the worker. It would also keep Stevens occupied. If he embarrassed the Government further, there was some consolation in the knowledge that the inquiry would end when Parliament prorogued in June or early in July.

We should not discount the possibility that Bennett himself had become more concerned about the effects of the depression. The day that Stevens submitted his resignation, the Prime Minister received a seventeen-page letter from W. D. Herridge, his brother-in-law and the Canadian ambassador in Washington. In Herridge's view, "the Canadian government should recognize that permanent changes in our social and economic structure have resulted over the past twenty years."[24] He agreed with the Government's policy of ignoring "the reckless and selfish demands which have been made upon it" for it had been imperative "that no action should be taken which would adversely affect the fulfilment of our foreign obligation." All that could be done "was to guide the ship as best we might through the storm." That storm was over; the United States was headed for recovery under its New Deal programme, and Canada could be, too, "if the government acted immediately. I would set up a committee of experts to gather all proposals and to conduct a preliminary examination of them." This was not Herridge's first letter in this vein, nor was it to be the last. They continued throughout the life of the Select Committee and culminated in Bennett's amazing New Deal broadcasts which burst upon the unsuspecting public in January, 1935, and died away soon after. It was probably due to Herridge's influence that Bennett did not interfere with Stevens' method of conducting the Price Spreads Inquiry. At times throughout the hearings, Stevens' emerging role as the defender of the little man must have seemed offensive and extreme to a Prime Minister who had been so successful as a financier and corporation lawyer. Some of his political associates urged Bennett to interfere. When Norman Sommerville of Toronto was suggested as counsel for the Select Committee, Arthur Meighen advised Bennett to veto his appointment because for many years Sommerville had been the counsel for the president of the Edmonton Stock Yards.[25] Yet Sommerville got the job. George Henry, the Conservative Premier of Ontario, complained to Bennett about one of the witnesses scheduled to appear before the committee, saying that "a man of this type who is definitely associated with the C.C.F. may use the information he gets for his own

[24] Bennett Papers, vol. F-244, W. D. Herridge to B., Jan. 16, 1934.
[25] *Ibid.*, vol. L-250-S, A. Meighen to B., Feb. 8, 1934.

purposes and not for the benefit of people generally, particularly ourselves."[26] The witness, Professor H. M. Cassidy of the University of
Toronto, later spent an entire day before the committee outlining the
results of a recent inquiry he and Professor Frank Scott of McGill had
made into labour conditions in the men's clothing industry. Their investigation, by the way, had been instigated by Warren Cook, in his capacity
as president of the Canadian Garment Manufacturers' Association.

It is not our intention to discuss the hearings of the Select Committee
on Price Spreads. It is perhaps enough to say that during the four months
of its life, Stevens made it clear that he intended to prove a case against
certain practices of the larger business firms, especially in the meat-
packing and merchandising fields. He directed the inquiry, selected the
witnesses, and scheduled the hearings. The press gave steady and often
prominent coverage, especially when Stevens had sharp exchanges with
Stanley McLean, president of Canada Packers, and with Gray Miller,
president of the Imperial Tobacco Company. In spite of the publicity,
Bennett could have allowed the inquiry to end when Parliament prorogued on July 5, 1934, although such a decision would have been
politically unwise. Instead, he agreed with the Committee's recommendation that the inquiry continue as a Royal Commission with Stevens as its
chairman.

The Commission was not scheduled to begin its hearings until October
29 but Stevens was unusually successful in keeping the subject before the
public. After directing the new secretary of the Commission, L. B.
Pearson, to call the members together for July 10, Stevens prepared a
speech on the Price Spreads Inquiry to be delivered on June 27 to the
Conservative Study Club. This was a group of forty Conservative members of Parliament who met occasionally while the House was in session
to hear speakers on current issues.

Stevens began his speech with a criticism of the many mergers that
had taken place over the past decade—criticisms he had often voiced
before. More specifically, he thought that "the bringing of the control of
the livestock industry into the hands of virtually one concern" was one
major reason for the distress in this industry.[27] After pointing out that
Canada Packers had had "their most prosperous years" from 1929 to 1934,
Stevens turned to what he called "The Story of Pat Burns." He claimed
that Dominion Securities of Toronto, which had refinanced this Calgary
packing firm, had used Burns's excellent reputation as a businessman to
get the public to invest. "Today the thing is practically a bankrupt concern." But "the classic one of all," according to Stevens, "was the Robert
Simpson Company." It had been "practically an ideal institution, profitable and well managed," until 1928 when Sir Joseph Flavelle, the major

---

[26] *Ibid.*, George Henry to B., Feb. 15, 1934.
[27] Stevens Papers, vol. 67, Study Club Speech, p. 12.

shareholder, headed a group to refinance the company. Among other things, a special type of stock was created so that the Simpson employees could participate. These employees "did not know that Sir Joseph Flavelle intended to back out of the company," after he had "extracted" several million dollars of his accumulated capital. Stevens declared that the bonds left in place of this capital "were not secured by the assets of the company." As a result, the firm had to raise the average mark-up on the cost of goods "to cover the added load of the overhead." This increase could not be passed on to the consumer, so pressure was applied on Simpson's suppliers to sell for less; sweatshop conditions resulted. In his concluding remarks, Stevens said that if real conservatism in politics was to survive, "it must get a new orientation of its views and fix them upon the well-being of the farmer" and the industrial worker. "The real health of the nation depends upon the success of these two groups."

Since Stevens' speech came near the end of the parliamentary session, a number of his colleagues were not present. At least a dozen wanted copies and Stevens told them that the speech would be distributed "as soon as it is cut down to a point where it can be properly handled." Except for a cover page and minor textual changes, the printed speech was the same. This was normal procedure, but most abnormal was Stevens' method of distribution. According to Chamberlain, a member of Stevens' staff who supervised the job, 3000 copies were to be printed and sent not only to interested Tory members, but to weekly newspaper editors as well.[28] Later, Stevens expressed surprise that so many were printed. "I had in mind only a few hundred."[29] The editing and mimeographing of the pamphlet form of the speech was done by James Muir of the Bureau of Statistics, who had been a member of the Parliamentary Press Gallery. He completed this work by the end of July, and sent all but six copies to Chamberlain. As Muir later explained it to Bennett: "in accordance with the usual practice carried on under arrangement with Mr. Stevens, I sent copies marked 'personal' to a few of his special friends who are editors of the daily newspapers in Canada, the general idea being to keep them in touch with the trend of events, but not for publication."[30]

Among the newspapers receiving copies of the pamphlet were the *Toronto Star,* the *Ottawa Citizen,* and the *Winnipeg Free Press*—all three strong Liberal supporters. The first two quoted briefly from the cover page, just enough to prompt C. L. Burton, the president of the Robert Simpson Company, to send a sharply worded telegram to the Prime Minister, threatening to sue for libel if publication was not withheld.

---

28 *Ibid.,* vol. 109, Major J. G. Parmelee, Deputy Minister of Trade and Commerce, to S., Aug. 10, 1934.

29 *Ibid.,* S. to J. G. Parmelee, Aug. 5, 1934.

30 Bennett Papers, vol. L-250-S, James Muir to B., Aug. 20, 1934.

After assuring him that every effort was being made to retrieve the six copies, Bennett began a frantic search for Stevens. He reached him at Winnipeg on his way to Vancouver. Stevens explained that he had arranged at his own expense to have the Study Club speech printed for distribution to club members "without thought of either giving [it] to the press or general circulation. Had no knowledge of the latter being done."[31] A short time later, Stevens learned from R. J. Manion that Burton might sue. Stevens was not worried. "He can serve me with his writ as soon as he likes."[32]

By August 7, 1934, the Stevens pamphlet was no longer just a cabinet affair. The *Winnipeg Free Press* published it in full, and, in an accompanying editorial entitled "The Pamphlet that was Suppressed," editor Dafoe declared that this was a public document "issued by a minister of the Crown for the furthering of the policies to which he is committed. . . . The glaring improprieties of Mr. Stevens' action . . . is not an argument against the publication of its contents, but instead a justification for publication."[33] No one sued the *Free Press;* Burton did not bring action against Stevens; and what is more surprising, Bennett did not request Stevens' resignation or replace him as chairman of the Royal Commission.

Two reasons may explain Bennett's decisions. On the one hand, he had more problems than Stevens and his pamphlet. Throughout most of July, the Prime Minister had been meeting with provincial government leaders over the growing problem of unemployment relief. Then on September 1, he was scheduled to sail for Europe to represent Canada at the Geneva meeting of the League of Nations. Among other things, he would leave behind him a miniature general election, for no less than five federal by-elections would be held in Ontario ridings on September 25. The other reason that may help to explain Bennett's actions is the fact that the pamphlet's publication created much publicity, most of it favourable to Stevens. A prominent Winnipeg Tory, John T. Haig, wrote Bennett that although it would have been better had the pamphlet not been published until the end of the investigation, Stevens deserved high praise for bringing out the facts.[34] One of Stevens' colleagues on the Royal Commission, W. W. Kennedy of Winnipeg, expressed his concern to Bennett over reports that Stevens would be replaced as Commission chairman. If that happened, "the commission might just as well fold up."[35] Still another letter, this one from W. D. Herridge in Washington, did not mention Stevens but it might as well have. Herridge urged Bennett to "declare for

31 Stevens Papers, vol. 109, S. in telegram to Bennett, Aug. 4, 1934.

32 Stevens Papers, S. to R. J. Manion, Aug. 5, 1934.

33 *Winnipeg Free Press,* Aug. 7, 1934.

34 Bennett Papers, vol. L-250-S, J. T. Haig to B., Aug. 9, 1934.

35 *Ibid.,* W. W. Kennedy to B., Aug. 21, 1934.

the new Toryism, for it means government in business [which] is the only fulcrum powerful enough to lift us from that wreck of capitalism which follows when demand falters and allows fast strengthening, unmanageable supply to over-run it. [The people] want action, and if government does not give it to them, action they will nevertheless have, and it will be action of their own making."[36]

It is impossible to estimate the influence these letters had on the Prime Minister, but Stevens became the chief Government spokesman in the by-election campaigns. His main opponent, W. L. M. King, emphasized the pamphlet episode practically every night for the next three weeks. Stevens frequently spoke in the same centres the night following the Liberal rally, but only one of his speeches was based on the pamphlet. It was given in Toronto in support of T. L. Church, the popular Tory candidate. This was the only riding the Conservatives won.

Three weeks later, Bennett returned to Canada and on October 25 held his first cabinet meeting. From the start, Stevens was the centre of attention. He was asked to state his views "in the light of complaints that had been made by those who claim to have been injured by misstatements contained in the pamphlet."[37] After a brief reply, Stevens was roundly criticized by C. H. Cahan. Bennett took no part in this exchange, and no other minister came to Stevens' defence. At length, he was asked to make a public apology to Sir Joseph Flavelle at the start of the Royal Commission hearings, scheduled to begin the next week. On this note, the meeting ended, to be resumed the following day. The Prime Minister emerged in an affable mood and chatted amiably with newsmen for fifteen minutes.[38]

Bennett's personal secretary, Miss Alice Millar, heard two versions of what happened next. "One is that Mr. Cahan gave information to the newspapers on what took place in the Council, stressing the request for an apology. When it was about to be published . . . Mr. Stevens became infuriated and sent in his resignation. The other story is that while discussing what took place in Council with one of his friends, [Stevens] overheard one of the press men say that the Cabinet Ministers were going to make him publicly apologize. This infuriated him and he sent in his resignation. I am also told on very excellent authority that if he had it to do over again today [two weeks later] he would not send in his resignation."[39] Bennett gave this version: "Greatly to our surprise, after a short discussion in Cabinet, he declined to come back, although the discussion

---

[36] *Ibid.*, vol. F-244, W. D. Herridge to B., Aug. 20, 1934.

[37] Stevens Papers, vol. 71, Bennett to S., Oct. 26, 1934. This letter was tabled in the House of Commons by C. H. Cahan on April 12, 1935. See House of Commons, *Debates*, April 12, 1935, III, 2671.

[38] William Marchington in Toronto *Globe*, Oct. 27, 1934.

[39] Bennett Papers, vol. L-250-S, Alice Millar to General J. S. Stewart, Nov. 9, 1934. Stewart was president of the Conservative Study Club.

was most amiable. I understand he did not expect his resignation to be accepted, but what else could we do when he had resigned twice in the same year."[40]

The writer could find no evidence to suggest that Bennett made Stevens resign from the cabinet and the chairmanship of the Royal Commission on Price Spreads. The many letters Stevens wrote at the time all named Cahan as the source for the press leakage. According to an account he gave to W. C. Pittfield of Montreal, who passed it on to Bennett, "his hand had been forced and realizing that certain elements in the cabinet were unfriendly to him, he decided that the only thing to do was to resign."[41] In all probability, these unfriendly elements and the "certain Conservative members" who had "cast aspersions" on Stevens in 1929 were one and the same.

Bennett's official acknowledgment of the resignations understandably made no mention of friction between Stevens and Cahan. Instead, it dwelt on Bennett's reasons for trying to suppress the pamphlet. It had been "fundamentally unsound" for Stevens to discuss publicly the proceedings of the inquiry before the final report.[42] Secondly, some of the statements were untrue. No doubt this referred to Sir Joseph Flavelle and the Robert Simpson Company. About a week before the eventful cabinet meeting, Bennett had received an unsigned memo describing Flavelle's relations with the company. It stated that Flavelle had had no knowledge of the plans for reorganization until "in common with the public, he saw the prospectus put out by Wood, Gundy, and Company."[43] A recent examination of the Flavelle Papers substantiates this.[44] It appears to be a case of an old man, without issue and in poor health, deciding to take his money out of a firm after an association of seventeen years.

Bennett's review of the affair, along with Stevens' letter of resignation, were published in the daily press, but one of Bennett's regular correspondents still blamed Cahan for the break. On November 4, 1934, R. A. Reid, a Toronto lawyer, wrote that he had information to indicate that the Prime Minister had been "grossly misled" by Cahan, who was described as the leader of a cabal formed "for the express purpose of injuring you personally . . . and to discredit your administration."[45] Reid had just learned that Cahan had been "laying plans since the preceding summer"

---

[40] *Ibid.*, B. to George Ferguson, Nov. 1, 1934.

[41] *Ibid.*, W. C. Pittfield to B., Jan. 2, 1935. (Pittfield was trying at this time to bring a reconciliation between Bennett and Stevens.)

[42] Stevens Papers, vol. 71, Bennett to S., Oct. 26, 1934.

[43] Bennett Papers, vol. L-250-S. (According to a letter Stevens wrote to B. on October 26, in which he referred to the cabinet meeting, this information was supplied to B. by C. L. Burton, president of the Robert Simpson Company.)

[44] This is the conclusion reached by Professor F. W. Gibson of Queen's University who has examined the Flavelle Papers.

[45] Bennett Papers, vol. F-114, R. A. Reid to B., Nov. 4, 1934.

to bring about a break between Bennett and Stevens. He thought it "a peculiar coincidence" that upon the eve of the investigation of "one of the greatest monopolies in Canada, namely the Dominion Textile Company, that this uproar and trouble in your cabinet takes place. The head and tail of that monopoly is Sir Charles Gordon, who is also president of the Bank of Montreal, for which institution Mr. Cahan and his law firm have been chief counsel and legal advisers for over twenty-five years."

Bennett discounted this thesis entirely, but there is considerable evidence to support it. During the summer of 1934, Stevens began a preliminary study of the textile industry, even though this was outside his terms of reference. Lengthy questionnaires were sent to all textile firms, and Sir Charles Gordon, as president of Dominion Textiles, wrote Bennett, saying that it would be impossible to complete the forms by the August 23 deadline. "I understand, however, that they are willing to grant a delay. . . . In the meantime, we will wait until we hear from you before going any further."[46] Whether Bennett did reply we do not know. When the inquiry resumed as a Royal Commission, Stevens' successor as chairman, W. W. Kennedy, asked Bennett to expand the terms of reference to include a textile investigation. Bennett agreed, but the subsequent textile hearing dealt mainly with the evidence of several garment workers dismissed for taking part in a strike. The Dominion Textile Company was rarely mentioned.

Stevens' name continued to occupy the front pages. At first, there was an effort to heal the breach between Bennett and his former minister, but by May, 1935, Stevens had all but talked himself out of the party. In July, he announced the formation of the Reconstruction party; the battle lines were joined. In the 1935 election, the Stevens movement had no chance, but neither had the Conservative party, torn as it was by internal dissension[47] and led by a man who refused to retire because it would have meant Stevens' succession.[48] If Stevens had assumed Bennett's mantle, the Conservative party might have fared better over the next two decades. It could scarcely have fared worse.

---

[46] *Ibid.*, vol. L-250-S, Sir Charles Gordon to B., Aug. 16, 1934.

[47] Eight of the eighteen members of the Bennett cabinet retired from active politics before the 1935 election. Of those who did run, only Bennett and four others were re-elected. Many private members of the party agreed with Stevens, but few joined him.

[48] In 1938, Bennett wrote to Lord Beaverbrook that he had intended to retire in 1935 "but Stevens' action prevented that and I had to remain." Cited in Lord Beaverbrook, *Friends* (London, 1959), 89.

28

The Great Debate of the 1930's: General Retrospect*

Arthur R. M. Lower

"WHEN CANADA became a police state," writes Professor A. R. M. Lower concerning that awesome autumn of 1939, "very few people knew what had happened." Yet writing about Canadians in the months leading up to September, 1939, he says, "Substantially what was happening was a slow gathering of courage and the re-emergence in something like their old form of the ancestral instincts, but this time with a considerable infusion of rationalism." Together these statements point up the incisiveness and still the enigma that is Professor Lower and that is, perhaps, the Canadian people whom he has so deeply loved and so bitterly and repeatedly chastised. In the following passages from one of his smaller books, the great prolific doyen of the liberal-nationalist historians deals with what he has always regarded "as the fundamental question in Canadian life": "where did loyalty lie for a Canadian?" According to Lower it was in the 1930s, during the depression, as Europe and hence the world slipped again toward massive bloodletting that Canadians finally engaged in "the Great Debate" over the basics of Canada's position. The national spirit was reinforced; the former colonial community was finally becoming a nation.

Yet the awareness of the date of the author's writing (1952), at the peak of liberal optimism about Canada's future, during the golden age of Canada's role in the United Nations and the world generally, repeatedly intrudes itself upon the reader. How disturbing today is the assertion that now Canada had "committed herself irrevocably to the western world against Russia" without "serious questioning" and that such questioning

* Portions of Chapters 13, 14, and 15 of *Canada: Nation and Neighbour* (Toronto: Ryerson Press, 1952), pp. 157–166, 178–182.

could only come "when the wisdom of the principal ally, the United States, came into question." Perhaps in some sense "loyalty" is still the great issue in Canada, but if it is, it is expressed in terms ever so different from those of the '30s and described in ways hardly imagined during the early '50s when complacency and near-consensus were ironically combined with the terror and certainty of the Cold War. Nevertheless, the Great Debate was real and important. Professor Lower writes both as a most active and committed participant and as a great historian reviewing and analysing it for both Canadians and Americans.

T HE GREAT DEPRESSION of the 1930's, bringing in its train the rise of Hitlerism and the grave weakening of British and French power, had almost as cataclysmic consequences as the World Wars themselves. It laid its finger of blight on Canada, as on most other countries, but while it provided the soil for a Canadian Communist party of some influence, it did not bring the country within serious range of civil disturbance. The normal Canadian mode of settlement for both internal and external problems—debate—continued to work reasonably well.

The decade of the 1930's could, in fact, appropriately be called "The Decade of the Great Debate," for it was during this eventful ten years that the fundamentals of Canada's position at last came in for thorough examination. A period which witnessed the rise of Hitlerism, the reversal of the verdict reached in the Great War, the advance of Japan to domination in the western Pacific, the débacle of British finance, the bitter defeat of England and France by Germany at Munich, a period during which an uneasy peace gradually died, and the world was plunged in blood once more, such a period could hardly pass over the heads of even so far-withdrawn a people as the Canadians without notice or comment. As it was, a rising nation, confronted by these great exterior threats to the familiar world in which it had been cradled, could hardly act otherwise than turn to an examination of the fundamentals of its life. How far into Canadian society, the debate carried, it is hard to say. It embraced virtually all the experts, and also many people who were not experts but simply intelligent and concerned. And when the storm signals of war began to stream out again, as they did from 1935 or 1936, more and more of the general populace were drawn in.

The precipitants of the debate were two: the first, the depression itself, and the second, the disturbances in Asia provoked by Japan, which necessitated the definition of Canadian attitudes towards Japan's conduct and towards collective action. But since, in the midst of great excitements, one subject is intertwined with another, it was not long before the topic of topics was projected into the forum: Canada's relations with

Great Britain. This subject has always been heavily charged with emotion in English Canada and those who have dared to deviate from orthodox attitudes have been made to pay heavily for their temerity. In the 1930's there were more deviationists, and bolder, than at any previous time in Canada's history. The debate eventually, therefore, became one upon the simple theme loyalty: where did loyalty lie for a Canadian? To Canada, or to Great Britain? This was (and perhaps still is) the fundamental question in Canadian life, as it is, indeed, the fundamental question in all politics.

It was during the Prime Ministership of R. B. Bennett that Japan in going into Manchuria forced upon the League of Nations a problem of first class importance, one involving the possible coercion of a Great Power. Both in the Manchurian crisis and in the Abyssinian crisis three years later, Canada's attitude at Geneva reflected little credit upon her. In both crises the representative on the spot was left virtually without instructions and had to improvise a policy and, in each case, his action was afterward disavowed by his government. It is impossible to resist the impression, as one reads the histories of these incidents, that the Canadian government was either not much interested in them (presumably because in this it reflected the Canadian people) or that alternatively, its diplomacy was extremely gauche. Canada at these times must have appeared in foreign eyes as the national backwoodsman that most of its people in their psychology, if not their actual mode of life, still were.

The Canadian representative to the League Assembly of the summer of 1932 was Hon. C. H. Cahan. Mr. Cahan stayed over for the special Assembly which was to meet December 5, 1932, to discuss the Lytton Report on Japanese conduct in Manchuria. In his own words, he "had had two months in which to study the questions involved." He came to the conclusion that the United States would not intervene by force against Japan and that if Great Britain did, she would soon lose everything she had, down as far as Singapore. This latter conclusion was based on the confidential Admiralty reports. In a letter to the writer, dated February 24, 1941, Mr. Cahan went on to say: ". . . In view of Canada's geographical situation, it was deemed advisable (he does not say by whom) that the representative of Canada should address the Special Assembly . . . I prepared my speech in writing and submitted it to the highest official of the British Foreign Office at Geneva, who returned it "approved." I did this that I might not unwittingly say anything that would preclude the closest co-operation between Canada and Great Britain. The time for the exercise of moral influence and expressions of "moral indignation" were (*sic*) then passed. We were face to face with the possibility and even the probability of war in the East should Great Britain intervene by force; and there was no available protection for ships conveying British or Canadian troops to police Manchukuo, as suggested in the Lytton Report. I have never seen any good reason for regretting that address. It was highly approved by eminent British and European statesmen, though grossly misrepresented at the time in the American and Canadian press . . ."

The address to which Mr. Cahan referred was one in which he pointed out the impossibility of interference, but chided Japan for her conduct. Mr. Cahan was right about its misrepresentation, though, under the circumstances, misrepresentation was not unnatural. The incident is crucial in our understanding of the whole Canadian attitude of the time.

Canadians had fought the First World War as a great crusade against despotism, tyranny, illegal aggression, and so on. Not one English-speaking Canadian in a million had taken any other attitude: in fact virtually the only exception had been J. S. Ewart, and he, too, had apparently been silent in the first three years of the war. The result was greatly to re-inforce the normal Puritan tendency of English Canadians to think of all foreign adventures as crusades for righteousness.

After the Great War, the League seemed to many of them, a nice, neat solution of the conflict between their urge to crusading and their urge to a peaceful domestic existence, for wrong-doers could simply be brought up before it, judged, and, if necessary, punished. It would be just like the way the courts worked at home. When the Japanese began to meddle in Chinese affairs and eventually clipped off the whole of Manchuria, the tendency of most Canadians was simply to say: this is burglary and the burglar must be arrested and punished. Consequently when Mr. Cahan, representing Canada, got up at Geneva and made a realistic speech about what should and should not be done with Japan (chiefly what should not and could not), the average man back home was first, puzzled, then ashamed, then angered. Here was the cause of the misrepresentation of which Mr. Cahan complained: Canadians had had their first brush with *realpolitik,* and they did not like it.

Incidentally there is nothing in what Mr. Cahan said at the time, nor in his private letters to the writer, to indicate that the content of his speech had been carefully considered by the government of which he was a member and which was eventually to disclaim responsibility for what he had said. In fact the writer possesses a letter from an official in a position to know, which states that "he went to Geneva without any particular instructions." A government and people which allows its attitude to be defined before the world by one minister may not unfairly be accused of what may be called political backwoodsmanship.

The result of the Manchurian crisis in Canada was to unleash the floodgates of talk, in the course of which various "schools" or segments of opinion became discernible. These rested primarily upon the traditional attitudes of the historic parties, but the existence of the League and Canada's place in a collective system complicated the otherwise relatively simple party-cum-emotion pattern.

The old Tory type, as has been said, had been caught off-guard by internationalism and took some years to recover its bearings. Left to himself the "true blue" would simply have quoted Tennyson—"Theirs but to do or die" and have fallen in at the word of command from Great Britain without concerning himself about complex international issues. The records of the 1930's are full of such sentiments.[1] But Mr. Meighen, one of the great men of Toryism, was not only a vocal, he was even an ardent, advocate of collectivism and the League way. He was not alone, though collectivist Conservatives were never overly common.

The Imperial Economic Conference of 1932, which assembled at Ottawa, thanks largely to the efforts of Prime Minister Bennett, had been intended by that gentleman not only to be an attempt to pull the British Empire together economically, but also to rekindle the old fires of British unity. Since it quickly became apparent at the Conference that the Imperial piety of Canadian manufacturers and other interested parties stopped at the point where their economic interests began to be affected, little progress could be made in economic bargaining. The Conference did not quite break up, but it has never been suggested that the British went home with a good taste in their mouths. It was too similar to the little difficulty over a small sum of borrowed money between two friends. The one who had borrowed it felt sure that he had paid it back, the other protested he had not. "And, after all," said he, as the first one, to keep his name in the clear, handed over what he was sure was a second ten dollars, "what's ten dollars between friends?"

Certain Canadians at Ottawa openly gloated at the British "defeat." This was hardly the way to re-cement the ties of Empire. For old-line Conservatives, consequently, the Imperial Economic Conference misfired, delaying the rally until the verge of war. At that time, in 1938 and 1939, right wing traditional sentiments revived, as it were, "with a bang," and in the hysteria of the first few days of war, there was talk from Toronto, if Prime Minister King did not act decisively, of some kind of wild march on Ottawa.

Next to traditional imperialistic and fighting Toryism stood the vast mass of Conservatives, the ordinary people of the small towns and villages, of the countryside, who in their hundreds of thousands, especially in New Brunswick, Ontario and British Columbia, shared a simple traditional faith, and when the hour of danger came would rally to it, men who scarcely had thought of their political position at all, which came to them as naturally as their religion, and their language, resting as easily in the traditions of their race and crown as a fish in the sea.

· And next to this vast mass were people who might belong either to Liberal or Conservative parties but who in reality were what might be called political empiricists—men who were not mere waiters on event, but whose main convictions were that one should do what circumstances

---

[1] See Soward, *et al.*, *Canada in World Affairs* (Toronto, 1941), pp. 66 ff.

permitted—"politics is the art of the possible"—and who do not seem to have been passionately attached to any one clear-cut political philosophy. There were probably far fewer of these on the Conservative side than the Liberal, and this has been one of the main reasons for the Conservatives having been out of power, with a five years' exception, since 1921. Easily the chief of the political empiricists was the man who made a record—in length of term—as Prime Minister, Mr. Mackenzie King. What Mr. King's inmost convictions were about the country of his birth, whose fortunes he was called on to shape, no one knows. He undoubtedly wished it well. He undoubtedly wished Great Britain well. He undoubtedly was a traditionalist. He undoubtedly was determined not to play second fiddle to any one in Great Britain—even if later on, he did talk about Canada being "at Britain's side." He undoubtedly believed with Pitt and Macdonald and every other successful politician that he "could save the country and no one else could." He undoubtedly was determined to stay in power. And when he died, his will showed how close to his heart Canada was, for did he not leave practically his entire estate to her public?

Liberalism in Canada has invariably had two wings, right and left. Right-wing Liberals, men of the school of Mr. W. S. Fielding or Mr. N. W. Rowell, have accepted most of the Conservative imperialist and royalist tradition, differing from Conservatives only in the less intense emotional quality, the more rational quality, in which they invested these subjects.

The left wing of Liberalism has always been farther in emotional detachment from Great Britain, apt to apply the touchstone of expediency and utility to the British connection and to the Crown. Men of this school are easily recognized political descendents of 18th century Whigs. As time wore on, a transfer of loyalties began to take place within this left wing of Liberalism and those who formerly had had their centre in Great Britain began to move it to Canada. As we have seen, the *Canada First* movement represented this attitude in the 1870's and Edward Blake was its uncertain prophet, a man who could not quite tear himself away from right wing Liberalism to go over to left, and consequently fell between two stools.

Insofar as external relations went, most French-speaking Liberals of the 1930's would have been comprehended within this group. French-speaking Liberals were all men whose centre was in Canada and whose loyalties towards Great Britain did not go beyond respectful deference. Among English-Canadians, the number of such men in the 1930's, men with hard, clear minds, was relatively small, if their impact was large. Ewart had been one of them, J. W. Dafoe was another, and others still were to be found in the law and the academic world. They represented the cutting edge of Liberalism. Such men, looking at the morass of world politics either decided that the only way out was a hard-headed collectivism—a virtual alliance with power to impose its will—or an equally hard-headed nationalism, which would play its cards in its own carefully thought-out interest and because no other country's interest, not even Great Britain's, could be Canada's.

Next to left-wing Liberals, in the political spectrum, and close to them, stood many in the various socialistic groups which in the 1930's were coalescing into the C.C.F. party. Persons in this category were both nationalist and internationalist in their outlook, like those in the previous group: they wished to see Canada get rid of the last trappings of colonialism, but there was nothing jingoistic in their outlook, for it was only as the country ceased to be a colony that it could effectively take its place among other nations, make its voice heard for peace and organize itself socially. The main difference between "Co-operative Commonwealth" intellectuals and left-wing Liberals was simply in the stress the former placed upon social reconstruction; the Liberals were possibly rather harder-hearted, and a little harder-minded, than the socialists, not quite so idealistic, more intent on nationalism as involving independence than on nationalism as an opportunity for service. One has only to contrast the parliamentary careers of Liberal Nationalists like Joseph Thorson with C.C.F. nationalists like Stanley Knowles to see these differences, or the non-parliamentary careers of men like J. B. Coyne of Winnipeg (now Mr. Justice Coyne) and Professor Frank Scott of McGill.

It used to be the fashion in the 1930's easily to classify most Canadians into "Imperialists" (or sometimes "interventionists"), "Collectivists" and "Isolationists." This classification was always too simple. "Isolationists" in English Canada were rare: most English Canadian nationalists were quite ready to see Canada play her part upon the world's stage, but not in a mere subordinate and helpless role: they were "isolationist" only in that they were unwilling to be dragged at the heels of British policy, especially during a period when British ministries were going from incompetence to catastrophe (or from Baldwin to Chamberlain).

In French Canada, on the other hand, most people were "isolationist" in some sense or other, for few were the French-speaking Canadians who did not wish to keep out of the troubles beyond their gates and few were those who had much emotional association with any part of Europe (except the Papacy). French Canada should never be compared with English Canada but with the United States—a North American community which, by the accidents of history, has turned its back upon the old world. But the United States is a great power, French Canada a small Province. Hence French Canada to this day feels little of the responsibility for the world's fate which now sits squarely on American shoulders. French-speaking Canadians have, therefore, been consistently "isolationist," or if willing to take part in military forays into Europe, anxious to keep them down to the lowest possible terms. Unlike English Canadians, they have not been charged with that acute sense of mission which marks the Protestant Evangelical and consequently if the world is out of joint, do not feel that it is their peremptory duty to set it right. Both as non-"Britishers" and as Catholics, they have deviated sharply in their attitude towards the outside world from their Protestant brethren, and the deviation forms one of the major problems of Canadian politics.[2]

The classification of groups of opinion during the divisive decade of the 1930's could go on indefinitely, for each of the main groups subdivided into many sub-groups. Nationalists, for example, include political realists at one end (again, Joseph Thorson might be named) and rather woolly nativists at the other. Socialism included the practical men like the second leader of the C.C.F., M. J. Coldwell, and the saints, like the first leader J. S. Woodsworth, who was a Canadian in every fibre and by religious conviction a pacifist. It included crusading, "interventionist" pacifists who would fight for peace with resolutions and sanctions but were unwilling to contemplate the armed strength which the logic of their position demanded. There is no end to shadings, and in the 1930's, nearly all of them managed to get some kind of public expression. The resultant clashing tide of opinion, which was to throw so much light on Canada's position in the world, may well be called the Great Debate. . . .

In 1936, the various alternatives for Canada in case war should break out in the Pacific between the United States and Japan had been examined by a Winnipeg Study Group of the C.I.I.A. In 1937, the national conference stressed the topic "Canada's Defence Policy." The two views of loyalty came out sharply. Was Canada merely a part of the Empire or was she an independent country taking her own decisions? In 1938, both in Institute meetings and many other places, the peril of war seemed close—a cold wind blew out of Czecho-Slovakia in the spring of 1938, with rumours of Hitler's troops all ready to strike, even as the Institute met in Ottawa and as Prime Minister King made one of his most important, if most evasive, foreign policy statements in parliament. Both the C.I.I.A. and the Canadian Institute of Politics chose this year, 1938, to debate the significant topic, Problems in Canadian Unity. This was also the period when the Rowell-Sirois Commission was conducting its grand inquest into the nature of the country's economy. The depression had shown up the weaknesses in the structure and the exposed position of the outlying regions. The great drought of the '30's had ravaged the countryside of the prairies as if an invading army had passed over it.[3] And now was added the possibility of another European blood-letting, with Canadian boys dying in the mud and blood of the trenches by their thousands.

War in 1938 would possibly have been more than the country could have stood, so many were the sectional interests opposed to each other, so

---

[2] There are today, 1952, signs that the gap is closing. For this reasons abound— see concluding chapter.

[3] Average wheat crop per acre for Saskatchewan in 1937: 2.7 bushels!

bitter the racial, so diverse the intellectual. On top of it all came the crashing victory of Hitler over Great Britain and France in the Munich negotiations of the fall of 1938, which stunned the average Canadian mind, reducing it apparently to passively waiting on events.

In reality what was going on was a gradual forming of resolution: there could be nothing unanimous about it of course, and finally it issued in a certain degree of compromise. Substantially what was happening was a slow gathering of courage and the re-emergence in something like their old form of the ancestral instincts, but this time with a considerable infusion of rationalism. Nothing could have been more effective in making up the Canadian mind than the half-mad voice of Hitler pouring out of the radio: few could understand what he said, all could understand what he meant.[4]

After the pre-war climax of Munich, events went in two directions. A statement signed by sixty representative English Canadians proclaiming Canada's right to make her own decision about peace or war was incorporated into a private bill by Mr. Joseph (later Justice) Thorson and presented for debate in the winter of 1939. Naturally it was talked out, but when war actually was declared by Great Britain on Germany, September 3, 1939, the Dominion of Canada remained at peace for a symbolical seven days until on September 10, it made its own declaration. The constitutional right of neutrality was thus asserted. Everyone knew it was merely symbolical at the time, but today, because of the changed power situation in the world, Canada's right to neutrality is at least as real as that of any other nation's.

Canada today (1952) has committed herself irrecoverably to the western world against Russia: every Canadian knows that and there is no serious questioning of the position: that would come only when the wisdom of the principal ally, the United States, came into question. Before the Second World War the wisdom of the principal ally, Great Britain, was in considerable doubt, at least to a not negligible number of informed people, and moreover, the feelings of a large section of Canada —French Canada—were against taking part in her wars. But Hitler's speeches, his victory at Munich, his further invasion of Czecho-Slovakia in the winter of 1939, all these evidences of things to come, were potent in reinvigorating the ancient feelings of English Canada and beating French Canada into acquiescence. Thus when the time came, a relatively

---

[4] The writer had a most vivid illustration of this. In September, 1938, driving from Ottawa to Montreal, he stopped at a service-station. The attendants were French-Canadian. A broadcast was blaring out into the open air—a little knot of men around the radio. It was the voice of Hitler. Not a man there, except the writer, understood anything of what was being said, and to a man they would have been against conscription, or even at that time against Canadian participation in a war. Yet nothing was clearer than that, scared by the shrieking voice, they were thoroughly aware of what the triumph of that voice would mean in the way of tyranny and madness.

united country could be swept into war. Towards this re-invigoration, the carefully timed and exquisitely managed visit of the King and Queen in the spring of 1939 greatly contributed.

Was the Great Debate, then, a mere intellectual exercise indulged in by those who could talk but had no influence on action?

How is the influence of talk, it may be asked, to be assessed? One of man's major distinctions from other animals is his ability to talk. "The pen is mightier than the sword," "Our echoes roll from soul to soul and grow forever and forever," etc. The Great Debate achieved its object because it had no specific object, except the clarification of a growing community's world position, and the reinforcing of the national spirit necessary to sustain such a community. When Canada was swept into a Second German War she at least went into it with her eyes wider open than in 1914, a little less as an act of colonial loyalty, a little more because she was becoming a national community with a will of its own.

In August, 1914, war burst on the world like a lion springing without warning out of the jungle: in September, 1939, the lion, before he eventually leapt, had long been roaring. People stood wearily again to arms. The war fever of the Canadian right had been mounting steadily and there was little possibility, even had there been the will or the desire, of keeping the country out of war. What happened was a symbolical compromise, a nod in the direction of nationalism signified by the delay of a week after the British declaration of war on Germany and then the separate Canadian declaration.

The week's neutrality was coincident with war preparations and the promulgation of a war-time constitution which suspended the traditional liberties. The War Measures Act, which had been sleeping in the statute book since 1919, was proclaimed, an act which constituted as complete a surrender of power by Parliament as well could be put into words. Under it, a ferocious set of "Defence of Canada Regulations" was promulgated. By these regulations and various others, less formal, which accompanied them, government acquired the arbitrary powers which Canadians had long been taught to reprobate when exercised by unregenerate Germans and Russians: the power of arbitrary arrest and imprisonment without trial, the power to punish with great severity virtually any exercise of freedom of speech, printing or assembly it thought expedient to punish, and a long list of minor powers. A set of regulations issued in mimeograph, apparently by the censorship authorities, was put out in such a hole-and-corner manner that few people really knew whether it was in force or not.

The Defence Regulations were drawn up by a committee of civil servants, though presumably inspected by the cabinet. Of this committee, it appears to have been the police members who pressed for the unqualified power of arbitrary arrest. It did not make much difference. Mr. Mackenzie King was no defender of Freedom, however ardently he may have loved her in theory, and as for the people of Canada few of them had gumption enough to know the difference between freedom and unfreedom: all the Communists and other aliens of the ilk had been "picked up" by the police and "put away," that was really what mattered. When Canada became a police state very few people knew what had happened.

However, it takes time and patience to break down the humane traditions drilled into a community, and luckily before they began to break down in Canada, enough people had become apprised of the situation to begin protests. It was lucky for Canada's liberties, though rather chilling to the crusading spirit, that the bizarre interlude of "the phony war" ensued. Mr. King's government had time to recover its nerves, and, thanks to pressure upon it, some provision was made to allay the worst rigours of arrest and imprisonment without trial.

When the German armies began that westward march which was to carry them to the English Channel—and almost across it—Canadian hearts began to beat in the old way. For both French and English Canada, voices called from the immemorial past, something deep and primitive woke up even in hearts which had believed themselves completely committed to North America. The tug of racial emotion outweighed the calculations of the intellect[5] and both peoples got ready to do their part in averting the hard stroke which, having destroyed France, seemed ready to descend on Great Britain. These harsh experiences of the lands overseas built a bridge of modest strength between the two peoples at home and, though the old distrust was to get possession of both of them before the war was over, Canada was not as badly split as she had been on the previous occasion.

---

[5] If a personal note may be interjected, the author can testify that this happened in his own case. Others confessed to similar experiences.

29

Canada and the Spanish Civil War*

Hugh MacLennan

THE 1930s were exciting years in Montreal with all its cosmopolitan strains and the bitterness bred by the depression. It spawned a wide variety of political organizations. Some of these such as the C.C.F. and the Union Nationale became directly involved in the party politics of Quebec or Canada. Other groups took their lead from ideological movements external to Canada.

The Spanish Civil War broke out in 1936 when a military junta attempted to overthrow the incumbent Republican government. Historically Canada had possessed few ties and exhibited little interest in Spanish affairs. Yet Canada sent over 1200 men to fight on the Republican side. They formed the famous Mackenzie-Papineau Battalion of the XV International Brigade. Dr. Norman Bethune, later famous for his work with the Communist forces in China, was one member. Many of these men were Canadian socialists who saw the Spanish war as a fight between two rival ideologies—socialism and fascism. With Hitler and Mussolini openly supporting General Franco and the Soviet Union backing the heterogeneous mixture which comprised the Republican forces, the Spanish Civil War was a preview to the Second World War.

In this section of the novel Dr. Jerome Martell, a brilliant young surgeon, is deeply involved in promoting the Republican cause in Montreal. He is an impulsive idealist who becomes obsessed with the war in Spain. Catherine is his wife; George Stewart, a close friend and teacher at a rural private school is the narrator.

---

* Excerpts from *The Watch that Ends the Night* (New York, 1961), pp. 206–7, 213, 226–33, 237–44.

CHAPTER ONE

THAT WINTER, increasingly after New Year, the atmosphere in the Martell household changed. Several times I noticed Catherine withdrawing herself. Often she made sharp, cutting remarks that surprised me. At the same time I noticed that Jerome talked with increasing obsession and violence about the political situation. I assumed that this was the sole source of disagreement between him and Catherine, and indeed I think it was the primary one. Catherine would not, and could not, be interested in politics even to the extent that I am interested in them now. She believed that Jerome's impetuosity caused him to be used by people unworthy of him, nor was she the only one who believed that. But this fixation of Jerome was real and sincere, and its very violence, oddly connected with his own violent history, undoubtedly had made him lonely with a wife who feared for him and for herself and for her daughter and dreaded where his impulsiveness might lead him. This was a time in which you were always meeting people who caught politics just as a person catches religion. It was probably the last time in this century when politics in our country will be evangelical, and if a man was once intensely religious, he was bound to be wide open to a mood like that of the Thirties. But why waste time explaining the pattern? It is obvious now, and dozens of books have been written about it. Less obvious have been some of the attendant passions that went along with this neo-religious faith. Passion has a way of spilling over into all aspects of the human mind and feelings. It is the most dangerous thing in the world whether it focuses itself on love, religion, reform, politics or art. Without it the world would die of dry rot. But though it creates it also destroys. Having seldom been its victim I have only pity for those who are, and I would be a hypocrite if I judged them by the standards you can safely apply to a man at peace with himself and his circumstances. . . .

"What's got into everyone these days I don't know. This damned Spanish War, you'd think it was happening here. All these meetings where the same people tell each other the same old things. What do they know about Spain? How the hell do they know whether what they say is true or not? At best they're guessing, at worst they're saying what they like to hear. Those Spanish War meetings are like revivals in a Methodist tent. What's Spain to a man like Jerome? He's never been there. That country's always been an impossible country. What's Spain to any of these people except an excuse for them to give free play to their neuroticism?" . . .

His voice changed. "But she doesn't understand the meaning of Spain and I can't make her see my side of it at all. If I didn't adore Kate—if I didn't worship her—" He turned away and then back again. "These people"—a sweep of his hand toward Montreal—"these people think I'm a Red because I want to help the Spanish Loyalists. My God, how stupid can they be! I'm not a revolutionary. I see a thing that has to be done— like tonight—and I do it. It gets damned lonely bucking the current all the time." His eyes stared into mine. "Have you the slightest idea how lucky you are, not being born with my temperament?"

Below us the city shimmered in its lights, around us the hospital was still. The sweet, gentle air of the April evening kept coming in.

Jerome, motionless and massive in the shadows, was silent for nearly a minute.

Then he said: "If I'd been raised like you and Kate maybe I wouldn't feel the way I do about all this. But do you know, George—it's always seemed to me an incredible privilege to belong to civilization."

I said nothing.

"You people take it for granted. I don't. One more big war and it can go so fast. A life can go so fast. And when it's gone?"

He lifted his hand and shrugged. A moment later she began talking again in a soft, gentle voice.

"In my work I often have to see old men die. They could live if—if they were younger. It's as simple as that. Old men are running our civilization now. Men like Rodgers. Well-meaning men, but old and tired. They want to be left in peace. They hope if they look the other way the tiger will eat somebody else." He hesitated. "I understand Kate better than she knows. I understand how hard it's been for her. With that heart of hers, of course she wants to be left in peace." Another pause. "But unless fascism is stopped in Spain, she won't be. There'll be a war we'll probably lose. I know that's what fascism is. It's not political at all, it's simply the organization of every murderous impulse in the human being."

He got up and I rose with him, and for a moment longer he brooded out over the city.

"George, I'm not clever. Maybe I'm wrong in this, but I really believe it. The old countries which gave us our civilization are tired of being civilized. But people like me, people born on the fringes, we really care. When I grew up in Halifax"—he turned and looked at me with a shy small smile—"do you know what I used to dream about? I used to dream of a city on top of a hill—Athens perhaps. It was white and it was beautiful, and it was a great privilege to enter it. I used to dream that if I worked hard all my life, and tried hard all my life, maybe some day I'd be allowed within its gates. And now I see the fascists besieging that city and a handful of Spanish peasants holding out inside. They're dying for lack of medical care. So what is my duty? Tell me that—what is my duty?"

CHAPTER TWO

In my years of work as a political commentator I have come to a conclusion which shocks some of my friends who think of politics as a rational occupation. I believe that most international crises are like gigantic mystery plays in which obscure and absolutely irrational passions are handled by politicians, and viewed by the public, in a form of ritual akin to primitive religious rites. Hardly anything anyone says or thinks in a time of political crisis is likely to be rational or a representation of the facts. The crisis is almost never about the outward things with which it professes to concern itself. Also no political crisis ever blows up quickly. It matures underground for years and months, the chemical ingredients are various and many. So it is within a nation, a human group or a city, and it often happens that the fulminate which fires the explosion is something nobody notices. We forget how in those days Spain was the stage on which a multitude of passions met. The big war which followed—very possibly because the powers refused to face what Spain meant—has made most of us forget what the very mention of the Spanish Civil War used to do to people's minds. It was the fulminate to so many conflicting fears and hopes that it caused explosions thousands of miles away from Madrid and Barcelona.

The night after Jerome operated on Shatwell's widow it caused an explosion in Montreal, and when it was over the newspapers pretended to be astonished that such an affair could happen in the city. But there was no reason why they should have been astonished, for the ingredients to make that particular explosion had been there for years.

My own part in the affair began quietly enough. Around noon the phone in my parents' flat rang and I discovered Arthur Lazenby on the other end of the line.

"I suppose you know tonight's the night when Jerome introduces this Spanish tank officer?" Arthur said. "Are you going?"

"I'd been thinking of it."

"Then let's eat some spaghetti first and go together."

Over our supper Lazenby talked with more excitement than I had ever heard from him. He looked lean, hungry and fanatical, something was on fire in him, but in a singular way he seemed happy and fulfilled. The successful, middle-aged Lazenby I know now has a dead face, but not the young one of that evening.

"There's going to be trouble tonight," he said over our coffee.

"What kind of trouble?"

"You remember that priest who stopped the Loyalist priest from speaking this winter?"

"I know who he is. Isn't that the time they had to hire a hotel suite and then the management was unable to get them out legally and turned out the lights to stop the meeting?"

"No, that was another meeting and another Spaniard. This priest orders his students to break up all meetings in favor of the Loyalists. He tells the priest-ridden fools the Loyalists are anti-Christ. You wait— there'll be trouble tonight."

The Mayor had evidently come to the same conclusion, for when we reached the hall we found police all over the place. They were stolidly good-natured in the way of most Montreal cops, but as we went in we had to pass between two men in plain clothes whose eyes were very sharp indeed.

"The R.C.M.P.," said Lazenby.

Inside the hall the atmosphere was electric because the communists had packed the house. There was a solid bloc of them in the middle, and they were ominously silent and disciplined. The hall filled up and there was no hint of trouble except for this unaccountable air of tension. Then half a dozen extra-large cops came in and posted themselves at the doors, where they stood impassively surveying the house.

Suddenly there was a loud, organized hissing and the cry: "The Cossacks!"

It sounded so foreign I was startled, and yet I should not have been. Most of the communists that night were Jewish; some had been born in Poland and Russia, and those who had not were the sons of parents who had emigrated to escape the pogroms. A considerable Jewish quarter had slowly emerged between the French and English sections of the city, and the depression had hit the Jews—at least in their minds—harder than it had hit any other racial group in the city.

I want to be clear about this. To me the Jews are the senior people of civilization and it annoys me that I am unable to say that some of my best friends are Jews without being accused of sneering at a people whose tradition I reverence. However, some of my best friends are, and one of them tells me that it is very easy for a Jew who leaves the synagogue, especially for one who left it in the 1930s, to become a communist. In Montreal quite a few had done this and had broken their parents' hearts, and the guilt they felt for having done so had made them all the more bitter. By no means all the communists in Montreal in those days were Jews, but I think it a fact that it was the Jews who provided the passion. Who could blame them? For they knew, while the French and English blocs did not, exactly what Hitler was preparing for all of us.

"The Cossacks!" the cry rang out again. "The Cossacks!"

When the platform party came out the hissing changed to applause, the applause to foot-stamping and the foot-stamping to cheers. The first man out looked like a middle-aged shoe-clerk, the second like a tallyman on the docks, the third was the Spanish tank officer and the fourth was Jerome. The Spaniard had a long scar down a swarthy cheek, he was lean and fanatic and as proud as a matador. The central bloc in the hall broke into the *Internationale* and looking down the aisle I saw the mild faces of a pair of Presbyterian ministers staring in surprise. The platform party stood at attention to the workers' hymn and all but Jerome raised their clenched fists. Then Jerome, seeing the others doing it, did the same. The hymn ended and silence fell with a crash.

The shoe-clerk in a toneless voice introduced Jerome as a great doctor, a great scientist, a great friend of the working class. He spoke as though Jerome was already a member of the Communist party, and as I listened I thought of what Jack Christopher had said about Jerome allowing himself to be used, and I felt cold and guilty. For that Jerome was being used now was obvious. The excitement of the crowd had worked on him. His own impetuosity, his own generous, reckless way of throwing himself into a moment and responding to the emotions of others—all this sucked him out of any restraint he might otherwise have had. He said things that night he would not have uttered had he kept his head. He sounded to an untrained ear more like a communist than the shoe-clerk had done, and at every point he made the crowd barked like dogs.

The Spaniard rose and for three-quarters of an hour he spoke in halting French all the more moving because of a certain grim naïveté in his manner and choice of words. He told us about horrors he had seen in Spain. He spoke of the murder of his parents by the fascists, of the hope the Spanish people had had before the Moors came in under Franco, and the passion of the Spanish war reached us even through the communist jargon he employed. He was arrogant, but in a way he was noble. I could not like him; I had the impression that if he ever achieved power he would be merciless. But he was obviously brave, he was fanatical, and he was literal. It was my impression that he had not been a communist for a long time and had become one only because the communists seemed to offer him hope. He ended his speech, raised his clenched fist and received a standing ovation. Then the central bloc, as though on a word of command, broke into the marching song of the German detachment of the International Brigade. It was called *Freiheit* and when they sang it in German it sounded like a Teutonic paean. They were still singing when the riot began.

The riot started with a ripe fruit which sailed over the heads of the crowd and squelched on the wall just behind Jerome's head. Jerome came to his feet with his bulldog jaw outthrust. Excited and stirred by the Spaniard, he had reverted to the primitive and if I ever saw a man thirsting for a fight it was Jerome at that moment. The Spaniard stood immobile and stately with folded arms, the shoe-clerk smirked and looked well pleased, but Jerome stepped forward to the edge of the platform and his very aspect was a challenge announcing that if there was anyone who wanted trouble, he was ready to oblige him. I turned and saw the black berets of French-Canadian students crowding in and the surge of the people in the back. Then I saw berets running down the central aisle toward the platform.

"The Cossacks have let the fascists in!" one of the communists screamed.

Fists began swinging and I heard French voices crying "*Sales Juifs*" while others responded with "*sauvage*," "fascist" and "peasoup." The flash bulbs of newspaper reporters began popping and a body of cops following the students down the aisle began to take control of the spectators. Three black berets climbed the platform and made for the speakers and Jerome, his eyes glittering, his body moving craftily despite his limp, slipped a punch and landed a solid right on a student's jaw. The student was knocked clean off the platform and disappeared and Jerome's eyes gleamed with joy. More students milled up and Jerome was in the center of a tangle of them, doing all right for himself, and then the police went up to the platform and began pulling the fighters apart.

"Let's get out of here!"

It was Lazenby talking and pointing to the cops with one hand and to a side door with another. He disappeared while I stood where I was, wondering what to do. By now the police had the riot under control and solid blue uniforms were marshalling the crowd from the center aisle to the side doors. I was pushed out in the mêlée and found myself next to Professor John David, who said excitedly that it was quite a night. In the street there were several paddy wagons, a crowd of loafers and about twenty cops, and everyone looked quiet and orderly except for one character who was being pushed by a pair of enormous cops into the back of a paddy wagon. His mouth was opening and closing very fast and I heard him scream that if they didn't let him go he would sue them for false arrest. The cops threw him in, closed the door on him and left him there.

I waited around thinking about Catherine and feeling shocked and rotten and wondering what to do. Now that the communists had made their demonstration, they were quiet and orderly. A few of them stood around, but most of them moved off singly or in small groups in an easterly direction. I saw no sign of Lazenby and forgot about him, and after a while I went to a cop and asked him what had happened to the platform party. He gave me a stolid look and did not answer. Then I walked around to the back of the building and saw a police automobile drawn up before the back door with one cop behind the wheel, and two more standing outside talking to a trio of students in black berets. I asked one of them in French what had happened to the platform party, but he did not answer. I waited about four minutes and then the door opened and they all came out: the shoe-clerk, the tallyman, the Spaniard and Jerome, and directly behind them was a woman I recognized as Norah Blackwell. Jerome had a mouse under his left eye and was laughing as though he had enjoyed himself. Norah came up to him and took his arm,

Jerome gave her a quick kiss, then all of them piled into the police car and were driven off. This happened in less than thirty seconds.

"What are you doing?" I asked the sergeant in French. "Arresting the speakers?"

He evidently thought I was a reporter, for he replied with courtesy.

"No, monsieur, we are protecting the speakers."

There was nothing more to see or do at this hall, so I walked away, and as I came around the corner I saw a familiar figure ahead of me, quickened my step and overtook Adam Blore.

"Were you at that goddamned meeting?" he asked me.

"I certainly was."

"Did you ever hear such crap in your life?" He let out a sneering laugh. "Well, was I right or wasn't I about Martell and that little Blackwell bitch? He's fallen for her like a tree in a swamp. Where are you going?"

"Home, I guess."

"I'm looking for a woman. There's nothing like a show like tonight's to serve as an aphrodisiac for some of these little puritan girls. Down on Dorchester Street it would cost me two bucks, but with them all I have to do is say I hate Franco . . ."

The following Monday morning, eating breakfast beside McNish in the Waterloo dining hall with my back to the admirals of the Red and my face to the admirals of the Blue, I learned from the morning paper that Saturday night's riot had outraged opinion in Montreal, and that the real cause of the outrage had not been the Spaniard, the students or the communists in the audience, but the presence of Jerome and the role he had played.

It is a curious city, Montreal, and in this story I keep returning to the fact that it is. Strangers never understand its inner nature, and immigrant families, even from other parts of Canada, can live here two generations without coming to know it in their bones. I am absolutely certain that Montreal is the subtlest and most intricate city in North America. With her history she could not have been otherwise and survived, for here the French, the Scotch and the English, over two centuries, have been divided on issues which ruin nations and civilizations, yet have contrived to live in outward harmony. This is no accident. They understand certain rules in their bones.

As a born Montrealer, I had been startled and shocked the night of Jerome's meeting even though I had gone to it in sympathy with its apparent aims. Now when I read the account of it in the Monday morning paper I trembled for Jerome and Catherine. This newspaper account could not possibly make a difference to the shoe-clerk, the tallyman or the mob which had shouted "Here come the Cossacks!" They were outsiders. But Jerome, no matter how much an outsider he might have felt himself to be, could not be dismissed as one because he was involved in the most respected institution the city has, the medical profession which has been great here since the days of Osler. By virtue of his position at the Beamis Memorial, Jerome had been at least half-way inside the Montreal Thing whether he wanted to be or not. Had he been a born Montrealer he would have realized what he had done, but he was not a born Montrealer and I was sure that even now he did not.

The press that morning had done something it seldom does here: it had featured a local riot. This I knew to be the result of a deliberate editorial decision to declare war on Jerome personally. Not only did they make a front page story of the riot; most of page three was covered with pictures of it, and the pictures made me feel cold all over. The caption under one of them was: "Dr. Martell Gives the Clenched Fist Salute." A lot of people at the meeting had given the clenched fist salute, and Jerome himself had given it too, but I remembered the instant when this particular picture was taken and the reason why Jerome's fist was up and clenched was that a rioter was making for him and he was making to hit the rioter on the jaw. In another picture the stage was a confusion of policemen, students and speakers, and in the middle of that mêlée was Jerome again. This picture was even more damning than the first, for there was something absolutely sordid and undignified about it. Jerome's eyes shone with the joy of battle, beside him the morose face of the Spanish tank officer looked sinister, and the last straw was Norah Blackwell. This picture, taken after I had left the hall, showed Norah clinging to Jerome's arm with a face rapt and staring at his. How she had got there I could not know, but I guessed she must have listened to the speeches from the wings and come out to stand by her hero when the fighting began.

Worse still was the story on the front page. It was under the by-line of a man called Irving Dublin, whom I knew to be a crypto-communist, and Dublin had worded his piece to make it appear to everyone that Jerome was not merely a humanitarian doctor with an interest in the Spanish Loyalists, but an actual member of the communist party. I realized that Dublin had done this deliberately in order still further to isolate Jerome and drive him all the way over into the arms of the communists.

I turned to the editorial page and found what I expected: a scandalized sermon asking how it was possible for a man with the educational advantages and public position of Dr. Martell to associate himself with such a disgraceful affair. And when I read all this I felt guilty and lacking, for I had known Montreal and I should have warned him of the danger he was entering. I should have listened to Jack Christopher, who also understood Montreal, and I should have recognized my own responsibility in even tacitly encouraging Jerome to behave as he did.

I had to wait a fortnight before I learned the details of the aftermath, for I was held at Waterloo on weekend duty. Every day I searched the papers, but they told me nothing. Their silence was also typical of the

Montreal technique in an affair of this sort: having fired their broadside the editors let the matter sleep. They printed a few letters expressing horror at Jerome's behavior, but none in support of him, and then they let the whole thing drop.

When I finally reached town, the first person I called was Jack Christopher, who was at home and asked me to drop around. Somehow the details of his story don't seem to matter, but here they are.

Dr. Rodgers, returning to the city from Detroit on the Monday morning after the riot, read about it while eating his breakfast on the train. It would be presumptuous of me to guess what the old man felt, but I can't believe that his feelings were simple. He may have felt a bitter pleasure because Jerome had finally delivered himself into his hands, but he came from an old Montreal family, he was the son of a judge, in his youth he had worked under Sir William Osler and he was a patrician by nature and training. It is impossible for me to believe that a man like Dr. Rodgers could ever have felt it necessary to prove his worth to Jerome or to anyone else in Canada. He was certainly outraged, and he may even have reproached himself for not having taken steps about Jerome long before.

But this is guess work; I never knew Dr. Rodgers and what I have is hearsay.

According to Jack Christopher, the old man did not reach the hospital until mid-morning, and by then Sir Rupert Irons, the chairman of the board, had twice called to speak to him. Rodgers knew what Irons wanted, and it was typical of him that even at this moment he ignored Irons' request that he get in touch with him the moment he arrived. In Rodgers' book a man like Irons, for all his wealth, was a parvenu. The old surgeon went to his office, read his correspondence, dictated a few letters and then made his customary rounds.

It was in the course of these that he discovered that on the night before the riot Jerome had operated on Mrs. Moffat. He at once consulted with Dr. Crawford, who had passed his kidney stone but was still resting in one of the hospital beds. After learning the details from Crawford, he returned to his office, read a report of the case and passed out the word that he would be pleased to see Dr. Martell at the Doctor's earliest convenience. As Jerome was then in the operating room, the two men did not meet until nearly noon.

With his capacity for sensing the hurt in another person, Jerome immediately understood that the old surgeon had been deeply humiliated by the Moffat case. What he had done or failed to do in the first operation I don't know, but it was obvious that he had slipped up somewhere.

Jerome, with the quick kindness which was the other side of his quick pugnacity, made the first move.

"Please don't concern yourself about this case," he said. "It's a thing that could have happened to anybody. I've had a thing like that happen to me once."

This remark, Jack told me, was the most unfortunate he could have made under the circumstances to an older and more experienced man.

The old doctor looked at the younger one, hated him, and said: "Since this case has been taken out of my hands, we will please not discuss it any further."

"But it's not been taken out of your hands." Jerome gave his gentlest and most sincere smile. "I just filled in because there was an emergency."

"We will not discuss it."

Then Dr. Rodgers picked up the morning paper, jogged it across the desk to Jerome and examined the younger man's face.

"Yes," Jerome said, "I've read it, too."

Rodgers continued to regard him, and Jerome, sensing implacable hostility, flared out.

"What I do outside the hospital is my own business, Dr. Rodgers. I don't happen to believe that the medical profession is a priesthood. That meeting was concerned with the most important subject in the world today. Look what happened in Germany. The men of science, the professors, the medical men—they were all so correctly professional they did nothing at all. They left what resistance there was to a handful of workers and unemployed. And now look what's happened to them."

The old man raised his eyebrows. "This is not Germany, this is Montreal. We have no Nazis here."

"No?"

"The name of this hospital, according to my count, appears five times in this morning's paper. I'm afraid that what you do in your spare time has a great deal of connection with this hospital."

"It wasn't us who started the riot." Suddenly Jerome began talking like a schoolboy. "It was a crowd of students duped by that fascist priest. It was a perfectly orderly meeting till they came in and started fighting."

After a moment's appraising silence, the old man put his finger down on the account of Jerome's speech.

"Did you actually say the things reported here?"

"I can't remember every word I said, but what's the matter with what's reported here? If you'd take your blinders off, you'd see it's true."

"You say it was an orderly meeting when you admit you made these statements? These are generalizations of the wildest kind. These are seditious accusations. These are statements no man of science should ever make anywhere. I shouldn't be surprised if they bring you within range of the courts."

Jerome looked at him and said: "Do you think you can stop fascism by closing your eyes and pretending it's not there?"

The old man looked back at him: "We will not argue, please. There have been quite enough generalizations. We will confine ourselves to some facts." His finger came down on one of the pictures. "Is it a fact that this young woman has been a nurse in this hospital?"

"Yes, she's Mrs. Blackwell."

"May I ask what she was doing in the middle of all this?"

"Isn't that her business?"

The old man leaned back in his chair and surveyed Jerome.

"What's come over you? You have often been rude and aggressive, but I put that down to your temperament and possibly to your background. You were a promising surgeon, and that was enough for me." A pause. "I have great respect for your wife and I have known her family for years." Another pause. "I am an old-fashioned man, as you have been heard to point out more than once in the corridors of this establishment, even to some of the housemen. I don't believe in washing dirty linen in public. I am even prepared to close my eyes to behavior I deplore so long as it does not expose the parties concerned to vulgar gossip. But"—again his finger came down on the photograph—"you have not only displayed your dirty linen in public, you have actually flaunted it in front of a newspaper camera." He stared at Jerome with his ascetic face, and Jerome flushed. "This particular sample of dirty linen, Dr. Martell, will no longer be associated with this hospital."

Jerome jumped to his feet: "Take that back, Dr. Rodgers."

The old man regarded him calmly and said: "No, I will not take it back. It was a considered statement. I will be even more explicit. I will inform you that Mrs. Blackwell has been discharged from the nursing staff of this hospital. She will probably find it very difficult to attach herself to the staff of any other."

"It's not her fault. You're unjust to her. She needs the job to live. She got mixed up in this riot the same way I did. What has she done wrong?"

The old man looked at Jerome and said: "I have received word that Sir Rupert Irons wishes me to get in touch with him immediately. I can guess what he wishes to talk about and what he will demand. So far I have not got in touch with him." A pause. "I am an old-fashioned man, Dr. Martell, as I have already mentioned. It is contrary to my principles that any hospital, school or university should have its policies and actions dictated by business men in any matter which lies outside a business man's competence." Another pause. "I dislike you, Doctor Martell, and for a reason which has not occurred to you. People like you place men of responsibility in an intolerable position. I have protected you for two years—not for your sake but for the sake of the principle. But you continue to make it intolerable for me. Moreover, you do this wilfully. You do it because you enjoy making trouble."

"That's absurd!" said Jerome.

"Is it? Please examine the situation more closely. If I discharge you from the staff, I will be vilified by you and by all your communist friends. You will say I am part of the capitalist conspiracy. You will say—and you will be right—that your work here has been satisfactory, and you will add that your private life is your own. But this propaganda"—again the finger tapped the newspaper—"aims at the destruction of the entire social order. Do you deny it?"

"Of course I deny it. Do you think—"

The old man waved his hand: "Medicine and science are sacred to me. They should be to you. No medical man or man of science ought to touch this—this vulgar filth."

Jerome sat in silence and after a while he said: "I will not vilify you if you demand my resignation. Instead I offer you my resignation. I'm sorry, for I was happy here. I think I did good work. I'm grateful for many things you've done for me. I never wanted to be your enemy, but you live in another world from mine, and I think mine is the real one."

The old man sat still, then shrugged: "We might have been friends. But as we are not friends, I will not shake hands with you now. I deplore your character and your behavior and your principles—or lack of them. As a surgeon you might have had a great career, but you will never have one now. I accept your resignation and I will inform the board it was given by you freely without my asking for it. You have ruined yourself."

30

Canadian Foreign Policy and the Whig Interpretation: 1936–1939*

K. W. McNaught

PROFESSOR MCNAUGHT is the author of *A Prophet in Politics: A Biography of J. S. Woodsworth* (Toronto, 1959). In this article, which appeared before the book, he criticizes the premise and rationale for Mackenzie King's approach to foreign affairs in the years immediately before World War II. In so doing he attacks the traditional whig historians who have extolled that approach. According to Ken McNaught, the man who claimed that Canada had no commitments and that he was preserving for Parliament the right to decide all matters of foreign relations was in fact the man who moved Canada some distance away from the historic parliamentary system in the direction of personal, plebiscitary executive rule. On the excuse of preserving or developing Canadian unity, King abandoned the League, passively supported appeasement of the dictators, and allowed matters to drift so that long before war actually came, Parliament had nothing to decide. Canada in effect had again become a colony of Britain.

Unlike the subject of his biography, Professor McNaught does not actually oppose Canada's early participation in World War II; he claims that even Woodsworth's C.C.F. had by 1937 accepted some participation. Instead he claims that Canadian unity would not have been strained by an open and frank discussion and enunciation of foreign and defence policy as Europe slipped again toward bloody conflagration. To do so would have been in keeping with Canada's post-Versailles position in the world and would in effect have matured rather than emasculated our parliamentary institutions.

The article therefore is part of the massive historiographic assault

* *Canadian Historical Association Report* (1957), pp. 43–54.

during our generation, from various points of view, on the role of the amorphous Liberal party during its 22 years of rule from 1935 to 1957 in promoting Canadian development and in facing and attempting to deal with Canada's basic problems.

THE POLITICAL UTILITY of history in Canada has been at least as obvious as it has been in other nations. Historical interpretation has frequently been used to justify past policies, to suggest present methods and even to define future purposes. Yet, curiously, this fact has received little attention. Professor Careless, in an illuminating article in 1954[1] undertook the difficult task of defining major schools of Canadian historical interpretation, and he produced an intriguing pattern. However, while he suggested some of the influences at work upon the writers of his four main schools, he did not stress any specific social or political influence of the opposing interpretations—other than an interaction amongst the historians themselves.

What have been the political effects of historical interpretation in Canada? Leaving aside French-Canadian historiography, where one need scarcely labour the point, they are observable in two phases. Prior to the first world war the writing of men like Kingsford, Parkin, Dent and Hannay worked chiefly to the advantage of the Conservatives—with their central themes of imperial unity and the struggles to keep Canada British in the face of American manifest destiny. After 1918 the old imperial theme was largely dropped. One might argue that from the 1920's the most effective function of Canadian historians has been the convincing of the majority of English-speaking Canadians of the validity of two major myths. The first myth is that Canada has enjoyed a steady, peaceful, constitutional evolution, as opposed to the violent, revolutionary and entirely undesirable development of Europe and the United States; that the only important revolutions to affect us were settled in England between 1660 and 1689, and in the United States in 1783. Thus, runs the first myth, Canadians can rest happily with the humdrum business of economic progress and mild assertions of national status. The second myth, proceeding logically enough from the first, is that Canada's greatest glory has been her ability to compromise. Murray and Carleton, Baldwin and Lafontaine, Macdonald and Cartier, Laurier and King, St. Laurent and Pearson are eulogized in this myth because of their compromising talents. The conclusion is that statesmanship in Canada, even more than

---

[1] J. M. S. Careless, "Frontierism, Metropolitanism, and Canadian History," *Canadian Historical Review*, XXXV (1), March 1954, 1–21.

elsewhere, must be displayed primarily in the ability to balance pressures—regional and racial, religious and economic.

Both of these myths are branches of the received, or whig interpretation of Canadian history. The first, that of peaceful, constitutional evolution is constructed by a consistent underplaying of the violence which actually has hovered close to the surface of our whole history: the 1837 rebellions were abortive and inconsequential compared to the Durham Report and the long paper war that followed it; the Riel rebellions have become affairs or incidents; the industrial warfare of the late nineteenth and early twentieth centuries has seemed scarcely worth the muck-raking effort to reveal it and has sunk comfortably out of view; the near civil war of 1917–1918, the Winnipeg strike, the prolonged industrial class war in Nova Scotia in the 1920's, and the series of engagements in the 1930's between provincial and federal police on the one hand and trade unionists or the unemployed on the other, merit scarcely a passing nod. By such an approach one can arrive at this whig formulation of the real theme of Canadian history:

Its essential drama does not lie in armed struggles in which the nation's destiny is at stake, or in political conflicts in which irreconcilable and contending forces press their quarrel to a decisive issue. It lies rather in the slow and tenacious advance from one step to another along the road to nationhood, the patient evolution of successive compromises in politics and government, the determined conquest of the physical obstacles to national economic development. In their very nature, few of Canada's crucial problems could be solved by violent methods. . . .[2]

The above is really a statement of the second myth: Canada's great achievement has been the avoidance of violent strife and of the diametric opposition of principles or policies. Thus, a compromise nationality is said to be the result. In the context of political utility this myth declares that those Canadians who oppose compromise and seek clear-cut enunciation of political and social purposes are un-Canadian, while those who adhere to compromise formulae and shun precise discussion of policy issues are essentially Canadian—and statesmen to boot.

Perhaps the argument can be summarized in another way—by paraphrasing in Canadian terms a well-known English statement of the underlying assumption of whig history:

It is part and parcel of the whig interpretation of history that it studies the past with reference to the present. Through this system of immediate reference to the present day, historical personage can easily and irresistably be classed into the men who furthered progress and the men who tried to hinder it. Working upon this system the whig historian can draw lines through certain events, some such line as that which leads through Robert Baldwin and a long succession of

---

[2] Edgar McInnis, *Canada, A Political and Social History* (Toronto, 1947) p. vii.

whigs to modern liberty. The total result of this method is to produce a scheme of general history which is bound to converge beautifully upon the present—all demonstrating throughout the ages the workings of an obvious principle of progress, of which Quebec and the Liberals have been the perennial allies while minority parties and tories have perpetually formed obstruction.[3]

The whig case is usually defended in the name of Canadian unity— which amounts to another version of the second, or compromise myth. Unity, as the central theme of Canadian history, and as the cardinal purpose of good policy, has been largely appropriated in the twentieth century by the Liberal party. Sir Wilfrid Laurier is reputed by his biographers, and by general historians discussing his career, to have made his most critical decisions in the light of this principle—and, indeed to have subordinated all other purposes to it. Where he is mainly criticized, it is not for holding to this purpose, but for alleged failure to achieve it. Certainly this was the interpretation of Laurier accepted by his successor in the leadership of the party. Mackenzie King, in fact, appropriated the principle of Canadian unity so comprehensively that *Le Canada* could write that he was the living incarnation of the principle. Even those historians, with a few notable exceptions, who are highly critical of specific aspects of the King governments end up in the apparently inevitable position of justifying all in the name of unity. Two quotations will serve to illustrate the point. Professor Lower, after a discussion of the divisions of opinion in Canada immediately preceding the second world war, concludes that, "Under the circumstances, the supreme task of statesmanship was to avoid enunciating a foreign policy."[4] Professor Mansergh, who has apparently imbibed from his chief Canadian sources the exported version of whiggery, arrives at much the same conclusion. King's policy, he writes, had "an air of indecision which misled even his friends, exasperated his opponents, and sowed doubts about his intentions in a wider world." But "the tribute can be paid his leadership that with a painstaking care that amounted almost to genius he fostered a unity of outlook which . . . brought a united people into a war against aggression on the side of Britain. . . ."[5]

Such is the generally accepted interpretation of Mackenzie King's foreign policy—at least on the basis of the interim reports. How does the same school interpret the opposition to King? The Government's chief thorn in the flesh in the area of pre-war external relations was J. S. Woodsworth, and here the pattern of interpretation is clear: Woodsworth was an impractical idealist heading toward, and perhaps even desiring

---

[3] With apologies to H. Butterfield, *The Whig Interpretation of History* (London, 1950), pp. 11–12.

[4] A.R.M. Lower, *Colony to Nation* (Toronto, 1946), p. 541.

[5] N. Mansergh, *Survey of British Commonwealth Affairs: Problems of External Policy*, 1931–1939 (Oxford, 1952), p. 136.

his inevitable martyrdom. Here are the phrases: "He was a kind of political saint."[6] Or, "It was the Munich crisis that revealed J. S. Woodsworth's dilemma most sharply . . . [while his colleagues in the C.C.F.] had been forced step by step to the conclusion that only collective military action by the rest of the world could stop the aggression."[7] And, more specifically, "Woodsworth's work had been in this world, his whole life of labour, poverty, and daily suffering had been devoted to the salvation of human beings here and now, and it had all been in vain."[8] Thus the whig interpretation argues that essentially King was right in helping to emasculate the League and in covertly endorsing Neville Chamberlain because he could thus avoid the issue of a Canadian foreign policy until *events* could coerce Canada, while Woodsworth was wrong in trying to force a declaration of policy from the Government and in finally refusing to vote for the address in September, 1939, because he thus threatened Canadian unity. Is this really a satisfactory interpretation of the years 1936–1939?

Perhaps the best way of answering the question is to define the main problems raised by the interpretation. They are, (1) Could Canadian unity have been maintained only by the King method? and, (2) Was unity preserved by implementing the doctrine of 'parliament will decide'? Let us attempt a selective examination of the period with these questions in mind.

In whig history these years represent the final statement of the supremacy of Parliament. And since all good whig history begins with the specific question of the relationship of the Crown to Parliament, let us begin with this problem, which in the Canadian case also involves external relations. In fact, the abdication crisis at the end of 1936 may be taken as a kind of symbol of the King method—because it is one of the subtlest, if most complete illustrations of what he meant by parliamentary decision.

In the United Kingdom, although Edward VIII signed the Instrument of Abdication on December 10, the action did not become final until the succession bill had been passed in Parliament and signed by the monarch on December 11. Throughout the critical period the British Prime Minister received Canada's views exclusively through Mr. King who was, of course, also Minister of External Affairs. Mr. King decided not to summon Parliament to express Canada's opinion in this matter (although this would have meant advancing the date by less than a month). Instead, with only an order-in-council as authority, he "requested and assented to" the British abdication and succession legislation. This action (as C. H. Cahan pointed out) had no Canadian statutory basis, and could only be justified by a very narrow interpretation of the British

[6] A.R.M. Lower, *op. cit.*, p. 513.
[7] Grace MacInnis, *A Man to Remember* (Toronto, 1953), pp. 244–246.
[8] Bruce Hutchison, *The Incredible Canadian* (Toronto, 1952), p. 255.

Statute of Westminster. Here King had, in effect, a choice between two procedures implied by the statute. He could follow that provided by the preamble which says that "any alteration in the law touching the Succession to the Throne or Royal Style and Titles shall hereafter require the assent as well of the Parliament of all the Dominions," in which case he would follow the United Kingdom example and obtain the prior consent of Parliament. Or, he could interpret the phrase "Dominion has requested and assented to," in section 4 of the statute, to mean that the Canadian cabinet could consent to a change in the succession, and obtain later endorsation by Parliament. It was, of course, the second procedure that King chose.

When the Canadian Parliament did assemble in January, 1937, the Government sought passage of an address of loyalty to George VI, and was at once criticized for its action by J. S. Woodsworth.[9] Woodsworth charged that the Prime Minister had usurped the powers of Parliament, that the loyalty address should not be passed until after the succession bill had been debated and passed, and that the oath of allegiance to George VI should not have been administered to the members. "Why," he asked, "should the Liberal party be in a position to decide who is to be King of the Canadian people?" Technically, he argued, if the Prime Minister could decide such matters as this, he could also declare war. Countering King's argument that there had been no time to call Parliament, Woodsworth said, "Surely if the King of the United Kingdom can be distinguished for legal purposes from the King of Canada, then the recognition of the King of the United Kingdom as King of Canada can wait until there is time to call parliament. If the selection of the King of Canada is of such minor importance, the question arises: why a King at all?" C. H. Cahan, for the Conservatives, also took exception to the procedure adopted, and although he did not agree with Woodsworth's emphasis on the divisibility of the Crown, he maintained that the order-in-council requesting and assenting to the United Kingdom legislation was invalid since it had no statutory foundation.

To the critics, Mackenzie King replied with a rather odd extension of his unity principle—but an extension that should reveal much to the historian. Prompt action, he declared, had been of the essence. "If there ever was a time in British history when it was of importance that the unity of the British Empire should be demonstrated to all the world, it was when a question affecting the crown itself was under consideration."[10] During the debate on the Canadian succession legislation Woodsworth again arraigned the Government for failing to give the House full information on the part played by Canada in advising the abdication. "The Minister of Justice," he said, "has referred to the con-

---

[9] Canada, House of Commons, *Debates,* 1937, I, 4, 13.
[10] *Ibid.,* 39.

fusion that might have arisen if the cabinet had not taken action. That is nothing to the confusion that might arise if this house showed some independence and did not endorse what has been done by the government."[11]

The explanation of King's policy in the abdication crisis is clear. The Statute of Westminster *was* open to his interpretation; and no doubt, from one point of view, it was highly desirable to demonstrate the unity of the British Empire. But how do these reasons square with King's declared central purposes throughout the period: maintenance of the unity of Canada, and supremacy of Parliament? To say that the unity of the Empire required fast cabinet action is a contradiction of every later statement he made, prior to the outbreak of war, on Canada's external relations; and it explicitly minimized the decisive powers of Parliament, if monarchical institutions were really to mean anything in this country. His policy at this point relied very heavily indeed on an extraordinary extension of prerogative right. It was an extension into the field of the constitution itself of what Harold Laski has called the "old and dubious tradition of secrecy" enshrined in foreign offices.[12] It may be true that even whigs concede a survival of prerogative power, but surely they must prefer that the use of such power should rest on the consent of at least the majority in the House of Commons. In this connection it is perhaps instructive to refer to the comment of an astute and well-informed Liberal M.P. who was later to become a member of King's Government. The comment appears in a letter written to J. W. Dafoe just two months prior to the abdication.[13] The writer was voicing disappointment at the way in which the House of Commons was being treated. He had thought that after the election of 1935 there would be a return to what he termed "Liberal principles." Instead, he wrote, "Under a Liberal regime the Prime Minister states the foreign policy and the Cabinet Ministers state the policy for internal affairs without consultation with any of the members."

In the conduct of external affairs the Government's relations with the House were exactly what they were during the abdication crisis. The key to the period is King's frequently reiterated refusal to expound his policy or to permit the clarification of issues. The point might be illustrated by any number of quotations, of which the following is a good example. In 1936, Ian Mackenzie, the Minister of National Defence, made an unguarded reference during a speech in Toronto to his opinion that Canada must stand by Britain. In the Commons Woodsworth declared, "He was speaking not for himself but for the government. It is a catchy slogan. . . . Has Canada no opinion of her own? We ought to know that. Otherwise it is a case, as in the last war, of 'Ready aye, Ready' . . . . Has the

---

[11] *Ibid.,* 82.

[12] H. J. Laski, *Parliamentary Government in England* (London, 1938), p. 245.

[13] Public Archives of Canada, J. W. Dafoe Papers, October 9, 1936.

Liberal government taken that stand? If it has not, I would like the Liberal government to say so." The reply was made by Ernest Lapointe, very briefly: "Does my honourable friend want to split the country right away?"[14] On this question, contemporary sources normally widely divergent in their views were in complete agreement. In March, 1937, Professor Underhill wrote, "We are getting close to the condition of mass hysteria that will make all sane discussion of our national policy impossible."[15] A year later *Saturday Night* observed that "for once the C.C.F. leader has a full legion of sympathizers" in his attempt to discover the Government's foreign policy.[16] It is nearly true to say that whatever Canadian opinion on foreign policy that was expressed during these years was unofficial: in the press, journals, conferences, on the radio, and much more briefly at the end of sessions by the opposition in the Commons.

As a result, Canadian opinion on external policy was gauged far more on the basis of what was said and written outside the Commons than by what went on *in* the House. This was as true of the Government as it was of most commentators and later historians. It is, for example, largely on the basis of the non-parliamentary discussion that Canadian opinion in these years has been divided into the over-neat categories of collectivist, imperialist and isolationist. There is little doubt that the Government charted its course on the basis of its estimate of public opinion rather than from any analysis of debate in the House—if for no other reason than that by far the most vocal group in the House on foreign policy was that led by Woodsworth. The Conservatives, to a marked degree, remained quiet, while the Liberal rank and file (save for one or two exceptional outbursts favouring neutrality) accepted whatever the Government said or refrained from saying. What evidence is available so far indicates very strongly that the Liberal caucus was not consulted. The conclusion is difficult to resist, therefore, that what Dr. E. A. Forsey has written concerning King's wartime policy and his method during the 1926 constitutional crisis is equally applicable to the area of pre-war external relations. That is, that Mackenzie King's basic creed was not really parliamentary democracy, but "plebiscitary democracy with a thin parliamentary veneer."[17]

The official line of Mackenzie King in external relations is not difficult to discover. After Ethiopia, at least, it was to withdraw from all commitments; and this held true right up to the summer of 1939. With respect to the League of Nations, J. W. Dafoe summed up the situation neatly in a letter in 1936:

---

14 Canada, House of Commons, *Debates,* 1938, III, 3214.

15 *Canadian Forum,* March, 1937.

16 Toronto *Saturday Night,* March 5, 1938.

17 E. A. Forsey, "Mr. King and Parliamentary Government," *Canadian Journal of Economics and Political Science,* XVII (4), 451–467.

The League of the future which Mr. King envisages will be a kind of recurrent conference with permanent organs functioning in the interim, at which there will be debate and more debate about world affairs. Mr. King's natural bias is in favour of procedures of this kind and in such an organization he would be apt to play a considerable role owing to his experience and his facility in making speeches of a certain kind. . . .[18]

On the question of Canada's obligation to participate in conferences dealing with violations of treaties to which she was a signatory, King was even more aloof. In 1936, after Germany's reoccupation of the Rhineland, King declared that Canada should keep out of the ensuing negotiations because she was not a signatory of the Locarno treaty. When J. S. Woodsworth pointed out that Versailles had also been violated, King replied that, "The attitude of the government is to do nothing itself and if possible to prevent anything occurring which will precipitate one additional factor into the all important discussions which are now taking place in Europe."[19] He concluded with the observation that his first duty was to keep Canada united.

In passing, it is interesting to note that correspondence in the Dafoe papers gives the very definite impression that the official line of withdrawal in these years was strongly influenced by Messrs. Loring Christie and O. D. Skelton.[20] Dafoe himself maintained that the advice of what he called "our own little foreign office" was one of the chief factors in producing the no-policy-at-all theme.

In any event, the line was maintained with care throughout 1937—especially when Woodsworth presented his motion, "that . . . in the event of war, Canada should remain strictly neutral regardless of who the belligerents may be."[21] Here King argued that it would be just as wrong to commit the country to neutrality as to automatic belligerency; in either case Parliament must be left free to decide. On this occasion, and during the debate on the increased defence estimates of that year[22] King, Ernest Lapointe, and Ian Mackenzie all asserted vigorously that Canada was arming only to be able to defend her own shores, and explicitly denied that the Government was preparing for any war that might occur outside Canada. When asked by Woodsworth against whom the Government intended to use the bombing planes provided for in the estimates, Lapointe retorted, "Can there be anything more ludicrous than that question? . . . Can the honourable member cite any country in the world where, when they organize their defence, they broadcast to the

---

[18] J. W. Dafoe Papers, Dafoe to Escott Reid, November 10, 1936.

[19] Canada, House of Commons, *Debates*, 1936, II, 1333.

[20] J. W. Dafoe Papers. See especially H. D. Hall to Dafoe, July 1, 1936; Dafoe to P. J. Noel-Baker, May 29, 1937.

[21] Canada, House of Commons, *Debates*, 1937, I, 237ff.

[22] *Ibid.*, 876ff.

world that they are arming against this or that country? . . . We have no enemies, I hope; in fact I know we have no enemies." The Minister of Justice then drove home his point by suggesting that Woodsworth was saying the same thing as the communists—a tack which was frequently favoured by Mr. Lapointe, and particularly so at this time when he was under heavy pressure from Woodsworth to disallow the Padlock Law.

Throughout the problems of non-intervention in Spain and China the Government's statements appeared more and more to confirm the no commitment line. There should be no embargo on arms to Germany, Italy or Japan after their respective aggressions, said King, because "we should wish at all costs to avoid making the present appalling situation on the two continents [in Europe and Asia] more embarrassing *for the countries faced with it,* in their efforts to work out a solution."[23] Time after time through the stages of the Czech crisis and the abortive Anglo-French negotiations for a defence pact with Russia, when pressed for a declaration of government policy, King elaborated the theme of no commitments. As late as August, 1939, the official line had not varied, and was distinctly re-drawn by King speaking at a banquet in his honour in Toronto, "One thing I will not do and cannot be persuaded to do is to say what Canada will do in regard to a situation that may arise at some future time and under circumstances of which we now know nothing."[24]

There is no room, then, for doubt about the official policy of no commitments—defended in the name of Canadian unity and the supremacy of Parliament. Even the 1939 Thorson motion to clarify Canada's *right* to declare neutrality in a British war was opposed on the same grounds as those taken to defeat the Woodsworth motion of the previous year—Parliament must be left unfettered.

Thus, when Hitler invaded Poland on September 1, the supremacy thesis was put to the test. But it was an ambiguous test. As Professor Brebner has written, "True to his promise Mr. King summoned Parliament for September 7 to discuss a declaration of war, with very curious results in terms of international law."[25] The results were curious—and for a very good reason. By the time Parliament met there was nothing left for it to decide; and an examination of the preceding three years suggests that King never intended that Parliament should have any real decision left to it. The conclusion that withdrawal from a positive League of Nations and from any other avowed policy meant in reality the conscious decision that Canada would be committed to the support of British policy wherever it led, is virtually unavoidable. Furthermore, the decision, clearly, was based upon an assessment of public opinion rather than any testing of the will of the Commons. Despite the elaborate explanations of

[23] Canada, House of Commons, *Debates,* 1938, II, 1407. Italics added.

[24] Quoted in F. H. Soward, *Canada in World Affairs* (Toronto, 1941), p. 148.

[25] J. B. Brebner, *North Atlantic Triangle* (Toronto, 1945), p. 318.

why Canada should not declare either a prior decision or a right to remain neutral, all the evidence indicates that the Government did not believe that Canada did, in fact, possess the right of neutrality in a British-declared war. Finally, the indications of prior implementation of the commitment to British policy decisions are not slight. What is the nature of the evidence to support these conclusions?

In 1937, in the debate on Woodworth's neutrality resolution[26] King carefully refrained from saying that Canada had anything more than the right of passive belligerency and, together with Lapointe, he accepted Laurier's well-known stand on this question. It was on this same occasion that King, for the first time, gave extravagant praise to British leadership and, as in the abdication crisis argued the dangers of weakening the unity of the British Commonwealth (using the correct designation this time). Partly because appeasement was foreshadowed at the 1937 Imperial Conference, and partly because the formula of emphasizing local defence was continued, King accepted British formulation of Canadian policy—in effect a common imperial policy. According to his own later statement he visited Hitler after the Imperial Conference specifically to tell the German dictator that, "if there was a war of aggression, nothing in the world would keep the Canadian people from being at the side of Britain."[27] It was, of course, precisely this kind of prior commitment that King denied, but whose existence was suspected by a large number of people. Woodsworth pressed vainly for greater use of the Commons committee on international affairs;[28] and, as Canada followed British policy step by step through the Spanish non-intervention, Munich and the recognition of the King of Italy as Emperor of Ethiopia, the lack of information about British-directed policy became increasingly irritating. Dafoe, writing from Ottawa, where he was undoubtedly better situated than any other editor in Canada to know what was really happening, noted privately just after Munich, ". . . we are going to see what is already under way—a permanent drive to induce Canada to tie herself in with Great Britain in armament and defence plans that will leave this country no option but to go the whole way when 'der tag' arrives. . . ."[29] A few days later, the same observer wrote "I find a growing feeling in circles on the inside here that King has been close to Chamberlain all through the piece, of which his visit to Hitler was the first outward sign . . . ."[30] And in November of 1938, Dafoe asserted that, ". . . the Chamberlain policy can be readily foreseen. It is to tie all the Dominion

[26] Canada, House of Commons, *Debates,* 1937, I, 237ff.

[27] *Ibid.,* 1944, VI, 6275. This unity of policy was known in advance to the British government according to (Sir) Anthony Eden. See N. Mansergh, *op. cit.,* p. 125n.

[28] See, for example, Canada, House of Commons, *Debates,* 1937, I, 701.

[29] J. W. Dafoe Papers, Dafoe to G. V. Ferguson, October 18, 1938.

[30] *Ibid.,* October 23, 1938.

governments to his chariot wheels. Identification with his policies will involve preparation to support those policies which will mean joint programmes of defence . . . . I begin to distrust King."[31]

As the defence estimates rose in 1938 and 1939, Woodsworth tried hard to wring an admission from the Government that its defence production and military-air training programmes were being worked out in consultation with Britain; but from the Minister of National Defence he never got more than the answer that "we have no more information than is in the possession of the hon. member who asked the question."[32] Yet the plans *were* made on the assumption of a united imperial war effort. As Ernest Lapointe finally revealed the position in March, 1939, Canada could not remain neutral in a major war involving Britain without "a civil war in Canada."[33] This was confirmed by King on the day of the British declaration of war when he said, commenting upon the appeal for unity made by George VI, "Canada has already answered that call."[34] In the week from September 3 to September 10, despite King's telephone denial of Canada's belligerent status to President Roosevelt,[35] the Government's action could be defended only on the assumption that Canada was at war. The enemy was defined, all armed services were put on a full war basis, enemy nationals were arrested, and trading with the enemy was prohibited by order-in-council. On September 7, the Governor-General's speech referred to "the state of war which now exists."[36]

In his speech during the debate on the Address in the emergency session,[37] King announced that the momentous question of peace or war "is not decided yet." He then proceeded to eulogize the Government's past policy of close co-operation with Britain in munitions production and air-training—a policy well developed which would make Canada the arsenal of democracy. While he stated later in the same speech that approval of the Address would be the Government's authority for "immediate participation in the war" he left it plain for all to see that the only basic thing remaining to be decided was the question of an expeditionary force (and this, as it turned out, was not really decided by Parliament). As Woodsworth noted in that debate, the Commons was being asked to endorse a policy already fully implemented and to give the Government a blank cheque for the future. The final turn of the screw came in the immediately succeeding months. On the basis of a $100 million War Appropriation Act, and without parliamentary direction, an

---

[31] *Ibid.*, November 5, 1938.

[32] Canada, House of Commons, *Debates*, 1938, IV, 3706.

[33] *Ibid.*, 1939, III, 2467.

[34] Quoted in F. H. Soward, *op. cit.*, 152.

[35] Bruce Hutchison, *op. cit.*, p. 250.

[36] Canada, House of Commons, *Debates,* Special War Session, 1939, p. 1.

[37] *Ibid.*, p. 19 ff.

expeditionary force was organized and dispatched, while innumerable orders-in-council were issued regulating the war effort. In January, 1940, the members of Parliament, expecting to examine and debate the Government's policy of the preceding months of war, were told that the Government would not go before the House, but before the people.[38] The policy foreshadowed in 1936, symbolized in the abdication procedure, and matured in the conduct of pre-war external relations, was now stratified. The civil war which Lapointe had professed to see lurking in any definite government statement of foreign policy had been avoided and Canada was successfully launched in the conflict at Britain's side.

Considering what happened to the status of Parliament behind the King-Lapointe smoke-screen it is surely worth asking two basic questions about all this whig mythology. First: was the unity of Canada worth the price of so sadly debased a Parliament: and, second: would that unity really have been dissolved had Parliament been taken into the Government's confidence in the formulation and execution of policy?

The first question would probably be answered in the negative by most Canadians: by French Canadians because for the majority of them the doctrine of unity has always seemed spurious; by English-speaking Canadians because of the long tradition of parliamentary institutions. But the second question is far more real and important. Did unity demand the King method? This, of course, is at the very core of the whig interpretation. Time had to be bought—bought so that Canada would still be intact when Britain declared war and events could coerce Canadian opinion. But what *were* the factors that operated to ensure that only three voices would be raised against participation in September 1939? They are obvious. The key to Quebec was Lapointe. The key to the so-called neutralists was the C.C.F. Apart from these two forces who could have "split the country down the middle" had the Government declared its policy, say in 1938?

As for Lapointe and his French-speaking colleagues in the cabinet, there was never any doubt after 1937; indeed, it was Lapointe who came closest of all to announcing the Government's actual policy. Again, the position of French-Canadians in 1939 has been well put by Professor Brebner. Their leaders "knew that they must choose France and Great Britain rather than the United States."[39] Concerning possible neutrality in a major European war, how could this statement be less true of 1937 or 1938 than it was of 1939?

In the C.C.F. there was equally little doubt after 1937. The significant modification of the party's Foreign policy plank in that year, and the debate in the emergency C.C.F. National Council meeting in September, 1939, constitute firm evidence that that factor was constant from 1937 to

[38] For a discussion of this, see E. A. Forsey, *op. cit.*
[39] *Op. cit.,* p. 319.

1939.[40] In short, it was not the divisions in the House of Commons, or in the nation that most threatened Canadian unity—it was the attitude of the Government toward Parliament. The refusal to declare its support of Chamberlain *as a Canadian policy,* the refusal to accept the Thorson resolution on the *right* of neutrality, the refusal to declare its decision to plan defence jointly with Britain, in fact its refusal to take Parliament into its confidence—these were the things that constituted a real threat to Canadian unity in the pre-war years. No historian of the period has done other than suggest that the overwhelming majority of Canadians accepted the general Chamberlain policy. The Government had only to declare itself, to establish the technical right of neutrality, and then defend itself on its well-chosen ground in the House. Refusal to do this made utter nonsense of the doctrine of parliamentary supremacy, was itself a cause of considerable disunity, and certainly debased Parliament.

Since Canadian participation in the second world war was a foregone conclusion, the question might well be asked whether the man who sought most insistently the use of Parliament for the clarification of Canadian policy made a greater contribution to the maturation of Canada than the man who subordinated Parliament to his personal (and inaccurate) interpretation of Canadian public opinion.

---

[40] Woodsworth House, Ottawa, C. C. F. National Council and Executive *Minutes,* 1937–42; C. C. F. National Convention *Minutes,* 1936–42. Correspondence in the Saskatchewan C. C. F. files (Regina) leaves no doubt that the C. C. F. leaders who defeated the Woodsworth-Farmer neutrality motion in the emergency National Council meeting in 1939 had concluded at least as early as September, 1938, that "it is already decided that if Britain declares war, Canada must accept the situation," but that for various reasons "our best contribution will be economic." (Letter of September 28, 1938). It was decided by these leaders at the time of Munich not to issue a statement to that effect "until we know whether it will be war."

part VI

Contemporary Canada

31

French Canada: The Interrelationship between Culture, Language, and Personality

Raymond Gagné

"THE INDEPENDENCE movement in Quebec," asserts Raymond Gagné, "springs from one prime malaise, and it is not essentially economic as most people believe, especially English Canadians. The independence movement in Quebec is out, first and foremost, to save the French culture, language and personality on the North American continent. In essence, it is a linguistic-cultural revolution."

In this thoughtful and daring article by a linguistic anthropologist is found both a serious attempt to explain the phenomena of the "Quiet Revolution" of the 60s in Quebec and also a demonstration of the interrelationship of the various social sciences, history, and linguistics. The comforting notion that knowledge can be neatly comprehended is shattered, and the danger of overspecialization exposed, while the individualistic scholar of the past is replaced by the team member of the future. To the young who wish to be the historians—or the sociologists—of tomorrow, the challenges would seem formidable. But Mr. Gagné is candidly describing his own society. He portrays the French Canadians of Quebec as a people who through their insecure historical experience now have their cultural backs to the wall. Some of them are conscious of this situation, while others react to it subconsciously. None can escape it.

In the 60s many of the new secular leadership in Quebec, somehow aware of the situation, concluded that the principal devise to prevent this collective death was their state, the one government which they could control, the government of the Province of Quebec. Here then, if one follows the Gagné analysis, is the meaning behind the phrase *maîtres chez nous* and the desire to replace the old world *survivance* with *épanouisse-ment. L'état, c'est nous.*

A shortened version of this paper appeared in *Canadian Dimension,* August–September, 1969.

I HAVE CHOSEN to divide this paper into two main parts. In the first, I shall attempt to define four fundamental concepts, namely, culture, language, personality, and structuralism in the light of modern social science. I shall try to show how the hypothetical construct of structuralism reveals the intimate and inextricable interrelationship between culture, language, and personality. In the second part, I shall present a broad outline of the fine interplay of the principal forces, that is, the sociodynamics, at work in given societies to maintain their identity in the face of the constant internal and external pressures to change their linguistic and cultural self-image. This will be done with specific reference to English Canada, French Canada, and France. In so doing, it is my purpose to demonstrate that the basic postulate, that is, the inextricable bonds between culture, language, and personality, is at the root of the social and political disturbances taking place in French Canada today, or more accurately, in Quebec.

Actually, it is not by chance that I shall discuss culture, language, and personality in that order but rather it is owing to a broad casual relationship among these entities. It is not a question of proving which came first, the chicken or the egg. In historical times, no living or extinct culture, great or small, has been found without having a language as its principal vehicle of expression. Therefore, language at least presupposes the existence of a culture whose main content it communicates among the members of the community. In turn, human personality, if stripped of the formative agents of culture and language, would be an empty vessel indeed. As for structuralism, as a working hypothesis it has become a foundation stone of the social sciences, to wit: anthropology, sociology, psychology, and linguistics. As a matter of fact, it has even crept into the sacrosanct field of literature or more specifically, literary criticism. Therefore, because structuralism is a concept so basic, overlapping and comprehensive, I shall deal with it first.

At the heart of structuralism is the idea that each unit, item, datum, function, manifestation, phenomenon, call it what you will, that we use to describe objective reality, does not exist independently, loose, as it were, in a void or vacuum. Each unit belongs to some system or structure, big or small, where it is intimately interrelated with like units to the extent that its very existence can be defined only in terms of its relationship with the other units. This interdependence among units of a particular structure or substructure extends to the various structures and substructures themselves. Consider, for example, the intimate interrelationship between society, the family, and the individual. In other words, everything hangs together: individual units, smaller and larger structures. No item, no pattern, no configuration is superfluous. Nothing is to be found floating at random. Nothing is absurd. All is relevant. Everything is integrated in one way or another into a highly intricate set of organized structures, within structures, within overlapping structures ad infinitum. Structuralism is a revolutionary idea in the sense that it is the major factor behind the growing emphasis being placed on interdisciplinary research. Nowadays, no anthropologist would dream of pursuing his research without a solid groundwork in linguistics. The same holds true in reverse. But no one can expect to be an expert in every field, hence the need for team work. The same trend has taken place within the physical sciences.

Even if most of the data of social science has the disadvantage of not being able to be studied neatly and tidily under a microscope, this does not mean that its findings are necessarily invalid. In linguistics, for example, what is immediately observable is found principally in the speech continuum but this does not prevent the linguist from positing the existence of a linguistic code, from defining its various functional units, and from describing its structures.

Culture, like language, has been likened to an iceberg, with only one tenth of its content observable. The material content of culture—housing, tools, implements, clothing, and the customary behaviour of its people expressed in its rituals, music, and dance forms, are on the surface of the iceberg, while the forces that animate their open manifestation lie latent and hidden below the surface. The sociodynamics at work in a given linguistic and cultural milieu are a set of powerful forces imperceptible to those who are caught up within them. Men are never aware of the ground rules of their environmental systems—their culture, their language, their psychology. Man responds to a set of automatic patterns that determine his linguistico-cultural personality. To paraphrase McLuhan, one might say that the total milieu is the message and in fact, the unconscious massage to which everyone is inescapably submitted. As McLuhan points out, the intellectual who says: "Personally I pay no attention to ads!" is simply kidding himself if he thinks that his perception and sensibility is not affected by them. However, it might be more appropriate to close these comments on structuralism with the words of Claude Levi-Strauss, the famous French anthropologist who is considered by many to be the father of structuralism: "Man's housing has a meaning that goes beyond its relationship to the center of his social and religious life . . . The structure of the village does not only reveal the fine interplay of the institutions: it sums up and determines the relation-

ship between man and the universe, between society and the super-
natural world, between the living and the dead."[1]

If linguistics does nothing else it makes one very wary of words,
especially broad abstractions like culture, language, and personality that
embrace a multitude of overlapping data. Fragile and vague as they may
be, man's predilection for such words as truth, beauty, justice, has not
been dampened by time and if they have achieved nothing else, they
have at least delimited vast areas of knowledge for his consideration and
exploration. Instead of the insistent plea heard among fastidious intellectuals engaged in serious conversation, to wit: "Please define your terms!,"
modern scientists prefer the more cautious exhortation: "Please state
explicitly and clearly your undefined terms!" The rapid multiplication of
our sources of knowledge from day to day make many of today's theories
as useless as yesterday's newspaper. This is why the contemporary man of
science prefers open-ended definitions. For instance, not all social scientists agree with the basic postulate presented in this paper. However, if in
his constant search for knowledge man is condemned to groping in the
dark, the least he can do is to equip himself with what he thinks are the
best searchlights available to him at a given time. Therefore, I hope to be
able to cast some light on the tangled skein of events that have taken
place in Quebec since 1960 with the help of the basic postulate implicit in
the title of this talk.

It is certainly easier for a nuclear physicist to define a *neutrino*, for
instance, than it is for a social scientist to define the abstract concepts
under study here because the word neutrino does not have first to be
cleansed and unburdened, as it were, of the popular meanings that have
accumulated around it in the course of history. Culture, language, and
personality are terms that have almost become household words, especially the first two, now that we are traversing the era of the B. and B.

First, then, let us turn our attention to culture, in its popular sense
before examining its anthropological definition. Generally speaking, the
people of the Western world use the noun *culture* and its adjective *cultured* with strict reference to the individual or at most to elite or priveleged
groups within a given society. The accent is always on individual accomplishment usually achieved with the help of specialized agencies such as
schools and universities although it is not uncommon to find a self-made
man who enjoys a high degree of culture obtained through his own
personal efforts, from reading, travelling, and acute observation of the
human comedy. In other words, culture in its popular usage, is not a gift
from the gods but implies conscious personal effort, will power, drive,
discipline—in fact, all that is involved in the individual's conscious search
and struggle for self-development. Modern anthropologists, on the con-

---

[1] Auzias, Jean-Marie, *Clefs pour le Structuralisme*. Paris, Seghers, 1967, p. 90,
(translation mine).

trary, apply the term culture, not to the individual as such but to the entire set of forces visibly and imperceptibly at work in the shaping of an entire society, all that goes into the information and formation of the individual. In this sense everyone born and brought up in the confines of a given society inherits a culture, a language and a collective personality that is freely and unconsciously transmitted from one generation to another. The formal educational system we wrongly identify as the chief repository and transmitter of culture and language is but one of the many substructures of the total set that constitutes culture. Family life, television, radio, and the cinema are other obvious examples. If schools were a *sine qua non* of culture and language, the Eskimos along with the great majority of the world's population would be meaningless nonentities since they have no formal school system. In its broadest anthropological sense, culture is the school par excellence of every human being, whatever culture he belongs to, and with no tuition fees to boot. It is learning without tears as Madison Avenue would no doubt advertise it, were it a good paying proposition. Briefly, one could summarize the essential difference between the popular and anthropological meaning of culture in the following formula: everyone *has* culture but not everybody *is* cultured. To put it another way, to be cultured is to be aware of one's culture.

For centuries, the Eskimos have transmitted their culture and language painlessly and unconsciously from generation to generation without benefit of formal schooling. However, the history of man shows that the transmission of culture and language was not always automatic, free, and untrammeled. As a matter of fact, the experience is often traumatic and dramatic as well. We need not go outside the boundaries of Canada or into ancient history to prove this. The central drama and trauma of the French-Canadian rest on this fact. The French-Canadian does not enjoy the traditional freedom of untrammeled transmission of language and culture exercised by the Eskimos until very recently. Rather he must spend the better part of his creative energies in a constant conscious struggle against debilitating odds to maintain what is taken for granted from the start in all normal societies—the free gift of language and culture. History has shown that his fight has born little fruit for his language and culture are in constant decline and rapid transformation, or if you will, mongrelization. But this is another story which I shall take up in greater detail later.

Anthropologically speaking, then, culture can be likened to a gift from the gods that each generation passes on to the next. It is the automatic transference of the creative efforts, knowledge, and skills distilled from the experience and wisdom of preceding generations to ensure the continuity of the group. In a sense, it is like an old recipe for living and indeed, for survival, bearing the stamp of experience and the test of time. In a word, the structures of culture contain the total historical consciousness of a given people. Culture represents a given people's particular set of preferences, predispositions, attitudes, objectives, goals; its particular way of perceiving, feeling, thinking, and reacting to objective reality.

This takes us to the intriguing notion of linguistic relativity commonly known as the Sapir-Whorf hypothesis.[2] By way of introduction, let us repeat that it is generally accepted that language is the most important vehicle of culture. There are other modes of cultural expression, notably art and music, but even these, at least in certain cultures, have been described and transmitted in part through the medium of words. In effect, language has its finger in every area of culture. It is all pervasive. The basic postulate of the Whorfian hypothesis can be summarized as follows: the very structure or grammatical categories of language imposes on its speaker a particular view of the universe and conditions his emotive responses to this distinct view of reality. According to Whorf, language is not merely an instrument to communicate ideas and feelings but it is itself the shaper of thought and emotion. It is a tool that limits the speaker's perception of objective reality. For Whorf, nature is divided and organized into concepts according to the grammatical categories of the language of the speaker. Since the structures of language, like those of culture, are for the most part latent and therefore lie outside the consciousness of the speaker, it means that even when we consider ourselves most free that our language imposes constraints on our interpretation of reality with the result that absolute impartiality and objectivity in our structuration of knowledge is impossible.

It must be pointed out that not all social scientists accept Whorf's ideas on linguistic relativity. Many have serious reservations and are waiting for more empirical evidence. In the last fifteen years, a great deal of research has been conducted to put this hypothesis to the test. The evidence so far seems to speak in its favour but it is still too early to make categorical pronouncements. My own findings with reference to the spatial categories of the Eskimo language would prove to be interesting ground for experimentation by the Whorfian group of researchers. It would seem that Eskimos view objective reality in two dimensions only. Everything they see, objects, people, areas are delimited and located in space in one of two ways: either the thing viewed is seen as being of two roughly equal dimensions like an igloo, a parka, or a human being, or it is of two distinctly unequal dimensions such as a gun, a harpoon, or a river.

Time, like space, is viewed very differently by the Eskimo. For one thing, he has no word for time. An Eskimo does not save time, lose time, kill time, and so on. His use of tenses converge on the present, immediate past, and immediate future. Since the Eskimo culture, unlike our own is

---

[2] Whorf, Benjamin Lee, *Language, Thought, and Reality.* Massachusetts Institute of Technology, 1956, 278 pages.

not future-oriented, it has little use for a remote future tense although it does exist but is seldom used. Furthermore, the Eskimo does not divide the colour continuum in the same way we do. The fact, that traditionally, the Eskimos did not distinguish between green and blue does not mean their eyesight was impaired. Their language simply did not take this distinction into account. The wide range of human emotions which we divide in one way, do not find their equivalent forms in Eskimo. Their notion of love and hate is different from ours. So are their likes and dislikes. Eskimo men who can show great tenderness and tolerance with children hardly notice the existence of flowers. What would a proper Englishman think of that especially if he were in the midst of tending his garden?

In fact, many examples could be given to illustrate the wide variety of emotional patterns from one culture to another. Generally speaking, the English are scandalized by bullfights yet not so with the fox hunt although a Spaniard might very well wonder why not. Broadly speaking, French-Canadians relish giving all the gory details of a long and painful illness, their own or someone else's, or to go into all the gruesome details of the pangs of death, the funeral, the internment, and any other dramatic incident connected with pain and sorrow. Recently, I witnessed a large French-Canadian audience killing themselves with laughter at a concert where a well-known French-Canadian chansonnier sang one of his own compositions—a long series of lamentations of this sort related in the form of a letter from a friend to another after twenty years' absence. This song revealed a basic psychological pattern which French-Canadians practise quite unconsciously but are quite able to recognize when a great artist has the insight and talent to make it manifest. Hence, its resounding success. Furthermore, United Nations translators have observed that different languages seem to imply different attitudes—the English pattern is said to be pragmatic and inductive, whereas the French pattern is generalizing and deductive. Anyone who has kept up with the great Canadian constitutional debate in recent years may have recognized that the French-Canadians want to revamp the sum and substance of the B.N.A. Act and inject it with broad declarations of principles and rights whereas the English-Canadians would be content to touch up certain details here and there. The custom of legal precedent is deeply rooted in British history but not so in the French. This might explain in part why the revolution of 1789 took place in France and not in England. It must never be forgotten that the manifestation of contemporary culture has deep historical roots, just as the language we use today echoes deep into the halls of time. All this, then, to show that we are all more or less unconsciously prisoners of our own linguistic and cultural patterns, which give us a particular view of the world and a particular way of reacting to it emotionally and rationally.

Edward Hall, the anthropologist, has written a superb book entitled

"The Silent Language"[3] whose main theme is that the hidden and latent patterns of culture constitute a nonverbal vehicle of communication quite separate from the spoken word. Let me cite an example from the area of study in modern anthropology called proxemics which has directly to do with this silent cultural language. Proxemics is concerned with analyzing the latent structures that control the use of space and distance in human contacts in various cultures. For instance, studies reveal that for an Englishman the tolerable distance separating him from his interlocutor is much wider than that between Latins. Just imagine the dangers of mixing Latins and Anglo-Saxons at cocktail parties. Can't you see the poor Englishman being literally pinned to the wall because for every step backwards he takes to keep at a tolerable distance from his Latin interlocutor, the Latin takes one step forward to adjust to his own comfortable distance. Can't you hear the Englishman fuming inwardly and wondering why these damned Latins are so aggressive in conversation, or for that matter, the Latin wondering why the English are so stand-offish or passive. So you can see that hidden culture patterns have their evil genius and can often lead to serious misunderstandings.

It is now time to turn our attention to spoken language as such. Here we face the danger of repeating ourselves since most of the general attributes of culture already discussed apply equally well to language proper, since culture is expressed mainly through language. Like culture, language can be likened to an iceberg whose surface structures, namely, the speech continuum, constitutes but one tenth of its entire structures. From a careful analysis of the speech patterns of individuals can be inferred the hidden patterns or deep structures. The hidden structures make up a highly complex linguistic code which contains all the unconscious rules and automatic patterns that animate the act of speech. If you want proof of this, try to explain to a foreigner or to yourself the multitude of rules that control English prepositions. For example, what are the rules underlying the following variations? "The man to whom I spoke about it"; "The man whom I spoke about it to"; "The man whom I spoke to about it." Whether you can formulate the rules coherently or not, one thing is certain and that is that you are absolutely sure that all the above are correct English statements if you are English-speaking, whereas the following is not: "The man about to I spoke it." And unless you know the rules consciously, you will be very hard put to explain why it is unacceptable English.

The bilingual epoch which is now upon us affords us ample opportunity of hearing people say: "It's funny, you know, I've studied French all through school and got excellent marks but because I've never learned to think in French I can hardly speak a word of it." Translated into the

3 Hall, Edward T., *The Silent Language*. Garden City, N.Y., Doubleday, 1959, 240 pages.

language of modern linguistics, this means simply: instead of responding to a set of unconscious automatic patterns I have to organize them at the conscious level. And I should like to add emphatically that *thinking about* a language is a very painful and inarticulate experience indeed. If you happen to be among those unhappy few, console yourselves for you have lots of company since most French-Canadians are past masters in the painful and inarticulate exercise of *thinking about* their language, especially the bilinguals. Normal societies, like the English-Canadians, the continental French, or the Eskimos, do not need to think about their language, they just simply speak it. Abnormal societies, like French-Canadians, are forced to think about their language because they cannot speak it. More about this further on.

Language, like culture, is made up of an intricate set of interwoven structures whose basic units are interdependent and definable only in terms of each other. Everything rests on contrasting patterns. Phonemes (basic functional sounds), morphemes (minimal units of meaning), syntagmemes (rules of syntax), and lexemes (vocabulary) are all functional units. Their function is determined in relation to each other within each of their substructures and in turn, all the substructures are interdependent. Let us illustrate this interdependence of units and structures.

The traditional four nasal basic functional sounds of French contained in the phrase *un bon vin blanc* "a good white wine" are now reduced to three in the speech patterns of the so-called Parisian French, even the elite (yes, including General de Gaulle). The *un* and *in* nasals have coalesced into a new nasal articulation which is different from either. The remaining two nasals have also slightly shifted in articulation as a result of this internal change. In turn, every other French vowel articulation, including the consonantal phonemes, have undergone slight modification, howsoever small. This in turn affects all the other linguistic structures since the phonemes are the building bricks of words and sentences. All this to show you once again, that everything hangs together in a set of structures, linguistic, cultural, or psychological. Now this change in the nasal vowels of Parisian French is the result of internal linguistic dynamics. By this, I mean, that it is not owing to the pressures of Arabic or Russian that this change was brought about.

The question of change as a result of languages in contact—an important source of pressures of external nature, can prove veritably devastating to the weaker language in certain cases. This is the situation of French in contact with English in Canada. French is the weaker language in this case not because its internal structure is deficient in itself but because the sociodynamics that prevail in the country at large, even in Quebec, is weighted heavily in favour of English. Visibly to the linguists, but imperceptibly to the masses, the French language spoken in Canada, not excepting Quebec—its fortress, is undergoing rapid transformation as a result of the pressures of Anglo-American culture and language. Even within the very walls of its fortress—Quebec, there is the Trojan horse of English Quebec centered at its very heart—Montreal. I shall be coming back to this matter later on.

We have seen that culture and language are intimately related; their point of intersection is the human personality. And the human personality is vital not only as the main repository of the content of culture and the code of language but also as their main instrument of communication and transmission. In other words, a dead language and an extinct culture are the net result of the total disappearance of the vessel of human personality in that particular language and culture. If the Beothuk Indian language and culture of Newfoundland have totally disappeared it is obviously because the Beothuk people were all annihilated. By the same token, if 500 million Chinese take over America and force us to speak Chinese and live *à la chinoise*, the net result will be the addition of 200 million white- red- and black-skinned Chinese to the Chinese cultural group and the veritable disappearance of Western culture in North America as we know it, even if the invading Chinese take to drinking Coca-Cola. In the same way, the thousands of French-Canadians who have been assimilated by the English in all parts of Canada, including 50,000 on the island of Montreal, can no longer claim to be transmitters of the French language and culture in Canada even though they may continue to enjoy pea soup for dinner once in a while.

Therefore, the human personality does not develop in a vacuum nor does it retain its identity by hanging on to a few traditional folksongs and favourite food recipes. Physically, the child is conceived and nurtured in his mother's womb. By virtue of heredity he will come into the world with a unique set of characteristics which will distinguish him from the other members of his group. However, the linguistico-cultural milieu, which is another kind of womb, will give him collective personality traits that will enable him to communicate more easily with his fellow members in the community and especially to feel at home within its structures. What else does this expression of *feeling at home* mean if not that the individual feels comfortable because he is within linguistico-cultural structures that he knows and understands unconsciously because he was shaped and nurtured within them, by them, and he is made to fit them. Ruth Benedict, the well-known American anthropologist, neatly summarizes the inseparability of culture and personality in this happy formula: "Culture is personality writ large; personality is culture writ small."[4]

The content of any particular mind comes from culture. No individual ever originates his culture any more than he invents his language. Culture is the collective side of personality; personality the subjective side of culture. Culture is a kind of suffused light that permeates subtly the

---

4 Kroeber, A. L. and Kluckhohn, Clyde, *Culture—a critical review of concepts and definitions*. New York, Random House, p. 218.

psychic and emotional make-up of each individual person that comes within its radius. The collective or linguistico-cultural personality, then, is the total set of latent patterns that predisposes the members of a particular group to behave in one way rather than another.

To conclude the considerations of Part I let us say that the sets of structures of culture, language, and personality are so inextricably interlocked that it is impossible to eliminate one set without doing violence to the others. For example, if the Eskimos lose their language, they no doubt will retain their slanted eyes and mongoloid spot, and perhaps their drum dance and caribou skin parka as well, but who would dare say that these scanty cultural and biological vestiges constitute Eskimo personality and culture?

PART II

It is my contention that if we accept the main thesis presented in Part I we can better understand the present crisis in French-Canadian society. Let us review a series of considerations and statements already expressed and examine their implications in relation to French Canada:

(1) the linguistico-cultural milieu is another kind of womb that nurtures and shapes human personality;

(2) language is the most important vehicle for the expression of culture and the human personality;

(3) language is the chief instrument to apprehend knowledge and to organize the reality that lies outside and inside the speaker;

(4) the structuring of human personality by the formative agents of culture and language is mainly a painless unconscious process and human behaviour expressed through the key channels of culture and language is also an unconscious automatic process;

(5) the linguistico-cultural milieu shapes the individual in order to fit him easily and comfortably into its own set of structures for the purpose of living, working, thinking, feeling, perceiving, developing, functioning, in a word, surviving at maximum efficiency within the structures that he feels at home in;

(6) a society can be said to be functioning and developing normally when its internal dynamics work towards maintaining an equilibrium within its cultural and linguistic structures in the face of constant change from internal and external pressures;

(7) a culture and a language embrace all aspects of human life: all of its institutions, not the least of which are, religious, educational, industrial, and commercial;

If we accept the validity of the foregoing remarks, we should be obliged to conclude that most French-Canadians are aliens on the greater part of Canadian soil, even in their own fortress—Quebec. Let us explain.

For a linguistico-cultural milieu to function normally, its structures must be reasonably homogeneous and its sociodynamics must be essentially self-propelled, creative, and self-perpetuating. Its institutions and national life must be the expression of this homogeneity and inner functional harmony. Its inventiveness and creativity must be fostered chiefly by the interplay of the total set of forces at work within its structures. It is realized that cultural change could not occur were it not for the creative activity of concrete individuals through whom both internal and external influences flow. However, if the foreign influence outweighs and overpowers the internal dynamics, a serious disequilibrium will result. We have indicated in Part I how the coalescence of two nasal vowels as a result of internal dynamics could alter, even though slightly, the entire set of French linguistic structures. If the disappearance of a phoneme can modify an entire set of language structures, the obsolescence or annihilation of an institution or any other single cultural pattern can have a similar effect on the total set of cultural structures. It is a well-recognized fact, well propagated by McLuhan and company, that the electronic age in which we live which allows for massive and rapid dissemination of knowledge cross-culturally, threatens the homogeneity and equilibrium of distinct cultures, especially the smaller and less powerful ones. One might immediately ask: if a normal, homogeneous and self-creating society such as France, for example, feels threatened by the influence of powerful foreign cultures, how can an abnormal, heterogeneous, and imitative society like French Canada possibly hope to survive? This is indeed a good question. One thing is certain, however, that if we choose to answer this question in the negative, then the solution to the French-Canadian problem would at least be simple. This solution would be to totally assimilate all French-Canadians into Anglo-American culture as soon as possible and forget once and for all the dream of a bilingual and bicultural Canada from coast to coast.

France and English Canada answer reasonably well to the description of normally functioning societies as described in the preceding paragraph. They do because their internal sociodynamics are still strong and vigourous enough to allow them each to evolve culturally and linguistically, in spite of powerful cross-cultural influences, at a rate that does not threaten their very life blood. To put it paradoxically, France and English Canada are allowed to change while remaining the same. This same notion is nicely expressed in Heidegger's prescription: since change is inevitable let it take place within the context of one's own roots and origins, that is, "Qu'on se dépayse dans ses origines!"

In contrast, we have termed French-Canadian society abnormal because its internal sociodynamics or forces of self-generation are too weak to allow it to change while remaining the same, or to change within its own self-image. It is terribly weakened by the heterogeneity of its linguistic and cultural structures—a kind of Franco-Anglo-American mishmash. It is threatened within its very own fortress—Quebec, indeed, at its very heart—Montreal, by a veritable Trojan horse—English Quebec, which in spite of its small numbers is infinitely more powerful than the French majority. At its very heart, then, French-Canadian society has a set of powerful foreign sociodynamics which creep visibly, imperceptibly, and inevitably into every facet of French life. Industry and commerce in the modern world are very powerful structures that reach like an octopus into every other structure that constitute the linguistic and cultural milieu. When a given language, in this case, French, is constantly under pressure to express the structures of a foreign culture, in this case, English, as well as the remnants of its own culture, it ill serves both groups and, in fact, is rejected by both.

This is exactly what is happening in Quebec and Canada at large today. The French-Canadians, themselves, look down upon their own language because they realize it is neither fish, flesh, nor fowl. They know it is hybrid and mongrelized and naturally it is so because it is the product of a hybrid culture. Has Prime Minister Trudeau not himself described it as "lousy French" not so long ago? By the same token, English Canadians and more particularly English Quebeckers have every reason to reject imitating and associating themselves with such a monster as this Frenglish; the more so, that it is their own creation. Human psychology teaches us that healthy individuals have no inclination to imitate or emulate the weak and infirm. So it goes also in the psychology of peoples. Therefore, English Canadians and especially English Quebeckers who may have obscure feelings of guilt for having kept themselves at a safe distance from French-Canadian society, should be able to find some relief in the fact that many French-Canadians understand their reactions since they themselves find wanting the quality of their linguistic and cultural inheritance. And the English who did learn French, naturally looked towards France—a healthy, normal, and prestigious model.

Always keeping in mind the inseparability of the three components of our basic postulate, we can state that the average French-Canadian scorns himself because he has contempt for the hybrid language he is forced to speak and the hybrid culture that necessarily shapes him. The self-contempt of the French-Candaian is increased by the fact that not only English Canadians reject him, his language, and his culture, but also all the various ethnic brands of New Canadians who naturally prefer to assimilate into the powerful and prestigious English minority group of Quebec. Worse still, when the French-Canadian is confronted with a truly healthy, normal French specimen, the continental French immigrant, that is, one born and brought up in a normal, healthy, and homogeneous linguistico-cultural milieu such as France, his feelings of self-hatred and of hate for the Frenchman, are both at once intensified (these feelings are in face much more violent vis-à-vis the Frenchman than the English Canadian or New Canadian) because in the presence of a healthy, normal, well-structured, and smooth functioning French personality, he tragically realizes that there is the person he might have been and should be but is not.

We have just touched the very heart of the French-Canadian crises. In brief, the French-Canadian today is saying: I do not like what I am and where I am going; now that I am beginning to understand the forces that made me so, I want to change the structures in order to become what I want to be. The sixty-four dollar question is, of course, is it too late? René Lévesque's new Parti Québécois does not think so although it certainly emphasizes the extreme urgency of the situation. It is now or never, they say. It is a huge gamble, they recognize, but they hasten to add, who has ever rejected a great risk when his very life is at stake? The independence movement in Quebec springs from one prime malaise, and it is not essentially economic as most people believe, especially English Canadians. The independence movement in Quebec is out, first and foremost, to save the French culture, language, and personality complex of structures on the North American continent. In essence, it is a linguistico-cultural revolution. It is based on the desire to transform the sociodynamics of Quebec into essentially French channels of expression and creation. The usual counter argument to this movement is as follows: have we not entered a new age with an enlightened French-Canadian at the helm in Ottawa who will guarantee French survival not only within the Province of Quebec but indeed from the Atlantic to the Pacific?

In this connection, it is important to note the following facts. French-Canadian demographers predict that within the next fifteen years there will be a majority of English-speaking people in greater Montreal if the present declining trends in French-Canadian birth rate continue and the present 95 percent rate of assimilation of New Canadians into the English minority group keeps up. If the French sociodynamics of Montreal are already endangered with a 63 percent French majority, what chance have they of gaining strength with an English majority on the island? Montreal is the heart of Quebec's cultural and industrial life. When the vital organ of an organism is seriously threatened what hope is there for those that depend on it? Here the counter argument usually is: but if everyone on the island of Montreal is bilingual then obviously French would no longer be in danger. Let us examine this last point of view briefly.

Bilingualism as a phenomenon usually relates to the individual and not to an entire society at large. In all societies it is the elite only that is bilingual, trilingual, or otherwise but not the whole society. Societal or collective bilingualism presupposes two sets of sociodynamics at work within one society in order to keep alive, functioning, and developing two different sets of culture, language, and personality structures. Wherever this is found, one set of structures must necessarily dominate the other. The predominance of one set of structures over another has been shown to be always the case in the study of individual bilinguals, no matter how they acquired their two languages. There are no exceptions here, not even for Prime Minister Trudeau.

It is clear that those who learn their French in Maillardville, British Columbia, do not have the same privilege of participation in a solid French set of linguistico-cultural structures as the persons who are born and brought up in relatively homogeneous Quebec City and highly homogeneous Paris, France. Even if Premier Bennett offered his French minority free French schooling from the cradle to the grave, he cannot alter the fact that French is not part of the institutional or total life of British Columbia. In effect, it would be like having the same privilege for French-Canadians in England, Italy, or Russia. At best, such a generous action could only somewhat ease the present struggle of the French minority of British Columbia. And even if the elite of Vancouver were to become as fluently bilingual as the British elite in England, for example, this would in no way change the absolute predominance of English sociodynamics in this Pacific province. One thing is certain, it would not in any way improve the French sociodynamics in Quebec. To be fanciful, I suppose one sure way of resolving this problem would be to have General de Gaulle invade the far western province with some 500,000 settlers and have the General himself settle down to govern it for the next generation. Then, roughly, we might have a repetition in British Columbia of what has taken place in Quebec since the British conquest in 1759, that is, a small minority enjoying all the privileges normally enjoyed by the majority and dominating the scene.

Montreal and the Ottawa-Hull region are excellent testing grounds for the study of languages and cultures in contact. Let us see how that affects the individual who belongs to the less stable set of linguistic and cultural structures. The massive infusion that French is constantly subjected to from English reaches into every structure. Dozens of verbs with English roots and French endings are used daily by French-Canadians, for example, *watch* becomes watch*er, bother* becomes bad*rer*. Nouns are literally borrowed by the hundreds such as *le wrench, le windshield, le file cabinet,* and so on. The coexistence of two linguistic structures in the French-Canadian bilingual's speech allows English pronunciation to alter French patterns, its rhythm, intonation, vocalic length, and stress. The French-speaking people of the Ottawa-Hull region consistently pronounce the initial *h* phoneme of *Hull* even though *h* is never pronounced in French, it is only written. Syntactic structures are also affected. An English sentence such as "the company that I work for" is literally translated to "la compagnie que je travaille pour" where the correct French would be "la compagnie pour laquelle je travaille." A nominalizing suffix such as *-ing* in *no smoking* is literally translated as *pas de fumage* in conversation instead of *défense de fumer* usually found in posters. These are but a few examples among hundreds, if not thousands, of similar cases found at all levels of language. But the most serious invasion and perhaps the most sinister one is at the semantic level. It is subtle and devastating. The semantic confusion in the mind of most French-Canadians is almost beyond description. The average bilingual, not the elite, is literally mutilated in the sense that he very seldom can express himself well and with confidence in either language.

Each word in a language has its own semantic field, that is, its meaning is actualized in various contexts, each with its own specific sense and nuance. It is hard enough to learn to use meanings accurately or to keep them apart within the context of one language for meaning is a world of shifting sands. It is even harder to master the shifting contours of meaning in two languages, especially when one language enjoys greater stability due to its higher frequency and greater creativity resulting from its more powerful sociodynamics. As just pointed out, it is not a question of greater English frequency alone. The fact is that most new concepts originate in English. One cannot expect every French-Canadian to walk around with a dictionary and, even if he did, the dictionary would be of little help for it does not reflect the milieu. Besides, a French-Canadian is not born a trained translator or interpreter any more than his English counterpart is. The trained official translators are like prisoners chained to their piles of dictionaries which are usually of continental French origin and very frequently prove insufficient to the task of translating North American Anglo-American realities. Their translations are heavily imitative of English thought and style because they, the translators, are not themselves involved in or are they products of a set of creative and homogeneous French sociodynamics and milieu. Only the best among them succeed in recreating an acceptable French style and thought in translation. Among the worst, who are not a small minority, there work amounts to writing English with French words. The laws of the Federal government and even of the Quebec legislature are classic examples of inelegant and clumsy translations and imitations of English thought, style and concepts.

Even if all the translations from English were first rate, let us never forget that language is not learned from the written word but from the spoken one. What we learn from reading is mostly technical and of low frequency in speech; it is, therefore, specialized knowledge. Even the French unilingual is not free from this heavy dosage of English patterns, for he, like everybody else, learns the use of language unconsciously from the milieu at large, so that in effect, the more bilinguals there are, the more open doors are there for the semantic confusion and general contamination that eventually reaches even the unilinguals. That explains why over the years, fairly homogeneous French regions of Quebec like Gaspé and the Saguenay have been tainted by English speech patterns as well.

In bilingual regions such as that of Ottawa-Hull where the English language and culture predominate, it is not only the French language which is undermined but the cultural patterns as well. As a matter of fact, as we have tried to show throughout this paper, the one reality cannot be altered without altering the other. French *sensibilité* which comprises the total set of emotive responses of this cultural group is under such pressure from the English patterns that a very large number of French-Canadians automatically turn on their television sets to the English channels, prefer going to English movies and generally prefer doing things in English without being aware that they act this way because they feel more at home in English. I know French-Canadians who always watch hockey night in English. When asked to explain such a gesture, they simply reply that they understand the English commentary better for there are too many strange and unfamiliar expressions in the French one. To many French-Canadian bilinguals and even unilinguals, radio and television French is an unfamiliar language with which they feel ill at ease and very frequently only half understand.

The net result of all this linguistic and cultural confusion is that the French-Canadian at large suffers from what I call linguistico-cultural psychoses of various kinds. These psychoses are created by the inner conflict resulting from the image of good French which the French-Canadian elite has presented him with, traditionally through the medium of the school, and more recently, through radio and television as well. This image is distorted all the more because the average French-Canadian is fed antiquated notions that have little in common with the findings of the social sciences to explain the reality of language and culture.

Social scientists agree that the basic patterns of culture, language, and personality are acquired by the child by the time he goes to school. In varying degrees, it is a hybrid linguistico-cultural milieu which shapes the French-Canadian child. When he enters school, over and above the normal psychological disarray of a school beginner, he faces the additional psychological burden of having most of his speech patterns challenged by a new set of rules which are tantamount to his learning a different language. It is as if he were being subtly told that all he stands for is not worth very much and that he must gently submit himself to what is literally a personality transplant. The minute he steps out the schoolroom door, he feels psychologically ill at ease to use such radically different patterns which his milieu does not reflect. In a very real sense he is being asked to perform the impossible duty of playing the hero every day of his future life in the valiant personal defense of his mother tongue. This task is beyond his powers as a simple individual because no single person can withstand the minute-to-minute struggle of swimming against the heavy tides of his linguistico-cultural milieu which in all normal societies is there to support the individual and not to drown him.

As a result, the French-Canadian wastes the better part of his creative energies trying to remake and re-create his language consciously by dint of personal effort, that is, trying to do something that in all normal societies just comes naturally, as a gift from the gods, as it were. The burden often becomes so heavy to bear, that many French-Canadian bilinguals prefer to speak English, even among each other. In this way, the French-Canadian, like poor Sisyphus, is condemned to a never-ending, wasteful, and fruitless struggle. Until very recent times, the power elite in Quebec thought that the school alone could undo all the evils brought about by an unhealthy and hybrid linguistico-cultural milieu. The various pronouncements of the old traditional parties are still so ambiguous that it is very hard to tell if they have really been enlightened by the findings of modern social science. The independence movement in Quebec has certainly not neglected these findings which form the basis of its language policies. Through ignorance or lack of moral courage or both, the traditional parties have never been able to come to grips with the core of the problem and take the bull by the horns to bring about a satisfactory solution. Their attitude can be likened to the man who chooses to bail a sinking boat with a thimble when there is a power pump available. This is why the independentists are interested in a fundamental restructuring of the sociodynamics in Quebec in favour of the French culture and language. It is the total milieu that must be restructured, not just the school.

The nefarious effects of the total linguistico-cultural milieu on the schools in French-Canada extend beyond undoing their positive efforts to improve the situation. Where, in normal societies, the school is a reflection and a reinforcement of the total milieu, in French Canada, the opposite holds true. This situation has devastating repercussions on the quality of individual achievement in the schools. For example, French is a deeply resented and hated subject among French-Canadian students for the simple reason that it is fighting a losing battle. Furthermore, in not reflecting the milieu adequately, it increases the students' traumas and psychoses. The constant pressures of bilingualism increase the linguistic uncertainty of the average speaker, that is, he is never quite sure that he is using the correct French word or pattern. Besides, if after long years of training in French, you are not even capable of working in that language except at second-rate jobs for the most part, this adds to the general frustration of studying French or *in* French, for that matter. What is even more serious, is that French-Canadians themselves after a while begin to doubt the utility of their own language. If a language is not used to express the fullness of a collective and individual personality at work and at play, the doubts just spoken of, like a subtle corrosive acid, sink into the subconscious of the French-Canadian with the serious evil effects we have been describing. The law of least effort is only human and it applies here as it does everywhere else. Why bother using a blunt instrument to make your way through life when there is a fine precision-sharp custom-made one at your immediate disposal?

Astounding findings in the B. and B. report that leaked out to the French press recently[5] demonstrated that even where French Quebeckers have equal education they still earn 35 percent less than their English-speaking counterparts. This report also reveals that French-Canadians in their own province come in twelfth place or third last on the list of comparative incomes among the various ethnic groups of Quebec. All those above them are either English born or have assimilated into the English minority. Interestingly enough, the report also shows that even the bilingual French-Canadians earn considerably less than their uni-lingual English-speaking counterparts. To my mind, such a state of affairs can only be explained by the theory of structures that I have been ex-pounding throughout this entire discussion. Your linguistic and cultural training is supposed to prepare you for living within those same struc-tures. It is not only ridiculous but also wasteful and even sadistic to train people in one set of structures and then oblige them to work in another. One might try to counter this statement by saying that most New Cana-dian bilinguals succeed, therefore, why can't the French? The crucial difference is that the New Canadians adopt wholesale the total socio-dynamics of English life and their retention of native linguistic and cultural patterns is but vestigial and folkloric. That is precisely what French Canadians refuse to do because they do not consider themselves New Canadians and in point of fact, are not. Immigrants to Canada know very well that they will be committing, in essence, cultural and linguistic suicide by leaving their native land. This was certainly not the case when the French first settled in Canada.

Statistics show the high rate of assimilation of French-Canadians outside the Province of Quebec. Actually, in time, even with enlightened legislation on bilingualism in English provinces, the small pockets of French life scattered throughout Canada with the possible exception of New Brunswick and those on the Ontario-Quebec border, are destined to a slow withering vestigial and folkloric end. New enlightened legislation might arrest the gradual assimilation of the French on these small and fragile islands but what it will certainly not do is to change the prevailing English sociodynamics of the milieu surrounding these islands. The French language and culture will have to be saved in Quebec or it will not survive at all anywhere in Canada.

I should like to close this discussion with a quotation from a leading French-Canadian intellectual and a former editor of the distinguished French-Canadian newspaper—*Le Devoir,* to wit, Jean Marc Léger:

The best educational system, the best programs of study, the best equipped and most modern schools, free tuition at all levels, will not change the fact that a nation will remain culturally underdeveloped, intellectually handicapped and

---

[5] *La Presse,* Montreal, October 25 and 26, 1968.

socially inferior, if it uses a kind of jargon to express itself. A people who know a language only half-well, that is, their own language, and who do not use it in every sphere of life are incapable of expressing themselves, of communicating, of inventing, incapable of profound and creative thought: at best, they are translators and imitators.[6]

<hr>

[6] *Le Devoir*, Montreal, Editorial, May 18, 1966.

32

Canadian-American
Economic Relations*

Melville H. Watkins

IN CANADA TODAY, there are few public issues which arouse passion as quickly as economic relations with the United States. From the Annexation Manifesto of 1849 to the present controversy over American ownership of Canadian companies there has always been plenty of heat on this question. In many instances anti-American prejudices were evident in Canadian reactions or the determination of Canadian businessmen to preserve their protected economic position by "National" policies or other expedients. Goldwin Smith suggested continental union as a goal in the late 19th century (see Chapter II) but few would accept his arguments today. Today most socialists have ideological reasons for weakening links with the United States.

In a simple lucid style Melville Watkins sums up the main factors he sees which have led to the integration of the Canadian and American economies. An economics professor at the University of Toronto he is an active participant in the current debate on Canadian-American economic relations. This paper was originally published in Russia and presented at Moscow State University. It appeared before the Waffle Movement was born.

The great dilemma faced by Canadians today is that most would like less American economic control but few have solutions which do not involve serious lowering of the Canadian standard of living, a cost most Canadians would consider too high.

* *South Atlantic Quarterly*, LXVI (1967), 382–94.

This paper was written to be given at Moscow State University and published in Russia. MR. WATKINS *is associate professor of economics, University of Toronto, and a member of the editorial board of the* Canadian Forum.

I T IS BELIEVED by some people in the world that Canada is, in fact
though not in law, a colony of the United States of America. Few
Canadians, however, would be prepared to describe their country as a
colony and to accept all of the connotations which are associated with
that term. But many Canadians, including both the present Minister of
Finance (Mitchell Sharp) and his immediate predecessor (Walter
Gordon), are prepared to state that Canada is an economic satellite of
the United States and to advocate that actions be taken to remedy this
state of affairs.

For reasons which I will try to explain, it is best to conceive of Canada
as an economic satellite of the United States rather than as a colony.
There is abundant evidence of a satellitic relationship. Canada's trade is
heavily oriented to the United States, with more than one-half of Canadian exports going to that country and approximately two-thirds of
Canadian imports coming from there. Furthermore, the composition of
that trade is such that most of the exports are of raw materials and
semiprocessed goods, while most of the imports are of manufactured
goods. The extent of Canadian reliance on American capital is even more
revealing. There is a persistent inflow of American investment into
Canada, and a substantial portion of the inflow takes the form of what is
called "direct investment," that is, it involves investment by American
corporations in branches or firms which they own in whole or in part, and
which they effectively control. Approximately 60 per cent of Canadian
manufacturing industry is controlled by non-residents, and Americans
control about three-quarters of that total.

One might well ask whether these statistics do not suggest that it
would be appropriate to regard Canada as a colony of the United States,
and that the Canadian reluctance to think in such terms is based on self-
deception. Most Canadians would be reluctant to accept such a description, because it implies economic backwardness and exploitation. By the
customary criteria of measuring economic development, Canada is not
backward, for it has a very high standard of living and a large and
technically advanced industrial sector. Nor would most Canadians believe that they are being exploited by the United States; rather, the
evidence is that they fear a decrease in their standard of living if the close
trade and investment ties were to be lessened—that is, they believe, at
least implicitly, that they are materially better off as a result of American
trade and investment.

Let us now look at the nature of the Canadian economy in general and
its relationship with the United States in particular.

The population of Canada is approximately twenty million, or about one-tenth that of the United States. While Canada is small relative to the United States, it is not small by world standards, for there are many countries with less than its twenty millions of inhabitants. The standard of living—or, more accurately, national income per capita—is one of the highest in the world. With the possible exception of a few oil sheikdoms, the United States has the world's highest standard of living, and Canada is second—about 25 per cent below that of the United States. The combination of an above-average population size and a very high standard of living means that the Canadian market is one of the largest in the world. While this explains the attractiveness of Canada to foreign investors, it also means that Canada is capable of supporting an indigenous industrial base.

Indeed, Canada does have a large and diversified secondary manufacturing sector, mostly concentrated in the St. Lawrence–Great Lakes area. The difference between Canada and the United States is one of degree rather than of kind; Canadian manufacturing industry is clearly recognizable as a small-scale version of the giant industrial economy of the United States. At the same time, primary manufacturing—or the processing of raw materials—bulks particularly large in Canada compared with most highly developed countries. But this primary manufacturing is as scientifically and technologically sophisticated as secondary manufacturing and generates as large gains in productivity. The image of Canada as a nation of hewers of wood and drawers of water—an image that Canadians have themselves fostered in order to promote the tourist trade—is only appropriate if it is understood that the wood is hewn with highly complex machinery and the water is drawn through giant turbines to generate hydroelectric power.

Canadian reliance on foreign trade is substantial—certainly much higher than for the United States or the U.S.S.R.—but not abnormal by world standards. Canadian reliance on trade is about the same as that of Britain, France, and West Germany, and less than that of such highly developed countries as Sweden, Denmark, and the Netherlands. Nor is Canadian trade heavily reliant on a small number of commodities; in spite of its world reputation as an exporter of wheat, newsprint, and minerals, the export trade is well diversified and even includes a number of highly complex manufactured commodities such as agricultural machinery, aircraft, and whisky. As already indicated, however, Canadian trade is heavily concentrated geographically as a result of close trade ties with the United States. It is by this measure that Canada looks like an underdeveloped export economy or even like a colony; the only developed country that has as high a concentration of trade with a single country is New Zealand vis-à-vis the United Kingdom.

Finally, Canada is a highly urbanized country, as would be expected given its high standard of living. A large proportion of the Canadian population lives in a small number of big cities. Partly for reasons of climate, these cities are all located in the southern part of Canada and hence lie close to the border with the United States. As a result, the great majority of the Canadian population lives within one hundred miles of the American border. This facilitates not only the exchange of goods, but also many other things, and has led to what one book calls "the mingling of the American and Canadian peoples."

All of us, and particularly economists, are interested not so much in facts about the state of affairs, as in deciding whether that state of affairs is good or bad. That is as it should be, though we should always be patient, and try to understand why a situation exists before we attempt to evaluate it. Why, then, is Canada so closely tied economically to the United States? That question can best be answered by lapsing into some historical generalizations about Canada.

The economic development of Canada should be viewed as an aspect of the spread of European civilization since about 1500. Traders and settlers from the Old World came primarily for reasons of economic gain. With only a limited population base in the New World, and therefore a limited domestic market, economic activity lay chiefly in exporting to more advanced industrial countries. Until the nineteenth century, the fisheries and the fur trade, directed toward European markets, were the dominant economic activities in what is now Canada. Traders in search of fur pushed across the continent to the Pacific Ocean and essentially defined what are today the boundaries of Canada. The existence of Canada as a country separate from the United States should not be regarded as a puzzle; the reason is the existence of the St. Lawrence River and the nature of the fur trade. The heartland of the area was controlled by the French to 1760 and thereafter by the British. The British North American colonies did not join in the American Revolution but rather provided a haven for American refugees. The result was to create a fresh population base that was Americanized, but not American in terms of its loyalty to the British crown and in terms of its generally greater conservatism. The emergence of timber and lumber as new staple exports, and the building of first canals and then railways, strengthened the economy of the St. Lawrence River and laid the basis for the emergence of Canada as a separate nation in 1867. In the colonial period, markets for exports were primarily in Europe, and the capital and labor needed to build a new country had to come largely from Europe.

After 1867, the building of transcontinental railways and the emergence of wheat from the Canadian prairie as the dominant export maintained ties with the Old World and facilitated the task of nation-building in Canada. But economic relations with the United States grew quickly, particularly in terms of reliance on imports. By the early twentieth century there had emerged a North Atlantic triangle in which Canada had a large export surplus with Europe and a large import deficit with the United States. Most of the immigrants who continued to flood into Canada, and most of the imports of capital, came from Europe.

Since World War I, American influence has waxed while British influence has waned. Canada has continued to import largely from the United States, while her exports—of such new commodities as newsprint and minerals—have gone to the United States rather than to Europe. The North Atlantic triangle has broken down and Canada has been drawn more closely into the American sphere of influence. In spite of a rising standard of living and an increasing capacity to generate domestic savings, Canada continued to rely on capital imports. These now came increasingly from the United States and were increasingly in the form of direct investment which carried with it the ownership and control of Canadian resources and Canadian industry.

While many people are concerned about this latter phenomenon, including many Canadians, it is not difficult to understand why it has happened. The basic reason is Canadian proximity to the United States in a world which is steadily being shrunk in size by technological advances in transportation and communication, and a world in which the influence of the United States has increased greatly relative to that of Europe, and particularly of Britain. The continuing industrialization of the United States has created enormous demands for raw materials; in spite of that country's own rich resources and the important developments which have taken place in synthetics, this has compelled the United States to rely on imports. Canada's closeness, and her own abundant resources relative to her population, have made Canada a happy hunting ground for American corporations in search of such raw materials as newsprint, iron ore, oil and gas, and so on. These American corporations frequently prefer to own the resources rather than to buy them on a trading basis, so what has been involved is not only increased exports to the United States but also increased American investment in Canada and ownership and control of Canadian resources.

A similar phenomenon has been at work with respect to imports as well. The desires of Canadians as consumers are more or less the same as those of Americans, a phenomenon which can be partly attributed to the pervasive influence of American advertising. In effect, Canada has been the first country to feel the wave of Americanization that has since spread to more distant parts of the globe. The result has been a substantial demand for American imports, both of consumer goods proper and of capital goods to produce American-style consumer goods. Some attempt has been made by the Canadian government to offset the consequences of this for Canadian trade by providing tariff protection for Canadian industry. While this protection has reduced the extent of imports from the United States, it has not prevented the situation now existing in which Canada buys two-thirds of its imports from the United States. At the same time, it has increased American investment in Canada in the form of ownership and control of secondary manufacturing industry. Unable to export to Canada because of the tariff wall, American corporations have simply built branch plants in Canada to sell behind the tariff wall.

This expansion of the American corporation into Canada can be seen as a natural spillover across the border. By natural I mean only that it was bound to happen in a situation in which both the United States and Canada have economies organized substantially on a capitalist basis. For reasons of proximity and of general similarities of ways of life, American corporations have tended not to regard investments in Canada as foreign investments proper. The spread of the American corporation into Canada has been an incident in the creation of the corporation as a spatially national entity within the United States.

The phenomenon has also been highly predictable in another sense. The twentieth century has been firmly in the grip of rapidly evolving science and technology. The United States has been one of the great centers of those developments, and notably in the field of consumer goods suitable to already developed economies. Only a small number of countries have made significant contributions to science and technology, and certainly not Canada. Yet economic development—which is today so highly valued everywhere in the world—rests fundamentally on science and technology. Countries which themselves do not innovate must be ready to absorb innovations if they are to keep abreast and to meet the demands of the people for a rising standard of living. Canadians are rich and want to stay that way, and close contact with the United States, including American direct investment in Canada, has been the major channel by which new technology has entered Canada. Though this investment has required the payment of interest and dividends, up to now most Canadians have regarded those payments as a reasonable price for the technical knowledge, the managerial skills, and the access to markets which are thereby obtained.

I now want to pose a number of questions which are intended to aid in evaluating the state of Canadian-American relations. What, if anything, has Canada done to lessen the closeness of its economic ties with the United States? Could Canada, if it wished, do more in this regard? Is it likely that in the foreseeable future Canadians will do more? Finally, should Canada do more?

To the first question, the short answer, as I have said, is the Canadians have not done much, but nevertheless they have done something. Canada has had a high protective tariff for almost a century. While this measure has probably facilitated the development of secondary manufacturing industry at the cost of marginally lowering the Canadian standard of living, it has also, as previously noted, increased the extent of American direct investment in Canada. It is arguable that trade ties are less serious than investment ties and hence that the Canadian tariff, unaccompanied by significant controls on foreign owners, has increased rather than decreased Canadian dependence on the United States. It is partly for this reason that some Canadians—and many Canadian economists—advocate that Canada move toward free or freer trade. In a capitalist economy, the rationale of the tariff is to provide protection, at least temporarily, for domestic entrepreneurship, but it is possible that the Canadian tariff has mostly provided protection for American enterpreneurship and may even have made more difficult the emergence of indigenous Canadian entrepreneurship.

Unlike the United States, Canada has some tolerance for public ownership, particularly in such key sectors as transportation and communication. Hence, while in the United States all railways and radio-television broadcasting are privately owned, Canada has both a publicly owned railway and a publicly owned radio-television network. Also in Canada, more than one-half of the electric power generated is produced by public utilities. While public ownership in Canada has not meant the complete nationalization of any of these activities, there is nevertheless evident a lesser commitment to the ideology of free enterprise than exists in the United States.

In the past decade a number of moves have been made by the federal government to offer some discouragement to foreign investors. Their effectiveness does not appear to have been great, and Canadian policy toward foreign investment remains one of the most liberal in the world. This is, however, one area which is politically very much alive in Canada. The recent issuance by the United States of guidelines to its corporations with respect to their investment abroad—for the purpose of strengthening the American balance of payments—has created considerable reaction in Canada and has led to Canada's issuing its own guidelines instructing American firms in Canada to behave like good corporate citizens of Canada.

As is well known, the most important changes in economic policy that have taken place in advanced capitalist economies in recent years have been in the area of monetary and fiscal policies designed to maintain full employment with stable prices. All political parties in Canada are committed to this objective and have shown some willingness when in power to pursue monetary and banking policies and taxing and spending policies that will minimize unemployment and curb inflation. I introduce this point because in the pursuit of these objectives, which many Canadians regard as the most important economic ones, close economic relations with the United States are not a seriously inhibiting factor. Certainly external trade and investment ties make more difficult the lives of policy makers, but they do not rule out the formulation and execution of effective policy.

Aside from these important developments that have followed from the application of the writings of John Maynard Keynes, there has not been in Canada any substantial interference with the operation of the capitalist system. That there has been some can be attributed to a general trend toward greater interference with the operation of the free market that has characterized all capitalist economies in this century. In Canada, this has been supplemented by the desire to define a national economy more sharply in the conviction that political identity would thereby be strengthened. That there has not been more interference reflects the fact that Canadians are basically committed to the liberal bourgeois ideology.

Can Canada, if it wishes, do more to lessen its economic ties with the United States? The answer, I think, is yes, though with certain qualifications. Canada is a sovereign state by law, and hence in all matters of economic policy, parliament—either at the national or provincial level—is sovereign. Though Canada, like all states, has international obligations, in matters of trade and investment there is very wide latitude, by law, for autonomous action. But, it might be asked, what would the United States do if Canada (let us say, by way of an extreme example) nationalized all American-controlled firms in Canada? We can agree that the United States would not like this, and that it would unquestionably bring its influence to bear to try to stop it. But if Canada stubbornly persisted, I have no doubt it would get its way—albeit at the risk of considerable economic cost.

By saying this, I am not denying certain realities about American foreign policy. Under the Monroe Doctrine, as recently restated and extended by President Johnson, the United States is committed to keeping what it regards as foreign ideologies out of the American hemisphere. Furthermore, Canada is an integral part of the North American military system, being on this critical level uniquely associated with the United States. These facts clearly impose ultimate limitations on the freedom of Canadian political action. At the same time, most Canadians show no unwillingness to live within these constraints.

The relevant constraints on autonomous Canadian action lie as much, if not more, within Canada than within the United States. If Canada took a strong position in economic affairs that would stand to damage the American economy, it is certainly possible that the United States would retaliate in a similar fashion. Indeed, Canada today has a uniquely preferred position within the American system in terms of special trade and investment arrangements, and should Canada unduly irritate the United States, it would risk losing that preferred status and would have to suffer the associated costs. The problem could be said to lie within the United States insofar as it is that country which might prove to be intolerant of too much Canadian autonomy. But the problem must also be seen as lying equally within Canada, for there is no doubt that Canadians fear a too drastic decrease in the standard of living, and that it is distinctly possible that a considerable number of Canadians would emigrate to the United States in that eventuality.

What if Canada simply stepped up its restrictions on foreign owners, but not in any extreme fashion? I have already implied that this is possible, and I shall shortly suggest that it is probable in the near future. As well as the risk of American retaliation, there are some specific problems which Canadians would have to face, though all of them should be manageable. Since Canada would become a less favorable climate for American corporations in search of raw materials, alternative markets would have to be sought. A decrease in the inflow of foreign capital would require an increase in the rate of domestic saving if the same level of domestic capital formation—and the associated rate of economic growth—were to be maintained. But this is surely possible. There is something strange about a country as rich as Canada having to import capital—indeed it is even scandalous given the terrible shortage of captial in the poor countries of the world. Changes in the structure of the capital market and more saving by the government should be possible by way of solving this problem.

Some mention must be made of the possibility that a significantly lower capital inflow would create serious balance-of-payments problems for Canada. Canada does have a large deficit on current account, and this would clearly have to be correspondingly reduced. While some short-run difficulties are possible in this area, there is reason to believe that no serious crisis would result. In part, this is because the capital inflow, by providing Canadians with American dollars, has been creating the deficit, rather than the deficit emerging independently and having to be covered by foreign borrowing. Hence, if the capital flow ceased, much of the deficit should disappear automatically. Also the historical evidence is that the Canadian balance of payments adjusts efficiently to changes in capital flows: that is, other items in the balance of payments tend to move so as to compensate for a change in any one component. The exchange crisis of 1962, which might seem to suggest that I am too optimistic, was, in fact, mostly the result of some serious blunders by the Canadian government.

To the extent that interferences with foreign investments would slow down the diffusion of new technology and skills into Canada, action could be taken to encourage scientific research within Canada, to facilitate contacts of scientists, engineers, and businessmen with foreign countries, and to improve the educational system which, though generally of high quality, is not yet accessible at the higher levels to a large enough proportion of Canadians. These are all areas in which Canadian governments have, in fact, shown greater interest in the last decade.

Finally, to answer the question whether Canada could do more if it wished about lessening its economic ties with the United States, it is impossible to avoid taking a stand on the issue of whether or not political independence is today really feasible at all for any but the very large countries. Perhaps everything I have been saying is irrelevant if one assumes that Canada as a nation has no future and will simply slip imperceptibly into the United States. There are some Canadians, not all of whom are silly people, who believe that this will happen. My own view is that such an event is improbable. While Canada is not an old country, it this year celebrates its centennial, and a century of history independent of the United States proves something about the viability of Canada as a nation.

Events at the world level similarly give cause for optimism. What we have witnessed in the last twenty years is the break-up of the European empires, and a wave of nationalism that has been evident around the globe. If Canada decides to annex itself to the United States, it would be in defiance of what most countries, many of whom have nothing like a century of national experience behind them, are doing. Indeed, as an aspect of this wave of nationalism there has been a sharp upsurge within Canada itself of demands for greater autonomy on the part of its French-speaking citizens. While this is a complex phenomenon which cannot be adequately dealt with under the heading of Canadian-American economic relations, it can be argued that the desires of the French-Canadians will ultimately lead to a stronger Canada, with a greater sense of national identity and a greater wish to pursue independent foreign policies.

Is it likely that Canada will take action in the foreseeable future to lessen the economic ties with the United States? My answer again would be: yes, though not of any extreme nature. In particular, I think this is true with respect to foreign investment. The extent of American ownership and control is a relatively recent phenomenon. It is only in the last decade that Canadians have shown real concern over this situation, and this concern seems to be steadily rising.

The present Canadian Minister of Finance, who has been known as generally favorable to business interests and as disposed to believe in the virtues of the capitalist economy, nevertheless said in a speech (May 4, 1966):

I believe that if we are to be reasonably independent, in any practical way, we must, as a nation, know more about the working of those large economic enterprises which dominate so many sectors of our economy, but which are controlled by foreigners. The inescapable fact is that no other country has such a large proportion of its production in the hands of corporations that take direction from parent firms in other countries. Without denying for an instant the great contribution such firms have made and continue to make to our standard of living, I suggest that no responsible government can look at the present degree of non-resident control over our economy with any great feeling of confidence, far less complacency.

His predecessor, who is still a powerful and respected politician in Canada, warned Canadians in a book published last year that there are enormous pressures exercised by Americans on Canadian policy that inhibit Canadian autonomy:

I was aware of these long before I entered politics . . . but I had not fully appreciated the depth and strength of these pressures until I became Minister of Finance . . . During the two-and-one-half years I held that office, the influence that financial and business interests in the United States had on Canadian policy and opinion was continually brought home to me. On occasion this influence was reinforced by representations from the State Department and the American Administration as a whole. It was pressed by those who direct American businesses in Canada, by their professional advisers, by Canadian financiers whose interests were identified directly or indirectly with American investment in Canada, by influential members of the Canadian civil service, by some representatives of the university community, and by some sections of the press. The effects of these pressures on the leaders and spokesmen of all the political parties in Canada are immense—and too often they are effective.[1]

These statements are symptomatic of a political climate in Canada in which some restrictions against foreign owners are a distinct possibility. A factor which has contributed to that climate is the balance-of-payments problem of the United States and its consequent guidelines on external investment by its corporations. On the one hand, Canadians are being compelled to think about the possibility of getting by with less American capital. On the other hand, they read statements by high American officials to the effect that large American corporations are the instruments of American foreign policy. Though many Canadians, but not all, are in agreement with American foreign policy, such blunt talk is not widely appreciated.

My final question is: Should Canada do more to lessen these ties? I cannot give any answer other than a personal one—for I do not pretend to speak for the Canadian government or for the Canadian people. My personal answer is yes, but for reasons that have little to do with narrow economic factors. We live in a world of great powers and competing ideologies. There is a role for smaller countries prepared to stand somewhere in between. For Canada, strong economic ties with the United States have been economically beneficial, but they have created a situation, partly real, and partly in Canadian minds, in which Canada is inhibited from taking independent actions because of a fear of the economic consequences. To lessen economic ties with the United States would be another step down the road toward a stronger national identity for Canada and a more independent foreign policy.

---

[1] Walter Gordon, *A Choice for Canada: Independence or Colonial Status* (Toronto, 1966).

33

Toward the Democratic Class Struggle*

Gad Horowitz

HISTORICALLY, argues Gad Horowitz, Canadians "have not moved as quickly or as consistently in the direction of democratic goals as either the liberal Americans or the socialist Britons. Our political elites operate, more clearly than theirs, on the periphery rather than the center of the structure of power." For Gad Horowitz and many of the younger left-wing intellectuals who share his viewpoint, Canadians "have not even approximated democracy." The party system should be the primary device which should move Canadian society toward democracy. Although he admits that "some form of elite rule is probably inevitable in a modern industrial society," he argues that because the political elite is the most sensitive to the needs of the masses, that elite must be strengthened so that it rather than the corporate and bureaucratic elites make the most important social decisions. This can only be accomplished through abandonment of the false myth of brokerage politics and acceptance of a right-left polarization. The important creative tension is the democratic class struggle, carried on intensely but peacefully in a civilized fashion, "within a society which is fundamentally at one." It is creative democratic class conflict not class war.

In this article we find articulate expression of an important viewpoint among committed Canadian social scientists and historians. Horowitz rejects both the accommodating liberalism, the drift toward the centre, and the "end of ideology" of many of the old social democrats and also the anarchistic and revolutionary dreaming of the so-called New Left. Horowitz's own call is for a genuine, realistic, updated, hard-nosed, mass-oriented socialism.

---

* *Journal of Canadian Studies*, I (November, 1966), pp. 3–10.

The historic argument made so popular by Mackenzie King and his followers that a country as tenuous as Canada simply could not afford class politics is directly refuted. A nation in danger of breaking up on ethnic-regional lines may be strengthened by a politics which joins people of various regions and ethnic groups around two poles. Professor Horowitz's views are further developed in his *Canadian Labour in Politics* (Toronto, 1968). Horowitz is linked with C. W. Gonick M.L.A., Charles Taylor, and many other nationalistic scholars of the left in the pages of the Winnipeg-based journal, the *Canadian Dimension*.

Introduction

THE TERM "DEMOCRACY" has, like many other honorific terms, fallen victim to twentieth century doublespeak, which is a device used by the practical minded for the purpose of "adjusting their ideals to reality," thereby obscuring the gap between the ideal and the real, and substituting the name for the thing. We no longer use the term "democracy" to refer to a situation in which masses of people participate, directly and meaningfully, in the making of the decisions which shape the basic conditions of their existence. We have discovered that this is an unattainable ideal—which means not that it is absolutely, inevitably, and eternally unattainable, but that all our efforts to attain it have failed: limited as we are by ignorance, or by original sin, or by what seem to be inexorable social and economic necessities, we do not know how to attain it. We have therefore decided to adjust the ideal to the reality, that is, we have given up the ideal. We now use the term "democracy" to refer to the *reality* of our way of life.

Of course there are large differences of opinion about the nature of that reality. Perhaps the most common view is that which was first formulated by Joseph Schumpeter, who defined democracy as "the rule of the politician," or, in a more extended phrase, as "that institutional arrangement for arriving at political decisions in which individuals acquire the power to decide by means of a competitive struggle for the people's vote." Those who hold this view believe that we have the second best thing to real democracy. The people do not have the power; their elected leaders have the power; the people act through their leaders. This is, surely, in this world, a satisfactory approximation to the real thing.

Assuming for the sake of argument that the people do act through their elected leaders—something that is not at all certain—and granting that the rule of politicians is a satisfactory substitute for the real thing— the question remains: is this really a description of the reality of our system? Is our system one in which elected leaders make the political decisions? Do we have even this second best approximation to democracy? That depends on how one defines "political." What are *political* decisions? If they are simply whatever decisions are made by politicians, the definition fits the reality. But tautology is never satisfying. What if the political decisions are less significant, less powerfully determining of the fate of the community, than non-political decisions? Can we then say that the community is *governed* by its political decision makers?

The only way of avoiding this difficulty is to define "political" non-tautologically, as "pertaining to the polity." Political decisions are decisions which are of importance to the community, decisions on public matters. And it is a fact that the most important of these decisions are not made by our political elite but by other elites which are *not* accountable to the community. The common or Schumpeterian definition of democracy is therefore not an accurate description of the reality of our system. We have not even achieved second best. We have not even approximated democracy.

I want to suggest that among the roles that the party system in our society can and should play, the most important is to move our society toward democracy—not the utopian democracy in which the people rule, but the attainable democracy in which an élite accountable to the people rules.

If the party system is to play the role of moving us closer to democracy; if, in other words, our political elite is to be strengthened to the point where it replaces the corporate and bureaucratic elites as the source of the most important social decisions, our party system must be polarized on a left-right basis, and the main issues raised for discussion in the political arena must be class issues. I will argue not only that this change in the party system ought to be brought about, but that it can be brought about, and with no evil side effects.

THE DEMOCRATIC CLASS STRUGGLE

We are interested in strengthening our political elite in relation to other elites not because we want politicians to have more power for themselves, but because we want ordinary people to have more power. Power is what it takes to get what there is to get. Power is valuable because it is a means to other values; Lasswell classifies them as security, income, deference. To move closer to democracy is to redistribute power, and with it all other values, downwards in the social system. Some form of elite rule is probably inevitable in a modern industrial society; the political elite is the one which is most sensitive to the needs of the mass of the people; therefore the rule of the politician is the form of elite rule which comes closest to democracy.

To move closer to democracy requires 1) that the political elite include a powerful party of the "left", which I will define provisionally as a party which is more responsive to the needs of the underprivileged than to those of the overprivileged; 2) that this party succeed in mobilizing popular support for programmes of social change, i.e., for policies which will reallocate social values in the interest of the underprivileged. This in turn requires attention to the latent—unexpressed—unarticulated needs of the masses as well as to their manifest needs, for the masses are seldom capable of expressing autonomously their need for power and the things that it can get. One of the techniques of oligarchy has always been to train the masses to be content with their lot, to minimize their demands, to want what they get. The task of a left party is to agitate—to train the masses to be discontented with their lot, to maximize their demands, to get what they want.

In a well ordered society, the privileged elites and the politicians responsive to them behave responsibly in the sense that they do not press their *resistance* to social change past the point where it would endanger the underlying consensus guaranteeing the stability of the society. The elite of the masses (the left) behaves responsibly in that it does not press the masses' *demands* for change past that same point, nor past the point of obvious impracticability. The political process is thus one of peaceful social change within a society which is fundamentally at one. The democratic class struggle is carried on within the framework of a broad integrating consensus; it is not a class *war*.

It should also be emphasized that change cannot proceed continuously at an intense rate without disrupting the society. Change in a well ordered society therefore comes in undulations or cycles. In the first stage of the cycle the left presses for change, the privileged elites resist. In the second stage the privileged elites absorb the change, while the left relaxes its pressure, whines that it has "run out of ideas," and one and all proclaim the "end of ideology" until the next undulation begins. The societal consensus is thus, as V. O. Key has pointed out, a *moving consensus*. It moves continuously from the stage of innovation, when social tension is great, to the stage of accommodation, when policy differences between left and right temporarily approach the vanishing point.

If popular support is to be mobilized for programmes of social change, the main issues which are raised in the political arena must be left-right issues, that is, *class* issues: issues which have to do with the allocation of values among the different classes of society. Under these conditions the political system can be used to some extent by non-elites as an instrument with which to counter the power of elites. Power and the things it can get can continually be redistributed downwards in successive first stages of the moving consensus. Without the dynamism provided by a left-right cleavage, the political system cannot initiate significant changes in the social order; it cannot radically alter the structure of comparative advantages and disadvantages in the interest of the underprivileged. It can only *reflect* the *existing* structure of power and coordinate to some extent the activities of the disparate component elements of that structure. In other words, when politics is not a democratic class struggle, the political elite cannot innovate in the interest of the non-elite; it can only serve as a broker among established elite groups. It cannot articulate the latent desires of the non-elite; it can only arrange compromises among the desires that are strong enough to assert themselves *without* the articulation services of politicians.

The social progress we have had in this country has not been the result of a left-right cleavage. It has been a result of the important but marginal pressure of the CCF-NDP together with the "demonstration effect" of reforms in Britain and the United States. That is why we have not moved as quickly or as consistently in the direction of democratic goals as either the liberal Americans or the socialist Britons. Our political elites operate, more clearly than theirs, on the periphery rather than the center of the structure of power. Our politicians are restricted, more clearly than theirs, to the tasks of adjustment and coordination. They make fewer new demands on behalf of the non-elite, because the leftists among them are a minor party which can never get close to the motor of the system.

I have argued that our party system should be polarized on a left-right basis. There are many who would agree in principle, but most of these would go on to take the line either that such a change is impracticable in this country or that if implemented it would have intolerable side effects. These people are operating with two erroneous theories which are epiphenomena of the conservative mood of the United States during the fifties. The first of these theories is the "end of ideology," which is the theory that the terms "left" and "right" have no relevance to the problems of the fifties and sixties. The second is the brokerage theory of party politics, the theory that North American parties are always and must always be nothing but coalitions of all the significant interests of society, and politicians nothing but brokers among these interests.

Both theories are false, or at the very best misleadingly half true; both theories, while purporting to be value free political science, are in fact conservative rationalizations; and both theories, while they reflected the mood of the fifties in the United States and Canada, are out of tune with the mood of the sixties. Since neither of these theories is stylish, both should be eschewed by our "new generation of urbane and intelligent people who live with a certain sense of style." Since neither of these theories is true, it is unfortunate that they have hobbled the political thought of left of center academics in Canada and thereby damaged the cause of social progress in this country.

THE END OF IDEOLOGY?

There is always a certain amount of confusion about the meaning of the terms "left" and "right." They are used to refer to a great many differing historical, ideological, and political phenomena. There have been suggestions that these terms have lost all meaning and ought therefore to be dropped. In my opinion, it would be better to cut away their useless meaning and retain the useful ones. The terms left and right are most useless and most confusing when they are used to refer to the content of particular policy proposals. Here is an example. In his study of the Canadian party system in *The Prospect of Change*, Jack McLeod defines "left" as more favorable to conciliation in international affairs, and more favorable to government intervention in the economy and public ownership than the "right." He then asserts that these criteria have little relevance to Canadian politics because both our major parties have implemented all three policies.

But—first of all—the fact that a party implements a "leftist" policy does not necessarily indicate that it is a left party. A policy—let us take government intervention in the economy as an example—is a means to an end. The same means can be used by people who have very different ends in mind, people who are operating with very different motives and responding to very different social stimuli. The German socialists pressed for welfare policies because they wanted the German people to have more of what there was to get. Bismarck implemented welfare policies because he wanted to steal the socialists' thunder and prevent revolution. Bismarck and the socialists favored the same policy. Was Bismarck a leftist?

Second of all, there is often disagreement on the right about the relative merits of alternative means of achieving rightist goals, and there is always disagreement on the left about the means of achieving leftist goals. Socialists, for example, have always disagreed among themselves about the appropriateness of nationalization and centralization as means to the distinctively socialist goals of community and equality of condition. Some socialists have preferred more decentralized forms of public ownership, and some have opined that very little public ownership of any kind is required. But these latter groups are just as socialist, just as leftist in this particular way of being leftist, as the nationalizers and centralizers.

To take another example, the goal of the American left, which is not socialist but liberal, has always been to protect the "little man"—the individual pursuer of happiness in the Great Competitive Society—against large concentrations of economic power, i.e., to preserve *equality of opportunity*. In the days of Andrew Jackson the means to this end were *laissez faire* and the destruction of monopolistic privileges. In the days of Franklin Roosevelt the means were government intervention and the regulation of concentrations of economic power. But Jackson and Roosevelt were both leftists, because they had the same broad ends in view. No one would call Jackson a right winger even though he believed in *laissez faire*. In 1830 *laissez faire* was the policy of the American left: it was a weapon against the privileged. In 1930 *laissez faire* was the policy of the American right: it was a weapon for the privileged.

Finally, the policy differences between left and right, since they occur within a moving consensus, are nearly always matters of degree. It therefore will not do to say that since both parties favor the same policy there is no longer a left-right distinction between them. Both the Tories and the Labor party in Britain—during this second or relaxed phase of the moving consensus in that country—are in favor of the policies of the welfare state and the managed economy. But the Labor party is still the left, because it was the originator of those policies, because it wants to implement them more thoroughly and swiftly, and because it has leftist motives for implementing them. The Tories are still the right because they first resisted those policies and then made peace with them, because they move less thoroughly and swiftly in implementing them, and because they have rightist motives for implementing them.

Because the same policy can be grounded in differing motives, and because the same motive can lead to differing policies, and because policy differences in a well ordered society are usually not very sharp, the terms left and right are least useful when they are applied to policy differences. They are most useful when they are applied to the broad, rather vague sets of attitudes—which we may call ideologies—which serve as one of the important grounds of policy (the other being expediency). Ideologies are in turn related, in a direct but complicated and ambiguous way, to the stratification system. We therefore define a left party as one which is more closely related to the lower strata and has an ideology oriented to redistributing social values to these strata; we define a right party as one which is more closely related to the higher strata and is ideologically oriented to resisting the redistribution of social values.

A leftist party believes that ordinary people should have more power in the society. To the degree that it is liberal it stresses equality of opportunity. To the degree that it is socialist it stresses equality of condition. A left party is the source of innovation, of social change on behalf of the non-elite. The parties of the right and center eventually adopt leftist innovations for their own reasons, but they do not for that reason deserve to be called leftist.

Now the theory of the end of ideology is itself unmasked as ideology in the following manner. To say that the distinction between left and right is no longer relevant to our social problems is to say that the unequal distribution of social values is no longer a problem. But that is always the opinion of the privileged. It is unfortunate that a leftist should find himself repeating it. If he requests merciful treatment on the ground that what he really meant was that inequality is still a problem, but that no one is excited about it, he may or may not be correct, depending on the stage of the moving consensus. But if no one is excited about the problem, the task of the leftist is surely to rouse a bit of excitement. The distinction between left and right will always be relevant—until the dream of equality is realized. We know that in all likelihood it will never be realized. The roles of left and right are therefore never ending.

Jack McLeod argues that the distinction between left and right is no guide to the solution of many troublesome Canadian problems—federal finance, regional development, bilingualism and biculturalism, American investment. In the first place, this is not so. An egalitarian ideology will have definite policy implications for these problems. In the second place, even if it were so, no one has ever maintained that leftism or rightism can be guides to the solution of *every* social problem; nor has anyone ever held that left and right must disagree about *everything*. They never do, in a well ordered society, which is the reason that blood is not flowing in the streets of London and Vancouver.

In the third place, the very fact that bilingualism and biculturalism and federal-provincial finance are more salient in Canada than the issue of inequality is itself an indication of the weakness of the left in this country. The distinguishing mark of a leftist is his belief that, ultimately, inequality is the most noxious of social problems, that the issue of inequality should be most salient in the political consciousness of a society, and that the party system should therefore be polarized on a left-right basis. If other issues are more salient, the leftist will try to minimize them. If the party system is not polarized, the leftist will try to polarize it. The non-leftist will always take the opposite view on these matters. His feeling will be that the masses already have enough power, or too much power, that class issues should therefore be non-salient and the party system unpolarized. He will, in other words, profess the ideology of the end of ideology and the brokerage theory of party politics.

BROKERAGE FOREVER?

The Brokerage Theory of Party Politics maintains that in North America, both major political parties are nearly identical coalitions of all the significant ideologies and social forces of the nation, that they must be coalitions of this type, and that all is for the best, in this best of all possible societies, when they are. We are told that the party system must have this character for these reasons: 1) North American societies are so heterogeneous, so diverse in their ethnic, religious, regional and economic composition, that the introduction of the additional element of class conflict would be intolerably divisive. In McLeod's words, there is "doubt whether Canada's people, already so sharply fragmented, could withstand yet another division into poles of the political left and right." Because North Americans are so sharply fragmented, the role of political parties must be to unify rather than to divide, to act as agents of consensus (brokers) rather than agents of dissensus (agitators). The function of *both* parties must be to "prevent new cleavages—to draw the divergent elements together into a majority by whatever means possible." 2) Again because North American society is so heterogeneous, electoral majorities are put together only with great difficulty. This *impels* each major party to appeal to all the elements of society for votes. In doing so, each party must either ignore or harmonize the differing views of various social forces. Both parties therefore end up with nearly identical social compositions, with nearly identical "lowest common denominator" approaches to the issues, unable to present the electorate with "a sharp set of alternatives."

But all is for the best. The price that is paid for this kind of party system, the brokerage theorists tell us, is merely a low level of intellectuality in political discourse and the absense of a "real choice" in elections. I say "merely" because for the brokerage theorist, the costs of such a system are far outweighed by the alleged gains: all significant elements of society are represented in each party—the demands of democracy are thus satisfied. Society is held together through moderation and compromise—the demands of social peace are thus satisfied.

The brokerage theory is unmasked as ideology in the following manner.

1. To say that a brokerage party is a "coalition" of all social forces, that it "represents" all social forces, is true only in the sense that its electoral support comes from all elements of the society. The language of "coalition" is a dangerously misleading language, because it obscures the differences which always exist between the leading or directing elements at the *core* of a political party and the heterogeneous elements in the electorate which support that core through their vote. The fact that a party is voted *for* by a heterogeneous grouping of voters does not make it the party *of* all those voters. For example, the fact that approximately forty per cent of the British working class votes for the Tories does not make the Tory party a "coalition" of labor and business, because the directing core of the Tory party has a much closer relationship with the British business community than with the British working class. To return to North America, what the brokerage theorists like to think of as a "party of all the people" is actually, as McLeod points out, "a middle class party financed by business and highly sensitive to commercial interests." The brokerage theory is in reality a class ideology, for it maintains that both our major parties must always be more closely related to the privileged elites than to the non-elites of our society.

2. To say that the role of a party system is to serve as a non-ideological broker among existing constellations of power, period, is first of all to conceal the fact that "non-ideological" is double-speak for "in accordance with the prevailing ideology," and second of all, it is to deny that the role of the party system is to move us closer to democracy, i.e., to *alter* existing constellations of power in the interest of the non-elite. It means that the party system must reflect rather than alter the present state of affairs in which non-political elites are the primary source of decision making and politicians are restricted to the task of mediating among elites. The brokerage theory is a rationalization of the interest of privileged elites in preserving their positions against the encroachments of politicians, i.e., against those who reflect the people's power.

3. To say that politicians must eschew class issues in order to avoid disrupting the society is to say that non-class issues must be salient. The people's vote must never be an expression of their desire for more power and the things that it can get; it must always be an expression of their non-class interests—region, ethnic group, etc.—and of their opinion on non-class issues such as the personality of Eisenhower, Communism-Corruption-Korea, Gerda Munsinger, the flag, and so on. To say that non-elite votes which are captured in this way make the party that gets them representative of the interests of the non-elite voter is the exact opposite of the truth, for these votes express all the interests of the non-elite voter *except* his interest as a *non-elite* voter. The brokerage theory is a rationalization of the privileged elites' interest in maintaining the non-saliency of class issues. Only the successful application of this strategy can keep a non-left party in power. The brokerage theory makes things very comfortable indeed for North American elites, for it insists that all major parties in North America must always follow this elite strategy.

The normative foundations of the brokerage theory are, I trust, exposed as bourgeois foundations and for that reason faulty. That the empirical foundations of the brokerage theory are also faulty will become evident through an examination of its false dichotomy of British-polarized and American-brokerage type party systems. According to the brokerage theory, a party system is *either* one in which the parties divide the electorate on a left-right basis, appeal to different classes, and present sharp policy alternatives to the voters *or* a system in which the parties unite the electorate on a lowest common denominator basis, appeal to the same classes, and present nearly identical programmes to the voters. A party system can perform *either* the function of building dissensus *or* the function of promoting consensus. It can *either* divide *or* integrate. It can be *either* British *or* American.

This is a false dichotomy because party systems that operate with any degree of efficiency—and this includes the British and the American, but not the Canadian—always perform both sets of functions; the consensus-building and the dissensus-promotion functions, though the relative emphasis given to these functions varies with the state of the moving consensus. The consensus model is *not* an accurate description of the American system and the dissensus model is *not* an accurate description of the British system. The party systems of both countries are really very similar in that both are polarized on a left-right basis (though the British is *more* polarized than the American) and in both all parties, left and right, perform both functions of consensus-building and dissensus-promotion.

The Labor and Democratic parties are both left parties; the Conservative and Republican parties are both right parties. The tendency of the left parties is to innovate in the interest of the lower strata; that of the right parties is to resist or retard innovation. The left parties receive much more electoral support from the lower than from the higher strata; the right parties receive proportionately much more from the higher than from the lower. The prerequisites for dissensus-promotion are thus satisfied. The electorate has a choice between a party which wants to move swiftly in redistributing social values, and which therefore tends to emphasize class issues, and a party which wants to move slowly or not at all and therefore emphasizes non-class issues.

At the same time, *all* these parties are coalitions of diverse interests, in these two senses: their directing cores are composed of factions representing differing interests which must be harmonized, and these directing cores, though they are broadly speaking *either* leftist *or* rightist, business oriented *or* labor oriented, are impelled by electoral exigencies to seek *votes* in every possible quarter. Thus, in Britain, the Tories do not call themselves "the party of the comfortable," but "the national party," and Labor does not call itself "the party of the down-trodden masses" but the party of "*all* who toil by hand and brain." In both countries, the right parties manage to get many votes from the lower strata, and the left parties get many votes from the upper strata. In both countries, the strength of the underlying consensus is such that left and right do not disagree on everything. In both countries non-class cleavages cut across rather than coincide with the class cleavage, thereby helping to integrate the society. In both countries most elections do not offer a very sharp set of alternatives to the voters except in the innovative stage—usually the briefest—of the moving consensus, and in freak elections such as the Goldwater-Johnson confrontation. In both countries, left and right do not press their differences past the point at which social peace would be endangered. The British and American systems thus prove that left-right polarization is not incompatible with social integration. The democratic class struggle does not cause a society to fall apart in class war.

One is often told that British society can "afford" a democratic class struggle only because it is a very homogeneous society. But the fact that American politics are also polarized on a left-right basis proves that polarization *can* be afforded by a heterogeneous society consisting of many diverse regional, ethnic, and religious interests. The idea that Canada, because it is a heterogeneous society, must forever be saddled with two major parties of the right or center is beginning to be recognized as erroneous. The relationship between the consensus and dissensus functions is always complex, but the following simplification may be helpful. A nation which is in danger of falling apart on class lines may be held together by a politics which emphasizes non-class issues; that is, class cleavage can be mitigated by emphasizing the non-class cleavages which cut across it. But by the same token a nation like Canada, which is in danger of falling apart on ethnic-regional lines, may be held together by a politics which unites the people of various regions and ethnic groups around the two poles of left and right. The contention of the brokerage theorists that our heterogeneous society can be held together only if an "additional" class cleavage is avoided is the exact opposite of the truth. The promotion of dissensus on class issues is a way of mitigating dissensus on many non-class issues.

A class politics in Canada would take for granted that the nation exists and will not be dismembered. Political debate would focus on the question: who gets what, when, how? The present non-class politics takes for granted that those who have the most of what there is to get will continue to get it, and political debate centers on the question of whether they will continue to get it in one nation or several, through the provincial governments or the federal. Class politics would translate popular discontent into demands for change in national social and economic policy. Non-class politics translates popular discontent into provincialism or separatism. Non-class politics perpetuates the power of established elites *and* endangers the existence of the nation.

The unity of this country will be assured only when a powerful party of the left operates at the center rather than the periphery of our political power structure. Such a party will emerge only if the regionally and ethnically segregated victims of our society can be united by a set of common ideals and symbols based on class. To say that this will never happen because Canadians aren't class conscious enough is to ignore the distinction between class consciousness *per se* and politicized class consciousness. Class consciousness exists in any stratified social system as a kind of natural resource which may or may not be mobilized by politicians. We are at least as class conscious as the Americans. The difference between our system and theirs is that their system mobilizes class consciousness, makes it relevant to politics, harnesses it to the political system, while ours lets class consciousness lie unused, an untapped resource. No one can convince me that the ordinary Manitoban feels his antipathy toward the Quebecois more deeply than he feels economically and socially disadvantaged by his non-elite status. He is class conscious, all right, and powerfully so; but he has to live with a political system which makes his ethnic identifications directly relevant to politics, and his class identifications irrelevant to politics.

What people feel most strongly is not automatically perceived as politically relevant. It is the political elite of a society that decides which feelings will be harnessed to the political system and which will be allowed to remain politically irrelevant. In C. Wright Mills' terms, politics is the transformation of personal *troubles* into public *issues*. There is no major party of the left in Canada not because our people are too stupid to be conscious of the disadvantages of non-elite status, but because our business oriented political elites have been reluctant to translate the personal trouble of non-elite status into the public issue of inequality.

When a major party of the left emerges in Canada, it will undoubtedly consist of leaders and voters who are now to be found in all four parties.

I believe that the best way to develop a *major* party of the left is to strengthen the only left wing party we already have—the New Democratic party. I respect the right of others to work for the same goal within the Liberal, Conservative or Social Credit parties, but I believe that on this question, they, not I, are the utopians.

34

The Canadian Political System*

John Porter

FEW CANADIAN BOOKS of the 60s have received greater acclaim than John Porter's much prized *The Vertical Mosaic*.

This sociological study of Canadian society presents a picture of relative class rigidity with the continued socio-economic supremacy of small portions of the British "charter group." The book shows the high degree of frustrating poverty which has existed in Canada and indicates a rather startling and alarming relationship between this vertical mosaic and the much hallowed myth of the cultural mosaic. In the section reproduced here, Professor Porter criticizes the uncreative, undynamic, and unprogressive nature of both the historic Canadian party system and the formal and especially the empirical Canadian federal system. Both have been manipulated, he asserts, by the small corporate elite and their allied, avocational political elite so as to preserve their relatively unchallenged position. Canadian federalism, he argues, with its "doubtful sociological assumptions, ". . . can provide an excuse for federal politicians not acting against the interests of the corporate economy." He agrees with Professor Mallory that those persons interested in entrenching economic power and opposing the development of the positive state have, with considerable effect, pragmatically backed whichever level of government in a jurisdictional dispute seemed least favourable to economic regulation. Thus, even the courts become a hidden ideological battleground as objection is often raised more to the purpose of legislation rather than to its source.

Porter has no patience with brokerage politics nor with those traditional political scientists and historians who have seen such politics as necessary or appropriate for the geographically and culturally diverse

* From *The Vertical Mosaic: An Analysis of Social Class and Power in Canada* (Toronto, 1965), pp. 373–383.

Canadian scene. For him, brokerage politics removes the creative dialectic which makes political progress possible and gives the electorate a chance to comprehend the issues and participate even indirectly in decision-making.

MAJOR PARTIES: THE CONSERVATIVE TONE

T HE MOST SIGNIFICANT CHARACTERISTIC of the two parties which have held power at the national level in Canada is the fact that they share the same conservative values. Both have at times been responsible for reform legislation which might suggest progressive values, but these steps to the left have been taken more with a spirit of opportunism than from a basic orientation to social progress and change. The Progressive Conservative party has been ingenious enough to incorporate the political dynamic within its name. As some of its opponents have suggested it is neither conservative nor progressive, but has remained opportunistic. Both parties have produced successive contingents of administrative politicians. The political dialogue, if it can be called such, in which they participate is not related to any basic class differences in the society from which the conservative-progressive dynamic might arise. It is not that Canadian social structure is so static that it has no immanent potential for dynamic politics; it is rather that Canada's basically opportunistic parties have not harnessed this potential in the political system. They have either ignored these basic social differences or covered them up in the pretence that they do not exist.

Both politicians and intellectuals, on those occasions when they deal with political issues, have defined the political task, not in terms of creative policies, but rather in terms of interstitial compromises between competing interests. In his introduction to Mackenzie King's diaries, Mr. J. W. Pickersgill states that "Mackenzie King genuinely believed and frequently said that the real secret of political leadership was more in what was prevented than what was accomplished."[1] Mr. Pickersgill did not elaborate on his own further statement, "yet his objectives were by no means negative," except to say that, between the Liberal convention of 1919 and the end of his political career, Mackenzie King had reached his destination.

According to Canada's two most outstanding political scientists, J. A. Corry and R. M. Dawson, Canada's two indistinguishable political parties are functionally appropriate for Canadian society. The views of these two men are important because it is mainly through their writings, and their

---

[1] J. W. Pickersgill, *The Mackenzie King Record*, vol. I (Toronto, 1960), 10.

students who have become teachers, that later generations of Canadian students are introduced to Canada's political system. Corry sees party politicians as brokers of ideas selecting among those that are current in the society the ones that appeal to the largest calculable number of voters.[2] They are brokers in another sense, too. They arrange deals between different sections of opinion, or interest groups, by working out the necessary compromises. If these are the tasks of political parties and political leaders their function is not to provide a conservative-progressive dialogue in terms of general social values, but simply to make available an "alternative" government. Elections become choices between one set of brokers and another. In a democracy there must be an alternative government to keep the incumbent government aware of its responsibilities. Corry makes the point that, if this alternative party was an ideological one deeply committed to principles, the social divisions which would follow would be so great that it would be difficult, if not impossible, to keep the nation together. Yet to obscure social divisions through brokerage politics is to remove from the political system that element of dialectic which is the source of creative politics. The choice between genuinely radical and genuinely conservative traditions could mean a period of creative politics followed by a period of consolidation as conservatives and radicals oscillated in and out of office. That at least would provide a two-party system suitable to parliamentary institutions, the debating of values, and the clarification of social goals.

To make brokerage politics work it is necessary at election time to rouse the voters from political somnolence and try to make them identify with one of the parties. When parties are without distinguishable social values voters have no commitments other than those arising from uncritical family traditions or habit. Consequently the parties require at election time an enormous "once for all" organization which takes large sums of money. On the whole these sums are not obtained from thousands of small individual contributions, but instead are obtained much more efficiently from wealthy benefactors. Because the parties do not differ in principle, the wealthy benefactors support both main parties. It is often suggested, although no evidence has ever been produced, that corporate benefactors, in particular, give 60 per cent of their contribution to the party in power and 40 per cent to the party that might succeed to power. In any case, the war chests of the two parties both seem to be full, allowing them to charter aircraft, print mountains of literature, rent fleets of limousines, and buy extensive advertising space on television and radio and in the newspapers. Millions of dollars spent on political education could be a good thing for the functioning of the political system, but when it is concentrated in a few weeks before elections and on devices scarcely designed to educate, the function is questionable.

---

[2] J. A. Corry, *Democratic Government and Politics* (Toronto, 1946), Chap. VI.

Corry accepts as inevitable these aspects of brokerage politics because in his view the role of the politician is simply to reflect the selfish aims of the various sections of the society and to make compromises between them. He recognizes that there are some unattractive features of this system but his strongest words of indictment are: "It would not be correct to say that party policy has been uninfluenced by contributions to party funds"; and "The parties deceive the public, but so do propagandists of every kind."[3] Corry's conclusion about the party system is that ". . . the evils in the party system are the outcome of general human frailties. Indeed it is hard to see how the parties which must woo the electorate with success can do other than reflect its vices and its virtues."[4] He sees little need for political education and political leadership.

Dawson, too, recognized and accepted the facts of Canadian political life, although he suggested that historically there have been differences between the parties which still influence their attitudes.[5] The Conservatives have been more conscious of the Empire tie, while the Liberals have been more nationalistic; the Conservatives have been a high tariff party and the Liberals a freer trade party; the Conservatives have been more concerned with strengthening the powers of the central government while the Liberals have been more anxious to maintain provincial rights; the Conservatives have been the party of free enterprise, while the Liberals have professed "to take the lead in public ownership and progressive social legislation."[6] Dawson claimed that these tendencies or biases still exist within the parties, although he admitted that their records on these issues have been confused and inconsistent.

Dawson also concluded that "a national party must take as its primary purpose the reconciliation of the widely scattered aims and interests of a number of areas."[7] Elections then are fought on minor issues and often the distinction between the parties is nothing more than a choice between personalities. "Finally the opportunism—and one may fairly say, the inescapable opportunism—embedded in the Canadian party system tends to minimize the importance of the platform and emphasize the importance of the party leaders. . . ."[8]

For more than thirty years, Frank H. Underhill has asked provocative questions about the Canadian political system. In his collected essays, *In Search of Canadian Liberalism*, he expresses conflicting views. One is the view of the orthodox political scientist: "a political party that aspires to the responsibility of government must not be a class party, but must be a

---

3 *Ibid.*, 138, 139.

4 *Ibid.*

5 R. M. Dawson, *The Government of Canada* (Toronto, 1948), 501 ff.

6 *Ibid.*, 506.

7 *Ibid.*, 508.

8 *Ibid.*, 510.

loosely knit representative collection of voters from all groups." "National unity is preserved by having every interest-group effectively inside the party which controls the government."[9] These quotations are from an essay written in 1950 praising the contributions of Mackenzie King to Canada. In other essays, too, he seems to feel that there is an inescapable logic in having, in the North American situation, all-embracing parties where the tensions within the society are resolved within the parties rather than between the parties.

On the other hand Underhill feels the need for creative leadership in political life. This can occur only when politicians have a vision that is greater than the sum of the special interests of particular groups. Underhill has deplored the lack of conservative thought in the Conservative party and of liberal thought in the Liberal party. He admired Franklin D. Roosevelt and regretted that Canada never had a New Deal. In 1932 Underhill pointed out the inadequacy of the Canadian party system: "a party which depends for success upon the different and often contradictory appeals which it must make to different sectional interests will become dependent upon and responsive to those interest-groups which are best organized and most strategically located for applying effective pressure upon the party leaders."[10] The two groups which could apply the most pressure he thought were the Catholic church in Quebec and big business. The real function of the two-party system since the Laurier era "has been to provide a screen behind which the controlling business interests pull the strings to manipulate the Punch and Judy who engage in mock combat before the public."[11]

In 1940 there appeared a book by Pendleton Herring, *The Politics of Democracy*,[12] which has influenced a whole generation of Canadian political scientists in their attitudes to political parties. It was Herring who expounded with great force the doctrine of brokerage politics. Underhill's estimate of Mackenzie King was that he had developed brokerage politics to a fine art. However, despite what he was to say about King in 1950, Underhill felt in 1943 that Herring's views about political parties were not altogether applicable to Canada, in part because the moderate polarization which had taken place between Republican and Democratic parties in the United States had not taken place between the two major parties in Canada despite the fact that World War I and the depression had created a new class structure. It was the new parties which appeared to give expression to this new class structure. "In dealing with these new conflicts among group interests the old parties were too

[9] Frank H. Underhill, *In Search of Canadian Liberalism* (Toronto, 1960), 136–37.

[10] *Ibid.*, 167.

[11] *Ibid.*, 168.

[12] Pendleton Herring, *The Politics of Democracy: American Parties in Action* (New York, 1940).

much under the control of one class group to function as honest brokers any more."[13]

By 1960 the two major parties were still trying to function as brokers. Not even a moderate polarization had taken place. Consequently dynamic politics to mobilize the creative energies of the society were still absent.

PARTIES OF POLITICAL PROTEST

In some respects the emergence of minor parties in the provinces can be viewed as populist protest against the established order. As a result of the social changes which have taken place in the country, some of which have been described in the earlier chapters on social class, there has always been a large number of people who experience deprivation. It is their feelings which can be exploited by the minor parties at the provincial level.[14] These populist reactions can also be seen at the federal level with the Progressives, the Social Credit, and the C.C.F. (New Democratic) parties. The existence of these minor parties has meant that only rarely does the victorious party acquire a majority of the popular vote. Mr. Diefenbaker's appeal in 1958 can also be interpreted as a populist one. His vision caught the imagination not only of the deprived, but also of the not so deprived but financially insecure, the heavily mortgaged suburban homeowner.[15] Because the appeals of the minor parties run the range of the rational-irrational continuum, from social democratic humanism to reactionary fundamentalism, as a political force they are fragmented even though they appeal to the same social groups.

The electoral success of the minor parties has been confined to the provinces. The Social Credit party in Alberta was in its early days a populist social movement led by its charismatic leader William Aberhart.[16] Its original aim was, through monetary and financial reforms, to free Alberta rural society from its indebtedness to eastern financial interest. Most of its goals were obstructed by disallowance and judicial decisions, and with the return of prosperity during and after World War II it became a traditional conservative party making occasional fanfares of Christian fundamentalism. In British Columbia the Social Credit party which has been in office since 1952 may also be labelled a conservative party even though it is, as described by some, opportunistic and nihilistic

---

[13] Underhill, *In Search of Canadian Liberalism*, 198.

[14] See the discussion in James Mallory, *Social Credit and the Federal Power in Canada* (Toronto, 1954), 153 ff.

[15] For an analysis along these lines see S. D. Clark, "Group Interests in Canadian Politics," in J. H. Aitchison, ed., *The Political Process in Canada* (Toronto, 1963).

[16] There has been a series of studies on Social Credit in Alberta. See particularly John Irving, *The Social Credit Movement in Alberta* (Toronto, 1959), and Mallory, *Social Credit and the Federal Power.*

to the point of being anti-ideological.[17] After the break-up of the Liberal-Conservative coalition which had been formed to keep the C.C.F. party from power in British Columbia there was no other political party to which the corporate and conservative elements could give their support. Although the C.C.F. never won an election in British Columbia the presence of a strong socialist movement, which it represents, has provided some polarization of politics in the province. The N.D.P., the successor to the C.C.F., has a social philosophy similar to that of the social democratic parties of Europe.

In Saskatchewan the C.C.F. party did acquire power in 1944 and retained it until 1964. In many respects it was an instrument of social change and a progressive force not only in the one province but in the country as a whole where it became a pace-setter in reform legislation. If there have been any creative politics in Canada in recent years, it was probably to be found in Saskatchewan. Even in Saskatchewan, however, the fact that the C.C.F. was in power for so long suggests that the conservative-progressive dialogue was weak because the opposing Liberal party had no counter-philosophy.

Except for one brief period, 1919 to 1923, Ontario has been ruled by Liberals or Conservatives. Parties with opposing values have made little headway. On one occasion the Liberal party harboured a leader of populist revolt, Mitchell Hepburn, but he soon became aligned to the corporate elite and so passed from the scene without any trace of political creativity. In Quebec, a similar populist appeal brought Maurice Duplessis' Union Nationale party to power in 1936 for three years, and again in 1944 for seventeen years. Duplessis was formerly a Conservative and his long regime in Quebec can best be described as a reactionary coalition with economic and ecclesiastical power. Some movement towards the progressive pole can be seen with the present Quebec Liberal party which won power in 1960 and which contains in its leadership some who claim to be socialists. Although it is by no means a socialist party it is strongly committed to reform, but its reformist values have become confused with its nationalist sentiments.

In all the other provinces Liberals and Conservatives have shared power while other parties have made scarcely a ripple on the political waters. What little polarization there has been in Canadian politics has remained within the provinces rather than within the national system.

CANADIAN FEDERALISM: SOME OBSERVATIONS

The one aspect of Canadian political structure which has received more attention than any other from historians, political scientists, and constitutional lawyers is the federal system. All the rationalizing on the

---

[17] See the interesting analysis by Donald V. Smiley, "Canada's Poujadists: A New Look at Social Credit," *Canadian Forum*, Sept. 1962.

part of royal commissions, politicians, and judges in Canada and the United Kingdom that has gone into constructing theories of Canadian federalism provides an unlimited field for scholarly activity. There is no intention here of reviewing this material.[18] It is important, however, to keep in mind that political parties and the careers of politicians are determined very frequently by the institutions in which they work. But at critical periods in a society's development political leaders can, if they have the ability, overcome institutional fetters and create new social arrangements. The relationship between political leadership and political institutions need not be a one-way influence; it can be a reciprocal one.

In the course of their histories most federal systems have seen a gradual lessening of the power of the individual states comprising them and an increase in the power of their central governments. With the conditions of modern industrial society and international relations it is almost essential that the central government acquire power at the expense of the provincial or state governments. Although this shift has taken place in Canada it has not taken place to the extent that it has, for example, in the United States or Australia. Moreover the shift that has taken place came so late that a rigidity of thought, both juridical and political, still governs the political processes. Social and political thought are partly the product of the social arrangements that exist, but if they were completely so, there would be no movement forward, no change. When Canadian politicians make pronouncements about Canadian federalism it is difficult to tell whether they are prisoners of a social mentality about federalism, or whether, in a machiavellian fashion, they are using federalism as an instrument of power or as an excuse not to exercise power.

A federal system is often seen as a device to decentralize power, but it can also be used as an instrument to acquire and consolidate power, and to maintain economically inefficient and socially out-dated and dysfunctional activities. It was suggested in an earlier chapter, for example, that because the Canadian educational system depends on the provinces it can not be geared to current demands of the labour force or to the principles of equality.

Most commentators on Canadian federalism seem to agree that as the system has developed there has been a turning back from the intentions of the creative politicians who brought about the federation and who governed it in the first thirty years of its existence. As Professor Wheare has pointed out, it is difficult to say whether Canada was provided with a federal constitution with unitary modifications or a unitary government

---

[18] More recent discussions of Canadian federalism which have been helpful are: the essays in A. R. M. Lower *et al.*, *Evolving Canadian Federalism* (Durham, N.C., 1958); D. V. Smiley, "The Rowell-Sirois Report, Provincial Autonomy, and Post-War Canadian Federalism," *C.J.E.P.S.*, XXVIII, no. 1 (Feb. 1962); and the papers by P.-E. Trudeau and F. R. Scott in M. Oliver, ed., *Social Purpose for Canada* (Toronto, 1961).

with federal modifications.[19] The unified judicial system, the federal powers of disallowance and appointment, and other elements suggest at least the intention of a strong central government. Yet gradually through the decisions of judges in the United Kingdom, whose knowledge of Canada could at the most be slight, the relative weight of responsibility went to the provinces and away from the central government. The federalism which resulted from the decisions of the Judicial Committee of the Privy Council left Canada after the 1930's politically and socially incapacitated.

Yet it must not be thought that judges alone were to blame, because judges make decisions on issues brought before them and issues are brought to the courts by people who have the power to bring them. In one of the most illuminating discussions of Canadian federalism,[20] Professor Mallory has shown how vested economic interests challenged both provincial and Dominion legislation as being *ultra vires,* if that legislation meant a regulatory encroachment on the economic system. With the growth of industrialization and a concomitant extension of the franchise, which in Canada became universal with the election of 1921, politicians were required to make appeals to, or heed the desires of, new social forces. When their policies became redistributive in character, these policies were vitiated through successful appeals to the courts.

In a federal country, those resisting [regulation] were able to cloak their economic motives in a concern for the public interest by raising doubts as to the power of the legislature to enact laws to which they objected. This course was most effective where the legislature whose jurisdiction they were defending was the least favourable to economic regulation or least able to make its regulation effective.

. . . Even in cases where a statute had been referred to the courts for an opinion on its validity there is reason to believe that objection often existed more to its purpose than to its source.[21]

Thus a federal constitution, although purporting to prevent the centralization of political power, can become an instrument for the entrenchment of economic power.

Although World War II saw a great increase in the activities of the central government, judicial pronouncements up until that time left Canadian governments incapable of dealing with contemporary problems or of assuming a creative role. They left Canadians with an attitude of despair and an outlook on their society as bleak as some parts of the land whose resources they were seeking to exploit. Moreover, these judicial decisions built up nine (ten with the entrance of Newfoundland in 1949)

---

[19] See the discussion in F. R. Scott, "French Canada and Canadian Federalism," in *Evolving Canadian Federalism.*

[20] Mallory, *Social Credit and the Federal Power.*

[21] *Ibid.,* 32.

strong provincial stages on which politicians could act out their roles, creating within the provinces systems of power which had a dissociative effect on the whole of the society, and particularly on the national political system. Provincial political leaders, their corresponding bureaucracies, and party organizations have acquired vested interest in their own power, and the themes of their political rhetoric emphasize local and provincial differences.

Because nobody has examined the problems with any thoroughness it is difficult to know whether or not provincial electorates who collectively make up the federal electorate share the views about federalism that are held by the political elite and the political scientists. It is often assumed without any evidence that they do.[22] Almost anyone who has taken part in electioneering can tell how confused the mass of the electorate is on which matters belong to provincial governments and which to the federal government. Because even in federal elections electorates seem more concerned with immediate, local problems, such as housing, health, and marketing, they address questions to federal candidates which should properly be addressed to their provincial members. In the absence of evidence from survey studies it might be speculated that federalism, in the sense that it divides powers between the provinces and the central government, cannot be comprehended by vast segments of the electorate.

The Dogma of Cultural Particularism

Some of the hallowed nonsense that goes into the theory of Canadian federalism is that each of the provinces constitutes a particular culture which federalism safeguards, but with the exception of Quebec it is never made clear just what these cultural differences are, or if the differences exist why they are more important than the similarities. It was suggested in an earlier chapter that Canadian history has taken place in a demographic railway station and that these were difficult conditions under which to develop collective sentiments and values. But neither are they the conditions that should result in strong sectionalism. Inter-provincial migration, modern means of travel and communication, economic integration through the growth of the national corporation, all suggest that any theory of sectionalism or cultural particularism needs to be re-examined. Most provinces, New Brunswick and Manitoba are striking examples, have a greater variety of particular cultures within them than

---

[22] Professor Jewett has provided some fairly thin evidence from answers to public opinion polls that: "Apparently 'provincial rights' was not the prerogative solely of status-seeking provincial politicians" (Pauline Jewett, "Political and Administrative Aspects of Policy Formation," in T. N. Brewis *et al.*, *Canadian Economic Policy* (Toronto, 1961), 295). The public opinion poll data which she uses were from the 1940's before the great social changes of the 1950's. Even so, 25 per cent of respondents were prepared to abolish the provincial governments!

between them. It is difficult to see how these intra-provincial cultures are protected by federal institutions *per se*. Another argument in favour of federalism is that regions and provinces have specialized economic activities and that these require strong provincial governments to safeguard and develop them. But equally strong counter-arguments could be made that regional economies could be better developed and better planned through integrative policies at the national level. National corporations undertake such integrative policies when, for example, coal mines are closed down in Nova Scotia from offices in Montreal.

One important value which is supported by federalism is the decentralization of government activity, and the prevention of the growth of a single monolithic state machinery. Federalism therefore safeguards liberty. Again a counter-argument could be made that liberties can be denied as well as safeguarded through strong provincial governments. What liberties Canadians have, in the absence of constitutional guarantees, have been defined in the decisions of the Canadian Supreme Court against provincial governments. There is no doubt that as the "mass society" develops, regionalism, local autonomy, and group differences should be fostered, but there is no reason to argue that they can be safeguarded and fostered only through a federal instrument which inhibits creative politics and prevents the emergence of that social power which lies in the creative energies of the whole society. There are many other ways in which the "evils" of centralized bureaucracy can be controlled.

Quebec without doubt is a special case where there is validity in the notion of cultural particularism, but as Quebec becomes more industrialized it will become culturally more like other industrialized societies. At that time the similarities in social characteristics which its urbanized population will share with other provinces may be far more important in terms of future social development than whatever differences remain. In the past, public sentiments in Quebec, which arise from the particular culture in that province, have been exploited in the interests of power as much as they have been protected by provincial autonomy. The low occupational level of French Canadians, the rigidity of French-Canadian class structure, and the authoritarian character of French-Canadian institutions are as much a consequence of the power enjoyed by French-Canadian provincial politicians in coalition with "alien" corporate powers as they are a consequence of domination by the British charter group.[23] In fact French-speaking Canadians and other Catholic groups outside of Quebec may well have fared better as provincial minorities, if education, for example, had been more a federal responsibility than a provincial one.

---

[23] Cf. Pierre-Elliott Trudeau, "Some Obstacles to Democracy in Quebec," *C.J.E.P.S.*, XXIV, no. 3 (Aug. 1958).

Co-operative Federalism

Since World War II Canadian federalism has acquired a new characteristic called "co-operative federalism" in which the federal and provincial governments participate in the provision of services particularly in the field of health and welfare. A wide range of governmental activity has grown up in this way without formal constitutional changes: "The federal aspects of the Canadian constitution, using the latter term in its broadest sense, have come to be less what the courts say they are than what the federal and provincial cabinets and bureaucracies in a continuous series of formal and informal relations determine them to be."[24] The question most frequently asked about these changes is whether provincial autonomy or federal "usurpation" has won out as a result of co-operative federalism. The answer seems to be that neither has, but rather that there is a "process of continuous and piecemeal adjustment between the two levels of government which is still going on."[25] There is little wonder that electorates are confused about where responsibilities lie when assessing the various services that come from provincial and federal governments, or from both.

Defenders of provincial autonomy will argue that if provincial governments do not produce the services electorates want (their wants are supposedly derived from their particular cultures) provincial electorates will throw out their governments. But provincial electorates collectively are also the federal electorate, and when they behave as such their cultural particularisms presumably do not operate. Yet federal politicians make the same kind of appeals for extensions of services as provincial politicians. Neither provincial nor federal politicians do much to clarify for electorates the "piecemeal" federal system which has emerged.

Because the distribution of powers that now exists between the two levels of government taxes the capacity of the constitutional lawyer and the political scientist to understand it, and because it provides for a series of courses in the political science departments of universities it is difficult to see what provincial autonomy means for vast segments of the electorate. Consequently, it may be speculated that federalism as such has meaning only for politicians and senior civil servants who work with the complex machinery that they have set up, as well as for the scholars who provide a continuing commentary on it, but that it has very little meaning for the bulk of the population. In this sense the myths that go to support the continued fragmentation of the political system need some critical examination.

In one important aspect, that is, in the responsibility which the central

---

24 Smiley, "The Rowell-Sirois Report, Provincial Autonomy, and Post-War Canadian Federalism," 59.
25 *Ibid.*, 58.

government has taken to stabilize the economic system, Canadian federalism has changed in the post World War II period. This change does not arise so much from changed attitudes to federalism on the part of elites as it does from the "Keynesian revolution" which has resulted in the assumption of these responsibilities in all western governments, federal or unitary. In Canada this increased role of the federal government has been possible because of its power over fiscal and monetary policy, and also over defence. In a federal system the policies of the various governments are always open to challenge through the courts. The recent increased power of the central government through economic policies has gone unchallenged, suggesting that there has emerged a new relationship between the federal government and the corporate elite.[26] The latter is interested in the stability that the former can provide. In addition, defence contracts, and also some of those arising from the co-operative activities between the two levels of government, have made the federal government directly and indirectly industry's best customer. The increase in foreign ownership and in the importance of international trade has also brought the corporate elite into a closer relationship with the federal government. One significant area in which this shift has not taken place is in labour relations. Here the corporate elite benefits from provincial powers which inhibit uniform labour standards across the country. Federalism can provide an excuse for federal politicians not acting against the interests of the corporate economy.

It is not the intention here to argue for the complete abandonment of federalism, but rather to point out that as it has developed Canadian federalism has imposed a conservative tone on the Canadian political system and political parties, and has inhibited creative political leadership. If Canada has any political charter it lies in a theory of federalism which has built into it some doubtful sociological assumptions. For federal political leaders, federalism may have a certain political reality which they feel they can ignore only at their peril. How much this political reality is a reflection of power interests within the provinces, and how much it is a reflection of general public sentiment cannot be said without further extensive investigation.

However real or unreal in sociological terms, and however it might be changing in the light of recent economic and social change, federalism has been for political parties, and the political elite we are about to examine, an important condition in the exercise of power. A system in which scope for political leadership is limited because of real, or assumed, cultural particularism or sectional interests, means that it is difficult for the professional political career to develop. Thus, as we shall see, along with brokerage politics, which is said to be appropriate for Canada, there is also avocational politics with a conservative tone.

---

[26] Cf. J. A. Corry, "Constitutional Trends and Federalism," in *Evolving Canadian Federalism*.

35

Canadian Literature and Canadian Society*

Northrop Frye

THIS ESSAY by Northrop Frye forms the concluding chapter of *The Literary History of Canada,* edited by Carl F. Klinck. As this work is usually not available except in libraries or reference collections the editors felt it deserved to be available on a wider basis for those interested in the development of Canada and its literature. Northrop Frye, formerly principal of Victoria College, University of Toronto, is currently Professor of English there.

This article ranks as probably the most brilliant and stimulating view of Canadian literature as a whole. Frye analyses literature for more than the forms and styles. He seeks out the many forces which have moulded and promoted the development of literature in this country. He assesses a whole range of these influences—mother Britain, the United States, the frontier, the harsh physical environment, nationalism—and shows how they converge to produce Canadian literature. There is much here that is of great interest to the historian, for often the forces moulding the evolution of Canadian society, are most graphically portrayed in literature. There is much here that is of interest to the scholar of literature and it should help to chase the lingering inferiority complex which some Canadians exhibit for their literature.

Many of the themes which run through the various articles in this volume are neatly summed up in this concluding essay.

---

* C. F. Klinck, *Literary History of Canada* (Toronto, 1965), pp. 821–849.

I T IS NOW several years since the group of editors listed on the title-page met, under Carl Klinck's leadership, to draw up the first tentative plans for this book. What we then dreamed of is substantially what we have got, changed very little in essentials. I expressed at the time the hope that such a book would help to broaden the inductive basis on which some writers on Canadian literature were making generalizations that bordered on guesswork. By "some writers" I meant primarily myself. I find, however, that this book tends to confirm me in most of my intuitions on the subject: the advantage for me is that this attempt at conclusion and summary can involve some self-plagiarism.

The book is a tribute to the maturity of Canadian literary scholarship and criticism, whatever one thinks of the literature. Its authors have completely outgrown the view that evaluation is the end of criticism, instead of its incidental by-product. Had evaluation been their guiding principle, this book would, if written at all, have been only a huge debunking project, leaving Canadian literature a poor naked *alouette* plucked of every feather of decency and dignity. True, the book gives evidence, on practically every one of its eight hundred odd pages, that what is really remarkable is not how little but how much good writing has been produced in Canada. But this would not affect the rigorous evaluator. The evaluative view is based on the conception of criticism as concerned mainly to define and canonize the genuine classics of literature. And Canada has produced no author who is a classic in the sense of possessing a vision greater in kind than that of his best readers (Canadians themselves might argue about one or two, but in the perspective of the world at large the statement is true). There is no Canadian writer of whom we can say what we can say of the world's major writers, that their readers can grow up inside their work without ever being aware of a circumference. Thus the metaphor of the critic as "judge" holds for the Canadian critic, who is never dealing with the kind of writer who judges him.

. This fact about Canadian literature, so widely deplored by Canadians, has one advantage. It is much easier to see what literature is trying to do when we are studying a literature that has not quite done it. If no Canadian author pulls us away from the Canadian context toward the centre of literary experience itself, then at every point we remain aware of his social and historical setting. The conception of what is literary has to be greatly broadened for such a literature. The literary, in Canada, is often only an incidental quality of writings which, like those of many of the early explorers, are as innocent of literary intention as a mating loon. Even when it is literature in its orthodox genres of poetry and fiction, it is more significantly studied as a part of Canadian life than as a part of an autonomous world of literature.

So far from merely admitting or conceding this, the editors have gone out of their way to emphasize it. We have asked for chapters on political, historical, religious, scholarly, philosophical, scientific, and other non-literary writing, to show how the verbal imagination operates as a ferment in all cultural life. We have included the writings of foreigners, of travellers, of immigrants, of emigrants—even of emigrants whose most articulate literary emotion was their thankfulness at getting the hell out of Canada. The reader of this book, even if he is not Canadian or much interested in Canadian literature as such, may still learn a good deal about the literary imagination as a force and function of life generally. For here another often deplored fact also becomes an advantage: that many Canadian cultural phenomena are not peculiarly Canadian at all, but are typical of their wider North American and Western contexts.

This book is a collection of essays in cultural history, and of the general principles of cultural history we still know relatively little. It is, of course, closely related to political and to economic history, but it is a separate and definable subject in itself. Like other kinds of history, it has its own themes of exploration, settlement, and development, but these themes relate to a social *imagination* that explores and settles and develops, and the imagination has its own rhythms of growth as well as its own modes of expression. It is obvious that Canadian literature, whatever its inherent merits, is an indispensable aid to the knowledge of Canada. It records what the Canadian imagination has reacted to, and it tells us things about this environment that nothing else will tell us. By examining this imagination as the authors of this book have tried to do, as an ingredient in Canadian verbal culture generally, a relatively small and low-lying cultural development is studied in all its dimensions. There is far too much Canadian writing for this book not to become, in places, something of a catalogue; but the outlines of the structure are clear. Fortunately, the bulk of Canadian non-literary writing, even today, has not yet declined into the state of sodden specialization in which the readable has become the impure.

I stress our ignorance of the laws and conditions of cultural history for an obvious reason. The question: why has there been no Canadian writer of classic proportions? may naturally be asked. At any rate it often has been. Our authors realize that it is better to deal with what is there than to raise speculations about why something else is not there. But it is clear that the question haunts their minds. And we know so little about cultural history that we not only cannot answer such a question, but we do not even know whether or not it is a real question. The notion, doubtless of romantic origin, that "genius" is a certain quantum that an individual is born with, as he might be born with red hair, is still around, but mainly as a folktale motif in fiction, like the story of Finch in the Jalna books.

"Genius" is as much, and as essentially, a matter of social context as it is of individual character. We do not know what the social conditions are that produce great literature, or even whether there is any causal relation at all. If there is, there is no reason to suppose that they are good conditions, or conditions that we should try to reproduce. The notion that the literature one admires must have been nourished by something admirable in the social environment is persistent, but has never been justified by evidence. One can still find books on Shakespeare that profess to make his achievement more plausible by talking about a "background" of social euphoria produced by the defeat of the Armada, the discovery of America a century before, and the conviction that Queen Elizabeth was a wonderful woman. There is a general sense of filler about such speculations, and when similar arguments are given in a negative form to explain the absence of a Shakespeare in Canada they are no more convincing. Puritan inhibitions, pioneer life, "an age too late, cold climate, or years"— these may be important as factors or conditions of Canadian culture, helping us to characterize its qualities. To suggest that any of them is a negative cause of its merit is to say much more than anyone knows.

One theme which runs all through this book is the obvious and unquenchable desire of the Canadian cultural public to identify itself through its literature. Canada is not a bad environment for the author, as far as recognition goes: in fact the recognition may even hamper his development by making him prematurely self-conscious. Scholarships, prizes, university posts, await the dedicated writer: there are so many medals offered for literary achievement that a modern Canadian Dryden might well be moved to write a satire on medals, except that if he did he would promptly be awarded the medal for satire and humour. Publishers take an active responsibility for native literature, even poetry; a fair proportion of the books bought by Canadian readers are by Canadian writers; the C.B.C. and other media help to employ some writers and publicize others. The efforts made at intervals to boost or hard-sell Canadian literature, by asserting that it is much better than it actually is, may look silly enough in retrospect, but they were also, in part, efforts to create a cultural community, and the aim deserves more sympathy than the means. Canada has two languages and two literatures, and every statement made in a book like this about "Canadian literature" employs the figure of speech known as synecdoche, putting a part for the whole. Every such statement implies a parallel or contrasting statement about French-Canadian literature. The advantages of having a national culture based on two languages are in some respects very great, but of course they are for the most part potential. The difficulties, if more superficial, are also more actual and more obvious.

Some of the seminal facts about the origins of Canadian culture are set down with great clarity near the beginning of this book. Canada began, says Mr. Galloway, as an obstacle, blocking the way to the treasures of the East, to be explored only in the hope of finding a passage through it. English Canada continued to be that long after what is now the United States had become a defined part of the Western world. One reason for this is obvious from the map. American culture was, down to about 1900, mainly a culture of the Atlantic seaboard, with a western frontier that moved irregularly but steadily back until it reached the other coast. The Revolution did not essentially change the cultural unity of the English-speaking community of the North Atlantic that had London and Edinburgh on one side of it and Boston and Philadelphia on the other. But Canada has, for all practical purposes, no Atlantic seaboard. The traveller from Europe edges into it like a tiny Jonah entering an inconceivably large whale, slipping past the Straits of Belle Isle into the Gulf of St. Lawrence, where five Canadian provinces surround him, for the most part invisible. Then he goes up the St. Lawrence and the inhabited country comes into view, mainly a French-speaking country, with its own cultural traditions. To enter the United States is a matter of crossing an ocean; to enter Canada is a matter of being silently swallowed by an alien continent.

It is an unforgettable and intimidating experience to enter Canada in this way. But the experience initiates one into that gigantic east-to-west thrust which, as Mr. Kilbourn notes, historians regard as the axis of Canadian development, the "Laurentian" movement that makes the growth of Canada geographically credible. This drive to the west has attracted to itself nearly everything that is heroic and romantic in the Canadian tradition. The original impetus begins in Europe, for English Canada in the British Isles, hence though adventurous it is also a conservative force, and naturally tends to preserve its colonial link with its starting-point. Once the Canadian has settled down in the country, however, he then becomes aware of the longitudinal dimension, the southward pull toward the richer and more glamorous American cities, some of which, such as Boston for the Maritimes and Minneapolis for the eastern prairies, are almost Canadian capitals. This is the axis of another kind of Canadian mentality, more critical and analytic, more inclined to see Canada as an unnatural and politically quixotic aggregate of disparate northern extensions of American culture—"seven fishing-rods tied together by the ends," as Goldwin Smith, quoted by Mr. Windsor, puts it. Mr. Kilbourn illustrates the contrast in his account of the styles, attitudes, and literary genres of Creighton and Underhill.

The simultaneous influence of two larger nations speaking the same language has been practically beneficial to English Canada, but theoretically confusing. It is often suggested that Canada's identity is to be found in some *via media,* or *via mediocris,* between the other two. This has the disadvantage that the British and American cultures have to be defined as extremes. Haliburton seems to have believed that the ideal for Nova Scotia would be a combination of American energy and British social structure, but such a chimera, or synthetic monster, is hard to achieve in practice. It is simpler merely to notice the alternating current in the Canadian mind, as reflected in its writing, between two moods, one romantic, traditional and idealistic, the other shrewd, observant and humorous. Canada in its attitude to Britain tends to be more royalist than the Queen, in the sense that it is more attracted to it as a symbol of tradition than as a fellow-nation. The Canadian attitude to the United States is typically that of a smaller country to a much bigger neighbour, sharing in its material civilization but anxious to keep clear of the huge mass movements that drive a great imperial power. The United States, being founded on a revolution and a written constitution, has introduced a deductive or *a priori* pattern into its cultural life that tends to define an American way of life and mark it off from anti-American heresies. Canada, having a seat on the sidelines of the American Revolution, adheres more to the inductive and the expedient. The Canadian genius for compromise is reflected in the existence of Canada itself.

The most obvious tension in the Canadian literary situation is in the use of language. Here, first of all, a traditional standard English collides with the need for a North American vocabulary and phrasing. Mr. Scargill and Mr. Klinck have studied this in the work of Mrs. Moodie and Mrs. Traill. As long as the North American speaker feels that he belongs in a minority, the European speech will impose a standard of correctness. This is to a considerable extent still true of French in Canada, with its campaigns against "joual" and the like. But as Americans began to out-number the British, Canada tended in practice to fall in with the American developments, though a good deal of Canadian theory is still Anglophile. A much more complicated cultural tension arises from the impact of the sophisticated on the primitive, and vice versa. The most dramatic example, and one I have given elsewhere, is that of Duncan Campbell Scott, working in the Department of Indian Affairs in Ottawa. He writes of a starving squaw baiting a fish-hook with her own flesh, and he writes of the music of Debussy and the poetry of Henry Vaughan. In English literature we have to go back to Anglo-Saxon times to encounter so incongruous a collision of cultures.

Cultural history, we said, has its own rhythms. It is possible that one of these rhythms is very like an organic rhythm: that there must be a period, of a certain magnitude, as Aristotle would say, in which a social imagination can take root and establish a tradition. American literature had this period, in the northeastern part of the country, between the Revolution and the Civil War. Canada has never had it. English Canada was first a part of the wilderness, then a part of North America and the British Empire, then a part of the world. But it has gone through these revolutions too quickly for a tradition of writing to be founded on any one of them. Canadian writers are, even now, still trying to assimilate a Canadian environment at a time when new techniques of communication, many of which, like television, constitute a verbal market, are annihilating the boundaries of that environment. This foreshortening of Canadian history, if it really does have any relevance to Canadian culture, would account for many features of it: its fixation on its own past, its penchant for old-fashioned literary techniques, its preoccupation with the theme of strangled articulateness. It seems to me that Canadian sensibility has been profoundly disturbed, not so much by our famous problem of identity, important as that is, as by a series of paradoxes in what confronts that identity. It is less perplexed by the question "Who am I?" than by some such riddle as "Where is here?"

Mr. Bailey, writing of the early Maritimes, warns us not to read the "mystique of Canadianism" back into the pre-Confederation period. Haliburton, for instance, was a Nova Scotian, a Bluenose: the word "Canadian" to him would have summoned up the figure of someone who spoke mainly French and whose enthusiasm for Haliburton's own political ideas would have been extremely tepid. The mystique of Canadianism was, as several chapters in this book make clear, specifically the cultural accompaniment of Confederation and the imperialistic mood that followed it. But it came so suddenly after the pioneer period that it was still full of wilderness. To feel "Canadian" was to feel part of a no-man's-land with huge rivers, lakes, and islands that very few Canadians had ever seen. "From sea to sea, and from the river unto the ends of the earth"—if Canada is not an island, the phrasing is still in the etymological sense isolating. One wonders if any other national consciousness has had so large an amount of the unknown, the unrealized, the humanly undigested, so built into it. Rupert Brooke, quoted by Mrs. Waterston, speaks of the "unseizable virginity" of the Canadian landscape. What is important here, for our purposes, is the position of the frontier in the Canadian imagination. In the United States one could choose to move out to the frontier or to retreat from it back to the seaboard. The tensions built up by such migrations have fascinated many American novelists and historians. In the Canadas, even in the Maritimes, the frontier was all around one, a part and a condition of one's whole imaginative being. The frontier was primarily what separated the Canadian, physically or mentally, from Great Britain, from the United States, and, even more important, from other Canadian communities. Such a frontier was the immediate datum of his imagination, the thing that had to be dealt with first.

After the Northwest passage failed to materialize, Canada became a colony in the mercantilist sense, treated by others less like a society than as a place to look for things. French, English, Americans plunged into it to carry off its supplies of furs, minerals, and pulpwood, aware only of their immediate objectives. From time to time recruiting officers searched the farms and villages to carry young men off to death in a European dynastic quarrel. The travellers reviewed by Mrs. Waterston visit Canada much as they would visit a zoo: even when their eyes momentarily focus on the natives they are still thinking primarily of how their own sensibility is going to react to what it sees. Mrs. Waterston speaks of a feature of Canadian life that has been noted by writers from Susanna Moodie onward: "the paradox of vast empty spaces plus lack of privacy," without defences against the prying or avaricious eye. The resentment expressed against this in Canada seems to have taken political rather than literary forms: this may be partly because Canadians have learned from their imaginative experience to look at each other in much the same way: "as objects, even as obstacles," to quote Miss Macpherson on a Canadian autobiography.

It is not much wonder if Canada developed with the bewilderment of a neglected child, preoccupied with trying to define its own identity, alternately bumptious and diffident about its own achievements. Adolescent dreams of glory haunt the Canadian consciousness (and unconsciousness), some naïve and some sophisticated. In the naïve area are the predictions that the twentieth century belongs to Canada, that our cities will become much bigger than they ought to be, or, like Edmonton and Vancouver, "gateways" to somewhere else, reconstructed Northwest passages. The more sophisticated usually take the form of a Messianic complex about Canadian culture, for Canadian culture, no less than Alberta, has always been "next year country." The myth of the hero brought up in the forest retreat, awaiting the moment when his giant strength will be fully grown and he can emerge into the world, informs a good deal of Canadian criticism down to our own time.

Certain features of life in a new country that are bound to handicap its writers are obvious enough. The difficulties of drama, which depends on a theatre and consequently on a highly organized urban life, are set out by Mr. Tait. Here the foreshortening of historical development has been particularly cruel, as drama was strangled by the movie just as it was getting started as a popular medium. Other literary genres have similar difficulties. Culture is born in leisure and an awareness of standards, and pioneer conditions tend to make energetic and uncritical work an end in itself, to preach a gospel of social unconsciousness, which lingers long after the pioneer conditions have disappeared. The impressive achievements of such a society are likely to be technological. It is in the inarticulate part of communication, railways and bridges and canals and highways, that Canada, one of whose symbols is the taciturn beaver, has shown its real strength. Again, Canadian culture, and literature in particular, has felt the force of what may be called Emerson's law. Emerson remarks in his journals that in a provincial society it is extremely easy to reach the highest level of cultivation, extremely difficult to take one step beyond that. In surveying Canadian poetry and fiction, we feel constantly that all the energy has been absorbed in meeting a standard, a self-defeating enterprise because real standards can only be established, not met. Such writing is academic in the pejorative sense of that term, an imitation of a prescribed model, second-rate in conception, not merely in execution. It is natural that academic writing of this kind should develop where literature is a social prestige symbol, as Mr. Cogswell says. However, it is not the handicaps of Canadian writers but the distinctive features that appear in spite of them which are the main concern of this book, and so of its conclusion.

II

The sense of probing into the distance, of fixing the eyes on the skyline, is something that Canadian sensibility has inherited from the *voyageurs*. It comes into Canadian painting a good deal, in Thomson whose focus is so often farthest back in the picture, where a river or a gorge in the hills twists elusively out of sight, in Emily Carr whose vision is always, in the title of a compatriot's book of poems, "deeper into the forest." Even in the Maritimes, where the feeling of linear distance is less urgent, Roberts contemplates the Tantramar marshes in the same way, the refrain of "miles and miles" having clearly some incantatory power for him. It would be interesting to know how many Canadian novels associate nobility of character with a faraway look, or base their perorations on a long-range perspective. This might be only a cliché, except that it is often found in sharply observed and distinctively written books. Here, as a random example, is the last sentence of W. O. Mitchell's *Who Has Seen the Wind:* "The wind turns in silent frenzy upon itself, whirling into a smoking funnel, breathing up top soil and tumbleweed skeletons to carry them on its spinning way over the prairie, out and out to the far line of the sky." Mr. Pacey quotes the similarly long-sighted conclusion of *Such is My Beloved.*

A vast country sparsely inhabited naturally depends on its modes of transportation, whether canoe, railway, or the driving and riding "circuits" of the judge, the Methodist preacher, or the Yankee peddler. The feeling of nomadic movement over great distances persists even into the age of the aeroplane, in a country where writers can hardly meet one another without a social organization that provides travel grants. Pratt's poetry is full of his fascination with means of communication, not simply the physical means of great ships and locomotives, though he is one of the best of all poets on such subjects, but with communication as message, with radar and asdic and wireless signals, and, in his war poems, with the power of rhetoric over fighting men. What is perhaps the most comprehensive structure of ideas yet made by a Canadian thinker, the structure embodied in Innis's *Bias of Communication,* is concerned with the same theme, and a disciple of Innis, Marshall McLuhan, continues to emphasize the unity of communication, as a complex containing both verbal and non-verbal factors, and warns us against making unreal divisions within it. Perhaps it is not too fanciful to see this need for continuity in the Canadian attitude to time as well as space, in its preoccupation with its own history (the motto of the Province of Quebec is *je me souviens*) and its relentless cultural stock-takings and self-inventories. The Burke sense of society as a continuum—consistent with the pragmatic and conservative outlook of Canadians—is strong and begins early. Mr. Irving quotes an expression of it in McCulloch, and another quotation shows that it was one of the most deeply held ideas of Brett. As I write, the centennial of Confederation in 1967 looms up before the country with the moral urgency of a Day of Atonement: I use a Jewish metaphor because there is something Hebraic about the Canadian tendency to read its conquest of a promised land, its Maccabean victories of 1812, its struggle for the central fortress on the hill at Quebec, as oracles of a future. It is doubtless only an accident that the theme of one of the most passionate and intense of all Canadian novels, A. M. Klein's *The Second Scroll*, is Zionism.

Civilization in Canada, as elsewhere, has advanced geometrically across the country, throwing down the long parallel lines of the railways, dividing up the farm lands into chessboards of square-mile sections and concession-line roads. There is little adaptation to nature: in both architecture and arrangement, Canadian cities and villages express rather an arrogant abstraction, the conquest of nature by an intelligence that does not love it. The word conquest suggests something military, as it should —one thinks of General Braddock, preferring to have his army annihilated rather than fight the natural man on his own asymmetrical ground. There are some features of this generally North American phenomenon that have a particular emphasis in Canada. It has been remarked—Mr. Kilbourn quotes Creighton on the subject—that Canadian expansion westward had a tight grip of authority over it that American expansion, with its outlaws and sheriffs and vigilantes and the like, did not have in the same measure. America moved from the back country to the wild west; Canada moved from a New France held down by British military occupation to a northwest patrolled by mounted police. Canada has not had, strictly speaking, an Indian war: there has been much less of the "another redskin bit the dust" feeling in our historical imagination, and only Riel remains to haunt the later period of it, though he is a formidable figure enough, rather like what a combination of John Brown and Vanzetti would be in the American conscience. Otherwise, the conquest, for the last two centuries, has been mainly of the unconscious forces of nature, personified by the dragon of the Lake Superior rocks in Pratt's *Towards the Last Spike:*

> On the North Shore a reptile lay asleep—
> A hybrid that the myths might have conceived,
> But not delivered.

Yet the conquest of nature has its own perils for the imagination, in a country where the winters are so cold and where conditions of life have so often been bleak and comfortless, where even the mosquitoes have been described, Mr. Klinck tells us, as "mementoes of the fall." I have long been impressed in Canadian poetry by a tone of deep terror in regard to nature, a theme to which we shall return. It is not a terror of the dangers or discomforts or even the mysteries of nature, but a terror of the soul at something that these things manifest. The human mind has nothing but human and moral values to cling to if it is to preserve its integrity or even its sanity, yet the vast unconsciousness of nature in front of it seems an unanswerable denial of those values. I notice that a sharp-witted Methodist preacher quoted by Mr. Cogswell speaks of the "shutting out of the whole moral creation" in the loneliness of the forests.

If we put together a few of these impressions, we may get some approach to characterizing the way in which the Canadian imagination has developed in its literature. Small and isolated communities surrounded with a physical or psychological "frontier," separated from one another and from their American and British cultural sources: communities that provide all that their members have in the way of distinctively human values, and that are compelled to feel a great respect for the law and order that holds them together, yet confronted with a huge, unthinking, menacing, and formidable physical setting—such communities are bound to develop what we may provisionally call a garrison mentality. In the earliest maps of the country the only inhabited centres are forts, and that remains true of the cultural maps for a much later time. Frances Brooke, in her eighteenth-century *Emily Montague*, wrote of what was literally a garrison; novelists of our day studying the impact of Montreal on Westmount write of a psychological one.

A garrison is a closely knit and beleaguered society, and its moral and social values are unquestionable. In a perilous enterprise ones does not discuss causes or motives: one is either a fighter or a deserter. Here again we may turn to Pratt, with his infallible instinct for what is central in the Canadian imagination. The societies in Pratt's poems are always tense and tight groups engaged in war, rescue, martyrdom, or crisis, and the moral values expressed are simply those of that group. In such a society the terror is not for the common enemy, even when the enemy is or seems victorious, as in the extermination of the Jesuit missionaries or the crew of Franklin (a great Canadian theme, well described in this book by Mr. Hopwood, that Pratt pondered but never completed). The real terror comes when the individual feels himself becoming an individual, pulling away from the group, losing the sense of driving power that the group gives him, aware of a conflict within himself far subtler than the struggle of morality against evil. It is much easier to multiply garrisons, and when that happens, something anti-cultural comes into Canadian life, a dominating herd-mind in which nothing original can grow. The intensity of the sectarian divisiveness in Canadian towns, both religious and political, is an example: what such groups represent, of course, vis-à-vis one another, is "two solitudes," the death of communication and dialogue. Separatism, whether English or French, is culturally the most sterile of all creeds. But at present I am concerned rather with a more creative side of the garrison mentality, one that has had positive effects on our intellectual life.

They were so certain of their moral values, says Mr. Cogswell, a little sadly, speaking of the early Maritime writers. Right was white, wrong black, and nothing else counted or even existed. He goes on to point out that such certainty invariably produces a sub-literary rhetoric. Or, as Yeats would say, we make rhetoric out of quarrels with one another, poetry out of the quarrel with ourselves. To use words, for any other purpose than straight description or command, is a form of play, a manifestation of *homo ludens*. But there are two forms of play, the contest and the construct. The editorial writer attacking the Family Compact, the preacher demolishing imaginary atheists with the argument of design, are using words aggressively, in theses that imply antitheses. Ideas are weapons; one seeks the verbal *coup de grâce,* the irrefutable refutation. Such a use of words is congenial enough to the earlier Canadian community: all the evidence, including the evidence of this book, points to a highly articulate and argumentative society in nineteenth-century Canada. Mr. MacLure remarks on the fact that scholarship in Canada has so often been written with more conviction and authority, and has attracted wider recognition, than the literature itself. There are historical reasons for this, apart from the fact, which will become clearer as we go on, that scholarly writing is more easily attached to its central tradition.

Leacock has a story which I often turn to because the particular aspect of Canadian culture it reflects has never been more accurately caught. He tells us of the rivalry in an Ontario town between two preachers, one Anglican and the other Presbyterian. The latter taught ethics in the local college on weekdays—without salary—and preached on Sundays. He gave his students, says Leacock, three parts Hegel and two parts St. Paul, and on Sunday he reversed the dose and gave his parishioners three parts St. Paul and two parts Hegel. Religion has been a major—perhaps the major—cultural force in Canada, at least down to the last generation or two. The names of two Methodist publishers, William Briggs and Lorne Pierce, recur more than once in this book, and illustrate the fact that the churches not only influenced the cultural climate but took an active part in the production of poetry and fiction, as the popularity of Ralph Connor reminds us. But the effective religious factors in Canada were doctrinal and evangelical, those that stressed the arguments of religion at the expense of its imagery.

Such a reliance on the arguing intellect was encouraged by the philosophers, who in the nineteenth century, as Mr. Irving shows, were invariably idealists with a strong religious bias. Mr. Irving quotes George as saying that civilization consists "in the conscience and intellect" of a cultivated people, and Watson as asserting that "we are capable of knowing Reality as it actually is. . . . Reality when so known is absolutely rational." An even higher point may have been reached by that triumphant theologian cited by Mr. Thomson, whose book I have not read but whose title I greatly admire: *The Riddle of the Universe Solved.* Naturally sophisticated intelligence of this kind was the normal means of contact with literature. Mr. MacLure tells us that James Cappon judged poetry according to whether it had a "rationalized concept" or not—this would have been a very common critical assumption. Sara Jeannette Duncan shows us a clergyman borrowing a copy of Browning's *Sordello,* no easy reading, and returning it with original suggestions for interpretation. Such an interest in ideas is not merely cultivated but exuberant.

But using language as one would use an axe, formulating arguments with sharp cutting edges that will help to clarify one's view of the landscape, remains a rhetorical and not a poetic achievement. To quote Yeats again, one can refute Hegel (perhaps even St. Paul) but not the *Song of Sixpence.* To create a disinterested structure of words, in poetry or in fiction, is a very different achievement, and it is clear that an intelligent and able rhetorician finds it particularly hard to understand how different it is. A rhetorician practising poetry is apt to express himself in spectral arguments, generalizations that escape the feeling of possible refutation only by being vast enough to contain it, or vapourous enough to elude it. The mystique of Canadianism was accompanied by an intellectual tendency of this kind, as Mr. Daniells indicates. World-views that avoided dialectic, of a theosophical or transcendentalist cast, became popular among the Canadian poets of that time, Roberts and Carman particularly, and later among painters, as the reminiscences of the Group of Seven make clear. Bucke's *Cosmic Consciousness,* though not mentioned by any of our authors so far as I remember, is an influential Canadian book in this area. When minor rhetorically-minded poets sought what Samuel Johnson calls, though in a very different context, the "grandeur of generality," the result is what is so well described by Mr. Beattie as "jejune chatter about infinity," and the like.

Mr. Watt's very important chapter on the literature of protest isolates another rhetorical tradition. In the nineteenth century the common assumption that nature had revealed the truth of progress, and that it was the duty of reason to accommodate that truth to mankind, could be either a conservative or a radical view. But in either case it was a revolutionary doctrine, introducing the conception of change as the key to the social process. In those whom Mr. Watt calls proletarian social Darwinists, and who represented "the unholy fusion of secularism, science and social discontent," there was a strong tendency to regard literature as a product and a symbol of a ruling-class mentality, with, as we have tried to indicate, some justification. Hence redicals tended either to hope that "the literature of the future will be the powerful ally of Democracy and Labour Reform," or to assume that serious thought and action would bypass the creative writer entirely, building a scientific socialism and leaving him to his Utopian dreams.

The radicalism of the period up to the Russian Revolution was, from a later point of view, largely undifferentiated. A labour magazine could regard Ignatius Donnelly, with his anti-Semitic and other crank views, as an advanced thinker equally with William Morris and Edward Bellamy. Similarly, even today, in Western Canadian elections, a protest vote may go Social Credit or NDP without much regard to the difference in political philosophy between these parties. The depression introduced a dialectic into Canadian social thought which profoundly affected its literature. In Mr. Watt's striking phrase, "the Depression was like an intense magnetic field that deflected the courses of all the poets who went through it." In this period there were, of course, the inevitable Marxist manifestos, assuring the writer that only social significance, as understood by Marxism, would bring vitality to his work. The *New Frontier*, a far-left journal of that period referred to several times in this book, shows an uneasy sense on the part of its contributors that this literary elixir of youth might have to be mixed with various other potions, not all favourable to the creative process: attending endless meetings, organizing, agitating, marching, demonstrating, or joining the Spanish Loyalists. It is easy for the critic to point out the fallacy of judging the merit of literature by its subject-matter, but these arguments over the role of "propaganda" were genuine and serious moral conflicts. Besides helping to shape the argument of such novels as Grove's *The Master of the Mill* and Callaghan's *They Shall Inherit the Earth*, they raised the fundamental issue of the role of the creative mind in society, and by doing so helped to give a maturity and depth to Canadian writing which is a permanent part of its heritage.

It is not surprising, given this background, that the belief in the inspiration of literature by social significance continued to be an active force long after it had ceased to be attached to any specifically Marxist or other political programmes. It is still strong in the *Preview* group in the forties, and in their immediate successors, though the best of them have developed in different directions. The theme of social realism is at its most attractive, and least theoretical, in the poetry of Souster. The existentialist movement, with its emphasis on the self-determination of social attitudes, seems to have had very little direct influence in Canada: Mr. Beattie's comment on the absence of the existential in Pratt suggests that this lack of influence may be significant.

During the last decade or so a kind of social Freudianism has been taking shape, mainly in the United States, as a democratic counterpart of Marxism. Here society is seen as controlled by certain anxieties, real or imaginary, which are designed to repress or sublimate human impulses toward a greater freedom. These impulses include the creative and the sexual, which are closely linked. The enemy of the poet is not the capitalist but the "square," or representative of repressive morality. The advantage of this attitude is that it preserves the position of rebellion against society for the poet, without imposing on him any specific social obligations. This movement has had a rather limited development in Canada, somewhat surprisingly considering how easy a target the square is in Canada: it has influenced Layton and many younger Montreal poets, but has not affected fiction to any great degree, though there may be something of it in Richler. It ignores the old political alignments: the Communists are usually regarded as Puritanic and repressive equally with the bourgeoisie, and a recent poem of Layton's contrasts the social hypocrisy in Canada with contemporary Spain. Thus it represents to some extent a return to the undifferentiated radicalism of a century before, though no longer in a political context.

As the centre of Canadian life moves from the fortress to the metropolis, the garrison mentality changes correspondingly. It begins as an expression of the moral values generally accepted in the group as a whole, and then, as society gets more complicated and more in control of its environment, it becomes more of a revolutionary garrison within a metropolitan society. But though it changes from a defence of to an attack on what society accepts as conventional standards, the literature it produces, at every stage, tends to be rhetorical, an illustration or allegory of certain social attitudes. These attitudes help to unify the mind of the writer by externalizing his enemy, the enemy being the anti-creative elements in life as he sees life. To approach these elements in a less rhetorical way would introduce the theme of self-conflict, a more perilous but ultimately more rewarding theme. The conflict involved is between the poetic impulse to construct and the rhetorical impulse to assert, and the victory of the former is the sign of the maturing of the writer.

III

There is of course nothing in all this that differentiates Canadian from other related cultural developments. The nineteenth-century Canadian reliance on the conceptual was not different in kind from that of the Victorian readers described by Douglas Bush, who thought they were reading poetry when they were really only looking for Great Thoughts. But if the tendency was not different in kind, it was more intense in degree. Here we need another seminal fact in this book, one that we have stumbled over already: Mr. Hopwood's remark that the Canadian literary mind, beginning as it did so late in the cultural history of the West, was established on a basis, not of myth, but of history. The conceptual emphasis in Canadian culture we have been speaking of is a consequence, and an essential part, of this historical bias.

Canada, of course, or the place where Canada is, can supply distinctive settings and props to a writer who is looking for local colour. Tourist-writing has its own importance (e.g., *Maria Chapdelaine*), as has the use of Canadian history for purposes of romance, of which more later. But it would be an obvious fallacy to claim that the setting provided anything more than novelty. When Canadian writers are urged to use distinctively Canadian themes, the fallacy is less obvious, but still there. The forms of literature are autonomous: they exist within literature itself, and cannot be derived from any experience outside literature. What the Canadian writer finds in his experience and environment may be new, but it will be new only as content: the form of his expression of it can take shape only from what he has read, not from what he has experienced. The great technical experiments of Joyce and Proust in fiction, of Eliot and Hopkins in poetry, have resulted partly from profound literary scholarship, from seeing the formal possibilities inherent in the literature they have studied. A writer who is or who feels removed from his literary tradition tends rather to take over forms already in existence. We notice how often the surveyors of Canadian fiction in this book have occasion to remark that a novel contains a good deal of sincere feeling and accurate observation, but that it is spoiled by an unconvincing plot, usually one too violent or dependent on coincidence for such material. What has happened is that the author felt he could make a novel out of his knowledge and observation, but had no story in particular to tell. His material did not come to him in the form of a story, but as a consolidated chunk of experience, reflection, and sensibility. He had to invent a plot to put this material in causal shape (for writing, as Kafka says, is an art of causality), to pour the new wine of content into the old bottles of form. Even Grove works in this way, though Grove, by sheer dogged persistence, does get his action powerfully if ponderously moving.

This brings us nearer the centre of Mr. Hopwood's observation. Literature is conscious mythology: as society develops, its mythical stories become structural principles of story-telling, its mythical concepts, sun-gods and the like, become habits of metaphorical thought. In a fully mature literary tradition the writer enters into a structure of traditional stories and images. He often has the feeling, and says so, that he is not actively shaping his material at all, but is rather a place where a verbal structure is taking its own shape. If a novelist, he starts with a story-telling impetus; if a poet, with a metaphor-crystallizing impetus. Down to the beginning of the twentieth century at least, the Canadian who wanted to write started with a feeling of detachment from his literary tradition, which existed for him mainly in his school books. He had probably, as said above, been educated in a way that heavily stressed the conceptual and argumentative use of language. Mrs. Fowke shows us how the Indians began with a mythology which included all the main elements of our own. It was, of course, impossible for Canadians to establish any real continuity with it: Indians, like the rest of the country, were seen as nineteenth-century literary conventions. Certain elements in Canadian culture, too, such as the Protestant revolutionary view of history, may have minimized the importance of the oral tradition in ballad and folk song, which seems to have survived best in Catholic communities. In Canada the mythical was simply the "prehistoric" (this word, we are told, is a Canadian coinage), and the writer had to attach himself to his literary tradition deliberately and voluntarily. And though this may be no longer true or necessary, attitudes surviving from an earlier period of isolation still have their influence.

The separation of subject and object is the primary fact of consciousness, for anyone so situated and so educated. Writing for him does not start with a rhythmical movement, or an impetus caught from or encouraged by a group of contemporaries: it starts with reportage, a single mind reacting to what is set over against it. Such a writer does not naturally think metaphorically but descriptively; it seems obvious to him that writing is a form of self-expression dependent on the gathering of a certain amount of experience, granted some inborn sensitivity toward that experience. We note (as does Mr. McPherson) how many Canadian novelists have written only one novel, or only one good novel, how many Canadian poets have written only one good book of poems, generally their first. Even the dream of "the great Canadian novel," the feeling that somebody some day will write a Canadian fictional classic, assumes that whoever does it will do it only once. This is a characteristic of writers dominated by the conception of writing up experiences or observations: nobody has enough experience to keep on writing about it, unless his writing is an incidental commentary on a non-literary career.

The Canadian writers who have overcome these difficulties and have found their way back to the real headwaters of inspiration are heroic explorers. There are a good many of them, and the evidence of this book is that the Canadian imagination has passed the stage of exploration and has embarked on that of settlement. But it is of course full of the failures as well as the successes of exploration, imaginative voyages to Golconda that froze in the ice, and we can learn something from them too. Why do Canadians write so many historical romances, of what Mr. McPherson calls the rut and thrust variety? One can understand it in Mr. Roper's period: the tendency to melodrama in romance makes it part of a central convention of that time, as Mr. Roper's discerning paragraph on the subject shows. But romances are still going strong in Mr. Pacey's period, and if anything even stronger in Mr. McPherson's.[1] They get a little sexier and more violent as they go on, but the formula remains much the

---

[1] Roper's Period, 1880–1920; Pacey's, 1920–1940; McPherson's, 1940–1960.

same: so much love-making, so much "research" about antiquities and costume copied off filing cards, more love-making, more filing cards. There is clearly a steady market for this, but the number of writers engaged in it suggests other answers. There is also a related fact, the unusually large number of Canadian popular best-selling fiction-writers, from Agnes Fleming through Gilbert Parker to Mazo de la Roche.

In Mr. Roper's chronicle not all the fiction is romance, but nearly all of it is formula-writing. In the books he mentions that I have read I remember much honest and competent work. Some of them did a good deal to form my own infantile imagination, and I could well have fared worse. What there is not, of course, is a recreated view of life, or anything to detach the mind from its customary attitudes. In Mr. Pacey's period we begin to notice a more consistent distinction between the romancer, who stays with established values and usually chooses a subject remote in time from himself, and the realist, who deals with contemporary life, and therefore—it appears to be a therefore—is more serious in intention, more concerned to unsettle a stock response. One tendency culminates in Mazo de la Roche, the other in Morley Callaghan, both professional writers and born story-tellers, though of very different kinds. By Mr. McPherson's period the two tendencies have more widely diverged. One is mainly romance dealing with Canada's past, the other is contemporary realism dealing with what is common to Canada and the rest of the world, like antique and modern furniture stores. One can see something similar in the poetry, a contrast between a romantic tradition closely associated with patriotic and idealistic themes, and a more intellectualized one with a more cosmopolitan bias. This contrast is prominently featured in the first edition of A. J. M. Smith's anthology, *A Book of Canadian Poetry* (1943).

This contrast of the romantic and the realistic, the latter having a moral dignity that the former lacks, reflects the social and conceptual approach to literature already mentioned. Here we are looking at the same question from a different point of view. Literature, we said, is conscious mythology: it creates an autonomous world that gives us an imaginative perspective on the actual one. But there is another kind of mythology, one produced by society itself, the object of which is to persuade us to accept existing social values. "Popular" literature, the kind that is read for relaxation and the quieting of the mind, expresses this social mythology. We all feel a general difference between serious and soothing literature, though I know of no critical rule for distinguishing them, nor is there likely to be one. The same work may belong to both mythologies at once, and in fact the separation between them is largely a perspective of our own revolutionary age.

In many popular novels, especially in the nineteenth century, we feel how strong the desire is on the part of the author to work out his situation within a framework of established social values. Mr. Roper notes that in the success-story formula frequent in such fiction the success is usually "emotional," i.e., the individual fulfils himself within his community. There is nothing hypocritical or cynical about this: the author usually believes very deeply in his values. Moral earnestness and the posing of serious problems are by no means excluded from popular literature, any more than serious literature is excused from the necessity of being entertaining. The difference is in the position of the reader's mind at the end, in whether he is being encouraged to remain within his habitual social responses or whether he is being prodded into making the steep and lonely climb into the imaginative world. This distinction in itself is familiar enough, and all I am suggesting here is that what I have called the garrison mentality is highly favourable to the growth of popular literature in this sense. The role of romance and melodrama in consolidating a social mythology is also not hard to see. In romance the characters tend to be psychological projections, heroes, heroines, villains, father-figures, comic-relief caricatures. The popular romance operates on Freudian principles, releasing sexual and power fantasies without disturbing the anxieties of the superego. The language of melodrama, at once violent and morally conventional, is the appropriate language for this. A subliminal sense of the erotic release in romance may have inspired some of the distrust of novels in nineteenth-century pietistic homes. But even those who preferred stories of real life did not want "realism": that, we learn, was denounced on all sides during the nineteenth century as nasty, prurient, morbid, and foreign. The garrison mentality is that of its officers: it can tolerate only the conservative idealism of its ruling class, which for Canada means the moral and propertied middle class.

The total effect of Canadian popular fiction, whatever incidental merits in it there may be, is that of a murmuring and echoing literary collective unconscious, the rippling of a watery Narcissus world reflecting the imaginative patterns above it. Robertson Davies' *Tempest Tost* is a sardonic study of the triumph of a social mythology over the imaginative one symbolized by Shakespeare's play. Maturity and individualization, in such a body of writing, are almost the same process. Occasionally a writer is individualized by accident. Thus Susanna Moodie in the Peterborough bush, surrounded by a half-comic, half-sinister rabble that she thinks of indifferently as Yankee, Irish, native, republican, and lower class, is a British army of occupation in herself, a one-woman garrison. We often find too, as in Leacock, a spirit of criticism, even of satire, that is the complementary half of a strong attachment to the mores that provoke the satire. That is, a good deal of what goes on in Mariposa may look ridiculous, but the norms or standards against which it looks ridiculous are provided by Mariposa itself. In Sara Jeannette Duncan there is something else again, as she watches the garrison parade to church in a small Ontario town: "The repressed magnetic excitement in gatherings of familiar faces, fellow-beings bound by the same convention to the same kind of behaviour, is precious in communities where the human interest is still thin and sparse." Here is a voice of genuine detachment, sympathetic but not defensive either of the group or of herself, concerned primarily to understand and to make the reader see. The social group is becoming external to the writer, but not in a way that isolates her from it.

This razor's edge of detachment is naturally rare in Canadian writing, even in this author, but as the twentieth century advances and Canadian society takes a firmer grip of its environment, it becomes easier to assume the role of an individual separated in standards and attitudes from the community. When this happens, an ironic or realistic literature becomes fully possible. This new kind of detachment of course often means only that the split between subject and object has become identified with a split between the individual and society. This is particularly likely to happen when the separated individual's point of view is also that of the author, as in the stories of misunderstood genius with which many minor authors are fascinated. According to Mr. Tait this convention was frequent in the plays put on in Hart House during the twenties; it certainly was so in fiction. But some of the most powerful of Canadian novels have been those in which this conflict has been portrayed objectively. Buckler's *The Mountain and the Valley* is a Maritime example, and Sinclair Ross's *As for Me and My House* one from the prairies.

Mr. Conron quotes B. K. Sandwell as saying: "I follow it [society] at a respectful distance . . . far enough away to make it clear that I do not belong to it." It is clear that this is not necessarily any advance on the expression of conventional social values in popular romance. The feeling of detachment from society means only that society has become more complex, and inner tensions have developed in it. We have traced this process already. The question that arises is: once society, along with physical nature, becomes external to the writer, what does he then feel a part of? For rhetorical or assertive writers it is generally a smaller society, the group that agrees with them. But the imaginative writer, though he often begins as a member of a school or group, normally pulls away from it as he develops.

If our general line of thought is sound, the imaginative writer is finding his identity within the world of literature itself. He is withdrawing from what Douglas LePan calls a country without a mythology into the country of mythology, ending where the Indians began. Mr. Tait quotes John Coulter's comment on his play, or libretto, *Deirdre of the Sorrows:* "The art of a Canadian remains . . . the art of the country of his forebears and the old world heritage of myth and legend remains his heritage . . . though the desk on which he writes be Canadian." But the progress may not be a simple matter of forsaking the Canadian for the international, the province for the capital. It may be that when the Canadian writer attaches himself to the world of literature, he discovers, or rediscovers, by doing so, something in his Canadian environment which is more vital and articulate than a desk.

IV

At the heart of all social mythology lies what may be called, because it usually is called, a pastoral myth, the vision of a social ideal. The pastoral myth in its most common form is associated with childhood, or with some earlier social condition—pioneer life, the small town, the *habitant* rooted to his land—that can be identified with childhood. The nostalgia for a world of peace and protection, with a spontaneous response to the nature around it, with a leisure and composure not to be found today, is particularly strong in Canada. It is overpowering in our popular literature, from *Anne of Green Gables* to Leacock's Mariposa, and from *Maria Chapdelaine* to *Jake and the Kid*. It is present in all the fiction that deals with small towns as collections of characters in search of an author. Its influence is strong in the most serious writers: one thinks of Gabrielle Roy, following her *Bonheur d'occasion* with *La poule d'eau*. It is the theme of all the essayists who write of fishing and other forms of the simpler life, especially as lived in the past. Mr. Conron quotes Mac-Mechan: "golden days in memory for the enrichment of less happier times to come." It even comes into our official documents—the Massey Report begins, almost as a matter of course, with an idyllic picture of the Canada of fifty years ago, as a point of departure for its investigations. Mr. Bailey speaks of the eighteenth-century Loyalists as looking "to a past that had never existed for comfort and illumination," which suggests that the pastoral myth has been around for some time.

The Indians have not figured so largely in the myth as one might expect, though in some early fiction and drama the noble savage takes the role, as he does to some extent even in the Gothic hero Wacousta. The popularity of Pauline Johnson and Grey Owl, however, shows that the kind of rapport with nature which the Indian symbolizes is central to it. Another form of pastoral myth is the evocation of an earlier period of history which is made romantic by having a more uninhibited expression of passion or virtue or courage attached to it. This of course links the pastoral myth with the vision of vanished grandeur that comes into the novels about the *ancien régime*. In *The Golden Dog* and *The Seats of the Mighty* the forlorn little fortress of seventeenth-century Quebec, sitting in the middle of what Madame de Pompadour called "a few arpents of snow," acquires a theatrical glamour that would do credit to Renaissance Florence. Mr. Klinck gives a most concise summary of the earlier literary romanticizing of this period, and Mr. Pacey studies its later aspects. The two forms of the myth collide on the Plains of Abraham, on the one side a

solitary man with caution, a group of men with trepidation, and a nation of men with terror." The same theme also forms part of the final cadences of Hugh MacLennan's *The Watch That Ends the Night:* "In the early October of that year, in the cathedral hush of a Quebec Indian summer with the lake drawing into its mirror the fire of the maples, it came to me that to be able to love the mystery surrounding us is the final and only sanction of human existence."

It is the appearance of this theme in D. C. Scott which moves Mr. Daniells to call Scott one of the "ancestral voices" of the Canadian imagination. It is much stronger and more continuous in Lampman, who talks less than his contemporaries and strives harder for the uniting of subject and object in the imaginative experience. This union takes place in the contact of individual poet and a landscape uninhabited except for Wordsworth's "huge and mighty forms" that are manifested by the union:

> Nay more, I think some blessèd power
> Hath brought me wandering idly here.

Again as in Wordsworth, this uniting of individual mind and nature is an experience from which human society, as such, is excluded. Thus when the poet finds a "blessèd power" in nature it is the society he leaves behind that tends to become the God-forsaken wilderness. Usually this society is merely trivial or boring; once, in the unforgettable "City of the End of Things," it becomes demonic.

The two aspects of the pastoral tradition we have been tracing are not inconsistent with each other; they are rather complementary. At one pole of experience there is a fusion of human life and the life in nature; at the opposite pole is the identity of the sinister and terrible elements in nature with the death-wish in man. In Pratt's "The Truant" the "genus *homo*" confronts the "great Panjandrum" of nature who is also his own death-wish: the great Panjandrum is the destructive force in the Nazis and in the Indians who martyred Brébeuf, the capacity in man that enables him to be deliberately cruel. Irving Layton shows us not only the cruelty but the vulgarity of the death-wish consciousness: as it has no innocence, it cannot suffer with dignity, as animals can; it loses its own imaginary soul by despising the body:

> Listen: for all his careful fuss,
> Will this cold one ever deceive us?
>   Self-hating, he rivets a glittering wall;
> Impairs it by a single pebble
> And loves himself for that concession.

We spoke earlier of a civilization conquering the landscape and imposing an alien and abstract pattern on it. As this process goes on, the writers, the poets especially, tend increasingly to see much of this process as something that is human but still dehumanized, leaving man's real humanity a part of the nature that he continually violates but is still inviolate.

Reading through any good collection of modern Canadian poems or stories, we find every variety of tone, mood, attitude, technique, and setting. But there is a certain unity of impression one gets from it, an impression of gentleness and reasonableness, seldom difficult or greatly daring in its imaginative flights, the passion, whether of love or anger, held in check by something meditative. It is not easy to put the feeling in words, but if we turn to the issue of the *Tamarack Review* that was devoted to West Indian literature, or to the Hungarian poems translated by Canadians in the collection *The Plough and the Pen,* we can see by contrast something of both the strength and the limitations of the Canadian writers. They too have lived, if not in Arcadia, at any rate in a land where empty space and the pervasiveness of physical nature have impressed a pastoral quality on their minds. From the deer and fish in Isabella Crawford's "The Canoe" to the frogs and toads in Layton, from the white narcissus of Knister to the night-blooming cereus of Reaney, everything that is central in Canadian writing seems to be marked by the imminence of the natural world. The sense of this imminence organizes the mythology of Jay Macpherson; it is the sign in which Canadian soldiers conquer Italy in Douglas LePan's *The Net and the Sword;* it may be in the foreground, as in Alden Nowlan, or in the background, as in Birney; but it is always there.

To go on with this absorbing subject would take us into another book: *A Literary Criticism of Canada,* let us say. Here we can only refer the reader to Mr. Beattie's able guidance and sum up the present argument emblematically, with two famous primitive American paintings. One is "Historical Monument of the American Republic," by Erastus Salisbury Field. Painted in 1876 for the centennial of the Revolution, it is an encyclopaedic portrayal of events in American history, against a background of soaring towers, with clouds around their spires, and connected by railway bridges. It is a prophetic vision of the skyscraper cities of the future, of the tremendous technological will to power of our time and the civilization it has built, a civilization now gradually imposing a uniformity of culture and habits of life all over the globe. Because the United States is the most powerful centre of this civilization, we often say, when referring to its uniformity, that the world is becoming Americanized. But of course America itself is being Americanized in this sense, and the uniformity imposed on New Delhi and Singapore, or on Toronto and Vancouver, is no greater than that imposed on New Orleans or Baltimore. A nation so huge and so productive, however, is deeply committed to this growing technological uniformity, even though many tendencies may pull in other directions. Canada has participated to the full in the wars, economic expansions, technological achievements, and internal stresses of the modern world. Canadians seem well adjusted to the new world of technology and very efficient at handling it. Yet in the Canadian imagination there are deep reservations to this world as an end of life in itself, and the political separation of Canada has helped to emphasize these reservations in its literature.

English Canada began with the influx of defeated Tories after the American Revolution, and so, in its literature, with a strong anti-revolutionary bias. The Canadian radicalism that developed in opposition to Loyalism was not a revival of the American revolutionary spirit, but a quite different movement, which had something in common with the Toryism it opposed: one thinks of the Tory and radical elements in the social vision of William Cobbett, who also finds a place in the Canadian record. A revolutionary tradition is liable to two defects: to an undervaluing of history and an impatience with law, and we have seen how unusually strong the Canadian attachment to law and history has been. The attitude to things American represented by Haliburton is not, on the whole, hostile: it would be better described as non-committal, as when Sam Slick speaks of a Fourth of July as "a splendid spectacle; fifteen millions of freemen and three millions of slaves a-celebratin' the birthday of liberty." The strong romantic tradition in Canadian literature has much to do with its original conservatism. When more radical expressions begin to creep into Canadian writing, as in the poetry of Alexander McLachlan, there is still much less of the assumption that freedom and national independence are the same thing, or that the mercantilist Whiggery which won the American Revolution is necessarily the only emancipating force in the world. In some Canadian writers of our own time—I think particularly of Earle Birney's *Trial of a City* and the poetry of F. R. Scott—there is an opposition, not to the democratic but to the oligarchic tendencies in North American civilization, not to liberal but to laissez-faire political doctrine. Perhaps it is a little easier to see these distinctions from the vantage-point of a smaller country, even one which has, in its material culture, made the "American way of life" its own.

The other painting is the much earlier "The Peaceable Kingdom," by Edward Hicks, painted around 1830. Here, in the background, is a treaty between the Indians and the Quaker settlers under Penn. In the foreground is a group of animals, lions, tigers, bears, oxen, illustrating the prophecy of Isaiah about the recovery of innocence in nature. Like the animals of the Douanier Rousseau, they stare past us with a serenity that transcends consciousness. It is a pictorial emblem of what Grove's narrator was trying to find under the surface of America: the reconciliation of man with man and of man with nature: the mood of Thoreau's Walden retreat, of Emily Dickinson's garden, of Huckleberry Finn's raft, of the elegies of Whitman, whose reaction to Canada is also recorded in this book. This mood is closer to the haunting vision of a serenity that is both human and natural which we have been struggling to identify in the

Canadian tradition. If we had to characterize a distinctive emphasis in that tradition, we might call it a quest for the peaceable kingdom.

The writers of the last decade, at least, have begun to write in a world which is post-Canadian, as it is post-American, post-British, and post everything except the world itself. There are no provinces in the empire of aeroplane and television, and no physical separation from the centres of culture, such as they are. Sensibility is no longer dependent on a specific environment or even on sense experience itself. A remark of Mr. Beattie's about Robert Finch illustrates a tendency which is affecting literature as well as painting: "the interplay of sense impressions is so complicated, and so exhilarating, that the reader receives no sense impression at all." Marshall McLuhan speaks of the world as reduced to a single gigantic primitive village, where everything has the same kind of immediacy. He speaks of the fears that so many intellectuals have of such a world, and remarks amiably: "Terror is the normal state of any oral society, for in it everything affects everything all the time." The Canadian spirit, to personify it as a single being dwelling in the country from the early voyages to the present, might well, reading this sentence, feel that this was where he came in. In other words, new conditions give the old ones a new importance, as what vanishes in one form reappears in another. The moment that the peaceable kingdom has been completely obliterated by its rival is the moment when it comes into the foreground again, as the eternal frontier, the first thing that the writer's imagination must deal with. Pratt's "The Truant," already referred to, foreshadows the poetry of the future, when physical nature has retreated to outer space and only individual and society are left as effective factors in the imagination. But the central conflict, and the moods in which it is fought out, are still unchanged.

One gets very tired, in old-fashioned biographies, of the dubious embryology that examines a poet's ancestry and wonders if a tendency to fantasy in him could be the result of an Irish great-grandmother. A reader may feel the same unreality in efforts to attach Canadian writers to a tradition made up of earlier writers whom they may not have read or greatly admired. I have felt this myself whenever I have written about Canadian literature. Yet I keep coming back to the feeling that there does seem to be such a thing as an imaginative continuum, and that writers are conditioned in their attitudes by their predecessors, or by the cultural climate of their predecessors, whether there is conscious influence or not. Again, nothing can give a writer's experience and sensitivity any form except the study of literature itself. In this study the great classics, "monuments of its own magnificence," and the best contemporaries have an obvious priority. The more such monuments or such contemporaries there are in a writer's particular cultural traditions, the more fortunate he is; but he needs those traditions in any case. He needs them most of all when what faces him seems so new as to threaten his identity. For present and future writers in Canada and their readers, what is important in Canadian literature, beyond the merits of the individual works in it, is the inheritance of the entire enterprise. The writers featured in this book have identified the habits and attitudes of the country, as Fraser and Mackenzie have identified its rivers. They have also left an imaginative legacy of dignity and of high courage.